Critical Marketing

Critical Marketing

Contemporary Issues in Marketing

Edited by

Mark Tadajewski
and
Douglas Brownlie

John Wiley & Sons, Ltd

Email (for orders and customer service enquiries): cs-books@wiley.co.uk
Visit our Home Page on www.wiley.com

Reprinted with corrections July 2008

Other Wiley Editorial Offices

John Wiley & Sons Inc., 111 River Street, Hoboken, NJ 07030, USA

Jossey-Bass, 989 Market Street, San Francisco, CA 94103-1741, USA

Wiley-VCH Verlag GmbH, Boschstr. 12, D-69469 Weinheim, Germany

John Wiley & Sons Australia Ltd, 42 McDougall Street, Milton, Queensland 4064, Australia

John Wiley & Sons (Asia) Pte Ltd, 2 Clementi Loop #02-01, Jin Xing Distripark, Singapore 129809

John Wiley & Sons Canada Ltd, 6045 Freemont Blvd, Mississauga, ONT, L5R 4J3

Wiley also publishes its books in a variety of electronic formats. Some content that appears in print
may not be available in electronic books.

Library of Congress Cataloging in Publication Data

Critical marketing : contemporary issues in marketing / edited by Mark Tadajewski
    and Douglas Brownlie.
        p.   cm.
    Includes bibliographical references and index.
    ISBN 978-0-470-51200-5 (cloth) — ISBN 978-0-470-51198-5 (pbk.)
    1. Marketing.   2. Green marketing.   3. Social marketing.   4. Consumer behavior.
    5. Marketing research.   I. Tadajewski, Mark.   II. Brownlie, Douglas T.
    HF5415.C72 2008
    658.8—dc22

                                                                            2007046841

British Library Cataloguing in Publication Data

A catalogue record for this book is available from the British Library

ISBN 978-0-470-51200-5 (H/B)
ISBN 978-0-470-51198-5 (P/B)

Typeset in 9/13pt Kunstler by Integra Software Services Pvt. Ltd, Pondicherry, India
Printed and bound in Great Britain by Antony Rowe Ltd, Chippenham, Wiltshire

For Ruth (from MT)

Contents

Acknowledgements   xi

Chapter 1   Critical Marketing: A Limit Attitude   1
            Mark Tadajewski and Douglas Brownlie

Chapter 2   Rethinking the Development of Marketing   29
            Mark Tadajewski and Douglas Brownlie

**Chapter 3   Prejudice V. Marketing? An Examination of some
            Historical Sources**   33
            Donald F. Dixon

**Chapter 4   Early Development of the Philosophy of Marketing
            Thought**   45
            D.G. Brian Jones and David D. Monieson

**Chapter 5   Consumer Sovereignty, Democracy, and the Marketing
            Concept: A Macromarketing Perspective**   67
            Donald F. Dixon

Chapter 6   Critical Reflections on Consumer Research   85
            Mark Tadajewski and Douglas Brownlie

**Chapter 7   Remembering Motivation Research: Toward an Alternative
            Genealogy of Interpretive Consumer Research**   91
            Mark Tadajewski

Chapter 8   Evolution, Biology and Consumer Research: What
              Darwin Knew that We've Forgotten   131
              Elizabeth C. Hirschman

Chapter 9   Ethnopsychology: A Return to Reason in Consumer
              Behaviour   157
              John O'Shaughnessy

Chapter 10   Marketing and Society   183
              Mark Tadajewski and Douglas Brownlie

Chapter 11   Marketing, the Consumer Society and Hedonism   187
              John O'Shaughnessy and Nicholas Jackson O'Shaughnessy

Chapter 12   Antiglobal Challenges to Marketing in Developing
              Countries: Exploring the Ideological Divide   211
              Terrence H. Witkowski

Chapter 13   On Negotiating the Market?   245
              Mark Tadajewski and Douglas Brownlie

Chapter 14   Sustainable Marketing   253
              Ynte K. van Dam and Paul A.C. Apeldoorn

Chapter 15   An Ecofeminist Analysis of Environmentally Sensitive
              Women Using Qualitative Methodology: The
              Emancipatory Potential of an Ecological Life   271
              Susan Dobscha and Julie L. Ozanne

Chapter 16   Past Postmodernism?   301
              Mark Tadajewski and Douglas Brownlie

Chapter 17   Introspection as Critical Marketing Thought, Critical
              Marketing Thought as Introspection   311
              Stephen J. Gould

Chapter 18   The Function of Cultural Studies in Marketing: A New
              Administrative Science?   329
              Adam Arvidsson

Chapter 19 **Thinking through Theory: Materialising the Oppositional Imagination**   345

Pauline Maclaran and Lorna Stevens

....

Chapter 20 **Postcolonialism and Marketing**   363

Gavin Jack

....

Index   385

....

Acknowledgements

I would like to acknowledge all of the authors that have contributed to the volume and also those with whom I have had discussions regarding critical marketing over the past year. Specifically, I would like to thank Barbara Stern, Craig Thompson, Pauline Maclaran, Stephen Brown, Brian Jones, Nick Ellis, Ming Lim, Matthew Higgins, James Fitchett, Gavin Jack, Stephen Dunne, Chris Hackley, Gibson Burrell, Martin Parker, Robert Tamilia, Daragh O' Reilly, Stan Shapiro and Terry Witkowski. Last, but not least, I would like to thank Sarah Booth, Anneli Mockett, Kim Stringer and Emma Cooper for the professionalism they have shown in helping Douglas and I put the critical marketing collection together.

Mark Tadajewski

I would like to thank Johan Arndt, Nik Dholakia, A.F. Firat, A. Venkatesh, Morris Holbrook and Robin Wensley for their inspiring work over the many years they have inadvertently contributed to the formation of the ideas that occupy my marketing imaginary.

Douglas Brownlie

1
Critical Marketing: A Limit Attitude

Mark Tadajewski[1] and Douglas Brownlie[2]

[1]*University of Leicester and* [2]*University of Stirling*

Introduction

As a practical exercise, marketing is concerned with meeting and satisfying customer needs, provided, that is, such an exercise would be profitable to the organisation. Satisfying customer needs, it is argued, forms the moral foundation of the marketing concept (Crane, 2000; Crane and Desmond, 2002; Kotler and Levy, 1969). However, even with marketing scholars signalling their 'customer focus' and commitment to customer satisfaction, since the 1960s there has been greater attention directed to the 'dark-side of marketing'. Rather than focusing on the beneficial aspects of the marketing system in ensuring the distribution of an ever widening assortment of goods and services, the ecological impact of marketing has garnered greater interest. By promoting goods and services, marketing is implicated in ecological despoliation and the stimulation of envy and consumer discontent (Richins, 1995). As Crane (2000: 13) correctly notes, marketing activities weigh upon the social environment in a variety of ways:

> . . . marketing activities can be seen to have further contributed to environmental deterioration through its reliance on enormous quantities of packaging, the creation of out-of-town shopping centres and the resource-sapping movement of consumer goods across the globe. The demands of the grocery and fast food industries for standardization and predictability in food products in the name of customer satisfaction has also led to myriad ecological problems associated with the use of agrochemicals, industrial pesticides and genetically modified crops

The importance of marketing activities, the continued enrolment of students on marketing courses in ever greater numbers and thus the diffusion of marketing discourse throughout society, means that marketing is a socially, politically and economically potent force in the world today (Hackley, 2003; Kangun, 1972; Laczniak and Michie, 1979).

In view of this power, it is an appropriate time to call attention to marketing theory and practice, revealing those background assumptions that pervade the discipline and the effects of marketing as a societal practice. Attention should be directed to highlighting how this discipline and practical endeavour have developed and continue to change. Such a project would be similar to the immanent criticism described by Theodor Adorno (1967), so that those values that the marketing student is exposed to through their 'mainstream' marketing education are illuminated for what they are, namely culturally and geographically contingent phenomena that should not be uncritically subscribed to or exported throughout the globe (Dholakia *et al.*, 1980).

But it would also go beyond Adorno's version of critique, perhaps in the direction of an 'intimate critique'. In the latter form of critique, marketing should be viewed from an appropriately historical dimension, with us all – as students and scholars – asking questions about the development of marketing, about whether it is developing in a way that we would like. This type of critique is about 'resisting resignation and accommodation to what is'. To be critical of marketing is not to be negative and dismissive of all that marketing activities have given to society (see also Shultz, 2007). Our vision of the relationship between marketing and critique is more affirmative. To be critical is to 'prevent the foreclosure of possibility, to keep the future of a different future open' (Kompridis, 2005: 340).

To take one example of the foreclosure of possibility – that is, the foreclosure of an alternative way of thinking about and engaging in marketing practice – we need only refer to the recent redefinitions of marketing. Before we touch upon this, a brief excursion into the history of marketing is necessary. Only then can we begin to sketch out more thoroughly what we mean by 'critical' marketing, illustrating this by reference to work that we think deserves this label. Let us begin.

Marketing as a Managerial Discourse

Even before the emergence of marketing as an academic discipline in the early twentieth century, marketing practitioners had articulated a managerialist agenda by focusing on business needs rather than, say, the detrimental effect of marketing on society (Coolsen, 1960/1978; Karlinsky, 1987; Tadajewski and Jones, 2008). In an important study, Coolsen documented the business activities and theoretical contributions of a number of nineteenth century economists who argued that business practitioners should produce and market those goods that consumers required in both domestic and international marketing contexts (i.e. the marketing concept[1]) (see also Dixon, Chapter 5; Jones and Richardson, 2007). This managerialist emphasis remains central to the identity of the discipline.

Yet, in the early twentieth century, marketing scholars also played socially activist roles, addressing issues beyond business concerns. Two of the earliest contributors to academic marketing thought, Henry Charles Taylor and Edward David Jones at the University of Wisconsin, demonstrated 'an explicit concern with ethics, sometimes manifested in social activism' (Jones, 1994: 70). Taylor, for example, was interested in what was called 'the marketing problem'. This related to the issue of whether middlemen were manipulating the prices for consumer goods, in this case, the prices obtained for farm products (i.e. the price received by the farmer was far less than the consumer paid). Highlighting his activist position, Taylor founded in 1917 'the American Association for Agricultural Legislation for the purposes of studying agricultural legislation and making recommendations on policy matters to government' (Jones, 1994: 76). The task of research conducted under the auspices of this association was to critically examine marketing legislation and issues related to producer and consumer protection, among others.

During the 1920s, this concern for the marketing problem was complemented by an interest in the 'consumer problem', that is, with improving marketing activities, in order to clear the market more effectively of the glut of consumer goods made available by the massive growth in production facilities following the First World War. The impact of this shift has been that since the turn of the twentieth century there has been increasing attention given to managerial issues such as improving marketing and consumer research (Frederick, 1959) and producing more effective advertising (Tipper et al., 1917), rather than concerted interest in distributive justice or other societal concerns, as Dixon illustrates in Chapter 5.

The social activist role that Jones and Taylor exhibited has continued to be espoused periodically throughout the past century. Of course, it would appear in different guises, some reinforcing and encouraging the stimulation of consumption, others not. Promoting higher levels of consumption in the 1950s, for instance, was believed to be desirable, as it was thought that this would strengthen the United States (US) economy and enable the US and free markets to triumph over state controlled production and consumption in Russia (Cheskin, 1960; Dichter, 1960). In the 1960s there was the 'broadening' of the boundaries of marketing to include nonprofit activities (Kotler and Levy, 1969; Laczniak and Michie, 1979). The 1970s witnessed the articulation of ecological marketing and in-depth research relating to the relationship between marketing, public policy and disadvantaged consumers (Kangun, 1972). By the 1980s the voluntary simplicity and green consumer movements began to rise to prominence.

Despite being buffeted by these movements in theory and practice marketing has, at the same time, undoubtedly become increasingly managerially-focused (Firat and Dholakia, 1982; Firat, 1985; Firat et al., 1987). Wilkie and Moore (2006) have done an admirable job of drawing out how the changing definition of marketing is circumscribing the issues that are of concern to scholars and practitioners. What they underscore is the progressive elimination of marketing and society related issues from the definition of marketing. Specifically, they note the definitions of marketing in the work of Arch Shaw, Wroe Alderson and Ralph Breyer, contrasting these with a recent American Marketing Association (AMA) definition. These authors each defined marketing in the following ways:

> (1) The accepted system of distribution was built up on the satisfying of staple needs ... this sort of activity has ... contributed to the progress of civilization; (2) Society can no more afford an ill-adjusted system of distribution than it can inefficient and wasteful methods of production; and (3) the middleman is a social necessity. (Shaw 1912: 708, 706, and 737)

> It is the responsibility of the marketing professor, therefore, to provide a marketing view of competition in order to guide efforts at regulation and to revitalize certain aspects of the science of economics ... For surely no one is better qualified to play a leading part in the consideration of measures designed for the regulation of competition. (Alderson 1937: 189, 190)

> Marketing is not primarily a means for garnering profits for individuals. It is, in the larger, more vital sense, an economic instrument used to accomplish indispensable social ends ... A marketing system designed solely for its social effectiveness would move goods with a minimum of time and effort to deficit points ... [and] provide a fair compensation, and no more, for the efforts of those engaged in the activity. At the same time it would provide the incentive needed to stimulate constant improvements in its methods. These are the prime requisites of social effectiveness (Breyer 1934: 192). (Wilkie and Moore, 2006: 225)

Wilkie and Moore note that from the first AMA definition outlined in 1935 which would be unmodified until 1985, only to change again in 2004, marketing has moved from being

> ... the performance of business activities that direct the flow of goods and services from producers to consumers. (1935) [To marketing as] the process of planning and executing the conception, pricing, promotion, and distribution of ideas, goods and services to create exchanges that satisfy individual and organizational objectives. (1985) [And most recently] Marketing is an organizational function and a set of processes for creating, communicating and delivering value to customers and for managing customer relationships in ways that benefit the organization and stakeholders. (Wilkie and Moore, 2006: 227)

There are a number of problems with this shifting definition of marketing as Moorman (1987) registers. Marketing, she proposes, has been reduced to the level of 'technique', that is, to the uncritical application of various methods, tools and ways of thinking in relation to marketing activities. 'Technique is results oriented' and this 'preoccupation with results fixates the performer on achieving the results to the near exclusion of recognizing other benefits and problems derived from the process itself' (Moorman, 1987: 194). Because of this results focus, 'technique is also amoral', as there is 'less of a concern with what is right', what is ethical, and 'more interest in what will work'. Connecting this with the historical development of marketing Moorman opines that the 1985 definition of marketing was one further step toward making marketing more like the amoral technique she describes.

She outlines her argument in a variety of ways. Firstly, given that marketing is depicted in the above definition as an organisational activity, it will be concerned with results (i.e. customer satisfaction, achieving organisational objectives etc.). This becomes problematic because 'marketers operate in an environment where there is an overwhelming emphasis on achieving results [which] may in fact lead them to neglect the consequences of their acts. Most important is the tendency to ignore the implications of results. Marketing practitioners have been criticized for this tendency by pursuing short-term results without considering the repercussions of such results on the environment' (Moorman, 1987: 198).

While marketing ethicists have been quick to outline sets of guidelines for ethical and socially responsible marketing, it is also often pointed out that pragmatic company level goals will work against ethical guidelines. Marketing managers, Laczniak and Murphy (2006) acknowledge, are responsible for ensuring the efficiency of marketing activities. They are likely to focus primarily on the managerial effectiveness of any given activity (i.e. will it get the job done quickly and effectively), rather than on its moral basis.

Desmond (1998) focuses on a significant issue here when he notes that as 'organisational actors' we are 'rarely faced directly with the consequences of our actions' (Desmond, 1998: 179). Thus, we are not faced with the child slave labour that has produced our highly priced, expensively marketed sports shoe. Nor do we witness the environmental waste discharged into a river as a result of the manufacturing process. As he puts it, once 'the face of the other has been "effaced", employees are freed from moral responsibility to focus on the technical (purpose centred or procedural) aspects of the "job at hand"' (Desmond, 1998: 178).

Putting this into marketing terms, macro questions about the impact of a firm's actions on society are likely to be neglected – as Wilkie and Moore (2006) and Moorman (1987) also suggest (cf. Bartkus and Glassman, forthcoming; Gaski, 1999; Thompson, 1995). Affirming Desmond's (1995, 1998) comments, Laczniak and Murphy maintain that,

> Not surprisingly, the pragmatics of company goals, as well as the defined job responsibilities of individual managers, directs the majority of marketing outcome evaluation toward micro (firm-level) practices . . . It is not so much that the consideration of ethics is actively opposed in organizations; rather, it is somewhat forgotten in the . . . quest to achieve economic and financial goals. (Laczniak and Murphy, 2006: 155)

So, what we see here is a shift in the definition of marketing so that it moves from being 'transferable to more aggregated issues such as competition, system performance, and contributions to human welfare' to a narrow focus on individual firm-based concerns (Wilkie and Moore, 2006: 227). Such a micro-level focus is not necessarily bad, although as Laczniak and Murphy (2006) indicate, it can have negative consequences. What is problematic is the fact that this definition of marketing serves to marginalise questions relating to the interaction between marketing and society beyond the proximate concerns of the firm. Marketing must be based on a 'larger conception' of its role in society (Tadajewski and Jones, 2008; Wilkie and Moore, 2006).

The AMA appears to have realised that their most recent definition bore a distinct managerial bias. In a recent communication via the ELMAR email distribution list (24th December, 2007), we are presented with an updated definition of marketing. It reads: 'Marketing is the activity, set of institutions, and processes for creating, communicating, delivering, and exchanging offerings that have value for customers, clients, partners, and society at large' (Lib, 2007).

To be charitable, the new definition is a first move in the right direction. It might not signal the complete rethinking of the role of marketing in society that some might like, and the 'devil is certainly in the details' regarding how this definition is enacted in practice (Witkowski, 2005). But, in the interests of critical reflection, let us pose some questions that we hope students and scholars alike will bear in mind while reading this book. Firstly, to what extent is the definition window-dressing for the academy in the face of the vociferous criticism found in recent issues of the *Journal of Public Policy and Marketing*? Only time will tell. But, if the definition functions in the same way as corporate codes of ethics, that is, in terms of providing an ethical salve for our conscience, while we continue with business as usual, we might rightly be cautious in heralding this definition as indicative of a greater macro emphasis in marketing.

In addition, we all operate – much like the marketing practitioners discussed earlier – in a specific intellectual and cultural climate. The new definition of marketing will be of little use if it does not fundamentally alter the moral and ethical compass of the academy. This, in itself, is unlikely to happen. As Shapiro has remarked, an intellectual focus on the relationship between marketing and society has 'been and today remains a relatively neglected domain of marketing' (Shapiro, 2006: 250). The reason why is that 'prevailing opinion seems to be that managerial, behavioral, and methodological concerns and courses have dominated academic marketing for a number of decades and will continue to do so for the foreseeable future' (Shapiro, 2006: 250). This focus continues to be reflected in the Marketing Science Institute's research priorities which make no mention of societal related issues (see http://www.msi.org/research/index.cm?id=43). We wonder how soon these will change to better reflect the new definition of marketing?

To be sure, there are alternative readings of the history and future of marketing that could, it might be claimed, suggest that marketers are less technique oriented and more socially responsible. The emergence of the social, societal and ecological marketing concepts in the 1960s, 1970s and 1980s would figure prominently here. The so-called 'broadening' of the marketing concept in the form of 'social marketing' was one response by scholars to make marketing relevant in a social climate that was beginning to register the detrimental effect of marketing activities on society (Andreasen, 2003; Kotler, 2005). But before we uncritically valorise social marketing, positioning it as part of any critical marketing project as some have done (e.g. Hastings and Saren, 2003), let us look at social marketing more closely.

Critical Social Marketing?

Recently redefined as 'the adaptation of commercial marketing technologies to programs designed to influence the voluntary behavior of target audiences to improve their personal welfare and that of the society of which they are a part', social marketing is currently prominent in research and teaching agendas (Andreasen, 1994: 110). The characteristics of social marketing programmes consist of the application of 'commercial marketing technology', 'have as its bottom line the influencing of voluntary behavior' and 'primarily seek to benefit individuals/families or the broader society and not the marketing organization itself' (Andreasen, 1994: 112).

Understandably, social marketing has received government and non-governmental support across the world (Andreasen, 2003). To assume that the positive benefits of social marketing are actually translated into practice is, however, a mistake. Certainly, while there are papers that register some of the difficulties associated with using commercial marketing theory in social marketing studies (e.g. Bloom and Novelli, 1979), social marketing is usually depicted in positive terms (Dholakia and Dholakia, 2001), sometimes for perfectly valid reasons (Witkowski, 2005). By contrast, Moorman (1987) sees the emergence of social marketing as a further augmentation of marketing as 'technique', bringing behavioural and social change into the purview of marketing practitioners.

If social marketing was to be part of the critical marketing project that Hastings and Saren (2003) and Hastings (2007) appear to think it is, we would expect social marketers to exhibit some degree of reflexivity about their presuppositions and regarding the limitations of social marketing (Brenkert, 2002; Brownlie, 2006). The fact that the aforementioned scholars exhibit little reflexivity regarding the ideology that social marketing surrounds itself with, failing to juxtapose this against societal reality is uncritical by its very nature.

Outside of the marketing literature we find a less positive representation of social marketing (although cf. Dholakia, 1984). In an important work, James Pfeiffer has detailed the complex interrelationships between condom social marketing in Sub-Saharan Africa and structural adjustment programmes. He notes how the 'diffusion' of social marketing practices across the globe are not, in fact, 'driven by a thoroughly demonstrated efficacy in improving health by motivating behavior change' (Pfeiffer, 2004: 77).

Social marketing (SM) campaigns, he claims, are rarely independently evaluated. More specifically, 'the widespread embrace of SM by many international nongovernment organizations (NGOs) and ministries, especially in Africa, can be traced more directly to the promotion of privitization and free-market economics in the era of structural adjust-ment across the region' (Pfeiffer, 2004: 78). Social marketing is not, therefore, simply a neutral tool to promote behavioural change, but in Africa fundamentally tied to neolib-eral economic policies. According to Pfeiffer, historically the support of social marketing in Africa has been linked with institutions (i.e. The World Bank) promoting structural adjustment programmes that require governments to reduce their levels of spending on public services. In Africa, 'this rollback in public service has coincided with the deepening AIDS crisis' (Pfeiffer, 2004: 78). It was in this context that the benefits of social marketing were touted by Western nongovernmental organisations who arrived with 'a prepackaged approach to AIDS prevention that could be easily integrated into ongoing economic reform programs that emphasized "cost-effectiveness" as the bottom line for priority setting in health' (Pfeiffer, 2004: 78).

In particular, Pfeiffer notes how the social marketing campaign he studied (which aimed to promote the use of condoms) was interpreted by the target audience and other stake-holders (i.e. church pastors) as 'promoting promiscuity'. By contrast to the argument that social marketing programmes should begin with extensive consumer and market research (Andreasen, 1994), the marketers in this case neglected to examine their target market in sufficient detail. Church pastors who were influential in the backlash against the marketing programme 'spoke angrily of the campaign that they believe has helped contribute to the AIDS crisis. This clash of messages illustrates how SM approaches to changing behaviours as complex and socially volatile as sexuality may not only be ineffective, but may actu-ally be harmful, because genuine community participation, dialogue, and monitoring are excluded from the process, while structural determinants and social context of "high-risk" behaviors are left unaddressed' (Pfeiffer, 2004: 79).

In this case, no real attempt was made to determine how community relations could be fostered, and this was ultimately harmful both to community–social marketer relations but also in terms of encouraging the socially beneficial behaviours that form the axiology of social marketing (see BBC News, 2007). Is social marketing, therefore, morally neutral or of a higher moral order than traditional marketing, as Hastings (2003) appears to gesture? We would suspect that a response to this depends on which side of the fence one sits.

Social marketers would, by and large, support Hastings' view. But even here we are faced with some equivocation. As Lusch *et al.* (1980) note, there are certain areas where social marketing might be considered more ethical than others (see also Laczniak and Michie, 1979). From their survey of professors of ethics, social-psychology academics and marketing practitioners they concluded that marketing 'techniques applied to areas like conservation, preventative health, and auto safety were generally perceived to be much more ethical than were applications to homosexual rights, political candidates and their platforms, and pornographic entertainment' (Lusch *et al.*, 1980: 161).

Lusch *et al.* raise a number of key questions such as 'who is the villain when ethic-ally sensitive issues are promoted or marketed? Are marketers *or* those that hire them to promote the issues to blame? Those on the side of the marketers might argue that social marketing techniques are merely *tools* which, when used properly, can aid effective communication or when misused, can compound social abuse' (Lusch *et al.*, 1980: 162; emphases in original). Consumer advocates would, they indicate, approach the issue differently, arguing that the marketers should take at least 'partial responsibility for the impact of any social marketing program or idea which has been professionally marketed' (Lusch *et al.*, 1980: 163).

Pfeiffer's (2004) work clearly indicates how the rhetoric of social marketing is not consistent with its actual enactment in the field. The point of Lusch *et al.*'s work for this discussion is that it highlights how essential it is that uncomfortable questions such as these do get raised. It is equally crucial that we continue to question the changing boundaries of the definition of marketing, scrutinising which issues are subsequently marginalised as a result. Critique *of* marketing theory and practice should, we believe, take the form of a readiness to ask such difficult questions. It is, to paraphrase Kompridis (2005), a continual process of revealing unquestioned assumptions and of re-evaluating the values that marketing is founded upon. In the next section, we want to examine this proposal in more detail.

Critical Marketing is . . .

Let us start to flesh out what the label 'critical marketing' might actually refer to. In management disciplines over the last thirty years there has been a surge of interest in 'critical' approaches (e.g. Burrell and Morgan, 1979/1992; Clegg and Dunkerley, 1980). The publication of Alvesson and Willmott's (1992) collection, *Critical Management Studies*, is believed to have heralded the explicit branding of a diverse range of scholars, subscribing to a range of critical positions under one label (Fournier and Grey, 2000). It might be expected that critical marketing would be closely affiliated with this area of scholarship. This would be largely correct.

Assuming this connection, what then is critical marketing? Following the articulation of critical management by Fournier and Grey (2000), the grammar of critical marketing could bear the hallmarks of theoretical pluralism, methodological pluralism and boundaries delineated by a commitment on three fronts: ontological denaturalisation, epistemological reflexivity and a non-performative stance (Brownlie, 2006; Dholakia *et al.*, 1980; Firat *et al.*, 1987; Monieson, 1981; O'Shaughnessy and O'Shaughnessy, 2002; Parker, 1995; Whittle and Spicer, 2008). What this latter criterion signals is that critical marketing research is not undertaken with the *sole* interest of developing knowledge to enable marketing managers to maximise the sales of goods or services with minimal expenditure (i.e. non-performative).

This non-performative criterion is shared to some extent with those involved with 'Consumer Culture Theoretics' (CCT) (Arnould and Thompson, 2007) – except that there appears to be more of a concern for managerial relevance in this area than we would support (e.g. Arnould and Thompson, 2005: 869, 870, 876; Thompson *et al.*, 2006). But, then, to assume that any critical marketing research could never be co-opted or not necessarily used in a beneficial manner by any stakeholder is, nonetheless, too strong a position to hold. We would add, though, that the very definition of 'beneficial', and to whose benefit such knowledge was being invoked, should be subject to critical scrutiny.

What we do have concerns about is the overriding profit motive adopted by many companies which can be detrimental to the interests of society. As Kilbourne (2002) has remarked, there are other goals in life that marketers should foster and which the market often does not (Hudson and Hudson, 2003). Broadly speaking, these include human solidarity, distributive 'justice, community, [and] human development, [and] ecological balance' and these 'should be brought to bear on the governance of economic activity. We are fundamentally critical of the notion that the pursuit of profit will automatically satisfy these broader goals' (Adler, 2002: 387) – as the comments by Desmond (1995, 1998), Jacques *et al.* (2003), Moorman (1987), Thompson (2004) and Laczniak and Murphy (2006) testify.

Continuing through Fournier and Grey's (2000) criteria, ontological denaturalisation involves the recognition that the way our 'consumer society' is structured is not an inevitable historical development; it is a very specific event and could be rethought of along different lines. In this case, critical marketing asserts the prevalence of power relations structuring reality, knowledge and human interests that determine how we view the role of marketing in society and whether or not it is possible to envision an alternative structure of market relations. Critical marketing would thus attempt to question the extent to which specific claims made in support of marketing practice affect society.

Finally, critical marketing scholarship should exhibit a degree of reflexivity. It should refuse the positivist idealisation that reality can be apprehended via the hypothetico-deductive method, and that this somehow allows us to determine THE true perspective. Science is invariably political and our own views influence the knowledge produced. Of course, these three criteria are clearly going to continue to develop (Whittle and Spicer, forthcoming) and at this point most marketing scholarship cannot be considered critical, if by critical it must meet all three of the above criteria. There are, nonetheless, multiple lines of research, across a diverse range of paradigmatic perspectives that do exhibit elements of the qualities that Fournier and Grey (2000) gesture toward.

Registering the much slower speed that critical approaches have diffused through marketing scholarship (Burton, 2001; McDonagh, 1995) and the 'easy complacency of mainstream thought on a variety of marketing topics' that the contributors to the edited collections, *Changing the Course of Marketing: Alternative Paradigms for Widening Marketing Theory* (Dholakia and Arndt, 1985), *Philosophical and Radical Thought in Marketing* (Firat *et al.*, 1987) and the *Rethinking Marketing* conference in the early 1990s diagnosed (e.g. Brownlie *et al.*, 1999: 4), we prefer to depart from Fournier and Grey's

(2000) work. It is a useful introduction to what a critical marketing studies approach could take, but at this point the practice of critique in critical marketing studies is united more by a problematising style of thinking and reflection and the adoption of a 'limit attitude', as we shall see (Healy, 2001).

Critical Theory and Marketing: Back to the 1940s

Scholarship that we believe constitutes the basis of 'critical marketing studies' is, for us, underscored by the question 'to what extent it might be possible to think differently, instead of legitimating what is already known?' (Foucault, 1992: 9). This is an attempt to adopt a 'limit attitude' towards marketing. It is not a simple rejection of all marketing theory and practice per se. Rather it involves an attempt to probe the limits of what marketing currently stands for as an intellectual and practical endeavour.[2] As Foucault (1984: 45) puts it, 'Criticism . . . consists of analyzing and reflecting on limits'.

Now, of course, this can be interpreted as a fairly traditional form of critique, as when a logical empiricist reflects on the limits of a specific theory. The perspectives we list below can be differentiated from the 'received view' of knowledge production in marketing by the explicit oppositional stance that they take to 'mainstream' marketing theory and practice and by the use of critical social theory in some form. The range of literature that we reference is only indicative of critical perspectives in marketing, but should provide enough of an outline to destabilise the idea that marketing is as woefully bereft of engagement with critical perspectives as Alvesson (1994) and Alvesson and Willmott (1996) opine (see Tadajewski and Maclaran, 2009a, 2009b, 2009c).

Marketing and Critical Theory in the 1940s

Marketing has actually been 'critical', if we mean critical in the sense of the Frankfurt School version of 'unmasking critique' (e.g. Adorno and Becker, 1999: 23), for quite some time. As early as 1941 the work of the critical theorists was described via the use of a number of marketing examples by Paul Lazarsfeld (1941). In this paper, Lazarsfeld contrasted administrative and critical communications research. Administrative research was research conducted for some public or private group and whose overriding emphasis was usually on solving problems relating to business activities. The majority of research, he suggested, fell into this category. By contrast, Lazarsfeld argued that critical research can be distinguished from administrative research in two key ways. Critical research 'develops a theory of prevailing social trends of our times . . . and it seems to imply ideas of basic human values according to which all actual or desired effects should be appraised' (Lazarsfeld, 1941: 9).

Using a number of examples, Lazarsfeld proposed that from a critical perspective 'our times are engulfed by a multitude of promotional patterns . . . coupled with the feeling that human beings, as a result, behave more and more like pawns on a chessboard, losing the spontaneity and dignity which is the basic characteristic of human personality' (Lazarsfeld, 1941: 10). In outlining an example of the way in which what has varyingly been called the 'promotional culture' (Lazarsfeld, 1941), 'consciousness industry' (Klein and Leiss, 1978), 'culture industries' (Horkheimer and Adorno, 2002) and 'distraction factories' (Kracauer, 1989) shape our perception, Lazarsfeld draws upon an example sketched by Theodor Adorno. Imagine, says Lazarsfeld,

> . . . you find a large brewery advertises its beer by showing a man disgustedly throwing aside a newspaper full of European war horrors while the caption says that in times like these the only place to find peace, strength, and courage is at your own fireside drinking beer. What will be the result if symbols referring to such basic human wants as that for peace become falsified into expressions of private comfort and are rendered habitual to millions of magazine readers as merchandising slogans? Why should people settle their social problems by action and sacrifice if they can serve the same ends by drinking a new brand of beer? To the casual observer the advertisement is nothing but a more or less clever sales trick. From the aspect of a more critical analysis, it becomes a dangerous sign of what a promotional culture might end up with. (Lazarsfeld, 1941: 11)

In concluding this early paper, Lazarsfeld called for studies that attempt to leverage the benefits of administrative and critical approaches, while at the same time registering that the introduction of critical approaches might not be easy. We should, nonetheless, 'learn to be hospitable to criticism and find forms in which more patience can be exercised to wait and, in the end, to see what is constructive and what is not' (Lazarsfeld, 1941: 14).

Moving closer to the present, as a critique of business marketing in the 1960s and 1970s we could turn to 'reconstructionist' marketing scholars, as these come close to adopting a limit attitude in the sense discussed above. The two other categories that Arnold and Fisher (1996) detail are, by contrast, the apologists who refused to listen to any critique of marketing as contributing to social ills, preferring instead to emphasise the economic benefits of marketing activities and the social marketers who exhibited little tension in using marketing tools and techniques to promote social behavioural change. In the case of the social marketers, Arnold and Fisher write, 'These scholars placed less emphasis than the reconstructionists on redefining the nature of marketing, which they viewed as primarily a management technology' (Arnold and Fisher, 1996: 126).

Diverging from the above two groups, the reconstructionists sought to rethink marketing activities and core marketing values in light of the 'social concerns for the general welfare of society, the consequences of ecological ambivalence, [and] the awareness of ethical dimensions of resource-use decisions' (Arnold and Fisher, 1996: 130). It was this group that attempted to provide a 'thoroughgoing critique or reconceptualization of the fundamental nature of marketing', registering the charges that marketing promoted materialism and environmental despoliation.

This form of critique still remains limited. The reconstructionists, in the form of Kotler and Levy (1969) among others, still remain within what Kilbourne *et al.* in their discussion of 'critical macromarketing' have called the dominant social paradigm. This refers to 'a society's belief structure that organizes the way people perceive and interpret the functioning of the world around them' (Kilbourne *et al.*, 1997: 4). Central to the dominant social paradigm in Western economies is an ideology of consumption, a faith in technology to avert environmental destruction, support for liberal democracy, defence of private property ownership, free markets and limited government intervention in the economy (Kilbourne *et al.*, 2002). What Kilbourne *et al.* (1997) mean when they refer to an ideology of consumption is that people view their quality of life in terms of their ability to consume ever greater quantities of goods. In other words, they are materialistic in orientation.

According to Spratlen (1972) the broadening of the concept of marketing does not actually involve any substantive change in marketing's relationship to society. Social costs, 'externalities, conservation in the use of resources, and other "macro," environmental and humanistic concerns' are still marginalised (Spratlen, 1972: 405). Instead, he calls for marketing to take a humanistic turn, balancing managerial, technical interests with 'greater humaneness (passionate concern for life-enriching qualities), responsibility (acceptance of obligations imposed by [the] consequences of marketing decisions), and rationality (openness to examination, experimentation and change in order to gain new insights in marketing thought and action)' (Spratlen, 1972: 408).

By contrast, more explicitly critical orientations attempt to deposition any exclusive focus on a managerial orientation, along with the usual 'positivistic' emphasis on predicting and controlling consumer behaviour, while attempting, at the same time, to move beyond the dominant social paradigm (e.g. Dholakia and Firat, 1980; Firat 1985; Hetrick and Lozada, 1999; Holbrook, 1985; Monieson, 1981). Given that the critical theory associated with the Frankfurt School is most often mentioned in connection with this form of critical reflection on marketing, it is appropriate to briefly consider what exactly critical theory refers to using Horkheimer's classic position piece.

Critical Theory

As Horkheimer (1972) would see it, the task of a critical theory is to scrutinise present reality indicating, for example, how industrial production does not necessarily serve the interests of the majority. This would thereby problematise the equality of exchange relationships that form the ideological basis of the capitalist system (and, in turn, marketing), highlighting how these serve the profit interests of a small minority whose interests continue to be reaffirmed by property relations. As Horkheimer (1972: 207) puts it,

> The aim of this activity is not simply to eliminate one or another abuse, for it regards such abuses as necessarily connected with the way in which the social structure is organized. Although it itself emerges from the social structure, its purpose is not, either in conscious intention or in its objective significance, the better functioning of any element in the structure. On the contrary it is suspicious of the very categories of better, useful, appropriate, productive, and valuable, as these are understood in the present order, and refuses to take them as nonscientific presuppositions about which one can do nothing.

While there have been a number of studies that aimed to promote the use of critical theory in marketing (Burton, 2001, 2003; Hetrick and Lozada, 1994; Hudson and Ozanne, 1988; Kilbourne, 1992, 1995, 2002; Morgan, 1992, 2003; Murray and Ozanne, 1991; Rogers, 1987), it remains the case that this paradigm continues to be under-utilised by the marketing academy. One reason given for this is that consumer researchers were interested in producing research that was 'fun' rather than being intent on 'making the world better' (Kernan, 1995: 553).

Broadly speaking, research inspired by critical theory assumes that social reality is socially manufactured, but asserts that individual consciousness is dominated and subservient to ideological superstructures. Critique in this case functions in 'unmasking' inequalities in exchange relationships (Horkheimer, 1972), questioning the privileging of 'having', that is consuming, over 'being' and relatedness to the world (Fromm, 1976/2007), scrutinising the role of marketing and advertising in the repression of individuality and the expansiveness of human existence (Adorno, 1989; Horkheimer and Adorno, 2002; Marcuse, 1964/1972), highlighting the importance of advertising and marketing as socialisation agents and drawing implications for public policy from this (Klein and Leiss, 1978; Leiss, 1983), developing a critical theory of needs (Leiss, 1978), critiquing the emergence of the marketing character and the failure to articulate humanist alternatives (Fromm, 1976/2007, 1998) and more generally in providing an extensive critical analysis of science, truth and objectivity (Habermas, 1968/1987, 1990; Horkheimer, 1947/2004). The ultimate goal of critique in this sense was to fuel positive social transformation (Leiss, 1978; Marcuse, 1964/1972).

Critical Marketing Thought

Taking a somewhat similar approach to that of the critical theorists Firat, Venkatesh and Dholakia have been central contributors to the development of critical marketing. As Firat (1985) noted some time ago, critique is beneficial for the discipline. Self-criticism of marketing and consumer research will, he argues, 'contribute to the discipline's growth' (Firat, 1985: 3). Nonetheless, marketing, Firat and Dholakia stressed, lacked a critical perspective. The implication of this was that any analysis of 'marketing phenomena has stopped at those explanatory boundaries which represent the ideologically accepted limits of knowledge. Probes into the dominant values, ideologies, worldviews, and institutions affecting marketing are conspicuous by their absence' (Firat and Dholakia, 1982: 14). Continuing in this vein they suggest: 'An analytical and critical understanding of the marketing system may open new and provocative avenues in the study of the human condition' (Firat and Dholakia, 1982: 14).

Marketing and consumer research, they maintain, uncritically supports the existing structure of consumption, serves 'techno-managerial' interests and focuses on consumer behaviour 'only when the consumer enters a buying situation in the market'. In addition, they assert that marketing scholarship reifies certain concepts such as consumer 'needs', rather than subjecting them to critical scrutiny. What this means in practice is that the category of the 'consumer' (Arnould and Thompson, 2005), a concept like consumer 'needs' (Firat, 1985; Leiss, 1978), an assumption such as 'consumer choice' (Dholakia and Dholakia, 1985) or specific consumption imagery (Holt, 2003) should be scrutinised much like concepts of 'freedom' (Horkheimer, 1966), 'static and dynamic' (Adorno, 1961) and 'revolution' (Marcuse, 1968) were analysed by the critical theorists.

To take one example, Firat notes that an individual is typically represented in mainstream marketing texts as a *homo-consumicus*, whose needs are depicted as innate to human nature (Firat, 1985; see Jones and Monieson, 1990: 110). The problem with this view is clearly that if all human needs are innate to the individual then what is the role of marketing in society? It would surely relegate marketers to simply identifying consumer needs and then producing the requisite products commensurate with these requirements (O'Shaughnessy and O'Shaughnessy, 2002). Marketing, arguably, functions more as a 'facilitator of consumcrism' (O'Shaughnessy and O'Shaughnessy, 2007).

On a more critical note, Firat diagnoses a clear omission in such a conceptualisation of the consumer. There is, he adds, little mention of how certain consumption patterns (e.g. the use of private-transportation) in society are structured by interconnected choices made at the political level (i.e. lobbying by business interests), 'at the level of production (what to produce), distribution (how to allocate the products within society), information dissemination (how is the existence of products going to be communicated?), and pricing (at what cost will the exchange take place?)' (Firat, 1977: 291).

This concentration on the individual consumer thereby ignores the more aggregate structures that influence consumption. More macro-level consumption research is thus desirable which would incorporate 'discussion of the social and cultural determinants of individual psychology', for instance (Leiss, 1978: 43). Pointing in this direction, Firat argues that other disciplines such as anthropology and sociology develop macro-theories that present a 'system perspective for the phenomenon in its entirety', and use these as the basis for developing micro-theories consistent with those developed by scholars schooled in the interpretive research tradition. Lears (1985) is even more critical of research that focuses on individual consumption behaviour. He, like Leiss (1978) and Klein and Leiss (1978), calls for studies that 'target the systemic features of consumer culture – the pressures organized to promote a way of life characterized by getting and spending, at the expense of human and natural resources, for the primary benefit of a managerial elite'.

Despite the fact that critical approaches to marketing and consumer research still remain marginal, the clarion calls for critical approaches are easily discernible. There are scholars who explicitly assert the value of critical marketing (Benton, 1985; Desmond, 1995; Firat and Dholakia, 1982; Hansen, 1981; Monieson, 1988), critical consumer research (Belk, 1995; Dholakia and Firat, 1980), critical macromarketing (Kilbourne *et al.*, 1997), structuration-ideology analysis (Schneiderman, 1998; Williamson, 1978), analyses of consumer culture that draw upon rhetorical, iconographic and cultural-historical approaches (Lears, 1985), critical hermeneutics (Arnold and Fischer, 1994), Marxist and feminist critiques of consumer research (Hirschman, 1993), Liberal feminism, women's voice/experience feminism, poststructuralist feminism and consumer research (Bristor and Fischer, 1993), critical ecofeminism (Dobscha and Ozanne, 2001), feminist poststructuralist critiques of exchange relationships (Fischer and Bristor, 1994), feminist reflection on the problems raised by the incorporation of feminist theory in consumer research (Bristor and Fischer, 1995) and calls for a return to materialist feminism (Catterall *et al.*, 2005).

The range of critical perspectives that have been used to examine marketing phenomena also include Marxist critiques of advertising (Lee and Murray, 1995), Post-Marxist perspectives on green marketing (Prothero and Fitchett, 2000), autonomist Marxist interpretations of branding (Arvidsson, 2005), Postmodern Marxist interpretations of consumer behaviour (Pietrykowski, 2007), dialectical and negation critiques of the structuring of consumer behaviour (Dholakia and Firat, 1980), Foucauldian consumption studies (Humphreys, 2006; Rosengarten, 2004; Shankar *et al.*, 2006), Foucauldian non-consumption studies (Moisander and Personen, 2002), Foucauldian histories of marketing thought (Tadajewski, 2006a, 2006b), Bachelardian consumption studies (Lane, 2006), literary-critical interpretations of marketing theory (Stern, 1990), deconstruction and consumer research (Stern, 1996; Thompson, 1993), radical deconstruction and economic development (Joy and Ross, 1989), poststructuralist consumer research (Thompson and Hirschman, 1995), explications of the evolution of critical theory (Poster and Venkatesh, 1987), critical theory and marketing education (Benton, 1985), critical theoretical interpretations of consumer behaviour (Alvesson, 1994; Burton, 2002; Hetrick and Lozada, 1994; Klein and Leiss, 1978; Leiss, 1978; Murray and Ozanne, 1991, 2006; Ozanne and Murray, 1995; Rogers, 1987; Schipper, 2002; Shankar and Fitchett, 2002; Varman and Vikas, 2007; Vikas and Varman, 2007; Wright and Shapiro, 1992),

Habermasian interpretations of marketing ethics (Nill, 2003; Nill and Schultz, 1997) and critical theoretic examinations of consumer research (Murray and Ozanne, 1997) to name but a few.

'The value of radical approaches', suggest Joy and Ross (1989: 27), is that 'they allow us to question and challenge the very premises and assumptions of marketing, as well as explore other alternatives for generating new ideas'. Again, Firat (1988a) has examined the place of marketing in capitalist society and the way in which certain features of marketing discourse work to structure and delimit consumption options (see also Klein and Leiss, 1978; Leiss, 1978). Taking the concept of consumer 'need' he works through a careful analysis that destabilises existing conceptualisations of need in society by showing how what is needed is structured by 'ecological, cultural and historical human experience'.

One simple example used by Firat will suffice to provide a flavour of his work in this area. He suggests that we reflect on the nature of movement in advanced industrial society. Moving from one city to another, he asserts, reveals certain structural features that delimit possible life choices – a so-called 'political economy of social choice' (Dholakia *et al.*, 1980: 28). Using a sample of three communities in the US, he writes, 'public transportation is either nonexistent or thoroughly inadequate. Consequently, this consumer unit is left with little choice but to buy a car' (Firat, 1988b: 290). There may be other options for the consumer in this example but these carry certain social, psychological and economic costs that are ameliorated by the use of a car. Is the ownership of a car in this example a real, authentic need or is it an indulgence, an irrational need that does not really require satisfaction, Firat rhetorically asks? No. Where the behaviours of consumers are so constrained by systemic logic it makes little 'sense to call such behaviour irrational', at an individual level.

What does make sense, he avows, is that marketing scholars continue to examine the way that the market system has come to be structured in the manner that it appears and the role that marketers play in reproducing the systemic logic that delimits the life choices that consumers can make. Firat writes, 'we need to seek to understand how phenomena interacted historically to produce the present conditions that surround us' (Firat, 1988a: 102). Only then can marketing scholars contribute to thinking about how marketing could work otherwise, and what interests we may want to promote over those of capital reproduction that the dominant managerialist emphasis at present supports (Firat, 1988a, 1988b).

If we are to pull two key arguments from the foregoing discussion, what we must register is that the interaction between individual consumer life choices and social, political and economic forces will invariably be complex and should not be judged positively or negatively on an *a priori* basis. The most useful way we can approach consumer behaviour and the marketing system therefore, would be from a postmoralist position. By this we mean that, as students and researchers, we should not celebrate consumer culture in an uncritical fashion (Schudson, 2007), but examine it critically, identifying its benefits and costs.

So, to summarise our position: we do not think that marketing theory and practice will cohere into a critical marketing 'theory' (Burton, 2001). The commonality that we perceive amongst the diverse range of perspectives gestured toward above is that they take critical perspectives on marketing to involve a continual effort to question the self-evidences that are concretised as the boundaries of marketing or as 'appropriate' contributions to marketing thought. Connected with this, is the recognition of the historicity of marketing theory and practice. Critical marketing cannot thus be equated with one brand of critical thought. It is better conceived in terms of an 'ethos' or an 'attitude'. We think of it as a 'critique of what we are' which is 'at one and the same time the historical analysis of the limits that are imposed on us and an experiment with the possibility of going beyond them' (Foucault, 1984: 50).

Each of the various approaches above has attempted to do this in some way and each would articulate their own way of critically engaging with marketing. To avoid closing down the boundaries of what critical marketing might be, we would venture that to be engaged in 'critical marketing' is to explicitly question hegemonic modes of thought wherever they appear, even if they emerge from scholars interested in critical marketing. Offering alternative views that explicitly question authorities of any kind will not be easy. Even so, it should be done. As Said (1996) argues, the function of the intellectual in our society is to dare to speak the truth to power, even though this might lead to criticism of the individual commentator (see also Foucault, 2001).

Critical Marketing as an Emancipatory Social Science?

It is probably a little early to argue that critical marketing could contribute to emancipation, if by emancipation we are going to describe a programme that points out the kinds of changes needed in market economies in order to eliminate oppression and exploitation. We would hope that critical marketing and transformative consumer research would have a part to play in moving society towards a state where the minority do not have to subsidise their lifestyles by means of the exploitation of the majority. We are only beginning to develop a sense of how the critical marketing agenda has started to be conceived. Currently, it would be fair to say that it is at stage one of Erik Olin Wright's (2006) sketch of the tasks of an emancipatory social science. These entail: 'first, to elaborate a systematic diagnosis and critique of the world as it exists; second, to envisage viable alternatives; and third, to understand the obstacles, possibilities and dilemmas of transformation' (Wright, 2006: 94).

Fleshing this out further, an emancipatory oriented critical marketing will begin by diagnosing what is wrong with the present conception of marketing and what we would need to do to rectify this. It then provides a critique of the relationship between marketing and society and why we need to reconfigure this beyond the boundaries of the existing social paradigm – not within it. To be able to reconfigure the marketing system, we would need a number of 'viable alternatives' for the reconstruction of the marketing–society relationship. Finally we require a 'theory of transformation that tells us how to get from here [the present status quo] to there a viable, sustainable world' (Wright, 2006: 99). Critical marketing cannot, realistically, hope to accomplish all of these steps without moving beyond the disciplinary boundaries of marketing and consumer research.

There will need to be a concerted effort by scholars to move beyond their disciplinary comfort zones to develop the solutions to the problems that continue to plague society and for which marketing is partly responsible. Here critical marketing scholars could work productively with those involved with the 'Real Utopias Project' in economics. This group of interdisciplinary scholars aims to question the extent to which the market can be supplemented or supplanted with alternative ways of organising exchanges between people. The Real Utopias Project aims to stimulate 'serious discussion of radical alternatives to existing institutions. The objective is to focus on specific proposals for the fundamental redesign of basic social institutions rather than on vague, abstract practices' (Wright, 1998: x). It aims to offer specific guidelines about how markets and property relations could be recast, in order to foster more egalitarian relations between people. Marketing, surely, has some role to play here. Whether scholars take up this call, only time will tell; emancipation for critical marketing will remain, nonetheless, never a final end in itself. It, like any critical marketing project, is 'an ongoing process' (Brownlie, 2006).

Conclusion

In this chapter we have attempted to indicate our interpretation of what constitutes critical marketing. While we appreciate the value of the criteria that Fournier and Grey (2000) sketched out for critical management studies, at this stage much of the critical literature in marketing would not cohere completely with the standards they articulate. This is not to say that marketing does not have a substantial body of critical marketing scholarship, far from it.

In writing this chapter and producing this book we would like to think that individuals of any philosophical or political persuasion will be willing to feed off the ideas generated by scholars with different paradigmatic viewpoints to their own (Arnould and Thompson, 2005). This said, rather than assuming that marketing theory will end up at some consensus position, we should acknowledge that there will always be a certain degree of antagonism between people with diverse research and practical interests.

If we are serious about pluralism in marketing – and scholars from across the discipline seem to indicate that they are – we can expect nothing less. As Chantal Mouffe has argued, 'one cannot take seriously the existence of a plurality of values without recognizing they will conflict. And this conflict cannot be visualized merely in terms of competing interests that could be adjudicated or accommodated without any form of violence. Many conflicts are antagonistic because they take place among conflicting interpretations of the ethico-political values embodied in liberal democratic institutions' (Mouffe, 1996: 8). As the democratic process will never run smoothly without dispute, we cannot ever expect marketing theory or practice to do so either. And it is for this reason that the field of critical marketing can never be easily defined, as some would like to do (e.g. Saren *et al.*, 2007).

Notes

1. The reader is probably horrified that such a mistake could be made so early on in the collection. The usual gesture here would be to point to the case of the Pillsbury Company (e.g. Keith, 1960) and their turn to the marketing concept in the 1950s and argue as Vargo and Lusch (2004) and Vargo and Morgan (2005) incorrectly do, that the marketing concept and marketing management functions appear during this period. The idea that the marketing concept emerges in the 1950s is completely incorrect. Close readers of the work of Borsch (1958) or especially McKitterick (1957) would have noted that both make the case that themes associated with the marketing concept are found routinely in the 1920s and 1930s. McKitterick (1957) even explicitly points to the work of Oswald Knauth (1948, 1956) who frequently uses similar language regarding exchange relationships to that found in the relationship marketing literature and discussions of the marketing concept. Coolsen (1960/1978), Fullerton (1988), Hollander (1986), Jones and Richardson (2007), Tadajewski (2008, 2009), Tadajewski and Saren (2008) and Tadajewski and Jones (2008) all develop this point further.
2. Given space limitations we do not include a discussion of the critiques levelled at marketing practice by Marx, Lenin, Veblen, C.W. Mills, or Galbraith.

References

Adler, P.S. (2002) 'Critical in the Name of Whom and What?', *Organization* 9(3): 387–395.
Adorno, T.W. (1961) '"Static" and "Dynamic" as Sociological Categories', *Diogenes* 9: 28–49.
—— (1967) *Prisms*. Cambridge: MIT Press.
—— (1989) 'The Culture Industry Revisited' in S.E. Bronner and D.M. Kellner (eds) *Critical Theory and Society: A Reader*, pp. 128–135. New York: Routledge.
Adorno, T.W. and Becker, H. (1999) 'Education for Maturity and Responsibility', *History of the Human Sciences* 12(3): 21–34.
Alvesson, M. (1994) 'Critical Theory and Consumer Marketing', *Scandinavian Journal of Management* 10(3): 291–313.
Alvesson, M. and Willmott, H. (1992) *Critical Management Studies*. London: Sage.
—— (1996) *Making Sense of Management: A Critical Introduction*. London: Sage.
Andreasen, A.R. (1994) 'Social Marketing: Its Definition and Domain', *Journal of Public Policy and Marketing* 13(1): 108–114.
—— (2003) 'The Life Trajectory of Social Marketing: Some Implications', *Marketing Theory* 3(3): 293–303.
Arnold, M.J. and Fisher, J.E. (1996) 'Counterculture, Criticisms and Crisis: Assessing the Effect of the Sixties on Marketing Thought', *Journal of Macromarketing* 16(Spring): 118–133.

Arnold, S.J. and Fischer, E. (1994) 'Hermeneutics and Consumer Research', *Journal of Consumer Research* 21(June): 55–70.

Arnould, E.J. and Thompson, C.J. (2005) 'Consumer Culture Theory (CCT): Twenty Years of Research', *Journal of Consumer Research*, 31(4): 868–882.

—— (2007) 'Consumer Culture Theory (and We Really Mean Theoretics): Dilemmas and Opportunities Posed by an Academic Branding Strategy', in R. Belk and J.F. Sherry Jr. (eds) *Consumer Culture Theory*. Research in Consumer Behavior, Vol. 11, pp. 3–22. Oxford: Elsevier.

Arvidsson, A. (2005) 'Brands: A Critical Perspective', *Journal of Consumer Culture* 5(2): 235–258.

Bartkus, B.R. and Glassma, M. (forthcoming) 'Do Firms Practice What They Preach? The Relationship Between Mission Statements and Stakeholder Management', *Journal of Business Ethics*.

BBC News (2007) 'Shock at Archbishop Condom Claim'. Available http://news.bbc.co.uk/1/hi/world/africa/7014335.stm Accessed 26/09/2007.

Belk, R.W. (1995) 'Studies in the New Consumer Behaviour', in D. Miller (ed.) *Acknowledging Consumption: A Review of New Studies*, pp. 58–95. London: Routledge.

Benton, R. Jr. (1985) 'Micro Bias and Macro Prejudice in the Teaching of Marketing', *Journal of Macromarketing* Fall: 43–58.

Bloom, P.N. and Novelli, W.D. (1979) 'Problems and Challenges in Social Marketing', *Journal of Marketing* 45(Spring): 79–88.

Borsch, F.J. (1958) 'The Marketing Philosophy as a Way of Life', in F.J. Kelley and W. Lazer (eds) *Managerial Marketing: Perspectives and Viewpoints: A Source Book*, pp. 18–24. Homewood: Richard D. Irwin.

Brenkert, G.G. (2002) 'Ethical Challenges of Social Marketing', *Journal of Public Policy and Marketing* 21(1): 14–25.

Bristor, J. and Fischer, E. (1995) 'Exploring Simultaneous Oppressions: Toward the Development of Consumer Research in the Interest of Diverse Women', *American Behavioral Scientist* 38(4): 526–536.

Bristor, J.M. and Fischer, E. (1993) 'Feminist Thought: Implications for Consumer Research', *Journal of Consumer Research* 19(March): 518–536.

Brownlie, D. (2006) 'Emancipation, Epiphany and Resistance: On the Underimagined and Overdetermined in Critical Marketing', *Journal of Marketing Management* 22: 505–528.

Brownlie, D., Saren, M., Wensley, R. and Whittington, R. (1999) 'Marketing Disequilibrium: On Redress and Restoration', in D. Brownlie, M. Saren, R. Wensley, and R. Whittington (eds) *Rethinking Marketing: Towards Critical Marketing Accountings*, pp. 1–22. London: Sage.

Burrell, G. and Morgan, G. (1979/1992) *Sociological Paradigms and Organisational Analysis*. Aldershot: Ashgate.

Burton, D. (2001) 'Critical Marketing Theory: The Blueprint?', *European Journal of Marketing* 35(5/6): 722–743.

—— (2002) 'Towards a Critical Multicultural Marketing Theory', *Marketing Theory* 2(2): 207–236.

—— (2003) 'Rethinking the UK System of Doctoral Training in Marketing', *Journal of Marketing Management* 19(7/8): 883–904.

Catterall, M., Maclaran, P. and Stevens, L. (2005) 'Postmodern Paralysis: The Critical Impasse in Feminist Perspectives on Consumers', *Journal of Marketing Management* 21(5–6): 489–504.

Cheskin, L. (1960) *Why People Buy: Motivation Research and its Successful Application*, Business Publications Limited, London.

Clegg, S. and Dunkerley, D. (1980) *Organization, Class and Control*. London: Routledge.

Coolsen, F.G. (1960/1978) 'Appraisal of Contributions to Marketing Thought by Nineteenth Century Liberal Economists', in H. Assael (ed.) *Early Development and Conceptualization of the Field of Marketing*, pp. 160–210. New York: Arno.

Crane, A. (2000) *Marketing, Morality and the Natural Environment*. London: Routledge.

Crane, A. and Desmond, J. (2002) 'Societal Marketing and Morality', *European Journal of Marketing* 36(5/6): 548–569

Desmond, J. (1995) 'Reclaiming The Subject: Decommodifying Marketing Knowledge', *Journal of Marketing Management* 11: 721–746.

—— (1998) 'Marketing and Moral Indifference', in M. Parker (ed.) *Ethics & Organizations*, pp. 173–196. London: Sage.

Dholakia, R.R. (1984) 'A Macromarketing Perspective on Social Marketing: The Case of Family Planning in India', *Journal of Macromarketing* 4: 53–61.

Dholakia, N. and Arndt, J. (1985) (eds) *Changing the Course of Marketing: Alternative Paradigms for Widening Marketing Theory*, Research in Marketing Supplement 2. Greenwich: JAI Press.

Dholakia, N. and Dholakia, R.R. (1985) 'Choice and Choicelessness in the Paradigm of Marketing', in N. Dholakia and J. Arndt (eds) *Changing the Course of Marketing: Alternative Paradigms for Widening Marketing Theory*, pp. 173–185. Greenwich: JAI Press.

Dholakia, N. and Firat, A.F. (1980) 'A Critical View of the Research Enterprise in Marketing', in R.P. Bagozzi, K.L. Bernhardt, P.S. Busch, D.W. Cravens, J.F Hair Jr, C.A. Scott (eds) *Marketing in the 80's: Changes & Challenges*, pp. 316–319. Chicago: American Marketing Association.

Dholakia, N., Firat, A.F. and Bagozzi, R.P. (1980) 'The De-Americanization of Marketing Thought: In Search of a Universal Basis', in C.W. Lamb and P.M. Dunne (eds) *Theoretical Developments in Marketing*, pp. 25–29. Chicago: American Marketing Association.

Dholakia, R.R. and Dholakia, N. (2001) 'Social Marketing and Development', in P.N. Bloom and G.T. Gundlach (eds) *Handbook of Marketing and Society*, pp. 486–505. Thousand Oaks: Sage.

Dichter, E. (1960) *The Strategy of Desire*. New York: Doubleday.

Dobscha, S. and Ozanne, J.L. (2001) 'An Ecofeminist Analysis of Environmentally Sensitive Women Using Qualitative Methodology: The Emancipating Potential of an Ecological Life', *Journal of Public Policy and Marketing* 20(2): 201–214.

Firat, A.F. (1977) 'Consumption Patterns and Macromarketing: A Radical Perspective', *European Journal of Marketing* 11(4): 291–298.

Firat, A.F. (1985) 'A Critique of Orientations in Theory Development in Consumer Behavior: Suggestions for the Future', *Advances in Consumer Research* 12(1): 3–6.

—— (1988a) 'A Critical Historical Perspective on Needs: The Macro or Micro Rationale?', in S. Shapiro and A.F. Walle (eds) *1988 AMA Winter Educators' Conference Marketing: A Return to the Broader Dimensions*, pp. 289–295. Chicago: American Marketing Association.

—— (1988b) 'Consumption as Production: The End Result of a Marketing Practice', in S. Shapiro and A.F. Walle (eds) *1988 AMA Winter Educators' Conference Marketing: A Return to the Broader Dimensions*, pp. 395–399. Chicago: American Marketing Association.

Firat, A.F. and Dholakia, N. (1982) 'Consumption Choices at the Macro Level', *Journal of Macromarketing* 2(Fall): 6–15.

Firat, A.F., Dholakia, N., and Bagozzi, R.P. (1987) 'Introduction: Breaking the Mold', in A.F. Firat, N. Dholakia and R.P. Bagozzi (eds) *Philosophical and Radical Thought in Marketing*, pp. xii–xxi. Lexington: Lexington Books.

Fischer, E. and Bristor, J. (1994) 'A Feminist Poststructuralist Analysis of the Rhetoric of Marketing Relationships', *International Journal of Research in Marketing* 11(4): 317–331.

Foucault, M. (1984) 'What is Enlightenment?', in P. Rabinow (ed.) *The Foucault Reader: An Introduction to Foucault's Thought*, pp. 32–50. London: Penguin.

—— (1992) *The Use of Pleasure: The History of Sexuality: 2*. Tr. R. Huxley. London: Penguin.

—— (2001) *Fearless Speech*. Ed. J. Pearson. Los Angles: Semiotext(e).

Fournier, V. and Grey, C. (2000) 'At the Critical Moment: Conditions and Prospects for Critical Management Studies', *Human Relations* 53(1): 7–32.

Frederick, J.G. (1959) *Introduction to The Art and Science of Motivation Research*. Liverpool: The Bell Press.

Fromm, E. (1976/2007) *To Have or To Be?* New York: Continuum.

—— (1998) *On Being Human*. New York: Continuum.

Fullerton, R.A. (1988) 'How Modern is "Modern" Marketing? Marketing's Evolution and the Myth of the Production Era', *Journal of Marketing* 52(1): 108–125.

Gaski, J.F. (1999) 'Does Marketing Ethics Really Have Anything to Say? – A Critical Inventory of the Literature', *Journal of Business Ehtics* 18: 315–334.

Habermas, J. (1968/1987) *Knowledge & Human Interests*. Tr. J.J. Shapiro. Cambridge: Polity Press.

—— (1990) 'The Hermeneutic Circle Claim to Universality', in G.L. Ormiston and A.D. Schrift (eds) *The Hermeneutic Tradition: From Ast to Ricoeur*, pp. 245–272. Albany: State University of New York Press.

Hackley, C. (2003) '"We Are All Customers Now": Rhetorical Strategy and Ideological Control in Marketing Management Texts', *Journal of Management Studies* 40(5): 1325–1352.

Hansen, F. (1981) 'Contemporary Research in Marketing in Denmark', *Journal of Marketing* 45(3): 214–218.

Hastings, G. (2003) 'Relational Paradigms in Social Marketing', *Journal of Macromarketing* 23(1): 6–15.

—— (2007) 'The Diaspora has Already Begun', *Marketing Intelligence and Planning* 25(2): 117–122.

Hastings, G. and Saren, M. (2003) 'The Critical Contribution of Social Marketing Theory and Application', *Marketing Theory* 3(3): 305–322.

Healy, P. (2001) 'A "Limit Attitude": Foucault, Automy, Critique', *History of the Human Sciences* 14(1): 49–68.

Hetrick, W.P. and Lozada, H.R. (1994) 'Construing the Critical Imagination: Comments and Necessary Diversions', *Journal of Consumer Research* 21(3): 548–558.

—— (1999) 'Theory, Ethical Critique and the Experience of Marketing', in D. Brownlie, M. Saren, R. Wensley, and R. Whittington (eds) *Rethinking Marketing: Towards Critical Marketing Accountings*, pp. 162–176. London: Sage.

Hirschman, E.C. (1993) 'Ideology in Consumer Research, 1980 and 1990: A Marxist and Feminist Critique', *Journal of Consumer Research* 19(March): 537–555.

Holbrook, M.B. (1985) 'Why Business is Bad for Consumer Research: The Three Bears Revisited', in E.C. Hirschman and M.B. Holbrook (eds) *Advances in Consumer Research* 12, pp. 145–156. Provo, UT: Association for Consumer Research.

Hollander, S.C. (1986) 'The Marketing Concept: A Déjà vu', in G. Fisk (ed.) *Marketing Management as a Social Process*, pp. 3–29. New York: Praeger.

Holt, D.B. (2003) 'What Becomes an Icon Most?', *Harvard Business Review* 81(3): 43–49.

Horkheimer, M. (1966) 'On the Concept of Freedom', *Diogenes* 14: 73–81.

—— (1972) *Critical Theory: Selected Essays*. Tr. M.J. Connell and Others. Herder and Herder, New York.

—— (1947/2004) *Eclipse of Reason*. London: Continuum.

Horkheimer, M. and Adorno, T. (2002) *Dialectic of Enlightenment: Philosophical Fragments*. G.S. Noerr (ed.) E. Jephcott (Tr.). Stanford: Stanford University Press.

Hudson, I. and Hudson, M. (2003) 'Removing the Veil? Commodity Fetishism, Fair Trade, and the Environment', *Organization & Environment* 16(4): 413–430.

Hudson, L.A. and Ozanne, J.L. (1988) 'Alternative Ways of Seeking Knowledge in Consumer Research', *Journal of Consumer Research* 14(4): 508–521.

Humphreys, A. (2006) 'The Consumer as Foucauldian 'Object of Knowledge"', *Social Science Computer Review* 24(3): 296–309.

Jacques, P., Thomas, R., Foster, D., McCann, J. and Tunno, M. (2003) 'Wal-Mart or World-Mart? A Teaching Case Study', *Review of Radical Political Economics* 35(4): 513–533.

Jones, D.G.B. (1994) 'Biography and the History of Marketing Thought: Henry Charles Taylor and Edward David Jones', in R.A. Fullerton (ed.) *Research in Marketing*, Supplement 6: Explorations in Marketing Thought, pp. 67–85. Greenwich: JAI Press.

Jones, D.G.B. and Monieson, D.D. (1990) 'Early Development of the Philosophy of Marketing Thought', *Journal of Marketing* 54(1): 102–113.

Jones, D.G.B. and Richardson, A. (2007) 'The Myth of the Marketing Revolution', *Journal of Macromarketing* 27(1): 15–24.

Joy, A. and Ross, C.A. (1989) 'Marketing and Development in Third World Contexts: An Evaluation and Future Directions', *Journal of Macromarketing* Fall: 17–31.

Kangun, N. (1972) 'Introduction', in N. Kangun (ed.) *Society and Marketing: An Unconventional View*, pp. 2–4. New York: Harper & Row.

Karlinsky, M. (1987) 'Changing Asymmetry in Marketing', in A.F. Firat, N. Dholakia and R.P. Bagozzi (eds) *Philosophical and Radical Thought in Marketing*, pp. 39–55. Lexington: Lexington Books.

Keith, R.J. (1960) 'The Marketing Revolution', *Journal of Marketing* 24(3): 35–38.

Kernan, J.B. (1995) 'Declaring a Discipline: Reflections on the ACR's Silver Anniversary', in F. Kardes and S. Mita (eds) *Advances in Consumer Research*. 22, pp. 553–560. Provo, UT: Association for Consumer Research.

Kilbourne, W.E. (1992) 'On the Role of Critical Theory in Moving Toward Voluntary Simplicity', in F. Rudmin and M. Richins (eds) *Meaning, Measure, and Morality of Materialism*, pp. 161–163. Provo, UT: Association for Consumer Research.

—— (1995) 'Green Advertising: Salvation or Oxymoron?', *Journal of Advertising* 24(2): 7–19.

—— (2002) 'Globalization and Development: An Expanded Macromarketing View', *Journal of Macromarketing* 24(2): 122–135.

Kilbourne, W.E., Beckmann, S.C., Thelen, E. (2002) 'The Role of the Dominant Social Paradigm in Environmental Attitudes: A Multinational Examination', *Journal of Business Research* 55: 193–204.

Kilbourne, W.E., McDonagh, P. and Prothero, A. (1997) 'Sustainable Consumption and the Quality of Life: A Macromarketing Challenge to the Dominant Social Paradigm', *Journal of Macromarketing* Spring: 4–24.

Klein, S. and Leiss, W. (1978) 'Advertising, Needs and "Commodity Fetishism"', *Canadian Journal of Political and Social Theory* 2(1): 5–30.

Knauth, O. (1948) *Managerial Enterprise, Its Growth and Methods of Operation*. New York: W.W. Norton.

—— (1956) *Business Practices, Trade Position, and Competition*. New York: Columbia University Press.

Kompridis, N. (2005) 'Disclosing Possibility: The Past and Future of Critical Theory', *International Journal of Philosophical Studies* 13(3): 325–351.

Kotler, P. (2005) 'The Role Played By the Broadening of Marketing Movement in the History of Marketing Thought', *Journal of Public Policy and Marketing* 24(1): 114–116.

Kotler, P. and Levy, S. (1969) 'Broadening the Concept of Marketing', *Journal of Marketing* 33(January): 10–15.

Kracauer, S. (1989) 'The Mass Ornament', in S.E. Bronner and D.M. Kellner (eds) *Critical Theory and Society: A Reader*, pp. 145–154. New York: Routledge.

Laczniak, G.R. and Michie, D.A. (1979) 'The Social Disorder of the Broadened Concept of Marketing', *Journal of the Academy of Marketing Science* 7(3): 214–232.

Laczniak, G.R. and Murphy, P.E. (2006) 'Normative Perspectives for Ethical and Socially Responsible Marketing', *Journal of Macromarketing* 26(2): 154–177.

Lane, J.F. (2006) 'Towards a Poetics of Consumerism: Gaston Bachelard's 'Material Imagination' and a Narrative of Post-War Modernisation', *French Cultural Studies* 17(1): 19–34.

Lazarsfeld, P.F. (1941) 'Remarks on Administrative and Critical Communications Research', *Studies on Philosophy and Social Science* 9: 2–16.

Lears, T.J.J. (1985) Beyond Veblen: Remapping Consumer Culture in Twentieth Century America, in Hollander, S.C. and Nevett, T. (eds) *Marketing in the Long Run: Proceedings of the Second Workshop on Historical Research in Marketing*, pp. 456–469. Michigan State University, Michigan.

Lee, R.G. and Murray, J.B. (1995) 'A Framework for Critiquing the Dysfunctions of Advertising: The Base-Superstructure Metaphor', *Advances in Consumer Research* 22: 139–143.

Leiss, W. (1978) 'Needs, Exchanges and the Fetishism of Objects', *Canadian Journal of Political and Social Theory* 2(3): 27–48.

—— (1983) 'The Icons of the Marketplace', *Theory, Culture and Society* 1(3): 10–21.

Lib, A. (2007) 'Definition of Marketing', *ELMAR: Electronic Marketing*. December 24.

Lusch, R.F., Laczniak, G.E. and Murphy, P.E. (1980) 'The "Ethics of Social Ideas" Versus The "Ethics of Marketing Social Ideas", *The Journal of Consumer Affairs* Summer: 156–164.

Marcuse, H. (1964/1972) *One Dimensional Man*. London: Abacus.

—— (1968) 'Re-Examination of the Concept of Revolution', *Diogenes* 16: 17–26.

Marion, G. (2007) 'Customer-Driven or Driving the Customer? Exploitation Versus Exploration', in M. Saren, P. Maclaran, C. Goulding, R. Elliott, A. Shankar and M. Catterall (eds) *Critical Marketing: Defining the Field*, pp. 99–113. Amsterdam: Butterworth-Heinemann.

McDonagh, P. (1995) 'Radical Change Through Rigorous Review? A Commentary on the Commodification of Marketing Knowledge', *Journal of Marketing Management* 11(7): 675–679.

McKitterick, J.B. (1957) 'What is the Marketing Management Concept?', in F.M. Bass (ed.) *The Frontiers of Marketing Thought and Science*, pp. 71–81. Chicago: American Marketing Association.

Moisander, J. and Personen, S. (2002) 'Narratives of Sustainable Ways of Living: Constructing the Self and the Other as a Green Consumer', *Management Decision* 40(4): 329–342.

Monieson, D.D. (1981) 'What Constitutes Usable Knowledge in Marketing?', *Journal of Macromarketing* Spring: 14–22.

—— (1988) 'Intellectualization in Macromarketing: A World Disenchanted', *Journal of Macromarketing* Fall: 4–10.

Moorman, C. (1987) 'Marketing as Technique: The Influence of Marketing on the Meanings of Consumption', in A.F. Firat, N. Dholakia and R.P. Bagozzi (eds) *Philosophical and Radical Thought in Marketing*, pp. 193–215. Lexington: Lexington Books.

Morgan, G. (1992) Marketing Discourse and Practice: Toward a Critical Analysis, in M. Alvesson & H. Willmott (eds) *Critical Management Studies*, pp. 136–158. Sage, London.

—— (2003) Marketing and Critique: Prospects and Problems, in M. Alvesson & H. Willmott (eds) *Studying Management Critically*, pp. 111–131. Sage, London.

Mouffe, C. (1996) 'Deconstruction, Pragmatism and the Politics of Democracy', in C. Mouffe (ed.) *Deconstruction and Pragmatism*, pp. 1–12. London: Routledge.

Murray, J. and Ozanne, J.L. (2006) 'Rethinking the Critical Imagination', in R. Belk (ed.) *Handbook of Qualitative Research Methods in Marketing*, pp. 46–55. Cheltenham: Edward Elgar.

Murray, J.B. and Ozanne, J.L. (1991) 'The Critical Imagination: Emanicipatory Interests in Consumer Research', *Journal of Consumer Research* 18(2): 129–144.

—— (1997) 'A Critical-Emancipatory Sociology of Knowledge: Reflections on the Social Construction of Consumer Research', in R. Belk (ed.) *Research in Consumer Behavior*, pp. 57–92. Greenwich: JAI Press.

Nill, A. (2003) 'Global Marketing Ethics: A Communicative Approach', *Journal of Macromarketing* 23(2): 90–104.

Nill, A.L. and Schultz, C.J. (1997) 'Marketing Ethics Across Countries: Decision-Making Guidelines and the Emergence of Dialogic Idealism', *Journal of Macromarketing* Fall: 4–19.

O'Shaughnessy, J. and O'Shaughnessy, N. (2002) 'Postmodernism and Marketing: Separating the Wheat from the Chaff', *Journal of Macromarketing* 22(1): 109–135.

—— (2007) 'Reply to Criticisms of Marketing, the Consumer Society and Hedonism', *European Journal of Marketing* 41(1/2): 7–16.

Ozanne, J.C. and Murray, J.B. (1995) 'Uniting Critical Theory and Public Policy to Create the Reflexively Defiant Consumer', *American Behavioral Scientist* 38(4): 516–525.

Parker, M. (1995) 'Critical in the Name of What? Postmodernism and Critical Approaches to Organization', *Organization Studies* 16(4): 553–564.

Pfeiffer, J. (2004) 'Condom Social Marketing, Pentecostalism, and Structural Adjustment in Mozambique: A Clash of AIDS Prevention Messages', *Medical Anthropology Quarterly* 18(1): 77–103.

Pietrykowski, B. (2007) 'Exploring New Directions for Research in the Radical Political Economy of Consumption', *Review of Radical Political Economy* 39: 257–283.

Poster, M. and Venkatesh, A. (1987) 'From Marx to Foucault – An Intellectual Journey Through Critical Theory', in R.W. Belk and G. Zaltman (eds) *Marketing Theory, AMA Winter Educators' Conference*, pp. 20–26. Chicago: American Marketing Association.

Prothero, A. and Fitchett, J.A. (2000) 'Greening Capitalism: Opportunities for a Green Commodity', *Journal of Macromarketing* 20(1): 46–55.

Richins, M. (1995) 'Social Comparison, Advertising, and Consumer Discontent', *American Behavioral Scientist* 38(4): 593–607.

Rogers, E.M. (1987) The Critical School and Consumer Research, in M. Wallendorf & P. Anderson (eds) *Advances in Consumer Research*, Vol. 14, pp. 8–11. Provo, UT: Association for Consumer Research.

Rosengarten, M. (2004) 'Consumer Activism in the Pharmacology of HIV', *Body and Society* 10(1): 91–107.

Said, E.W. (1996) *Representations of the Intellectual*. New York: Vintage.

Saren, M., Maclaran, P., Goulding, C., Elliott, R., Shankar, A., and Catterall, M. (eds) (2007) *Critical Marketing: Defining the Field*. Amsterdam: Butterworth-Heinemann.

Schipper, F. (2002) 'The Relevance of Horkheimer's View of the Customer', *European Journal of Marketing* 36(1/2): 23–35.

Schneiderman, D. (1998) 'Constituting the Culture-Ideology of Consumerism', *Social and Legal Studies* 7(2): 213–238.

Schudson, M. (2007) 'Citizens, Consumers and the Good Society', *The Annals of the American Academy of Political and Social Science* 611: 236–249.

Shankar, A., Cherrier, H. and Canniford, R. (2006) 'Consumer Empowerment: A Foucauldian Interpretation', *European Journal of Marketing* 40(9/10): 1013–1030.

Shankar, A. and Fitchett, J.A. (2002) 'Having, Being and Consumption', *Journal of Marketing Management* 18: 501–516.

Shapiro, S.J. (2006) 'A JMM-Based Macromarketing Doctoral-Level reading List', *Journal of Macromarketing* 26(2): 250–255.

Shaw, Arch, W. (1912) 'Some Problems in Market Distribution', *The Quarterly Journal of Economics*, 26(4): 703–765.

Shultz, C.J. II (2007) 'The Unquestioned Marketing Life? Let Us Hope Not', *Journal of Macromarketing* 27(3): 224.

Spratlen, T.H. (1972) 'The Challenge of a Humanistic Orientation in Marketing', in N. Kangun (ed.) *Society and Marketing: An Unconventional View*, pp. 403–413. New York: Harper & Row.

Stern, B.B. (1990) 'Literary Criticism and the History of Marketing Thought: A New Perspective on "Reading" Marketing Theory', *Journal of the Academy of Marketing Science* 18(4): 329–336.

—— (1996) 'Deconstructive Strategy and Consumer Research: Concepts and Illustrative Exemplar', *Journal of Consumer Research* 23(September): 136–147.

Tadajewski, M. (2006a) 'The Ordering of Marketing Theory: The Influence of McCarthyism and the Cold War', *Marketing Theory* 6(2): 163–200.

—— (2006b) 'Remembering Motivation Research: Toward an Alternative Genealogy of Interpretive Consumer Research', *Marketing Theory* 6(4): 429–466.

—— (2008) 'The Foundations of Relationship Marketing: Reciprocity and Trade Relations', *Marketing Theory*.

—— (2009) 'Relationship Marketing in Consumer Markets: The View from Philadelphia in the Nineteenth and Early Twentieth Centuries', *Journal of Macromarketing*.

Tadajewski, M. and Jones, D.G.B. (2008) 'The History of Marketing Thought: Introduction and Overview', in M. Tadajewski and D.G.B. Jones (eds) *The History of Marketing Thought*, Volume I. London: Sage.

Tadajewski, M. and Maclaran, P. (2009a) *Critical Marketing Studies. Vol. I*. London: Sage.

—— (2009b) *Critical Marketing Studies. Vol. II*. London: Sage.

—— (2009c) *Critical Marketing Studies. Vol. III*. London: Sage.

Tadajewski, M. and Saren, M. (2008) 'Rethinking the Emergence of Relationship Marketing', *Journal of Macromarketing*.

Thompson, C.J. (1993) 'Modern Truth and Postmodern Incredulity: A Hermeneutic Deconstruction of the Metanarrative of 'Scientific Truth' in Marketing Research', *Journal of Public Policy and Marketing* 10(3): 325–338.

—— (1995) 'A Contextualist Proposal for the Conceptualization and Study of Marketing Ethics', *Journal of Public Policy and Marketing* 14(2): 177–191.

—— (2004) 'Marketplace Mythology and Discourses of Power', *Journal of Consumer Research* 31(June): 162–180.

Thompson, C.J. and Hirschman, E.C. (1995) 'Understanding the Socialized Body: A Poststructuralist Analysis of Consumers' Self-Conceptions, Body Images, and Self-Care Practices', *Journal of Consumer Research* 22(September): 139–153.

Thompson, C.J., Rindfleisch, A. and Arsel, Z. (2006) 'Emotional Branding and the Strategic Value of the Doppelgänger Brand Image', *Journal of Marketing* 70(January): 50–64

Tipper, H., Hollingworth, H.L., Hotchkiss, G.B. and Parsons, F.A. (1917) *Advertising: Its Principles and Practice*. New York: The Ronald Press Co.

Vargo, S.L. and Lusch, R.F. (2004) 'Evolving to a New Dominant Logic for Marketing', *Journal of Marketing* 68(1): 1–17.

Vargo, S.L. and Morgan, F.W. (2005) 'Services in Society and Academic Thought: An Historical Analysis', *Journal of Macromarketing* 25(1): 42–53.

Varman, R. and Vikas, R.M. (2007) 'Freedom and Consumption: Toward Conceptualizing Systemic Constraints for Subaltern Consumers in a Capitalist Society', *Consumption, Markets and Culture* 10(2): 117–131.

Vikas, R.M. and Varman, R. (2007) 'Erasing Futures: Ethics of Marketing an Intoxicant to Homeless Children', *Consumption, Markets and Culture* 10(2): 189–202.

Whittle, A. and Spicer, A. (forthcoming) 'Essai: Is Actor Network Theory Critical?', *Organization Studies*.

Wilkie, W.L. and Moore, E.S. (2006) 'Macromarketing as a Pillar of Marketing Thought', *Journal of Macromarketing* 26(2): 224–232.

Williamson, J. (1978) *Decoding Advertisements: Ideology and Meaning in Advertising*. London: Marion Boyars.

Witkowski, T.H. (2005) 'Antiglobal Challenges to Marketing in Developing Countries: Exploring the Ideological Divide', *Journal of Public Policy and Marketing* 24 (Spring): 7–23.

Wright, E.O. (1998) 'Introduction', in S. Bowles and H. Gintis (eds) *Recasting Egalitarianism: New Rules for Communities, States and Markets*, pp. xi-xiii. London: Verso.

—— (2006) 'Compass Points: Towards a Socialist Alternative', *New Left Review* Sept–Oct: 93–124.

Wright, N.D. and Shapiro, J. (1992) 'Consumption and the Crisis of Teen Pregnancy: A Critical Theory Approach', *Advances in Consumer Research* 19: 404–406.

2
Rethinking the Development of Marketing

Mark Tadajewski[1] and Douglas Brownlie[2]

[1]*University of Leicester and* [2]*University of Stirling*

A s our introductory chapter made clear, we see the historical study of marketing as an important component of any attempt to critically reflect on the nature of marketing. The way we think about marketing as academics and students is invariably a product of history. And history, as Thomas Kuhn (1962) reminds us, is usually written by the winners. For this reason, we should begin to examine the history of marketing in a cautious manner.

We should not simply accept that the way marketing has developed is necessarily the most appropriate; nor should we accept the existing conceptualisations, values and goals of marketing as an inviolable given (Benton, 1985). We should question them, seeing them as *nomoi*, that is, as the foundational beliefs of the discipline that have become so well entrenched that they are the background supports 'against which all else is judged. Critical thinking about marketing begins with the questioning of marketing's nomoi' (O'Shaughnessy and O'Shaughnessy, 2002: 130).

In an interesting paper, Steiner (1976) makes the case that antipathy to marketing has an 'ancient origin'. He argues that when we consult the work of scholars like Plato, Aristotle and Cassiodorus as well as that of more recent origin such as the work of Veblen and Galbraith, we find marketing, retailing and distributive activities denounced as 'unnatural and base', treated 'scornfully' and referred to with a 'derisive tone' (Steiner, 1976: 2). Advertising in the latter works is depicted as 'satanically powerful' (Steiner, 1976: 3) and domestic marketing roles when discussed in the former are generally given to the 'less prestigious members [of society] – slaves, women, the weak, Jews, [and] nationals of inconsequent nations' (Steiner, 1976: 8).

These are serious allegations and the chapter that follows by Dixon subjects Steiner's representation of marketing to extended critique. Dixon returns to the original sources of the literature that Steiner sometimes does not do and argues, *contra* Steiner, that market exchange and marketers have historically been viewed as performing a socially beneficial role. The fact that the weak were allocated the role of marketer in the work of Plato, for example, was not because it was a less prestigious role necessarily, but rather more a function of the division of labour. Plato, quite naturally, thought that those who were strongest should perform the most strenuous tasks. Those that could not, were allocated less arduous roles. Hence, the weak were found sitting trading in the market place. When marketing was represented in a more negative light, it was not the marketing system that was at fault, blame was usually attributed to traders who desired to amass an 'unnatural' amount of wealth.

This theme of marketers performing socially beneficial roles is further developed by Jones and Monieson who trace the 'origins' of marketing thought. Going beyond the analysis provided by Bartels (1988), they highlight the impact of the German Historicist School on early marketing thought. As was relatively common in the late nineteenth century, many marketing scholars undertook some training in Germany. While studying there a number of these individuals adopted the research philosophy of this school. In practice, this meant that their research utilised an 'inductive, statistical methodology with a historical perspective and [demonstrated] a concern for the application of knowledge and skills to social ends'. Some of these scholars were socially activist in that they attempted to examine issues of consumer protection, the fairness of prices for agricultural products and the functions of the middleman, with a concern to solve distributive problems as they arose.

To some extent such societal concerns are mirrored, Dixon argues in the next chapter, throughout much of early marketing scholarship. Again, from an historical perspective, Dixon highlights how early marketing scholars argued that profit was not simply the end of all business activity, but instead more of an incentive to satisfy the customer, by providing products that fulfilled human requirements. Those products that were not in the interest of the customer should not be produced, it was maintained. In this fascinating chapter, he examines the relationship between consumer sovereignty and the marketing concept, perhaps the key foundations of marketing thought, and critically evaluates two key ideas. Firstly, he examines the proposal that businesses produce what customers want and secondly, that marketing activities will maximise social welfare. In both cases, he finds the arguments that underpin these key tenets of marketing theory and practice – or more appropriately marketing ideology (Brownlie and Saren, 1992) – wanting.

What we hope the reader will take from these chapters is that marketing has not consistently been viewed as necessarily unproductive, nor are marketers essentially the nefarious characters that social critics have often presented them as. Early scholars were socially activist, as Jones (1994) indicates, and interested in examining the functioning of the economy in order to make it more equitable to market participants, whether these were middlemen whose contribution to economic and distributive efficiency was undervalued

(Shaw, 1915), or in order to protect the consumer from product adulteration (King, 1913; Kallett, 1934).

References

Bartels, R. (1988) *The History of Marketing Thought*, Third Edition. Columbus: Publishing Horizons.

Benton, R. Jr (1985) 'Micro Bias and Macro Prejudice in the Teaching of Marketing', *Journal of Macromarketing* Fall: 43–58.

Brownlie, D. and Saren, M. (1992) 'The Four Ps of the Marketing Concept: Prescriptive, Polemical, Permanent and Problematical', *European Journal of Marketing* 26(4): 34–47.

Jones, D.G.B. (1994) 'Biography and the History of Marketing Thought: Henry Charles Taylor and Edward David Jones', in R.A. Fullerton (ed.) *Research in Marketing*, Supplement 6: Explorations in Marketing Thought, pp. 67–85. Greenwich: JAI Press.

Kallett, A. (1934) 'Foods and Drugs for the Consumer', *The Annals of the American Academy of Political and Social Science* 173: 26–34.

King, C.L. (1913) 'Can the Cost of Distributing Food Products be Reduced?', *The Annals of the American Academy of Political and Social Science* 48: 199–224.

Kuhn, T.S. (1962) *The Structure of Scientific Revolutions*. Chicago: University of Chicago Press.

O'Shaughnessy, J. and O'Shaughnessy, N. (2002) 'Postmodernism and Marketing: Separating the Wheat from the Chaff', *Journal of Macromarketing* 22(1): 109–135.

Shaw, A.W. (1915) *Some Problems in Market Distribution*. Cambridge: Harvard University Press.

Steiner, R.L. (1976) 'The Prejudice Against Marketing', *Journal of Marketing* 40(July): 2–9.

3

Prejudice V. Marketing? An Examination of some Historical Sources*

Donald F. Dixon

Temple University

I t is a commonplace in the marketing literature that not only is there widespread hostility toward marketing, but that this hostility is rooted in ancient theoretical works. A recent statement of this position begins by defining marketing in terms of time, place, and possession utility, and it identifies prejudice against marketing as an attitude which denigrates the economic role of these three utilities as distinguished from form utility.[1]

This paper is not concerned with value judgments which may be identified as "hostile" to marketing. Rather, it intends to demonstrate that prejudice, as defined above, did not exist in the conceptual models of economic activity presented by ancient scholars. It should be noted that the notion that marketing created utilities which differ from those created by other economic activities was introduced by marketing writers in the early twentieth century. However, at the time when this occurred, economists had long been arguing that such a distinction made no sense at all. A quotation from Marshall's *Principles of Economics*, which must be ranked among the greatest works of economic analysis, clearly demonstrates this:

> Man cannot create material things ... He really only produces utilities; or in other words, his efforts and sacrifices result in changing the form or arrangement of matter to adapt it

* Article originally published in the *Akron Business and Economic Review* 1979; Fall:37–42. Reproduced by permission of Akron Business and Economics Review.

better for the satisfaction of wants . . . It is sometimes said that traders do not produce; that while the cabinet-maker produces furniture, the furniture dealer merely sells what is already produced. But there is no scientific foundation for this distinction. They both produce utilities, and neither of them can do more.[2]

This paper is concerned with the analytical roots of this position, which are found in the works of the classical philosophers of ancient Greece and the medieval scholastics.

The Contribution of Marketing to Social Welfare

It is alleged in the article mentioned above that "The philosophers of ancient Greece were among the earlier disparagers of marketing."[3] To support this statement the author cites two articles in the *Journal of Marketing*. Let us see what the original sources say.

Plato finds that the origins of the state lie in the relationship between man's many wants and his inability to satisfy these without the cooperation of others. The state arises "out of the needs of mankind; no one is self sufficing," and it consists of individuals who exchange with one another "under the idea that the exchange will be for their good." Social benefits arise because of specialization: "We are not all alike; there are diversities of natures among us which are adapted to different occupations . . . we must infer that all things are produced more plentifully and easily and of a better quality when a man does one thing which is natural to him."

The marketer is an example of this specialization; his duty is to be in the market place and to "give money in exchange for goods to those who desire to sell and to take money from those who desire to buy." Because the marketer does this work, "the farmer or artisan who brings the goods to the market need not 'sit idle in the marketplace, taking a holiday from his work' while waiting for customers."[4] This position, that the marketer performs socially useful work by sitting in the market place and buying and selling goods, hardly demonstrates a conceptual bias against marketing. Further, Plato remarks that:

> The natural purpose for which all retail trading comes into existence in a State is not a loss, but precisely the opposite; for how can any man be anything but a benefactor if he renders even and symmetrical the distribution of any kind of goods which before was unsymmetrical and uneven? . . . And we must declare that the merchant is ordained for this purpose.[5]

Again, the contribution of the marketer is clear, and does not seem to refer to any alteration in the physical form of products.

Aristotle also appreciates the role of the exchange process in a state where men specialize in different tasks, and understands that exchange activity involves both physical distribution and offering goods for sale. Moreover, he stresses the social significance of market activity. "One of the essential activities of states is the buying and selling of goods to meet their varying needs."[6]

Thus, the ancient Greek philosophers based their concept of the aggregate social system, the state; upon the division of labor, which Schumpeter refers to as the "eternal commonplace of economics."[7] With the division of labor there must be social exchange. Some social exchange is economic in nature, and some economic exchange takes place in the markets. The specialists who make markets work, that is, who do the work of marketing, have an important place in the system, and perform socially beneficial work.

The classical analytical system provided the foundation for the detailed analysis of marketing functions undertaken by the medieval writers in their efforts to determine whether marketing was a morally justifiable activity. This was a perplexing question. On the one hand Aristotle's reasoning showed that marketing conferred benefits on society. But on the other hand, the mechanism which produced this result was difficult to understand. To St. John Chrysostom (345–407) for example, a marketer seemed to be one "who buys an article to make a profit by selling it whole and unchanged."[8] That is, unlike a craftsman, who converts raw materials into finished goods, the marketer does not seem to add any value to the goods which he sells.

Under these circumstances it appeared to writers such as St. Jerome (340–420) that the seller's gain must be the buyer's loss, so that marketing was a sinful activity.[9] Yet the issue was not at all clear. Leo the Great (390–461) did not condemn marketing, but argued that "The nature of a gain either convicts or excuses a man doing business, for there is a gain which is honest, another which is disgraceful."[10]

It was St. Augustine (354–430) who discovered a means of demonstrating that marketing activities made a social contribution. He identified two aspects of the issue: first, the person who performed the task of marketing, and second, the task itself. Once this distinction was made, it became possible to focus upon the activity of marketing and determine if it contributed to the public good. In his discussion, St. Augustine presents an imaginary conversation with a merchant, who says: "I bring merchandise from afar to those places in which there are not the things which I bring." Here the work of marketing is identified as transportation, and the social benefit is that people have goods which would not otherwise be available. The merchant continues by saying "I ask a wage for my labor, so that I buy more cheaply than I sell." That is, the merchant's profit is simply a wage, and the marketer deserves this profit because "The laborer is worthy of his hire." It is important to note that St. Augustine does not distinguish between the value of the work done by the merchant and that done by other laborers.[11]

Hence, by the fall of the Western Roman Empire (c. 476), the best known of the early church writers not only had demonstrated that the marketer made a social contribution by creating "place utility" but he also had shown that the profit earned represents nothing more than a wage paid for the labor expended. Steiner's statement that "By the fall of the

Roman Empire, the major foundations of the anti-marketing bias had been sunk deep into intellectual soil" is not supported by the evidence.[12]

Subsequent writers developed a more complete analysis of marketing functions. Alexander of Hales (1175–1245) adds a recognition of the storage function to that of transportation, and notes that the marketer incurs risks of product deterioration, fire and theft. In his analysis, the marketer earns a profit both for the labor performed and the risks incurred.[13]

John Duns Scotus (1265–1308) adds a third factor, *industria* (diligence) which the marketer contributes and for which he deserves to earn a profit.[14] Next, San Bernadino (1380–1444) adds a fourth factor, *sollicitudo* (apprehension or anxiety), which the marketer faces because he must take care "concerning predictions."[15] That is, the marketer must forecast both price and value, as well as suitable opportunities for buying and selling goods. It was also fully recognized that the marketer undertook risks, not only of damage or theft of his goods, but of the price at which he might sell these goods. Thus the marketer earned a profit to compensate himself for his labor, diligence, anxiety, and the risks incurred.

It is apparent then that the medieval scholars not only developed a precise understanding of those marketing functions associated with "time and place utility," but achieved an even broader comprehension of the marketing process. Furthermore, there was no question that the performance of the work of marketing represented a social contribution, for there are numerous explicit statements to this effect in the literature. Alexander of Hales remarks that trading is in harmony with the law of nature. St. Thomas says that "Buying and selling seem to be established for the common advantage of both parties, one of whom requires that which belongs to the other, and vice versa."[16] Duns Scotus says that "Trade is necessary and useful for the well-being of society." Martin Luther remarks that "It cannot be denied that buying and selling are necessary. They cannot be dispensed with . . . "[17]

Hence neither the analysis of the medieval scholastics nor their explicit statements are consistent with the argument that they viewed marketing as a zero sum game. Indeed, Richard of Middletown (1249–1306) fully describes the mechanism by which both parties gain in exchange. The merchant buys in one market and sells in another. Since the market price rules in each market, the exchange is equal in each case. The merchant's gain is achieved because of price differences between markets, and as a result of his transactions, supply is equalized, and everyone benefits.[18]

Although the Scholastic system of thought demonstrated that exchange was not a zero sum game, other views were held. However, the typical examples do not suggest an anti-marketing bias. Montaigne (1533–1592) contends that "no profit can be made except at another's expense . . .The merchant only thrives on the extravagance of youth." But this does not represent prejudice against marketing since Montaigne's rule condemns every sort of gain: the farmer benefits from the high price of grain, the architect on the collapse of houses, ministers on men's deaths and vices, physicians on the illness of others, even their friends, and soldiers of war.[19]

There is also the well known statement of Francis Bacon (1561–1626): "Whatsoever is somewhere gotten is somewhere lost". This doctrine is derived from the mercantilist emphasis upon money as a measure of wealth. Within such a system of thought the world's money supply is considered fixed, so that a gain in money by one nation means an equivalent loss to the rest of the world. But, this is not a condemnation of marketing. On the contrary, Bacon recognizes three types of productive activity; extraction, manufacture and "vecture" or carriage: "If these three wheels go, wealth will flow as a spring tide. And it cometh many times to pass . . . that the work and carriage is more worth than the material, and enricheth a state more."[20]

Social Costs of Marketing

Although the social benefits of marketing were well understood, the social costs were also recognized. But, the tendency to confuse discussions of social costs with prejudice must be resisted. The word "prejudice" refers to the judgment made without regard to the facts of the case: "A prejudice is a vagrant opinion without visible means of support."[21]

Marketing writers who contend that it is prejudice which leads Plato to assign weak men to marketing activity in his ideal state are incorrect.[22] Plato assigns people to tasks according to their abilities. The principle of comparative advantage requires that the strongest citizens be assigned to tasks which require strength, and the weakest to tasks where physical strength is not required, such as sitting in the market. The placing of the weakest in the market is the result of the logic of the system, and is unrelated to the public attitude toward physical strength, or marketing as an activity.

Plato clearly appreciates this distinction, and carefully examines the public antagonism to marketing both to determine its cause and to develop remedies: "Let us see them wherein trade is reputed to be a thing not noble nor even respectable, and what has caused it to be disparaged, in order that we may remedy by law parts of it at least, if not the whole."[23] He wishes to cure the evil because marketing is important and must be conducted so that it "will benefit everyone, and do the least possible injury to those in the state who practice it."

The social costs of marketing are many and complex. Some writers understood that marketing fulfilled a need, but wished that the need did not exist. A good statement of this position is that of Aquinas, who prefers that a nation be self-sufficient rather than dependent upon supplies from other countries:

> The State which needs a number of merchants to maintain its subsistence is liable to be injured in war through a shortage of foods if communications are in any way impeded. Moreover, the influx of strangers corrupts the morals of many of the citizens . . . whereas, if the

citizens . . . themselves devote themselves to commerce, a door is open to many vices . . . the pursuit of a merchant is as contrary as possible to military exertion. For merchants abstain from labors and while they enjoy the good things of life, they become soft in mind and their bodies are rendered weak and unsuitable for military exercises.[24]

Thus, although there are economic benefits from the division of labor and market exchange, there are political and social benefits from self-sufficiency. But, a preference for non-economic benefits does not constitute a prejudice against marketing.

Some writers disapprove of certain types of human activity, and marketing is disparaged because it is a subset of this general category. In early Greece and Rome, manual labor and working for pay were denigrated. Herodotus lists the many peoples who hold handicrafts in less esteem than the rest of society, adding that this opinion "is held by all Greeks."[25] Similarly, Dionysius reports that "No Roman citizen was permitted to earn a livelihood as a tradesman or artisan."[26] Cicero's discussion is explicitly derived from "what we have been taught:"

Unbecoming to a gentleman, too, and vulgar are the means of livelihood of all hired workmen whom we pay for mere manual labour . . . Vulgar we must consider those also who buy from wholesale merchants to retail immediately . . . And all mechanics are engaged in vulgar trades; for no workshop can have anything liberal about it.[27]

Cicero is not prejudiced against marketing *per se*, since his proscription includes activities which contribute form utility. Moreover, he distinguishes between retailing and wholesaling: "Trade, if it is a small scale, is to be considered vulgar, but if wholesale and on a large scale . . . is not to be greatly disparaged."

Marketing may also have a detrimental effect upon the environment. For example, by A.D. 92, the shops of Rome had become very obtrusive, and Domitian enacted legislation forbidding the encroachment of retailers on the streets. Martial, a first century poet, provides a description of the situation:

They were stealing the whole city—
those audacious shopkeepers.
There wasn't a single establishment
that didn't spill over its doorsill
into the streets themselves.[28]

Here we have a straightforward statement of the excesses of competition, and the need for social control. Once again, no prejudice seems to be involved.

There also was concern about the effectiveness of marketing. To be effective, any activity must be conducted justly, and setting rules under which social activity must be conducted has long been recognized as a legitimate function of the political system. Laws for the conduct of marketing appear in the Code of Hammurabi, and in Biblical sources. An example of the latter concerns weights and measures:

> You shall not have in your bag two kinds of weights, a large and a small. You shall not have in your house two kinds of measures, a large and a small. A full and just weight you shall have, a full and just measure you shall have.[29]

Plato follows in this tradition by suggesting laws which would prohibit adulteration, price discrimination, or "praising" goods.

If we accept the story of Diogenes with his lantern searching for an honest man, it seems that there was a certain lack of morality in early Athens. And the Agora was no exception; there were complaints that Athenian retailers adulterated their goods, gave short weight and short changed their customers. Aristotle mentions the practice of dishonest tradesmen shifting the fulcrum of their scales toward the pan in which the weights lay.[30] Further, satirists in both Greece and Rome often commented on the dishonesty of merchants as well as others.

The Scholastic writers, too, were concerned with the moral behavior of all members of society. Many sermons were instructional, intended to keep the listener from evil. Berthold describes the manner in which a seller might fall into sin:

> Yet now thou swearest so loudly how good thy wares are, and what profit thou gives the buyer thereby; more than ten or thirty times takest thou the names of all the saints in vain . . . thou swearest laud and boldly: "I have been already offered far more for these wares," and that is a lie.[31]

But the sermon was not solely proscriptive; an example of appropriate seller behavior is also provided: "Thou shouldst say: 'If thou will not buy it, perchance another will; and should thus sell honestly without lie or deceit.'"

By the Fourteenth and Fifteenth centuries, there were several manuals of religious teachings for laymen as well as the clergy. The strategems found in one of these include selling a different article for more than was first bargained, hiding the fault of a thing, as horse dealers do, and making a thing look better than it is, as do cloth sellers who choose dim places to sell their cloth.[32] Another example of sinful seller behavior is even more precise:

> Then I went to the drapers to learn their ways, stratching the selvedge till the cloth seemed longer. I got hold of a trick with a good striped cloth, to prick it with a needle and join the pieces, lay them flat in a press, all pinned together, till ten or twelve yards had turned into thirteen.[33]

Yet, throughout the literature there was a clear distinction drawn between the sinful and proper marketer. As Gower states: "There is a difference between the merchant whose thoughts are set on deceit, and he whose day is spent in honest work; both labor alike for gain, but one cannot be compared with the other."[34]

Marketing is Not the Cause of Sinful Marketers

Steiner argues that marketing as a process was looked down upon, and that this view "rubbed off" on marketers.[35] It has been demonstrated above that the premise of this argument is incorrect, so that the conclusion is erroneous. Moreover, there is a further objection. Not only did the scholastics and others note that some marketers were good, and others bad, but they also recognized that the market was not the cause of sinful behavior. Rather, the causal relationship was the reverse of the "rub off" hypothesis. Marketing as an activity was looked down upon not because of the process itself, but because the participants in the market were by nature open to temptation.

Plato remarks:

> The class of men is small . . . who, when assailed by wants and desires, are able to hold out and observe moderation and when they might make a great deal of money are sober in their wishes, and prefer a moderate to a large gain. But the mass of mankind are the very opposite; their desires are unbounded, and when they might gain in moderation they prefer gains without limit; wherefore all that relates to retail trade and merchandise, and the keeping of taverns is denounced and numbered among dishonorable things.[36]

And Plato's conclusion "If all such occupations were managed on incorrupt principles they would be honored"[35] certainly suggests that it is the marketers who corrupt marketing, not vice versa.

Aristotle holds a similar position. "Some persons are led to believe that making money is the object . . . and that the whole idea of their lives is that they ought either to increase their money without limit, or at any rate not to lose it. . . . Some men turn every quality or art into a means of making money; this they conceive to be the end."[37] And this is the very point that caused the philosophical objection to some kinds of marketing activity. In *Nicomachean Ethics*, the underlying principle of human virtue was moderation; avoiding excesses was an important rule of human conduct.

Some kinds of exchange, such as barter, and the sale of produce from an estate, were "natural" because the purpose of such exchange was to obtain the necessities of life.

Only exchange undertaken for profit was "unnatural," and this was not because it was "marketing" but because the motivation of the participants was viewed as an immoderate acquisition of wealth.

Plato's remedy was to devise some way to prevent marketers from falling into habits of "shamelessness and meanness." And since this could not be completely successful, a limitation on the number of participants would reduce the number who might be injured. Also, where possible, the work would be assigned to that class of men whose corruption would cause the least injury to the state.

The medieval Schoolmen fully recognized that marketing activity should not be condemned because of the sinfulness of the participants. As noted above, St. Augustine argues that if lies and perjuries arose in marketing, they were the fault of the person, not the profession:

> I do not approve of covetous traders... but those failings are in the man and not in his trade, which can be carried on honestly. In all vocations... sins are committed, but it is not the vocations which are at fault, it is the man who sins.[38]

And the sins are many and varied. Markets were held on feast days, so that men failed to attend church, and "some merchants, kept by their voyaging so long away from their wives, seek satisfactions where they should not... and some are careful enough to keep the laws of the market which man has made but are not so careful to keep the laws which are from God."[39] Of course it was not only the merchants who were open to temptation. St. Cyprian complains of the many bishops who "after abandoning their thrones and deserting the people... wandered through foreign provinces and sought the market places for gainful business... they wished to possess money in abundance."[40]

Several of the early Church Councils decreed that no members of the clergy should engage in business or other secular activities. But these decrees did not condemn secular activity; the issue was one of discipline, and had no bearing on the attitude toward marketing or other business pursuits. What was condemned was "the secularity of the motive back of the occupation" and the consequent interference with the clergy's ministerial duty.[41] Moreover, marketing was not the only opportunity for temptation; it was only a part of the whole set of dangers in the outside world. This is seen in the *Ancre Riwle*, a Thirteenth Century religious handbook which states that a nun "ought not to have any thing that draweth her heart outward." Among the numerous prohibitions intended to avoid this danger is "Carry ye on no traffic."[42]

The merchant, of course, faced the temptations of the outside world, so that his character and motivations were of great significance in determining the goodness of his activity. It has been seen above that it was not earning a profit which was sinful, but the adoption of profit as the sole objective of one's behavior. This is consistent with the Biblical admonition against overemphasis upon worldly needs.[43]

Conclusion

The marketing practioner is ill served by professional literature which not only denies his rich heritage but compounds the felony by presenting myths such as "a tradition of prejudice against marketing." There is ample evidence that the role of marketing was appreciated in the earliest literature.

When criticisms of marketing are attributed to non-existent "prejudice," there is the danger of ignoring the underlying issue that marketing, as any social activity, has a social cost as well as benefit. An appreciation of marketing activity by the practitioner, the household buyer and consumer, or the policy maker, requires a recognition of the net social contribution. An evaluation of this net contribution ought to be a part of the formal education of practitioners, as was the case in previous generations.

The problem is that current texts present forty-year-old micro-economics as marketing theory. The present generation has seized upon Chamberlin's model of the manager as a manipulator of marketing variables (price, the product, including place, and promotion) in a quest for sales.[44] But these four "P's" provide no analytical framework for placing marketing activity in a context which links individual and social goals. The foundation of such a framework does exist, having been painstakingly constructed through the efforts of scholars over a score of centuries. It is well past time for the practioner to be informed of this heritage, rather than having such knowledge limited to occasional Ph.D. courses in the History of Marketing Thought.

Notes

1. Robert L. Steiner, "The Prejudice against Marketing," *Journal of Marketing*, Vol. 40 (July 1976), p. 2.
2. Alfred A. Marshall, *Principles of Economics* (1890) New York: The Macmillan Company, 1920, p 63.
3. Same reference as footnote #1.
4. Plato, *The Republic*, Book II.269–371, in *The Dialogues of Plato* Benjamin Jowett, tr. New York: Random House, 1937, Vol. I, pp. 632–634.
5. Plato, *Laws*, XI, 918, R.G. Bury, tr. The Loeb Classical Library, p. 405.
6. Aristotle, *The Politics*, IV, 8, J.A. Sinclair, tr. Harmondsworth, Middlesex: Penguin Books Ltd., 1962, p. 250.
7. Joseph A. Schumpeter, *History of Economic Analysis* New York: Oxford University Press, 1954, p. 56.
8. Quoted in Alexandri de Hales, *Summa Theologica*, Pars II, Ing. III, Tract. II, Sec. II, Quaest, II, Tlt. III Florence: Quaracchi, 1948, Tomus IV, p. 722.
9. Quoted in W.A. Ashley, *An Introduction to English Economic History and Theory*, Longmans, Green, and Co., 1909, Vol. I, Pt. 1, p. 129.
10. Sancti Leonis Magni, *Epist. ad Rusticum*, c. IX., Tr. The Fathers of the Church, V. 34, p. 294.

11. Sancti Aurelii Augustini, *Ennarratio in Psalmum LXX*, 17. Patrologiae Cursus Completus, Series Latina. Paris, 1844–1865, Vol. XXVI, pp. 836–837.
12. Same reference as footnote #1, p. 3.
13. Same reference as footnote #8, p. 723.
14. Joannis Duns Scoti, *Quaestiones in Quartum Librum Sententiarum*, IV. Distinctio 15, Questio, 23, In *Opera Omnia*, Paris, 1894, Vol. 18, p. 320.
15. S. Bernardini Senensis, *Quadragesimale de Evangello Aeterno, Sermon* 33, Art. 2, in *Opera Omnia*. Florence: Quaracchi, 1941, Vol. IV. p. 145.
16. Sancti Thomae Aquinatis, *Summa Theologica*, II, II, Qu. 77, Art, 1, The Fathers of the Church, Vol. 10, p. 328.
17. Martin Luther, *Trade and Usury* (1524). T.G. Tappert, ed., Selected Writings of Martin Luther. Fortress Press, Philadelphia, 1967, Vol. 3, p. 86.
18. Ricardus de Media Villa, *Quodllbeta* II, Questio 23, Art. 1; Sententia III, Distinctio 38, Art. 3, Questio 4, quoted in M. Beer, *Early British Economics*. London: George Allen & Unwin, 1938, pp. 42–43.
19. "Le Profit de L'Un est Dommage de L'Autre," in *Essais de Montaigne*, I, 22. M.J.-V. Le Clerk, ed. Paris: Garnier Frères, 1865, p. 127.
20. "Of Seditions and Troubles" Essay xv, in *The Essays of Francis Bacon*, Samuel H. Reynolds, ed. Oxford: Claredon Press, 1890, p. 99.
21. Ambrose Bierce, *The Devils Dictionary*.
22. Same reference as footnote #1, p. 2; and William T. Kelly, "The Development of Early Thought in Marketing and Promotion," *Journal of Marketing*, Vol. 21 (July 1956) p. 62. Cf. J.M. Cassels, "The Significance of Early Economic Thought on Marketing," *Journal of Marketing*, Vol. 1 (October 1936) pp. 129–130.
23. Same reference as footnote #5, p. 407.
24. Sancti. Thomae Aquinatis, *De Regimine Principum*, ii, 3, quoted in George O'Brien, *An Essay on Medieval Economic Teaching* (London: Longman's Green and Co., 1920, p. 147.
25. Herodotus, *Historiae*, II, 167. A.D. Godley, tr., Loeb Classical Library, Vil. 1, p. 481.
26. Dionysius, Book IX, XXV, 3, in Earnest Carry, tr. *The Roman Antiquities of Dionysius of Halicarnassus*, Loeb Classical Library p. 5.
27. Cicero, *De Officiis*, I, XL, ii., Walter Miller, tr. Loeb Classical Library, p. 153.
28. Marital, Epigram VII, 61[sic], in *Epigrams from Martial*. Barris Mills, tr. Lafayette, Indiana: Purdue University Studies, 1969, p. 125.
29. Deuteronomy 25:13–16.
30. William T. Sedwick and H.W. Tyler, *Short History of Science*. New York: Macmillan, 1927, p. 102.
31. Berthold von: Regensburg. "Sermons," in G.G. Coulton, *A Mediaval Garner*: London: Constable and Company, 1910, p. 349.
32. *Jacob's Well*, Capitulum XX, De Cupiditate, Arthur Brandais, ed. London: Early English Text Society, 1900, pp. 133–134.
33. *The Vision of William Concerning Piers: The Plowman*, V. 209–214, Margaret Williams tr. New York: Random House, 1971, p. 118.
34. John Gower, "Miraur de I'Omne" 25213–25236 in G.C. Macaulay, ed., *The Complete Works of John Gower*. Oxford: Clarendon Press, 1899, p. 279.
35. Same reference as footnote #1.
36. Same reference as footnote #5.
37. Aristotle, *Politics*; I, 9: Benjamin Jowett, tr. London: Oxford University Press, 1905, p. 44.
38. Same reference as footnote #11.

39. Humbart de Romans, *Sermons*, xci, "In Nundinis," 1508.

40. St. Cyprian, *De Lapsis*, 6 (The Fathers of the Church) Vol. 36, p. 61.

41. Henry J. Schroeder, *Disciplinary Decrees of the General Councils*. London: B. Herder Book Co., 1937 p. 91.

42. James Morton, *The Nun's Rule*. London: Chatto & Windus, 1924 p. 316.

43. Matthew 6: 25–34.

44. Edward Chamberlin, *The Theory of Monopolistic Competition*. Cambridge: Harvard University Press, 1933, p. 71.

4

Early Development of the Philosophy of Marketing Thought*

D.G. Brian Jones[1] and David D. Monieson[2]

[1]University of Prince Edward Island, [2]Queen's University, Kingston, Ontario

ABSTRACT *An extensive study of archival materials is used to examine the philosophic origins of marketing thought at two centers of early development, the University of Wisconsin and the Harvard Business School. Evidence suggests that the German Historical school of economics provided much of the philosophic foundation of the discipline.*

I n this article, we attempt to examine some of the currents from which twentieth century marketing thought emerged in order to provide a correct account of its philosophic origins. Marketing historians have identified the first associations, books, and articles pertaining to marketing as we know it today (Bartels 1962). However, these elements reflect marketing once it had been labeled as such. We do not take issue with the accepted wisdom about who the first marketing scholars were, what constitutes the earliest marketing literature, or which university courses were the first in the field of marketing. Nor do we attempt to redefine marketing as it was conceived initially. These facts about the early history of marketing ideas were certainly considered. However, ideas do not develop in a vacuum. We therefore look beyond this patch-work of surface facts

* Article originally published in the *Journal of Marketing* 1990; **54** January: 102–113, American Marketing Association. Reproduced by permission of the American Marketing Association.

and identify some common threads. More precisely, the purpose of our article is to identify and describe some of the philosophic underpinnings of marketing.

Method

Significant historical research involves the collection, analysis, and reporting of primary data (Savitt 1983, p. 30). Therefore, archival research was an essential part of our study. Previous historical research in marketing has identified the significant contributors to the discipline (Bartels 1951, p. 4; Converse 1959; Wright and Dimsdale 1974), the earliest published literature (Converse 1933; Hagerty 1936), and the first university courses (Maynard 1941; Monieson 1981, p. 14). This literature provided many potential sources of primary data.

Inasmuch as the University of Wisconsin and Harvard University were the original centers of influence on the development of marketing thought (Bartels 1962, p. 34), those two institutions were chosen as the major sites of primary research. The collections of Edwin Francis Gay, first dean of the Harvard Business School, and of Richard T. Ely, first director of the School of Economics at the University of Wisconsin, were major sources of data, as were the collections of several other scholars associated with those institutions (see References section). Specifically, data sources included diaries, journals, correspondence, autobiographies, school essays, research notes, and unpublished papers and books.

We do not compare the influences derived from economics with those possible from other social sciences. Such a task is beyond the scope of our study. Instead, we limit our focus to the major influences apparent through economics at two original centres of development of marketing thought.

Origins of the Institutional Approach

During the nineteenth century many American students seeking higher education were attracted to Germany. Various estimates place the number of American students there between 1820 and 1920 at approximately 10,000 (Herbst 1965, p. 1; Thwing 1928, p. 40). This academic migration was impressive, not only in absolute numbers, but also in relation to the American attendance at other European institutions (Thwing 1928, p. 76).

In American colleges the emphasis was on uniformity and discipline. Instruction followed the lecture-and-recitation method. By contrast, the German universities were professional schools. They provided an atmosphere of academic freedom and equality between students and professors. When the first business school associated with the

University of Berlin began classes in 1906, seminars rather than lectures were thought to be a partial answer to the unique educational needs of business students (Redlich 1957, p. 62). During the 1890s and perhaps even earlier, students in economics often went on excursions to various industrial establishments to study firsthand the institutional forces in the economy (Brooks 1906). The academic atmosphere in Germany created in American students a "craftsman's regard for technical expertise, an unfailing respect for accuracy, and a concern for the application of knowledge and skills to social ends" (Herbst 1965, p. 19).

In the latter part of the nineteenth century, a scientific model of historicism, which became identified with the Historical school, began to dominate the social sciences in Germany (Herbst 1965). The Historical school of economics emerged during the middle of the nineteenth century as a reaction to classical economic thinking (Myles 1956). The founders of the Historical school were dissatisfied with the inability of classical economics to resolve the problems associated with the rapid growth of the German economy at that time, such as poverty, industrial development, and development of a banking system (Hildebrand 1848). This preoccupation with solving real economic problems was to rein-force a unique and consistent set of philosophic assumptions about teaching as well as studying economics. The Historical school was distinctive for its historical, statistical methodology (e.g., Roscher 1843), its pragmatism (e.g., Conrad 1868), and its ideals (Herbst 1965, p. 145), rather than for theoretical or conceptual ideas.

A steady stream of German-trained economists began returning to North America during the 1870s. Columbia University hired J.B. Clark, R. Mayo-Smith, and E.R.A. Seligman. To the University of Pennsylvania went S.N. Patten, J.F. Johnson, E.J. James, R.P. Falkner, and E.R. Johnson. This movement also included F.W. Taussig and Edwin Francis Gay, who both went to Harvard, and Richard T. Ely and Henry C. Adams, appointed to positions at Johns Hopkins University. Later, Ely and Adams moved to the University of Wisconsin and University of Michigan, respectively. These individuals were among the most influential Americans to train under the German Historical school. Others followed until the onset of World War I, but the influence was probably strongest during the 1870s and 1880s (Dorfman 1955, p. 24). There are no estimates of the number of economists who trained in Germany during that period, but the total appears to have been substantial (Farnam 1908; Myles 1956, Appendix 2).

Richard T. Ely was a vocal and enduring disciple of the Historical school. On returning from Germany, he accepted a position at Johns Hopkins University and established a reputation as one of America's most reform-minded economists. Ely led an attack on orthodox economic doctrine, ideology, and methodology. In "The Past and Present of Political Economy," Ely proclaimed the succession of the "New School," the German Historical school, over the old school of orthodox, classical economics (1884). He criticized the rigidity and determinism of classical economics as well as its oversimplified notion of economic man (1884, p. 10–12). Ely claimed enthusiastically that "the younger men in

America are clearly abandoning the dry bones of orthodox English political economy for the methods of the German school" (1884, p. 64).

In 1885 Ely led a group of German-trained economists in forming the American Economic Association (AEA). In its founding statement of principles and in its early publications, the AEA revealed the influence of the German Historical school (Ely 1936, p. 144). According to Ely, the formation of the AEA represented both a protest against the system of *laissez-faire* economics and an emphasis on historical and statistical study (Ely 1931, Appendix B).

In 1892 Ely became the first director of the new School of Economics at the University of Wisconsin. Ely's belief in a strong role for the state in certain spheres of industrial activity fit well with the unique philosophy of education at the University of Wisconsin. That philosophy was represented by the term "Wisconsin Idea," which stood essentially for better government through better education. It involved a close working relation between the university and the state government whereby academic experts gave advice on matters of administration. More generally, the Wisconsin Idea was part of the Progressive Movement for which the state became noted during the late nineteenth century. Ely, later described as a "barometer of Wisconsin Progressivism" (Rader 1966, ch. 7), seemed to have been a perfect choice to head the new School of Economics at Wisconsin.

In 1904 Ely invited John R. Commons, who had been his student at Johns Hopkins, to join the faculty at Wisconsin. Commons was to become one of America's most notable institutional economists and his work became a legendary part of the Wisconsin Idea. Commons also was known for his pragmatic approach to teaching. He often brought civil servants, union officials, and other practitioners into his classroom to speak to students. Ely, too, followed this principle of pedagogical pragmatism by employing the seminar method, with which he had become familiar in his course work in Germany. He cited his German education for the realization that book knowledge and practical experience must be combined, especially for business education (Ely, undated). He also liked to quote Commons that "academic teaching... is merely brains without experience; the practical extreme [however] is experience without brains; one is half-baked philosophy, the other is rule of thumb" (Ely 1938, p. 186).

For graduate research, Ely felt the most appropriate topics were ones that were historical and descriptive. Theses supervised by Ely certainly reflected this notion – for example, B.H. Hibbard's (1902) "The History of Agriculture in Dane County, Wisconsin," Paul Nystrom's (1914) "Retail Distribution of Goods," and Theodore Macklin's (1917) "A History of the Organization of Creameries and Cheese Factories in the U.S." In addition, for one of his graduate courses in economics offered in 1899, Ely kept a book that listed suitable topics for student papers. These topics included "The Economic Effects of Changes in Fashion," "Advertising Considered From an Economic Standpoint," and "Competition in Advertising and Effects of Trademarks." Graduate students carried out these studies by applying an inductive method, adopting a historical perspective, and maintaining a concern for the general welfare of society in their search for solutions to economic (often marketing) problems. In this way, many of Ely's students were applying the institutional approach to the study of marketing.

Applying the Institutional Approach to Marketing

Among the first students in economics at Wisconsin were David Kinley (later head of the Economics Department at Illinois), E.D. Jones, Samuel Sparling, James Hagerty (later head of the Economics Department at Ohio State), M.B. Hammond (who later taught under Hagerty at Ohio State), H.C. Taylor, and B.H. Hibbard. These individuals also were among the first noted contributors to the development of marketing thought (Bartels 1951, p. 4).[1] Each had spent some time studying in Germany, as it became Ely's habit to encourage his students to do so whenever possible. In this way a direct link was formed between the German Historical school and many of the earliest contributors to marketing thought.

In 1894, for example, Jones, Sparling, and Hammond traveled together to Germany to study economics. Edward David Jones, though recognized for teaching the first university course in marketing (Bartels 1951, p. 3; Maynard 1941, p. 382), has been curiously overlooked by marketing historians. A recent biographical sketch of Jones describes his considerable contributions to the marketing literature and to teaching (Jones 1987). For example, Jones wrote about the evolution of marketing methods (Ely 1903), the efficiency of the marketing process (1912a), distributive justice (1911b), and the functional approach to marketing (1911c, 1912b, 1913a). He believed that marketing courses were basic to an education in business, along with instruction in administration and accounting/finance. To teach business, however, he believed that scientific investigation was necessary to discover the general principles of those subjects. He added that the appropriate methodology for such study is "the inductive form of the scientific method" (1913b, p. 188). Jones used that method in his own research in marketing, gathering historical, descriptive case studies of marketing processes.

Between 1911 and 1914 Jones published a series of articles in *Mill Supplies* that were remarkable for the tone in which they were presented as well as for the principles and concepts of marketing they identified. In the opening piece, "The Larger Aspects of Private Business," Jones stated that his purpose in presenting the work was to examine "some marketing problems," the most general of which, in Jones' estimation, was the apparent inefficiency of the marketing process (1911a, p. 2). For example, in the retail trade Jones had determined that marketing activity added 50% to the cost of goods and he felt that much of the added cost was waste due to advertising and an overabundance of retail stores (1912c, p. 461).

Jones believed that a philosophy or science of business, and similarly of distribution or marketing, could be developed. It would require the development of principles based on empirical data and would be practiced by professionals whose objective would be to promote the general welfare (Ely 1918). This vision of science was similar to that held by his mentor, Richard T. Ely, and by the German Historical school under which Jones had also studied.

Samuel Sparling returned from Germany with Jones to complete a thesis on public administration. He then taught that subject at Wisconsin until 1909. In 1906 Sparling published *Introduction to Business Organization*. In that volume (p. 3–4) he described how he believed a science of business could be developed:

> Science is based upon accumulated experience. Classification is the result of a comparison of differences and similarities . . . We may describe and classify the facts of business in such a way as to indicate their underlying tendencies and principles.

Sparling classified all business activity as extractive, manufacturing, or distributive. Distribution was divided further into marketing activities that facilitate exchange. Marketing proper was defined as "those commercial processes which are concerned with the distribution of raw materials of production and the finished output of the factory . . . Their function is to give additional value to these commodities through exchange" (p. 17).

In the section of Sparling's book covering "Organization of Distributive Industries" are chapters on the evolution of the market, exchanges, direct selling, wholesaling and retailing, traveling salesmanship, the mail-order business, advertising, and credits and collections. Sparling clearly viewed marketing as part of a science of business that would be developed by following the methodology of the German Historical school, that is, by using an inductive, comparative, historical approach. With its extensive discussion of marketing-related topics, Sparling's book later was credited by James Hagerty (1936, p. 22) as one of the earliest contributions to the literature of marketing.

Hagerty himself was a student of Ely's and also studied in Germany. Of this training he later commented, "I believe that I have been influenced as much by American as by German teachers in the methods of the German economists. I make to mention Professor Ely especially whose influence has been in that direction" (1906).

Another of Ely's students, Henry C. Taylor, was even clearer on the influence of Ely and the German Historical school. Following Ely's advice, Taylor went to England in 1899, then to Germany where he studied under Johannes Conrad at the University of Halle and Max Sering at the University of Berlin. Conrad's courses in agricultural economics were described by Taylor as "historical and descriptive in character," concentrating on the political economy of agriculture rather than on the technical aspects of farming. At Berlin he also took courses from Wagner and Schmoller of the Historical school.

When Taylor returned from Germany to Wisconsin in 1901, he began teaching economic history and economic geography. One of Taylor's first moves was to give the course in economic geography more emphasis on agriculture and marketing. As he later described it (1941, p. 23):

From two-thirds to three-quarters of the time in the course in economic geography was spent in describing where each of the important agricultural products was grown, where it was consumed, and the transporting, merchandising, and processing which it underwent as it passed from producer to consumer.

The text used in this course was Volume VI of the Report of the United States Industrial Commission of 1900, entitled, "Distribution and Marketing of Farm Products" (Taylor 1941, p. 23). It provided descriptions of the distribution of cereals, cotton, and dairy products and of the marketing of livestock, as well as a discussion of the significance of cold storage and refrigeration in the marketing of perishable products. In Taylor's opinion (Taylor and Taylor 1974, p. 517), Volume VI of the Industrial Commission Report was:

... by all odds the best book on agricultural marketing available to students of agricultural economics at the beginning of the twentieth century ... The facts assembled and the methods of presentation made it possible for the reader to develop in his mind a fairly clear picture of marketing processes and price-making forces.

In presenting statistical facts from original and official sources in a descriptive way, the approach used in that report was consistent with the general approach to the study of economics at Wisconsin.

In 1906, as the interest of Wisconsin farmers in the activities of middlemen grew, Taylor began studying the cooperative creameries and cheese factories in southern Wisconsin. In 1910 he published an article on the prices of farm products. Taylor's conclusions about the prices of eggs, butter, and cheese were consistent with the notion that middlemen serve an essential function for which a price must be paid. Nevertheless, there was continued skepticism and the state legislature wanted further investigation.

As part of those investigations, two senior students in agricultural economics were given the task of studying the marketing of Wisconsin cheese. Together with Taylor, in 1913, they published the results of their investigations as "The Marketing of Wisconsin Cheese" (Taylor, Schoenfeld, and Wehrwein 1913). Using extensive descriptive statistics and maps, they illustrated where cheese was produced and where it was consumed. Most of the study, however, described the middleman processes: the advantages and disadvantages of a cheesemaker versus a sales agent in carrying out the selling function, the various types of retailers and wholesalers, the operation of dairy boards, retail prices, and the services rendered by various middlemen. Taylor commented that "while our findings tended to sober those persons who had been speaking excitedly about the marketing problem, they made it perfectly clear that, in certain stages in the marketing of Wisconsin cheese, the agencies were not functioning satisfactorily" (1941, p. 16).

This early research on the marketing of Wisconsin cheese was significant in several ways. It signified the beginning of a specialization by the Department of Agricultural

Economics in marketing and cooperatives, which is considered to be its single most important contribution to the study of agriculture (Pulver 1984, p. 7). Also, a flurry of graduate research inspired by this initial study led to numerous theses in agricultural marketing, including G.S. Wehrwein's (1913) "The Dairy Boards of Wisconsin," W.A. Schoenfeld's (1914) "Seasonal and Geographical Distribution of Wisconsin Cheddar Cheese for the Year 1911," H.R. Walker's (1915) "The Cooperative Marketing of Livestock in Wisconsin," E.T. Cusick's (1916) "The Raising and Marketing of Wisconsin Tobacco," and P.A.C. Eke's (1920) "Marketing Wisconsin Potatoes."

This research led to the return to Wisconsin of B.H. Hibbard (from the University of Iowa) in 1913 and Theodore Macklin (from Kansas State College) in 1917 as faculty members in agricultural economics to specialize in cooperation and marketing (Taylor 1941, p. 19). Hibbard, Taylor, and several of the graduate students in the department published a series of studies including "Agricultural Cooperation" (1914), "Markets and Prices of Wisconsin Cheese" (1915), "The Marketing of Wisconsin Butter" (1915), "Cooperation in Wisconsin" (1917), and "Marketing Wisconsin Milk" (1917). The latter study led to a thesis and subsequent book entitled *The Marketing of Whole Milk* (1921), by H.E. Erdman. That book, as well as Hibbard's (1921) *The Marketing of Agricultural Products* and Macklin's (1921) *Efficient Marketing for Agriculture*, were seminal contributions to the marketing literature.

Taylor observed that the series of articles published between 1913 and 1917 all followed a common pattern. Each study was designed "to picture the marketing process clearly in order that the true character of the problems of marketing might be discovered" (1941, p. 22). Each study proceeded from a perceived marketing problem and the method was always the same: to observe the facts, to look and see, and then formulate principles and recommendations.

From its inception in 1892, the School of Economics at the University of Wisconsin developed an institutional approach to the study of economics. This approach included an inductive, statistical methodology with a historical perspective and a concern for the application of knowledge and skills to social ends. Directly and indirectly this approach was derived from the German Historical school of economics. Therefore, as a center of the early development of marketing thought, the University of Wisconsin provided the emerging discipline with a distinctive and well-developed philosophic foundation.

Origins of Scientific Marketing Management

Harvard University, and in particular the Graduate School of Business, was the other center of early influence on the development of marketing thought. Founded in 1908, the School was based on a vision of business as a profession, an art, and a science. As such, it became one of the first truly academic, professional business schools in the world.

As at Wisconsin, the seeds of teaching and research in marketing at Harvard were planted by the Economics Department. For example, the Harvard economists Frank W. Taussig and Edwin Francis Gay have been recognized for their contribution to the development of marketing thought (Bartels 1951, p. 4). Both were instrumental in the planning of the Harvard Business School and Gay became the School's first dean. As dean of the Business School, Gay was the major instigator of research and teaching in marketing.

Taussig studied at the University of Berlin in 1879 and 1880. He was less enthusiastic than some, however, about the ideas of his German teachers, claiming (1906) to have been influenced more by Alfred Marshall. During the early twentieth century many American marketing scholars turned to the more deductive approach of the neoclassical economists such as Marshall in their attempts to develop marketing theory (Sheth and Gross 1988, p. 10). The most popular sources of these ideas were Marshall's *Principles of Economics* (1890) and *Industry and Trade* (1919).

In 1911 Taussig published his own *Principles of Economics*. Nonetheless, he was an economic historian, as demonstrated in his first book, *Tariff History of the United States* (1886). Though he may have been influenced more by Alfred Marshall, he would at least have appreciated the positive contributions of the Historical school. As Marshall himself stated (Pigou 1956, p. 165):

> It would be difficult to overrate the importance of the work that has been done by the great leaders of this school in tracing the history of economic habits and institutions.

Taussig was also a friend and colleague of Ignaz Jastrow, who became the first Rector of the business school founded at Berlin in 1906. Under Jastrow the Berlin Handelshochschule shared an educational philosophy with Harvard that "focused on the real world of business and at the same time was truly academic in nature" (Redlich 1957, p. 35).

As a member of the committee formed in 1906 by Harvard President Charles W. Eliot to plan the Harvard Business School, Taussig singled out the German business schools for comparison with existing American ones. He wrote the following comments to Gay in 1907:

> The movement for advanced instruction of this kind is active throughout the world, most so in Germany and in the U.S. In Germany it has resulted in at least two large institutions of high grade, liberally supported at Berlin and Cologne. In this country, the Universities of Pennsylvania, Michigan, Wisconsin, Illinois, California and Dartmouth College.

Undoubtedly, Taussig's opinions about the formation of the Business School were influenced by his familiarity with developments in Germany and by his own training there.

Much more profound was the impact of the School's first dean, Edwin Francis Gay, on the development of marketing thought. Like Taussig, Gay was very familiar with developments in Germany. He had studied history at the University of Leipzig during 1890–91, then political economy at the University of Berlin from 1891 to 1893 under Wagner and Schmoller of the Historical school. He later studied in Zurich during 1894 before returning to Berlin to finish his doctoral degree under Schmoller in 1901–02. According to Heaton (1949, p. 12–13):

> It was Schmoller who really fired Gay's enthusiasm: first by belief that economics could be made into a real social science by being brought into close relation with psychology, ethics, history and political science; second, by his faith, accompanied by hope, charity and hard work – that economics could be converted into an inductive science through the patient study of economic phenomena past and present . . . Private conversations with Schmoller were among Gay's treasured memories of his Berlin days; the phrase "Schmoller says" appears occasionally in letters when Gay was interpreting some part of the European scene; and when Gay began to have graduate students of his own he tried to model his treatment of them on the example of his German master.

Indeed, Gay once commented, "If I could only transfer some of Schmoller's qualities into my work as a teacher I would be happy" (Heaton 1949, p. 61). That wish apparently was realized. One of Gay's students in economic history later observed that "he was not given to vague theorizing. . . hardly ever paused to generalize" (Cole 1970, p. 34).

Gay credited the German Historical school for founding the discipline of economic history (1941). He singled out Wilhelm Roscher as the "original formulator" of the Historical school and cited Karl Knies' principle of historical relativity as well as the use of a comparative method as highlights of the school's contribution to research methodology. He also recognized the intense struggle of the Historical economists, especially Schmoller, with the manner in which generalizations could be developed from the mass of economic facts being collected, summarized, and synthesized. The reason for that struggle was the inherent complexity of economic events. Gay commented (1923, p. 2) that:

> . . . the longer I live, the more inclined I am to agree with the late Professor Schmoller of Berlin that the world of political, social-psychological, and economic phenomena is a terribly complicated business.

Nevertheless Gay maintained, as the Historical school had, that the ultimate objective of inductive research is to produce generalizations and principles. Consistent with his German training, Gay believed that the scientific principles and generalizations of business should be "built up by observation and induction from widely gathered and carefully sifted facts" (1927a).

In Gay's words, the Harvard Business School was to become a "simple scientific endeavor" (Cruikshank 1987, ch. 2). This modest objective, however, was to lead to some fundamental achievements that became Harvard's principal contributions to the development of marketing thought. First, Gay had to determine what was essential to be taught; he had to define the subject matter of business. Second, he had to determine how that subject matter would be taught.

Gay's answer to the first of these challenges was to divide business into "two fundamental functions of industrial management [production] and commercial organization or marketing" (Gay quoted by Hanford 1954, p. 7). During the time when the Business School was being planned, Frederick W. Taylor and his associates were developing a body of knowledge about the industrial management aspect of business and Gay adopted it enthusiastically for the School. Taylor used time and motion studies of work activity and the detailed observation and measurement of work to develop his principles of scientific management. Those principles were considered scientific because they were "generalized rules of conduct based on law . . . a summary statement of fact or a description of a tendency common to a class of things" (Thompson 1917, p. 5). Apparently, as a member of a committee drafting a detailed plan of programs, courses, and arrangements, Gay was searching for and identifying materials for the Business School's courses. Taylor's seminal articles on the "Art of Cutting Metals" (1906) and "Shop Management" (1903) were among the first to be noted in that connection (Gay 1907).

Industrial management was only one of the two basic functions of business. The other, as Gay defined it, was distribution or marketing. When the School opened in 1908, there were three required courses: Principles of Accounting, Commercial Contracts, and Economic Resources of the United States. According to Copeland (1958, p. 3), the general idea for the latter course was developed by Gay on the basis of his background in economic history and his interest in marketing methods. The course first was taught by Paul Cherington and later (in 1914) evolved into the course titled "Marketing."

The distinctive philosophy of marketing science being developed at Harvard was manifested in three specific forms: the case method of teaching, the Bureau of Business Research, and Arch W. Shaw's description of the basic functions of marketing.

The Case Method

The case method often is cited as a significant and distinctive contribution of Harvard to the development of marketing thought. On the basis of his 1945 survey of marketing scholars, Converse reported that the case method was voted one of the most important concepts or techniques in marketing (1945, p. 20). Bartels also concluded that the case method was Harvard's "principal contribution throughout the years to the development of marketing thought" (1951, p. 11) and cited Copeland (1920), Tosdal (1921), McNair and David (1925), and Borden (1927) as examples.

Consistent with his vision of business as a profession, a science, and an art, Gay recognized from the outset the need for a unique means of teaching business (1908, p. 161):

> The teacher of business . . . must discover the fundamental principles of business system, and then, in a scientific spirit, teach not only those principles, but the art of applying them after investigation, to any given enterprise. This means, then, that new courses of study must be organized and that a laboratory-system of instruction must, as far as possible, be introduced.

The term "laboratory method" was derived from the method of teaching in the natural sciences on which the seminar method, used so successfully in Germany, was modeled. In a 1927 speech about the founding of the Business School, Gay further described this conception of the laboratory method as an "experimental laboratory studying genetically and theoretically the institutions and processes of our economic organization and practically [applying] the new insights for the continued betterment of our business practise" (1927b, p. 400).

Another emphasis in Gay's early thinking about business training was the role of historical study. Certainly here his training under the Historical school was influential. The following reflections were jotted down in Gay's personal journal in 1910 shortly after the School opened.

> For most business men do not know enough history to make analogies, those who do, know enough to make analogies . . . Some influence of the historical method in spirit. Gaining of perspective, realization of changing character of institutions apparently stable . . . sense of proportion . . . relation to principles . . . realization of complexity and interrelations and their modification of too rigid and simple standards of judgement.

Though these notes are only fragments of Gay's thinking on the matter, they indicate the importance he attributed to historical study in a business school. Therein lay the foundation of the case method at the Harvard Business School. As Harvard business historian Alfred Chandler recently observed, "Don't forget, the heart of this school's curriculum has always been the case study, and the case study is precisely what a historian does, what a historian is trained to do" (Kantrow 1986, p. 82).

Research in Marketing

Gay's training as an economic historian probably influenced his views on research methodology even more than those on pedagogy. Much of that methodological perspective is described in the preceding section. The first clear example of its application to the field of marketing, however, was probably the Bureau of Business Research. The Bureau was formed in 1911 with the financial assistance and urging of Arch W. Shaw.

In 1911 Gay remarked to Shaw, "What is needed is a quantitative measurement for the marketing side of distribution," to which Shaw replied in writing, "I wish to give for use in this School a fund which shall be applied for the purpose of investigation of business problems, primarily for the problem of distribution of products" (Cruikshank 1987, p. 59). The result of Shaw's initiative was the establishment of the Bureau of Business Research under the direction of staff members of the Business School.

The first director of the Bureau was Seldin O. Martin and the first studies carried out were of the shoe industry. As Martin explained (1916, p. 266):

> The field of marketing seemed especially promising for research. It has apparently received less scientific attention than production in the field of manufacturing at least. Why was there such a variety of methods of selling and in channels of distribution? The concrete fact that from one-fourth to one-half of the retail selling price of an article is consumed in getting the article from the producer to the consumer seemed of itself worthy of study without prejudice for or against the existing order.

In the more industrialized economy of the eastern United States, the distribution or marketing problems being studied were different from those of the Midwest. Whereas agriculture provided most of the subject matter for research on marketing problems at the University of Wisconsin, retailing and manufacturing were the focus of similar work at Harvard. Hence, studies of the shoe industry were the first to be carried out and were followed by the study of grocery retailing. Following from this research, class-room discussion in marketing courses often centered on such topics as the department store, retailers' work and methods, and marketing problems as factors in industrial development.

The problems studied at Harvard were also different from those studied at Wisconsin in that they were the problems faced by individual marketing managers. In Arch W. Shaw's words, they were concerned with the "how to" of marketing. Marketing scholars at Wisconsin tended to be more concerned with whether the entire system was working "properly." At Harvard the emphasis was on the marketing policies of business firms.

In commenting on the research being carried out by the Bureau, Gay drew a parallel between the research methodology of the School and its pedagogy (1912a, p. 1215–17):

> There are laboratories for the natural sciences both pure and applied; there are agricultural experiment stations for the farmer; why not a laboratory for business? The primary object of this research is the development of instruction in the school. But it should also give to the business man a partial basis for judgement in meeting his particular problems.

This use of an inductive, historical method was not confined to the Bureau of Business Research, though. One of the earliest student research papers to apply the historical approach was one that identified the basic functions of marketing.

Basic Functions of Marketing

The concept of "marketing functions" has been hailed as one of the most significant theoretical developments of early contemporary marketing thought (Hunt and Goolsby 1988). Indeed, it has been compared with the discovery of atomic theory (Converse 1945, p. 19). There is some consensus that Arch W. Shaw originated the functional approach in his 1912 article, "Some Problems in Market Distribution" (Converse 1945, p. 18; Faria 1983, p. 162; Hunt and Goolsby 1988, p. 36). Shaw used the term "functions" to refer to acts or services performed by middlemen (1912, p. 731). In describing these as "general" functions, Shaw clearly had in mind that they were universal, that the performance of such functions was a principle or law-like generalization of marketing. To study such marketing problems, Shaw advocated what he called the "laboratory method," which included the use of observation, statistics, comparison, and an historical perspective (1912, p. 754). The product of such a scientific method, in Shaw's view, would be general principles, exemplified by the functions of middlemen.

On the surface Shaw's 1912 statement of marketing functions appears to be a series of simple assertions. In fact, Shaw had used the laboratory method in the form of a historical, statistical study of the role of merchants in the British economy. The findings of that study led to the writing of "Some Problems in Market Distribution." As a student of Gay's in 1910, Shaw undertook a research project that led directly to his seminal 1912 article. Shaw (1950) described that sequence of events in the following way:

> Dean Gay of Harvard had the knack of challenging the energies of students. In one of his lectures on the economic history of England he put special emphasis on the contribution of the merchant in the extension of the British economy both at home and around the world. The emphasis to me was, in effect, a challenge to trace the development of distribution stage by stage starting with the role of the British merchant as the handicraft period came to a close . . . So it seemed of significance also to trace through the functions supplementing those of the merchant, which together with his functions made up the compound of the British economy and then to search for some simple concept by means of which these functions would fall naturally into definite classifications and their interdependence disclosed.

At about the same time as Shaw's 1912 article was published, Gay presented an address to the American Historical Association in which he stated (1912b, p. 7):

> One of the most interesting problems which the historian of domestic trade will face is that of the organization of the domestic market, and with this goes the study of the middleman, the morphology of the merchant . . . It is of importance to know how this orthodox system of market distribution came into existence, what needs it met, how far and in what industries

those needs have persisted. We ought to know more definitely what has been the evolution of the merchant and his various functions.

Gay's research agenda apparently had been accepted by Shaw, as was evident in the latter's description of the evolution of distribution in England and in his seminal article on the basic functions of marketing.

Gay's use of the term "morphology" in his address is especially interesting as it reflects a tendency to anthropomorphize the phenomena of economics, a tendency very characteristic of the German Historical school. For example, in his lecture notes on the Historical school, Gay often referred to their "organic conception of society" (undated). In fact, Wilhelm Roscher referred to the historical method as yielding the anatomy and physiology of the economy (1878, p. 111):

> Our aim is simply to describe man's economic nature and economic wants, to investigate the laws and the character of the institutions which are adapted to the satisfaction of these wants, and the greater or less amount of success by which they have been attended. Our task is, therefore, so to speak, the anatomy and physiology of social or national economy.

But for the last sentence, that quotation could have appeared in any modern-day marketing text. Similarly, Gay saw the task of marketing scholars to be the description of the morphology of the merchant. Shaw's contribution in that area was the basic functions of middlemen.

Conclusion

During the early part of the twentieth century, when marketing thought began to emerge in its contemporary form, North American economics was divided fairly clearly into neoclassical and institutional schools of thought (Arndt 1981, p. 38). Neoclassical economics was the offspring of English classical economics. Institutionalism has been traced to the German Historical school of economics (Dorfman 1955; Myles 1956).

The German Historical school developed a particular version of a positivistic philosophy of science. Their approach to economics might well be considered a paradigm or a research tradition. That research tradition was an inductive-statistical version of positivism. It combined the exploratory, descriptive, process orientation of nineteenth century German Idealism with a faith in the objectivity of facts and a concern with problem solving. Together, these intellectual threads were woven into a relatively sophisticated vision of science, one that was used by scholars at the University of Wisconsin and at Harvard to intellectualize marketing practice.

The Intellectual Genealogy of Marketing

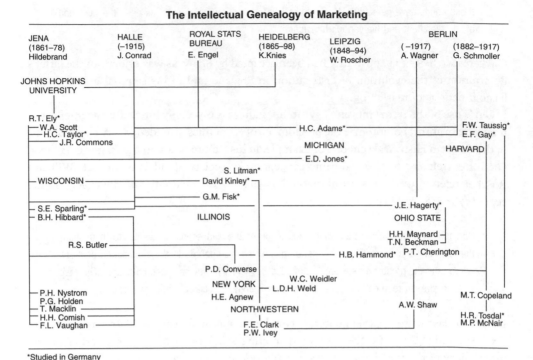

*Studied in Germany

Figure 1 The Intellectual Genealogy of Marketing

The courses taught and literature written by many of the earliest marketing scholars at the University of Wisconsin and the Harvard Business School reflected the philosophic assumptions and ideals we have described. This evidence, combined with the fact that many of the early marketing scholars actually studied in Germany under the Historical school or under American economists who had studied there and who had adopted that philosophic position, would be enough to suggest that the German Historical school provided a philosophic foundation for many of our early marketing scholars (Figure 1). In addition, several scholars clearly identified with the field of marketing, as well as economists with a major interest in marketing, explicitly acknowledged that the German Historical school influenced their thinking.[2]

We do not suggest that scholars at these two institutions were not influenced by other individuals or ideas not associated with the Historical school. The Progressive Movement and the relatively large German population in Wisconsin at the turn of the century provided a receptive environment for Ely's German-inspired institutionalism. Also, the relatively well-developed doctrine of scientific management, together with the popular philosophic movement of Pragmatism at Harvard, undoubtedly reinforced the philosophy followed by Taussig and especially by Gay. The extent of other such influences and the nature of philosophic underpinnings at other institutions in North America are topics for further research. We examine only the major sources of philosophic influence at the two recognized centers of early development of marketing thought.

Many marketing scholars today believe that the discipline only recently has become aware of its underlying philosophy of science and, hence, to debate the status of marketing as a science. Most date the beginning of this discussion to Converse's 1945 article. However, we now can see more clearly that the earliest scholars of this century believed marketing could be developed into a science – one based largely on the philosophy of the German Historical school.

Notes

1. We do not discuss L.D.H. Weld because no strong, direct links could be demonstrated between Weld and either of the two American institutions used as data collection sites. However, we can speculate on Weld's indirect connection with the German Historical school by virtue of his having studied economics at the University of Illinois (MA Economics 1907) and Columbia (PhD 1908) and having taught at Wharton (1909–1910). Both Columbia and Pennsylvania were popular with German-trained economists during the late nineteenth century. The University of Illinois also had the potential for such influence through George Fisk, Simon Litman, and David Kinley (Figure 1). An institutionalist and prominent early marketing scholar, Weld may have been influenced through his association with these institutions.
2. We speculate that marketing courses may actually have been offered in Germany before those offered at American institutions around the turn of the century. A report sent to Benjamin Hibbard at the University of Wisconsin from the American Consulate-General in Berlin indicates that courses in agricultural marketing were offered as early as 1912 and possibly earlier (Thakara 1913). A course description in the 1912/13 catalogue for the University of Berlin read (Thakara 1913, p. 5):

> General course in business management. Includes credit, competition, speculation, the methods
> and psychology of advertising, selling methods and organization tariff technique. Organization
> of commercial establishments in particular branches. The grain trade and the marketing of grain.

The report concluded, ". . . in most, if not all, of the universities there are opportunities for the study of various phases of economics bearing in a broad way on the subject of marketing" (Thakara 1913, p. 2).

References

Arndt, Johan (1981), "The Political Economy of Marketing Systems: Reviving the Institutional Approach," *Journal of Macromarketing*, 1 (Fall), 36–47.
Bartels, Robert (1951), "Influences on the Development of Marketing Thought, 1900–1923," *Journal of Marketing*, 16(1), 1–17.

—— (1962), *The Development of Marketing Thought*. Homewood, IL: Irwin Press.

Borden, Neil H. (1927), *Problems in Advertising*. New York: A. W. Shaw Co.

Brooks, Robert (1906), Brooks to Henry W. Farnam, unpublished correspondence, *Farnam Family Papers*. New Haven, CT: Yale University Library Archives.

Cole, Arthur (1970), "The First Dean: A Wondrous Choice," *Harvard Business School Bulletin* (May–June), 32–34.

Conrad, Johannes (1868), "Die Statistik der Landwirthschaftlichen Production," *Jahrbucher fur Nationalokonomie und Statistik*, 10, 81.

Converse, Paul D. (1933), "The First Decade of Marketing Literature," *NATMA Bulletin* (November), 1–4.

—— (1945), "The Development of the Science of Marketing," *Journal of Marketing*, 10 (July), 14–23.

—— (1959), *The Beginning of Marketing Thought in the United States*: Austin: Bureau of Business Research, University of Texas.

Copeland, Melvin T. (1920), *Marketing Problems*. New York: A. W. Shaw Co.

—— (1958), *And Mark an Era: The Story of the Harvard Business School*. Boston: Little, Brown & Co.

Cruikshank, Jeffrey L. (1987), *A Delicate Experiment: The Harvard Business School 1908–1945*. Cambridge, MA: Harvard Business School Press.

Dorfman, Joseph (1955), "The Role of the German Historical School in American Economic Growth," *American Economic Review*, 45 (May Supplement), 17–39.

Ely, Richard T. (1884), "The Past and Present of Political Economy," in *Johns Hopkins University Studies in Political Science*. Baltimore: Johns Hopkins University, 1–64.

—— (undated), "Economics and Social Science in Relation to Business Education," unpublished manuscript, *Ely Papers*. Madison: State Historical Society of Wisconsin.

—— (1891), Ely to E. A. Ross, June 23, unpublished correspondence, *Ely Papers*. Madison: State Historical Society of Wisconsin.

—— (1903), E. D. Jones to Ely, March 18, unpublished correspondence, *Ely Papers*. Madison: State Historical Society of Wisconsin.

—— (1906), Ely to Henry W. Farnam, unpublished correspondence, *Farnam Family Papers*. New Haven, CT: Yale University Library Archives.

—— (1918), E.D. Jones to Ely, February 3, unpublished correspondence, *Ely Papers*. Madison: State Historical Society of Wisconsin.

—— (1931), Remarks of Richard T. Ely at the Annual Meeting of the AEA. unpublished manuscript, *Ely Papers*. Madison: State Historical Society of Wisconsin.

—— (1936), "The Founding and Early History of the American Economic Association," *Proceedings of the American Economic Association*, 26 (December), 141–50.

—— (1938), *Ground Under Our Feet*. New York: Macmillan Publishing Co.

Faria, A.J. (1983), "The Development of the Functional Approach to the Study of Marketing to 1940," in *First North American Workshop on Historical Research in Marketing*, Stanley Hollander and Ronald Savitt, eds. East Lansing: Michigan State University, 160–9.

Farnam, Henry W. (1908), "Deutsche-amerikanische Bezie-hungen in der Volkswirtschaft-slehre," in *Die Entwicklung der Deutschen Volkswirtschaftslehre im Neunzehnten Jahrundert*, Gustav Schmoller, ed., Leipzig, 25–9.

Fullerton, Ronald A. (1987), "The Poverty of Ahistorical Analysis: Present Weakness and Future Cure in U.S. Marketing Thought," in *Philosophical and Radical Thought in Marketing*, F. Firat, N. Dholakia, and Richard Bagozzi, eds. Lexington, MA: Lexington Books.

Gay, Edwin Francis (1907), Diaries 1907–1914, unpublished diaries, *Edwin Francis Gay Collection*. San Marino, CA: The Huntington Library.

—— (1908), "The New Graduate School of Business Administration," *Harvard Illustrated Magazine*, 9, 159–61.

—— (1912a), "The Scientific Study of Retailing," *Hardware Dealer's Magazine* (December), 1215–17.

—— (1912b), "The History of Modern Commerce as a Field of Investigation," unpublished address to Historical Association, *Edwin Francis Gay Collection*. San Marino, CA: The Huntington Library.

—— (1923), "The Rhythm of History," *Harvard Graduate Magazine*, 2.

—— (1927a), "Social Progress and Business Education," Gay's Addresses, Address delivered at the Dedication of Weiboldt Hall, Northwestern University, June 16, *Edwin Francis Gay Collection*. San Marino, CA: The Huntington Library.

—— (1927b), "The Founding of the Harvard Business School," *Harvard Business Review*, 5 (July), 397–400.

—— (1941), "The Tasks of Economic History," *Journal of Economic History*, 1.

Hagerty, James E. (1906), "Hagerty to Henry W. Farnam," unpublished correspondence, *Farnam Family Papers*. New Haven, CT: Yale University Library Archives.

—— (1936), "Experiences of Our Early Marketing Teachers," *Journal of Marketing*, 1 (July), 20–7.

Hanford, G.H. (1954), "About the Formative Years," *Harvard Business School Bulletin*, 219–24.

Heaton, Herbert A. (1949), "The Making of an Economic Historian," *Journal of Economic History*, Supplement 9, 1–18.

Herbst, Jurgen (1965), *The German Historical School in American Scholarship*. New York: Cornell University Press.

Hildebrand, Bruno (1848), *Die National Okonomie der Gegenwart and Zukunst*. Frankfurt: J. Rutten.

Hunt, Shelby D. and Jerry Goolsby (1988), "The Rise and Fall of the Functional Approach to Marketing: A Paradigm Displacement Perspective," in *Historical Perspectives in Marketing: Essays in Honor of Stanley Hollander*, Terence Nevett and Ronald Fullerton, eds. Lexington, MA: Lexington Books, 35–51.

Jones, D. G. Brian (1987), "Edward David Jones: A Pioneer in Marketing," in *Marketing in Three Eras*, Stanley Hollander and Terence Nevett, eds. East Lansing: Michigan State University, 126–34.

Jones, Edward David (1911a), "The Larger Aspects of Private Business," *Mill Supplies*, 1, 2–4.

—— (1911b), "Quantity Prices Versus Classified Lists," *Mill Supplies*, 1, 245.

—— (1911c), "Functions of a System of Grades," *Mill Supplies*, 1, 529–30.

—— (1912a), "Cost of Living and the Retail Trade," *Mill Supplies*, 2, 577.

—— (1912b), "Functions of the Merchant," *Mill Supplies*, 2, 575–7.

—— (1912c), "Principles of Modern Retail Merchandising," *Mill Supplies*, 2, 461–2.

—— (1913a), "Function of Trade Marks," *Mill Supplies*, 3, 69–70.

—— (1913b), "Some Propositions Concerning University Instruction in Business Administration," *Journal of Political Economy*, 21, 185–95.

Kantrow, Alan M. (1986), "Why History Matters to Managers," *Harvard Business Review*, 64 (January–February). 81–8.

Knies, Karl (1853), *Die Politische Ockonomie vom Standpunkte der Geschichtlichen Methode*. Braunschweig: C.A. Schwetschke.

Marshall, Alfred (1890), *Principles of Economics*. London: Macmillan & Co.

—— (1919), *Industry and Trade*, 2nd ed. London: Macmillan & Co.

Martin, Seldin O. (1916), "The Bureau of Business Research," *Harvard Alumni Bulletin*, 266–9.

Maynard, Harold H. (1941), "Marketing Courses Prior to 1910," *Journal of Marketing*, 5 (April), 382–4.

McNair, Malcolm P. and D.K. David (1925), *Problems in Retailing*. Chicago: A. W. Shaw Co.

Monicson, David D. (1981), "What Constitutes Usable Knowledge in Marketing?" *Journal of Macromarketing*, 1 (Spring), 14–22.

Myles, Jack C. (1956), "German Historicism and American Economics—A Study of the Influence of the German Historical School on American Economic Thought," PhD dissertation, Princeton University.

Pigou, A. C., ed. (1956), *Memorials of Alfred Marshall*. New York: Kelley & Millman Inc.

Pulver, Glen C. (1984), "Improving Agriculture and Rural Life," in *Achievements in Agricultural Economics 1909–1984*. Madison: University of Wisconsin.

Rader, Benjamin (1966), *The Academic Mind and Reform: The Influence of Richard T. Ely in American Life*. Lexington: University of Kentucky Press.

Redlich, Fritz (1957), "Academic Education for Business: Its Development and the Contribution of Ignaz Jastrow (1856–1937)," *Business History Review*, 31 (Spring), 35–93.

Roscher, Wilhelm (1843), *Grundriss zu Vorlesungen uber die Staatswirthschaft nach Geschichtlichen Methode*. Gottingen: Dieterich.

—— (1878), *Principles of Political Economy*, translated by John J. Lalor, Vol. 1. Chicago: Callaghan & Co.

Savitt, Ronald (1980), "Historical Research in Marketing," *Journal of Marketing*, 44 (Fall), 52–8.

—— (1983), "A Note on the Varieties and Vagaries of Historical Data," *First North American Workshop on Historical Research in Marketing*, Stanley Hollander and Ronald Savitt, eds, East Lansing: Michigan State University, 30–4.

Shaw, Arch W. (1912), "Some Problems in Market Distribution," *Quarterly Journal of Economics*, 26, 703–65.

—— (1950), "Acceptance Speech at the 1950 Converse Award," unpublished manuscript, *Edwin Francis Gay Collection*. San Marino, CA: The Huntington Library.

Sheth, Jagdish N. and Barbara L. Gross (1988), "Parallel Development of Marketing and Consumer Behavior: A Historical Perspective," in *Historical Perspectives in Marketing*, Terence Nevett and Ronald Fullerton, eds. Lexington, MA: Lexington Books, 9–33.

Sparling, Samuel E. (1906), *Introduction to Business Organization*. New York: Macmillan Publishing Co.

Taussig, Frank (1906), Taussig to Henry W. Farnam, unpublished correspondence, *Farnam Family Papers*. New Haven, CT: Yale University Library Archives.

—— (1907), Taussig to Gay, unpublished correspondence, *C.W. Eliot Papers*. Cambridge, MA: Harvard University Archives, Pusey Library.

Taylor, Henry C. (1908), Taylor to B. H. Hibbard, unpublished correspondence, *Henry Charles Taylor Papers*. Madison: State Historical Society of Wisconsin.

—— (1910), "The Prices of Farm Products," *University of Wisconsin Agricultural Experiment Station Bulletins*, 209 (May), 1–29.

—— (1920), "The Development of Research and Education in Agricultural Cooperation and Marketing at the University of Wisconsin 1910–1920," unpublished manuscript, *Henry Charles Taylor Papers*. Madison: State Historical Society of Wisconsin.

—— (1922), "What's Back of Marketing?" unpublished manuscript, *Henry Charles Taylor Papers*. Madison: State Historical Society of Wisconsin.

—— (1941), "Plus Ultra," unpublished autobiography, *Henry Charles Taylor Papers*. Madison: State Historical Society of Wisconsin.

——, W. A. Schoenfeld, and G. S. Wehrwein (1913), "The Marketing of Wisconsin Cheese," *Agricultural Experiment Station Bulletins*, 231 (April), 1–36.

—— and Ann Dewees Taylor (1974), *The Story of Agricultural Economics in the U.S. 1840–1932*. Westport, CT: Greenwood Press.

Thakara, A. M. (1913), "German Educational Courses in Cooperation and Marketing," unpublished report, *Benjamin Hibbard Papers*. Madison: University of Wisconsin Library Archives.

Thompson, Clarence B. (1917), *The Theory and Practice of Scientific Management*. Boston: Houghton-Mifflin Company.

Thwing, Charles F. (1928), *The American and the German University*. New York: The Macmillan Co.

Tosdal, H. R. (1921), *Problems in Sales Management*. New York: A. W. Shaw Co.

Wright, John and P. B. Dimsdale (1974), *Pioneers in Marketing*. Atlanta: Georgia State University.

5

Consumer Sovereignty, Democracy, and the Marketing Concept: A Macromarketing Perspective*

Donald F. Dixon

Penn State University

Marketing students are taught that managers manipulate marketing instruments to earn profit: "The purpose of the marketing concept is to help organizations achieve their goals. In the case of private firms, the major goal is profit" (Kotler, 1991, p. 20). However, besides inducing the purchasing behavior from which profits are derived, marketing efforts have many other effects.

First, marketing efforts affect many aspects of human behavior, not just purchasing. The activity of purchasing agents in the market affects their other roles, their interactions with other household and organization members, and other members of society. Second, the transformation and consumption of purchased goods and services have derivative effects upon both the persons involved and the environments within which households and organizations operate. Third, marketing efforts directly affect persons who are neither

* Article originally published in the *Canadian Journal of Administrative Sciences* 1992; **9(2)** 116–125. Reproduced by permission of John Wiley & Sons Ltd on behalf of ASAC.

buyers nor consumers, since marketing efforts alter a society's cultural and social environment. For example, those who do not have the means to acquire goods and services offered in the market may experience feelings of inadequacy. Fourth, changes in behavior, social institutions, and the material environment caused by marketing efforts have an impact upon marketing itself.

Considerations such as these are the concern of macromarketing. Macromarketing issues tend to be noted, but essentially ignored, in current textbooks. Kotler, for example, refers to "the societal marketing concept" that includes a mention of "society's well-being" (1991, p. 26), but there is no reference to this term in the index. The societal marketing concept ostensibly takes "public interest" into account (1991, p. 27) but there is no further mention of this term in the book.

Macromarketing issues are not only ignored, but distorted, by textbooks that repeat the myth that the pursuit of profit by marketing managers maximizes social welfare (Kotler, 1980, pp. 32–33; McCarthy, 1981, p. 666). This purported identity of private and social interests is presented without explanation, but its origins are ostensibly historical, since reference is often made to Adam Smith. The obvious flaws in this mythical identity become apparent when the origins of the underlying concepts are traced, and their treatment by early marketing writers is examined.

"The Consumer is King"

Early American marketing writers considered marketing a process of responding to demand, sometimes using the phrase "the consumer is king." Adam Smith made this point in an embryonic statement of the marketing concept: "The real and effectual discipline which is exercised over a workman is . . . that of his customer" (1776, Vol. I, p. 161). The statement often cited in marketing textbooks, "consumption is the end and aim of all economic action" (1789, p. 625), did not appear until the third edition of *The Wealth of Nations*.

By the nineteenth century, Adam Smith's proposition was widely accepted. A standard American economics textbook notes that no one would make an effort to produce a good without the promise of a reward: "Production goes forward satisfactorily only when there is a reasonable prospect of consumption for the producer" (Ely, 1889, p. 267). The concept of consumer direction also achieved public acceptance. A popular magazine explained that "the producing man is essentially the servant of the consuming man, and the final direction of industry lies with the consumers." The implications of this principle for the household purchasing agent also were understood:

> The homemaker in her capacity as buyer for a family is largely responsible for that which is made as well as for the conditions under which it is made. Here she must act single-handed, and decide what it is worthwhile to buy. (Hunt, 1903, p. 275)

Taussig, whose *Principles of Economics* dominated the American market from 1911 to 1931, emphasized the purpose rather than the motive of production: "The essence of production is that it leads to satisfactions or utilities" (1911, p. 18).

Early American marketing textbooks also held that profit was a means, not an end; the purpose of marketing was not to earn a profit for the firm but to satisfy human wants. Moriarty repeats Ely's statement that "the ultimate reason for production receiving any reward is that others will pay for the privilege of consumption" (1923, p. 10). Converse both accepts Taussig's view that "the object of all business is to supply human wants," and extends the argument. From society's perspective, "profit is not the object of business, but the incentive for business to supply human wants" (1929, p. 2).

The societal perspective is still apparent in the late 1930s: "The end of all marketing activities is the satisfaction of human wants. The earning of profits is the incentive which induces businessmen to attempt to satisfy wants." (Barker & Anshen, 1939, p. 6). Emphasis upon the relationship between marketing and society continued after the Second World War. For example, Converse and Huegy state: "Consumption is the object of production – the goal of the economic system . . . If an operation is not in the interest of the consumers, it is not justified, no matter how profitable it may be to its owners. "He profits most who serves best" (1946, p. 21).

Converse and Huegy translate the principle of consumer direction into a decision rule for the seller, noting that the emphasis upon marketing activity serving consumers leads to the "consumer minded" businessman who "looks at his own business from the viewpoint of the consumers" (1946, p. 21). The subsequent introduction of the "marketing concept" simply introduced a new term for an idea that had been implicit in the economics and marketing literature since the eighteenth century.

The phrase "the consumer is king" also refers to the principle of a consumer-directed economy. One popular marketing text begins a discussion of consumer behavior with a section dealing with "marketing from the consumer's point of view," stressing "the dominant position of the consumer:"

> "The Customer is King." Under our economic system the ultimate consumer, within the limits set by his income, is relatively free to consume what he pleases. (Phillips & Duncan, 1949, p. 45)

Later textbooks begin to adopt a new term, "consumer sovereignty," that enters the economics literature in the 1930s. Eventually this term is associated with the marketing concept. These developments are the subject of the next section of this paper.

Consumer Sovereignty and the Marketing Concept

The mechanism through which business responds to consumer demand is the market, viewed as a system in which "dollar votes" are cast: "The market is a democracy where every penny gives a right of vote" (Fetter, 1911, p. 394). This political analogy led to the phrase "sovereignty of consumers," to represent the concept of a consumer-directed economy.

Hutt introduces the phrase in a discussion of the concept of market structure; monopoly is seen as "the frustration of consumer's sovereignty" (1934, p. 17). In the following year, Ropke contrasts the Fascist military economy with Britain's economic system that was "governed, roughly speaking, by the democracy of the consumers." (1935, p. 93) Hayek speaks of a centrally planned economy as the "abrogation of the sovereignty of the consumer" (1935, p. 214). By the end of the decade the term appeared in a popular economics textbook. (Brenham, 1939).

Hoyt, one of the first marketing writers to adopt the term, defines consumers' sovereignty as "the final authority which consumers as a group exercise over the amount and kind of production" (1939, p. 75). However, the term was not widely used in marketing textbooks until after the Second World War. Fisk defines consumer sovereignty as "the right to choose among a sufficient range of products so that the particular demand specifications of a particular consumer can be reasonably matched" (1967, p. 680). Narver and Savitt emphasize the societal implications, stating that consumer sovereignty "means simply that consumer demand determines what a society produces" (1971, p. 401).

Hartley links "dollar votes" with consumer sovereignty: "Customers vote daily with their sales dollars," and with the phrase "the consumer is king," holding that "essentially, consumer sovereignty signifies that the consumer is in fact the ultimate king with a right to buy or not to buy." The societal implications are also recognized: "Production in a market economy is ultimately oriented toward meeting the wants of consumers" (1972, pp. 97–98).

The underlying theme associated with consumer sovereignty is that an individual's productive effort is driven by the promise of a reward in the form of goods and services that the individual wishes to consume. When generalized, the argument is that all productive activity is a response to the perceived demand for goods and services. In this sense, consumption drives production activity.

The next step in the argument, that consumption is the purpose of productive activity, follows from the General Systems paradigm. If the market is a subsystem of the societal system, the goods and services produced can be envisioned as the output of the subsystem to the system. Business serves society by providing goods and services; the profit derived from the provision of appropriate goods and services is the incentive for production.

Consumer sovereignty is a useful description of the principles of a market system. However, it can be employed to describe the functioning of a market only as long as its limitations are understood. These limits were recognized over a half century ago: "In practice today, as we shall see, it is exercised only partially... It implies that consumers must have the utmost freedom in their choices" (Hoyt, 1938, p. 75). Most marketing textbooks indicate these limitations. For example, Duddy and Revzan note that

"The restrictions on the actuality of perfect competition do, of course, make the concept of consumer sovereignty invalid to the extent that what people actually buy differs from what they want" (1953, p. 486).

Many of these limitations arise from the actions of sellers in the market. Thus, the marketing concept represents a constraint upon consumer sovereignty. Unfortunately, some authors overlook this constraint and link the concept of a consumer-directed economy with the marketing concept:

> The importance of a customer orientation for marketing managers is reflected in the axiom, "The Consumer is King." . . . The concept of customer satisfaction as the basis for marketing activity is often referred to as the "modern" marketing concept. (Buzzell et al., 1972, pp. 50–51)

Those who identify the marketing concept with consumer sovereignty fail to recognize that the ends of buyers and sellers are not identical. This obvious point is clear in *The Wealth of Nations*: "The interest of dealers . . . in any particular branch of trade or manufacturers, is always in some respects different from, and even opposite to, that of the public" (Vol. I, p. 316).

One popular textbook that points out the potential connection between a firm's marketing effort and social welfare, refers to a " 'macro-micro dilemma' – what is 'good' for some producers and consumers may not be 'good' for society as a whole" (McCarthy, 1981, p. 11). Later in the book this dilemma disappears, and the outcome of the marketing activity of individuals seeking their own interests automatically contributes to the welfare of society as a whole. It is alleged that an increase in the profit earned by a seller not only increases the satisfaction attained by that seller's customers, but also that "satisfaction can be loosely measured by company profits" (1981, p. 666). This argument also appears in Kotler's work:

> The marketing concept is the company's commitment to the time-honored concept in economic theory known as consumer sovereignty. The determination of what is to be produced should not be in the hands of the companies or in the hands of government but in the hands of consumers. The companies produce what the consumers want, and in this way maximize consumer welfare and earn their profits. (Kotler, 1980, pp. 32–33)

There are two fatal objections to the statement that companies produce what consumers want and thus maximize consumer welfare. First, many limitations to the descriptive statement that companies produce what consumers want have been recognized during the past two centuries. Moreover, as N. Craig Smith notes, consumer sovereignty maximizes consumer welfare. The following two sections discuss the validity of both the descriptive and normative statements.

Companies Produce What Consumers Want: The Descriptive Statement

The statement that "companies produce what consumers want" contains three elements: wants must be identified by consumers, these wants must be transformed into demand expressed in the market, and the market must be responsive to demand. Each of these elements will be considered in turn.

Consumer wants

Two issues must be clarified. First, wants are not "individual." Since people live in groups, an individual's wants are learned in household and other group settings, and ultimately in the context of the society as a whole. Second, although the term "consumer" refers to a single role, wants refer to an individual's entire role set. Since wants refer to people rather than roles, "consumer" wants cannot be separated from "human" wants.

People's wants involve interactions with other people. Goods and services acquired by households make this interaction possible and give it meaning. Since one's wants are defined in terms of other members of society, conflicts may arise from social interaction. Moreover individuals may perceive ethical conflicts among different ends; what one "wants" may not be what one "ought" to want.

Since a person's life is so closely tied to others, the very definition of wants is derived from the society and its culture. The ideas communicated by marketing organizations are a part of this culture, so that wants are not independent of, but are influenced by, marketing effort.

This relationship between marketing effort and human wants is widely recognized. A recent newspaper article argues that today's parents have to spend a great deal of time and effort trying to counter the effect of the culture on their children:

> Once the chorus of cultural values was full of ministers, teachers, neighbors, leaders. They demanded more conformity, but offered more support. Now the messengers are Ninja Turtles, Madonna, rap groups and celebrities pushing sneakers. (Goodman, 1991, p. 7A)

At the time marketing textbooks were beginning to appear in the U.S., a prominent American economist argued that wants are "merely the raw material" that buyers bring into the market. These wants are then transformed by producers "just as truly as rubber heels, tennis balls, fountain pens, and automobile tires are manufactured out of the same crude rubber." Business firms produce two kinds of products; both wants, and the means of satisfying them: "The wheels of industry grind out both kinds of products. In a single business establishment one department furnishes the desires which other departments are to satisfy" (Clark, 1918, p. 8).

Some marketing textbooks explicitly recognize that marketing activity influences the very wants that it helps satisfy. Vaile, Grether, and Cox state that a basic task of marketing is "making consumption dynamic." One "contribution" of marketing is "persuading people to want and to buy more and different things. This contribution of marketing to the dynamics of living is now widely conceded to be socially desirable, but people have not always thought so" (1952, p. 252).

The influence of marketing effort on wants significantly limits the argument that companies produce what people want. But whatever the source of wants, before producers can respond, these wants must be transformed into market demands for specific goods and services.

Wants are transformed into market demand

Not all wants are transformed into market demand. Some wants are satisfied by individual behavior, others by transfers, such as gifts, and still other wants are satisfied by various non-market forms of social exchange.

When wants are to be met in the market, it is not the consumer who expresses demand; wants are interpreted and market goods acquired by purchasing agents. In some cases, such as young children, household purchasing agents act on the principle that consumers do not know what they want. In other cases the wants of household members are so poorly specified that the purchasing agent's interpretation may be incorrect. When purchasing agents make errors, the demand for goods and services does not reflect consumer wants.

Wants are not transformed into market demand when available resources are insufficient to purchase the appropriate goods and services. Since no one has sufficient income to satisfy all possible wants, the purchasing unit must choose which wants to satisfy, and which will remain unsatisfied. Thus only some wants that people wish to satisfy in the market can be transformed into market demand.

Limitations upon time, the ultimate scarce resource, also may prevent the purchase of goods and services to satisfy wants. If the needed goods are not readily available in the market, the purchasing agent may be unable to devote the time necessary for inspection and choice.

Goods not only must be available, but it also must be known that they are available. The acquisition of information is costly, and the evaluation of information available from advertising that is self serving, and sometimes false and misleading, is difficult.

For a market to function, purchasing agents must be intelligent and use reasonable decision rules. However, the qualities of many goods are not observable. In earlier times purchasing agents had first hand knowledge of goods and services, trade was local, and a local reputation was important. But when production is for the anonymous "market" rather than for individuals, and purchasers do not have the skills needed to evaluate complex products, purchasing agents are limited in their ability to represent household consumers. Mitchell's famous article, "Backward Art of Spending Money," (1912) shows the extent of this problem early in this century.

The situation has hardly improved in the intervening years as households have become capital intensive factories for the satisfaction of wants. Today the problem is increased as buyers are expected to identify the ecological attributes of goods and services (Schneider, 1991). Third parties provide some protection from information that individuals cannot verify, and from goods and services whose properties cannot be verified with the skills or facilities available to buyers. However, limitations remain. Thus the argument that companies produce what consumers want also is flawed because wants are not always transformed into demand. The third issue remains to be considered.

Producers respond to demand

Just as marketing efforts influence ends, these efforts influence demand. For example, Vaile, Grether, and Cox argue that "marketing often proceeds and flourishes on the assumption that whatever customers may be persuaded to accept is socially desirable as well as commercially profitable" (1952, p. 30). Thus it cannot be argued that producers simply respond to demand: "Private enterprise either adjusts itself to existing demands or attempts to influence demands through an elaborate system of research, estimating, planning, and promoting" (1952, p. 575).

Fisk includes the impact of marketing in his definition of marketing as "all activities intended to stimulate or serve demand" (1967, p. 10). Kotler lists five "influence strategies" to be used in selling (1991, p. 674). Dickinson, Herbst, and O'Shaughnessy argue that consumers "are much more open to persuasion than is commonly acknowledged under the marketing concept." (1986, p. 22).

The marketing concept identifies only one constituency that constrains a firm's decisions. Since there are constituencies other than stockholders, conflict may arise not only between producing a specific good and earning a profit, but also between producing the good and improving working conditions and wages, for example. The possibility of conflict exists at each stage of the channel, so that decisions not to offer the desired goods and services may be made at one or more channel stages. Finally, marketing intermediaries may base decisions on the availability of payments from sellers to sell particular goods rather than the demand of household purchasing agents.

Just as demand is limited by income, supply is limited by costs and available technology. The decision rule to produce those goods that are most profitable means that other goods are not produced. Since most goods are not produced to order, but in anticipation of orders, errors in demand estimation are made. Producers sometimes act on incorrect information or misinterpret available information. Retailers make similar errors and thus order goods that are not wanted. The economic resources that are wasted because of such errors are not available to produce goods and services that are wanted.

If the market is to be responsive to consumer demand, producers must be free to supply what consumers demand. However, there are ethical and legal limitations to the range of goods and services offered in the market. Licensing is one example. Within the limits of social and cultural restraints it is usually thought that competition will provide adequate assortments of goods and services for consumer choice to be meaningful. That is, it is believed that competition serves as a better incentive than monopoly power for economic benefit, or "good will" or benevolence.

However, the "meaningful choice" offered by competition actually represents a significant limitation to the response of the market to demand. Thus the unqualified statement that companies produce what consumers want is not a valid description of the operation of markets. Similarly, consumer sovereignty cannot be identical with the marketing concept.

Marketing and Social Welfare: The Normative Issue

Besides the question of how close the description comes to reality, Kotler's statement contains a normative issue. Here we are not concerned with the extent to which consumers direct production, but how well this direction works.

The previous section argued that the proposition that the marketing concept leads to the maximization of consumer welfare is invalid because the premise that "companies produce what consumers want" is an inaccurate description of the actual operation of the market. Besides its failure in the face of practical issues, the proposition that marketing effort maximizes social welfare lacks a conceptual foundation. The foundations for this link between consumer sovereignty and social welfare can be traced to Adam Smith's argument that "every individual necessarily labours to render the annual revenue of the society as great as he can." This result follows from the operation of an "invisible hand:"

> He generally indeed neither intends to promote the public interest, nor knows how much he is promoting it . . . He intends only his own gain, and he is in this, as in many other cases, led by an invisible hand to promote an end which was no part of his intention. (1776, Vol. II, p. 55)

Smith and the nineteenth century classical economists held that self-interest is the most significant human motive, and the competitive market transforms individual actions based on self-interest into the common good. Conceptually, competition leads to economic efficiency because resources flow to applications where they produce goods of greater value; resources are bid away by the higher rewards that can be paid because of the higher value of output produced. The general acceptance of this view is apparent in the economic reforms in China and Eastern Europe, and privatization in the United Kingdom and elsewhere.

Although the self-interest maxim holds freedom to be the rule and restraint the exception, in classical economics the conceptual model is clearly distinguished from reality. One early classical writer explicitly describes "competition" as a theoretical concept:

> When we speak . . . of a class of commodities as produced under circumstances of equal competition . . . we do not mean to state that any such commodities exist, but that, if they did exist, such would be the laws by which their price would be regulated. (Senior, 1836, p. 114)

It always has been recognized that there are limits to the transformation of self-interest into social welfare. John Stuart Mill, the premier classical economist, supports "the popular dictum, that people understand their own business and their own interests better, and care for them more, than the government does, or can be expected to do." However, he qualifies this support: "This maxim holds true throughout the greatest part of the business of life, and wherever it is true we ought to condemn every kind of government intervention that conflicts with it" (1848, p. 947). Mill understands that the buyer's limited ability to choose required intervention by the state, and that sometimes government intervention did not conflict with individual choice, but was necessary to give effect to this choice.

Alfred Marshall, whose work dominated neoclassical economics, offers only limited support to "the doctrine that the maximum satisfaction is generally to be attained by encouraging each individual to spend his own resources in that way which suits him best." Indeed, it is not universally true, and its limits have yet to be determined:

> Much remains to be done . . . to discover what are the limits of the work that society can with advantage do towards turning the economic actions of individuals into those channels in which they will add the most to the sum total of happiness. (1890, p. 475)

Modern welfare economics demonstrates that there are ways to adjust the results of a competitive market by government actions, such as taxation and subsidy, to maximize what Adam Smith called as "the annual revenue of the society." However, it is not simply the total output that is important, but also its distribution among the members of society. This issue of distributing the benefits of a competitive market, and the problem of measurement, have proved to be intractable.

There also is an underlying moral problem. Should the "optimum" distribution of economic goods and services be that in which there is no alternative outcome in which any individual is made better off without anyone being made worse off? This principle fails to recognize inequalities that exist in any society. An alternative rule is that those who are in a favored position ought to gain from their good fortune only on terms that improve the position of those who are less well off. Although this principle does not subordinate individual welfare to the common good, it is not universally accepted. Since social welfare cannot be defined until an ethical foundation is established, it cannot be argued that marketing activity maximizes social welfare.

Summarizing, the propositions that individual decisions are transformed into public benefit by the competitive market cannot be supported theoretically, and the theoretical conditions are not met in practice because of the inherent conflict between the marketing concept and consumer sovereignty. Nevertheless this proposition remains one of marketing's myths, probably because one of the "wants" of the marketing discipline is a justification of marketing activity beyond that of attaining organizational goals.

The necessity for such a justification of marketing is explicitly recognized by an early American marketing writer. Arch Shaw discusses the "external" problems of business, suggesting that society asks the businessman:

> What besides the market minimum of value and service at the price are you going to supply
> as my profit on my investment of community machinery and opportunity? (1915, p. 32)

An answer to Shaw's question has become particularly elusive since the 1950s when the accepted paradigm for marketing thought became organizational efforts to achieve their objectives by manipulating marketing instruments to influence buyer behavior. Interest falters once a purchase has been made and consumers typically are not distinguished from buyers.

The failure of the paradigm dominating current marketing thought suggests that a new approach is needed if a meaningful relationship is to be established between marketing effort and social welfare. The General Systems paradigm provides a means of examining the linkage between marketing effort and social welfare. If the market is perceived as a social institution, then its output consists of more than goods and services provided to consumers. Thus output can be evaluated in terms of its impact upon other elements of the society.

The conceptual linkage between marketing activity and other elements of the society is suggested by an examination of the political system that is closely linked to the concept of consumer sovereignty. The relevance of this linkage is apparent in the dramatic developments in Eastern Europe where movements toward democracy are closely linked to market reform.

Consumer Sovereignty and Democracy

Consumer sovereignty is closely tied to the democratic political system through the analogy of "dollar votes." A recent speech referred to consumer sovereignty as "America's second democracy" (Peterson, 1990). Many characteristics of democracy are analogous to those of a free market. Democracy means personal freedom and opportunities to exercise choice, including freedom of thought, speech, political activity, and personal life. Consumer sovereignty refers to the freedom to choose one's consumption goods, including one's residence, education for oneself and one's children, forms of recreation, and books one reads, and the movies one sees.

In the ancient Greek city states, sovereignty was vested in the entire body of citizens, and this sovereignty was vested through popular assemblies in which each citizen had one vote. In a free market, each dollar is equal and the right to spend it is guaranteed. The underlying concept of democracy is the equality of citizens, and the protection of people's basic rights. However, not all persons were equal in ancient Greece. Women and slaves were not considered "citizens," and were not part of the sovereign body. There is a parallel limitation of consumer sovereignty; although each dollar held by a buyer is equal, the buyers themselves are not equal. The number of "dollar votes" a buyer commands depends upon income and other economic resources, and these are not equally distributed.

After the decline of the Greek city states, democracy remained nothing more than a theoretical construct until the American and French revolutions. It is more than pure coincidence that the date of publication of *The Wealth of Nations*, the conceptual foundation of economic freedom, is the same as that of the Declaration of Independence.

The large population of a nation makes it impossible for citizens to exercise their sovereignty directly. What is required is representative democracy in which individuals exercise their sovereignty by electing representatives who choose the "wants" of the community that will be satisfied. Here the interests of political officials come into play, and the self interest of political representatives may conflict with the wants of the citizens. In a market, the demands of household buyers are represented through marketing intermediaries, and the interests of intermediaries may conflict with the wants and demands of consumers.

A democratic political institution interprets and implements the will of the majority of electors; thus the "sovereign" is the body of voters. But another aspect of sovereignty is the range of actions defined as natural rights that are not delegated to the state. Among these natural rights are those necessary for a free market to operate.

Democracy requires competent and responsible voters. But voters may not be able to understand the issues, just as a buyer may not be able to ascertain product quality. Moreover, the impact of the voters is limited because office seekers need only make plausible promises to voters, just as advertisers need only make plausible promises to customers.

Since freedom is a matter of choice among alternatives, a society ought to offer its members as large a sphere as possible to pursue their ends. But there is a dilemma; one person's freedom to act may interfere with another person's freedom. Probably most individual actions have an impact upon the environment and affect the alternatives available to others. Thus there must be a framework of compulsion and informal pressures to limit one's freedom.

These limitations upon human action may be divided into those that are impersonal and those that are arbitrary. Laws imposed by the State or other authority and social customs are established by impersonal forces and reflect the "public will." Thus they are likely to be considered "normal" so that one's feeling of freedom is not affected. A strong argument for competition as a constraint upon market behavior is that it is impersonal.

Constraints become a social problem when they are not accepted as inevitable, and one's preferred course of action is limited arbitrarily. Arbitrary constraints are an especially significant issue because one attribute of democracy is toleration. But social pressures and the opinion of others makes for conformity. These pressures can be resisted if one so chooses, and it can be argued that individuals who are unwilling to accept the poor opinion of others to attain their goals have not earned their freedom.

Criticism of market effort as an interference with consumer sovereignty is analogous to criticism of political campaigns as an interference with voter choice. If the characteristics of freedom include freedom of expression and toleration of behavior of others, then every restriction of these rights is a restriction of a person's ultimate right to make individual choices. Benham overstates the case when he denies that marketing effort limits the sovereignty of consumers because "a monarch may be advised and cajoled, as to some of his activities, even by his slaves, but he remains a monarch none the less" (1939, p. 160). Nevertheless, voters and buyers do have individual responsibilities that parallel their individual rights.

Consumer Sovereignty, Democracy, and the Marketing Concept

If one considers only the economics system in isolation, the argument for maintaining a wide range of consumer choice can be questioned. If wants cannot always be specified, if specific goods and services are not always necessary to the satisfaction of wants, and buyers are easily manipulated, perhaps production need not simply respond to demand. It might be more efficient to mass produce goods and services and manipulate demand to match the assortment produced.

The position of one marketing writer, once a staunch advocate of the marketing concept, reflects this argument. Levitt, whose "Marketing Myopia" article argued for the marketing concept, completely reversed his position. Now the prescription is to "force suitably standardized products and practices" on everyone to take advantage of the efficiencies of mass production (1983, p. 102). Never must it be assumed that "the customer is a king who knows his own wishes" (1983, p. 94).

It is no response to this argument simply to restate the myth that the marketing concept is identical with consumer sovereignty, and that marketing effort maximizes social welfare. A direction for analysis is suggested by the parallel between democracy and consumer sovereignty. It is perhaps significant that *The Wealth of Nations* was published when democratic political systems began to emerge, and the term consumer sovereignty was introduced when democracy was challenged by competing political systems. Both consumer sovereignty and democracy are based on ethical judgments about freedom as a desirable end for human society to attain.

It has long been recognized that freedom requires that individuals have opportunities to make choices, and the extent of freedom is indicated by the breadth of opportunities for choice. J.S. Mill holds that one of the strongest reasons for the exercise of individual choice is that the very process itself is important for the society. There always will be a need of "active talent and practical judgment in the affairs of life" so that "it is important that those endowments should be cultivated" (1848, p. 948). And this cultivation should be vigorous: "It is therefore of supreme importance that all classes of the community, down to the lowest, should have much to do for themselves; that as great a demand should be made upon their intelligence and virtue as it is in any respect equal to" (1848, p. 949).

From the General Systems perspective, political and economic systems interact. Mill saw economic freedom contributing to political freedom: "In proportion as the people are accustomed to manage their affairs by their own active intervention, instead of leaving them to the government, their desires will turn to repelling tyranny, rather than to tyrannizing" (1848, p. 950). A similar point was made by Hoyt, who argued that the concept of consumer sovereignty "does assume, however, that the value of free choice to a man is greater than the value of an arbitrary standard set by another. It emphasizes the development of men rather than the nature and quality of goods as such" (1938, p. 75).

One justification for freedom of choice thus lies in the social function performed by the choice process itself. The significance of consumer sovereignty lies in the type of choice. As Hutt stresses, the decisions made by buyers refer to the ends that are chosen. Each person is both a producer and consumer, "As a 'consumer,' each directs. As a 'producer,' each obeys" (1936, p. 258). The producer "obeys" by choosing the means by which the consumer's ends may be met. The consumer directs the production process by determining the ends to be achieved by productive activity.

The marketing concept refers to organizational decisions about the means of offering the goods and services that enable consumers to attain their ends. For buyers to have choices, producers must be free to offer choices in the market. That is, consumer sovereignty with respect to ends must be paired with producer sovereignty with respect to means.

In the free market model, both buyers and sellers are constrained by rules enforced by the political system and informal social pressures. Within the range of choices thus available a balance of interests is achieved. This model cannot maximize output; its attraction is that it gives full reign to freedom of choice. Whether the extent of this freedom is optimal is a different question. Although freedom of choice is an ethical "good," there are other ethical "goods" to consider.

Mill identified a relationship between economic and political freedom. But there are more than economic and political aspects of life. Moreover, democracy and consumer sovereignty refer to behavior that is constrained, but not completely specified. Since behavior is not completely specified, both consumer sovereignty and democracy are necessary, but not sufficient for social welfare.

This issue was addressed in the economics literature at the time Arch Shaw noted that society was asking businessmen what they were offering society besides the output of goods and services. Ingram argues that freedom is "the necessary condition precedent of the solution of practical problems," but freedom "is not in itself enough." In the future

> The individual point of view will have to be subordinated to the social; each agent will have to be regarded as an organ of the society to which he belongs and of the larger society . . . What is now most urgent is . . . the formation, in both the higher and lower regions of the industrial world, of profound convictions as to social duties, and some more effective mode than at present exists of diffusing, maintaining, and applying those convictions . . . The solution, indeed, must be at all times largely a moral one. (Ingram, 1915, pp. 297–299)

Shaw is concerned that "The average businessman, submerged in the activities of his undertaking, has at times either not caught society's drift or has not realized its vital bearing on his business" (1915, p. 35). The marketing concept, as presented in contemporary textbooks, guarantees the continual submergence of the marketer "in the activities of his undertaking" without considering the broader implications of marketing efforts because of its emphasis upon private means and limited concern with social ends.

The mythical identity of the marketing concept, consumer sovereignty, and social welfare arises from a complete misunderstanding of the conceptual foundations of a free market economy. References to Adam Smith ignore a clear statement that his model requires a "system of natural liberty." Smith asserts that "every man, as long as he does not violate the laws of justice, is left perfectly free to pursue his own interest his own way, and to bring both his industry and capital into competition with those of any other man or order of men" (1776, Vol. II, p. 288).

The "system of natural liberty," and "the laws of justice" within which the market operates are crucial elements of *The Wealth of Nations*. This work is characterized by a concern with the conflict between private interest and public welfare; it does not assert that this conflict is completely resolved by a competitive market. Misunderstandings of Smith's conceptual scheme arise from the neglect of the ethical foundations of the market system presented in his earlier work, *The Theory of Moral Sentiments*, in which he states: "How selfish so ever man may be supposed, there are evidently some principles in his nature, which interest him in the fortune of others, and render their happiness necessary to him" (1759, p. 1).

This interest in the fortune of others involves "fair play," and this ethical context underlies the conclusion that "in the race for wealth, for honours, the preferments" man "may run as hard as he can, and strain every nerve and every muscle, in order to outstrip all his competitors" (1759, p. 76). The spontaneous behavior of each person contributes to the common welfare only when the members of a society achieve a moral consensus and a system of rights and liberties, as well as reciprocal duties. Without this ethical foundation "the immense fabric of human society... must in a moment crumble into atoms" (1759, p. 79).

The emphasis upon the individual's ethical responsibility in Smith's works may be contrasted with the treatment of this topic in a modern marketing textbook. The term "ethics" appears once in Kotler's Marketing Management. The reader is informed that many techniques of competitive intelligence "involve questionable ethics" but these should be avoided (1991, p. 233). The term "moral" also appears once, in connection with "moral appeals" in marketing communication. These "are often used to exhort people to support social causes" (1991, p. 575).

One contribution of macromarketing is the identification of marketing myths that direct attention away from fundamental issues. It must be understood that freedom implies burdens as well as rights, and that individual responsibility lies at the core of political and economic freedom. Some elements of a paradigm for understanding market systems have emerged since 1776. It remains to develop theory that will fulfil the promise of this paradigm.

References

Barker, C.W. & Anshen, M. (1939). *Modern marketing*. New York: McGraw-Hill.

Benham, F. (1939). *Economics*. London: Sir Isaac Pitman & Sons.

Buzzell, R.D. (1972). *Marketing: A contemporary analysis*. New York: McGraw-Hill.

Converse, P.D. (1929). *Marketing methods and policies*. New York: Prentice-Hall.

Converse, P.D. (1936). *Essentials of distribution*. New York: Prentice-Hall.

Converse, P.D., & Huegy, H.W. (1946). *The elements of marketing*. New York: Prentice-Hall.

Collins, G.R. (1930). *Marketing*. New York: Alexander Hamilton Institute.

Dickinson, R., Herbst, A., & O'Shaughnessy, J. (1986). Marketing concept and customer orientation. *European Journal of Marketing, 20*(10), 18–23.

Duddy, E.A., & Revzan, D.A. (1953). *Marketing - An institutional approach*. New York: McGraw-Hill.

Ely, R.T. (1889). *An introduction to political economy*. New York: Chautauqua.

Fetter, F.A. (1911). *The principles of economics*. New York: Century.

Fisk, G. (1967). *Marketing systems*. New York: Harper & Row.

Fraser, L.M. (1939). The doctrine of "consumers sovereignty." *The Economic Journal, 49*, September, 544–548.

Goodman, E. (1991, August 17). Media messages force parents to become persistent naysayers. *The Philadelphia Inquirer*, p. 7–A.

Hartley, R.F. (1972). *Marketing: Management and social change*. Scranton, PA: Intext Educational Publishers.

Hayek, F.A. von (1935). *Collectivist economic planning*. London: George Routledge & Sons.

Hoyt, E.E. (1938). *Consumption in our society*. New York, McGraw-Hill.

Hunt, C.L. (1903). More conscience for the consumer. *Chautauquan, 37*, 272–76.

Hutt, W.H. (1934). Economic method and the concept of competition. *The South African Journal of Economics, 2*(1), 23.

Hutt, W.H. (1936). *Economists and the public*. London: Jonathan Cape.

Hutt, W.H. (1940). The concept of consumers' sovereignty. *The Economic Journal, 50*, (March), 66–77.

Ingram, J.K. (1915). *A history of political economy*. London: A. & C. Black.

Kotler, P. (1980). *Marketing management*. Englewood Cliffs, NJ: Prentice Hall.

Kotler, P. (1991). *Marketing management*. Englewood Cliffs, NJ: Prentice Hall.

Levitt, T. (1983). The globalization of markets. *Harvard Business Review, 61*(3), May-June, 92–102.

McCarthy, E.J. (1981). *Basic marketing*. Homewood, IL: Richard D. Irwin.

Mitchell, W.C. (1912). The backward art of spending money. *American Economic Review, II*, 2, 269–281.

Moriarty, W.D. (1923). *The economics of marketing and advertising*. New York: Harper & Brothers.

Narver, J.C., & Savitt, R. (1971). *The marketing economy*. New York: Holt, Rinehart & Winston.

Peterson, W.H. (1990, October 1). America's second democracy-Consumer sovereignty. *Vital Speeches of the Day, 56*(24), 765–768.

Phillips, C.F., & Duncan, D.J. (1949). *Marketing principles and methods*. Chicago, IL: Richard D. Irwin.

Ropke, W. (1935). Fascist economics. *Economica, 2*, February, 85–100.

Schneider, K. (1991, July 14). Can shoppers tell if something is really good for the planet? *The New York Times*.

Senior, W.N. (1836). *An outline of the science of political economy*. London: Bradford and Dickens, 1938.

Shaw, A.W. (1915). *Some problems in market distribution*. Cambridge, MA: Harvard University Press.

Smith, A. (1759). *The theory of moral sentiments*. Reprinted in *Essays philosophical and literary*. London: Ward, Lock, & Co., n.d.

Smith, A. (1776). *An inquiry into the nature and causes of the wealth of nations*. London: W. Strahan & T. Cadell.

Smith, A. (1789). *An inquiry into the nature and causes of the wealth of nations*. New York: The Modern Library, 1937.

Smith, N.C. (1990). *Morality and the market*. London: Routledge.

Taussig, F.W. (1911). *Principles of economics*. New York: MacMillan.

Vaile, R.S., Grether, E.T., and Cox, R. (1952). *Marketing in the American economy*. New York: Ronald.

6
Critical Reflections on Consumer Research

Mark Tadajewski[1] and Douglas Brownlie[2]

[1]*University of Leicester and* [2]*University of Stirling*

The following three chapters represent, in their own distinctive ways, attempts to prevent the foreclosure of possibility that we depicted as central to critical marketing. Each of the chapters is historical to a certain extent in that Tadajewski, for example, demonstrates an alternative reading of the development of consumer research, illuminating how interpretive research actually emerged far earlier in the history of marketing thought than is often acknowledged.

What Tadajewski does not signal in actual fact is that this historical account can be pushed back even further. In his 1959 work on motivation research, J. George Frederick makes the case that he had been conducting motivation research studies since 1909. Where Tadajewski argues that his account of motivation research resituates the emergence of this discourse by some 60 years, when we factor in Frederick's claim it would indicate that interpretive consumer research is actually closer to 85 years older than previously thought.

In her chapter, Beth Hirschman undertakes a close reading of the contribution of evolutionary theory to consumer research. Using papers published in the *Journal of Consumer Research* as her foil she highlights how certain evolutionary perspectives can enlarge our understanding of consumer behaviour and also serve to question the basis of much of the behavioural decision research that currently dominates the discipline (see Payne *et al.*, 1992). Clearly there is much to be learnt from recent developments in evolutionary theory and genetic research. It is perhaps not wholly unexpected that the biological basis for consumer behaviour has been ignored for so long.

While the stream of research that Hirschman indicates as her basis is derived from the work of Charles Darwin, Francis Galton was equally interested in the role of nature versus nurture in determining the development of specific behavioural traits. Such work steadily accumulated acolytes, but unfortunately it was the particularly undesirable focus of the Nazis and their abuse of genetics, along with the rise of behaviorism, which stalled the development of genetic science (Plomin and Asbury, 2005).

Nonetheless, research in the area of genetic science has sought to connect genetic and environmental influences on behaviour and it should accordingly merit the interest of consumer researchers. As Plomin and Asbury (2005: 96) suggest, 'the importance of genes as well as environment in the etiology [cause] of individual differences in behavior is increasingly accepted in science as well as in society. We predict that this trend will accelerate'. This view is reaffirmed by Rabinow and Rose (2006) who believe the twenty-first century will be known ultimately as the biological century, given the advances in biomedicine, neuroscience and genomic mapping likely to occur within a foreseeable time horizon.

Scholars tapping into this vein of thought have provided extensive reviews of Darwinian theory as it relates to consumption behaviours (Saad, 2004; Saad and Gill, 2000, 2003) and examined topics such sun-bathing, using Darwinian theory to design social marketing intervention strategies (Saad and Peng, 2006), and have also studied mate-choice strategies, using personal advertisements as their data source (Pawlowski and Dunbar, 1999a, 1999b). Recent research has, moreover, demonstrated some interesting implications for those involved with studying so-called brand communities. Utilising an evolutionary psychology approach Dunbar (2007: 41–42) has established

> ... that neocortex volume (essentially the thinking part of the brain) correlates directly with social group size across a wide range of primate species, and this relationship predicts extremely closely the size of human social groups. The predicted size for human social groups is approximately 150 individuals, and this turns out to be extremely common in a wide range of circumstances ... In addition, we have been able to show that human social networks are highly structured, such that they have the form of concentric circles (the 'circles of acquaintanceship'): each successive circle of acquaintanceship includes more individuals, but involves relationships of markedly reduced intimacy and frequency of contact.

This latter point might not really be surprising. What is more interesting is that 'the size of these successive circles has a very characteristic ratio: each grouping is exactly three times larger than that contained within it' (Dunbar, 2007: 42). Now, Dunbar is not sure why this should be the case, but such structured interaction, along with the recognition of the interconnection of nature and nurture in fostering consumer behaviour and the nearly complete neglect of these issues in consumer research signals a clear limitation placed around the boundaries of what constitutes a valid theoretical perspective in consumer research. Of course, there are plenty of opportunities for this theory to be used in a way that develops performative marketing knowledge, useful to business organisations, but equally this does not have to be the case. It does foreground the possibility that we are not thinking about marketing and consumer phenomena in all their genetic, environmental and theoretical complexity and this self-imposed limitation is a mistake.

Without doubt, if evolutionary perspectives on consumer behaviour can clarify 'individuals' strategic decision-making under the constraints of circumstance' (Dunbar, 2007: 46), then they can further develop insight into the effects of the 'political economy of social choice' that delimits consumer agency in the marketplace (e.g. Dholakia and Dholakia, 1985). This, in turn, would contribute to the ontological denaturalisation of the ordering of our consumer society. It should go without saying that such a theoretical contribution warrants further investigation not simply from a buyer behaviour perspective, which it will no doubt receive, but in order to better understand the complex interplay between multi-level social systems, individual cognitive decision-making and relevant biological processes. It should, in other words, further encourage theoretical pluralism and reflexivity among consumer researchers.

John O'Shaughnessy's chapter constitutes a challenge to postmodernism in marketing. It also, importantly, highlights an aspect of the cognitive revolution that may have passed many marketing scholars by and thus represents another attempt at limiting the foreclosure of possibility to think otherwise. O'Shaughnessy has rallied against the impact of certain limited understandings of postmodernism in marketing previously, specifically in relation to the issue of interpretation and the extent to which interpretation is inevitably viewed as underdetermined, he alleges, by postmodernists. In case we have forgotten, O'Shaughnessy and O'Shaughnessy (2002a) have explicitly challenged methodological monism. Support for monism – that is, the restriction of marketing and consumer research to research questions that could only be answered by natural scientific methods – is overly restrictive and not particularly useful for the social sciences, they posit.

By contrast, O'Shaughnessy and O'Shaughnessy (2002b) called for marketing scholars to embrace methodological pluralism which 'rejects the view that there is just one set of methods or one way of knowing that gives privileged access to all that can be validly asserted' (O'Shaughnessy and O'Shaughnessy, 2002b: 150). This support for pluralism is a function of the belief that 'We need an infusion of theory in marketing in order to conceptualize, provide sensitizing concepts, give direction, and allow talk about marketing to be conducted in an intelligent manner. To rule out judgments of better and worse [in terms of interpretations of consumer phenomena] reduces marketers to merely expressing differences' (O'Shaughnessy and O'Shaughnessy, 2002a: 127).

Rather than following a similar path to that of much mainstream marketing theory and methodological discussion, O'Shaughnessy does not single-mindedly support a technical interest in the manipulation, prediction and control of the social and natural environment that Habermas (1968/1987: 302) connects with the 'positivistic self-understanding of the sciences'. Instead, O'Shaughnessy turns to the hermeneutic sciences and in keeping with the view that we presented in Chapter 1 regarding the key attributes of critical marketing, hermeneutics 'is . . . a deeply self-reflexive and self-critical process' (Prasad, 2002: 12).

According to Habermas, hermeneutic inquiry does not involve producing law-like generalisations. For these sciences, 'theories are not constructed deductively and experience is not organized with regard to the success of operations. Access to the facts is provided by the understanding of meaning, not observation. The verification of lawlike hypotheses in the empirical-analytic sciences has its counterpart here in the interpretation of texts' (1968/1987: 309; cf. Gadamer, 1989: 274). In his chapter, O'Shaughnessy suggests that we seek plausible interpretations of consumer behaviour and that our view of the plausibility of any given interpretation will be influenced by our own attitudes, values and 'fused' with the text we are interpreting.

Understanding and interpretation will never be concluded definitively from a hermeneutic perspective and the value of Gadamer's exposition of hermeneutics and of O'Shaughnessy's version of this in the form of ethnopsychology, is that it is founded upon self-reflection and our own attention to the pre-suppositions guiding our interpretation of a specific text or phenomenon. There will never, it could be argued, be one true definitive interpretation of a text. Similar to the argument developed in Chapter 1 in relation to the limit attitude, Gadamer was well aware of 'human finitude' (Bernstein, 2002). But Gadamer does not take this point far enough for Moran (2000: 283) who writes, 'the project of human understanding should never be understood as Hegel, and, Gadamer claims, even Dilthey thought; namely as a historical progression towards a totality of truth. Gadamer believes we must follow Heidegger in recognising that human understanding is shot through with finitude and historicity. There is no end to interpretation when all the interpretations have been synthesised together'.

In an important gesture away from the stereotyped understanding of the natural sciences, particularly in relation to the objective nature of scientific inquiry, Gadamer, in a manner similar to Kuhn (1977), views our prejudices as productive, as without such a foundation, we cannot even begin to understand others. For Habermas (1990a), Gadamer, nonetheless, places too much emphasis on prejudice without significant reference to the power of reflection. This is a point of much dispute (e.g. Gadamer, 1989). Habermas's criticism is worth noting, even so, when he makes the case that hermeneutic understanding will prove inadequate in the face of systematically distorted communication.

Not only does 'Gadamer's prejudice for the rights of prejudices certified by tradition [deny] . . . the power of reflection. The latter proves itself, however in being able to reject the claim of tradition. Reflection dissolves substantiality because it not only confirms, but also breaks up dogmatic forces' (Habermas, 1990a: 237). In equal measure, hermeneutics, in Habermas's opinion, will be 'shaken when . . . patterns of systematically distorted communication are also evident in "normal" . . . speech. This is the case in the pseudo-communication in which the participants do not recognize a breakdown in their communication; only an external observer notes that they misunderstand each other' (Habermas, 1990a: 254; cf. Honneth, 2003).

This is, of course, where Habermas's theory of communicative action is useful but is beyond the scope of our attention here. Suffice to say that Gadamer is not convinced by Habermas's attempted problematisation of hermeneutics via reference to distorted communication (e.g. Habermas, 1990b: 257), preferring instead to make continued reference to 'fusion of horizons' and 'dialogue' throughout his work. This is an over-optimistic view that needs to be reflected on in more detail. Dialogue, as Burrell (2001) has argued, is a weapon of the powerful; likewise, establishing consensus, while possibly a result of mutual understanding and dialogue, can also easily be the result of ideological distortions, as Feminist critics of Gadamer have argued (Moran, 2000; see also Arnold and Fischer, 1994: 65). Even acknowledging these limitations, Gadamer and O'Shaughnessy both make the point, in different ways, that we need to be vigilant when certain views of 'science', 'scientific method' or the 'cognitive revolution' present themselves as received wisdom.

To conclude this overview, each of these three chapters thus represents a challenge to mainstream interpretations of consumer research, in some respect.

References

Arnold, S.J. and Fischer, E. (1994) 'Hermeneutics and Consumer Research', *Journal of Consumer Research* 21(June): 55–70.

Bernstein, R.J. (2002) 'The Constellation of Hermeneutics, Critical Theory and Deconstruction', in R.J. Dostal (ed.) *The Cambridge Companion to Gadamer*, pp. 266–282. Cambridge: Cambridge University Press.

Burrell, G. (2001) 'ephemera: Critical Dialogues on Organization', *ephemera: critical dialogues on organization* 1(1): 11–29.

Dholakia, N. and Dholakia, R.R. (1985) 'Choice and Choicelessness in the Paradigm of Marketing', in N. Dholakia and J. Arndt (eds) *Changing the Course of Marketing: Alternative Paradigms for Widening Marketing Theory*, pp. 173–185. Greenwich: JAI Press.

Dunbar, R.I.M. (2007) 'Evolution and the Social Sciences', *History of the Human Sciences* 20(2): 29–50.

Frederick, J.G. (1959) *Introduction to The Art and Science of Motivation Research*. Liverpool: The Bell Press.

Gadamer, H.G. (1989) *Truth and Method*, Second Edition. Tr. J. Weinsheimer and D.G. Marshall. London: Sheed & Ward.

Habermas, J. (1968/1987) *Knowledge & Human Interests*. Tr. J.J. Shapiro. Cambridge: Polity Press.

—— (1990a) 'A Review of Gadamer's *Truth and Method*', in G.L. Ormiston and A.D. Schrift (eds) *The Hermeneutic Tradition: From Ast to Ricoeur*, pp. 213–244. Albany: State University of New York Press.

—— (1990b) 'The Hermeneutic Circle Claim to Universality', in G.L. Ormiston and A.D. Schrift (eds) *The Hermeneutic Tradition: From Ast to Ricoeur*, pp. 245–272. Albany: State University of New York Press.

Honneth, A. (2003) 'On the Destructive Power of the Third: Gadamer and Heidegger's Doctrine of Intersubjectivity', *Philosophy & Social Criticism* 29(1): 5–21.

Kuhn, T.S. (1977) 'The Essential Tension: Tradition and Innovation in Scientific Research', in T.S. Kuhn (1977) *The Essential Tension: Selected Studies in Scientific Tradition and Change*, pp. 225–239. Chicago: The University of Chicago Press.

Moran, D. (2000) *Introduction to Phenomenology*. London: Routledge.

O'Shaughnessy, J. and O'Shaughnessy, N. (2002a) Postmodernism and Marketing: Separating the Wheat from the Chaff, *Journal of Macromarketing* **22**(1): 109–135.

—— (2002b) Ways of Knowing and their Applicability, *Marketing Theory* 2(2): 147–164.

Pawlowski, B. and Dunbar, R.I.M. (1999a) 'Impact of Market Value on Mate Choice Decisions', *Proceedings of the Royal Society* 266B: 281–285.

—— (1999b) 'Withholding Age as Putative Deception in Mate Search Tactics', *Evolution and Human Behavior* 20: 52–59.

Payne, J.W., Bettman, J.R. and Johnson, E.J. (1992) 'Behavioral Decision Research: A Constructive Processing Perspective', *Annual Review of Psychology* 43: 87–131.

Plomin, R. and Asbury, K. (2005) 'Nature and Nurture: Genetic and Environmental Influences on Behavior', *The Annals of the American Academy of Political and Social Science* 600: 86–98.

Prasad, A. (2002) 'The Contest Over Meaning: Hermeneutics as an Interpretive Methodology for Understanding Texts', *Organizational Research Methods* 5(1): 12–33.

Rabinow, P. and Rose, N. (2006) 'Biopower Today', *Biosocieties* 1(2): 195–217.

Saad, G. (2004) 'Applying Evolutionary Psychology in Understanding the Representation of Women in Advertisements', *Psychology and Marketing* 21(8): 593–612.

Saad, G. and Gill, T. (2000) 'Applications of Evolutionary Psychology in Marketing', *Psychology and Marketing* 17(12): 1005–1034.

—— (2003) 'An Evolutionary Psychology Perspective on Gift-Giving Among Young Adults', *Psychology and Marketing* 20(9): 765–784.

Saad, G. and Peng, A. (2006) 'Applying Darwinian Principles in Designing Effective Intervention Strategies: The Case of Sun Tanning', *Psychology and Marketing* 23: 617–638.

7

Remembering Motivation Research: Toward an Alternative Genealogy of Interpretive Consumer Research*

Mark Tadajewski

University of Leicester

ABSTRACT   *This article traces the emergence and subsequent decline of motivation research. It argues that contrary to recent opinion that interpretive consumer research emerged in the mid-1980s, an embryonic form of interpretive research can actually be found in the 1930s in the form of motivation research. It demonstrates that there are clear and distinct parallels regarding the ontology, axiology, epistemology, methodology and view of human nature between motivation research, interpretive research and, to a limited extent, critical theory. Not only is motivation research presented as an early form of interpretive consumer research, but in addition, Holbrook's and Hirschman's experiential analysis is shown to be a possible take-off point to make the case that motivation research represents an early root of Consumer Culture Theory. This genealogical exercise resituates the emergence of the CCT discourse by 80 years and interpretive research by 60 years.*

* Article originally published in *Marketing Theory* 2006; **6(4)**: 429–466, Sage Publications. Reproduced by permission of Sage Publications Ltd. www.sagepub.co.uk

The maddening fact about motivation research from its very inception has been the difficulty
of separating the real from the glittering. (Martineau, 1961: 198)

Introduction

In a recent article, Shankar and Patterson (2001) argued that the dominant paradigmatic position in consumer research has historically been some variant of 'positivism'
(compare with Calder and Tybout, 1989; Hunt, 1991). They acknowledge the explicit
bifurcation of paradigm allegiance in consumer research as stemming largely from the
contributions of the Consumer Behavior Odyssey, whose naturalistic research strategy
at swap meets and flea markets (among other sites) across the United States has been
an important catalyst for the interpretive turn (Wallendorf and Belk, 1989). At the risk
of generalization, proponents of the subjective world (i.e. interpretive) paradigm view
the social world as having a precarious ontological status. In questioning the ontological status of social reality, the emphasis in interpretive research is on the de-emphasis
of an external concrete social world. In place of assuming an external, concrete reality,
interpretive researchers seek to investigate the social world at the level of subjective
experience (Arndt, 1985a, 1985b). For interpretive researchers, social reality is seen to
be inter-subjectively composed, so that epistemologically, knowledge is not approached
from the standpoint of an external, objective position, but from the lived experience of
the research co-participant. As a methodological strategy to 'understand' the lived experience of consumers', interpretive researchers generally – although not exclusively – use
qualitative methods (e.g. Hudson and Ozanne, 1988; Moore and Lutz, 2000; Thompson
et al., 1989).

A more recent turn in this debate has been made by Arnould and Thompson, who have
argued in reference to the 'paradigm wars' that one major feature of these debates has been
the introduction of 'many nebulous epithets' (Arnould and Thompson, 2005: 868). These
include, 'relativist, post-positivist, interpretivist, humanistic, naturalistic, postmodern'
labels (Arnould and Thompson, 2005: 868). Where they see a problem with the use of
such terms is that they obfuscate, rather than clarify the discussion by failing to 'signify the
theoretical commonalities and linkages' (p. 868) within a research tradition that Arnould
and Thompson label 'Consumer Culture Theory' (CCT). While this label, like that of
interpretive research, represents a variety of research traditions, the common theoretical
orientation among them concerns the study of cultural complexity:

> Rather than viewing culture as a fairly homogenous system of collectively shared meanings,
> ways of life, and unifying values shared by a member of society (e.g. Americans share this kind
> of culture; Japanese share that kind of culture), CCT explores the heterogeneous distribution
> of meanings and multiplicity of overlapping cultural groupings that exist within the broader

sociohistoric frame of globalization and market capitalism . . . Owing to its internal fragmented complexity, consumer culture does not determine action as a causal force. Much like a game where individuals improvise within the constraints of rules . . . consumer culture – and the marketplace ideology it conveys – frames consumers' horizons of conceivable action, feeling, and thought, making certain patterns of behavior and sense-making interpretations more likely than others. (Arnould and Thompson, 2005: 869)

As we shall see later, while Arnould and Thompson's analysis is an important contribution to the paradigm debate(s), at the moment, however, what is interesting for our present purposes is how Shankar and Patterson (2001) offer an important paradox in their opening of a discursive space for their own work. They write, 'The dominant position within consumer research has been, and still is, occupied by positivism and its variants. However this position has been questioned *consistently* within consumer research since the mid-1980s' (Shankar and Patterson, 2001: 482; emphasis added). This, of course, is the chronological point at which interpretive research is generally positioned (e.g. Arnould and Thompson, 2005; Belk, 1995; Goulding, 1999; O'Shaughnessy and O'Shaughnessy, 2002; Sherry, 1991; Tadajewski, 2004). Note, however, that they write that it is only recently that the dominant position of positivism has been consistently questioned (Shankar and Patterson, 2001). It follows that at some time in the history of consumer research that the paradigmatic dominance of positivism has been questioned, albeit on an inconsistent basis. As a variety of scholars, from postmodern history (Jenkins, 2003), the history of systems of thought (Foucault, 1984), historical theological studies (de Certeau, 1988), organization studies (Parker, 1998, 2000, 2002) and marketing (Fullerton, 1988; Hollander, 1986) have argued, a closer examination of such narratives often reveals less linear progression than we might expect. In a similar vein, it can be maintained that motivation research has largely been forgotten by consumer researchers. What we mean by this, is that motivation research has been progressively forgotten in relation to more institutionalized forms of knowledge associated with logical empiricism. Indeed, a series of recent papers by Barbara Stern are indicative of precisely how forgotten this history is, with Stern repeatedly drawing attention to the neglect of this discourse within the canon (Fullerton and Stern, 1990; Stern, 1990, 2001, 2004). More recently, Stern (2004) laments the clear neglect of motivation research and Ernest Dichter's contribution to consumer research. Stern, however, is not to be deterred in her project of extending our understanding of motivation research and its central proponent although, as she registers, her earlier research 'is more aimed at justifying his [Dichter's] neglect than on evaluating his contributions and ongoing influence' (2004: 165).

Certainly, when we turn to the literature, those sources that have attempted to establish the paradigmatic position of motivation research are far from reaching a consensus position. Here we might recall Kassarjian's (1989) insightful book review in which he proposed that the motivation research of Herta Hertzog and Ernest Dichter could 'perhaps' be seen as a forerunner of interpretive, qualitative research. Similarly, Levy suggests that motivation research 'died, but, of course, continued to grow as qualitative research' (Levy, 2003a: 104). Likewise, Kernan (1992) sees motivation research as simply qualitative research (see also, Bartos, 1986a; Fullerton and Stern, 1990). This equation of qualitative with motivation research has, however, been questioned by Sampson (1978) who noted that motivation research was not simply qualitative research but was equally amenable to quantification. This narrative does not end here. When we turn to the pages of Murray et al. (1997) these authors suggest that the foundations of motivation research were 'historical-hermeneutic' based (Murray et al., 1997: 101). Similarly, Arndt (1985a, 1985b) offers us further clues that motivation research may indeed be an interpretive approach, by positioning motivation research in the subjective world paradigm (compare with Alvesson, 1994). Arndt's proposal also appears to have the support of Fullerton (1990) who, in his review of Paul Lazarsfeld's early studies of consumer behaviour, asserted that these studies share similar characteristics to phenomenological research in that Lazarsfeld used open-ended questions, required specific concrete examples from respondents and drew upon theory from experimental psychology and psychoanalysis in the interpretation of transcripts. In light of these comments, it seems fair to suggest, despite Shankar and Patterson's (2001) insistence that the early history of interpretive consumer research has been elevated to the status of 'received wisdom', that the general consensus regarding the historical development of interpretive consumer research is somewhat less clear. Given this ambiguity, it is an appropriate moment to determine the paradigm with which motivation research is most consistent. Now clearly, the worldview presented as embodying the axiological, ontological, epistemological, methodological characteristics of motivation research is a generalization. This is to be expected and has not prevented previous commentators from delineating positivist or interpretivist research in this way (e.g. Burrell and Morgan, 1992[1979]; Holbrook, 1997; Hudson and Ozanne, 1988; Keat and Urry, 1975; Mick and Demoss, 1990; Morgan and Smircich, 1980; Murray and Ozanne, 1991; Szmigin and Foxall, 2000).

Having discussed the recent developments in the paradigm debate and the turn towards CCT, we will now examine the emergence of motivation research. Following this, the axiology, ontology, epistemology and methodology of motivation research is delineated and its historical relationship to interpretive research and CCT outlined.

Researching the Consumer

After the Second World War, the growth in standards of living meant that many consumers found themselves within striking distance of middle-class prosperity, with access to consumer goods that far surpassed those available to even the most prosperous of past centuries (Dichter, 1964; Packard, 1960). In spite of such economic changes, the ability of advertisers to sell their wares to the buying public was being challenged, with consumers becoming ever more discernable customers (Green, 1952). As Green pointed out:

> Consumers are beginning to save their money rather than buy merchandise. Durable good sales are down, nondurable sales are slightly up . . . Long accepted advertising techniques are being reviewed in light of new selling concepts. Rapidly changing market patterns are requiring marketing decisions to be made ever more quickly. (Green, 1952: 30)

These difficulties were further compounded by the increasing saturation of the market for consumer durables, thereby leading marketers and advertisers alike to acknowledge that this was indeed a 'buyer's market' (Britt, 1950). In this state-of-affairs, an understanding of buying motives increased in importance, with the growing complexity of the business environment leading many to assert that the early descriptive focus of consumer research was an unsuitable research strategy for use in a dynamic marketplace (Converse et al., 1958).

It was in this context that consumer research as a distinct discipline emerged when a confluence of factors came together (Levy, 2001). Important here is the *wider* acceptance of the marketing concept by the business community (see Hollander, 1986; Klass, 1964; Twedt, 1964). Commensurate with this turn was the realisation among the practitioner and academic communities that very little attention had been devoted to researching what consumers want to buy (see Karesh, 1995). This lacunae stimulated researchers from a variety of disciplines to fill what were 'highly disturbing voids' in relation to consumer needs, wants and general consumption behaviours (Newman, 1955). This focus on actual consumer behaviour was accentuated by the growing awareness that the existing conceptual foundations of consumer research were of dubious veracity, based as they were on notions of rational, economic man; an abstraction that was being challenged by a growing quantity of evidence (see Breyer, 1934; Katona, 1954; Levy, 1959; Mueller, 1954). It was this increasing concern among marketing and advertising professionals that they were losing contact with the marketplace that encouraged them to turn to the methods developed in the social and behavioural sciences as a means to understand consumer needs, wants, desires and fears. In particular, advertisers and marketing managers highly prized the insights available from sociologists, psychologists and psychoanalysts who could provide ideas on conscious and unconscious human motivations. Information that was especially sought after, in particular, related to 'the unconscious or hidden ideas, associations or attitudes of the consumer in connection with . . . [a] particular product' (Weiss and Green, 1951: 36).

It is the translation of psychological theory and concepts into consumer research that is our focus here and this process did involve some subtle changes in emphasis. Psychology, for example, had traditionally placed greater emphasis on the psychological features of motivation at an individual level and devoted far less attention toward the manner in which these motivations reflected wider social values, beliefs and conventions (Cofer and Appley, 1964). The interest in the influence of the structural environment was, in contrast, seen to be the remit of sociologists and anthropologists. Bringing these two distinct areas together was the work of the early motivation researchers. These researchers had received extensive psychological training and perceived the opportunities available in the market and consumer research industry for the application of psychological theory to actual market problems. In addition, they were well placed by virtue of their training to appreciate the epistemological and methodological limitations of consumer research (Dichter, 1979).

While motivation research is frequently seen to be the product of Ernest Dichter, the reality is that by the time Dichter arrived in the United States motivation research was already well underway, having been developed in an embryonic fashion by Paul Lazarsfeld in the 1930s (Lazarsfeld, 1935, 1969). Lazarsfeld's importance here cannot be understated given his formative influence in initiating qualitative motivation studies. Of equal importance in terms of the conditions of possibility that contributed to the emergence and sedimentation of this discourse in the United States was the wider political environment that affected Lazarsfeld and, in turn, Dichter. While Lazarsfeld was in the United States pursuing a travelling fellowship provided by the Rockefeller Foundation, in his home country the Conservative Party of Austria rejected their constitution, 'outlawed the Socialist Party, and established an Italian-type fascism' (Lazarsfeld, 1969: 276). This was to have a profound impact on Lazarsfeld when his position in the secondary school system was cancelled, while his university role remained 'nominally unaffected'. More importantly, 'most members' of his family living in Vienna were imprisoned, a turn of events that gave 'the sympathetic officers of the Rockefeller Foundation the pretext for extending [Lazarsfeld's] . . . fellowship another year' (Lazarsfeld, 1969: 276). This shift in the political environment in Vienna, the imprisonment of family members, the extension of his Rockefeller fellowship ultimately led Lazarsfeld to remain in the United States where he had begun to publish articles devoted to motivation research in the *National Marketing Review*, the precursor to the *Journal of Marketing* (Lazarsfeld, 1935). The Viennese political climate would also influence another important figure in motivation research to move to the relative political and racial stability of the United States. In 1936 Ernest Dichter was working on a research project at the University of Vienna in the *Wirtschafts Psychologisches Institut* (Psychoeconomic Institute) studying the milk-drinking habits of the Viennese. Describing the day he had completed his depth interviews, Dichter (1979: 16–17) recalled entering the department:

> The man who stood behind the door . . . was a peculiar looking guy. He asked me whether I was connected with the Institute and what my name was. He had a tone of authority so I did not feel like telling him off. 'You are under arrest,' he growled . . . Without my knowledge, the Institute was used during the Dollfuss & Schuschnigg Fascist rule of Austria as a secret mailing centre from where information was sent to Brno, Czechoslovakia.

Not only was Dichter arrested and imprisoned for a week as a 'subversive', his wife reported to him that the current newspapers 'were full of stories about how market research and public opinion research had been used to cleverly disguise the subversive socialist activities of the underground' (Dichter, 1979: 17). These activities would be reported in the official Nazi newspaper, *Volkische Beobachter*, a move that hints at the potential danger in which these activities placed Dichter, especially given the political, ideological and ethnic tensions at the time. Not only was Dichter Jewish, and thus in a precarious position, his arrest was noted in a list of other subversive influences (some of whom would later flee from the Nazis) including 'Sigmund Freud, Albert Einstein, Karl Marx, [and] Engels' (Dichter, 1979: 18). It was during a meeting with a colleague, who was the head of the Aptitude Testing Institute of the City of Vienna (ATICV), that Dichter realized his time and prospects for business success in Vienna were limited. When, for example, he asked the head what his chances of earning an internship at the ATICV were the response was: 'I would love to give you a job. You have developed a number of new ideas, but you are Jewish are you not?' 'His advice contributed considerably to my leaving the country in early 1937' (Dichter, 1979: 18); a view further compounded by 'some ill brown wind from across the German border' (Dichter, 1979: 21). In his attempt to leave Austria, Dichter discussed his view of motivation research with the American consulate, where he stressed his contribution to the United States:

> 'I am sure that America is a wonderful country,' I answered. 'But I also know that it has just as many problems as most other countries. Many of these problems need solutions.' We have to understand the real reasons why people do things . . . obviously we all want fewer criminals; we want people to be happy, interested in their work, we want them to increase their productivity. Some companies want people to buy their products rather than those of their competitors. (Dichter, 1979: 24)

It was the last point with which motivation research has been most closely associated and on the basis of his meeting with the consulate (who assisted Dichter in his application to enter the United States), Dichter was able to transplant himself from Vienna to the United States where he would become the foremost proponent of motivation research.

Motivation Research

Concerned with understanding the motives underpinning consumer (buying and consuming) behaviours, motivation researchers believed that the most pressing task facing researchers was to establish the 'real' motives underpinning consumer behaviour from those that were espoused. Broadly speaking these motives are classifiable, as Converse et al. (1958) proposed, into three broad categories: (1) those of which the consumer is consciously aware and willing to disclose to the researcher; (2) those of which they are aware but are unwilling to divulge to the researcher; and (3) those motives of which the consumer is unaware. For example:

> A consumer buys food because her children like it or because it is low in calories. Usually she is willing to give the reasons for such purchases. A middle-income family buys an expensive car because they want to outdo the next-door neighbors. Often they will not disclose the real reason but will say they bought the car because it is heavier and rides easier . . . We often do not know the real reason for many of our actions. Why do we trade at one store rather than another. (Converse et al., 1958: 535)

It is these hidden motives that posed the greatest difficulties for conventional consumer research at the time. While such research typically involved the use of experimental-statistical tools, pre-coded questionnaires and large samples, motivation research questioned the wholesale support of such methods to the neglect of qualitative methods. Dichter's response was unequivocal. Americans, Dichter lambasted, were 'still using outmoded and inefficient methods to determine and understand consumer motivations' (Dichter, 1947: 432). 'They are only scratching the surface of the motivations underlying why humans behave as they do' (Dichter, 1947: 432). For Dichter, this meant that marketers should recognize that when they use such 'outmoded' direct methods such as consumer surveys, they are at 'about the same stage as botany used to be before Linnaeus', that by classifying people by their 'outward phenomenological appearance instead of looking at the general type a person may look and apparently belong to . . . [they may be missing important features because] at a different level, he may be entirely different' (Bartos, 1986b: 19). This, Dichter argued, required consumer researchers to rethink the way they practiced consumer research and in response, he outlined a suitable direction that he thought offered a fruitful way of understanding consumer behaviour – motivation research.

Axiology

Awareness of the limitations of current (logical empiricist) research practice and the ambiguity of the term 'motivation research' led to intense academy interest, with the University of Michigan sponsoring a conference dedicated to motivation research, as well as this topic occupying an afternoon of debate at the American Marketing Association in Atlantic City in 1953 (Blake, 1954). Given their willingness to borrow the conceptual tools of other disciplines, it was not long before Freud's work and the implications of this for the conceptualization of the consumer were being discussed seriously by scholars (Collins and

Montgomery, 1970). Dichter, on the other hand, was quick to dispel interpretations of his work as indicative of a wholesale subscription to Freudian thought, preferring instead to stress the eclectic nature of his own axiological, epistemological and methodological influences (compare with Blankenship, 1965; Kelne, 1955): 'I have often been accused of being a Freudian. I don't see quite why this should be an accusation rather than a compliment. In reality I am not; I am much more of an eclectic. By popular opinion Freud is always associated with sex' (Dichter, 1979: 92). What Dichter's remarks serve to forewarn here is the complex constellation of epistemic values that underpin motivation research. As a discreet community of discourse, however, its main focus is on 'why' questions, with a primary interest towards establishing a better understanding of why consumers engage in certain types of behaviour, and why they view particular products in the manner that they do. As Britt saw the task, 'It is not enough to know that young women use more hand lotions than older women. The point is to find out *why* people have these preferences' (1950: 669; emphasis in original). Communicating the rationale behind the need for marketers to understand their consumer base in greater depth, Britt maintained that '*the consumer is king today*. Our nation has moved from an era of scarcity to an era of plenty, and this makes the role of the consumer more important than ever . . . Because of his "dollar ballots" the consumer will continue to be king. Everyday he casts his ballots at the cash registers' (Britt, 1960: 36; emphasis in original). Since the actual behaviour of consumers was believed to be the key to greater organizational prosperity and since textbook representations of consumer behaviours were increasingly problematized, motivation researchers (primarily) adopted a research strategy that bore resemblance to 'cultural anthropology'. What this meant in practice was that the major axiological tenant underpinning this form of consumer research was that 'the day-to-day behavior of twentieth century man – even when he lives in Brooklyn, on the outskirts of Paris, or in the south of Italy – is as worthy of study as the Samoans or the Trobrianders' (Dichter, 1971: 2). No more were consumers seen to be 'nice, [and] rational', as this could only lead to disappointment 'when we meet the walking and talking master mold' (Dichter, 1979: 113). What was required to counterpoint such idealistic representations was the careful observation of the consumption behaviour of interest. As an example, Dichter recalled how he used observation, supplemented with extensive photography, when he was interested in the 'why' and 'how' people smoked. He recalled:

> Considering myself an anthropologist, I decided to use film clippings, Getch [Dichter's employer] gave me a couple of hundred dollars and I went out and became a roving photographic reporter. I still have the film. I went to Rockefeller Plaza and photographed people in a candid camera fashion while they were ice skating and smoking at the same time. Some people warmed their hands on the cigarette which they held in inverted fashion. Another type smoked and chewed gum at the same time. Some Western Union boys whom I caught in the act were

lighting each other's cigarettes in a secretive fashion while goofing off and standing behind the corner. Observing human behavior in this fashion became a hobby and a scientific discovery trip for me. Why did people smoke? Obviously not just because of the addiction to nicotine, but for many other reasons, too. Tightening your lips around a cigarette gives you a feeling of security . . . Therefore, cigarette smoking was a way of combating stress. (Dichter, 1979: 42)

Human behaviour, on this reading, is not only determined by outside forces acting on the individual. Instead, Dichter stressed the complex interplay between the individual, the group and the society in which they are placed. Having gestured towards this, there is far more nuance to the axiology of motivation research than would make this a paradigmatic case of either positivist or interpretive research. Dichter, for instance, evinced little belief in the possibility of explaining consumer behaviour by subsuming it under a universal law.

What motivation theorists did actually propose, is that it is possible for consumer behaviour to be explained and from such explanations that it will become possible to predict what a given cohort of consumers will do in any specific consumption situation. But their attempts to do so are not consistent with what would be the case if this paradigmatic community were positivist. Rather, motivation researchers looked for some underlying thematic association between various consumer segments in order to explain why any given community will view – using the example provided by Haire (1950) – a buyer and consumer of instant coffee as lazy, a bad wife, single and so forth. This type of thematic analysis is undertaken so that the motivation researcher can 'understand' the phenomena that they are investigating by way of identifying the individual associations, meanings and symbolism attached to a given product or consumer environment (e.g. department store). This is achieved via a process of between 50 (Yoell, 1952), 100 to 150 (Yoell, 1950), 500 (Dichter, 1960), 2000 (Dichter, 1964) and 5000 interviews (Dichter, 1955b) in order to discern the pattern of shared meanings in the chosen sample:

the verification or refutation of our hypotheses based on approximately 200 or 250 individual histories, still does not lead us to the same variety and numerical accuracy, e.g., the ability to distinguish between a brand recognition-index of 68 percent or 73 percent, that 2,000 or 5,000 interviews would do. However, what we have is a really thorough understanding of a basic motivational pattern among enough people to indicate that the pattern is significant and lends itself to practical applications. In finding that 80 mothers out of 100 reveal, in multiple waves and multiple tests, when talking about food for their babies that they are as concerned about their own convenience as the nutritional value of the food, we have a finding valid enough to permit any practitioner in advertising or public relations to take advantage of it and act accordingly. (Dichter, 1955a: 32)

Table 1 A summary of positivism, interpretivism, critical theory and motivation research (Table adapted from Murray and Ozanne, 1991)

	Positivism	Interpretivism	Critical theory	Motivation research
Ontological assumptions (nature of reality)	Objective; tangible; ahistorical; fragmentable; divisible	Socially constructed; multiple; holistic; contextual	'Force-field' between subject and object; dynamic; historical totality	Historically and socially constructed; multiple; contextual
Nature of social being	Deterministic; reactive	Voluntaristic; proactive	Suspend judgment; emphasize human potential	Historically influenced, but voluntaristic emphasis
Axiological assumptions (overriding goal)	'Explanation' via subsumption under general laws; prediction	'Understanding' via interpretation but not necessarily in order to confirm hypotheses	'Emancipation' via social organization that facilitates reason, justice and freedom	Understanding via interpretation; understanding as prerequisite to explanation and prediction
Epistemological assumptions (knowledge generated)	Nomothetic; time-free; context-independent; value-free	Idiographic; time-bound; context-dependent; value-laden;	Forward looking; imaginative; critical/unmasking; practical	Largely idiographic time-bound; value-laden; forward-looking; critical
View of causality	Real causes exist	Multiple; simultaneous; shaping	Reflection; exposure of constraints through dialogue; reconstruction	Multiple; shaping; exposure of potential constraints
Research relationship metaphor	Dualism; separation; detached observer	Interactive; co-operative; translator	Continuing dialogue; liberator	Interactive; co-operative but tempered with suspicion; Dichter as liberator

The 'patterns' that the motivation researcher excavated were not expected to remain stable in the sense of a law-like generalization.[1] Dichter is instead using this term to describe the way that general motivational patterns emerge from qualitative data and to indicate that there are certain norms adhered to by a substantial proportion of the population. Depending on the requirements of the client:

> Whenever it is desirable and practical, there is no reason why such a pattern cannot be tested on the basis of 5,000 cases. In practice, however, at the end of a study a client will much more frequently accept our recommendation, if it provides him with new insight into his sales and advertising problem. (Dichter, 1955a: 34)

This said, some similarity can still be discerned between motivation research and logical empiricism in the sense that motivation research does aim to demonstrate the underlying systematic association between variables. In conducting depth interviews and observing the consumer segment of interest, Dichter stressed the need to verify, corroborate or refute initial hypotheses. Having made this case, motivation researchers did place very concrete bounds on the extent to which generalization is possible: 'Things that may be learned about one buyer situation in one locality with respect to one kind of product may have little or no applicability to another buyer situation in another locality with respect to another kind of product' (Britt, 1960: 20). Emphasizing these limitations further, 'Actually, every social situation is different from every other and requires a separate analysis' (Britt, 1950: 667). One consequence of this limited generalizability is that the research process can never authoritatively conclude: '*Re-search* is a continued search with the emphasis on the search' (Dichter, 1961: 2; emphasis in original). The task for motivation researchers is that they accept 'the need for continuous testing and observation' if an adequate understanding of a specific consumer behaviour is to be elicited however provisional this will remain (Dichter, 1960: 2).

Ontological Assumptions

Although little discussed in the literature, there are brief ontological references relating to the nature of reality for motivation researchers. Conventional research at this time subscribed to a variant of realism and the view that the external, physical world has an existence independent of human perception. In this context, observation was assumed to be fallible, but theory-neutral, rather than theory-laden (Bayton, 1958). Here theories do not impinge on observation, which is seen to be pure and untainted by mediating influences. Subscription to this view, while largely implicit, led consumer researchers to assume that the description of behaviour based on 'directly observable [and] . . . directly ascertainable collections of facts' were likely to corroborate current hypotheses (Dichter, 1978: 54).

There is little, if any, ontological depth presumed here, with surface phenomena seen to be connected in directly observable, causal fashion and whose empirical regularities are assumed to be measurable: 'It relies on observations, answers to questions, and recording and registrations of various forms of behaviour. It is, in the sense of modern semantics, based on naïve empiricism' (Dichter, 1978: 55). In practice, this meant consumer researchers emphasized the utility of direct questions in the research process, with causal relationships assumed to be identifiable between what consumers say they do, and what they actually do, in practice (Politz, 1957). In contrast to this empiricism, motivation researchers espoused an ontological position that is closer to interpretivism than to positivism, although it shares certain aspects of each. For motivation researchers, the social world is seen to embody emergent, historically and temporally stable properties with certain behaviours dating 'back tens of thousands of years' (Dichter, 1979: 107). As Dichter registered, human behaviour is influenced 'by instinctive responses and social norms, or cultural values', and in response to the complexity of their lives consumers create cognitive shortcuts that enable them to move through and manage their everyday lives (Dichter, 1960: 80). One pertinent example of what Dichter is gesturing toward here can be found in a discussion of consumer choice behaviour.

Examining the choice behaviour associated with buying behaviours for soap, Cheskin and Ward attempted to explain why one style of packaging was more popular than another. They concluded: 'it is self-evident that the average housewife does not consciously go to the grocery store to buy package designs; she goes to buy ham, vegetables, soap, canned fruit, and so on. Only rarely does she consciously consider the container in which these items are sold' (Cheskin and Ward, 1948: 573). The implication of this view is that consumers are not necessarily rational information processors or wholly beholden to deterministic forces that dictate appropriate behaviours. Instead, they are capable of exhibiting a degree of voluntarism in that they can refuse their extant categorization systems. Even allowing that this was possible, many consumers will not engage in an extended refusal of all previous knowledge, since as Britt (1960) suggested, this kind of individual would be in need of serious therapy given the decision-making paralysis that such a state would induce. More likely, as a consequence of environmental complexity, consumers will remain willing to engage in sub-optimal behaviours (what Szmigin and Foxall (2000) equate with a mid-point between the determinism of positivist research and the voluntaristic perspective of interpretivism) because it serves a useful purpose in enabling them to negotiate the complexity of everyday life.

In line with this mid-point position, the primary interest for the motivation researcher is how consumer behaviour is determined in part by the environmental conditions and the subjective perception of the consumption situation for the respondent(s). Consistent with this view of the social, whenever we are interested in understanding why a consumer, a group, or a cultural unit behaves in the way that they do, Dichter writes, 'I must use interpretative research. I cannot exclusively rely on asking the people or groups involved why they are doing what they are doing' (Dichter, 1978: 54). Where research seeks to ask a 'why' question (in contrast to the 'what' questions asked by conventional researchers), what they are asking for is an '*interpretation* of human behavior' (Dichter, 1978: 54; emphasis in original). 'We want to find out what motivated, what moved, what influenced these people to do what they did' (Dichter, 1978: 54). Clearly motivation researchers do not ask these 'why' questions directly, given that a very clear methodological aim of motivation research is concerned with the attempt to sidestep those rationalizations that are likely to emerge when the respondent feels that they have been placed in position where they are being prejudged by the researcher (discussed below). In methodological terms, this involves the formulation of hypotheses, which are:

> developed for the purpose of theoretically explaining a particular behavior. It then tests the validity of these various hypotheses, rejecting those which are not confirmed through further research and substituting others until several reasonable and supportable explanations for the behavior to be interpreted have been established. (Dichter, 1978: 55)

After the initial sets of hypotheses have been established, the motivation researcher then uses a battery of projective tests to elicit a description of the subjective processes that a consumer goes through when purchasing specific goods or services. Yoell described his research approach in the following manner:

> The technique for discovering . . . buying motives . . . is based on the discovery of behavioral processes . . . To find the motive, I insist, examine the experiences. What I do in interviewing consumers is to uncover the most recent experience the consumer has had with the product. Then I gradually take the consumer back into experiences – back even until the first usage and experience . . . Reliving the experience gets the individual back into the exact atmosphere under which the events took place. (Yoell, 1952: 86)

Here, the 'objective' external world is ontologically marginalized in favour of the subjective interpretation of the behaviour of consumers (Dichter, 1960). The espoused interpretations of their own behaviours by the respondents will not 'always correspond with reality' and it is the task of the motivation researcher to negotiate espoused beliefs in favour of those repressed 'real', subjective beliefs, opinions and motivations (Britt, 1960).

In a reflection on the process of ontological co-creation Dichter proffers what appears to be an ontological position more in line with social constructionism than logical empiricism. Reflecting on the last stages of the research process, Dichter noted how those involved play a central part in the social construction of the 'world in which we live, the motivation researcher and the communicator who applies his findings are at the same time participants and formulators of the future world' (Dichter, 1960: 63). And these players in the business community are ultimately responsive to the consumer. As Britt affirms in his book on motivation research: *'American business is not your callous master...but rather the servant of you, the American consumer – the spender'* (Britt, 1960: xii; emphasis in original). It is the spender, the consumer, who is consequently a central participant in the ontological creation of the consumerist society that Dichter (1960, 1971) applauded and Packard (1960) lamented.

Epistemological Assumptions

While Dichter does stress the complimentary nature of motivation research to conventional statistical research, he continues to emphasize the importance of motivation research as a counterpoint for the limitations of conventional consumer research. 'The advertiser has gradually come to realize that by using this tool [statistical methods] alone he has received only part of the information which he requires to make an intelligent and scientifically based decision' (Dichter, 1955a: 27). This said, Dichter is critical of the naïve empiricism that underpins statistical 'nose counting research' that drew upon demographic variables to categorize consumers (Dichter, 1979). More than the use of statistics alone, it is the argument that research could be objective in the sense of being theory-neutral that most perturbed Dichter (compare with Dichter, 1947: 438). By objective research, Dichter (1979) gestured towards research that suggested it was devoid of any interpretation, or otherwise assumes that 'all that is necessary is that the facts speak for themselves' (Bayton, 1958: 289). Rather, what is more scientific is the acknowledgement that researchers will – as the primary research instrument – introduce certain assumptions into their research projects: 'To state the existence of these assumptions, instead of pretending that they are not there, frees the researcher from naïve empiricism' (Dichter, 1961: 2). Commensurate with the positions put forward by Fleck (1979[1935]), Hanson (1960), Kuhn (1962) and Feyerabend (1975) against the possibility of a theory-neutral observation language, an important quotation highlights Dichter's position in relation to naïve empiricism. Let us quote it in full:

> Studying human motivation is not unlike Herodotus' problem of studying the reason for the inundation of the Nile. By merely observing a person's behavior it is close to impossible to determine why he does what he does. Herodotus approached his problem by picking out, on the basis of previous knowledge, certain elements in the subject matter which he thought were significant. He felt that the distance covered by the flowing waters, the time at which the inundation began, the time at which the overflow reached its maximum, and the fact that there were no winds or breezes at the river surface were all interesting phenomena, although he did not know what they had to do with each other. In this form they were all meaningless facts, not susceptible to interpretation. Why did he pick these facts rather than others? The

answer was he was familiar with certain theories dealing with the behavior of the rivers . . . In the field of human motivation, we approach problems with certain general theories about why people behave as they do. For example, we believe that most people are more concerned with their own egos than with other people; that most people suffer from a degree of insecurity and have as one of their main goals in life self-protection against dangers and anxiety. Applying this theory to a specific problem, we develop a hypothesis. (Dichter, 1955a: 28–9)

To further illustrate the clear divergence between the epistemological presuppositions associated with the 'naïve' empiricism of the 1950s, it is appropriate to acknowledge the use of a version of free association in motivation research. Where free association is used in a clinical environment to treat psychologically maladjusted patients, when translated into motivation research it is used to encourage the spontaneity of response by the interviewee. This is because 'encouraging a person with some slight guidance to simply pour out his feelings about a particular subject brings out true motivations [and is] . . . much more reliable . . . *than predetermining the framework in which the answers are to be given*' (Dichter, 1960: 285; emphasis added). Here the respondent is asked 'to summarize for us his own motivations and to give us the interpretation of what he considers normal, usual, average, etc. What we insist instead is that he report actual events' (Dichter, 1960: 284). This process, however, still needs further qualification because despite the openness of the interpretive framework, motivation researchers did not trust the responses of their respondents. Instead, they subscribed to an 'epistemology of suspicion'.

In *Freud and Philosophy: An Essay on Interpretation*, Ricoeur (1970) calls Freud a 'master of suspicion'. By this, Ricoeur is trying to position psychoanalysis as a form of suspicious interpretation. For the psychoanalyst, for instance, the object of interest is distorted in the sense of the repression of sexual or aggressive wishes that are outside the bounds of acceptable behaviour and consequently find themselves manifested in dreams where the censorship of the ego is less influential. In such cases it is the task of the dream analyst to translate the dream language (Freud, 1965[1900]). What this means is that the dream analyst has to unravel the complexity and ambiguity that will be inherent in the complex network of meaningful associations that are condensed in the dream, so that it can be understood. In a similar fashion, Dichter's research style (and that of motivation research) bears the hallmarks of epistemological 'suspicion', where he suggests his own research position in relation to his research co-participants is similar to that of an 'archaeologist', while the personality of the respondent is akin to an 'onion' (Dichter, 1979: 159, 188). What he means is that the espoused responses might not reveal very much because people prefer to make their behaviour appear more rational and more reasonable, so the motivation researcher has to peel away the various layers of ego protection, much like one would peel an onion, in order to reveal the 'true', 'real' beliefs and behaviours.

> Psychology has demonstrated that there are several permanent distortion factors which interfere with the objective observation of the motivational field. The most important one is our desire to appear rational to ourselves and to others. When confronted with an investigation of our motives we first search actively for rational explanations. The danger is great, however, that this desire to act rationally results in a pseudo-rational cause for our behavior. (Dichter, 1955a: 36)

While consumers may strive to hide or modify what they might consider irrational behaviours, this is not to suggest that motivation research is concerned only with irrational buying needs, or that all behaviours *have* to be explained with reference to emotion (compare with Holbrook and Hirschman, 1982). Rather, what this epistemological stance holds is that 'people do behave rationally. But rational behaviour also includes acceptance of emotions, such as the fear of embarrassment, as a motivator' (Dichter, 1979: 114). This is not necessarily a function of consumer irrationality, but serves to illustrate that the motivation researcher must devote greater time to making what is normally dismissed as irrational consumption behaviour understandable in terms of the standards of rationality acceptable at the time (Britt, 1960). In a similar manner to the concept of *verstehen* that underwrites interpretive research, motivation research sees buying behaviour as never completely irrational in itself, but only from a particular point of view.

Methodological Assumptions

The realization that the subjective beliefs of consumers might not mirror those they espoused heralded an important turn within consumer research regarding the conception of 'man', that is, the understanding of human nature that was adopted as a methodological presupposition. Here, Eliasberg (1954) made the important point that since the popularization of Veblen's (1934) conspicuous consumption thesis, it had become clear that consumers were not simply satisfied with the essential products that they must consume such as food or shelter. Instead, their consumption becomes a way of satisfying other socially related ego needs and from this, Eliasberg reasoned, the latest psychological and psychiatric techniques are of particular importance for those interested in consumer behaviour (Eliasberg, 1954; Vicary, 1951). One way that these techniques can be acquired and utilized efficiently, Eliasberg suggested, was for companies to employ psychologists, sociologists and other trained behavioural experts in their consumer research departments.

Despite the occasional direct importation of Freudian thought as an interpretive heuristic (e.g. Bayton, 1958), motivation researchers did not generally import psychoanalytic theory or method *in toto* into consumer research despite accusations otherwise (e.g. Rothwell, 1955; Scriven, 1958; Westfall et al., 1957; Williams, 1957). Nor was motivation research an attempt to uncover and repair neuroses implanted in childhood (Dichter, 1979). A 'much better' description of the relationship between psychoanalysis and motivation research is that both are forms of psychological 'detective' work in which the researcher is viewed as a 'psycho-detective' charged with uncovering consumer motivations through extended depth interviews (Dichter, 1979: 79): 'For the first time in my life I realized that a detective's job was similar to that of a motivational researcher... I often call myself the "Columbo" of human motivations' (Dichter, 1979: 18). Clearly the kind of detective work this involved and the environment in which it took place does not resemble a 'proper' psychoanalytic counselling session but bears more resemblance, Dichter suggested, to a form of 'mini-psychoanalysis' utilizing qualitative research and small samples (Dichter, 1979: 45, 49).

When a particularly interesting behaviour has been discovered in the initial exploratory research, these themes are explored further through lengthy interviews 'in order to prove or disprove our original hypothesis' (Dichter, 1979: 49). Each of these interviews is recorded verbatim and 'every phrase, every gesture, and every intonation of the respondent' noted by the researcher (Dichter, 1960: 285). As an example of the way in which Dichter used such information to support his arguments, let us examine a paper published in the *Harvard Business Review* that investigated word-of-mouth advertising where Dichter and his colleagues conducted depth interviews with 255 consumers in 24 different locations in the United States: 'Respondents were encouraged to recall freely (and in full detail) conversations in which products, services, and advertising had been discussed, including recommendations made as well as received' (Dichter, 1966: 149). In describing the major themes that emerged from these interviews, Dichter provided a variety of examples that demonstrated how a particular thematic structure is played out in the text. For example, in relation to the theme of product involvement, Dichter writes:

> Of the 352 talking episodes reported by our respondents, 33% belong in this category. This category includes incidents of strongly felt, gratifying experiences with a product or service which make the speaker 'flow over' . . . In many instances it is talk which confirms for the speaker his ownership and joy in the product, or his discovery of it. For example: 'She asked if I'd ever used Guardsman. She said, "You ought to get some — it's terrific!" ' Well, I said I'd try it, and I did. I mentioned to this friend later that I had used it, and she seemed anxious to know if I'd liked it. I told her it seemed to be pretty good, but she was hardly satisfied with that comment, and began to rave about it all over again. I don't rave much as a rule anyway. She seemed convinced she'd done me a huge favor by recommending it, and if I wouldn't get all excited after using it, she had to get excited for me. (Dichter, 1966: 149; emphasis in original)

Extrapolating from his numerous interviews, Dichter concluded:

> I consider the establishment of a close link between successful, everyday Word-of-Mouth recommendations and effective advertising to be one of the . . . findings of the present study.

It emphasizes the new role of the advertiser as that of a friend who recommends a trusted product, as against that of a salesman who tries to get rid of merchandise . . . People mold opinion. The glossy, brightly colored magazine page can never replace the influence and the value of a personal recommendation. Were that the case, the consumer public would have to be very passive – simply sitting back and receiving information, and enough of it to permit a proper evaluation. However our recent studies [as indicated in the above citation] have shown quite the opposite: the consumer public is in fact active. Consequently in a buying situation a dynamic interpersonal relationship – where ideas are discussed, opinions are exchanged, questions are asked, and answers given – will frequently exist. (Dichter, 1966: 166)

The logic of this depth approach is succinctly explicated by Newman (1958), who proposed that free association encouraged the consumer to avoid recourse to any extensive logical analysis of the narrative they espoused, and instead permitted the skilled interviewer to uncover those thoughts that have somehow been repressed by the respondent. For instance, in a project that sought to understand why men read the magazine *Esquire*, which at the time Dichter was conducting his study resembled *Playboy* or *Penthouse*, he explained his research approach. 'I would go out and talk at great length to a number of men, but I would not ask them why they did or did not read *Esquire*. I would simply let them tell me their associations, their experiences, their ideas and thoughts while talking and thumbing through the magazine' (Dichter, 1979: 34).[2] In this context, the task of the motivation researcher is to reassure the respondent by 'developing rapport . . . [by] inserting delicate probes, where necessary, to encourage fuller discussion' (Dichter, 1958: 28; compare with Wallendorf and Belk, 1989: 81).

Discussing the depth interview towards the end of his life, Dichter again reminds us how distinct motivation research remains from psychoanalysis – 'it isn't really putting somebody on the couch . . . It's very simple. We don't tell our interviewer what we are interested in, just as the physician does not tell the lab assistant that he suspects that the patient has liver disease' (Bartos, 1986b: 17). Here the emphasis is on the analysis of the subjective accounts that are generated by researcher immersion in the consumption history of the individuals sampled, with importance placed on letting the emergent nature of the phenomena reveal its characteristics to the researcher. This is in stark contrast to what we would expect if this were a positivist study, whereby the researcher typically works through a conceptual framework identified prior to the fieldwork. Instead, the guiding methodological assumption adopted for the purposes of a motivational research study was an emergent research design alongside an ethos of openness and sensitivity to the nature of the phenomena is all pervasive: 'Researching is a process where open-mindedness, the ability to see seemingly unrelated things as related and in a new light, is the major requirement' (Dichter, 1960: 70). Tools central to examining consumer behaviours in this way included qualitative methods such as depth interviewing, word association tests, sentence completion, role playing, cartoon tests, Thematic Apperception Tests and Rorschach personality tests, which provided the answers to managerial requirements that conventional techniques had failed to yield namely, meaningful results (see, Blake, 1954).

Having noted the variety of tools that were used in motivation research, two, including the Thematic Apperception Tests and the depth interview were often singled out for criticism. Most notably, the depth interview was frequently critiqued as little more than an open-ended interview otherwise semantically cloaked. The idea that these interviews would provide more depth of understanding was, for some, apparently ludicrous (Paradise and Blankenship, 1951; Politz, 1957). Dichter, however, explicitly argued that the depth interview began where open-ended interviewing concluded. Where the open-ended interviewer has faith in the validity of the responses that the respondent provides, the views espoused by the respondent are not, as was noted above, to be taken at face value. At this point, the researcher and the interviewee are equally important *dramatis personae*, with the researcher seen to be the instrument, the 'living seismograph' in this process, who should be sensitive to the comments, gestures and other inflexions that consumers provided during the interviews (Dichter, 1960). As a co-participant in the research process, the researcher is charged with the task of phenomenologically bracketing their own assumptions and this required that the researcher put themselves 'into the shoes of the other person' (Dichter, 1979: 179). This, Dichter admitted, is 'difficult but important' because the further the researcher removes themselves from the actual consumption situation or from the person engaged in the consumption behaviour of interest, then the less likely the desired ideographic knowledge will be generated (Dichter, 1979).

Despite the now obvious appeal of this type of research strategy, it was almost immediately criticized for failing to generate any 'more depth than the "depth" of any conversation with friends, journalists, lawyers' (Politz, 1956–1957: 670). This criticism appears unwarranted when it is counter-pointed with the actual depth interview process as related by Smith (1954). Contrary to the criticism that where the psychoanalyst might take days, weeks, months, or even years to analyse a client, whereas motivation researchers spend very little time on the doorstep with their interviewee (Rothwell, 1955), the psychoanalytic-inspired interviews discussed by Smith (1954) took a minimum of 40 hours and were spread over a two-week period (see also Britt, 1950). And this could, it might be assumed, *ceteris paribus*, have provided a level of detail slightly more in-depth than Politz or Rothwell were prepared to have acknowledged.

The Politics of Translation

As Robertson and Ward (1973) and Hudson and Ozanne (1988) have noted, one problem with the translation of Freud's work into consumer research is that there is some difficulty in operationalizing it. For those consumer researchers who tried to use this body of theory in an applied setting it was, quite naturally, steadily more diluted according to the needs of

Table 2 Four methodological approaches to research[3] (Table adapted from Murray and Ozanne, 1991: 136)

Research process	Positivism	Interpretivism	Critical theory	Motivation research
Initial stage	Review of existing literature to identify a gap; development of an a priori conceptual framework	Identification of general phenomenon of interest; phenomenon's boundaries are left open and undelineated	Identification of a concrete practical problem; identification of all groups involved with this problem	Research stimulated by practitioners concrete, but often general problem; phenomenon's boundaries are left open; review of existing literature
	Empirically testable hypotheses	'Bracketing' of prior conceptions	The interpretive step: construction of an intersubjective understanding of each group	'Bracketing' of prior or textbook conceptualizations; multiple-perspectival analysis; empirically testable hypotheses
	Hypotheses are tested in a fixed design	Immersion in natural setting for extended time period	The historical-empirical step: examination of the historical development of any relevant social structures or processes	Immersion in as natural a setting as possible
	Data are gathered	Design, questions, and sampling strategies evolve as the phenomena is studied	The dialectical step: search for contradictions between the intersubjective understanding and the objective social conditions	Not usually an a priori framework before fieldwork; design, questions, and sampling strategies evolve as the phenomena is studied

Table 2 (Continued)

Research process	Positivism	Interpretivism	Critical theory	Motivation research
Data collection stage (cont.)	Strict adherence to scientific protocol	Reliance on the human instrument for generating 'thick description'	The awareness step: discuss alternative ways of seeing their situation with the repressed group(s)	Reliance on human instrument, especially the sensitivity of the researcher for understanding motives
	Statistical analysis of data to yield an explanation	Content or textual analysis to yield an interpretation	The praxis step: participate in a theoretically grounded programme of action to change social conditions	Content or textual analysis to yield an interpretation
Standard data-gathering techniques	Laboratory experiment; large scale survey	Participant observation; in-depth interviews;	In-depth interviews; historical analysis	Depth interviews; participant observation; projective techniques; possible large scale survey
Sample evaluation criteria	Validity and reliability	Length of immersion and creation of thick description	Improvement of the quality of life	Understanding of consumer behaviour; prediction as a benefit of adequate understanding; for Dichter, affirmation of the American Way (see note 3)

the client, usually resulting in the use of concepts and methods that were related to 'less-than-conscious motivation, projection and free association' (Newman, 1992: 12). In spite of this, the use of psychological and psychoanalytic tools was frequently misinterpreted and read by critics of motivation research as the direct incorporation of clinical methods into consumer research or otherwise depicted as a 'hodge-podge of jabberwocky, or the line of a glib psycho-salesman bent on selling fifty "depth" interviews for $50,000' (Scriven, 1958: 65).

In this heated debate, the responses of motivation researchers were not enough to ameliorate the profusion of criticism that coalesced in *The Journal of Marketing* throughout the 1950s (Rothwell, 1955; Westfall et al., 1957; Williams, 1957). While criticism of new and emerging paradigms is a sign of a healthy academic community, much of the criticism directed towards motivation research tended to ignore the substantive content of its intended target. The article by Rothwell (1955) is illuminating in this regard. From the very start, the reader is left in no uncertain terms regarding Rothwell's view of motivation research, when told that the conclusions proffered by motivation researchers are often 'irritatingly round-about' and that their research tools such as projective tests had had doubts cast on their validity for predicting overt behaviour in the clinical literature. More problematic, for Rothwell, was the fact that the interpretations derived from these techniques can be affected by the mood and disposition of the researcher, leading to multiple interpretations of the same data by different researchers. Finally, she adds, there is little available response 'norm' data for participants other than the maladjusted, students or the rich. What this suggested, Rothwell maintained, was that the scientific status of these tools reduced the search for knowledge 'to a mere parlor game' and how, Rothwell questioned, 'could it be otherwise? What market research firm could administer a Thematic Apperception Test or a sound version of it in a few minutes on the door step or in the parlor, to a distracted housewife?' (Rothwell, 1955: 152). Despite the comprehensive discussion above which serves to indicate how Rothwell is misinterpreting the practice of motivation research, Krugman's (1956–7) response is important here: in an important counterpoint in support for motivation research, he made the case that perhaps advertising and marketing executives have added motivation research to their armoury of tools because the scientific rigour associated with statistics was not impressive unless they can contribute to interpreting and explaining consumer marketplace behaviours. What executives want, according to Krugman, is a 'little more education with their facts and figures. Facts and figures are very concrete, very hard, yet easy to give with a minimum of explanation' (Krugman, 1956–7: 723). Perhaps, he suggests, conventional consumer researchers will eventually thank the motivation researchers for pointing out that the overriding goal of science is not, in actual fact, *prediction*, but instead, *understanding*. Prediction, on his reading, is simply the test of understanding and the control over any behaviours that result is the reward for the systematic researcher.

The Transformation of Motivation Research

Clearly admitting that bias is introduced into research as a function of our own historical and cultural position was never likely to be a popular view in a discipline wedded to logical empiricism. Moreover, when such comments emanated from outside of the academy, primarily from practitioners who flouted the extant rules of discursive formation by criticizing the excessive quantification of consumer research, motivation research was ripe for discipline. This was not necessarily a bad thing either, as Dichter himself argued,

> There is no doubt that motivational . . . research needs discipline. But it has to be the discipline appropriate to its specific nature as a science. To insist that because you have to research 2,000 people to know how many people have stomach disorders at a given time, that therefore any scientifically proven explanation of the real causes of stomach disorder based on experimentation and an entirely different set of inductive and deductive inferences is invalid, is in itself proof of lack of scientific discipline of a much wider consequence. Prediction of consumer behavior necessitates first understanding his behavior today. (Dichter, 1955a: 37)

Stressing his belief in the value of paradigm pluralism, Dichter appealed for a disciplinary movement towards paradigmatic accommodation, where no one perspective is viewed as the one proper route to scientific truth:

> If we can, within the ranks of the broad family of researchers, begin to see that different problems require different research solutions, and that our problems, as researchers, *are* different in . . . many ways, then we shall be in a position at last to unite around a common scientific philosophy which nevertheless recognizes the utility of different approaches and tools. (Dichter, 1958: 23; emphasis in original)

As Dichter (1958) registered at the time, although there was a variety of good and bad motivation research available, unfortunately it was the less rigorous and less systematic research that led to a profusion of criticism from more quantitatively oriented empiricists. Where Dichter called for tolerance and for researchers to assess motivation research on its own paradigmatic basis, those attacking motivation research (e.g. Rothwell, 1955; Scriven, 1958) attacked straw-figures, presenting motivation research and its use of qualitative methods as unscientific, often on the basis of partial readings of the original texts. This was largely a political move with motivation research 'denied, berated, despised . . . [with] Attempts by marketers to disown this child . . . [were] wily and nefarious' (Jameson, 1971: 189). Despite such political and academic pressures Dichter appears to have taken such criticism in his stride:

The accusations and counteraccusations currently rampant in research circles represent more than the healthy, 'competitive' claims and counterclaims or robust research organizations. Instead, they are signs of a dangerous confusion and unease – an unease which may very well be communicated to the ultimate consumer who simply will not know which (if any!) of these techniques to choose or reject. The more we do, therefore, within our own family of researchers to dispel these confusions and doubts among our consumers and ourselves, the more we advance our profession as a whole. It is true that the only kind of research 'worth doing' is research that meets the most rigorous canons of scientific accuracy and honesty. (Dichter, 1958: 23)

In a somewhat surprising development, Theodor Adorno, of Frankfurt School fame, oscillated between praising and criticizing motivation research. He did so by, on the one hand, applauding motivation research for directing attention to the qualitative, subjective reactions of consumers; but he was also equally emphatic in his criticism of what he saw to be the excessive focus on the subjective reactions of consumers without equal attention being given to the extent to which these are conditioned by the cultural climate and societal structures (Adorno, 1969). Adorno's support and criticism appears to have been largely ignored at the time, with the debate organized around two main camps. On one side, we have Ernest Dichter, the President of the Institute for Research in Mass Motivations, Incorporated and the largest purveyor of motivation research in the world (Dichter, 1979). And on the other, Alfred Politz, the President of Alfred Politz Research Incorporated, an organization dedicated to survey research, accompanied by a heavy emphasis on quantitative, statistical analysis which aimed to produce 'predicts of the causal type' (Politz and Deming, 1953: 1; compare with Packard, 1960: 139). Again, a familiar pattern of animosity and criticism is evident between authors associated with the Institute for Research in Mass Motivations (e.g. Henry, 1958; Vicary, 1951) and those affiliated with Alfred Politz Research (e.g. Politz and Deming, 1953; Politz, 1957; Williams, 1957). Nor was the partisan nature of this critique-rebuttal lost on book reviewers at the time (see also, Blake, 1954: 33). Stryker's comments, in his review of Harry Henry's book, *Motivation Research*, are typical:

It is not surprising that Mr. Henry is a firm advocate of motivation research, since the advertising agency for which he is a director of research (McCann-Erickson) has long used M.R. Techniques; and one of his American colleagues, Dr. Herta Hertzog, is among the most experienced M.R. practitioners in the U.S. (Stryker, 1959: 344)

Newman highlights these political tensions most clearly where he recalls that the lines of 'intense' intellectual 'hostility' were drawn largely along agency lines (1992: 13). New thinking, in this case, was 'not popular, it will be resisted because it typically threatens vested interests – either intellectual or financial or both' as it was, Newman maintained, with motivation research (1992: 13). This hostility was further compounded by the criticism that Dichter faced because he failed to satisfy 'the more rigid scholars and the business-hating intellectuals who tend to see his work as "not really psychological", "not moral"' (Martineau, 1961: 108).

Ultimately, however, the scholarly Dichter of his early writing (e.g. Dichter, 1947, 1949, 1957) became subsumed under the messianic figure of Ernest Dichter with the following comment appearing in print: 'I could cure cancer, solve international conflicts eliminating wars, or to put it very modestly, become a messiah who could use his talents in almost all areas' (Dichter, 1979: 13). This immodesty, Collins and Montgomery (1970) suggest, is one reason for the active turn against motivation research towards the end of the 1950s, early 1960s with Dichter's 'pentacostally fervent advocacy of motivation research . . . [obscuring] its possible usefulness' (Collins and Montgomery, 1970: 10). Certainly, the time came when marketing and consumer scholars were simply not seeing what motivation research had to offer, only the discursive pyrotechnics that Dichter continued to perform. Nonetheless, to simply place the demise of what was an embryonic form of interpretive research at the feet of Dichter is to over-emphasize internal disciplinary conditions to the marginalization of the wider social, economic and political changes that were taking place and affecting the academy in formative ways. Important here are the Ford and Carnegie reports (Gordon and Howell, 1959; Pierson, 1959) and the funding that followed as an institutional support for the vision of business education that these reports demanded (see, Cochoy, 1998; Hunt and Goolsby, 1988; Kassarjian, 1981; Sheth and Gross, 1988; Staelin, 2005). As Tadajewski (2006) has argued, the Gordon and Howell report was part of a larger institutional move by the Ford Foundation – as the most important financial contributor to marketing at the time (Bartels, 1988) – to avoid the criticism that a number of House of UnAmerican Committees and their McCarthyite political pressures had levelled at the Foundation. Commensurate with these pressures, the Ford Foundation engaged in a deliberately cautious philanthropic strategy, whereby they funded the reorientation of marketing theory towards logical empiricism and quantitative methods because business-related subjects and quantitative methods were politically neutral; pressures that were also felt within the university (McCumber, 2001; Schrecker, 1986) with researchers in the social sciences avoiding issues that could be seen as politically contentious (Lazarsfeld and Thielens, 1958). It is hard to understate the influence that McCarthyism had on the academy through the Ford Foundation sponsoring the successful courses run at the Institute of Basic Mathematics for Application to Business. These, Wilkie argued, had 'a *huge impact* on the course of research in marketing' (2002: 144; emphasis in original). As Staelin (2005: 146) registers, the influence of this seminar series 'helped solidify the infusion of scientific theory, methods and analysis into the field of marketing'. With this change in intellectual climate towards 'scientific marketing' and the support of research that adopted the symbolism of advanced mathematics (Kernan, 1995) the motivation researchers were marginalized because the intellectual climate was not yet ready for the propagation of a scientific style that was so different from the extant research culture. Here the comments by Collins and Montgomery (1970) are important in that they acknowledge the 'risk' element involved in motivation research.

Where more statistical and logical empiricist inspired research has its 'anxiety-dissipating rituals' such as formalized procedures for interpreting statistical descriptions, any similar attempts to formalize qualitative motivation research 'tends to inhibit the diagnostic function in hand; the supporting structure they provide is inimical to authentic exposure to the phenomena of study' (Collins and Montgomery, 1970: 9). The inability of researchers like Dichter and Vicary to agree on interpretations of consumer behaviour (see Blake, 1954; Kornhauser, 1941), together with the fact that they still remained reluctant to publish their entire transcripts due to the proprietary nature of the material (see Blake, 1954; Karesh, 1995; Vicary, 1951), meant that it was hardly unexpected that the desire to negotiate the interpretive creativity associated with motivation research was communicated. In light of such calls, motivation research *was* methodologically formalized (Collins and Montgomery, 1970). This type of operation was commonplace at the time, particularly where European perspectives were transplanted into the US context. Like Adorno who experienced similar attempts to operationalize his research in questionnaire format, Dichter was equally reluctant to subscribe to the 'prescriptive right of way given to quantitative methods of research, to which both theory and individual qualitative studies should at best be supplementary' (Adorno, 1969: 347). While Dichter was equally aware of the potential benefits accruing from both qualitative and quantitative research (Dichter, 1947), motivation research nevertheless rapidly became a supplement to quantitative research (Collins and Montgomery, 1970; Converse et al., 1958; Kelne, 1955).

Reluctant to ignore the opportunities offered by motivation research in understanding complex consumer behaviour, motivation research was not completely replaced and then ignored in the way that the functional paradigm was replaced by a marketing management orientation (see Hunt and Goolsby, 1988). Rather, the influx of social scientists into consumer research following the Ford and Carnegie recommendations whose own research interests were related to the development of qualitative variables that could be tested quantitatively, contributed to the combination of the humanistic orientation of motivation research with the experimental, quantitative survey tradition, thereby creating a composite of the two (Demby, 1974). Given a variety of names, but most frequently termed psychographics, motivation research morphed into one facet of a quantitative research programme that sought to 'place consumers on psychological – as distinguished from demographic dimensions' in order to explain why consumers, in large isolatable market segments, behave in the way they do (Wells, 1975: 197). Where motivation research used small samples and primarily qualitative research, psychographic research used 'precoded, objective questionnaires that can be self-administered or administered by ordinary survey interviewers [since this] . . . Precoding makes the data amenable to complex multivariate statistical analysis' (Wells, 1975: 197); statistical analysis that only became possible due to the greater availability of computer technology in the 1960s and 70s, along with the skills to use such technology (see Alderson and Shapiro, 1963; Belk, 1987; Tadajewski, 2006; Wilkie, 1986).

From Psychographics to Experiential Consumer Research

As Holbrook and Hirschman (1982) noted, it was the 'poor performance' of personality measures in predicting consumer behaviour that encouraged the turn towards psychographics, the use of lifestyle variables and the information processing view of the consumer. However, in time, the information processing perspective was also perceived to leave certain aspects of consumer behaviour largely untapped. In order to augment the perceived deficiencies of the information processing approach, Holbrook and Hirschman argued forcefully for a focus on the experiential aspects of consumer behaviour. Their experiential view, they maintained, is 'phenomenological in spirit [regarding] . . . consumption as a primarily subjective state of consciousness with a variety of symbolic meanings, hedonic responses, and esthetic criteria' (Holbrook and Hirschman, 1982: 132). Now, in promoting a turn towards a more phenomenological scientific style, Holbrook and Hirschman's article is particularly important as it links motivation research with CCT (Arnould and Thompson, 2005). Since it has already been demonstrated that motivation researchers not only investigated the experiential, social and cultural dimensions of consumer behaviour based on an interpretive paradigmatic style, we now want to argue that motivation research is the historical root of Holbrook and Hirschman's article and, therefore, a historical rhizome of CCT (cf. Arnould, 2006). For the purposes of brevity we will take two examples from Holbrook and Hirschman's analysis – that of consumer cognition and behaviour – which connects motivation research, the experiential view and CCT. In terms of cognition, Holbrook and Hirschman described their experiential perspective thus:

> In its treatment of cognitive phenomena, particularly material of a subconscious nature, the experiential view borders somewhat on motivation research (e.g. Dichter, 1960). However, there are two methodological differences. First we believe that much relevant fantasy life and many key symbolic meanings lie just below the threshold of consciousness – that is, that they are subconscious or preconscious as opposed to unconscious – and that they can be retrieved and reported if sufficiently indirect methods are used to overcome sensitivity barriers. Second we advocate the use of structured projective techniques that employ quantitative questionnaire items applicable to samples large enough to permit statistical testing. (Holbrook and Hirschman, 1982: 136)

In this quotation, the second point is moot, as motivation researchers have argued that symbolic meaning could be elicited from just below the threshold of consciousness. Such meaning could, Dichter surmised, be deduced using projective techniques and the thematic patterns which emerged, could then used to formulate hypotheses that 'should then be put to test in a second market-analysis' (Eliasberg, 1954: 52). Nor is the first point made by Holbrook and Hirschman particularly problematic because Dichter typically made reference to the unconscious, either in regard to advances in the social sciences or via vague allusions to general human activities. For example,

> The social sciences, too, are full of new discoveries, comparable to those of atomic physics and the field of biology. These discoveries seem to violate all common sense and direct observation as stipulated by Aristotle and others as the basis for scientific endeavor [like the] . . . discovery of the unconscious. (Dichter, 1957: 161)

Whereas in other instances, he made ambiguous statements to the 'unconscious desire not to remember' (Dichter, 1947: 432), what would, however, appear to be a common feature in all of Dichter's and the other motivation researchers' work is perhaps best characterized as a movement away from postulating unconscious factors in favour of distinguishing 'between symptoms expressing the superficial rational explanations of an action, and the real, deeper reasons which form the basis of the actions' (Dichter, 1949: 64). Let us take three representative examples. Firstly, in his review of motivation research Blake opined that 'The psychologist scrutinizes the interviews, specializing on individual reactions to conscious and subconscious experience', without making reference to the unconscious (1954: 31). Likewise, Yoell argued that:

> It is impossible to bring anyone to remember consciously all his experiences by random digging and probing, no matter how many questions the consumer is asked, and no matter how much time he is given to answer them . . . [this is because] The brain has at least two sections: the *conscious* and *subconscious*. When a new experience or new combination of experiences enters the conscious, it is assimilated and passed on to the subconscious, where it is stored away for future use and reference. That use or reference is seldom conscious. But once the correct stimulus has been presented or exposed to the brain or mind, the *subconscious* immediately reacts to it. Within these experiences lies the key to inducing the consumer to buy your brand. (Yoell, 1950: 38–9; emphases added)

Similarly, in a critique of Packard's representation of motivation research, Bauer argued that motivation research might connect with purchases made for '*non-economic* reasons, but such motives are not necessarily unconscious. It is a serious mistake to equate the two' (1964: 43; emphasis in original), as he believed Packard (1960) did.

As our second main example, Holbrook and Hirschman proposed that:

> In exploring the nature of that overall [consumption] experience, the approach envisioned here departs from the traditional positivist focus on directly observable buying behavior and devotes increased attention to the mental events surrounding the act of consumption. The investigation of these mental events requires a willingness to deal with the purely subjective aspects of consciousness. The exploration of consumption as conscious experience must be rigorous and scientific, but the methodology must include introspective reports, rather than relying on overt behavioral measures. The necessary methodological shift thus leads towards a more phenomenological approach – i.e., 'a free commentary on whatever cognitive material the subject is aware of'. (Holbrook and Hirschman, 1982: 137)

The parallels with motivation research are undeniable here, especially if we reflect on the preceding analysis where axiologically, Dichter was concerned with understanding why consumers buy – or, in this context – what subjective benefit consumers derive from consumption (e.g. Dichter, 1979: 42, 44). Ontologically, direct observation of consumer behaviour was, the motivation researchers bemoaned, largely misleading (e.g. Dichter, 1979: 38) and there was a need to understand the subjective processes that consumers moved through in a buying and consumption situation. This was achieved through the use of a version of free association (e.g. Yoell, 1950, 1952). Epistemologically, Dichter was a master of suspicion, and therefore more critical than Holbrook and Hirschman of the reliability of the espoused views of consumers. It would therefore appear valid to suggest that motivation research is both an embryonic form of interpretive consumer research and a historical root of CCT given its consonance with Holbrook and Hirschman's experiential perspective. To stress these arguments once more, let us conclude with comments from Levy, who in reflecting on the development of consumer research recalled:

> Because of the desire to examine consumers' actions, motivations, and perceptions more closely and richly than is done by the usual surveys, statistical regressions, and cognitive experiments, the use of qualitative methods to study consumer behavior has recently grown. (Actually, I have been making that remark optimistically for 50 years.) Use of the more obvious or candid introspections of researchers at work using ethnography, discursive interviewing, or the interpretation of projective techniques arouses anxiety and controversy, with disparagement and defensiveness on all sides. Some of this noise sounds like the verbal flailing that went on in the 1950s, when . . . motivation research . . . became visible and threatening to the entrenched surveyor. (Levy, 1996: 172)

More recently Levy has attempted to reaffirm this point in still stronger terms, acknowledging like Arnould et al. (2004), Chakarvarti and Staelin (2001), Kassarjian (1994) and Sherry and McGrath (1989) that:

all the methods that have been despised and sneered at as 'motivation research' in the 1950s have rebounded. Group interviews became focus groups and depth interviews became phenomenological and hermeneutic, projective techniques propagated collages, and the ancient method of ethnography came into its own . . . The old qualitative research methods, long practiced in the study of history, in anthropology, in the Chicago School of sociology, and by projective psychologists, have become the 'interpretive turn;' which, by its recognition of the constructing nature of human experience and the importance of subjectivity and introspection, has morphed into post-modernism . . . with a continuing struggle between nomothetic and idiographic approaches, a perpetual conflict that was lively when I was a student 50 years ago. (Levy, 2001; compare with Levy, 2003a, 2003b, 2005)

Where Levy talks about the recent turn towards qualitative research, introspection, ethnography and discursive interviewing, we could easily acknowledge Dichter's use of these, in addition to an emergent research design, his use of photography, while adopting an anthropological perspective with attention directed towards consuming, often as part of a multi-method research strategy. Nor are Levy's comments unrepresentative of those held by other influential consumer researchers (see also, Holbrook, 1997; Mick and Demoss, 1990; Sherry and McGrath, 1989; Wallendorf and Belk, 1989). Holbrook, for example, has argued that a psycho-analytically informed research strategy can make the latent meanings of consumption objects available for study. As he concluded,

I believe that the insights drawn from psychoanalytic interpretation can provide rich supplementary explications of the material uncovered by naturalistic inquiry. Through photographs, videotapes, depth interviews, and other field methods, naturalistic inquiry can reveal important themes that permeate consumption experiences. However, the full explication of these themes may require the use of approaches that move beyond the relatively surface level of meaning accessible to the ethnographer to explore the psychoanalytic interpretation of consumption. (Holbrook, 1988: 541)

While Dichter was wary of association with any single theoretical perspective, all of the elements of an embryonic form of interpretive consumer research were present in Dichter's and the other motivation researchers' work. Not only does this suggest a new date for the emergence of this paradigm by 60 years, but it also resituates the emergence of CCT, some 80 years prior to our existing understanding of the emergence of these forms of inquiry.

Conclusion

In this article, the emergence and subsequent decline of motivation research was traced. It was demonstrated that contrary to recent opinion that interpretive consumer research emerged in the mid 1980s, an embryonic form of interpretive research can be found in the 1930s in the form of motivation research. It was not so much the methods that Dichter and his fellow motivation researchers used that made motivation research an embryonic form of interpretive consumer research, but the complete range of:

> thinking, the concepts, the hypotheses and the total range of modern scientific thought processes which characterize the *interpretative* approach in research. But people still say, 'Yes, but what is it that you exactly do?' The detailed discussion of all the steps and the techniques used in interpretive research can fill, of course, a separate textbook. (Dichter, 1960: 283; emphasis in original)

As the summaries of the various research traditions put forward as the main paradigmatic options within the literature suggest, when we compare motivation research against the common characteristics of interpretive research (see Table 1) there are clear and distinct parallels in relation to ontological, nature of social being, axiological, epistemological, views of causality and research metaphors between motivation research, interpretive research and to a limited extent critical theory. As we demonstrated, motivation research gradually developed into psychographics, and with the development and large scale use of the computer, the information processing view of the consumer emerged. In response to the limitations of the information processing approach, Holbrook and Hirschman were seen to make the case for more experientially and phenomenologically oriented research and they indicated a place for motivation research in this tradition. Where, however, Holbrook and Hirschman argued that motivation research focused on unconscious consumer beliefs and rationalizations, and was therefore distinct from their experiential perspective, it was pointed out that while Dichter may have mentioned the unconscious on occasion, a more widespread view (which Dichter supported) was that motivation research tapped into subconscious thought and non-economic values (e.g. symbolic values). In this regard, it was posited that when we reflect on the assumptions underpinning motivation research, that motivation research is one possible early root of CCT. This retraces the emergence of this discourse by 80 years and interpretive research by 60 years. In the context of the transformation of consumer research stimulated by the Ford and Carnegie reports and the subsequent reorientation of the intellectual culture that these occasioned, motivation research was transformed into a scientific style that cohered with the scientific vision of the time. Given this, it is hard not to agree with Fleck (1979 [1935]) that a break with a particular 'thought style' is a rare occurrence and one which, we submit, would again be occasioned by the invisible college that formed around 1969 with the Ohio State Workshop on consumer behaviour and the formation of the Association for Consumer Research in the 1970s (Kassarjian, 1981). It would be around this time that interpretive styles of research would re-emerge and a greater importance accorded to qualitative methods.

Notes

My thanks to Stan Shapiro, Craig Thompson, Sidney Levy and Avi Shankar for comments on a previous draft of this paper. Any mistakes that remain are my own.

1. Although it should be acknowledged that Dichter does make occasional reference to 'causal laws' or 'psychological laws' in one paper (1961: 79).
2. Packard (1960), presented motivation researchers as using advanced psychological techniques to probe the inner workings of consumers' minds, which in conjunction with subliminal advertising (the two were often seen to be related) could motivate consumers in ways that were advantageous to the specific organization funding the research. Motivation researchers were, Packard asserted, 'doctors of commerce' who 'were called upon to get to the roots of our [consumption] resistance and proscribe corrective measures' (Packard, 1960: 116). Of course to some extent, motivation research, when applied to commercial problems, must have been successful, for Packard lists a variety of cases where following the advice of motivation researchers the sales of products rose. Dichter, never a reluctant marketer (see Collins and Montgomery, 1969, 1971), was somewhat more tempered in his view arguing that 'Motivational thinking, even when applied to commercial problems, does not motivate people, talk them into buying things that they do not need, by twisting their unconscious' (1960: 256). Instead, Dichter (1955a) is concerned with being able to differentiate rationalizations from reason. The criticism directed towards the motivation research community by Packard bore, somewhat paradoxically, similarities to the social conscience communicated by Dichter. Where Packard saw the changing nature of the American character in terms of the decline of the protestant ethic and the growing valorization of materialism and hedonism attributable to marketing, advertising and motivation research; a shift, he believed, made the United States 'unfit for global leadership and placed it in the very real danger of being deposed by a thrifty, self-reliant and hard-working Soviet Union' (Brown, 2001: 32). Dichter espoused a similar radical agenda that Horowitz (1998) equates with a peculiar inflexion of the sentiment espoused by critical theorists, whereby individual consciousness is seen to be subservient to external pressures that imprison the individual. Where the role of the critical marketing scholar involves the critique of these structures in order to emancipate those inhabiting a 'false consciousness' (Alvesson, 1994), Dichter supports a similar perspective albeit given his own twist. Having seen the pernicious influence of state Communism first hand and believing he was participating in the reconstruction of American society in the post-war world, Dichter's (axiological) views reflect common sentiment at this time when the social and political climate was characterized by an internal terror in the form of McCarthyism. This was a context in which McCarthyism was rife and anti-Communist paranoia evoked with movies like *The Invasion of the Body Snatchers* playing at cinemas in 1956 and Soviet technological superiority was keenly felt (Castronovo, 2004). To do this, he made the case that the increased consumption of consumer goods and services was one way of keeping the free enterprise system at the heart of America's economic engine running, when the alternative – economic stagnation or Russian dominance – appeared to be a very real alternative with the Soviet Union 'riding its Sputnik's to new heights' (Dichter, 1960: 277). In his attempt to reaffirm the need to consume, and thereby enhance the American economy, Dichter adopted a stance that sought to emancipate consumers, but in a direction that does not question the logic of capital accumulation or the continuing spiral of consumer goods and services. Instead he wanted to

motivate American consumers to consume increased quantities of durables and services (Dichter, 1955a, 1979).

3. Table adapted from Murray and Ozanne (1991: 136).

References

Adorno, T.W. (1969) 'Scientific Experiences of a European Scholar in America', in D. Fleming and B. Bailyn (eds) *The Intellectual Migration: Europe and America, 1930–1960*, tr. D. Fleming, pp. 338–70. Cambridge: The Belknap Press.

Alderson, W. and Shapiro, S.J. (eds) (1963) *Marketing and the Computer*. Englewood Cliffs, NJ: Prentice-Hall.

Alvesson, M. (1994) 'Critical Theory and Consumer Marketing', *Scandinavian Journal of Management* 10(3): 291–313.

Arndt, J. (1985a) 'On Making Marketing Science More Scientific: Role of Orientations, Paradigms, Metaphors, and Problem Solving', *Journal of Marketing* 49(3): 11–23.

Arndt, J. (1985b) 'The Tyranny of Paradigms: The Case for Paradigmatic Pluralism in Marketing', in N. Dholakia and J. Arndt (eds) *Changing the Course of Marketing: Alternative Paradigms for Widening Marketing Theory*, pp. 3–25. Greenwich, CT: JAI Press.

Arnould, E.J. (2006) 'Service-dominant Logic and Consumer Culture Theory: Natural Allies in an Emerging Paradigm', *Marketing Theory* 6(3): 293–295.

Arnould, E. and Thompson, C.J. (2005) 'Consumer Culture Theory: Twenty Years of Research', *Journal of Consumer Research* 31(4): 868–82.

Arnould, E., Price, L. and Zinkhan, G. (2004) *Consumers* (2nd edn). New York: McGraw-Hill.

Augier, M., March, J.G. and Sullivan, B.N. (2005) 'Notes on the Evolution of a Research Community: Organization Studies in Anglophone North America', *Organization Science* 16(1): 85–95.

Baker, M.J. (2001) 'Introduction', in M.J. Baker (ed.) *Marketing: Critical Perspectives on Business and Management*, pp. 1–25. London: Routledge.

Bartels, R. (1988) *The History of Marketing Thought* (3rd edn). Columbus, OH: Publishing Horizons.

Bartos, R. (1986a) 'Ernest Dichter: Motive Interpreter', *Journal of Advertising Research* Feb/March: 15–20.

Bartos, R. (1986b) 'Qualitative Research: What it is and Where it Came From', *Journal of Advertising Research* 26(3): RC-3–6.

Bauer, R.A. (1964) 'The Limits to Persuasion: The Hidden Persuaders are Made of Straw', in M.M. Grossack (ed.) *Understanding Consumer Behavior*, pp. 39–52. Boston, MA: The Christopher Publishing House.

Bayton, J.A. (1958) 'Motivation, Cognition, Learning – Basic Factors in Consumer Behavior', *The Journal of Marketing* 22(3): 282–9.

Belk, R.W. (1987) 'A Modest Proposal for Creating Verisimilitude in Consumer-Information-processing Models and Some Suggestions for Establishing a Discipline to Study Consumer Behavior', in A.F. Firat, N. Dholakia and R.P. Bagozzi (eds) *Philosophical and Radical Thought in Marketing*, pp. 361–72. Lexington, MA: Lexington Books.

Belk, R.W. (1995) 'Studies in the New Consumer Behaviour', in D. Miller (ed.) *Acknowledging Consumption: A Review of New Studies*, pp. 58–95. London: Routledge.

Beyer, R.F. (1934) *The Marketing Institution*. New York: McGraw Hill.

Blake, J.K. (1954) 'Consumer Motivation Research', *Dun's Review and Modern Industry* July: 30–46.

Blankenship, A.B. (1965) 'Freud in Consumerland . . .', *The Journal of Marketing* 29(1): 116.

Breyer, R.F. (1934) *The Marketing Institution*. New York: McGraw-Hill.

Britt, S.H. (1950) 'The Strategy of Human Motivation', *The Journal of Marketing* 14(5): 666–74.

Britt, S.H. (1960) *The Spenders*. New York: McGraw-Hill.

Brown, S. (2001) *Marketing – The Retro Revolution*. London: SAGE.

Brown, S. (2005) *Writing Marketing*. London: SAGE.

Burrell, G. and Morgan, G. (1992[1979]) *Sociological Paradigms and Organisational Analysis*. Aldershot: Ashgate.

Calder, B.J. and Tybout, A.M. (1989) 'Interpretive, Qualitative, and Traditional Scientific Empirical Consumer Behavior Research', in E.C. Hirschman (ed.) *Interpretive Consumer Research*, pp. 199–208. Provo, UT: Association for Consumer Research.

Castronovo, D. (2004) *Beyond the Gray Flannel Suit: Books from the 1950s that Made American Culture*. New York: Continuum.

Chakravarti, D. and Staelin, R. (2001) 'Remembrance: Joseph W. Newman', *Journal of Consumer Research* 28(3): 512–13.

Cheskin, L. and Ward, L.B. (1948) 'Indirect Approach to Market Reactions', *Harvard Business Review* 26(5): 572–81.

Cochoy, F. (1998) 'Another Discipline for the Market Economy Marketing as a Performative Knowledge and Know-how for Capitalism', in M. Callon (ed.) *The Laws of the Markets*, pp. 194–221. Oxford: Blackwell.

Cofer, C.N. and Appley, M.H. (1964) *Motivation: Theory and Research*. London: Wiley.

Collins, L. and Montgomery, C. (1969) 'The Origins of Motivation Research', *British Journal of Marketing* 3(2): 103–13.

Collins, L. and Montgomery, C. (1970) 'Whatever Happened to Motivation Research? End of the Messianic Hope', *Journal of the Market Research Society* 12(1): 1–11.

Converse, P.D., Huegy, H.W. and Mitchell, R.V. (1958) *Elements of Marketing*. London: Sir Issac Pitman and Son.

de Certeau, M. (1988) *The Writing of History*, tr. T. Conley. New York: Columbia University Press.

Demby, E. (1974) 'Psychographics and from Whence it Came', in W.D. Wells (ed.) *Life Style and Psychographics*, pp. 11–30. Chicago, IL: American Marketing Association.

Dichter, E. (1947) 'Psychology in Market Research', *Harvard Business Review* 25(4): 432–43.

Dichter, E. (1949) 'A Psychological View of Advertising Effectiveness', *The Journal of Marketing* 14(1): 61–7.

Dichter, E. (1955a) 'Scientifically Predicting and Understanding Consumer Behavior', in R.H. Cole (ed.) *Consumer Behavior and Motivation*, pp. 26–37. Urbana: University of Illinois Bulletin.

Dichter, E. (1955b) 'What are the Real Reasons People Buy', *Sales Management* 74(Feb): 36–89.

Dichter, E. (1957) 'Thinking Ahead', *Harvard Business Review* Nov-Dec: 19–162.

Dichter, E. (1958) 'Toward an Understanding of Human Behavior', in R. Ferber and Hugh G. Wales (eds) *Motivation and Market Behavior*, pp. 21–30. Homewood, IL: Richard D. Irwin.

Dichter, E. (1960) *The Strategy of Desire*. New York: Doubleday.

Dichter, E. (1961) 'Seven Tenants of Creative Research', *The Journal of Marketing* 25(4): 1–4.

Dichter, E. (1964) *Handbook of Consumer Motivations: The Psychology of the World of Objects*. New York: McGraw-Hill.

Dichter, E. (1966) 'How Word-of-Mouth Advertising Works', *Harvard Business Review* Nov/Dec: 147–66.

Dichter, E. (1971) *Motivating Human Behavior*. New York: McGraw-Hill.

Dichter, E. (1978) 'Interpretive versus Descriptive Research', in J.N. Sheth (ed.) *Research in Marketing, Volume 1*, pp. 53–78. Greenwich, CT: JAI Press.

Dichter, E. (1979) *Getting Motivated by Ernest Dichter: The Secret Behind Individual Motivation by the Man Who Was Not Afraid to Ask "Why?"*. New York: Pergamon Press.

Eliasberg, W. (1954) 'Freud, Veblen and Marketing', *Printers' Ink* February 12: 46–52.

Feyerabend, P. (1975) *Against Method*. London: New Left Books.

Fleck, L. (1979[1935]) *Genesis and Development of a Scientific Fact*, trs F. Bradley and T.J. Trenn. Chicago, IL: University of Chicago Press.

Foucault, M. (1984) 'Nietzsche, Genealogy, History', in P. Rabinow (ed.) *The Foucault Reader*, pp. 76–100. London: Penguin.

Freud, S. (1965[1900]) *The Interpretation of Dreams*, tr. J. Strachey. New York: Avon.

Fullerton, R.A. (1988) 'How Modern is Modern Marketing? Marketing's Evolution and the Myth of the Production Era', *Journal of Marketing* 52(1): 108–25.

Fullerton, R.A. (1990) 'The Art of Marketing Research: Selections from Paul F. Lazarsfeld's "Shoe Buying in Zurich"', *Journal of the Academy of Marketing Science* 18(4): 319–27.

Fullerton, R.A. and Stern, B.B. (1990) 'The Rise and Fall of Ernest Dichter', *Werbeforschung and Praxis* June: 208–11.

Gordon, R.A. and Howell, J.E. (1959) *Higher Education for Business*. New York: Columbia University Press.

Goulding, C. (1999) 'Consumer Research, Interpretive Paradigms and Methodological Ambiguities', *European Journal of Marketing* 33(9/10): 859–73.

Green, H.E. (1952) 'Chicago Tribune Ad Forum Relates Social Sciences to Sales', *Printers' Ink* May 30th: 30.

Haire, M. (1950) 'Projective Techniques in Marketing Research', *The Journal of Marketing* 24(5): 649–56.

Hanson, N.R. (1960) *Patterns of Discovery: An Inquiry into the Conceptual Foundations of Science*. Cambridge: Cambridge University Press.

Henry, H. (1958) *Motivation Research: Its Practice and Uses for Advertising, Marketing, and Other Business Purposes*. London: Crosby Lockwood and Son.

Hirschman, E.C. (1985) 'Scientific Style and the Conduct of Consumer Research', *Journal of Consumer Research* 12(2): 225–39.

Hirschman, E.C. (1986) 'Humanistic Inquiry in Marketing Research: Philosophy, Method and Criteria', *Journal of Marketing Research* 23(3): 237–49.

Holbrook, M.B. (1988) 'Steps Towards a Psychoanalytic Interpretation of Consumption: A Meta-Meta-Meta-Analysis of Some Issues Raised by the Consumer Behavior Odyssey', in M.I. Houston (ed.) *Advances in Consumer Research 15*, pp. 537–42. Provo, UT: Association for Consumer Research.

Holbrook, M.B. (1997) 'Romanticism, Introspection, and the Roots of Experiential Consumption', *Consumption, Markets and Culture* 1(2): 97–164.

Holbrook, M.B. and Hirschman, E.C. (1982) 'The Experiential Aspects of Consumption: Consumer Fantasies, Feelings and Fun', *Journal of Consumer Research* 9(2): 132–40.

Hollander, S.C. (1986) 'The Marketing Concept: A Déjà vu', in G. Fisk (ed.) *Marketing Management Technology as a Social Process*, pp. 3–29. New York: Praeger.

Hollander, S.C., Rassuli, K.M., Jones, D.G.B. and Dix, L.F. (2005) 'Periodization in Marketing History', *Journal of Macromarketing* 25(1): 32–41.

Horowitz, D. (1998) 'The Émigré as Celebrant of Consumer Culture: George Katona and Ernest Dichter', in S. Strasser., C. McGovern and M. Judt (eds) *Getting and Spending: European and American Consumer Societies in the Twentieth Century*, pp. 149–66. Cambridge: Cambridge University Press.

Hudson, L.A. and Ozanne, J.L. (1988) 'Alternative Ways of Seeking Knowledge in Consumer Research', *Journal of Consumer Research* 14(4): 508–21.

Hunt, S.D. (1991) 'Positivism and Paradigm Dominance in Consumer Research', *Journal of Consumer Research* 18(1): 32–44.

Hunt, S.D. and Goolsby, J. (1988) 'The Rise and Fall of the Functional Approach to Marketing: A Paradigm Displacement Perspective', in T. Nevett and R.A. Fullerton (eds) *Historical Perspectives in Marketing: Essays in Memory of Stanley C. Hollander*, pp. 35–51. Lexington, MA: Lexington Books.

Jameson, C. (1971) 'The Theory and Nonsense of Motivation Research', *European Journal of Marketing* 5(4): 189–97.

Jenkins, K. (2003) *Re-Thinking History*. London: Routledge.

Karesh, M.A. (1995) 'The Social Scientific Origins of Symbolic Consumer Research: Social Research, Inc.', in K.M. Rassuli, S.C. Hollander and T.R. Nevett (eds) *Marketing History: Marketing's Greatest Empirical Experiment: Proceedings of the 7th Conference on Historical Research in Marketing & Management Thought*, pp. 95–111. East Lansing, MI: Michigan State University.

Kassarjian, H.H. (1981) 'Presentation of the ACR award: "Fellow in Consumer Behavior" to J.A. Howard and James F. Engel', in K. Monroe (ed.) *Advances in Consumer Research* Volume 8, pp. 6–8. Provo, UT: Association for Consumer Research.

Kassarjian, H.H. (1989) 'Review of Philosophical and Radical Thought in Marketing', *Journal of Marketing* 43(1): 123–6.

Kassarjian, H.H. (1994) 'Scholarly Traditions and the European Roots of American Consumer Research', in G. Laurent, G.L. Lillien and B. Pras (eds) *Research Traditions in Marketing*, pp. 265–79. Boston, MA: Kluwer.

Katona, G. (1954) 'A Study of Purchase Decisions: Part 1. The Research Design', in L.H. Clark (ed.) *Consumer Behavior Volume I: The Dynamics of Consumer Reaction*, pp. 30–6. New York: New York University Press.

Keat, R. and Urry, J. (1975) *Social Theory as Science*. London: Routledge and Kegan Paul.

Kelne, N. (1955) 'Politz vs. Dichter on Motivation', *Printers' Ink* July 22: 37–40.

Kernan, J.B. (1992) 'On Debts Due: Presentation of ACR Fellow-in-Consumer-Behavior Awards', in *Advances in Consumer Research* 19, pp. 7–8. Provo, UT: Association for Consumer Research.

Kernan, J.B. (1995) 'Declaring a Discipline: Reflections on the ACR's Silver Anniversary', in F. Kardes and S. Mita (eds) *Advances in Consumer Research* 22, pp. 553–60. Provo, UT: Association for Consumer Research.

Klass, B. (1964) 'Understanding Why They Buy', in M.M. Grossack (ed.) *Understanding Consumer Behavior*, pp. 67–76. Boston, MA: The Christopher Publishing House.

Kornhauser, A.W. (1941) 'The Role of Psychological Interpretation in Market Research', *Journal of Consulting Psychology* 5(July): 187–93.

Krugman, H.E. (1956–7) 'A Historical Note on Motivation Research', *The Public Opinion Quarterly* 20(4): 719–23.

Kuhn, T.S. (1962) *The Structure of Scientific Revolutions*. Chicago, IL: University of Chicago Press.

Lazarsfeld, P.F. (1935) 'The Art of Asking WHY in Marketing Research', *National Marketing Review* 1(1): 32–43, reprinted in Lazarsfeld, P.F. (1972) *Qualitative Analysis: Historical and Critical Essays*, pp. 183–202. Boston, MA: Allyn and Bacon.

Lazarsfeld, P.F. (1969) 'An Episode in the History of Social Research: A Memoir', in Fleming, D. and Bailyn, B. (eds) *The Intellectual Migration: Europe and America, 1930–1960'*, pp. 270–337. Cambridge, MA: The Belknap Press of Harvard University Press.

Lazarsfeld, P.F. and Thielens, W. (1958) *The Academic Mind*. Illinois: Free Press.

Levy, S.J. (1959) 'Symbols for Sale', *Harvard Business Review* 37(4): 117–24.

Levy, S.J. (1983) 'Interdisciplinary Marketing Study', in R. Bagozzi and A. Tybout (eds) *Advances in Consumer Research 10*, pp. 9–11. Provo, UT: Association for Consumer Research.

Levy, S.J. (1996) 'Stalking the Amphisbaena', *Journal of Consumer Research* 23(3): 163–76.

Levy, S.J. (2001) 'Whence and Whither Consumer Research', *ACR News* Fall. URL: (consulted December, 2004) http;//www.acrweb.org/acrnews/FALL-01/WISD.html

Levy, S.J. (2003a) 'Roots of Marketing and Consumer Research at the University of Chicago', *Consumption, Markets and Culture* 6(2): 99–110.

Levy, S.J. (2003b) 'An Interview with Sidney J. Levy', *Consumption, Markets, and Culture* 6(2): 111–13.

Levy, S.J. (2005) 'The Evolution of Qualitative Research in Consumer Behavior', *Journal of Business Research* 58: 341–7.

Martineau, P.D. (1961) 'Respectable Persuasion', *The Journal of Marketing* 25(4): 108–10.

McCumber, J. (2001) *Time in the Ditch*. Evanston, IL: Northwestern University Press.

Mick, D.G. and Demoss, M. (1990) 'Self-Gifts: Phenomenological Insights from Four Contexts', *Journal of Consumer Research* 17(3): 322–32.

Moore, E.S. and Lutz, R.J. (2000) 'Children, Advertising, and Product Experiences', *Journal of Consumer Research* 27(1): 31–49.

Morgan, G. and Smircich, L. (1980) 'The Case for Qualitative Research', *Academy of Management Review* 5(4): 491–500.

Mueller, E. (1954) 'Part 2. The Sample Survey', in L.H. Clark (ed.) *Consumer Behavior Volume I: The Dynamics of Consumer Reaction*, pp. 36–87. New York: New York University Press.

Murray, J.B and Ozanne, J.L. (1991) 'The Critical Imagination: Emancipatory Interests in Consumer Research', *Journal of Consumer Research* 18(2): 129–44.

Murray, J.B., Evers, D.J. and Janda, S. (1997) 'Marketing, Theory Borrowing and Critical Reflection', *Journal of Macromarketing* 15(2): 92–106.

Newman, J.W. (1955) 'Looking Around', *Harvard Business Review* 33(1): 135–44.

Newman, J.W. (1958) *Motivation Research and Marketing Management*. Boston, MA: Harvard Business School, Division of Research.

Newman, J.W. (1992) 'Some Observations on a Developing Field', in J. Olson (ed.) *Advances in Consumer Research 19*, pp. 12–14. Provo, UT: Association for Consumer Research.

O'Shaughnessy, J. and O'Shaughnessy, N.J. (2002) 'Postmodernism and Marketing: Separating the Wheat from the Chaff', *Journal of Macromarketing* 22(1): 109–35.

Packard, V. (1960) *The Hidden Persuaders*. Harmondsworth: Penguin.

Paradise, L.M. and Blankenship, A.B. (1951) 'Depth Questioning', *The Journal of Marketing* 15(3): 274–88.

Parker, M. (1998) *Organizational Culture and Identity*. London: SAGE.

Parker, M. (2000) 'The Sociology of Organizations and the Organization of Sociology Some Reflections on the Making of a Division of Labour', *The Sociological Review* 48(1): 124–46.

Parker, M. (2002) 'Future Challenges in Organization Theory? Amnesia and the Production of Ignorance', in J. S. Jung (ed.) *Rethinking Administrative Theory: The Challenges of the New Century*, pp. 37–52. Westport, CT: Praeger.

Pierson, G.W. (1959) *The Education of American Businessmen*. New York: McGraw-Hill.

Politz, A. (1956–1957) ' "Motivation Research" from a Research Viewpoint', *The Public Opinion Quarterly* 20(4): 663–73.

Politz, A. (1957) 'Science and Truth in Marketing Research', *Harvard Business Review* 35(1): 117–26.

Politz, A. and Deming, W.E. (1953) 'On the Necessity to Present Consumer Preferences as Predictions', *The Journal of Marketing* 18(1): 1–5.

Ricoeur, P. (1970) *Freud & Philosophy: An Essay on Interpretation*, tr. D. Savage. New Haven, CT: Yale.

Robertson, T.S. and Ward, S. (1973) 'Consumer Behavior Research: Promise and Prospects', in S. Ward and T.S. Robertson (eds) *Consumer Behavior: Theoretical Sources*, pp. 3–42. Englewood Cliffs, NJ: Prentice Hall.

Rothwell, N.D. (1955) 'Motivational Research Revisited', *The Journal of Marketing* 20(2): 150–4.

Sampson, P. (1978) 'Qualitative Research and Motivation Research', in R.M. Worcester and J. Downham (eds) *Consumer Market Research Handbook* (2nd edn), pp. 25–48. New York: Van Nostrand Reinhold Company.

Schrecker, E.W. (1986) *No Ivory Tower*. New York: Oxford University Press.

Scriven, L.E. (1958) 'Rationality and Irrationality in Motivation Research', in R. Ferber and Hugh G. Wales (eds) *Motivation and Market Behavior*, pp. 64–74. Homewood, IL: Richard D. Irwin.

Shankar, A. and Patterson, M. (2001) 'Interpreting the Past, Writing the Future', *Journal of Marketing Management* 17(5/6): 481–501.

Sherry, J.F. (1991) 'Postmodern Alternatives The Interpretive Turn in Consumer Research', in T.S. Robertson and H.H. Kassarjian (eds) *Handbook of Consumer Research*, pp. 548–91. Englewood Cliffs, NJ: Prentice-Hall.

Sherry, J.F. and McGrath, M.A. (1989) 'Unpacking the Holiday Presence: A Comparative Ethnography of Two Gift Stores', in E.C. Hirschman (ed.) *Interpretive Consumer Research*, pp. 148–67. Provo, UT: Association for Consumer Research.

Sheth, J.N. and Gross, B.L. (1988) 'Parallel Development of Marketing and Consumer Behavior: A Historical Perspective', in T. Nevett and R.A. Fullerton (eds) *Historical Perspectives in Marketing: Essays in Honor of Stanley C. Hollander*, pp. 9–33. Lexington, MA: Lexington Books.

Smith, G.H. (1954) *Motivation Research in Advertising and Marketing*. New York: McGraw-Hill.

Smith, G.H. and Vitriol, H.A. (1952) 'Why We Use Group Explorations', *Printers' Ink* 18 July: 46–8.

Staelin, R. (2005) 'Eras III and IV My Reflections', *Journal of Public Policy and Marketing* 24(1): 146–9.

Stern, B.B. (1990) 'Literary Criticism and the History of Marketing Thought: A New Perspective on "Reading" Marketing Theory', *Journal of the Academy of Marketing Science* 18(4): 329–36.

Stern, B.B. (2001) 'Book Review: The Why of Consumption: Contemporary Perspectives on Consumer Motives, Goals, and Desires', *Journal of Advertising Research* 41(4): 83–5.

Stern, B.B. (2004) 'The Importance of Being Ernest: Commemorating Dichter's Contribution to Advertising Research', *Journal of Advertising Research* 44(2): 165–9.

Stryker, P. (1959) 'Motivation Research, by Harry Henry', *The Journal of Marketing* 23(3): 344–5.

Szmigin, I. and Foxall, G. (2000) 'Interpretive Consumer Research: How Far Have We Come?', *Qualitative Market Research* 3(4): 187–97.

Tadajewski, M. (2004) 'The Philosophy of Marketing Theory: Historical and Future Directions', *The Marketing Review* 4(3): 307–40.

Tadajewski, M. (2006) 'The Ordering of Marketing Theory: The Influence of McCarthyism and the Cold War', *Marketing Theory* 6(1): 163–99.

Thompson, C.J., Locander, W.B. and Pollio, H.R. (1989) 'Putting Consumer Experience Back into Consumer Research', *Journal of Consumer Research* 16(2): 133–47.

Twedt, D.W. (1964) 'The Consumer Psychologist', in M.M. Grossack (ed.) *Understanding Consumer Behavior*, pp. 53–63. Boston, MA: The Christopher Publishing House.

Veblen, T. (1934) *The Theory of the Leisure Class*. New York: Random House.

Vicary, J.M. (1951) 'How Psychiatric Methods can be applied to Market Research', *Printer's Ink* 11 May: 39–48.

Wallendorf, M. and Belk, R.W. (1989) 'Assessing Trustworthiness in Naturalistic Consumer Research', in E.C. Hirschman (ed.) *Interpretive Consumer Research*, pp. 69–84. Provo, UT: Association for Consumer Research.

Weiss, E.H. and Green, H.E. (1951) 'Unique Human Motivation Library is Centre of Thought in this Agency', *Printers' Ink* 6 February: 36–7.

Wells, W.D. (1975) 'Psychographics: A Critical Review', *Journal of Marketing Research* 12(2): 196–213.

Westfall, R.L., Boyd, H.W. and Campbell, D.T. (1957) 'The Use of Structured Techniques in Motivation Research', *The Journal of Marketing* 22(2): 134–9.

Wilkie, W.L. (1986) *Consumer Behavior*. New York: John Wiley.

Wilkie, W.L. (2002) 'On Books and Scholarship: Reflections of a Marketing Academic', *Journal of Marketing* 66(3): 141–52.

Williams, R.J. (1957) 'Is it True What They Say About Motivation Research?', *The Journal of Marketing* 22(2): 125–33.

Yoell, W.A. (1950) 'Base Your Advertising on the True Buying Motive', *Printers' Ink* 8 September: 38–9.

Yoell, W.A. (1952) 'Make Your Advertising Themes Match Consumer Behavior', *Printers' Ink* 21 March: 82–7.

8

Evolution, Biology and Consumer Research: What Darwin Knew that We've Forgotten

Elizabeth C. Hirschman

Rutgers University

Because of the complexity of human behavior . . . it is essential that our research be theoretically driven and that care be taken to integrate biological as well as environmental factors in our explanations . . . A reader might well ask, 'why the theory of evolution?' The reason is that it is the most general theory we have in the life sciences. It unifies the disciplines of microbiology, medicine, psychology, anthropology and sociology. (Burgess, 2005: 1)

ABSTRACT *One of the great uncharted areas of consumer behaviour is the biological underpinning of human thought and action. I present a review and critique of the past six volumes of the* Journal of Consumer Research (JCR) *from the perspective of evolutionary biology. Several ways in which aspects of current consumption inquiry can be productively reframed from a biological perspective are suggested. In addition, an evolutionary model of the development of cognitive and behavioural capabilities crucial to modern consumption is presented.*

Introduction

In this chapter I want to highlight the long-neglected, but vitally important, evolutionary aspects of consumer behaviour. Consumers have not suddenly come into being 'fully formed' during the 20th century. A review of the consumer research literature from a major journal like the *Journal of Consumer Research* (*JCR*) would, nonetheless, lead us to conclude that this was indeed the case. As a first move in critiquing the consumer research literature from an evolutionary perspective, I will present a review and critique of the past six volumes of the *JCR* from the perspective of evolutionary biology. Several ways in which aspects of current consumption inquiry can be productively reframed from a biological perspective are suggested. In addition, an evolutionary model of the development of cognitive and behavioural capabilities crucial to modern consumption is presented.

In what was to prove one of the most eventful naturalistic inquiries in modern history, Charles Darwin returned from a five year voyage spent documenting the behaviour of several species in their natural habitat to write *The Origin of Species* (1859). He proposed that a process of 'natural selection' gave members of various species best suited to their environment a higher probability of surviving to produce offspring. Through heredity, the offspring carried forward these same biological features and subsequently survived to reproduce. If the environment changed, then a different set of features might be more appropriate, and the better adapted members carrying those biological traits would survive to reproduce.

Subsequently, Darwin turned his attention to the human species and in two large volumes, *The Descent of Man and Selection in Relation to Sex* (1871) and *The Expression of the Emotions in Man and Animals* (1872), discussed the similarities in social and emotional expression between humans and particular animal species, including monkeys, apes and dogs. Despite Darwin's insights regarding natural selection and the passing forward of adaptive genes, it was Herbert Spencer's book, *The Ascent of Man* (1894), that coined the term 'survival of the fittest' so often associated with Darwinism.

Within the social sciences, however, a contrary movement was under way. Led by Franz Boas (1940/1995) and students Margaret Mead (1928/1992) and Ruth Benedict (1946), these researchers argued against the Darwinian–Spencerian perspective, and instead championed Nurture over Nature (i.e., culture over genetics) – an intellectual conflict over causality which continues into the present day. Because consumer behaviour research is grounded in the social sciences, which have largely embraced cultural and social constructs as explanators of human behaviour, theorisation based upon biological and/or genetic causation is virtually invisible in the field. To date, fewer than a handful of researchers, most notably Dickson (2000), Loewenstein (2001), Wright (2002) and Zaltman (2000), have begun to explore biological bases for consumer behaviour. The vast majority of consumer researchers remain grounded in various forms of *cognitive decision theory*, focusing upon choice and information processing studies; while a minority segment of critical culture/interpretive/ethnographic investigators utilises a Boasian cultural-determinism foundation.

I believe that both these paradigms of inquiry could benefit greatly from increased familiarity with biological and evolutionary theories, especially those concerning individual and group behaviour. I examine seven topics currently 'in play' in the *JCR* (2000–2005) and develop an agenda for reframing and extending each from an evolutionary vantage point.

Gender Differences and Mate Choice

Both social psychology and sociology are turning increasingly to biological/evolutionary studies to explain observed behavioural differences between human males and females (Buss, 1994), yet consumer researchers appear to be unaware of these findings. In the 2000–2005 volumes of *JCR*, there were five articles that touched upon gender differences and which could likely be enhanced by the incorporation of biological causation. In 'When Good Brands Go Bad' (2004), Aaker, Fournier and Brasel cast the relationships consumers have with brands as intimate partnerships noting, 'Status, warmth and vitality . . . underlie peoples' conceptions of ideal partners in intimate relationships and thus exert particular influence on relationship strength potential' (2004: 2). Within this relationship paradigm they found differing responses for consumers who felt betrayed by what had seemed to be a sincere brand versus those who viewed their relationship with an exciting brand as 'fling-like' (Aaker *et al.*, 2004: 13). As I discuss below, evolutionary theory can further enrich this construal of consumer-brand pairing.

Holt and Thompson in 'Man-of-Action Heroes' (2004) call forth a series of character-istics associated with maleness and masculinity: 'riding a Harley, hunting wild game, or brandishing a body-by-Soloflex physique' (Holt and Thompson, 2004: 425). They note that male icons such as the cowboy, the adventurer and the big game hunter are part and parcel of American cultural mythology and propose that men are socially expected to display a certain set of personality traits: 'rugged individualism, an adventurous spirit, risk taking, displays of physical prowess and . . . a high degree of personal autonomy' (2004: 426). I will argue that such iconography and personality structure is likely to be rooted in evolutionary adaptation.

A third article (Henry, 2005) on social class relies upon several ideas that are foundational in evolutionary theory on human mating patterns including, for example, the struggle for resources with which to provision one's family, economic and social power, authority relationships, personal autonomy, estimates of relative prestige constructed from lifestyle markers, and the like. Evolutionary theorists posit that these entities are core phenomena within modern societies, because they emerged from a process of genetic-cultural co-evolution.

A fourth article, by Fisher and Dube (2005), explicitly addresses gender differences in response to emotional advertising, noting that females are stereotypically expected to be more emotionally responsive than males, while men are culturally conditioned to display agentic (competitive, hierarchical, emotionally distanced) behaviour and attitudes in public, and to avoid exhibiting emotions such as tenderness, sadness or sympathy. These researchers found that men avoided such displays only when in the presence of other men – an outcome consistent with evolutionary theory. Finally, a fifth article, (Commuri and Gentry, 2005) began with the statement that, 'It is often asserted that a husband's role and worth are identified with his ability to earn a living for his family' (2005: 185), a proposition supported by evolutionary research not only on humans, but also relevant to several species ranging from bluebirds to bonobos (Trivers, 1972). I will now consider how evolutionary theory may enhance and extend our understanding of the above findings.

Evolutionary theory proposes that our primary biological adaptation occurred during the Pleistocene era (roughly the past 2.5 million years), but likely experienced additional selective pressures in response to the advent of symbolic reasoning (about 40,000 years ago) and even more recently during the development of agriculture, approximately 10,000 years ago (Mithen, 1996). This implies that certain physical, mental and behavioural characteristics would be favoured in men and women, and that persons having these characteristics would be more likely to successfully reproduce (Jobling *et al.*, 2004). These individuals would, in turn, pass on these characteristics to future generations, namely, modern day consumers.

For example, MacDonald (2005: 221) summarises several studies to report that males are significantly higher than females in sensation seeking:

> Sensation seeking . . . and aggression peak in late adolescence and young adulthood, followed by a gradual decline during adulthood . . . This 'young male syndrome' is highly compatible with evolutionary thinking: sex-differentiated [behavioural] systems are expected to be strongest at the time of sexual maturation and maximum divergence of reproductive strategies. Because mating is theorized to involve competition with other males, tendencies toward sensation seeking, risk taking and aggression are expected to be at their peak during young adulthood, when males are attempting to establish themselves in the wider group and accumulate resources necessary for mating.

Further, from infancy onward males exceed females in rough and tumble play and large-motor, physically intense activity; in social interactions, boys are more likely to exhibit dominance and forceful, demanding styles. MacDonald (2005: 222) further notes that 'evolutionary theory predicts that females will be more sensitive to danger than males [in order to protect their offspring]. Females [are found to] be more prone to most anxiety disorders, including agoraphobia and panic disorder'.

Human males appear to have evolved certain physical features that affect their desirability as mates to females. Among these are beards and muscular upper torsos, both of which are believed to be phenotypic (physically observable) signals of well-adapted genes. Taller men are typically seen by women as more desirable mates and, indeed, tend to exhibit lower mortality than shorter or average height men (Barber, 1995). Female preference for larger, more muscular men may also be due to cultural evolution, as these males may have social advantages in obtaining and maintaining high levels of economic resources. In several studies of 'dating advertisements' across diverse cultures, males commonly offered evidence of economic and financial success including the possession of advanced educational credentials, high status jobs and expensive goods such as automobiles and houses (Buss, 1994). Correspondingly, women usually offered physical and emotional resources, when seeking prospective mates.

Evolutionary theory also suggests that women's primary assets from a male perspective are fertility and long-term nurturing ability. In affluent cultures, this is believed to lead to a preference for women having 'hourglass' figures with a low waist-to-hip ratio (Barber, 1995). Conversely in societies and communities characterised by subsistence living and uncertain food resources, women with a high body-mass-index (BMI) appear to be preferred, as their fertility and parental performance is more likely to be ensured by greater fat reserves (Barrett et al., 2002: 109). Younger women are proposed to be more sought after as potential mates across cultures due to their higher potential fertility (Barrett et al., 2002). From a modern consumer behaviour standpoint, these evolutionary tendencies may be strong impetuses for the beauty and fitness industries found in Western societies.

Mating Strategies

Continuing in this theoretical vein, males and females may also exhibit markedly different strategies in mating, according to evolutionary theory. It is believed that women choose mates based upon (1) the male's genetic quality (e.g., as exhibited by physical appearance and courage); (2) the male's presumed ability to contribute to childcare (e.g., through direct parenting or provision of economic, financial, social and other resources) (Barrett et al., 2002). In addition, evolutionary theorists propose that modern male displays of material resources such as expensive automobiles, cell phones, computers and sophisticated audio and video equipment may be part of a strategy to signal their competitiveness to other males and their desirability to females. Correspondingly, they propose that young, single women's apparel, which emphasises narrow waists with ample hips and bosoms, the use of eye shadow (which mimics ovulatory eyelid darkening), rouge/blusher (an indicator of health), hair oils, pomades and glossers (also to signal health) are cultural adaptations with biological roots as indicators of fertility (Barrett *et al.*, 2002).

Let us extend our discussion of the evolutionary basis of consumer acquisition behaviours in more detail by examining consumer tribal identity.

Tribal Identity: Ethnicity, Race, Possessions and Brands

During the human species' long sojourn in the Pleistocene, people survived by forming interrelated units or 'tribes' numbering between ten and one hundred and fifty persons (Jobling *et al.*, 2004). Evolutionary biologists propose that humans evolved elaborate ways of determining group membership in order to guarantee provisioning and protection to those who belonged to the tribe and to exclude free-loading persons who did not. Within the recent (2000–2005) *JCR* article set, the paper on 'Brand Community' (2001) by Muniz and O'Guinn provides a compelling example of tribal structures underlying current consumption practices. As those authors state: 'A brand community is a specialized non-geographically bound community, based on a structured set of social relationships among admirers of a brand. It is specialized because at its center is a branded good or service. Like other communities, it is marked by a shared consciousness, rituals and traditions, and a sense of moral responsibility' (Muniz and O'Guinn, 2001: 412).

Consistent with evolutionary notions, Muniz and O'Guinn found that brand community members share a 'consciousness of kind . . . Members feel an important connection to the brand, but more importantly, they feel a stronger connection to one another. Members feel that they "sort of know each other" at some level, even if they have never met' (2001: 418). They continue by noting that brand communities establish norms by which they 'differentiate between true members of the community and those who are not' (2001: 419), construct 'rituals and traditions' (2001: 421), engage in story telling (2001: 423) and are 'marked by shared moral responsibility' (2001: 424). As I discuss subsequently, these tribal features evolved in human groups over an extended period and are believed to be intrinsic to our species.

Kozinets has examined similar themes specifically in relation to the culture of consumption surrounding the *Star Trek* science fiction series. Drawing upon earlier work by Schouten and McAlexander (1995), Kozinets' (2001) research documents the deeply tribalised nature of the Star Trek community. Notably, this community is assisted by the presence of multiple, ongoing narrative series, specialised languages and ethnic props, diverse material culture artifacts and the archetypal notion of utopia, all of which contribute to group cohesiveness, according to evolutionary theory. In a later study of the Burning Man anti-consumption community, Kozinets (2002) documents the importance of humans returning to collectivist, primeval ideologies to construct a sense of localised oneness and freedom from larger, overarching cultural structures. Within evolutionary theory, smaller, more cohesive social structures are proposed to be innately preferred, because they represent a higher likelihood of interpersonal commitment and mutual support.

An article titled 'The Limits of Fungibility' (McGraw et al., 2003) also tapped into tribal consciousness. In this study, consumers were 'asked to sell an object whose acquisition was symbolically linked to a communal-sharing, authority-ranking, or equality-matching relationship' (McGraw et al., 2003: 237). Notably, their participants experienced 'a surge in distress' in response to being asked to sell objects that represented communal sharing (McGraw et al., 2003: 227). I will argue that this is likely to be due to the evolution of tribal in-group norms of sharing and reciprocity.

As McGraw et al. observe, 'people judge the value of things through the prism of interpersonal relationships, and these effects may extend even to experimental demonstrations of allegedly pure cognitive processes' (McGraw et al., 2003: 228). Among ancient humans, tribal survival often ensured personal survival, hence evolutionary theory predicts that such norms are fundamental to human behaviour. Adopting brands that signify membership in a social group, especially on a local level, is likely to be one manifestation of tribal behaviour in contemporary society.

From an evolutionary standpoint, I believe, the postmodern notion of disconnected, rootless individuals would seem fallacious (e.g. Funk, 2003). Unless, that is, they are emotionally disabled in some way, it is probable that all humans are biologically predestined to form group memberships. As an example of this, Tian and Belk's (2005) article on personal possessions in the workplace can be interpreted from an evolutionary viewpoint. The 'corporate red clothing' which the company encouraged its employees to wear might not be merely 'corporate signage' (2005: 308), but also a deeply embedded way of signaling tribal membership: 'a familial body', a 'big happy family' as the authors describe it. Tribes from the Paleolithic onward were believed to be founded as family and extended kinship groupings (Trivers, 1971), so the family metaphor employed by Tian and Belk (2005) is fundamentally rooted in biological kinship. A final study by Escalas and Bettman (2005) brings us even closer to evolutionary understandings of the tribe. As they note, the possession of certain brands is used socially to signify not only to which groups one belongs, but also those to which one does *not* belong, i.e., I am in this tribe; I am not in that tribe. The in-group/out-group distinction is central to evolutionary construals of tribal functioning.

It is believed that approximately 50,000 years ago, the humans who were destined to become East Asians, Native Americans, Europeans, and Australians migrated out of Africa (Jobling et al., 2004). Upon their departure from that continent, they were likely brown skinned, brown eyed and black haired. As they migrated, their genotypes (i.e., genetic characteristics) and phenotypes (i.e., physical characteristics) shifted due to random and environmental factors. Among those who went northward, skin colour, hair colour and eye colour lightened – a process termed de-pigmentation (Jobling *et al.*, 2004). Body hair increased in some Northern European populations; while tooth forms were altered in some Asian populations.

The epicanthic eyelid fold (a secondary skin fold above the eye, common in many Asian populations) carried out of Africa was lost in Europe, but maintained by several Asian and Australian peoples. Body shapes became adapted to cold, hot, arid and moist conditions by becoming thinner, taller, shorter or heavier. Noses became arched and elongated, or flattened and shortened; hair texture took on myriad forms. As a result, human groups no longer resembled each other as they once had, but instead exhibited physical similarities based on kinship and geographic proximity. Humans came to view those who looked most like their group as being most like themselves, most likely to be kin, and therefore most likely to be trustworthy and helpful (Barrett *et al.*, 2002).

In support of this view, Hamilton (1964) proposed that human beings have been adaptively selected to aid persons with whom they share genetic ancestry; therefore the closer the genetic relationship, the higher the probability of two individuals assisting one another. Termed 'kin selection', such behaviour is found in species as diverse as lions and prairie dogs. By assisting those to whom one is related, one's genes are more likely to be passed onward to future generations. Further, humans may consciously extend kin boundaries to non-kin individuals in order to 'draw them into our circle of obligation and, hopefully, influence their behavior towards us' (Barrett *et al.*, 2002: 239).

Once language entered the human repertoire, it further facilitated the formation and maintenance of group boundaries; dialects have been found by linguists to evolve very quickly (in under two generations) and can be used by group members to quickly identify one another and also to just as quickly recognise interlopers. The rapidity with which human groups can create and circulate jargon among group members – effectively creating verbal barriers to entry – is also believed to be due to evolutionary adaptation (Barrett *et al.*, 2002). The brand communities described earlier appear to generate and perpetuate a language system similarly used to identify users of the brand and alert members to the presence of novice arrivals.

Altruism, Sharing and Selection for Group Welfare

We have already noted that humans are social animals and that evolutionary biologists propose that we have undergone selection over time for personality traits and emotional structures suitable for group living (Geary, 2005; Lafreniere, 2005). Within consumer research, several studies provide evidence of this phenomenon. For example, Ariely and Levav (2000) found that group members may alter their selections in response to other members' stated preferences, foregoing their own first choice selections. They note that 'the variety seeking we find might be the outcome of a strong normative social influence that governs behavior' (Ariely and Levav, 2000: 289).

A fundamental evolutionary precept is that group cohesion is supported through adapted norms of resource sharing and reciprocity (MacDonald, 2005). The extensive literature in consumer research on gift giving practices, I believe, is ultimately grounded in this evolved behaviour. For example, Joy's (2001) study of gift giving within the Chinese culture examines the social expectations of reciprocity, which involve gift giving and the emotional ties that are established thereby. Notably, the 'kin/family' notion predominates as a gift giving context, and this is believed to be the evolutionary origin of the practice.

Briley and Wyer (2002) extend this argument in a study on group membership and negative outcomes. They report, 'people who become aware of their membership in a group are likely to feel a sense of responsibility to its members; people are often more concerned about the negative consequences of their behavioral decisions than about positive consequences . . . This bias is likely to be magnified when decisions affect other persons as well as themselves' (Briley and Wyer, 2002: 401). This bias, from an evolutionary perspective, is due to the selective adaptation of humans to act in ways that promote group survival. Seen in this context, negative outcomes, such as the loss of food, failure to find water and poor preparation for hunting arc likcly to be much more deleterious to group welfare than are potential positive outcomes, like acquiring an especially large animal during a hunt.

It is also believed that human selection for group living led to the development of social ethics and norms of fairness. These norms may be then projected onto external actors in order to determine if they are acting fairly (Flinn, 2005). For instance, a paper by Bolton, Warlop and Alba (2003) found that consumers use group-level fairness judgments in deciding whether firms are receiving a 'fair' return or are engaging in price gouging. The latter perception is likely to lead to negative attitudes toward the company, whereas beliefs that an appropriate profit is being received do not damage consumer attitudes toward the firm. In essence, the firm's actions are being evaluated as if it is a group member: i.e., each member is permitted to do well, but not at the expense of other members' welfare. Following the same line of reasoning, a study by Grayson and Martinec (2004: 310) reported that 'in the minds of consumers . . . authenticity is associated with evidence and truth. Consumers . . . become circumspect, if they discover that standards for authenticity have been manipulated for the purpose of making a profit'. In evolutionary terms, such firms are viewed as acting selfishly, flouting accepted standards of equity, and should be shunned and ostracised as a deviant group member would be.

Equity, cooperation and community norms are clearly vital from an evolutionary viewpoint, as Jobling *et al.* (2004) have argued. They point out that the advent of agriculture (i.e., farming and the domestication of animals such as cattle, sheep and goats) about 10,000 years ago led to a radical alteration in human community size and structure.

For the first time in our history, the presence of an economic surplus created the possibility of sedentary communities and social hierarchies. Because successful crop cultivation and animal husbandry were assisted by larger community size, genetic selectivity would have favoured the development of more advanced social skills and cooperative tendencies. Large-scale cooperative endeavours would permit self-sufficient communities to be established and the population to be adequately provisioned and defended against attack. Specialised skills such as pottery-making, metal working, leather tanning and carpentry developed; fertility levels also increased. As Jobling *et al.* observe, 'The development of trade specialization, structured societies, and complex economies eventually precipitated the birth of civilization. The earliest evidence for writing is . . . economic transactions on clay tablets' (2004: 306).

At this point, evolutionary adaptation embraced the individual, the group and culture simultaneously (Sober and Wilson, 1998). Individuals were favoured (in a genetic sense) who could function well within groups; and groups evolved which could function well within culture (Barrett *et al.*, 2002). Interaction between the individual, community and culture meant that social influence and social relationships were important to humans in evolutionary terms. Likewise, a compelling case could be made that with the growth of large-scale industry and non-familial relationships, these are even more so in contemporary consumer culture.

Social Influence and the Theory of Mind

It is not unexpected that because consumer research originated as a subdiscipline of marketing, inquiries into persuasion and social influence (e.g., by advertisers, by reference groups) have been one of the field's stock-in-trades. Over 20 articles were published in *JCR* during the past six years on this topic. I discuss several of these and then present a core evolutionary explanation – the Theory of Mind – which in evolutionary theory is the theory of how the mind functions in solving problems and achieves conscious thought.

One study (Moon, 2000) examined the degree to which consumers were willing to self-disclose personal information to a computer. She found that if the computer played the role of a self-disclosing person first, consumers were willing to reciprocate and provide personal information in return. An extension of consumer attempts to interpret and respond to others' communicative efforts is their own attempt to be influential in an interpersonal context: i.e., just as we are aware that others may try to persuade us, so also are we aware of our own desire to persuade them (Bearden *et al.*, 2001). A paper by Wooten (2000) describes how consumers try to manage the impressions they make on others through gift giving, for example. Relatedly, Dahl *et al.* (2001) describe the emotion of embarrassment that occurs when one feels his/her behaviours are being negatively evaluated by others. Evolutionary theorists argue that in order to feel such social concerns, humans must be able to reason about what is 'going on' in another person's mind and to place themselves in that person's position as an observer, that is, we must possess a 'theory of mind' regarding other individuals' thoughts and intentions (Flinn, 2005).

Holt (2002) extends this application in consumer research to a novel platform by introducing a critique of Marxist theorising regarding the persuasive hegemony of the contemporary marketing system: 'These accounts are dominated by the cultural authority narrative. Marketers are portrayed as cultural engineers, organizing how people think and feel through branded commercial products. Omnipotent corporations use sophisticated marketing techniques to seduce consumers to participate in a system of commodified meanings embedded in brands' (Holt, 2002: 71). Here I would point out that in several ways evolutionary biology is contradictory to Marxist thought. To take one major example, according to evolutionary theory 'commodity fetishism', that is, a fixation on acquiring material possessions and the idolisation of possessions, would not be viewed as necessarily a product of capitalism, but rather as an innate evolutionary feature of human symbolic thought, dating back at least 50,000–30,000 years (see Mithen, 1996). Evolutionary theorists further argue that humans have adapted to deal with persuasive efforts for millennia, and while they are certainly capable of occasionally being deceived, deceptions are more likely to come from fellow humans whom they know or interact with, than they are from marketing communications on behalf of a particular brand.

In a 2002 article Schlosser and Shavitt bring up a significant issue regarding the Theory of Mind: because consumers may anticipate having to justify a particular action to other persons, say a colleague, friend or family member, they may develop internal (mental) arguments in support of that action that are appropriate for convincing someone else, but are not the actual reasons they chose to engage in the behaviour. Because humans are mentally capable of seeing themselves from another's perspective (and temporarily abandoning their own), it is possible that the act of taking the role of observer may disrupt their original position. To my knowledge, this possibility has not been investigated by evolutionary theorists and may constitute a contribution of consumer research to that field.

A final enlightening example of Theory of Mind comes from Rose and Wood's (2005) paper on reality television show viewing. As they describe this process:

> If the reality television show genre is perceived to resonate with authenticity, what process accounts for this resonance? . . . Viewer responses . . . were characterized by wondering. They wondered why the cast members acted or spoke as they did, they wondered what they would do if in the cast members' place, they wondered what the producers were 'up to', they wondered about what actually happened and what might have been . . . This is evocative of a naïve move toward deconstructionist textual critique. (Rose and Wood, 2005: 294)

It is likely that from an evolutionary perspective, all consumers are deconstructionists, to a certain extent.

Now, let us consider in more detail the evolutionary perspective regarding social influence, persuasion and the Theory of Mind. Flinn (2005) and other theorists (e.g., Geary, 2005) believe that human mental capacities evolved largely in response to the demands of social interaction with other persons, rather than the physical environment in which they lived. As Flinn states, 'Human social relationships are complex. Predicting the future moves of a competitor-cooperator and appropriate countermoves amplified by multiple relationships, shifting coalitions and deception makes social success a difficult undertaking' (Flinn, 2005: 87). Consumers are capable of sophisticated reasoning with regard to marketers' influence attempts and I would simply add that strategic reasoning ability most likely grew historically out of our need to anticipate other persons' influence attempts and now has been extended to evaluating those of social institutions.

Extending this, evolutionary biology also proposes that from infancy onward, humans will be especially attuned to developing their social interpretation skills. Research has shown that by age three months, infants are able to distinguish familiar from unfamiliar faces and to interpret the emotional state of the faces they observe (Nelson, 1997). Primates, including humans, have been shown by neurological imaging to possess specialised collections of neurons for processing face recognition and facial emotions. Building upon this, the Social Brain Hypothesis (Barton and Dunbar, 1997; Dunbar, 1998) proposed that the relative size of the neocortex (the thinking part of the brain) in primates was indicative of the extent to which evolutionary adaptations have been made in response to social performance demands: the larger the size of the neocortex, the larger the average social group size for a given primate species (Barrett *et al.*, 2002: 139).

Within this same brain region is believed to be seated the Theory of Mind capacity discussed earlier that enables persons to reason about other people's thoughts and to plan strategies in response to others' strategising (Leslie, 2000; Baron-Cohen, 2000a, 2000b). Through a process of anthropomorphising animals and inanimate objects, humans also attempt to interpret the perceived strategies and intentions of non-humans. To take a few examples: 'the weather is not letting me get a suntan'; 'my dog is trying to be really good, so I will take him to the beach'; 'the Ford Motor Company is trying to trick me into buying one of their new trucks'.

There also appear to be interpersonal and gender variations in the complexity with which individuals can reason about others' strategies. Some persons are able to reason through highly intricate multi-level strategies (for instance, as depicted in the motion pictures 'Dangerous Liaisons' or 'Syriana'), while others are baffled by such narratives. In general, women appear to be more adept than men at interpreting and responding to others' thoughts (Swarbrick, 2000). If this is correct, then consumer research studies directed towards understanding persuasion and influence would perhaps be better designed if they segregated samples by gender and tested for both main and interaction effects (those found in the standard analysis of variance model used in experiments).

Metaphor and the Modular Mind

Evolutionary biologists have divided opinions in relation to the development of modern human mental capabilities, with some arguing that the mind has specialised modules for specific functions (Cosmides and Tooby, 1992), while others emphasise the general unity of cognitive function (Fodor, 1983). Discussions of metaphor and symbolism in consumer research are usually the domain of interpretive researchers. These mental operations are generally considered to be advanced, domain-general constructions, because they evolved only 50,000–30,000 years ago and were concurrent with the first appearances of art, religion and self-adornment in human prehistory (Mithen, 1996). In Grayson and Shulman's (2000) article on irreplaceable possessions, they note that 'prior consumer research . . . explanations for why people value objects as special possessions . . . focus on the meanings that special possessions signify for consumers . . . Such [special] possessions can represent personally relevant events, people, places and values' (Grayson and Shulman, 2000: 17). To imbue material objects with such meanings requires the intellectually advanced ability of taking attributes found in one domain of experience and transferring them to another, while still preserving their original meaning.

Consumers are, in other words, active creators of abstract meanings that are then tied to events and objects in the social environment. As Peñalosa registers, 'Consumers negotiate western cultural meanings signifying naturalism, competition, freedom and independence' (Peñalosa, 2001: 395). Indeed, the fact that consumers (and consumer researchers) are able to generate abstract concepts such as these from life experiences supports a domain-general reasoning ability capable of scanning across different types of social and physical experiences and extracting their common characteristics. Murray (2002: 428) ties this symbolic activity to human social efforts to influence others, as well as to communicate group membership: 'Using fashion to express symbolic statements of membership and demarcation assumes that semantic codes are open discursive systems'. Murray further argues that such symbolic construction efforts are analogous to linguistic systems (another uniquely human skill) which 'have shared rules, but can still be played with in imaginative ways'.

Humans are also uniquely able to create and respond to aesthetic images (Mithen, 1996), a characteristic which has received some attention in the recent literature (see Schroeder, 2006). For example the article by Bloch et al. (2003) not only addresses product design aesthetics, but links them to the larger domain of cultural production: 'Visual aesthetics also have a symbolic function that influences how a product is comprehended and evaluated. Images of elegance, ease of use, youthfulness, durability and innovativeness all may stem from choices marketers make' (Bloch *et al.*, 2003: 561).

The discussion of symbolism and aesthetics leads us to a core point of theoretical tension in evolutionary biology. This is whether the human mind is *domain general* or *domain specific*. As Barrett *et al.* (2002: 271) put it, 'The issue here is whether the mind is composed of a number of essentially innate modules, each designed to solve problems of a particular kind – the "Swiss Army Knife" model of Cosmides and Tooby (1992) – or alternatively, is it a single "domain general" reasoning device that we apply flexibly to many different situations?'

Let me clarify this point. Fodor, a philosopher-linguist, first proposed the term 'modularity of mind' in 1983. He argued that many basic perceptual and mental processes were genetically pre-coded within special purpose modules; these included vision, hearing, and language production and comprehension. Fodor proposed that each of these functional systems operated independently and was keyed to take in specific forms of sensory stimulation from the environment (Fodor, 1983). In Fodor's view, each modular processing system was 'hard wired' or rigidly programmed and had little or no flexibility or adaptability.

The lack of module adaptability is attributed to evolutionary responses intended to ensure the species' survival. During the Pleistocene period, humans faced many violent and potentially fatal situations in which instant, automatic (and appropriate) responses were required. Those humans survived to reproduce who, without conscious thought, spontaneously acted appropriately to escape the danger. But, according to Fodor (1983), not all mental functions are modularised and automatic. Our species also possesses central cognitive processes that are subject to conscious control and direction, can adapt to information gained from the social and physical environment, construct reasoned strategies and evaluate alternative responses (Fodor, 1983).

By contrast, Cosmides and Tooby (1992), both of whom are evolutionary psychologists, have argued against the existence of domain-general central processing. They propose that human response to several recurring social problems is genetically hardwired within our species; among the areas they believe are modularised in this fashion are complex tool use and construction, interpersonal persuasion, choosing a mate, learning and using language, and interpreting others' motives and intentions (Cosmides and Tooby, 2000).

Sperber (1994) opposes Cosmides and Tooby's model as unnecessarily inflexible. He proposes that function-specific modular areas of the human mind ultimately feed into a *meta-representational module*. As Barrett *et al.* (2002: 276) comment, 'An organism endowed with such a module could form representations of concepts across all potential domains . . . [Such] modular functioning could give rise to imaginative, creative and holistic thought. It would also allow for cultural differences to have an impact on individuals' thoughts and behavior'. Such a conceptualisation would be consistent with recent research on consumer behaviour. It could account well for the personalities consumers attribute to objects and brands, the use of clothing, automobiles, foodstuffs and the like to represent self, consumer ponderings about peer and advertiser intentions, cultural differences in social influence effects and so forth (Geary, 2005; MacDonald, 2005). While consumer researchers have not deeply investigated the implications of the Modular Mind for consumption, they have devoted enormous energy to consumer decision-making over the past several decades. We now turn to an examination of recent research on this important topic.

Automatic and Unconscious Choice, Fast and Frugal Algorithms and Two Routes to Emotion: Or Why White Matter Doesn't Always Matter

Individual decision-making was the most heavily investigated topic in consumer research during the 2000–2005 time frame considered here. An article by Johar and Simmons (2000) exemplified some of the foundational thinking in this research stream. As they note, 'Based on the information integration literature, we suggest that adequate levels of elaboration on a disclosure are required to facilitate appropriate integration... into judgments. Such elaboration is likely, given processing capacity, which in turn depends on ability, motivation and opportunity' (Johar and Simmons, 2000: 307). In this model of human thinking, mental activities are conscious and under the direction and control of the consumer, who decides how much cognitive energy to invest in a given thought task.

Subsequently, Van Osselaer and Alba (2000) presented a study that initiated a revision process to the standard cognitive processing model. They stated, 'Our results are inconsistent with a currently prominent explanation that relies on normative causal reasoning processes. A central premise of the causal reasoning explanation is that consumers retrospectively retrieve instances of relevant experiences and perform a causal analysis on those experiences... [However] our results are consistent... with theories that view learning as a forward-looking process... Evaluative learning is dominated by a satisficing process' (2000: 13).

The first empirical study I encountered in *JCR* that explicitly used the evolutionary literature was Pham *et al.* (2001). This article not only incorporated a role for emotion in the decision-making process, but also argued that 'Affective responses involve processing structures that are phylogenetically and ontogenetically older' (Pham *et al.*, 2001: 170). What they mean by this is that emotional response patterns are believed to have preceded those involving conscious, deliberative thought in both humans and related species on an evolutionary basis. With regard to consumers, they identify three types of affective response: Type 1 'innate somatic structures', Type 2 'matching of emotional schematics', and Type 3 'controlled appraisal processes', noting that the first two are likely universal across humans due to evolutionary adaptation, whereas the third type may be personally and culturally idiosyncratic, that is, unique to the consumer and his/her cultural setting.

An article by Loewenstein (2001) challenged the premises of the prevailing decision models: 'A number of researchers have argued that deliberative, calculated decision making is the exception, and that most behavior is relatively automatic' (2001: 500). He continues, 'the brain consists of specialized modules and most brain functions are broadly distributed across multiple modules' (2001: 500). Furthermore, 'an account of behavior should not exaggerate the role of consciousness. Rather than actually guiding or controlling behavior, consciousness seems mainly to make sense of behavior after it is executed' (2001: 503). Surely this is a stunning challenge to over 30 years of accumulated decision-making research in consumer behavior which assumes that most decision-making results from conscious, deliberative thought processes.

Empirical articles actually incorporating unconscious or automatic processes in consumer decision-making are sparse, however. An exception is Menon and Raghubir (2003). Using a series of experiments, these researchers documented the 'automatic use of ease of retrieval in judgments' (Menon and Raghubir, 2003: 230). Subsequently, Yorkston and Menon (2004) found that they were able to demonstrate 'the automatic use of sound symbolism . . . If phonetic effects manifest even partially automatically, this automatic effect will exert a more consistent influence over attitudes and behavior over time' (2004: 49). Thus sounds may be processed on a subconscious level and therefore will be less able to be evaluated by the consumer in a conscious manner.

Let us take a closer look at how evolutionary biologists conceive of human mental activities. Flinn (2005: 83) suggests a model consistent with current consumer research that proposes individuals are able to mentally construct alternative courses of action and choose among them: 'Humans . . . have developed complex forms of learning that involve behavior modification based on mental representation and scenario building. We use mental "games" to predict possible outcomes of alternatives'. These kinds of cognitive problem-solving tasks can be tracked using brain-imaging.

However, Geary (2005) further notes that the human brain exhibits response 'systems [which] include implicit (below the level of conscious awareness) decision-making heuristics . . . These are cognitive 'rules of thumb' that represent evolved behavioral responses to evolutionarily significant conditions'. Barrett et al. (2002) term these *fast and frugal algorithms*, because they are used to reach satisfactory, acceptable, 'good enough' outcomes, rather than requiring excessive mental, emotional and time resources to achieve optimal outcomes. Such an approach to choice represents bounded rationality and likely evolved because humans needed to focus on overall survival, rather than maximising outcomes in one particular area of activity.

Humans also appear to have evolved at least two routes of emotional response: a rapid, holistic, unconscious route via a brain structure called the amygdala (a brain organ believed to be responsible for instinctive emotional response, especially of the 'approach-avoidance' type) and a slower, conscious, evaluative route via the cortex (Damasio, 1994; LeDoux, 1998). Within consumer research, then, a fruitful path for inquiry would be separating the emotional aspects of decision-making emanating from the ancient, holistic amygdala route from those aspects emanating from the more recently evolved, feature-based processing found in the cortex. We now turn to a consideration of how evolution and genetics may play a role not in fostering cross-human similarities, but in creating consumer response differences.

Individual Differences and the DRD4 7-Repeat Allele

In recent years, consumer researchers have directed little attention towards investigating individual differences (for exceptions see Simonson and Nowlis, 2000). Even less inquiry has been directed towards hereditary or genetic origins for these differences. Yet evolutionary biology has made important progress on these issues during the past two decades, and several findings are directly relevant to consumer research. Among these are the validation of a five dimensional model of human personality structure which is hereditable (Buss, 1996). Another series of studies has identified a particular genetic mutation, the DRD4 7-repeat allele, which appears to be linked to innovativeness, variety seeking and creativity (Chang et al., 1996).

Within recent consumer research, variety seeking behaviour is the most often studied personality dimension. Simonson and Nowlis (2000) investigated a trait termed 'Need for Uniqueness' that appears related to novelty seeking, autonomy and independence. They state that, 'buyers with high need for uniqueness... are not concerned with others' criticism and tend to make unconventional choices' (Simonson and Nowlis, 2000: 49). Further, 'unconventional, novel reasons may show the individual is capable of original, creative and analytical thinking' (2000: 51). A second paper on the need for uniqueness (Tian et al., 2001) linked this trait to nonconformity, the purchase of original, novel or unique consumer goods, risk taking, rule breaking and challenging of existing consumer norms. While these researchers propose that such behaviours may spring from early childhood socialisation, a more likely cause is genetic predisposition.

Drolet (2002) notes that individuals may desire to vary their selection processes simply to achieve 'change for change's sake' and that this indicates an alternative form of variety seeking. Related to this at the purchasing level, Steenkamp and Gielens (2003) investigated dispositional innovativeness – the predisposition to purchase new products and brands. As they note, innovative consumers have key identifying traits, including 'high optimum stimulation level, openness to change, independence, risk taking, venturesomeness, tolerance for ambiguity, low dogmatism and low conservatism' (Steenkamp and Gielens, 2003: 370). Burroughs and Mick (2004), studying consumer creativity, extended this line of reasoning by noting that innovative consumers were also able to construct novel mental representations and enjoyed being curious. Let us now turn to look at these issues in more detail, examining the consumer behaviour literature from our evolutionary perspective.

The Role of Genetics

Specifically I now want to take a look at a particular allele (gene) and its several variants (mutations). There are several dopamine (a neurotransmitter) receptors in the human brain; one of these, Dopamine Receptor 4 (DRD4), has a most common version of 4 repeats (DRD4 4-repeat) and less common versions of 7-repeats and 2-repeats (DRD4 7-repeat and 2-repeat, respectively). The DRD4 4-repeat version is believed to be the ancestral type, while the 7-repeat and 2-repeat versions are believed to have arisen via mutations approximately 50,000 to 30,000 years ago (Swanson et al., 2000). Both the 7-repeat and 2-repeat versions are associated with ADHD, novelty-seeking, stimulation seeking, curiosity, risk taking, impulsiveness and independence (Ding et al., 2002).

It is believed that the DRD4 allele and its set of mutations represent 'a model system for understanding the relationship between genetic variation and human cultural diversity' (Harpending and Cochran, 2002: 11). What I mean by this is that specific populations are likely to prosper when they have a majority of persons carrying the 4-repeat version, which is associated with altruistic behaviours and a minority representation of either the 7-repeat or 2-repeat versions, which are associated with innovativeness and independence. In essence, the 4-repeat population majority is theorised to serve a stabilising, cooperative function, creating population cohesion, while the 7- or 2-repeat minority stimulates cultural change, competition and openness to new ideas. It is interesting to speculate that within the US population there may be a larger than average minority carrying the 7-repeat and 2-repeat versions due to the high venturesomeness of immigrants to these shores over the centuries, and that the presence of high levels of these alleles may account, in part, for American cultural innovativeness. It is also likely that consumer innovators and early adopters carry either the 7-repeat or 2-repeat DRD4 allele.

But the genetic aspects of personality are not restricted to the DRD4 allele. As Baumgartner (2002) has pointed out, there is substantial evidence that five personality traits – (1) extroversion, energy and enthusiasm, (2) agreeableness, altruism and affection, (3) conscientiousness, self control and self constraint, (4) neuroticism, negative affect and nervousness and (5) openness to experience, originality and open-mindedness – are all influenced by heredity (see Jang *et al.*, 1998; Loehlin *et al.* 1998). Let us now consider how all of this could impact upon current cultural theory conceptions of consumer behaviour.

Incorporating Evolutionary Biology in Consumer Research

In a recent review article, Arnould and Thompson (2005) develop the framework of CCT as a model for conceptualising 'the sociocultural, experiential, symbolic and ideological aspects of consumption' (2005: 868). Within this perspective, culture is depicted as 'the very fabric of experience, meaning, and action' (2005: 869). Where my view differs from this proposal is not in denying the importance of culture to consumer behaviour, but rather in arguing for the inclusion of biology as an equally potent causative force. Culture, when conceptualised as consciously shared social meanings, has been present within only the most recent portion of human development. Certainly, it has had an extraordinary impact in shaping modern consumption; but for hundreds of millennia prior to the advent of cultural consciousness, humans were constructing tools, dwelling in kinship groups, hunting animals and gathering plants in order to survive and pass forward their genetic legacy. If evolutionary theory is correct, much, likely almost all of our present behaviour as consumers, was influenced by processes of selective adaptation prior to the existence of the modern marketplace.

Similarly, I would take issue, as others recently have (Zaltman, 2000), with the other dominant paradigm in the field which focuses on the conscious, deliberative, evaluative thought processes of (usually) adult humans and construes these to be the essence of consumer behaviour. Just as culture represents a recent event in human history, guided conscious reasoning represents a very recent addition to human mental and emotional response capacity. If we are to study how and why consumers behave as they do now, the most promising place to start would seem to be examining the evolutionary course they followed to get here.

Figure 8.1 provides a rough (and substantially simplified) map of consumer behaviour development in evolutionary perspective. As it suggests, one potential extension to current consumer behaviour inquiry would be studies directed toward family formation and the mate choice process which probe structural issues such as economic asset acquisition, resource bequests across and within generations and expectations regarding spousal roles in financial and nurturing contributions. Economic acquisitiveness among males may be recast as evolutionarily rooted and gender differences regarding materialism may be constructively examined in an evolutionary context. Let us now turn to the question of what the above discussion might mean in terms of symbolic consumption.

Pre-consumer Behaviour 2.5 Million Years ———————————→	Symbolic Consumption ———————————→	Modern Consumption 50,000–30,000 Years ———————————→
• Pleistocene Era	• Cognitive Revolution	• Cultural Revolution
• Kinship groups, tribes are primary social structures	• Meta-representational mind module evolves	• Humans form sedentary communities characterised by economic surplus, labour specialisation, social, political and economic hierarchies
• Mind modules for social comprehension and coopera-tion, tool use and construction are present	• Capacity for abstract, symbolic and metaphoric thought appears	
• Amygdala-based emotional response pattern: automatic appraisal of external events	• Appearance of art and religion; grave-goods signal possible belief in afterlife	• Possession of quality and quantity of goods and services used to signal position in hierarchies
• Absence of syntactical language, abstract thought, metaphoric reasoning, art, and religion	• Use of objects and body designs to communicate personal and tribal identity	• Gene-culture co-evolution
• Gender differences: males aggressive and exploratory; females nurturing and cautious	• Development of syntactical speech and identifying dialects	
• Likely use of physical appearance (e.g., body colouring, size, shape) to judge kinship	• DRD4 7-repeat and 2-repeat mutations lead to greater innovativeness and creativity	

Figure 8.1 **Consumer Cognitive, Emotional, and Behavioural Development in Evolutionary Perspective.**

Symbolic Consumption

Approximately 50,000 to 30,000 years ago, humans evolved the capacity to combine knowledges that were previously processed and stored in different brain areas (Mithen, 1996). This was a significant advance and likely the origin point for what most would consider fully human behaviours and capabilities. Now able to form mental abstractions and construct metaphors and analogies, humans could create art and imagine supernatural phenomena and construct personal and tribal identities. Persons were buried in specific positions with ornamental and practical objects (for example, shell beads and spear points) placed nearby, suggesting these items were seen as personal property and also in the anticipation of an afterlife. It is at this stage that humans became both symbol makers and symbol consumers.

It was also at this stage that the DRD4 7-repeat and 2-repeat allele mutations occurred and led to increased exploratory and experimental behaviours in certain humans. Specific communities began wandering widely across the landscape, carrying new ideas, practices – and genes – with them (Jobling *et al.*, 2004). It would be interesting to consider consumer innovativeness and need for uniqueness as evolutionarily allied traits which serve as sources of 'creative destruction' (Schumpeter, 1942/1962) in human societies. Desiring to differentiate oneself from others and purposely seeking out novel stimuli are both boundary breaking activities – social and experiential – respectively. The motivation to challenge existing patterns can have both negative and positive social consequences. This may be the reason why the mutated alleles have evolved to characterise only a fraction of any given populations. Future studies may find that consumer subcultures carrying the mutated forms of the DRD4 allele at above average levels are more fluid, unstable and unpredictable, than those having lower levels.

Conclusion

The aim of this chapter has been to draw attention to the long-neglected, but vitally important, evolutionary aspects of consumer behaviour. Consumers did not suddenly come into being 'fully formed', so to speak, during the 20th century. This, however, is precisely the view that a review of the recent literature published in the *JCR* might lead us to believe. What I have attempted to indicate, as a first move in explicitly criticising the literature examined above from an evolutionary perspective, is that consumers were moulded via evolutionary forces for millennia in ways that still exert a large degree of influence on their lives and consumption patterns. I should add, of course, that there are numerous other scholars conducting similar research at present, only that the work of a major consumer research journal has yet to have undergone such sustained scrutiny. To conclude this chapter, while I do not advocate the privileging of biological findings over those generated by the methods traditionally used in consumer research, I propose that the inclusion of the novel and potentially unifying perspectives offered by evolutionary theory can be a valuable supplement to current practice. In particular, the developmental concepts offered may help us to reframe current lines of inquiry in ways that can enrich the results obtained.

References

Aaker, J., Fournier, S. and Brasel, A. (2004) 'When Good Brands Go Bad', *Journal of Consumer Research* 31(1): 1–16.

Ariely, D. and Levav, J. (2000) 'Sequential Choice in Group Settings: Taking the Road Less Travelled and Less Enjoyed', *Journal of Consumer Research* 27(3): 279–290.

Arnould, E.J. and Thompson, C.J. (2005) 'Consumer Culture Theory (CCT): Twenty Years of Research', *Journal of Consumer Research*, 31(4): 868–882.

Barber, N. (1995) 'The Evolutionary Psychology of Physical Attractiveness', *Ethology and Sociobiology* 16: 395–424.

Baron-Cohen, S. (2000a) 'Autism: Deficits in folk psychology exist alongside superiority in folk physics', in: S. Baron-Cohen, H. Tager-Flusberg and D.J. Cohen (eds) *Understanding Other Minds: Perspectives from Developmental Neuroscience*, pp. 73–82. Oxford: Oxford University Press.

—— (2000b) 'The Cognitive Neuroscience of Autism: Evolutionary Approaches', in M. Gazzaniga (ed.) *The New Cognitive Neurosciences*, pp. 1249–1258. Cambridge, MA: MIT Press.

Barrett, L., Dunbar, R. and Lycett, J. (2002) *Human Evolutionary Psychology*. Princeton: Princeton University Press.

Barton, R.A. and Dunbar, R.I.M. (1997) 'Evolution of the Social Brain', in A. Whiten and R.W. Byrne (eds) *Machiavellian Intelligence II*, pp. 240–263. Cambridge: Cambridge University Press.

Baumgartner, H. (2002) 'Toward a Personology of the Consumer', *Journal of Consumer Research* 29(2): 286–291.

Bearden, W.O., Hardesty, D.M., and Rose, R.L. (2001) 'Consumer Self-Confidence: Refinements in Conceptualization and Measurement', *Journal of Consumer Research* 28(1): 121–134.

Benedict, R. (1946) *The Chrysanthemum and the Sword*. Houghton-Mifflin, Boston.

Bloch, P.H., Brunel, F.F. and Arnold, T.J. (2003) 'Individual differences in the Centrality of Visual Product Aesthetics: Concept and Measurement', *Journal of Consumer Research* 29(4): 551–565.

Boas, Franz (1940/1995) *Race, Language and Culture*. Chicago: University of Chicago Press.

Bolton, L.E., Warlop, L. and Alba, J.W. (2003) 'Consumer Perceptions of Price Unfairness', *Journal of Consumer Research* 29(4): 474–491.

Briley, D.A. and Wyer, R.S. (2002) 'The Effect of Group Membership Salience on the Avoidance of Negative Outcomes', *Journal of Consumer Research* 29(3): 400–415.

Burgess, R.L. (2005) 'Evolutionary Theory and Human Development', in R.L. Burgess and K. MacDonald (eds) *Evolutionary Perspectives on Human Development*, pp. 1–21. Thousand Oaks: Sage.

Burroughs, J.E. and Mick, D.G. (2004) 'Exploring Antecedents and Consequences of Consumer Creativity', *Journal of Consumer Research* 31(2): 402–411.

Buss, D.M. (1994) *The Evolution of Desire: Strategies of Human Mating*. New York: Harper Collins.

—— (1996) 'Social Adaptation and Five Major Factors of Personality', in J.S. Wiggins (ed.) *The Five-Factor Model of Personality: Theoretical Perspectives*, pp. 180–287. New York: Guilford.

—— (1999) *Evolutionary Psychology: The New Science of the Mind*. London: Allyn and Bacon.

Chang, F.M., Kidd, J.R., Livak, K.J., Pakstis, A.J. and Kidd, K.K. (1996) 'The World-Wide Distribution of Allele Frequencies at the Human Dopamine D4 Receptor Locus', *Human Genetics* 98: 91–101.

Commuri, S. and Gentry, J.W. (2005) 'Resource Allocations in Households With Women as Chief Wage Earners', *Journal of Consumer Research* 32(2): 185–195.

Cosmides, L. and Tooby, J. (1992) 'Cognitive Adaptations for Social Change' in J.H. Barkow, L. Cosmides and Y. Tooby (eds) *The Adapted Mind: Evolutionary Psychology and the Generation of Culture*, pp. 163–228. Oxford: Oxford University Press.

—— (2000) 'The Cognitive Neuroscience of Social Reasoning', in M. Gazziniga (ed.) *The New Cognitive Neurosciences*, pp. 1259–1270. Cambridge: MIT Press.

Dahl, D.W., Manchanda, R.V. and Argo, J.L. (2001) 'Embarrassment in Consumer Purchase: The Roles of Social Presence and Purchase Familiarity', *Journal of Consumer Research* 28(3): 473–481.

Damasio, A. (1994) *Descartes Error: Emotion, Reason and the Human Brain*. London: Papermac.

Darwin, C. (1871/1981) *The Descent of Man and Selection in Relation to Sex*. London: Princeton University Press.

—— (1872/1998) *The Expression of the Emotions in Man and Animals*. London: John Murray/Harper Collins.

Dickson, P.R. (2000) 'Understanding the Trade Winds: The Global Evolution of Production, Consumption and the Internet', *Journal of Consumer Research* 27(1): 115–122.

Ding Y.C., Chi, H.C., Grady, D.L., Morishima, A., Kidd, J.R., Kidd, K.K., Flodman, P., Spence, M.A., Schuck, S., Swanson, J.M., Zhang Y.P. and Moyzis R.K. (2002) 'Evidence of Positive Selection Acting at the Human Dopamine Receptor D4 Gene Locus', *Proceedings of the National Academy of Sciences USA* 99: 309–314.

Drolet, A. (2002) 'Inherent Rule Variability in Consumer Choice: Changing Rules for Change's Sake', *Journal of Consumer Research* 29(3): 293–305.

—— (1998) 'The Social Brain Hypothesis', *Evolutionary Anthropology* 6: 178–190.

Escalas, J.E. and Bettman, J.R. (2005) 'Self-Construal, Reference Groups and Brand Meaning', *Journal of Consumer Research* 32(3): 378–390.

Fisher, R. and Dube, L. (2005) 'Gender Differences in Response to Emotional Advertising: A Social Desirability Perspective', *Journal of Consumer Research* 31(4): 850–858.

Flinn, M.V. (2005) 'Culture and Developmental Plasticity: Evolution of the Social Brain' in R.L. Burgess and K. MacDonald (eds) *Evolutionary Perspectives on Human Development*, Second Edition, pp. 73–98. London: Sage.

Fodor, J.A. (1983) *Representations: Philosophical Essays on the Foundations of Cognitive Science*. Cambridge: MIT Press.

Funk, R. (2003) 'Man for Himself: A Classic?', in E. Fromm (1947/2003) *Man For Himself*, pp. vix-xii. London: Routledge.

Geary, D.C. (2005) 'Evolution and Cognitive Development', in R.L. Burgess and K. MacDonald (eds) *Evolutionary Perspectives on Human Development*, Second Edition, pp. 99–134. London: Sage.

Grayson, K. and Martinec, R. (2004) 'Consumer Perceptions of Iconicity and Indexicality and Their Influence on Assessments of Authentic Market Offerings', *Journal of Consumer Research* 31(2): 296–312.

Grayson, K. and Shulman, D. (2000) 'Indexicality and the Verification Function of Irreplaceable Possessions: A Semiotic Analysis', *Journal of Consumer Research* 27(1): 17–30.

Hamilton, W.D. (1964) 'The Genetical Evolution of Social Behaviour', *Journal of Theoretical Biology* 7: 1–52.

Harpending, H. and Cochran, G. (2002) 'In Our Genes', *Proceedings of the National Academy of Sciences* 99(1): 10–12.

Henry, P.C. (2005) 'Social Class, Market Situation, and Consumers' Metaphors of (Dis) Empowerment', *Journal of Consumer Research* 31(4): 766–778.

Holt, D.B. (2002) 'Why Do Brands Cause Trouble? A Dialectical Theory of Consumer Culture and Branding', *Journal of Consumer Research* 29(1): 70–90.

Holt, D.B. and Thompson, C.J. (2004) 'Man-of-Action Heroes: The Pursuit of Heroic Masculinity in Everyday Consumption', *Journal of Consumer Research* 31(2): 425–440.

Jang, K.L., McCrae, R.R., Angleitner, A., Riemann, R. and Livesley, W.J. (1998) 'Heritability of Facet-Level Traits in a Cross-Cultural Twin Sample: Support for a Hierarchical Model of Personality', *Journal of Personality and Social Psychology* 74(6): 1556–1567.

Jobling, M.A., Hurles, M.E. and Tyler-Smith, C. (2004) *Human Evolutionary Genetics*. New York: Garland Science.

Johar, G.V. and Simmons, C.J. (2000) 'The Use of Concurrent Disclosures to Correct Invalid Inferences', *Journal of Consumer Research* 26(4): 307–322.

Joy, A. (2001) 'Gift Giving in Hong Kong and the Continuum of Social Ties', *Journal of Consumer Research* 28(2): 239–256.

Kozinets, R.V. (2002) 'Can Consumers Escape the Market? Emancipatory Illuminations from Burning Man', *Journal of Consumer Research* 29(1): 20–38.

Lafreniere, P. (2005) 'Human Emotions as Multipurpose Adaptations', in R.L. Burgess and K. MacDonald (eds) *Evolutionary Perspectives on Human Development*, Second Edition, pp. 189–206. London: Sage.

LeDoux, J. (1998) *The Emotional Brain*. New York: Simon and Schuster.

Leslie, A.M. (2000) 'Theory of Mind as a Mechanism of Selective Attention', in M. Gazzaniga (ed) *The New Cognitive Neurosciences*, pp. 1235–1247. Cambridge, MA: MIT Press.

Loehlin, J.C., McCrae, R.R., Costa, P.T., Jr and John, O.P. (1998) 'Heritabilities of Common and Measure-specific Components of the Big Five Personality Factors', *Journal of Research in Personality* 32: 431–453.

Loewenstein, G. (2001) 'The Creative Destruction of Decision Research', *Journal of Consumer Research* 28(3): 499–505.

MacDonald, K. (2005) 'Personality, Evolution and Development', in R.L. Burgess and K. MacDonald (eds) *Evolutionary Perspectives on Human Development*, Second Edition, pp. 207–242. London: Sage.

McGraw, A.P., Tetlock, P.E. and Kristel, O.V. (2003) 'The Limits of Fungibility: Relational Schemata and the Value of Things', *Journal of Consumer Research* 30(2): 219–229.

Mead, M. (1928/1992) *Coming of Age in Samoa*. New York: William Morrow and Co.

Menon, G. and Raghubir, P. (2003) 'Ease of Retrieval as an Automatic Input in Judgments: A Mere-Accessibility Framework?', *Journal of Consumer Research* 30(2): 230–243.

Mithen, S. (1996) *The Prehistory of the Mind*. New York: Thames and Hudson.

Moon, Y.M. (2000) 'Intimate Exchanges: Using Computers to Elicit Self-Disclosure from Consumers', *Journal of Consumer Research* 26(4): 323–339.

Muniz, A.M. and O'Guinn, T.C. (2001) 'Brand Community', *Journal of Consumer Research* 27(4): 412–432.

Murray, J.B. (2002) 'The Politics of Consumption: A Re-Inquiry on Thompson and Haytko's "Speaking of Fashion"', *Journal of Consumer Research* 29(3): 427–440.

Nelson, M. (1997) 'Children by Choice: The Evolutionary Implications of Childlessness', Unpublished MSc Thesis: University of Liverpool.

Peñalosa, L. (2001) 'Consuming the American West: Animating Cultural Meaning and Memory at a Stock Show and Rodeo', *Journal of Consumer Research* 28(3): 369–398.

Pham, M.T., Cohen, J.B., Pracejus, J. and Hughes, G.D. (2001) 'Affect Monitoring and the Primacy of Feelings in Judgment', *Journal of Consumer Research* 28(2): 167–188.

Rose, R.L. and Wood, S.L. (2005) 'Paradox and the Consumption of Authenticity through Reality Television', *Journal of Consumer Research* 32(2): 284–296.

Schlosser, A.E. and Shavitt, S. (2002) 'Anticipating Discussion About a Product: Rehearsing What to Say Can Affect Your Judgments', *Journal of Consumer Research* 29(1): 101–115.

Schouten, J.W. and McAlexander, J.H. (1995) 'Subcultures of Consumption: An Ethnography of the New Bikers', *Journal of Consumer Research* 22(1): 43–62.

Schroeder, J.E. (2006) 'Introduction to the Special Issue on Aesthetics, Images and Vision', *Marketing Theory* 6(1): 5–10.

Schumpeter, J.A. (1942/1962) *Capitalism, Socialism and Democracy*. New York: Harper and Row.

Simonson, I. and Nowlis, S.M. (2000) 'The Role of Explanations and the Need for Uniqueness in Consumer Decision Making: Unconventional Choices Based on Reasons', *Journal of Consumer Research* 27(1): 49–68.

Sober, E. and Wilson, D.S. (1998) *Unto Others: the Evolution and Psychology of Unselfish Behavior*. Cambridge: Harvard University Press.

Sperber, D. (1994) 'The Modularity of Thought and the Epidemiology of Representations', in L. Hirshfeld and R. Gelman (eds) *Mapping the Mind*, pp. 39–67. Cambridge: Cambridge University Press.

Steenkamp, J.-B. and Gielens, K. (2003) 'Consumer and Market Drivers of the Trial Probability of New Consumer Packaged Goods', *Journal of Consumer Research* 30(3): 368–384.

Swanson, J.M., Flodman, P., Kennedy J., Spence, M.A., Moyzis, R., Schuck, S., Murias, M., Moriarty, J., Barr, C., Smith, M. and Posner, M. (2000) 'Dopamine Genes and ADHD', *Neuroscience and Behavioral Reviews* 24: 21–25.

Swarbrick, R. (2000), 'A Social Cognitive Model of Paranoid Delusions', PhD Thesis, University of Manchester.

Tian, K.T., Bearden, W.O. and Hunter, G.L. (2001) 'Consumers' Need for Uniqueness: Scale Development and Validation', *Journal of Consumer Research* 28(1): 50–66.

Tian, K. and Belk, R.W. (2005) 'Extended Self and Possessions in the Workplace', *Journal of Consumer Research* 32(2): 297–310.

Trivers, R.L. (1971) 'The Evolution of Reciprocal Altruism', *Quarterly Review of Biology* 46: 35–57.

—— (1972) 'Parental Investment and Sexual Selection', in B. Campbell (ed.) *Sexual Selection and the Descent of Man, 1871–1971*, pp. 136–179. Chicago: Aldine.

Van Osselaer, S. and Alba, J.W. (2000) 'Consumer Learning and Brand Equity', *Journal of Consumer Research* 27(1): 1–16.

Wooten, D.B. (2000) 'Qualitative Steps Toward an Expanded Model of Anxiety in Gift-Giving', *Journal of Consumer Research* 27(1): 84–95.

Wright, P. (2002) 'Marketplace Metacognition and Social Intelligence', *Journal of Consumer Research* 28(4): 677–682.

Yorkston, E. and Menon, G. (2004) 'A Sound Idea: Phonetic Effects of Brand Names on Consumer Judgments', *Journal of Consumer Research* 31(1): 43–51.

Zaltman, G. (2000) 'Consumer Researchers: Take a Hike!', *Journal of Consumer Research* 26(4): 423–428.

9
Ethnopsychology: A Return to Reason in Consumer Behaviour

John O'Shaughnessy

Columbia University

ABSTRACT *This chapter describes ethnopsychology as the systematisation of folk psychology or, in simpler language, the psychology that people use in their everyday lives. Folk psychology is what people use to guide their interpretations and to impute reasons for action as well as to manipulate others and judge the credibility of proposals. Marketers accept that we need to take account of consumer perceptions without recognising that such perceptions are best understood from the point of view of folk psychology. Ethnopsychology in marketing seeks out the rules that consumers bring to bear in creating meanings as they go about buying. It is 'meaning' in the sense of significance for the consumer that is of interest. When we say something has high meaning for the consumer, we are saying that the consumer believes that something has high significance for her wants or what concerns her.*

Ethnopsychology views meaning as directing buying action and talks of buying action in terms of wants, beliefs, intentions and the meaning (significance) of things for the consumer. This chapter, therefore, sets out various views on the methods lying behind folk psychology as well as the assumption being made about inter-subjective understanding. It also discusses whether wants and beliefs are both reasons and causes of action, with action defined as voluntary behaviour. Ethnopsychology is advocated to answer certain questions. It makes no claim to answer questions on, say, neurotic behaviour. It is however an important perspective for understanding consumer actions from the consumer's point of view. It does not aim to displace other viewpoints since it endorses a *multi-perspective* approach as well as methodological pluralism in the study of consumer behaviour. Its interpretations may make use of concepts developed in the social sciences since these concepts can sensitise us to things we might otherwise miss. Ethnopsychology comes under *hermeneutics* or interpretive psychology since the focus is on understanding actions through interpreting them.

Introduction: Ethnopsychology as the Study of Folk Psychology

Jerome Bruner (1990), in his book *Acts of Meaning*, argues that the cognitive revolution was initially intended to establish 'meaning' as the central concept of psychology: the aim being to nudge psychology to join forces with the interpretive disciplines in the humanities and social sciences such as ethnomethodology, ethnography, symbolic interactionism, action research, discourse analysis and cultural anthropology (Bruner, 1990). But slowly there was a change of course from this original conception of cognitive psychology. The move was from the search for 'meaning' (significance and/or intentions) to viewing the mind as a software program to the brain's hard drive.

It was Gardner who coined the term 'cognitive revolution'. It was a revolution when contrasted with what it aimed to replace, namely, behaviorism which eschewed all talk of mental concepts. In the cognitive revolution the study of mind returned to psychology with the metaphor of the mind as a computer. As for behaviorism itself, its real emergence arose with the work of John Broadus Watson (1878–1958) who sought to expunge all introspection and mentalist concepts from scientific psychology. Watson claimed that lying behind all behaviour lay causal stimuli, resulting from conditioning. This causal-type explanation conflicts with teleological (towards a predetermined goal) explanation that talks of purposive behaviour. Watson eschewed the concept of purpose from his behaviorism, with the consequence that the dependent variables in all his studies were *physical* movement and not action. For marketing it meant focusing on conditioning consumers and refraining from asking any questions about what was happening in the mind as the consumer goes about buying. But it was the behaviorism in terms of operant conditioning, associated with Burrhus Frederic Skinner, that initially dominated psychology after World War II (Skinner, 1974). *Operant conditioning* asserts that we emit behaviour all the time and those emitted behaviours that are reinforced recur while those that are not reinforced die away. According to operant conditioning, all behaviour is contingent on (dependent upon) being reinforced. Reinforcement is anything in the *environment* that increases the probability of a response and a reinforcer is anything that increases the probability of *occurrence* of a given *class* of responses.

Skinner's operant conditioning, like Watson's, limited the questions that could 'legitimately' be asked about the consumer. Skinner's behaviorism is not concerned with happenings in the mind like beliefs, attitudes, motives and so on. (A 'motive' to Skinner is some property of the stimulus by which it gains control over the behaviour.) While initially denying the very existence of subjective entities, Skinner later spoke of behaviour being both overt (public) and covert (private) with all thoughts being regarded as covert (private) events. Skinner abstained from looking at mental events as a stage along some causal chain of S-O-R (stimulus→mental event→response) on the ground that, if the mental event ('mental way station') itself fails to divert attention from the first stage (the stimulus), it would surely divert attention from the last stage (the response). Behaviorism's legacy is to remind us of the importance of external influences on behaviour and the consumer's intense desire for instant gratification.

Cognitive psychology was a revolution in that it acknowledged that only by addressing what is occurring in the mind could psychologists come to understand voluntary behaviour as opposed to involuntary movement. The major approach in cognitive psychology imputes an interpretation of behaviour through the metaphorical model of the computer; viewing the brain as hardware and the mind as software. With its computer metaphor, thinking is viewed as symbol manipulation and cognition as information processing. Thinking is the focus, not human action per se, as the computer metaphor fits better with the idea of people being information processors. Cognitive psychology has never dealt satisfactorily with emotion and motivation: key concepts for the marketer. Consciousness cannot be captured by this metaphor while our intentions are more than mere neural states. A more recent approach in cognitive science is to find the neural correlates of consciousness but few are convinced that knowing neural correlates will explain consciousness.

Bruner, as one of the leaders of the cognitive revolution, was in a position to know this early history. Yet in Howard Gardner's (1985) *The Mind's New Science: A History of the Cognitive Revolution*, there is no mention of any initial phase where the emphasis of cognitive psychology was on 'meaning' (Gardner, 1985). This is surprising as Gardner studied under Bruner at Harvard and it was George Miller, with Jerome Bruner, who established the Center for Cognitive Studies at Harvard. Another surprise. In John Horgan's *The Undiscovered Mind*, an interview with Gardner revealed he was surprisingly critical of cognitive science which he had done so much to popularise (Horgan, 1999).

Gardner argues that strictly scientific approaches to the mind have not advanced our understanding of psychology's core topics like consciousness, the self, free will and personality. He contended that psychologists may advance their discipline by following a more 'literary' style in both investigation and discourse. He is finally quoted as saying: 'By the way, 95 per cent – you can quote me on this – 95 per cent of psychologists are not deeply intuitive about others – They come to psychology out of chemistry because they weren't good enough in chemistry'. This last comment seems a little odd particularly as in his recent (2004) book on persuasion there is no strong sense that Gardner is anything other than a card-carrying member of the cognitive science profession (Gardner, 2004).

Even so, Bruner (1990) claims a culturally sensitive psychology would give a central role to ethnopsychology which is the systemisation of folk psychology into a discipline. As he says:

> A culturally oriented psychology neither dismisses what people say about their mental states, nor treats their statements only as if they were predictive indices of overt behavior. What it takes as central, rather, is that the relationship between action and saying (or experiencing) is, in the ordinary conduct of life, interpretable. It takes the position that there is a publicly interpretable congruence between saying, doing, and the circumstances in which the saying and doing occur. (Bruner, 1990: 19)

Few would subscribe to the doctrine of solipsism which asserts that the individual human mind has no grounds for believing in anything but itself: that we can only be aware of our own mental states and actions. We recognise we possess some ability in the form of a 'folk psychology' that allows us to interpret others; to recognise their actions and the reasons for those actions. Folk psychology is what guides our interpretations of behaviour. It is folk psychology that allows us to anticipate what others will do and lead those others to believe what we intend them to believe. Those with Asperger's syndrome (synonymous with high-functioning autism), for instance, are deficient in this respect and, although they may possess high IQs, as normally measured, they lack the rudiments of social skills. If we set out all that social science has taught us about human actions – how people act and react to others – the memorising of this knowledge would not make up for the absence of folk psychology in those who suffer Asperger's syndrome (see Cole, 1998).

Fritz Heider (1958) argues, like Bruner, that humans act and react to each other in terms of their own psychology, rather than the psychologist's psychology, and this fact must be taken into account in any methodology that is meant to lead to a human psychology (Heider, 1958). The methodology adopted by any discipline must be tied to the type of understanding sought, that is, tied to the type of questions the discipline tries to answer. The different paradigms in social science address different questions or offer different perspectives on a problem. Differences in questions asked commonly demand differences in methodology. As a consequence, there is a need to justify why, say, mathematical physics should be adopted as the model for psychology. Nor is the rational choice model of the economist necessarily enlightening when interest lies in behaviour that is primarily expressive, or behaviour tied to social norms, roles played and moral rules. Human attach-ments can take precedence over self-interest.

When behaviorism was viewed as the only truly 'scientific' way to go, this limited the questions being asked. It is the same with cognitive psychology. Differences in subject matter give rise to different questions needing to be asked and this necessitates diversity in methodologies. All the disciplines in the social sciences can be viewed as different conceptual lenses on behaviour or at least different windows on to a problem, with some windows clearer than others for the problem at hand. Each disciplinary paradigm is a way of seeing but also a way of not-seeing. As a consequence, they do not all address the same questions. Ethnopsychology is the psychology of every man and woman. It is how *they* describe *their* actions, *their* wants and beliefs. Consumer research must focus on folk psychology if it is to understand the perceptions of the consumer. Ethnopsychology is, in other words, the layperson's way of understanding the world. In marketing, it means observing and listening to consumers. This is in line with what Kagan (2006) says about the importance of observation.

Kagan takes to task those researchers who start with a lot of abstract concepts, semanti-cally linked together through sense-meanings and, if they seem true, construct a coherent semantic argument to support a model without giving referential meaning to the concepts via operational definitions. This has been a common approach in consumer research, stretching back to what is now regarded as a seminal work in the field, namely, Howard and Sheth's *The Theory of Buyer Behavior* (Howard and Sheth, 1968). In contrast, Kagan recommends proceeding from observational data to appropriate concepts:

> I was critical of concepts that bubbled up from intuition, rather than plucked from the red-hot kiln of direct observation . . . I cannot think of one theoretically important psychological concept originating in intuition, without the support of reliable observations, that survived more than twenty-five years . . . Psychologists like abstract words – 'emotion,' 'memory' and 'learning' – that bury the natural phenomena under a blanket of semantic networks. Too many investigators begin their research with concepts like 'intelligence' or 'reactivity' and look for evidence to prove their existence. (Kagan, 2006: 179)

Constructs inferred from direct observations, he argues, are the ones that have proved most fruitful. He refers to Danish physicist, Niels Bohr, who took for granted that the mathe-matics of quantum theory were correct and then imagined what reality corresponded to the equations. On the other hand, Albert Einstein started with the facts and only then created the mathematics that would explain the experimental evidence. We can be supportive of Kagan while acknowledging that conceptual deprivation limits what we observe.

Bruner reminds us that an interpretive psychology like ethnopsychology does not mean that it 'Need be unprincipled or without methods, even hardnosed ones. It seeks out the rules that human beings bring to bear in creating meanings in cultural contexts. These contexts are always contexts of practice: it is always necessary to ask what people are doing or trying to do in that context' (Bruner, 1990: 118). For Bruner, the quest for meaning or personal significance lies behind human action. He points out that when the mind is equated with a program, there is no need for 'mind' in the sense of intentional states like believing, wanting, intending or grasping meaning. Bruner claims that 'folk' psychology must be the basis of any 'cultural' psychology, a basic premise of which is that people act intentionally in accordance with their beliefs and wants. We would expect this claim to be endorsed by academics in marketing where talk about wants and beliefs is pervasive. But the urge to join the ranks of 'scientific' psychology has led to the most idiosyncratic models of the consumer's information processing system or, alternatively, a focus on attitude measures based purely on self-report about beliefs. But beliefs alone are not very predictive unless beliefs and wants cohere. Thus people often point out that some religious believers do not act in line with their beliefs. But unless their motives/wants/desires are in line with the action the beliefs further, the action will be stymied. Of the three elements of beliefs, wants and action, we need at least two of them for predictive purposes. As Lyons (2001) says in a review of successive theories of mind in psychology, the most useful and informative explanation of any action will always be because of 'what I believed and wanted' (Lyons, 2001: 156).

Bruner also rejects the methodological monism (the notion that any discipline that aspires to be a science must follow the methodology of the natural sciences) implicit in the claim that social science, to be science, needs to focus on causal explanation. As he says: 'To insist upon explanation in terms of "causes" simply bars us from trying to understand how human beings interpret their worlds and how we interpret their acts of interpretation' (1990: xiii). Bruner eschews the notion of the atomic individual in favour of the concept of agency or agents who are essentially socially and culturally involved.

Bruner argues that psychology must link up with culture because human actions are tied to culturally shared meanings and concepts; to shared 'modes of discourse' by which differences in meaning and interpretation are negotiated among people and because, most important of all, actions are tied to a culture's account of what makes humans tick. The culture's account of what makes humans tick is 'folk psychology' with the term ethnopsychology used to refer to its formal study. The very survival of an individual may depend on his or her understanding of this psychology. We depend on concepts like beliefs, wants, intentions and so on for social interaction and conducting our lives generally. It is through folk psychology that people anticipate, predict and judge one another, draw conclusions about the 'worthwhileness' of their lives (and so on) and their decisions are inevitably influenced by how they view things.

For Charles Taylor (1983) the crucial difference between people and machines is not consciousness, but the fact that 'We also enjoy consciousness, because we are capable of focusing on the significance things have for us . . . Once you do see the importance of the significance feature, it is evident that computing machines can at best go some of the way to explaining human computation, let alone intelligent, adaptive performance generally' (Taylor, 1983: 157–160).

We see the significance of things for us through our capacity for 'reflexive consciousness' – the consciousness of consciousness. It is through this reflexive consciousness (i.e. self-observation) that we develop our understanding of others (Humphrey, 1983). It seems that by the end of the second year of a child's existence, a consciousness of consciousness has started to develop so folk psychology evolves in that the ability to infer the thoughts and feelings of others begins to develop (Kagan, 2006).

Methods Involved in Ethnopsychology: How do People Interpret and Predict the Actions of Others?

Goldman (1995) offers us three methods of how people interpret the actions of others. First is interpretation based on the assumption that people conform to some ideal or normative model of inference and choice. Dennett, discussed later in this chapter, shares a similar view to this, adopting an intentional stance in interpreting behaviour. Second is interpretation based on 'folk psychology' which Goldman views as the situation where people possess some set of law-like generalisations that relate stimulus inputs to certain mental states or, alternatively, mental states to other mental states or mental states to action outputs. But Goldman (1995) rightly argues there is no set of 'laws' shared by people in general, though this does not mean that people may not act as if such generalisations exist. People do implicitly use folk psychology generalisations to interpret behaviour and there may be a good deal of agreement within a culture on such interpretations. Marketing is inevitably interested in the generalisations used by consumers as they go about buying a certain product. Third is interpretation based on the simulation approach, whereby we interpret the actions of others by mentally simulating the context (situation and conditions) that these others are in and interpret accordingly; the simulation approach assumes others are like us.

Folk psychology, to reiterate, is commonly viewed as embracing roughly the second and the third methods for interpreting the actions of others.

Meaning as Directing Action

A large part of the vocabulary of consumer behaviour consists of 'action concepts' that are 'doings' like buying, not 'happenings' like a fall from a horse (Fay, 1996). Action concepts express behaviour that is done for a purpose like buying and that purpose is tied to the meaning of the action.

Those who focus on the meaning of action, talk of meaning directing action. How does this view of 'meaning' as directing action relate to talk of reasons and psychology which talks of 'motive'? If a 'motive,' as commonly conceived, is a disposition to seek certain goals and/or relieve certain inner tensions, then a 'motive' can be viewed as a psychological term for a general category of 'want'. 'Meaning', in this context, is more than a motive, but involves a set of beliefs.

When a social scientist says that meaning directs behaviour, she is saying in effect that it is beliefs about what something signifies for a person's wants that determine his or her actions. On this basis, 'meaning' is not something distinct from wants and beliefs, but a convenient way of capturing in one construct the idea of wants, beliefs and the intentions directing action. When we speak of what something means to the consumer, unless otherwise specified, we refer to the significance of that something for the consumer. This concept of 'significance' has the advantage of embracing wants and beliefs into meaning for the individual. To say something has high meaning for the consumer implies she believes it has high significance for her wants.

'Beliefs' act to tell us how the world is; 'wants' aim to tell us how we would like the world to be. Beliefs, though sometimes overridden by the emotions, generally track truth as a matter of survival. Thus to be curious is to search for beliefs that may be significant for personal welfare. The reason-giving explanation views reasons as comprising the beliefs and wants that lie behind intentions. While wants motivate, beliefs do the steering. In contrast to this notion, Bittner (2003), in the behaviourist tradition, would have us locate reasons for action entirely outside the mind on the ground that reason-giving explanations in terms of wants and beliefs are too vague and obscure. He claims it is difficult to make sense of the motivating–steering distinction since, if a desire moves us to act, it moves us to act in a certain way. This is erroneous thinking since it ignores the fact that a desire/want state is simply a dispositional/tendency state that needs to be supplemented by beliefs about the options open to the consumer. The fallacy lies in assuming that a 'want' on its own is something more than a disposition to seek some broad goal. If I am hungry, I desire something to satisfy my hunger, and am predisposed to seek that something. However, beliefs about my tastes and what is available within my price bracket are needed to actually make a specific choice.

Cognitive psychologists focus on the processes of perceiving, recognising, naming, classifying, speaking, generalising, reasoning and solving problems rather than explaining human action per se. Cognitive psychologists as a group tend to avoid the folk psychology language of wants and beliefs even if most philosophers regard wants and beliefs as bed-rock concepts for explaining human action. In the view of Bennett (a neuroscientist) and Hacker (a philosopher), folk psychology comprises a set of concepts that cannot be ignored as they characterise human beings (Bennett and Hacker, 2003).

Folk Psychology, Intention and Prediction

'Folk psychology', then, is the framework people use to guide their interpretations and to impute reasons for action. Folk psychology is what we use to understand and manipulate the behaviour of others and to judge, say, in a movie, whether the behaviour is credible. Folk psychology involves consideration of context, since predicting behaviour commonly occurs on the basis of knowing a person's habits and expectations as to adherence to social norms.

In social science, interpretive methods are typically tied to the search for meaning in terms of significance but embrace the search for the intentions that lie behind the action. Though intentions can result from different combinations of wants (desires) and beliefs, if we know the relevant wants and beliefs of an individual, this may be predictive of intentions. Having an intention to take some action has been compared with going into gear, with the need to have the 'will' to press the accelerator to action (McGinn, 1982). 'Having the will' to press the accelerator suggests some emotional commitment to goals. Although cognitive psychology accepts the notion of goal-directed behaviour, Bruner (1990) claims it generally bypasses the notion of agency, that is, where people are viewed as being guided by intentional states arising from wants and beliefs – unless it describes a purely normative or stipulated scenario like Dennett's intentional stance.

Dennett (1989) describes his intentional stance in the following manner:

> Here is how it works: first you decide to treat the object whose behavior is to be predicted as a rational agent; then you figure out what beliefs that agent ought to have, given its place in the world and its purpose. Then you figure out what desires it ought to have, on the same considerations, and finally you predict that this rational agent will act to further its goals in the light of its beliefs. A little practical reasoning from the chosen set of beliefs and desires will in most instances yield a decision about what the agent ought to do; that is what you predict the agent will do. (Dennett, 1989: 17)

In the intentional stance we thus postulate ideal rationality or cognitive/conative optimality to structure our interpretation of people's or other entities' behaviour (Dennett, 1986). Goldman (1995) undermines this as a basis for ethnopsychology in pointing out that there has been a good deal of work showing that subjects violate accepted norms of rationality (e.g., Tversky and Kahneman, 1983). On the other hand, the argument that the norms of ideal rationality should be watered down to understand folk psychology, as proposed by Cherniak's (1986) concept of minimal rationality, he regards as flawed and much too vague.

Auyang takes Dennett (1989) to task for extending intentional concepts like beliefs and desires to all manner of artifacts such as talk of lightning in the sky desiring to strike a particular object; water desiring to go downhill and magnetic needles believing that a certain direction is north. Dennett conceived his 'intentional stance' as the perspective typically adopted in undertaking interpretation as we attribute intentional mental states both to ourselves and to others. Dennett contrasts this intentional stance with the 'physical stance' of the natural sciences and the 'design stance' in describing artifacts. Dennett would defend his position by arguing that the concept of an 'intentional stance' is helpful in understanding things other than human actions, since even with humans it is only 'as if' they possess desires and beliefs. We might argue in reply that the 'as if' in the case of humans can be defended but, in the case of artifacts, the term 'function' is more appropriate in that artifacts perform functions not actions.

Dennett (1996) also talks of our having 'Popperian' minds (after Karl Popper) in that we spend much of our time generating and testing ideas and learning by experimenting with inner representations. This seems an echo of George Kelly's (1963) 'constructive alternativism', captured in the following quote:

> Might not the individual man, each in his own personal way, assume more of the stature of a scientist, ever seeking to predict and control the course of events, with which he is involved? Would he not have his theories, test his hypotheses, and weigh his experimental evidence? And, if so, might not the difference between the personal viewpoints of different men correspond to the differences between theoretical points of view of different scientists? (Kelly, 1963: 5)

This perspective, man as scientist, has never been fully explored in interpreting the behaviour of consumers. In terms of folk psychology, it might qualify as being one facet of the simulation method we might use to understand others.

The Appeal of Viewing the Mind as Software to the Brain's Hardware

William Lyons (2001) explains why psychologists would be anxious to view the mind as an information processor. Such a model allows a clear autonomy of psychology from physiology and neuroscience (so there would be no question of putting the psychologist out of a job!), with the psychologist needing only to take account of input information (sensory impressions), internal processing of information (thinking) and output of information (verbalisation of thought). The information processing view had the backing at one time of philosophers of the caliber of Hilary Putnam (1975) and Jerry Fodor (1981) as it seemed to solve the mind–body problem by viewing the human mind as a set of cognitive programs realised by the brain's neural hardware (the dualist view asserts that mind and body are distinct things but this view is overthrown if mind is simply software to the brain's hardware).

However, Fodor (like Bruner) never abandoned the need for psychology to explain human action (voluntary behaviour) in terms of wants and beliefs, as in 'folk' psychology. It is a system of explanation that marketing managers understand. But if this system of explanation were to be adopted by marketing academics involved in consumer research, there would be a need in ethnopsychology to refine concepts like wants, beliefs and intentions even though much of this work has been done for them by philosophers in their theory of action; refinements which I sought to incorporate in *Why People Buy* (O'Shaughnessy, 1986). The conceptual analysis of our everyday folk psychology terms yields insights and makes us sensitive to the nuanced distinctions in the language. The current level of discourse in the marketing literature is no more precise than would be expected in shop floor conversations.

So, while no marketing manager or transformative consumer researcher for that matter could fall back uncritically on social science findings for all the answers he seeks, even so it is the insights from folk psychology that are often decisive. Folk psychology interprets action in terms of reasons for the action. It does this without subscribing to any assumption that the reasons must necessarily be rational. It is only necessary that they be intelligible to make sense of them and folk psychology is what can make them intelligible.

This is not to suggest that in approaching the consumer from the perspective of ethnopsychology we necessarily ignore the vast number of concepts that have been developed by social scientists. We record and reflect on what the consumer has to say but may, for certain marketing purposes, re-interpret some of it in terms of sensitising concepts from the behavioural sciences. We can listen to the consumer before, during and after any given consumption experience and get a deeper understanding through the directions given to us by these concepts which essentially sensitise us to things to look for. We see better when we have been taught to see better. Social science gives us sensitising concepts that can be used to understand, augment and categorise in moving to ethnopsychology from purely folk psychology. This is not the same as saying social science provides universal laws, since there are no universal laws in social science as contexts are so different.

Ethnopsychology as Culturally Based

Bogdan (2001) shows how the ability to interpret others has evolved under communal, political and epistemic pressures to help humans cope with social life and this interpretation of behaviour has evolved by natural and cultural selection. It has been a survival tactic necessary when life is social. What is central would be the recognition that the relationship between expressed feelings, expressed wants and expressed beliefs and subsequent actions is, in the ordinary conduct of life, interpretable and valid. For Bruner ethnopsychology, as a cultural psychology, should be the major thrust of psychology; an interpretive psychology in much the same way that history, anthropology and linguistics are interpretive disciplines.

What it would seek are the rules that people bring to bear in creating meaning in cultural contexts.

The term rule-governed as applied to behaviour may be viewed as (or like) an instruction consciously obeyed and in this sense deciding behaviour. But human action in general cannot be said to arise from a conscious application of rules. An alternative view is behaviour as rule-following which suggests simply regularity in behaviour, in which case the behaviour itself describes the rule. Those endorsing the rule-following or rule-governed approach to understanding action, regard the rules as underpinned by social norms. Peters (1958) views people as chess players writ large, with overall actions constrained by the rules of the game. The individual moves, incorporating individual creativity, become impossible to predict beyond that offered as a consequence of assuming rational behaviour. This is analogous to language. Language is governed by an overall structure of rules, but such rules cannot predict exactly how the rules will be applied in the individual case, without knowledge of an individual's linguistic history. Where action is intentional, explanation in ethnopsychology explains the action by showing the action to be part of a purposeful pattern, intelligible in the context. The inclusion of the word 'context' is important in that there are no universal laws of behaviour: all explanations presuppose a certain context.

While the overall action of going to play a particular tune on the piano may be a deliberate intentional act, the sequence of actual notes played happens automatically without conscious control or attention. The idea of two complementary processes – one lacking conscious control and the other where conscious control initiates and guides action – is a claim made by Norman and Shallice (1986). Not all actions are, however, intentional even though they are not simply involuntary movements either. Thus I non-intentionally read print material on a billboard or on the TV screen (La Berge, 1975).

Just as with playing the piano, we act intentionally in shopping, governed not by causal laws but by the concepts relevant to shopping. Winch (1958), a student of Wittgenstein, directed attention to understanding a society through identifying the concepts of the culture, on the ground that underlying these concepts are the rules being followed. For example, if a consumer says she buys brand X because it is familiar, the concept of familiarity suggests the rule being followed (other things being equal) is that she buys the brand with which she is familiar.

Action Concepts

Action concepts are 'doings' that have an explanation in terms of values, wants, beliefs, decisions and intentions. The criteria for applying action concepts involve more than just looking at physical movements alone. A wink (a voluntary action) is not the same as a blink (an involuntary movement) even if they cannot be distinguished physically but only by knowing the context.

To interpret an action presupposes first and foremost an understanding of the concept under which the action falls. If someone lacks the concept of 'shopping', it is conceptually impossible to shop or describe an act as shopping since what counts as 'shopping' is determined by the rules governing the use of the concept and not by the attributes of the movements themselves. We absorb the implicit rules that allow us to say that some movement counts as shopping. We cannot, in fact, identify movements as action without understanding the social rules and institutions within which the actions take place. As Hartnack (1972: 111) says:

> It is from the behavior a person displays that I am able to infer what kind of act he is performing. I observe that he is walking and I infer that he is taking a walk (and not just going to the grocer's). I observe that he is looking at an open book and that his eyes are moving in a special way, and I infer that he is reading a book (and not just heeding the kinesthetic sensations caused by the movements of the eyes)... It is only because I already understand the language of acts that I am able to infer an act from a particular instance of behavior Behavior is a necessary but not a sufficient condition for inferring another person's acts.

All action cannot be equated with conscious action. Many things are done non-consciously, simply as a matter of habit, indoctrination or conditioning, where we act as if on automatic pilot. In fact, between stimuli and responsive action, no conscious reflection need intervene at all. Consumers may on occasions be more reactive rather than proactive, simply reacting to the meaning of the situation, in terms of like or dislike. Consumers may buy a product or into an idea (e.g. environmental friendliness) purely on the basis of the likeability heuristic: I like, therefore I buy.

Reason-giving May Not be Enough

In daily life we seek reasons for people's actions. The reason-giving explanation is the natural starting place for explaining action not only in courts of law but also in social life and history. Reasons lead to intentions or a commitment to action. If we are to capture the salient features of mental life, those investigating human action must frame their explanations in terms of reasons using the concepts of beliefs and wants (or cognates of these terms). Marketing managers who are skilled at answering questions about customer behaviour have context-sensitivity to likely reasons for action and come to recognise certain patterns of behaviour as related to future actions. But many psychologists eschew the reason-giving type of explanation on the grounds that:

- It does not lend itself to theory development as per the natural sciences. They may even argue that such teleological explanations were abandoned with Newton when the focus shifted to causal explanation. But the question arises whether the methods of natural science are the most suitable model for understanding human action or at least capable of answering all the questions of interest. Those researchers who confine their methods to the methods of the natural sciences inevitably restrict what questions to ask and what behaviour to explain.
- The reason-giving explanation is not one that is falsifiable and the possibility of falsification is the mark of scientific explanation. This view is questionable since reason-giving explanations can be tested against different types of evidence while universal scientific laws cannot be absolutely proved or (contrary to Popper) disproved.
- Reason-giving explanation inhibits the search for causal laws, that is, the factors causing the action (e.g. poverty causes crime). In reply, it is argued that external causes like poverty do enter into reason-giving explanations, but to restrict explanations to just push-forces like poverty will always result in the explanation being inadequate unless the findings can be related to wants and beliefs. Thus we can still ask 'why?' poverty causes crime to try and identify the motives and beliefs at work.
- Reasons would not capture non-conscious influences or all the other influences at work. Unconscious influences can be at work and not all the influences affecting behaviour are likely to be captured in the reasons given for undertaking some action.

In spite of the limitations of the reason-giving explanation it is still true that, for consumer action to be intelligible, explanations must directly or indirectly be tied to wants and beliefs as knowledge of the wants and beliefs lying behind action gives meaning to the action. Reasons give meaning to action because wants and beliefs are tied to the rationality principle viz.: 'If any person wants to achieve goal "A" and believes that action "B" is a way to achieve goal "A" in the circumstances, then that person will be predisposed to take action "B", other things remaining equal'. Both wants and beliefs are involved. This is important to say since many social science approaches assume one or the other is all that is needed for explanation. Attitude measures are usually built up from statements of beliefs though beliefs are unlikely to be predictive without knowing wants. Motivation concepts like 'achievement need' are unlikely to be predictive in themselves without knowledge of beliefs and so on.

Assumption of Inter-subjective Understanding

If consumers were completely illogical and there were no reasons for their actions, marketers would simply have no idea where to start to discover what they wanted or why they wanted it. The prediction of buying action rests on the assumption of fairly rational buyers even if their rationality is highly flawed. Predicting buying action also presupposes some inter-subjective understanding. Thus we have no problem predicting consumers will not want to eat mud pies, would not want to return to sundials for telling the time, but would like to have self-cleaning spectacles, cheaper air fares and to have cars that can slide sideways from awkward parking slots.

Motives and Self-Interest

Unlike the economist, ethnopsychology does not assume that the reasons for choosing action 'A' rather than 'B' will always be self-interested reasons, since reasons can be more tied to social appropriateness and personal integrity than tied to what is most efficient for achieving narrow (material) self-interest. Reflection allows us to put desires at a distance to evaluate them. Intentional action is not just a dependent variable to be predicted simply from knowledge of the relative strength of wants. Consumers do not always act on the strongest desires but may exercise self-control and 'savour' the long term payoff.

It is also true that consumers pay attention to more than the observable attributes of products. Consumers worry, for example, about whether food is safe and consumers in different industrialised nations can view safety very differently. Thus consumers in Europe worry much more about genetically modified food than they do in the USA. Only one per cent of the world's modified food is grown in Europe while 55 per cent of the world's acreage in genetically modified crops is in the USA (Rosenthal, 2007). In one survey, 70 per cent of Germans claimed that they did not want genetically modified organisms in their food, and as Rosenthal says, the German food industry 'does everything it can to avoid using the stuff'.

The strongest motive is that which is stronger than any other single motive, but it need not be stronger than any other two or more motives in alliance. The relative strength of all the reasons to do X rather than Y depends substantially on what other desires people have and beliefs about how satisfactions will be changed by choosing to satisfy X rather than Y. Typically, the consumer contrasts what she wants to do most with what she believes she should do, whether for reasons of duty or practical necessity. Beliefs plus desires/wants constitute reasons for action and make a coordinated contribution to determining what action to take. Desire is a synonym for a species of motive but reasons for action involve more than motive. Thus in the case of a decision as opposed to an automatic or non-deliberated choice:

If we have a motive (or desire) to do X (buy brand X)
And
We have the ability (e.g., financial)
And

The opportunity (e.g. brand availability) to do X
And
The belief that doing X makes most sense in the circumstances, then we come to have an expectation of doing X which in turn
Leads to
An intention to do X that, other things remaining equal, leads to the 'will' to do X and the actual doing of X.

Motive + ability + opportunity + beliefs about means lie behind a deliberated buy – though the role of motive versus belief can vary widely. Yet without a motive (desire/want) there is no action.

Although, as shorthand, we speak of a motive for doing something, in practice there are likely to be several motives at work. Thus a mother may take her children to church, not only to affirm a belief in God and to acknowledge a faith, but also as an attempt to bring up her children as good citizens and to show unity with others in the community. Similarly, people can take the same action for very different motives, just as consumers may buy identical makes of car for different reasons.

The above discussion inevitably raises the issue of the relationship between reasons and causes of action. Typically, we endorse the notion that the reason-giving explanation is tied to practical reasoning whereby people typically do what they have good reasons for doing. But Bennett and Hacker (2003), as do many, regard the relation between reasons and action as conceptual (not causal) since to grasp the connection is not to understand any law-like generalisation but simply to grasp the concepts of belief, want, intention and action. As indicated earlier, Bruner also supports this position. In contrast, Brown (2001), a philosopher of science, argues that philosophers today generally hold that 'reasons are causes and reason explanations are causal explanations' of action (2001: 152).

Fay's (1996) view on reasons as causes is more nuanced than Brown's. He argues, in line with Bennett and Hacker, that reasons in themselves cannot possibly be the cause of anything, as the content of thought is neither a state, nor an event, nor a process. Those who argue similarly usually go on to claim reasons are simply justifications for action. But Fay does not go down this route, arguing that the real (causal) reasons for action must be understood to mean the practical reasoning process that caused the person to act. In other words, an ethnopsychologist would try to identify this process through listening and observing, not by seeking the mental processes occurring in the mind. But Fay agrees that the reasoning process that causes the person to act may not always be conscious or amenable to recall or even capable of verbalisation. This is often recognised in marketing and acknowledged when we say respondents may rationalise when the real reasons are lost in time.

Although a reason for action involves both belief and want/desire, either belief or desire may on occasions be more determining. In fact, the phrase 'impulse buys' suggests that affect-driven choice (desire) has been dominant as opposed to belief-driven choice. But all affect-driven choices need not be impulse buys since emotion plays such an important role in tradeoffs. De Sousa (1990) claims emotions, by being tied to values, determine what is considered important; what options are considered; the patterns of salience among options; the relative importance of attributes, while limiting the inferences actually drawn from a potential infinity of possible inferences. The beliefs associated with pure rational thought (if such exists) would engage the cognitive but not the values anchored in the emotions.

Reasoning may tell consumers a good deal about the features of a product, but it is the link between rationality and emotion that decides the actual tradeoffs made. The multiplicity of values or goals that are considered worth pursuing cannot all be reduced to a common money metric so tradeoffs need to be made. For de Sousa it is the linking of values to the emotions that determines the importance given to various considerations and therefore decide what tradeoffs are made. Values are both emotionally grounded and emotionally developed. While arguing that emotion limits the range of information and the range of options taken into account, de Sousa points out that emotion fills the gaps left by pure reason in the determination of action. Without emotion, non-trivial decision making would suffer paralysis for the decision maker would be unable to make up his or her mind (see also Damasio, 1994).

Traditionally there is controversy over which – emotion or reason – is generally domi-nant, with Kant (1724–1804) arguing that a person can act against his present desires, but Hume (1711–1776) claiming that action Y is chosen at time X rather than some alternative action Z, because the desire to do Y instead of another is because a particular desire has the most force at the time. We now accept that beliefs alone seldom motivate any specific action without a corresponding supportive desire, while desire itself does not lead to a specific action without a corresponding supportive belief, even if it is a 'default' belief. Certainly, if desire is interpreted as sensory pleasure, desire is not the only motive at work.

What ethnopsychology also registers is that it is not only wants/desires and beliefs that are tied to motivation but also fantasies and wishes. Here Velleman (2000) substitutes 'fantasies' for the role of beliefs and 'wishes' for the role of desires. Wishes, unlike wants, are unrestricted as to feasibility – we can just go ahead and wish for anything we like, regardless of whether it is obtainable or whether it exists. As Velleman says, fantasies and wishes are able to motivate behaviour expressive of emotion.

However, Jerome Kagan (1999) rejects the notion of human action being mostly moti-vated by the (narrow hedonistic) desire for sensory pleasure and argues that a universal motive is a wish to regard the self as possessing good qualities. Advertising occasionally assumes this is so. Human beings tend to act to avoid experiencing regret which follows from loss, rather than to obtain the immediate pleasure or gratification from attaining a desired immediate goal. People are inhibited from actions that are likely to bring about guilt, embarrassment or shame, contributing to what Kagan calls a motive for virtue. Adherence to ethics or moral norms is tied to feelings of self-respect, while the violation of these norms gives rise to the emotion of guilt.

For example, a growing number of consumers take account of the environment in their buying and choose manufacturers who exhibit social responsibility in that they do not, for example, exploit child labour, pollute the environment and so on. It also violates a person's sense of integrity to accept an unfair transaction, so consumers ask what something is worth in some objective sense, rather than just what it is worth to them. A consumer may forgo buying, not because the utility of the product to her is less than the price to be paid, but because the price is considered a 'rip-off' (Frank, 1988). Consumers are emotional animals and emotions are not just turned on by the narrow hedonistic desire for possessions, but by just about anything that concerns them.

Operative Reasons and Auxiliary Reasons, Conclusive and Absolute Reasons

There are operative reasons and auxiliary reasons for buying. Operative reasons for buying cover the functions sought, while auxiliary reasons cover the means for fulfilling the functions sought. Different markets compete whenever they tempt buyers to change their operative reasons (e.g., to buy a new golf cart instead of taking a holiday cruise) but rival brands compete by focusing on auxiliary reasons (e.g., by showing the firm's brand best matches the consumer's auxiliary reasons).

There are conclusive and absolute reasons for buying. A conclusive reason for buying is a sufficient reason for choosing one product or brand rather than another, given the circumstances. An absolute reason is a sufficient reason for choosing one product or brand rather than another, regardless of circumstances. A conclusive reason does not override all other possible reasons but an absolute reason does. A conclusive reason for choosing brand XYZ may be its price but, given a change in circumstances (e.g., increase in income), price may no longer be a conclusive reason to buy. Reasons for buying a particular brand may be conclusive but rarely (if ever) absolute. Invariably some change in the conditions of purchase will lead a buyer to change her mind as to which product or brand to buy. We assume 'loyal' buyers have absolute reasons for staying with our brand when they only have conclusive reasons, typically tied to emotional attachment. We should always ask ourselves whether change in the total offering will do anything to unbalance brand loyalty.

Categories of Reasons

In interpreting action, folk psychology points to reasons but what sort of reasons? Answers to the question: 'Why did she buy that particular brand of detergent?' could involve several types of reason. Thus I might locate the reason in the external world by saying that it was prompted by the discounted brand of detergent being the last one on the shelf. A second reason might be in terms of the consumer's internal goals, namely, she bought it to fulfil her goal of doing all the laundry the next day. A third reason might invoke a moral principle in saying it was wrong to leave dirty clothes hanging around. Each of these reasons can enter into a reason-giving explanation, as there can be several reasons (motives) involved.

The reason-giving explanation is composed of wants and beliefs: the consumer wanted the detergent to do her laundry the next day as she hated to leave dirty clothes hanging around and believed that the particular brand of detergent was the best for her purposes and also believed the price at which it was being offered was a bargain too good to miss. In framing a reason-giving explanation we start with knowledge of a set of choices under consideration as these provide the set of contrasts and contextual cues for understanding the action chosen. But if the reason-giving explanation is to capture real reasons (and not just any reasons) there is a need to record the dynamics of deliberation by listening as the consumer talks 'off the back of her head' as she goes about buying.

In the situation where the consumer is talking 'off the back of her head', there is likely to be less confabulation and rationalisation. The explanation takes the form of a narrative, interpreting the cognitive and affective components that led to the intention to buy, before buying, during buying and after buying. In this way the logic of the explanation is revealed (Lewis, 1973). Interpretation is aided by mentally simulating what has occurred to ensure the sequence in the narrative captures the temporal and contextual detail of the decision.

Another way of categorising reasons is on the basis of the choice criteria employed. This has been the form of categorisation that I have favoured. We all have reasons for choosing one product rather than another which implies we have criteria against which we may compare options. Choice criteria can be complex or a single criterion such as which brand has most immediate appeal. It can apply to just the product itself or to all elements of the offering: product, price, promotion and distribution. Emotion influences the weighting of choice criteria and these point to the need to give emotional significance to the choice criteria that fit the firm's competitive position.

As we listen to the consumer before, during and after buying, we can interpret her beliefs and the choice criteria she employs in choosing what she wants. There are six categories of decision criteria (technical, economic, legalistic, integrative, adaptive and likeability) that may singly or in combination be evaluated by whatever indicators are used to judge the magnitude of their presence (O'Shaughnessy, 1986). These choice criteria are universal but need to be interpreted for different applications: consumer behaviour is not the only application for the criteria. An example that makes it easy to remember the six criteria is their application to the problem of capital punishment:

1. Technical criteria e.g., is capital punishment a deterrent?
2. Economic criteria e.g., 'if you can't save souls, can we save money?' in that it costs a lot to house a prisoner over a life sentence (note how this notion repels us unless said as a joke).
3. Legalistic criteria e.g., does capital punishment conflict with laws that ban abnormal forms of punishment?
4. Integrative criteria e.g., will capital punishment weaken integration within society if its adoption falls disproportionately on minority groups or, alternatively, its non-adoption provokes outrage at justice being ill-served?
5. Adaptive criteria (coming to terms with decision uncertainty and fear of regret) e.g., will the condemned prisoner after execution turn out to have been innocent?
6. Likeability or intrinsic appeal is the criterion that enters into most decisions e.g., do many people find taking a life abhorrent in a civilised society?

To illustrate with a consumer example, the following criteria were extracted from an analysis of a buying episode of one woman buying a shampoo: the whole of the buying episode being recorded before buying (anticipatory account), during buying (contemporaneous account) and after buying (retrospective account):

Choice Criteria (on which rules of buying are based)

Technical criteria applied

1. Core-use function: to wash the hair. Although Lisa had not yet tried Ultra Suave (the shampoo being bought) and so was unable to evaluate its effectiveness in performing this function, she inferred effectiveness from the perceived expertise of Garnier in hair products.
2. Ancillary-use functions

    (a)   Softness (avoids use of hair softeners)
    (b)   High frequency use without harm to hair (needed because consumer plays tennis every day)
    (c)   Brightness and strength
    (d)   Volume look
    (e)   Flexible/less brittle

3. Convenience-in-use functions

    (a) Easy to wash out the shampoo
    (b) Easy to comb the hair after use
    (c) Allows daily washes
    (d) Advice on package emphasises suitability for different types of hair

Integrative criteria applied

1. Convention (cleanliness)
2. Ego (self-image)

Economic criteria applied

1. Prepared to pay a premium price to avoid risk: low price/high quantity shampoo to be avoided
2. Sensitive to the time/effort involved in buying the product

Adaptive criteria applied

1. Advice of hairstylist
2. Reputation of Garnier as trustworthy French firm with a wide expertise in hair products
3. Guarantees: Bottle translucent (allows the possibility for checking that the bottle is full) and shampoo must also contains natural plant extracts

Likeability (intrinsic criteria)

1. Pleasant smell after use
2. Attractive bottle (O'Shaughnessy, 1995: 188).

All choices do not involve reflecting on choice criteria. In this sense, all choosing is not deciding in that deciding assumes deliberation on choice criteria. Some choices merely arise from habit, impulse or simply reflect 'picking' in that the consumer is indifferent as to which brand to choose, just as the smoker is indifferent as to which cigarette he takes from the packet.

Hermeneutics and Ethnopsychology: Concluding Comments

Ethnopsychology is, as I have described it, an interpretive approach to understanding others and hence would seemingly fall under 'hermeneutics'. I regard ethnopsychology as a species of hermeneutics in that hermeneutics is now used in a general sense of covering all methods of interpreting. While this is so, hermeneutics has developed certain methods (see below) which may or may not be employed in ethnopsychological investigations. What ethnopsychology does share with the modern hermeneutic approach is an acknowledge-ment that no 'interpretation' of action can ever be declared the one and only, no more than any scientific law can claim to be the last word. Although hermeneutics is commonly viewed as the interpretation of written texts, it is used to cover the interpreting of anything at all, since everything can be regarded as a 'text' for interpretation. The word 'text' can cover any form of communication and any type of behaviour.

Many attempts have been made to find a set of general principles for the interpretation of texts as a foundation for hermeneutics. Friedrich Schleiermacher (1768–1834) conceived the 'hermeneutic circle' which stresses interpreting the parts of a text by reference to the whole, and understanding the whole by reference to the parts. This posed the problem of knowing where to start, but Schleiermacher argued the problem is resolved intuitively by a 'leap' into the circle, moving from parts to whole and whole to parts in an iterative way. The hermeneutic circle is part of today's hermeneutics though it does not solve the problem of determining the meaning of a text.

Heidegger's (1889–1976) reformulation of the hermeneutic circle defined the circle, not as a problem to be resolved by an intuitive leap into the circle, but as interplay between the traditions reflected in the text and the interpreter. Hans-Georg Gadamer (1979), a student of Heidegger, argues that this reformulation concedes that the interpreter is not neutral, but positioned vis-à-vis the tradition 'out of which the text speaks' (Warnke, 1987). The interpreter's own slant on the tradition in the text is part of the interpreter's 'horizon', set against the different and possibly distant 'horizon' of the text. He claimed that what is needed is a fusion of horizons – of text tradition and interpreter.

Gadamer (1979) is the major figure in 20th century hermeneutics, a position established by his *Truth and Method*. Gadamer argues that hermeneutics is dominant in science as well as cultural contexts. Like many philosophers, Gadamer speaks of understanding actions rather than explaining them to emphasise what he considers the difference between the natural and the social sciences. He rejects the notion of objectivity and open-mindedness in interpreting action on the ground that it is only our preconceptions that make under-standing of others possible. It is not possible to interpret in a completely objective way. The mind is not a tabula rasa, a clean slate upon which experience records impressions without distortion. Understanding others arises not from abandoning our own sets of meanings or even trying to put ourselves in another's shoes. Any depth of understanding only arises from fusing, or integrating our meanings with those meanings we want to understand. Gadamer calls this the 'fusion of horizons'. But if 'fusion' carries the notion of the horizons becoming one single unity this is not what Gadamer has in mind. He accepts a tension is likely to remain since whatever is being interpreted may belong to a different context and different conceptual schemata than that of the interpreter.

Gadamer's view leaves no room for reaching back to the time of the action to understand people's minds at the time and context. Gadamer argues that, while the text parts constitute the elements to be interpreted, the whole is best viewed as a relationship between these elements or parts and the different audiences that undertake the interpretation. Closing the hermeneutic circle links author, text and readers. As such, the meaning of the interpreted parts or elements will differ with different interpreters. The various interpretive audiences and the actions being interpreted form an interacting system; new interpretations of the action change the viewpoint of the interpretive audience while this new viewpoint leads the interpretive audience to re-interpret the meaning of the action.

For Gadamer, it is inadequate simply to recover meanings in studying an alien culture (or sub-culture), since the need is to illuminate that culture by fusing its concepts with one's own way of thinking. It is the interplay of the social scientist's own perspective and set of beliefs and those being studied that gives rise to depth of understanding. In studying the consumer it is the interplay of the researcher's set of concepts and beliefs and those of the consumer that result in understanding. It is thus a great help to understanding if both marketer and target customer group are part of the same subculture. Whether the meaning of interest is significance or whatever, it is not static but varies between interpreters and with the same interpreter at different times or within different contexts. This is also true for interpreting the meaning of advertisements; context, like location, is important, as is the time of day. Someone at home doing the housework in the morning does not view an advert on television in the same way that that same someone would in the evening after dinner.

For Gadamer, the meaning of action is never fixed in stone since the meaning of action and its consequences change as new interpreters come along and new perspectives come on board. *Truth and Method* opposes simply going back to original historical meaning, since just to understand historical meanings is to fail to perceive the possible truth for us at present. It amounts to the recovery of dead meaning. Thus to understand Plato's *Republic* is not simply a matter of understanding the way Plato understood the *Republic* but for us to be induced to think deeper about the issues raised by Plato's text. There needs to be a 'conversation' between text and readers whose prior perspective (and prejudices) makes up their horizon of understanding, something that is apt to change as it melts in with the horizon of the text. The total effect is to bring about a new understanding.

So, to conclude, we have *reasons* for our actions and the actions of others. As I have argued in this chapter, if we are to capture the salient features of consumer behaviour, marketers must first frame explanations in terms of reasons using the concepts of beliefs and wants (or cognates of these terms) with the recognition that the meaning or significance of things for the consumer is what guides their actions. When we say that something has high meaning for the consumer, we are saying the consumer believes it has high significance in terms of his or her wants. For buyer action to be intelligible, therefore, explanations must directly or indirectly be tied to wants and beliefs as knowledge of the wants and beliefs lying behind action gives *meaning* to the action. If consumers were completely illogical and there were no reasons for their action, marketers would simply have no idea where to start to discover what consumers really wanted or why they wanted it. Predicting consumer behaviour presupposes *some* inter-subjective understanding and this understanding is in terms of reasons and what things mean to others. Unlike the economist, ethnopsychology does not assume that the reasons for choosing action 'A' rather than 'B' will always be self-interested reasons since reasons can be tied to social appropriateness and personal integrity rather than tied to what is most efficient for achieving narrow (material) self-interest.

References

Auyang, S.Y. (2000) *Mind in Everyday Life and Cognitive Science*. Cambridge: MIT Press.

Bennett, M.R. and Hacker, P.M.S. (2003) *Philosophical Foundations of Neuroscience*. Oxford: Blackwell.

Bittner, R. (2003) *Doing Things for Reasons*. Oxford: Oxford University Press.

Bogdan, R.J. (2001) *Interpreting Minds*. Cambridge: A Bradford Book/MIT Press.

Brown, J.R. (2001) *Who Rules in Science*. Cambridge: Harvard University Press.

Bruner, J. (1990) *Acts of Meaning*. Cambridge: Harvard University Press.

Cherniak, C. (1986) *Minimal Rationality*. Cambridge: A Bradford book/The MIT Press.

Cole, J. (1998) *About Face*. Cambridge: The MIT Press.

Damasio, A. (1994) *Descartes Error: Emotion, Reason and the Human Brain*. Papermac, London.

Dennett, D.C (1986) *Brainstorms: Philosophical Essays on Mind and Psychology*. Cambridge: MIT Press.

—— (1989) *The Intentional Stance*. Cambridge: MIT Press.

—— (1996) *Kinds of Minds*. New York: HarperCollins.

De Sousa, R. (1990) *The Rationality of Emotion*. Boston: MIT Press.

Fay, B. (1996) *Contemporary Philosophy of Science*. Oxford: Blackwell.

—— (1981) *Representations: Philosophical Essays on the Foundations of Cognitive Science*. Cambridge: MIT Press.

Frank, R.H. (1988) *Passions Within Reasons*. New York: W.W. Norton.

Gadamer, H.-G. (1979) *Truth and Method*. J. Cumming and G. Barden (eds.) Tr. William Glen-Doepel. London: Sheed and Ward.

Gardner, H. (1985) *The Mind's New Science: A History of the Cognitive Revolution*. New York: Basic Books Inc.

—— (2004) *Changing Minds*. Cambridge: Harvard University Press.

Goldman, A. (1995) 'Interpretations Psychologized', in M. Davies and T. Stone (eds) *Folk Psychology*, pp. 74–100. Oxford: Blackwell.

Hartnack, J. (1972) *Language and Philosophy*. Paris: Mouton.

Heider, F. (1958) *The Psychology of Interpersonal Relations*. New York: John Wiley and Sons.

Horgan, J. (1999) *The Undiscovered Mind: How the Brain Defies Explanation*. London: Weidenfeld and Nicolson.

Howard, J.A. and Sheth, J.N. (1968) *The Theory of Buyer Behavior*. New York: John Wiley.

Humphrey, N. (1983) *Consciousness Regained*. Oxford: Oxford University Press.

Kagan, J. (1999) *Three Seductive Ideas*. Cambridge: Harvard University Press.

—— (2006) *An Argument for Mind*. New Haven: Yale University Press.

Kelly, G.A. (1963) *A Theory of Personality*. New York: W.W. Norton and Company.

La Berge, D. (1975) 'Acquisition of Automatic Processing in Perceptual and Associative Learning', in P.M.A. Rabbitt and S. Dormic (eds) *Attention and Performance*, Volume 5, pp. 1–44. London: Academic Press.

Lewis, D. (1973) 'Causation', *Journal of Philosophy* 70(17): 556–67.

Lyons, W. (2001) *Matters of the Mind*. Edinburgh: Edinburgh University Press.

McGinn, C. (1982) *The Character of Mind*. Oxford: Oxford University Press.

Norman, D.A. and Shallice, T. (1986) 'Attention to Action: Willed and Automatic Control of Behavior', in R.J. Davidson, G.E. Schwartz andD. Shapiro (eds) *Consciousness and Self-Regulation: Advances in Research and Theory*, Vol 4, pp. 1–18. New York: Plenum Press.

O'Shaughnessy, J. (1986) *Why People Buy*. New York: Oxford University Press.

—— (1995) *Competitive Marketing: A Strategic Approach*, Third Edition. London: Routledge.

Peters, R. (1958) *The Concept of Motivation*. Atlantic Highlands: Humanities Press.

Putnam, H. (1975) 'Minds and Machines', in H. Putnam, *Mind, Language and Reality: Philosophical Papers*, Volume II, pp. 362–384. Cambridge: Cambridge University Press.

Rosenthal, E. (2007) 'A Genetically Modified Potato, Not for Eating, is Stirring Some Opposition in Europe', *The New York Times*, 24 July: C.3.

Skinner, B.F. (1974) *About Behaviorism*. New York: Knof.

Taylor, C. (1983) 'The Significance of Significance: The Case of Cognitive Psychology', in S. Mitchell and M. Rosen (eds) *The Need for Interpretation*, pp. 141–169. London: The Athlone Press.

Tversky, A. and Kahneman, D. (1983) 'Extensional versus Intuitive Reasoning: The Conjunction Fallacy in Probability Judgment', *Psychological Review* 90: 293–315.

Velleman, J. D. (2000) *The Possibility of Practical Reason.* New York: Oxford University Press.

Warnke, G. (1987) *Gadamer: Hermeneutics, Tradition and Reason*. Stanford: Stanford University Press.

Winch, P. (1958) *The Idea of a Social Science and its Relation to Philosophy*. London: Routledge & Kegan Paul.

10
Marketing and Society

Mark Tadajewski[1] and Douglas Brownlie[2]

[1]University of Leicester and [2]University of Stirling

With the failure of the Socialist project and the marketisation of Russia, neoliberalism, free markets and concomitantly marketing essentially became the pre-eminent economic doctrines by default. Many years ago now, Farmer (1977) was making a similar point. He argued that Communist states were losing the economic battle against the Capitalist West. An important figure in spreading the economic doctrines that triumphed was, of course, the marketing professional, whose role and position in society was further supported by the growing network of business schools and the growth in the popularity of marketing courses across the world (Kangun, 1972).

Multinational companies, in particular, were singled out by Farmer. He argued that these 'have done more than anyone to show that good management including very importantly marketing, really pays off, and they have done this so well that they have scared many poorer countries to death' (Farmer, 1977: 16). Of course, poorer nations are now welcoming large multinationals with relatively open arms, hoping that they will provide the stimulus to economic growth that will raise their populations out of poverty. This view can be juxtaposed with an alternative picture of the exploitation of the natural and social world and the movement of multinational corporations from one less developed country to another, as wages rise in one country, in relation to the others.

Many of those companies singled out for anti-corporate critique are well known marketing organisations like Nike, to take a prominent example. While such companies strive to alter public perception of their activities through corporate social responsibility reports, ethical guidelines and the regular inspection of production facilities, marketers face a similar uphill struggle of changing public perceptions of their profession.

We have seen in Chapter 1 that pragmatic business concerns will cloud ethical decision-making (Desmond, 1995, 1998; Laczniak and Murphy, 2006). The 'moral decay' that

Farmer (1977) discusses is, it would appear, still with us. Indeed, the critique of marketing that Farmer acknowledged in 1977 is more prominent today than it ever has been. Farmer asserted that marketing was accused of pushing 'silly consumption while scarce resources are running out' (Farmer, 1977: 15).

Whether or not we agree with this sentiment, as human beings we do try to be ethical in our everyday activities. Most people, Farmer opines (1977: 17), want a 'world that avoids human greed, and that is peaceful, tranquil, and decidedly uninterested in marketing. It makes us feel good to see love and brotherhood, while greed, corruption and exploitation upset us'. Our very humanness can be conducive to making the world a better place. The problem is that marketing activities are so central to many people's lives and marketing, for Farmer

> ... essentially deals with greed and selfishness and base human desires. It is realistic, which gets the field into trouble, since no one interested in true ethics is really interested in reality. We prefer not to face what we really are, but rather dream of what we could be. I suspect that the most vicious criticisms of marketing and its ethics stem from this frantic effort to avoid who we are. Better to plan and dream along the lines of what we should be rather than face the awful truth. (Farmer, 1977: 18)

In their chapter, O'Shaughnessy and O'Shaughnessy avoid the polemical tone that Farmer (1977) adopts, preferring instead to carefully examine the arguments that critics of marketing proffer in relation to marketing's alleged stimulation of hedonism. Defining hedonism as 'the view that pleasure (which includes the avoidance of pain) is the only good in life', they problematise a number of key issues. These include the claim that marketing stimulates a materialistic orientation. That the accumulation and display of material possessions is encouraged by marketing; that marketing stimulates and then fulfils transitory desires; encourages the consumption and display of positional goods; that consumers use products to define their identities; that consumption elides class differences; that fantasy and imagery influence consumer decision-making and that marketing promotes superficial values. In a nuanced reading of the impact of marketing on society they move through these issues in turn and find varying levels of support for each.

In an equally close reading of a contemporary issue Witkowski examines the antiglobal criticism of marketing. Drawing from a wide range of literature, Witkowski notes that whether or not marketing is actually guilty of the charges levelled at it by a variety of environmental, political, labour and religious groups, the fact that these groups perceive marketing to play a role in perpetuating inequality in the world needs careful, considered analysis. Specifically, Witkowski directs his attention to four key questions: whether marketing undermines local cultures, the extent to which private intellectual property rights override human rights, how and to what extent marketing is implicated in the promotion of poor dietary patterns and potentially dangerous food technologies, and finally, that marketing promotes unsustainable levels of consumption.

His balanced account introduces these questions and then counterpoints the antiglobal arguments with those that we might expect marketers to respond with. So, for example, in relation to criticism regarding marketing's implication in the promotion of poor diets, Witkowski notes that one line of defence marketers might rely on would include assertions of consumer sovereignty, combined with the view that if market segments demanding healthy foods were of sufficient size, then marketers would respond by producing the products consumers desire. Using the criticism of the antiglobal commentators, Witkowski concludes his chapter with a series of recommendations that responsible marketers should consider when operating in emerging markets. His account thus represents a critique of marketing practice, juxtaposed with a response by marketers, and, in turn, with some normative guidance for marketing managers.

While the latter managerial focus might render this non-critical in Fournier and Grey's (2000) discussion of critical management, Witkowski's reflexivity and attempt at ontological denaturalisation regarding the presuppositions of marketing theory and practice, along with his affirmative stance in recognising the benefits of marketing activities in a global world, make this chapter an important contribution to any attempted engagement between the anti-corporate movement and marketing.

References

Desmond, J. (1995) 'Reclaiming the Subject: Decommodifying Marketing Knowledge', *Journal of Marketing Management* 11: 721–746.
—— (1998) 'Marketing and Moral Indifference', in M. Parker (ed.) *Ethics & Organizations*, pp. 173–196. London: Sage.
Farmer, R.N. (1977) 'Would You Want Your Son to Marry a Marketing Lady?', *Journal of Marketing* January: 15–18.
Fournier, V. and Grey, C. (2000) 'At the Critical Moment: Conditions and Prospects for Critical Management Studies', *Human Relations* 53(1): 7–32.
Kangun, N. (1972) 'Introduction', in N. Kangun (ed.) *Society and Marketing: An Unconventional View*, pp. 2–4. New York: Harper & Row.
Laczniak, G.R. and Murphy, P.E. (2006) 'Normative Perspectives for Ethical and Socially Responsible Marketing', *Journal of Macromarketing* 26(2): 154–177.

11
Marketing, the Consumer Society and Hedonism*

John O'Shaughnessy[1] and Nicholas Jackson O'Shaughnessy[2]

[1]*The Judge Institute of Management Studies, University of Cambridge, Cambridge, UK, and* [2]*Department of Management, Keele University, Keele, UK*

ABSTRACT   *Marketing is commonly assumed to be responsible for the consumer society with its hedonistic lifestyle and for undermining other cultures by its materialistic stance. This, for many critics, is the dark side of consumer marketing, undermining its ethical standing. This paper considers the connection between marketing, the consumer society, globalization and the hedonistic lifestyle, and whether marketing is guilty as charged. After all, anything that affects the image of marketing as a profession is important, as this influences both recruitment and social acceptance.*

The Charge: A Hedonistic Society Attributable to Consumer Marketing

This paper discusses the claim that today's consumer society is hedonistic, due largely to modern day marketing practices. To its critics, the implicit claims made by consumer marketing are that the meaning of life is discovered through acquisition; that the hedonistic

* Article originally published in the *European Journal of Marketing* (2002); **36(5/6)**: 524–547. Published by Emerald Insight.

experience of material accumulation is the core object of existence on earth. As hedonism in this context is meant to suggest a degenerate influence, it is important to assess whether the charge against marketing is true or the extent to which it is valid. This is the purpose of this paper. Consumer culture, and the ideology of consumerism, generally get a bad press today. The public visibility of goods is seen as becoming the core of social identity, achieved at the expense of other values such as family orientation and so on. This has now become a public issue. One piece in the *Sunday Telegraph* (McCartney, 2000) states:

> Every night, on the television advertisements, you see smooth-jawed men driving £30,000 cars, attracting the envious, admiring glances of their peers and attractive women . . . Values, however, percolate through our culture (or our lack of it). Witty, moneyed advertisers have always sought to sell us more and more expensive possessions, but they now also choose to do so by relentlessly mocking any 'value' which is not material: usually those found in either marriage or religion.

This process of acquiring, consuming and discarding is viewed as a novel and forbidding cultural form. Hedonism-consumerism has rapidly acquired the status of a modern bogeyman, and is seen as intimately associated with the parallel phenomenon of globalization. In fact, consumerism and globalization have become metaphors for human acquisitiveness in a revolt that is intellectual, moral and even physical. And such thinking is becoming conventional orthodoxy. Nor are such reservations entirely new: anti-materialism has a tradition and a history. The thrust of most of the world's religions is anti-materialistic, where materialism is seen as being against spiritual values. Consumption and possession-driven hedonism find no support here, and much condemnation. Though Calvinism may at one time have associated material prosperity with a sign of being one of the 'elect', this is not the same as endorsing hedonism.

A consumer society is defined as one directed largely by the accumulation and consumption of material goods. The term 'consumer society' is used in a pejorative sense, coming from the perception that such a society will inevitably be hedonistic. It is the search for instant gratification that we traditionally associate with hedonism. Hedonism viewed in this way is the opposite to puritanism, associated with antipathy to all pleasures of the flesh. Yet hedonism is the more natural of these two positions. If there is one thing we have learned from behaviorism (Foxall, 1996), it is the strong desire for instant (egoistic) gratification. If explanations are sought, it is puritanism that requires explanation, not hedonism. Nonetheless hedonism is regarded as the least attractive feature of Western society: constructions such as 'doing one's own thing' or 'dumbing down' connect with the idea of an egoistic, individualistic culture distinguished – or degraded – by materialism, introversion and self-obsession. Phrases such as the 'me-generation' and 'the culture of narcissism' have entered the language of popular discourse with individuals viewed as standing apart from their community obligations, less aware of any connectedness to the larger whole, beguiled by the ceaseless medley of consumer offerings.

While many cultural forces – not least, Hollywood – have been indicted as having a role in this, the blame is frequently attributed to the supposed ingenuity and insistence of consumer marketing. When the term 'marketing' is used by critics in this context, it is meant to cover all the ways used by marketing to tempt the consumer into buying, whether through product design, brand name, packaging or promotion. Yet this concept of marketing by critics rests on a purely outsider's view of marketing, not recognizing that the key decision areas of marketing embrace at least the following:

- identifying actual/potential wants within a market or markets; segmenting the market into want categories and selecting market segments suited to the firm's thrust and core competencies;
- determining the offering to match the want of each segment selected;
- making the offering available;
- informing and persuading those within the market segment or segments to buy or rebuy;
- deciding on a continuous basis what offerings to add, subtract, modify and upgrade; and
- cooperating with others to secure resources and support marketing plans.

These decisions have to be made by every company. They are not optional but need to be carefully considered, if a company is to be successful. A knowledge of marketing as a discipline provides useful approaches, concepts and findings that help in making these decisions. But there is no guarantee of success.

The criticisms of marketing overwhelmingly refer to consumer marketing with next to nothing to say on business-to-business marketing. Not-for-profit marketing is similarly ignored. Advertising in particular is singled out as acclaiming acquisition and celebrating consumption at the expense of other values, with advertising being described as the most value-destroying activity of Western civilization (Schudson, 1994). The genius of advertising, it is claimed, is to provide an alibi for self-indulgence. Advertising may, for example, seek to assuage guilt through reinterpretation, particularly of rules acquired from past authority figures such as parents, so what might initially be perceived as, say, an extravagance is reinterpreted as an investment. Kentucky Fried Chicken saw guilt as a problem to be overcome in selling fast food and sought to sell the notion of guilt-free fast food. This gave rise to the advertising slogan: 'It's nice to feel so good about a meal'.

The gospel of hedonism, it is claimed, is spread via globalization with marketing regarded as the engine used to propel acceptance. Marxist dogma regards marketing-directed hedonism as having been created by power structures to maintain dominance, with the mass media responsible for creating the 'false consciousness' (beliefs out of line with true self-interests) of a consumption ideology (Adamson, 1980; Gramsci, 1971). Advertisements are seen as being produced by the dominant group for approval by the suppressed group, envisioning a process that is gratifying to the masses yet contributes to their enslavement. These claims are not irrelevant for marketing practitioners or marketing academics, since they relate intimately to the perceived ethical status of marketing.

Hedonism: Definitions and Meanings

If the major charge against consumer marketing lies in bringing about a hedonistic society, there is a need to define what is meant by hedonism.

As any etymological dictionary will tell us, the word hedonism is from the Greek *hedone*, which means pleasure, enjoyment or delight. Hedonism is the view that pleasure (which includes the avoidance of pain) is the only good in life. In philosophical discourse there are variations on this theme. Psychological hedonism claims that pleasure is the only possible object of desire, because all motivation is based on the prospect of pleasure. If pleasure is interpreted as selfish gratification, then this is consistent with a traditional view of man. Thus Descartes (1596–1650) argued that man is first and foremost regulated by selfish passion and Hobbes (1588–1679) viewed man as self-seeking, atomistic and not by nature (contrary to Aristotle) even social. Ethical hedonism claims pleasure (more broadly defined) is what we ought to pursue. Universal hedonism (which lies behind utilitarianism) has the moral edge in arguing that every man ought to act in whatever manner brings about the most pleasure to the greatest number in the long run. Finally, rationalizing hedonism argues that it is the pursuit of pleasure that makes action rational by making it purposeful; that the criterion of rationality and intentional action demands a foundation in terms of pleasure. Systems of psychology such as behaviorism whose categories stress materialistic satisfactions are, by definition, hedonistic. Hedonism is pleasure-seeking, though, to leave it at that, makes hedonists of us all, since a preference for pleasure, in the very broadest sense, is what structures our lives.

These various philosophical positions are lost on the general public. Hedonism, in popular usage, is typically regarded as a form of egoism where pleasure and the avoidance of pain dominate as motives for action. Consumers are assumed to ask only: 'Does it feel good?' without making any serious attempt to calculate the full consequences of action. This is narrow hedonism, which, it is argued, is the hallmark of today's consumer society. Bourdieu (1984) regards the ethic of hard work as being replaced by narrow hedonism as the fun ethic of modern day society, with sellers exploiting this trend by focusing on selling through emotive words and images instead of product substance (Bourdieu, 1984). There is even a resort company with the name Hedonism that offers precisely that! It claims the highest return rate of customers of any resort.

Yet, even in popular usage, hedonism connotes not just any pleasure. Few would describe, for example, listening to the orchestra as a hedonistic experience. Ideas of a self-gratificatory sensuality are linked to hedonism in the popular mind, with the implicit idea of excess, even of a kind of compulsion. Nor would popular usage refer to hedonistic behaviour as anything but selfish.

Hedonism, among critics of the consumer society is tied to popular usage since it is viewed as pleasure-seeking that is driven, and the notion of its compelling nature is contained in criticisms of consumerism. Hedonism is seen as something less than addiction, something more than ideology, something that victimizes consumers, even though they may understand its dysfunctional consequences at the detached intellectual level. As Rohatyn (1990, p. 78) comments:

> Yet we continue to 'buy' expensive products, cheap slogans, corrupt candidates and (above all) the ideology of ceaseless consumption of material goods as a way of life . . . Even when we know that it benefits corporations far more than ourselves, that every new acquisition generates disappointment, restlessness and another round of conspicuous (hence pointless) consumption . . . To live in North America today is to endure more propaganda in 24 hours than our ancestors faced in a lifetime.

Hedonism as popularly conceived is not a sustainable experience. If hedonism domi-nates the consumer society, its pleasures are fleeting and uncertain. Campbell (1987) distinguishes pleasure-seeking from satisfaction-seeking. Satisfaction-seeking is to fulfill biological needs to relieve discomfort arising from deprivation (e.g. hunger). In contrast, pleasure-seeking aims for a quality of experience arising from certain patterns of sensation. For Campbell the pleasures of consumption reside in imagination. Consumers imagina-tively anticipate the pleasure that a novel new product might bring, though the reality never lives up to what they anticipate. It is all a tragic saga of continuous hope and continuous disappointment, with true pleasure typically lying only in the imagination. According to Campbell, understanding today's hedonistic buyers means understanding how consumers use (and came to use) fantasizing to generate feelings. While no great pleasure can be derived from just imagined sensations, it is easy to imagine situations (e.g. love making) and events (e.g. meeting one's lost love) that have the capacity to stimulate emotional experience. For Campbell, when consumers feel something to be true (even when they know it to be false), that feeling may be all that is needed to determine a brand preference.

The Campbell view of modern day hedonism differs from the narrow hedonism used by critics of the consumer society. Campbell does not suggest that modern hedonism equates with self-indulgence. He acknowledges that the self-illusory pleasure-seeker may be led in the direction of idealistic commitment. Campbell thus moves from narrow hedonism to a broader view.

While we accept that humans, like all animals, seek pleasure and avoid pain, it is somewhat strained to argue that seeking pleasure/avoiding pain covers all motivations for buying. If every intentional action can be interpreted as driven by self-interest and self-interest is viewed as pleasure-seeking/pain-avoiding, it is extremely reductionist. Even sacrificing one's life to save others becomes acting for purely selfish reasons.

'Consumerism' and 'hedonism' are part of a rhetoric of reproval and reprobation, suggesting that selfish, irresponsible pleasure-seeking has come to dominate life. These terms do not have a definitive and primordial meaning but are loose conceptual bundles covering multiple diverse phenomena. They are, or have become, rhetoric – and politicized rhetoric at that. They are not exact terms but emotional resonant rhetorical brands conscripted in an ideological war. But they affect attitudes to marketing as a social force in equating the simple desire for acquisition with greed. What is perhaps important is not so much the meaning of terms like 'hedonism' and 'consumerism' as the dominant public idea of what they mean. We have come to see them as anathematizing all those values that, at least at the level of public discourse, we hold dear. They have become a convenient shorthand for multiple and diverse threats.

Hedonism and Consumerism

At the heart of the debate about hedonism and marketing responsibility lies the question of social consequences and the role of marketing in creating 'new' products and the culture of consumption. Phrases such as 'shop till you drop' reflect popular appreciation of this phenomenon. The stimulation of consumption is the most tangible expression of attempts at marketing-directed hedonism. In making this connection, marketing is blamed for social consequences; parents, for example, seen as too concerned with earning money to pay for the goods that marketing promotes, spending too little time with their children but, instead, buying their affection. The consumer society embraces consumerism, not in the sense of protecting and advancing the interests of consumers, but in vigorously promoting a culture of consumption. The alleged characteristics of this consumer society approximate those associated with postmodernity (Lyon, 1994; Brown, 1995; Rosenau, 1992; Best and Kellner, 1997). These alleged characteristics constitute descriptive hypotheses, which (unlike scientific hypotheses, which can never be proved absolutely) can be shown to be true or false, provided that there is agreement on operational definitions and a sampling plan. No such research has been carried out. The claims made by critics are taken to be self-evident from observation. However, they are by no means self-evident and, in any case, cannot be taken necessarily as an indictment of modern society. The claims and our responses are as follows:

The Accumulation and Display of Material Possessions

Western societies are criticized for their materialistic orientation and focus on material possessions (Belk, 1985). Marxists like Marcuse (1964) view Western societies as characterized by conspicuous consumption with critical thought overthrown in a 'one-dimensional' culture of mass conformity. There is the claim that the orientation of modern capitalist societies is toward the marketing and consumption of goods with societal members extraordinarily concerned with the accumulation and display of material possessions. Baritz (1989) sums up this fever to accumulate possessions with the bumper sticker slogan: 'Whoever dies with the most toys wins'. Consumer lifestyles together with mass consumption are said to control the lives of ordinary citizens.

We would argue that the accumulation of material possessions is simply a consequence of wealth and has been throughout the ages, since one purpose of possessions and 'conspicuous consumption' is to serve as a live information system to signal to others the owner's self-image, rank and values (Douglas and Isherwood, 1979). Except that more people in society are able to indulge, there is nothing new about the display motive. While marketing facilitates the accumulation of goods and status emanating from their display, the basic motive is already there: people may not need many possessions but want them all the same. Without marketing, society would appear less materialistic but, without the opportunity to choose, there would be no merit in virtue.

John Stuart Mill (1806–1873) made the distinction between 'self-regarding actions' and 'other-regarding actions', arguing that individuals should be free to do what they want to do, provided that their actions are purely self-regarding and do no harm to others. In practice Mill's distinction has never been as operational as it appears (e.g. would you not feel that a person should be stopped from committing suicide, even if it brings no harm to others?). Mill never approved the various applications of his principle (see later on globalization). Nonetheless, as applied here, Mill's principle has applicability in relation to consumer choice: what people want to spend their money on is their own decision and critics have no right to impose their own 'better' values. This is not to suggest that there is no meaningful difference between high and low culture as postmodernists claim but simply that freedom to choose is a matter of individual liberty. Rawls (1972) in *A Theory of Justice* puts liberty as the foundation value for all else and sets out to establish a rational basis for the personal and civil liberties, which are held to be inviolable rights by twentieth century liberals.

Satisfying Transitory Appetites and Created Wants

It is argued that the primary motivation of those in a consumer society is satisfying the transitory appetites and wants created by advertising. Frank (1999), like Campbell, argues that the pleasures from consumption are both relative and fleeting. Moving to a relatively better house provides pleasure only for a short time, namely, until the new level of luxury seems routine or one's neighbor goes one better. The pleasure derived from owning any house or any other possession is tied to the status attached to owning such a house relative to those owned by neighbors. Frank uses the metaphor of the arms race to characterize conspicuous consumption, because it is motivated by a desire to keep up with the Joneses. He concludes that consumers in affluent societies would be more content, if less was spent on luxury goods, resulting in less of a need to work long hours and more time spent with families.

We agree. Pleasures, like all pleasurable emotions, tend to be short-lived. But whether satisfying transitory appetites is desirable or not depends on the context and a person's values. No one who claims to support a democratic society would deny people the right to make choices for themselves. But the real charge is against advertising with its assumed ability to create wants (see, for example, Galbraith, 1977). But wants cannot be created. There must be an underlying appetite for the product. Galbraith, like other economists before him, claimed that firms are less preoccupied with want-satisfying than with want-creating, which involves some element of manipulation. Galbraith sees corporations as a powerful force in shaping wants, arguing that the myth that holds that the great corporation is the puppet of the market, the powerless servant of the consumer, is one of the devices by which power is perpetuated.

The controversy over whether wants (market demand) can be created or molded at will is important (O'Shaughnessy, 1995). A firm that believes that wants can be created, or demand can be molded, is less concerned with discovering wants but will adopt something close to a promotion-cum-manipulation orientation. If the orientation is wrong, resources are misdirected. The assertion, however, assumes that consumers are motivationally empty until injected by marketers with wants created by advertising (Campbell, 1987). It seems truer to say that there are wants that are latent until activated by promotion. All persuasion, to be effective, taps into the target audience's motives. As Walter Reuther, the US automobile union leader, is once reputed to have said: 'You can automate the production of cars but you cannot automate the production of customers'.

Seeking Positional Goods for Social Status and Social Bonding

In a consumer society, consumers seek 'positional' goods to demonstrate group membership, to identify themselves and mark their position. With positional goods, satisfaction arises in large part from a product's scarcity and social exclusiveness (Hirsch, 1977). It is argued that advertising stimulates this perversion of values by dramatizing the satisfactions of positional goods and status; with an implicit claim that the advertiser can soothe the consumers' floating discontent at the deepest of levels through the ownership of goods.

This Baudrillard (1968) calls the ideology of consumption. As Holbrook and Hirschman (1993) remark, such an ideology holds that social meaning is attached to and communicated by commodities. In line with this, it is argued that accumulation, consumption and disposal become the core of existence to give life meaning: advertising in the aggregate is seen as a proselytisation for this ideology. The search, purchase, using and discarding of products become the great aim of life and an alternative self-articulation. As the close bonds of communities wither away, people survive the new order of weak communities by a continuous re-expression of self to transient audiences. They dress up, now as skiers who never ski, now as pilots who cannot fly, now as soldiers who never see army life, in a search for the expression of individualism bound up in a fantasy status. They discover community through the community of shared brands: brands link consumers via promotion to similar others. Branding pulls things together into one tangible attractive symbol, while advertisements differentiate the brands. On this reading, the hedonistic need satisfied by marketing is dramaturgical; a need to self-present in the theater of life, and to refine our act. The hedonistic pleasure satisfied is a need to be socially admired and envied, and to maintain a sense of connection.

The continual process of search, purchase, savoring, using and finally replacing goods is seen as masking what is ultimately a search for social bonds covering social integration, the display of power or status, and the attainment of friendship. For Gottdiener (1990) and others, social meaning is attached to and communicated by commodities. Schudson (1984) suggests that through consumption people seek social membership and social acceptance as much as anything else. Commodities become means for acquiring social ends such as love and friendship. Consumers seek, through symbolic material artifacts, what could be experienced in more satisfactory ways: all a consequence of the need for social communication in a rootless world. Marketing-driven hedonism is seen as a response to this need. As Fiske (1990) stresses, in line with Douglas and Isherwood (1979), in a world where appearances matter enormously, most cultural artifacts have a communication as well as a technological function, so possessions and acquisitions really count.

We argue that consumers do desire to be accepted by their social milieu, but also desire visibility and social status and positional goods help in this. If the search for status and power are base motives, they are also basic motives, which are pervasive throughout the animal kingdom. People in affluent democracies, whatever the education system, seek the symbols of status and power in their purchases and there is no way of denying them this choice without abandoning democracy itself. Marketing does not create these motives but, in recognizing them, serves them.

Consumers take their Identity from their Possessions

A postmodernist claim is that self-identity is no longer a matter of social ascription but individual choice. It is a short step from this to arguing that people take their self-identity from their possessions or at least their social self (Belk, 1988). This is a position well defended by Dittmar (1992), drawing on extensive social science findings. The movement is from ascribed to personally achieved identity (Belk, 1984). Dittmar views possessions as material symbols of identity; as expressive symbols of identity and as reflections of identity in terms of gender, and social-material status. This view of possessions and self-identity connects to positional goods, as both are quoted to explain a move away from assembly-line mass production to niche marketing.

There would be something wrong with society, if the whole of a person's self-identity were defined by his or her possessions. But it is a parochial view to equate self-identity with possessions. Self includes a life history (Schiffer, 1998). Many other factors enter into self-identity such as personal history, socio-economic status, religion, ethnicity, roles in life, job and so on. In fact, as Flanagan (1996) argues, the whole narrative of our lives and what concerns us enters into our self-identity. Self-identity is something more than the sum of our appetites. As Erving Goffman (1971) says, no one's self-identity is limited to a singular 'core image', as people have many different sides to their personalities, revealed on different occasions. This is not to deny that consumers use goods as a way to express some aspects of their social identity and to distinguish themselves from others 'in a world in which traditional social bonds and class boundaries are weakening' (Gronow, 1997).

With regard to the claim that self-identity is now more a matter of individual choice than social ascription, this ignores the fact that self-identity is not developed in a vacuum but is very much influenced by how others view us in social interactions. Similarly with possessions, there is a limit to the extent that consumers can express a completely distinct self-identity. There is the matter of time and financial resources while consumers, non-conforming to societal norms, may be conformative to the norms of subcultural groups. Subcultural social pressures are likely to produce a strong family resemblance in possessions among the members of the subgroup.

Consumption Cleavages Being Less Based on Social Class

Another claim is that consumption cleavages (social divisions in consumption) are becoming less based on social class than on differences in patterns of consumption. Clothes, for example, are less apt to reflect social class than personal choices. This is consistent with the earlier claim that the construction of self-identity is more a matter of personal choice than social class ascription. It suggests the declining importance of social classes.

If the importance of social class is declining, it is of considerable importance to marketing, since social class is considered vital in defining target audiences in advertising and in segmentation. Whether social class has significantly declined in importance for these purposes must, in the final analysis, be a matter for empirical inquiry. But there are strong reasons for doubt. When economic status varies widely among the citizens of a society (and it is very wide in Western societies), sharp divisions in social class inevitably exist, as people seek status and visibility in possessions that reflect income level.

More Commodification of Social Life

It is claimed that the market is extending its reach with more and more aspects of social life becoming commodified, that is, offered for sale. Everything from religion to government services is presented and segmented as various offerings from which the public is to choose; a distinct move away from the 'one size fits all' view. This is said to bring with it a move away from the welfare state and all public ownership that offers 'freebies'.

While there is truth in this, it is not clear how extensive it is. The evidence in support is mainly anecdotal, which gives no order of magnitude. In any case, many would welcome a move away from any welfare system that has come to be perceived as encouraging dependency and feckless behavior.

The Impact of Fantasy and Imagery in Influencing Buying

According to Campbell (1987), modern hedonism is characterized by day-dreams (fantasy), giving rise to illusions known to be false but felt to be true. Featherstone (1991) in a similar vein identifies three facets of consumption in the consumer society:

(1) that consumption is continuously encouraged as an inducement to work;
(2) that consumption patterns are a significant source of status differentiation; and
(3) that consumption is a source of fantasy and pleasure.

We agree that advertising attaches to brands culturally symbolic images in the hope that a fusion of the two enhances a brand's desirability. All consumer marketers emphasize the importance of symbolic meaning. As Eliade (1991, p. 168) says:

> We may even wonder whether the accessibility of Christianity may not be attributable in great measure to symbolism, whether the universal images it takes up in its turn have not considerably facilitated the diffusion of its message.

Baudrillard (1975, 1981) argues that, through the manipulation of the symbolic code, any object can take on any symbolic meaning regardless of its physical attributes. For Baudrillard the new electronic media introduce a world of pure simulacra, where the distinction between the 'real' world and images is eroded and where people are regarded as non-rational with an orientation toward instant gratification, feelings, emotions and the deviant.

The claim that consumers may be so immersed in the imagery that this becomes the reality for consumers is not backed by evidence. The fact that people often buy purely on the basis of brand image is no proof, since brand image acts as a summary evaluation, which can on occasions determine choice simply because it saves time. In any case, whatever symbolic code exists, it needs to be known (codified), that is, the relevant bits need to be identified in some way if a code is to be used by advertisers. Until then advertisers must rely on their own intuitions as to what is likely to symbolize what. Not all associations (however pleasant) are compelling and advertisers can seldom ensure in advance those that will be.

Privileging Ephemeral and Superficial Values

Critics see marketing as privileging the material surfaces of life . . . the ideology of consumption as a way of life, supported by a set of value perspectives . . . over the deeper things that dignify humanity. Self-identity, as we have seen, becomes the assemblage of possessions; signals to define status, social involvement and stylistic intelligence. An individual's intellect, wisdom, decency, erudition and personal accomplishment, it is claimed, do not figure in the advertising universe. Advertising concentrates on what we have, not what we are, in any profound sense.

More important, according to the critics, advertising speaks to current ephemeral values and the very latest in household knick-knacks that enunciate style over substance. In effect, advertising exhibits a cult of what is contemporary, the passing insubstantial style, the chic and the trendy, often clothed in a sort of pseudo-sophistication, a worldly know-knowingness. Certain personality characteristics are highlighted for approval such as being sexy, powerful, to be in control and, above all, 'cool'. Much advertising is about the loss and restoration of control (e.g. in love) via the agency of the product. Selfless deeds, dedication to community, sensitivity to the elderly and so on are conspicuous by their absence. Those human values which, it is claimed, advertising leaves out are as important as those which it leaves in. There are, for example, no references to religion, except humorously or satirically in the form of the genial sky pilot vicar, or to erudition, intellect, creativity – none of the corpus of human traits considered traditionally to ennoble mankind; nothing which reaches the higher octaves of spiritual and intellectual striving. On the other hand, bad habits are advocated with eloquence.

To critics, the values thus promoted by advertising celebrate narrow hedonism, because, while much differentiates us as individuals, lower order passions such as greed, lust and power are all we have in common. For Pollay (1986), advertising is a 'distorted mirror' in that it provides only reinforcement of shallow hedonistic values and thereby strengthens them and expands their domains of salience. This projection of hedonistic values, it is argued, is not something incidental to advertising, but central to advertising's ability to persuade. Schudson (1984) sees advertising as based on a kind of Utopianism characteristic of Soviet art or 'socialist realism', what he calls in contrast 'capitalist realism', an edited version of life based on the upbeat and stereotypical, which claims to picture reality not as it is, but as it should be, showing people only as incarnations of larger social categories. He quotes one study of 500 magazine advertisements in which couples were pictured. There are no old, poor, sick or unattractive couples in the advertisements. Along the lines of Campbell, it is thus claimed that advertising reflects not how people are acting, but their dreaming: advertising wraps up these dreams and sells them back to its target audience. For otherwise undifferentiated products, copywriters tend to converge, in various ways, on the idea of constructing illusions, images and fantasies round the product, and such projections are never value-free. When, as in many mature markets, technical and other performance factors such as service are all equal, image becomes the basis of differentiation, with the projection of these images tied to hedonistic values.

We agree that advertising seeks to persuade. All ways of promoting a brand are meant to persuade. This is because advertising is advocacy of the brand designed to influence buying behavior. If the provision of lots of accurate information helps in this advocacy role or is needed to ensure successful use of the product, such information will be provided. Sometimes in fact all that needs to be done in advertising is to provide a compelling logic as to why the brand is best for the function being served. More commonly, however, in persuading the consumer, there is a need to get the consumer on to the 'right wavelength', to have the right perspective. This changing of perspectives is never simply a matter of logic but of appeals to the imagination (e.g. to savor an experience with the product) and emotive words that resonate with the target audience. All persuaders need to put 'their best foot forward' and advertising is simply doing this. What there should be, however, is a way of reinforcing the 'will to be good' by ensuring that there are penalties for lying and misrepresentation.

Image-saturated Environment Pressing Consumers to Buy

Another focus by critics has been the sheer insistence and multiplication of marketing messages. To live in the West today, and increasingly in other parts of the world, is to inhabit a message-saturated environment. The claim is made that the aggregate effects of mass consumer messaging on this scale press consumers in a hedonistic direction. Some see advanced capitalist society as self-subverting, in effect needing to continually stimulate self-indulgence to expand market share and, in the process, undermining notions of self-discipline and self-denial that made advanced capitalism possible in the first place. What might appear threatening in a radical newspaper, left-wing poster or pornographic text is neutered by advertising, which has the ability to stylize and domesticate the perverse, bringing it into the cultural mainstream.

Marketing communications thus stand accused of creating strong social pressure to consume; that the icons of our age are manufactured by marketing's processes; that seductive images, designer labels, slick packaging, the product's self-proclamation as the gateway to a sophisticated lifestyle and so on constitute a live information system about what the élite have now become. By this argument, the social pressure to acquire is immense and, conversely, a marketing-arbitered social ecology, arousing envy among those who cannot purchase these things, and leading ultimately to increased criminality.

We agree that we live in a message-saturated environment concerned with exhortations to consume. But consumers are selective in what they perceive and tune out the vast majority of messages coming their way. Consumers attend to what concerns them. Advertising provides information and creates the initial awareness of innovative new products and services. If advertising were to disappear tomorrow, there would be a perception of loss, because, as with newspapers, advertising provides a sense of what is happening in the world, while many ads have intrinsic appeal, all of their own.

Globalization as Transmitting the Consumer Society

Hedonistic marketing, according to critics, bleaches out the indigenous cultures of traditional societies, emptying them of content and filling the vacuum with sensually glazed materialism. The advertising promise is of a costless cornucopia, a sensual nirvana, and it is marketing's disguise of the true cost of earning the delights it proffers that encourages the association made between marketing and hedonism. Marketing on this view, in its global expansion, is concerned with hedonistic appetite and its stimulation: hidden from view is the amount of work and skill necessary to pay for what is offered, or the social and emotional costs of indulging some of the desires that advertising summons forth.

A good deal has recently been written about global capitalism and the accompanying spread of the consumer society with its dysfunctional consequences, a by-product of a materialistic, throw-away transient society promoted by marketing. LaFeber (1999) quotes the case of Nike and the way it used Michael Jordan's celebrity status and the seductiveness of US culture to influence everything from eating habits, clothes, TV viewing and even language to push its products around the world. According to LaFeber, this globalization of the consumer society has had the unintended consequence, not only of undermining other cultures, but of strengthening anti-US feeling around the globe. Even if freely seduced, the seduced still feels hatred with the recognition that something has been lost, in this case, a dilution of culture. In a book, edited by Jameson and Miyochi (1999), contributors suggest that the global dominance of Western societies, with their ideology of consumerism, not only has been undermining foreign cultures but has led to a weakening of national governments in controlling both capital and the transnational corporations themselves. Thus the radical dynamism of global free markets is seen as sanitizing the authenticity of cultures and demolishing traditional authority structures, killing indigenous industries; the organizational form of this radical dynamism, the global corporation, is seen as an unchallenged extraterritorial force of immense power, switching manufacturing apparently at whim from country to country. And this is seen as being intimately connected with questions of equity, particularly the unfairness of the deal for poor countries. The paradigm case is the problem of treating AIDS in South Africa, given the monopolistic prices Western countries charge for their drugs. John le Carré's novel, *The Constant Gardener*, thus expounds the theme of pharmaceutical imperialism.

Pankaj Mishra (1999), while paying tribute to the deceased writer Nirad Chaudhuri, acknowledges that Hindu xenophobia flourishes in India but argues that the most dominant culture in India is made up of borrowings from the West. He claims that the main emblems of these borrowings are not Pascal or Mozart but MTV and Coca-Cola! Even countries that shout the loudest anti-US slogans still exhibit the iconography of consumer hedonism, McDonald's and all the designer labels. On the global scene the charge, too, against marketing is that it has fostered the wrong (i.e. hedonistic) values.

If a nation's culture is its total way of life: its institutions, values, ideas, art, music, literature and all the other socially constructed aspects of society (Kammen, 1999), then trade and all other interactions with foreign nations have always had an impact on culture. Without the export of technology, books and medicines from the industrialized West, countries around the world would be far more impoverished than they are today. Every nation benefits from the inventions and innovations of other nations. What is really at issue is a value judgment as to what is good for a nation and what is bad. This is a cultural issue, as culture reflects societal values. To the French, US computers are worthy of import but not US movies or fast food, as these undermine French culture, while the Anglicizing of the French language strikes at the most cherished value of all, French 'Frenchness'!

Many countries look at the USA as a mirror of their own future and worry that it will not be the dynamism of the USA that will be adopted but rampant individualism. It is easy to whip up feeling on this issue, given the speed with which ethnicity and chauvinism can be mobilized (Mayhew, 1997). In the shadow of globalization, as Crossette (1999) says, there is a revival of intense provincialism in unlikely places. However, Lal (1999) claims that non-Western countries such as those in Asia can import the best of US practices without undermining cultural values. Lal argues that the individualism and instrumental rationality that are the fountain of science in Western societies, have undermined the social values that held these societies together. The breakdown of family life and the general hedonism of consumerist culture are simply illustrative. Lal claims that such dysfunctional consequences need not arise in non-Western countries intent on scientific and technological progress. This is because, elsewhere in the world, cultures such as Hinduism, Islam and Confucianism are 'shame' cultures, where cultural mores are enforced by social pressure.

This is not a new claim. The difference between Western culture and that of Japan has often been seen in terms of the difference between a guilt and shame culture. In Japan the sense of shame has traditionally been strong and the radical act of hara-kiri or suicide is associated with it. The same goes for many other Asian cultures. In Urdu there are few words so heavily loaded as *sharam* (shame), except perhaps *izzat* (honor), which is reflective of cultural value priorities. Western cultures, Lal argues, are in contrast 'guilt' cultures. Guilt cultures work fine, while a belief in God and Christian teaching prevails but the move towards secular societies in the West has meant that feelings of guilt have begun to dissolve. In contrast, non-Western cultures can adopt the technology and science of modernity without diluting their own value systems, as conformity is brought about by shame not guilt.

While shame is a powerful emotion in Japan and in other Asian countries, it is also a strong emotion in the West. Elster (1999) is particularly persuasive on this. Elster gives the key role to shame in bringing about compliance with all social norms. For him social norms always operate through the emotions of shame and contempt. As he says, if shame is a negative emotion triggered by a belief about one's own character, the emotion of shame is not only *a* support of social norms but *the* support.

Similarly, in spite of all the efforts of psychological self-help books and the decline in religious observance, guilt has not gone away. These emotions simply get attached to new concerns brought about by cultural drift. It is far-fetched to explain the failings of Western societies purely on the decline of religious belief, as this assumes that religion rather than social conditioning is the major force in social behavior. Gellner (1994) reminds us of the comment made by Hume (1711–1776) that classical antiquity inculcated civil duty and social virtues conducive to communal wellbeing in the real world, while Christianity replaced this with an egotistical concern for personal salvation in another world. We can disagree with the Christianity part, while recognizing that the role of cultural indoctrination is ethical conditioning. Education in particular is important in increasing the likelihood that people will adhere to socially desirable goals and feel shame if they do not. Thus Hyman and Wright (1979) show the enduring effects of education on values that can be far removed from narrow hedonism. In any case, we cannot ignore causal social factors such as the pill, the social mobility of labor, and the social emancipation of women in making for a less culturally restrained society.

Micklethwait and Wooldrige (2000) look at globalization as the current economic reality and tabulate its flaws like the consumer society, while at the same time claiming that its superiority lies in its promise of increasing individual liberty. The authors draw on John Stuart Mill in arguing that globalization brings with it the liberal ideal of personal freedom by ultimately bringing about a world-wide open society. Theirs is a defensible position, though it is illicit to quote Mill in support, as Mill rejects any implication that his principles on personal liberty can be used to justify a universal free market. In his *On Liberty* (1859), Mill argued that all forms of trade are social acts which can harm the interests of others and so are other-regarding actions, with the consequence that his principle of liberty cannot be used in defense. On the other hand, we do find that global flows of information, made possible by the Internet, are enhancing personal liberty around the world. Global flows of capital, however, are more problematic. George Soros is reputed as saying that deregulated financial markets can behave more like wrecking-balls than pendulums. In other words, the picture is mixed. Certainly, it cannot be claimed that a democratic society equates with a market economy and that free markets (as is commonly claimed) are the engine for democracy, though many of us feel that it helps. There are winners and losers in the wake of globalization. Some of those winners are the wretched of the earth. Globalization has also meant more freedom of information and its development could contribute to the sum of human freedom. Moreover, the displacement of cultures is not necessarily true: new artefacts, new product forms do not necessarily banish old cultures and their forms, but are merely absorbed by them, interpreted within the parameters of the particular culture.

Hedonism and the Pleasure Motive Revisited

Narrow hedonism is but one among many motives for human action: it would be strange therefore if it were the only motive for marketing to tap. Hedonism is one of those simple-sounding concepts that tends to remain unanalyzed in debates. Upon analysis, the concept is rather elusive. What, for example, is the role of altruism? What if human beings receive pleasure largely through indirect ways, say, through fantasy? Those seeking to nuance and qualify the notion of hedonism in effect considerably qualify the responsibility of marketing for much of that hedonism: hedonism becomes less negatively charged as a moral concept and marketing is seen as less blameworthy.

Csikszentmihalyi (2000) argues that humans have a need to keep consciousness in an ordered state and this experiential need to keep consciousness tuned is what influences a good deal of consumer behavior. Sometimes it does not matter what we are shopping for – the point is to shop for anything regardless, as consuming is one way to respond to the void in consciousness, when there is nothing else to do. This is something different from narrow hedonistic shopping.

Campbell (1987) argues that human motivation involves not only self-interest but perceptions of moral obligations, since embarking on any action has to be justified to the consumer's moral self. We have a sense of ourselves as moral agents. Morally idealized self-images can be sources of pleasure. Similarly, there is aesthetic pleasure. It is by no means demonstrated that the pleasures associated with narrow hedonism are what life is about or what people really want most of all. This in fact is known as the hedonistic paradox, which is the paradox that the deepest pleasures in life, such as maternal love, come about from undertaking actions for reasons other than pleasure. 'Happiness' encompasses something broader than pleasure and it is happiness which is the more natural end of human activities. Seeking pleasure directly is commonly not the best way to achieve happiness.

Csikszentmihalyi (1990), in his discussion of the attainment of what he calls 'flow' (a state of contentment or happiness), finds it necessary to distinguish 'pleasure' from 'enjoyment'. Csikszentmihalyi views enjoyment as optimal experience and distinguishes this enjoyment from mere pleasure, which he sees as resulting from a reflex response built into the genes for the preservation of the species. Just as the pleasure obtained from eating when hungry ensures that the body will get the nourishment it needs, the pleasure that arises from meeting social expectations is related to the continuance of the 'tribe' for collective security. Though pleasurable experiences can on occasions be optimal experiences (enjoyment), pleasure is generally evanescent. Here we have an echo of Campbell. Only if the pleasurable experience involves intensity of attention, sense of achievement and psychological growth, does pleasure become enjoyment.

Rationalizing (non-narrow) hedonism has most relevance for marketing. Gosling (1969) points out that a hedonist, contrary to popular interpretations, does not claim that all actions are simply undertaken for pleasure but that, if an action is voluntary, the final reason for it will have some reference to pleasure. For Gosling, this gets round the paradox of hedonism, since he denies that the hedonist necessarily seeks pleasure directly in all his or her actions. He makes the nice distinction between hedonism, defined as the claim that people ought to pursue the achievements they contemplate with pleasure and the achievements they think will give them pleasure. Pleasure is a way of attending, not a sort of feeling, as most views on hedonism seem to assume. This is very much tied to Campbell's (1987) thesis that the modern hedonist obtains his or her pleasure from anticipating novel products as offering the hope of realizing some of the idealized pleasures imagined in daydreams (fantasies). However, since reality falls short of the dream, disappointment results. It is the contemplation of anticipated buys that is so pleasurable.

For Gosling, doing things for pleasure means doing things into which you can put your heart and soul without reservations. This implies that, for long-term success, marketing must aim at getting target audiences:

- to contemplate buying with pleasure; and
- to buy without reservations.

Anticipation, attending to and contemplation are conceptually related. Anticipating implies or extends into attending to and contemplation. From a marketing point of view, what both Campbell and Gosling are saying is that marketing should arouse or intensify the anticipation, attending to, contemplation in fantasizing about the product (including services/experiences), as this feeds the urge to buy.

On Gosling's view (and Campbell's) the consumer can contemplate with pleasure upholding social norms or some system of uplifting values in buying and still be acting in a hedonistic way. This claim is in direct opposition to what most of the critics of the consumer society say with their focus on narrow hedonism.

Is Marketing Really Responsible for the Hedonist Life Style?

There are many rival explanations for the Western hedonistic life style, made possible by increasing affluence. Bauman (1999) claims that pervasive insecurity, uncertainty and danger, plus the decline of the family, mean that people lose their traditional informational anchors and, as a consequence, turn to a hedonistic lifestyle. After all, the fact that society is more and more organized to offer more variety and individual choice for self-expression should, on the surface, incur no criticism, unless the aim (one that can be defended) is a more world-wide redistribution of wealth. However, what is being typically argued is that marketing encourages hedonism by creating wants. The claim that wants can be created, we have argued earlier, assumes that consumers are motivationally empty until injected by marketers with wants created by advertising. This is nonsense. We simply come to see what some product might do to enrich our lives. In other words, consumers have latent wants which can be activated.

In reversal theory, pioneered by Apter (1989), people, at any one time, can be in either a telic or a paratelic mode. In a paratelic mode people are in a mood to seek excitement to avoid boredom, while in a telic mode people focus on goals to avoid anxiety. Although people move from a telic to a paratelic mode and vice versa, it is possible to get locked into one state or the other. To be locked into a paratelic mode means to focus on pleasurable (exciting) experiences, not on any set of goals. Although, in a telic mode, people seek to avoid anxiety as being painful, it is not a mode associated with hedonism. In other words, reversal theory claims that narrow hedonistic pleasure-seeking is reserved for the paratelic mode. Reversal theory demonstrates that our lives are by no means concerned with just narrow hedonistic pleasure-seeking. Narrow hedonistic pursuits do not dominate our lives.

Many of the criticisms of marketing-induced hedonism are exaggerated. The hedonism that permeates society, the 'culture of narcissism', is viewed low on a scale of values, but it is often not a question of worse but only of different values. This is not to underwrite the relativism of postmodernism but simply to acknowledge that hedonism will characterize any affluent society where there is freedom of choice. As Posner (1999, p. 14) says:

> Unless we want to go the way of Iran, we shall not be able to return to the era of premarital chastity, low divorce, stay-at-home moms, pornography-free media and the closeting of homosexuals and adulterers . . . But it would be more accurate to speak not of a cultural revolution but of a transformation in morals and manners resulting from diverse material factors that include changes in the nature of work, growing prosperity, advances in reproductive technology, increasing ethnic diversity and a communications revolution that has created a far better informed population.

The whole attack on marketing promotions rests on a passive/reactive view of the consumer: a more precise image of marketing's impact would be that of negotiated meaning or co-production, rather than a hypodermic or stimulus-response model. Consumers are hard to persuade. They have a great ability to filter out the siren voices that beckon. Materialism and sex were not invented by consumer marketing: societies were highly materialistic before its advent. Moreover, marketing, as a set of techniques, is open to everybody. Religious leaders who complain about shopping-malls on an epic scale and the 'shop till you drop' culture have seized on the same techniques themselves to promote the gospel and have been equally accused of manipulation (Moore, 1994).

Marketers often chose hedonistic appeals, but marketing in itself is simply an orientation and a set of tools that are value-neutral and can be used to proselytize any perspective. Critics of marketing-hedonism, such as media critics generally, are apt to take marketing imagery and messages literally, and techniques such as content analysis reinforce this literalness of interpretation. There is so much in marketing promotions – product-irony, self-parody, subversion – which eludes these techniques of analysis, especially since it is contained in the surface decoration of texts or in the kind of paralanguage discussed by Cook (1992). What marketing often gives us is less a celebration of hedonism or an arousal of sensual and material passions that can be conscripted into the process of consumer stimulation, than something more complex, namely, the tongue-in-cheek invitation, the spoof, the bizarre and the anarchic. In fact the attitude to hedonism contained in most advertisements is at least ambivalent: not a rejection, but by no means an explicit, roaring endorsement either.

It is not clear what the alternative to the consumer society is when people become relatively affluent and seek freedom of choice. Bauman (1990) argues that a communist planned economy can only understand and cater to the logic of needs, not that of desires, and argues that the main reason for the collapse of the East European socialist states was the incompatibility of socialism with a modern society. Communist states could satisfy people's basic needs but could not contend with the more segmented and refined demands of consumers, as their discretionary incomes increased.

There are costs as well as benefits attached to every type of society and the consumer society is no exception. In the USA, the organization called 'Buy Nothing Day' (BND) argues that over-consumption is wrecking the environment and dragging down the quality of life (*The Economist*, 2000a). *The Economist* points out that personal borrowings in the USA went up from 26 per cent of personal income in 1985 to 34 per cent in 2000 and the number of bankruptcies have quadrupled over the same period. Marketing communications are not entirely blameless for this. However, marketing can in fact be used to reduce and not just increase consumption (Kotler, 1972). There is much waste. Susan Strasser (1999) talks of the 'disposable society', how affluent societies dispose of perfectly serviceable products, simply because newer models have come along. Strasser documents the cost of this waste. Marketing promotes psychological obsolescence, where the new models become, through promotion, a celebration of the modern way. Finally, Csikszentmihalyi (2000) quotes a number of studies showing that, beyond a low threshold, material does not correlate with subjective wellbeing. He goes on to say that research indicates that excessive concern with financial success and material values is associated with less satisfaction with life. In fact excessive concern for material goals is a sign of dissatisfaction with life: people report being happier in life when they are actively involved with a challenging task and less happy when they are passively consuming goods or entertainment. However, it is the consumer society which offers choices, convenience, the reduction in chores – and the excitement of contemplating buying of the new. Even the promotion of psychological obsolescence is the spur behind the innovation that, in particular, characterizes the US social scene.

Conclusion

Whatever influence marketing has had on the creation of a consumerism tied to the narrowest form of hedonism, it has been in the role more of facilitator than of manufacturer. If someone were to insist that we name a single culprit, it would be the development of a strong value orientation that puts unrestrained freedom to the forefront. Consumers, like people generally in Western societies, really do want to feel unrestrained by the social norms of the past and demand freedom to 'do their own thing'. As Kass and Kass (2000) argue, the more people grow to love their freedom, so as to regard it as the defining feature of the life style, the more they come to view themselves as having no obligation to do other than self-indulge, as long as it is a self-regarding action. But consumer values can change, as can the weighting of values. It may be that society's current values will change but the change must come from people themselves, as coercion only achieves minimum compliance and is incompatible with the value of liberty and freedom of choice. Marketing seldom tries to change values altogether, though it may seek to change value judgements through changing perspectives as to what is in line with values. Marketing can be enlisted to oppose the habits and addictions it is accused of sustaining. *The Economist* (2000b) records the enormous success of a shock advertising campaign in reducing smoking among the young in California; the point is significant, since one of the gravest charges laid at marketing's door is its world-proselytization of nicotine addiction. As a medium it is quite a mercenary to anyone who can hire it.

The arguments denouncing hedonism-consumerism represent a gross simplification of complex issues. Marketing does not create or invent wants but merely surfaces them: materialism became part of the human condition long before the first advertising executive. Man has always been, in all societies, materialistic but, in former days, poverty meant the absence of ability and opportunity to indulge in a hedonistic lifestyle. The global economy underpinning material advance has existed in prototype form for centuries.

Thousands of Roman artifacts have been discovered in India: the Phoenicians traded everywhere, and Japanese junks first visited South America in the early seventeenth century.

We said earlier that many of the assertions made by critics are matters of empirical inquiry. It follows that a limitation of this paper is the absence of relevant data. This would seemingly point to future research areas. But such research pre-supposes that many of the concepts used in the debate, like hedonism itself, are uncontroversial and easy to operationalize and measure. This is unlikely to be so. Similarly, there would be problems in obtaining relevant samples of consumers and seeking to gauge motivations and beliefs. On the other hand, as this paper shows, critics need not be answered by empty rhetoric but argument that draws on social science and our collective experience.

References

Adamson, W. (1980), *Hegemony and Revolution: Antonio Gramsci's Political and Cultural Theory*, University of California Press, Berkeley, CA.

Apter, M.J. (1989), *Reversal Theory*, Routledge, London.

Baritz, L. (1989), *The Good Life: The Meaning of Success for the American Middle Class*, Knopf, New York, NY.

Baudrillard, J. (1968), *Les Systems des Objets*, Gallimard, Paris.

—— (1975), *The Mirror of Production*, tr. Poster, M., Telos Press, St Louis, MO.

—— (1981), *The Critique of the Political Economy of the Sign*, tr. Levin, C., Telos Press, St Louis, MO.

Bauman, Z. (1990), "Communism: a postmortem", *Praxis International*, Vol. 10 No. 3–4, pp. 185–92.

—— *In Search of Politics*, Polity Press, Oxford.

Belk, R.W. (1984), "Cultural and historical differences in concept of self and their effects on attitudes towards having and giving", in Kinnear, T.C. (Ed.) *Advances in Consumer Research*, Vol. 11, Association for Consumer Research, Provo, UT, pp. 753–60.

—— "Materialism: trait aspects of living in the material world", *Journal of Consumer Research*, Vol. 12 No. 3, pp. 265–80.

—— "Possession and the extended self", *Journal of Consumer Research*, Vol. 15 No. 2, pp. 139–68.

Best, S. and Kellner, D. (1997), *The Postmodern Turn*, Guilford Press, New York, NY.

Bourdieu, P. (1984), *Distinction: A Social Critique of the Judgement of Taste*, Routledge & Kegan Paul, London.

Brown, S. (1995), *Postmodern Marketing*, Routledge, London.

Campbell, C. (1987), *The Romantic Ethic and the Spirit of Modern Consumerism*, Basil Blackwell, Oxford.

Cook, G. (1992), *The Discourse of Advertising*, Routledge, London.

Crossette, B. (1999), "Who needs anyone?", *The New York Times*, Sunday October 17.

Csikszentmihalyi, M. (1990), *Flow: The Psychology of Optimal Experience*, Harper & Row, New York, NY.

—— (2000), "The cost and benefits of consuming", *Journal of Consumer Research*, Vol. 27, September, pp. 267–72.

Dittmar, H. (1992), *The Social Psychology of Material Possessions*, St Martin's Press, New York, NY.

Douglas, M. and Isherwood, B. (1979), *The World of Goods*, Basic Books, New York, NY.

The Economist (2000a), "Baa or buy", November 18, p. 82.

The Economist (2000b), "Smoking: just say no", December 9, p. 72.

Eliade, M. (1991), *Images and Symbols: Studies in Religious Symbolism*, Princeton University Press, Princeton, NJ, p. 168.

Elster, J. (1999), *Alchemies of the Mind: Rationality and the Emotions*, Cambridge University Press, Cambridge.

Featherstone, M. (1991), *Consumer Culture and Postmodernism*, Sage, Beverly Hills, CA.

Fiske, J. (1990), *Introduction to Communication Studies*, Routledge, London.

Flanagan, O. (1996), *Self-Expressions*, Oxford University Press, New York, NY.

Foxall, G. (1996), *Consumers in Context*, Routledge, London.

Frank, R.H. (1988), *Passions within Reasons*, W.W. Norton, New York, NY.

—— (1999), *Luxury Fever*, Free Press, New York, NY.

Galbraith, J.K. (1977), "UGE: the inside story", *Horizon*, March.

Gellner, E. (1994), *Conditions of Liberty*, Penguin Books, London, p. 44.

Goffman, E. (1971), *The Presentation of Self in Everyday Life* Penguin, Harmondsworth.

Gosling, J.C.B. (1969), *Pleasure and Desire*, Clarendon Press, Oxford.

Gottdiener, M. (1990), "Hegemony and mass culture: a semiotic approach", *American Journal of Sociology*, Fall, pp. 979–1001.

Gramsci, A. (1971), *Selections from Prison Notebooks*, International Publishers, New York, NY.

Gronow, J. (1997), *The Sociology of Taste*, Routledge, London, p. 5.

Hirsch, F. (1977), *Social Limits to Growth*, Routledge & Kegan Paul, London.

Holbrook, M.B. and Hirschman, E.C. (1993), *The Semiotics of Consumption*, Mouton de Gruyer, New York, NY.

Hyman, H. and Wright, C.R. (1979), *Education's Lasting Influence on Values*, University of Chicago Press, Chicago, IL.

Jameson, F. and Miyochi, M. (1999) (Eds), *The Cultures of Globalization*. Duke University Press, Durham, NC.

Kagan, J. (1999), *Three Seductive Ideas*, Harvard University Press, Cambridge, MA.

Kammen, M. (1999), *American Culture, American Tastes: Social Change and the 20th Century*, Knopf, New York, NY.

Kass, A. and Kass, L.R. (2000), *Wing to Wing, Oar to Oar*, University of Notre Dame Press, Notre Dame, IN.

Kotler, P. (1972), "A generic concept of marketing", *Journal of Marketing*, Vol. 36, April, pp. 46–54.

LaFeber, W. (1999), *Michael Jordan and the New Global Capitalism*, Norton & Company, New York, NY.

Lal, D. (1999), *Unintended Consequences: The Impact of Factor Endowments, Culture, and Politics on Long-run Economic Performance*, MIT Press, Boston, MA.

Lyon, D. (1994), *Postmodernity*, Open University Press, Buckingham, UK.

McCartney, J. (2000), "Taylor's lament", *Sunday Telegraph*, December 10.

Marcuse, H. (1964), *One-Dimensional Man*, Beacon Press, Boston, MA.

Mayhew, L.H. (1997), *The New Public*, Cambridge University Press, Cambridge.

Micklethwait, J. and Wooldrige, A. (2000), *A Future Perfect: The Challenge and Hidden Promise of Globalization*, Heinemann, London and New York, NY.

Mishra, P. (1999), "Nirad Chaudhuri", *New York Review*, September 23.

Moore, R.L. (1994), *Selling God*, Oxford University Press, New York, NY and Oxford.

O'Shaughnessy, J. (1995), *Competitive Marketing*, Routledge, London and New York, NY.

Pollay, R.W. (1986), "The distorted mirror: reflections on the unintended consequences of advertising", *Journal of Marketing*, April, pp. 18–36.

Posner, R.A. (1999), "The moral minority", *The New York Times* Book Review, December 19, p. 14.

Rawls, J. (1972), *A Theory of Justice*, Oxford University Press, New York, NY.

Rohatyn, D. (1990), "The (mis)information society: an analysis of the role of propaganda in shaping consciousness", *Bulletin of Science, Technology and Society*, Vol. 10 No. 2, pp. 77–85.

Rosenau, P.M. (1992), *Postmodernism and the Social Sciences*, Princeton University Press, Princeton, NJ.

Schiffer, F. (1998), *Of Two Minds: The Revolutionary Science of Dual-Brain Psychology*, The Free Press, New York, NY.

Schudson, M. (1984), *Advertising, the Uneasy Persuasion*, Basic Books, New York, NY.

Strasser, S. (1999), *Waste and Want: A Social History of Trash*, Henry Holt, New York, NY.

12
Antiglobal Challenges to Marketing in Developing Countries: Exploring the Ideological Divide*

Terrence H. Witkowski

California State University

ABSTRACT *Antiglobalization critics have accused marketing in developing countries of undermining local cultures, placing intellectual property rights ahead of human rights, contributing to unhealthy dietary patterns and unsafe food technologies, and promoting unsustainable consumption. Following a brief review of the history of development theory and practice, the author describes these four challenges and presents rebuttals, drawing from the philosophy of marketing. Subsequent sections explore some areas of similarity between antiglobal and marketing thought, as well as some further ideological differences.*

I n recent years, a burgeoning political movement has developed a wide-ranging critique of the theory, institutions, and practices of economic globalization. This ideology, prominently represented by the International Forum on Globalization (IFG) (Cavanagh and Mander 2002), objects to privatization of public services and commodification of the global (atmosphere and oceans) and community (local water and biota) commons.[1] It fears the effects of "hypergrowth" on the environment, rampant

---

* Article originally published in the *Journal of Public Policy and Marketing* (2005); **24(1)** (Spring): 7–23. Reproduced by permission of the American Marketing Association.

consumerism on the social fabric, and cultural homogenization on diversity everywhere. It finds regional trade agreements, such as the North American Free Trade Agreement, and world trade and development bodies, such as the World Trade Organization (WTO), the World Bank, and the International Monetary Fund, undemocratic and slanted toward business interests. The Forum and other critics harbor strong reservations about international corporations as legal entities and voice great skepticism about free trade and the uncontrolled movement of investment capital into smaller, poorer countries. Above all, antiglobalism despairs over the continuing level of poverty and growing inequality in the world and roundly condemns the hypocrisy of rich countries that preach open markets while protecting their own workers and farmers and subsidizing their own corporations. The antiglobal political agenda has been forcefully stated through street protests, press coverage, seminars and conferences, books and journals, and Internet Web sites.

Antiglobalization philosophy deems marketing strategies and systems – brands and advertising, franchised distribution, and mass media – to be especially problematic (Jameson 2000; Johansson 2004; Klein 1999) and alleges that marketing has had negative influences on developing countries' quality of life (Ger 1992; Ger and Belk 1996; Kilbourne, McDonagh, and Prothero 1997).[2] In this view, marketing does not always serve the needs of poor people, poor countries, and indigenous cultures. For example, ill-conceived campaigns, such as the now infamous promotion of Nestlé's infant formula in the 1970s to mothers who were too impoverished and inadequately informed to use it properly, can harm consumers directly. Advertising and other elements of the marketing mix can have more indirect but equally serious consequences by encouraging standards of consumption to rise more quickly than incomes. Dissatisfaction and dysfunctional behavior often result (Ger 1997; United Nations Development Programme 1998).

Such appraisals should not be surprising, because the theoretical assumptions and political implications of antiglobalism contrast with those of marketing thought.[3] Whereas much antiglobal commentary draws from Marxist ideas (The Economist 2002b), marketing has deep intellectual roots in neoclassical economics (Shaw and Jones 2005; Wilkie and Moore 2003) with its emphasis on limited government regulation, the rule of law, and the free international movement of goods, services, and capital. Marketing has flourished under capitalism, and its teachings are naturally sympathetic to the creation of markets for allocating resources and organizing society. Whereas antiglobal policy recommendations typically lean toward collectivist solutions to social problems, including economic development, marketing theory adheres to the philosophies of individualism and utilitarianism. Marketing asserts consumer sovereignty as its most fundamental principle, and its texts tout consumer satisfaction as the primary goal. The less affluent countries have hundreds of millions of consumers, many with substantial discretionary income (The Economist 2003a; Prahalad and Hammond 2002). In the marketing worldview, state-of-the-art strategy and tactics can help satisfy the needs of emerging mass markets at a profit, and their continuing economic growth offers the prospect of even larger returns in the future. Marketing theory is compatible with development through private initiative and with government policies that foster economic freedom (Heritage Foundation 2004).

Antiglobal opinions about marketing in developing countries deserve close scrutiny. First, in general, the antiglobal program, which is championed by an international cadre of labor, environmental, religious, and left-of-center interests, has lofty purposes.[4] It emphasizes the needs of the weak and poverty stricken and finds inequality within and across countries to be shameful and in need of remedy. These ideals are not necessarily inconsistent with those of most marketing academics and managers. Indeed, advancing the economic development of poor countries is a major world policy objective and a profound intellectual challenge. Second, antiglobal criticism may stimulate new thinking that improves the relationships among corporate marketing, macromarketing systems, and economic and social development. The marketing literature has a long history of incorporating ideas from other disciplines. Third, whether and to what extent marketing practice may actually be deleterious to the interests of the poor, millions of people throughout the world believe this to be so. It would be foolish to ignore this opinion and fail to understand its underlying dynamics and political implications.

Among the many charges commonly made by antiglobalization writers, four are central to an assessment of marketing in developing countries:

- Marketing undermines local cultures.
- Marketing places intellectual property (IP) rights ahead of human rights.
- Marketing contributes to unhealthy dietary patterns and unsafe food technologies.
- Marketing promotes unsustainable consumption.

I have selected these particular challenges from the broader critique because they are closely linked to the effects of marketing activities, have been widely discussed, and are of current interest. Marketing managers have less control over other important issues. Some allegations, such as increases in local pollution caused by outsourcing production to countries with less stringent environmental regulations or the exploitation of poor country laborers, particularly women, children, and migrants who are working in sweat-shop conditions, are more properly questions of manufacturing, human resources management, and corporate social responsibility. The downsides of massive capital outflows and ruinous debt loads, often resulting from corrupt and irresponsible governments' excessive borrowing, are largely financial, political, and moral matters. Finally, trade agreement constraints on the exercise of national sovereignty and the sense and scope of democratic control (Bhagwati 2004) are more legal and legislative problems than marketing problems.

In this article, I adapt Singer's (2002) analytical approach. For each of the four challenges, I present a summary of the antiglobalization position, followed by counter-arguments that draw from the core political philosophy that is embedded in mainstream marketing thought. Next, I explore some areas of theoretical compatibility – consumer agency, social marketing, and customer orientation – and then analyze how the explosive combination of U.S. global marketing and rising anti-Americanism may be exacerbating the ideological divide. However, before I examine the four challenges and the other issues, some background in the recent political and intellectual history of economic development is necessary.

Three Eras in the History of Development Thought

Changing political environments and ideological trends have greatly influenced marketing in developing countries. Development history over the past sixty years can be divided into three eras: 1945–1979, 1979–1999, and 1999–today. The end of World War II is a good place to begin because it meant the resumption of more open trade and investment relations, the beginning of the end of Western colonization, the creation of many new but poor countries, and the founding of important global development organizations, including the United Nations, the World Bank, and the International Monetary Fund. The other two chronological divisions, 1979 and 1999, are also based on important political events and shifting ideological tides, namely, China's rejection of Maoism and the advent of mass antiglobalization protests. Admittedly, this periodization scheme may be a little presumptuous because the history it organizes is rather recent and the time spans are relatively short (Hollander et al. 2005). That said, the current approach should serve at least as a useful narrative framework.

1945–1979: Era of State-Directed Development

From 1945 until 1979, the preponderance of development thought and policy favored industrialization through government intervention. Influenced by the success of the Soviet Union in becoming a superpower, most third-world countries adopted local variations on the theme of state-directed development. Governments would control the major industries and infrastructure, the "commanding heights" of the economy (Lindsey 2002; Yergin and Stanislaw 2002). The largest developing country, China, confiscated private property and instituted Stalinist-inspired central planning to achieve its economic transformation. India adopted a democratic form of government, but it too pursued policies of socialism and centralization to the point at which eventually a "permit raj" enwrapped private initiative and business within an enormous, stifling bureaucracy. Many countries nationalized the property of Western foreign investors. Leaders, such as Burma's U Nu, Chile's Salvador Allende, Indonesia's Sukarno, and Uganda's Milton Obote, nationalized British, American, and Dutch enterprises (Chua 2004). Thus, different manifestations of state-dominated economic development became the norm throughout Africa, the Middle East, and Latin America.

However, not all countries took this path. Hong Kong thrived under laissez-faire capitalism (known locally as "positive nonintervention" by the government) that emphasized light manufacturing for export and strong financial and business service sectors (Hung 1984). In the 1960s, after a decade of failed import-substituting industrialization, Taiwan and South Korea also adopted export-led growth strategies, albeit with more trade protection than Hong Kong (Cohn 2003). However, such cases were few, and development theories of industrialization through economic protectionism and government ownership prevailed.

Dependency theories, or the historical structuralist perspective, identified the source of third-world problems in North–South linkages, wherein the terms of trade favored the finished goods made by advanced industrial states of the "core" over the raw materials and agricultural products of the "periphery" (Cohn 2003). To break exploitative linkages and foster autonomy, "import substitution" programs imposed punitive tariffs and other trade and investment barriers on foreign firms to protect domestic infant industries. Public enterprises in a variety of forms would serve as the engines of modernization, champions of national sovereignty, and providers of social welfare services (Lindsey 2002; Yergin and Stanislaw 2002). These policies made eminent sense within the larger political context, because many developing countries had just shaken off their colonial masters and wanted to control their own destinies. Better yet, these approaches appeared to work. Latin America, India, and a few African countries, such as Ghana, registered healthy rates of growth during the 1950s and 1960s (Cohn 2003).

Marketing activity was considered mostly irrelevant to such inward-oriented supply creation: "The general view of theorists and practitioners was that the marketing system, by definition, must follow the development of the industrial and agricultural sectors. Marketing also will automatically distribute this production if and when it becomes available" (Klein and Nason 2001, p. 265). Government officials and international aid specialists failed to consider marketing as a catalyst in development (Duhaime, McTavish, and Ross 1985). Moreover, marketing was sometimes considered potentially detrimental because of parasitic, predatory intermediaries who often came from ethnic minorities (Dholakia and Dholakia 1984; Kaynak 1986). Chua (2004) contends that nominally socialist policies have long been used as a cover for seizing the property of market-dominant minorities, such as the Chinese in Southeast Asia, who control an outsized proportion of developing country business and wealth.

1979–1999: Era of Development Through Neoliberalism and Globalization

The early successes of state intervention and protectionist barriers had begun to stall in the 1970s. Neglect of agriculture led to food crises in 1972–1973, and the energy crisis instigated by the Organization of Petroleum Exporting Countries added further external stresses. Moreover, attempts at industrialization foundered because of a lack of capital and advanced technology (Cohn 2003). The reforms that Deng Xiaoping presented to China in 1978 and 1979 marked a turning point for development thought and practice. Mao's experiments with utopian socialism had simply not done much to help the Chinese people improve their standard of living. Beginning with agriculture, "pragmatism" and "results" would be the new watchwords. As the payoff for China became so spectacular in terms of unprecedented economic growth, vast inflows of foreign direct investment, and, arguably, renewed cultural vitality, policy-makers in many countries experimented with economic liberalization. Inspired by Ronald Reagan and Margaret Thatcher, neoliberalism flourished in the 1980s and then found even more adherents after the fall of Communism in Central and Eastern Europe. In India, Southeast Asia, and Latin America, the policies that dependency theorists advocated were being abandoned in favor of privatization, markets, and free trade (Cohn 2003; Lindsey 2002; Yergin and Stanislaw 2002).

Between 1979 and 1999, the ascendancy of neoliberal thought and policy was reinforced by the apparent successes and future promise of "globalization," the myriad processes of economic, political, and cultural integration that were gaining momentum in much of the world. Trade figures soared, stock markets rose, and the *United Nations Human Development Index* showed improvements for the large majority of all people, including a majority of the people of developing countries (United Nations Development Programme 2004). On the marketing side, global products and brands, retail chains and store formats, and advertising and other mass communication became increasingly prominent and served new markets with rising spending power. Business writers bubbled with enthusiasm. Caslione and Thomas (2000) used the freighted term "global manifest destiny" to describe the inevitable economic integration of all humankind. Thomas Friedman (1999) wrote about shared consumer cultures unifying the world and preventing war.

In academia, the study of global business became more fashionable, a trend encouraged by the accrediting body now known as the Association to Advance Collegiate Schools of Business. In marketing, sales of international texts boomed, and several new journals were founded, including *International Marketing Review* (1984), *Journal of International Consumer Marketing* (1988), and *Journal of International Marketing* (1993). The marketing professoriate became increasingly confident about the potential contributions of their field to world development (see, e.g., Cundiff 1982; Duhaime, McTavish, and Ross 1985; Kotler 1988; Savitt 1988; Wood and Vitell 1986), and by the late 1990s, some even believed that applying strategic market management could become a key factor in building national wealth (Kotler, Jatusripitak, and Maesincee 1997). This work was largely based on different versions of modernization theory, all of which assume that third-world development depends on the adoption of the institutions and values of Western society (Joy and Wallendorf 1996). Levitt's (1983) seminal article, "The Globalization of Markets," proclaimed that technology was driving consumers toward the same goals, making the world into a single marketplace. This view provided a rationale for more globally standardized products that would reap the benefits of scale and scope economies (Johansson 2004).

Since 1999: Era of Antiglobal Backlash

However, not everyone benefited from neoliberal globalization policies. Many of the poorest countries were simply left out of the virtuous cycle of economic, social, and political development. All of the post-Communist countries of Central and Eastern Europe found the creation of free market economies and better living standards to be more difficult than expected. As happened in Southeast Asia in 1997, investment capital proved skittish, and the rapid withdrawal of large amounts could cause serious social hardship and disruption. Within countries such as Mexico, which had eagerly signed on to trade agreements, the forces of global competition inevitably created losses within some groups, such as small farmers, who could not compete with their state-subsidized, agribusiness competitors to the north. In other cases, autocratic governments suppressed democracy in favor of "crony capitalism," which successfully attracted development loans and foreign investments and produced nominally good macro results. However, although klepto-crats, such as Indonesia's General Suharto and his family – along with much of the Chinese minority – prospered greatly, the bulk of the indigenous (or *pribumi*, "of the soil") population had relatively little to show, at least by comparison (Chua 2004).

Criticism of corporate-driven globalization had been in the air for years (Bhagwati 2004), fed in part by the influential, postcolonial writings of the late Edward Said (1979, 1984) and other "poco" theorists. The term "antiglobalization" became well known worldwide following the heated demonstrations at the November 1999 WTO meeting – the "battle in Seattle" – and many such subsequent confabs. The general slowdown of the world economy in 2001 and 2002 may have further inflamed protectionist sentiments that challenged the rosy neoliberal worldview. Once again, there had been an ideological reversal of fortune, and as of this writing, neoliberalism seems increasingly to be on the defensive. Antiglobal, nongovernmental organizations have been adept at using the Internet to spread their message and mobilize protesters. Furthermore, at the September 2003 WTO ministerial meeting in Cancun, developing countries accused rich countries of supporting free trade for their own exports, while hypocritically protecting their own agricultural and textile industries.

Antiglobal thinking has sometimes been criticized for being too "anti" and for not having worked out an alternative to the present economic order (*The Economist* 2002b, c). Borrowing an analytical habit from the Marxist tradition, the antiglobalization movement takes a critical but sometimes impractical approach to social problems. Antiglobalism often verges toward the utopian. Ger's (1997) essay on human development and humane consumption advocates a selfless "love culture" as an alternative to self-interested "enterprise culture" and hopes for the emergence of "caring and aesthetic firms." Jameson's (2000, p. 68) dreams for perfection are even more unabashed:

> For the moment, we can use the word "utopian" to designate whatever programmes and representations express, in however distorted or unconscious a fashion, the demands of a collective life to come, and identify social collectivity as the crucial centre of any truly progressive and innovative political response to globalization.

Antiglobal proponents envision a world of social justice, living wages, fair (not free) trade, and environmental sustainability, but neoliberals argue that they do not present a comprehensive plan for getting there. The International Forum on Globalization disputes this contention – "The claim that the protesters offer no alternatives is as false as the other claims" (Cavanagh and Mander 2002, p. 3) – and makes dozens of policy proposals that range from the narrow (e.g., rewriting corporate charters) to socially transformative (e.g., alternative energy and transportation systems). The Forum and other critics dislike labels such as "antiglobal" and "antiglobalization," because such negative language detracts from what they consider their positive program for improving the human condition.

Some marketing academics have raised questions about the applicability of the modernization theories to marketing and development (Dholakia 1984; Dholakia and Dholakia 1982), whereas others have explored how the spread of consumerism through marketing activities has affected the less affluent world (Ger 1992, 1997; Ger and Belk 1996; Hirschman 1986). The group of scholars who would become the International Society for Marketing and Development held their first conference in 1986 and incorporated formally in 1993. In 2000, the membership voted to change the name to the International Society of Marketing and Development, a more neutral title that avoids giving the impression that the organization necessarily endorses marketing in developing countries (International Society of Marketing and Development 2004). The three presentations in the final plenary session of the 8th International Conference on Marketing and Development, held in Bangkok, Thailand, January 3–7, 2003, all contained reasoned but unflattering accounts of globalization. As then International Society of Marketing and Development President Russell Belk (2003, p. 661) stated, "Global markets undermine national sovereignty and create turmoil."

Four Challenges to Marketing

Table 1 summarizes the four primary challenges, antiglobal assertions, and responses that are implicit in marketing ideology. I have attempted to interpret and convey the majority or consensus opinion rather than the minority or more extreme arguments in each camp.

Table 1 Four Challenges to Marketing in Developing Countries: A Summary of Antiglobal Assertions and Marketing Responses

Challenge	Antiglobal Assertions	Marketing Responses
1. Marketing undermines local cultures.	• Imported products displace local cultural goods. • Cultural diversity is preferable to cultural homogenization. • Cultural trade barriers and subsidies for domestic cultural producers are useful remedies.	• Consumers should be able to choose their own cultural goods. • Cultural and other goods are adapted to local markets. • Standardized products provide operational efficiencies and consumer benefits. • Cultural change is inevitable, even desirable.
2. Marketing places IP rights ahead of human rights.	• Corporations should not have the same rights as people. • Global IP regimes do not benefit poor countries. • Pharmaceutical pricing should reflect ability to pay. • Large corporations are pirating indigenous knowledge.	• Private IP ownership is desirable because it stimulates innovation. • Local governments must enforce IP rights. • Counterfeiting and piracy damage business and societies everywhere.
3. Marketing contributes to unhealthy dietary patterns and unsafe food technologies.	• Marketing is a factor in the worldwide obesity epidemic. • Fast-food marketing targets vulnerable populations. • Genetically modified (GM) foods are potentially dangerous and are not authentic. • If GM foods are sold, they should be clearly identified.	• Food consumption choices are an individual responsibility. • Marketing of fast foods is a legitimate activity. • GM foods provide benefits for producers and consumers everywhere. • Food distribution is the real problem in poor countries.
4. Marketing promotes unsustainable consumption.	• Foreign corporations exploit weak laws and despoil local environments. • Long-distance transportation is polluting. • Renewable resources are the key to productivity. • Global warming is the paramount environmental problem.	• Managerial marketing asserts the right to consume and assumes that more is better. • Green marketing seeks to attach ecological riders to the marketing concept. • Economic growth creates resources that can protect the environment. • Privatization leads to better conservation of resources.

Marketing Undermines Local Cultures[5]

Antiglobal Assertions

The antiglobalization critique maintains that an influx of ideas, values, products, and lifestyles from the rich countries, above all, the increasingly hegemonic United States, unduly influences and ultimately debases developing countries' cultures (Barber 1995; Jameson 2000; Tunstall 1977). Traditional societies are in grave danger of displacement and homogenization. Their ethos – their unique perspectives on the world – is being weakened or destroyed by external commercial influences (Cowen 2002). When they are not being eradicated altogether, native languages are being tainted by English, the lingua franca of globalization. In addition, just as competition from large foreign manufacturers challenges smaller local firms, the forces of globalization cause economic loss to domestic cultural industries, especially film (Baughn and Buchanan 2001). Some critics describe these processes as "cultural imperialism." a new form of exploitation resulting from the export of popular culture to the developing world (Watson 1997). Theories of cultural imperialism first emerged in the 1970s (Tunstall 1977) and have been propounded under a variety of phrases (e.g., "structural imperialism," "cultural dependency," "electronic colonialism") by scholars from several disciplines (White 2001). Although it is problematic everywhere, foreign penetration particularly threatens the cultures of the smaller developing countries and groups of indigenous peoples. In contrast, large societies, such as Mexico or India, can maintain distinct identities better in the face of cross-cultural contact because they are regionally diverse and historically synthetic cultures (Cowen 2002).

Marketing management provides the strategies and tactics for spreading the dominant world culture. As Johansson (2004, p. 10) observes, global marketers are "the flag-bearers of free trade and globalization. To use a metaphor they are vassals in the service of capitalism, the first troops to attack when formerly closed markets open." Brand names in the form of embedded logos on clothing and other consumer goods or conveyed through carefully targeted advertising campaigns manipulate personal tastes (Klein 1999). Branding as a macro process shifts the balance away from the local, unique, and creative to the global, standardized, and bland. In the words of the International Forum on Globalization, the world's consumers

> are to be served by the same few global corporations, the same fast-food restaurants, hotel chains, and clothing chains; wear the same jeans and shoes; drive similar cars; receive the same films, music, and television shows; live in the same kind of urban landscape; and engage in the same kind of agricultural and industrial development schemes, while carrying the same personal, cultural, and spiritual values – *a global monoculture*. (Cavanaugh and Mander 2002, p. 23, emphasis in original)

This is more than just a question of cultural preeminence; it is one of real political power. One McDonald's or Starbucks may enhance diversity, but 100 or 1000 permeate markets and stifle competition (Barber 1995, 2003). Belk (1995) observes that the forces of global marketing, from Ronald McDonald to buying the world a Coke, are difficult to resist because they so often seem innocuous and benign. In the eyes of the most radical critics, marketing enables international corporations to wrest control of the distribution and consumption of goods and services from impoverished countries.

Thus, the antiglobal position favors measures that protect local cultures. Remedies for stemming the onslaught of global popular culture can take many forms. Government-imposed trade barriers include (1) censorship, such as Iran's ban on satellite television dishes or China's blocking of Web sites; (2) quotas, such as China's restrictions on the number of U.S. films that can be imported legally each year; and (3) high tariffs and other forms of discriminatory taxation, such as France's surcharge on non-European Union films. An alternative strategy is to subsidize domestic cultural productions. For example, the Mexican government funds a state-run school for cinema, finances films through the Instituto Mexicano de Cinematografía, and owns the Churubusco Azteca studio (Kraul and Muñoz 2003; Sheridan 1998).

Consumers in developing countries, often egged on by intellectuals, preachers, or opportunistic politicians, sometimes initiate boycotts of imported culture. The socialist Janata Dal Party chased Coca-Cola out of India in 1977 because it would not reveal its formula to local cola brands (Chua 2004; Yergin and Stanislaw 2002). When Coke returned in 1994 through a strategic alliance with an Indian soft drinks manufacturer, Janata Dal leaders threatened boycotts and picketing of bottling plants and delivery trucks (Dahlburg 1995). More recently, extreme right-wingers in India's Bharatiya Janata Party have called for more self-reliance (Bhagwati 2004), and consumers in Arab countries have shunned U.S. brands and fast-food restaurants to protest U.S. policies in the Middle East (Mroue 2002).

Does cultural protectionism work? Trade barriers, especially when vigorously implemented by autocratic regimes, can limit the influx of foreign goods and popular culture. Evidence suggests that local products can sometimes benefit as a result. The Korean film industry has profited financially from such regulations as the "106 day" rule, which mandates that local theaters screen Korean-language cinema the equivalent of 106 days a year. Korean blockbusters now dominate the local market (Lee 2004; Russell 2004), and Korean-language movies have begun to attract favorable reviews from international critics (*The Economist* 2003b). However, consumers often find ways to circumvent cultural trade barriers, such as by purchasing smuggled hard goods (printed materials, CDs, and DVDs) or downloading digital files from the Internet (Duda and Witkowski 2003). Moreover, local production to fill domestic quotas may turn out to be poor quality "quota quickies" (Baughn and Buchanan 2001).

Marketing Responses

The marketing response to these accusations begins with the principle of consumer sovereignty; that is, consumers should be allowed to make their own choices among products, including cultural products, regardless of origin. Free trade in cultural goods broadens the range of choices available to individual consumers within societies (Cowen 2002). In contrast, cultural protectionism serves special interests, not society at large. The interests of domestic publishers and film producers may not necessarily be tantamount to those of their audiences. Enforcing a homogenized status quo is itself inimical to diversity (Henwood 2003).

In general, the marketing literature respects cultural differences as an important environmental variable. Textbooks take great pains to explain that local adaptation of the marketing mix is the sine qua non of international marketing:

> Adaptation is a key concept in international marketing, and willingness to adapt is a crucial attitude. Adaptation, or at least accommodation, is required on small matters as well as large ones. In fact, the small, seemingly insignificant situations are often the most crucial. More than tolerance of an alien culture is required. There is a need for affirmative acceptance, that is, open tolerance of the concept "different but equal." Through such affirmative acceptance, adaptation becomes easier because empathy for another's point of view naturally leads to ideas for meeting cultural differences. (Cateora and Graham 2005, pp. 124–25)

Similarly, Czinkota and Ronkainen (2004, p. 248), whose text devotes an entire chapter to the topic, justify adaptation "because meeting and satisfying customer needs and expectations is the key to successful marketing." This is not just all "cheap talk"; evidence of marketer-driven adaptation is plentiful. Multinational firms, such as Nestlé, Procter & Gamble, and Unilever, manage large portfolios of brands that are sold in just one or two countries (Boze and Patton 1995). Companies modify their so-called global products to suit the tastes of consumers in different markets. A visit to the McDonald's Web site (www.mcdonalds.com) shows how menus vary from country to country. For example, McDonald's India promotes "McVeggies," "McAloo Tikkis," and "Maharaja Macs"; McDonald's Uruguay sells "Dulce de Leche" pancakes. Packaging, pricing, distribution, and advertising are all tailored for different cultures. KFC in China has switched from white meat to dark for its chicken burgers and is replacing coleslaw and mashed potatoes, both side dishes that work in the West, with seasonal vegetables, shredded carrot salads, fungus and bamboo shoots, and rice porridge (*congee*) (Adler 2003).

It can also be argued that standardization provides both operational and consumer benefits. Foreign fast-food chains can offer competitive value propositions to the world's less affluent consumers because of economical acquisition of inputs (e.g., raw and processed foods, food preparation and serving equipment), standardized production and management processes, and the ability to test new offerings. They provide sales training to service workers and frequently introduce higher marketing standards from the first world. More-over, consumers may prefer these global products. Chinese people who dine at KFC or McDonald's in Beijing can taste a bit of Americana within clean and cheerful surroundings (Yan 2000), and they will most likely have a similar experience at any other such restau-rant in their city. Watching a Hollywood film enables audiences in developing countries to sample a wider world, however distorted its depiction, than they would if they were restricted to domestic productions only. Global brands may confer some additional status on the user and his or her family in some cultures and may help enhance social ties and maintain traditional role relationships (Eckhardt and Houston 1998, 2001).

Embedded within the managerial literature are the assumptions that cultural change is inevitable and that innovation is desirable. For example, consider the following paragraph:

> Although cultures meet most newness with some resistance or rejection, that resistance can be overcome. Cultures are dynamic, and change occurs when resistance slowly yields to acceptance as the basis for resistance becomes unimportant or forgotten. Gradually there comes an awareness of the need for change, or ideas once too complex become less so because of cultural gains in understanding, or an idea is restructured in a less-complex way, and so on. After a need is recognized, it may be impossible to prevent the acceptance of a new idea. For some ideas, solutions to problems, or new products, resistance can be overcome in months; for others, approval may come only after decades or centuries. (Cateora and Graham 2005, p. 117)

The tone of this message is one of inexorability. The authors also explain that companies can choose between the strategies of "unplanned change" and the more proactive "planned change." They acknowledge that some change can be socially dysfunctional and that marketers have a responsibility for negative consequences of marketing efforts. However, the recommendation is not to refrain from cultural interference but "to design programs not only to gain acceptance for a product but also to eliminate any negative cultural effects" (Cateora and Graham 2005, p. 119).

Marketing Places IP Rights Ahead of Human Rights

Antiglobal Assertions

Antiglobal thought increasingly questions the legitimacy of privately owned IP rights and their imposition on poor countries through mechanisms such as the WTO Agreement on Trade-Related Aspects of Intellectual Property Rights (Mayer 1998). In part, this theoretical stance feeds on an antipathy toward the large, multinational corporations that typically control patents, copyrights, and trademarks. Legal rights to IP almost always belong to companies that are headquartered in Europe, North America, and Japan. Some of the more strident critics contend that these powerful firms are monopolists that exploit poor consumers, and therefore any losses due to piracy or counterfeiting can be dismissed as inconsequential. More commonly voiced – for example, by Consumers International, an umbrella organization for the world's consumer groups – is the argument that the exercise of IP rights reduces poor countries' access to knowledge in genetics, health, agriculture, education and information technology (Drahos and Mayne 2002; Mayer 1998). Many governments and their citizens simply cannot afford the imposition of first-world pricing. Thus, IP regulatory regimes that work in rich countries may not be applicable worldwide. Even the staunchly neoliberal *Economist* (2002a, p. 13), in reporting the findings of the U.K. Commission on Intellectual Property Rights, admits, "There is little evidence to show that truly downtrodden places which introduce robust intellectual-property protection reap any of the much-touted benefits."

A crucial problem is the pricing and distribution of pharmaceutical products, such as treatments for HIV/AIDS. This malady has reached epidemic proportions in eastern and southern Africa and has become a problem in several other countries, especially Thailand. The drug companies fear that lowering prices in poor countries will result in shipments being diverted for reexport to rich countries, where they can be sold below the set retail price. Thus, the less affluent do not receive their medication, and the companies lose revenues. Antiglobalists argue that basic human rights far outweigh this eventuality and that prices should reflect ability to pay. Besides, drug companies spend far more on marketing than on basic research (some of which is funded by public money), and reducing patent protection provides smaller, local suppliers a chance to compete (Cavanagh and Mander 2002).

Paradoxically, some patented, high-priced, Western pharmaceuticals may actually incorporate the "traditional knowledge" of developing countries, such as herbal remedies that have been used for centuries (*The Economist* 2003c; Shiva 2000). To the antiglobalists, this is an example of corporations raiding the commons, which can be defined as those "aspects of life that had been accepted since time immemorial as collective property, or the common heritage of all peoples and communities, existing for everyone to share as they have for millennia" (Cavanagh and Mander 2002, p. 81). In this view, the commons embrace air, water, and much of the land, as well as plant, animal, and human genetic material. In addition, many types of IP – product and process technologies, numerous literary and musical creations, and even some brand names – have entered the public domain over time.

Economists distinguish between rivalrous and nonrivalrous resources (Lessig 2002). If a logging company harvests trees from national forests, that activity may interfere with the access and enjoyment of hikers. In contrast, a nonrivalrous resource, such as academic research, is inexhaustible; after it is created it cannot be undone, and a person acquiring the knowledge does not stop another from doing the same. From an antiglobal perspective, much more IP should be considered a nonrivalrous resource. The claim that technology or content is private property is problematic and becomes more so the longer the claim remains in force. As I discuss in the section on unsustainable consumption, antiglobalists view air, water, and other natural endowments as rivalrous resources.

Marketing Responses

Marketing thought assumes that IP belongs to its creators, not to the commons. Those who develop IP should have the right to control and profit from it for a reasonable length of time. Ownership rights of some types of IP, such as the trade names and trademarks that are major components of brand equity, should extend indefinitely. Society benefits from the privatization of ideas because hope for financial gain drives innovation. Moreover, companies believe that their rights have been too often ignored. An example is the Indian Patent Act of 1970 (amended in 1999), which does not allow patents on the content of pharmaceuticals (it does permit patents on the methods of manufacture) and thereby encourages reverse engineering of drugs for purposes of local production (Embassy of India 2004; Mayer 1998).

Counterfeiting of tangibles and piracy of digital goods are especially serious problems. These acts take sales away from legitimate companies, reduce their brands' values, and force them to bear the costs of countermeasures. Jobs are lost, and because counterfeiters rarely pay taxes, governments are deprived of revenues (*The Economist* 2003c). Some counterfeit goods (bogus pharmaceuticals, shoddy airplane parts) may endanger the health and safety of consumers. Endemic piracy may not only drive away potential foreign investors but also perpetuate a climate of law breaking that is inimical to development. The process of economic development depends greatly on a society's observance of the rule of law, which includes respect for different types of property rights. When countries have fair and transparent legal systems, capitalism succeeds and economic growth is more likely (De Soto 2000).

The theft of IP, whether in the form of counterfeit branded clothing, toys, sports equipment, and pharmaceuticals or through pirated copyrighted materials, is a growing threat to international business (Nil and Shultz 1996). The International Intellectual Property Alliance (2004), a trade association that represents the music, motion picture, software, and book-publishing industries, believes that its US-member firms alone lose $20–$22 billion annually, not including Internet piracy. In its May 2003 "Special 301" review, the Office of the U.S. Trade Representative pegged U.S. losses for all industries as high as $200–$250 billion, and the International Chamber of Commerce estimates that from 7% to 9% of all world trade is in counterfeits (*The Economist* 2003c). In many developing countries, local vendors quite openly sell brand knockoffs of all kinds, as well as hard copies of software, music, and movies (Duda and Witkowski 2003). China has become the world capital of counterfeiting and piracy (Buckley 2003; *The Economist* 2003c; Iritani 2003), but many additional hotbeds can be found throughout the world.

Counterfeiting and piracy can damage local IP industries in developing countries. In Hong Kong, cheap video compact disc players were introduced in the early 1990s. By the end of the decade, a third of all households owned these players, and pirated media to play in them became much in demand. Box-office revenues declined 15%–20% a year throughout the 1990s, and the local film industry was reduced to a third of its 1990 size, when Hong Kong exported the second-largest number of films (after the United States) to the world market. Hong Kong cinemas closed for a day on March 17, 1999, to protest video piracy (*The Economist* 1999). India, which has both vigorous motion picture and growing software industries, may also be quite vulnerable.

Marketing Contributes to Unhealthy Dietary Patterns and Unsafe Food Technologies

Antiglobal Assertions

Rising levels of obesity have alarmed public health officials worldwide (World Health Organization 2003). The problem is especially acute in the United States and Britain, but it is expanding in many other countries. The causes of this epidemic, which range from a human genetic predisposition, to overeating, to increasingly sedentary lifestyles, to individual moral failings, are many, and their full examination is beyond the scope of this article. However, critics point out a major marketing dimension to the problem. Marketers have become quite adept at developing an endless variety of convenient, tasty foods that are widely available, reasonably priced, and sold through aggressive advertising that is often targeted at vulnerable populations, especially children and teenagers (Schlosser 2001). Results of a recent national survey (Bowman et al. 2004) indicate that fast-food consumption among U.S. children apparently has an adverse effect on dietary quality that plausibly could increase risk for obesity. A reason the French activist José Bové and his accomplices vandalized the construction site of a new McDonald's in Millau was their belief that it symbolized the proliferation of *le malbouf*, or junk food (Woodruff 2001).

Ironically, given the malnutrition and starvation that still plague many poor countries, obesity rates are increasing in Latin America, Central and Eastern Europe, and the Middle East and North Africa (Caballero 2001; Martorell 2001; World Health Organization 2003). According to a recent study by the Organization of Economic Cooperation and Development, 64% of women and 60% of men in Mexico are now overweight, and 24% of the population is considered obese (Boudreaux 2004). Good longitudinal data are limited, but estimates of Body Mass Index (BMI) – BMI measures weight relative to height – are suggestive. As I show in Figure 1, BMI trends in the developing world have been rising, perhaps dangerously so for some populations. Again, determinants are many.

Undernutrition in early life may trigger hormonal and metabolic changes that put a person at risk of excess fat accumulation. Some native peoples, such as American Indians

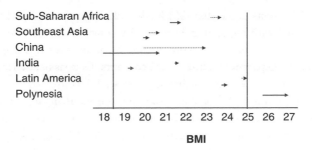

Figure 1   Trends in BMI in the Developing World, 1960–1990

Notes: Solid horizontal lines indicate changes in BMI for lower quartiles, and dotted lines indicate changes in BMI for upper quartiles. Vertical lines depict normal BMI range.

Source: Caballero (2001).

and Pacific Islanders, may have a "thrift gene" that makes them extra susceptible to obesity. Urbanization leads to lower levels of physical activity and loss of traditional diets. Finally, contact with imported fast-food culture is increasing. As one headline reads, "West Exports Obesity to Developing World" (*BBC News* 2000).

Fast-food chains are among the first Western companies to arrive when a country opens its market. Grand openings can be huge events. Thousands queued for hours when the first McDonald's opened in Beijing in 1992 (Yan 2000), and two years later, a line of cars waiting at the drive-through window of a new McDonald's in Kuwait stretched for seven miles (Schlosser 2001). Advertising strategies and executions that have worked in the West have been equally successful in developing countries. Children have been favorite targets (Schlosser 2001; Watson 1997; Yan 2000). In 2000, ACNielsen Media International conducted a survey in 30 Chinese cities, and on the basis of 16,677 questionnaires, it showed that KFC was the most famous international brand in China (*People's Daily Online* 2000).

Antiglobalization rhetoric has been even more disparaging of new biotechnologies, specifically the development and sale of genetically modified (GM) plants and animals. The long-term effects of ingesting these substances is unknown, and it is not yet possible to predict their ultimate environmental consequences. Antiglobal thought subscribes to a "precautionary principle":

> When a practice or product raises potentially significant threats of harm to human health or the environment, precautionary action should be taken to restrict or ban it, even if there is scientific uncertainty about whether or how it is actually causing that harm. Because it can take years for scientific proof of harm to be established – during which time undesirable or irreversible effects may continue to be inflicted – the proponents of a practice or product should bear the burden of proving that it is safe. (Cavanagh and Mander 2002, p. 76)

Furthermore, antiglobalists argue that GM foods lack the authenticity of more traditional agriculture. Compared with regional and organically grown foods, GM products are disparaged as impersonal and corporate. Finally, food companies have not been entirely forthcoming in regard to transparent labeling of GM contents. Dozens of advocacy organizations have been pressing for new legislation that requires such labeling.

Negative opinions about GM foods are especially prevalent in rich European countries (see, e.g., Scholderer *et al.* 1999), but they have also been voiced by many developing countries, ranging from Ethiopia, to Brazil, to India (*BBC News* 2003; Zane 2003). In December 1992 and again in July 1994, mobs ransacked the Bangalore office of Cargill, a Minneapolis-based company that sells hybrid sunflower and corn seed (Dahlburg 1995). Sensitivity to the introduction of new GM foods in developing countries should not be unexpected. Watson (1997) argues that dietary patterns, attitudes toward food, and notions of what constitutes a proper meal are central to maintaining local culture.

Marketing Responses

The principle of consumer sovereignty once again provides the first line of defense against antiglobal allegations about marketing programs being partly responsible for rising world obesity rates. As rational decision makers, consumers have the right to ingest whatever (legal substance) they choose, and if they overeat, that is their own personal responsibility. Consumers should be given sufficient information to make informed choices, but then they are on their own. In turn, food marketers have the right – and even a duty to shareholders – to compete for customers globally whether through new snacks, larger portion sizes, or lower prices. In countries where national regulations allow the practice, aiming advertising and promotions toward young consumers constitutes a legitimate strategy.

Marketing theory offers a second line of justification. According to the concept of market segmentation, if enough consumers are truly diet conscious and this group can be identified, targeted, and profitably served, marketers will respond with the appropriate marketing mix. Unmistakably, this has occurred. Diet foods and a plethora of slimming products and services have become a multibillion dollar industry in the rich world. Moreover, prominent packaged goods and fast-food companies, such as Kraft, Frito-Lay and McDonald's, have introduced new, "healthier" menu choices around the world. The threat of product liability lawsuits, at least in the United States, may be motivating their switch in marketing tactics, but these firms are also responding to trends in consumer demand.

In many of the world's poorest countries, the more pressing problem is insufficient food security – that is, physical and economic access to food – not food abundance and obesity (Bone and France 2003). The marketing problem here is inefficient distribution caused, in large part, by breakdowns in law and order. Developing countries agree with some of this analysis. In early 2004, the United Nations Food and Agricultural Organization along with the World Health Organization proposed a new strategy to combat global obesity by encouraging governments to discourage the intake of sugar and fat and instead to promote increased consumption of fruits and vegetables. Representatives from the Group of Seventy-Seven at the United Nations faulted the report for shoddy science and urged better nutrition education, not limits on foods (Ross 2004).

In general, the marketing literature supports the development and introduction of new products. Thus, from a marketing perspective, as well as that of research scientists and the agribusiness industry, GM foods should be considered a remarkable technological achievement. Crops can be designed to resist infestations and grow better in less favorable soil conditions, thus requiring fewer chemical pesticides and fertilizers. Costs can be reduced and the environment will benefit (Hart 1997; Magretta 1997; Scholderer *et al.* 1999). This and other new biotechnologies should be especially beneficial to countries that experience difficulty feeding their swelling populations. Genetically modified food products can also be exported, creating jobs and foreign exchange reserves. Proponents of GM foods have not found any credible evidence to suggest that these foods are unsafe, and several developing countries, including China, Brazil and Argentina, have adopted the technology. The overzealous application of the precautionary principle can result in real harm to the least affluent consumers who, according to GM food enthusiasts, stand to benefit most from this technology.

Marketing Promotes Unsustainable Consumption

Antiglobal Assertions

The term "sustainable consumption" and the closely related notion of "sustainable development" refer to the use of goods and services in ways that improve the quality of life yet do not irreparably harm the environment or society and thus jeopardize the needs of future generations (United Nations Development Programme 1998). Even "skeptical environmentalists," such as Bjorn Lomborg (2000), cannot completely dismiss the idea that development imperils the world's ecosystems. Threats include various forms of local pollution; depletion of renewable resources, such as forests and fish stocks; and, above all, global warming caused by the production of greenhouse gases beyond the earth's absorption capacity. Antiglobal and marketing thought disagree over the nature of these problems and how best to achieve sustainable consumption.

According to antiglobal doctrine, unregulated economic growth and increasing levels of consumption inevitably stress the environment. Fossil-fuel emissions in third-world cities are especially problematic. Beijing, Delhi and Mexico City already have high levels of air pollution, which may only become worse as their inhabitants use more power tools and appliances and drive more motorcycles and automobiles. At the same time, companies continue to relocate manufacturing facilities from richer to poorer countries. They do so not only to exploit cheaper labor but also to take advantage of laxer environmental regulation and law enforcement than in their home markets. Furthermore, the long-distance transportation systems that serve the global economy also contribute to environmental problems (Cavanagh and Mander 2002). Ocean shipping, which is fueled by low quality "Bunker C" oil, and seaports are notable polluters, as are cargo aircraft and diesel trucks. Thus, the emulation of Western consumerism in the less affluent world (Ger 1997; Ger and Belk 1996) and the movement of manufacturing to developing countries combine to diminish air quality, foul waterways, savage rainforests, and perhaps make global warming inevitable. In short, development will not be sustainable, either locally or globally.

Environmental issues can also accompany development in the supposedly more benign services sector. For example, Belk (1993) describes how trekking in Nepal has degraded local forests. Recently, Fonatur, the Mexican agency for tourism development, announced plans to develop a string of marinas along the Pacific and Gulf shores of Baja. Rich tourists will arrive by yacht, spread their money around, and create as many as 250,000 jobs within the next ten years. Environmentalists find these claims about economic benefits to be exaggerated, and they strenuously object to the project because of potential damage to the breeding grounds of whales, sea turtles, and other wildlife (Kraul and Weiss 2003).

Cavanagh and Mander (2002, pp. 62–63) present alternative principles for sustainable consumption:

> (a) [R]ates of renewable resource use do not exceed their rates of regeneration; (b) rates of consumption or irretrievable disposal of nonrenewable resources do not exceed the rates at which renewable substitutes are phased into use; (c) rates of pollution emission into the environment do not exceed the rate of their harmless assimilation.

Rich countries have addressed the first condition through new regulations that seek to preserve their forests and fisheries. Such niceties are widely ignored in poor countries, in which deforestation and other harvesting have been rampant (Harvey 1995). Condition b requires government mandates or tax incentives to either reduce consumption or favor alternative energy sources, such as windmills. Condition c, which is essentially about global warming, implies setting limits for emissions and finding ways to meet these limits, such as through the Kyoto protocols, carbon taxes, and new technologies. It is easy to imagine how, if rigorously implemented, these conditions could have tremendous impacts on all the elements of the marketing mix in countries everywhere.

Marketing Responses

Although few marketing studies support the antiglobal position for each of the first three challenges, marketing thought is more evenly divided on the topic of sustainable consumption. The managerial side of the discipline focuses on satisfying the needs of individual consumers. If buyers demand large houses, energy-inefficient appliances, and gasguzzling vehicles, then so be it. In general, marketing doctrine does not make moral judgments about consumer preferences, and therefore companies are fully justified in catering to, if not encouraging, this demand. Furthermore, in general, the field accepts sales growth as a primary marketing objective. Little, if any, attention has been paid to setting upper limits to marketing metrics, such as number of units sold, market share, and profitability. In practice, the marketing of savings (e.g., college funds and retirement accounts) rather than spending and the "de-marketing" of certain categories of objectionable consumption (e.g., cigarette smoking and other drug use) are important but relatively minor endeavors compared with the overwhelming encouragement to buy and consume more goods and services. Marketing management is deeply wedded to the "dominant social paradigm" of free markets, individual choice, and continuous economic growth (Kilbourne, McDonagh, and Prothero 1997). Even the concept of sustainable consumption is perhaps overly embedded within the dominant paradigm (Dolan 2002).

In contrast, a respectable number of marketing academics have closely examined the environmental consequences of marketing practices under rubrics such as "green marketing," "environmental marketing," "ecological marketing," "ecomarketing," and "sustainable marketing" (Fuller 1999). This now sizable literature comprises numerous articles and a small cottage industry of specialized texts (see Crane 2000). These writings have challenged micromanagerial assumptions (Kilbourne, McDonagh, and Prothero 1997), while attempting to add riders to the marketing concept. For example, Fuller (1999, p. 4) defines sustainable marketing as "the process of planning, implementing, and controlling the development, pricing, promotion, and distribution of products in a manner that satisfies the following three criteria: (1) customer needs are met, (2) organizational goals are attained, and (3) the process is compatible with ecosystems." The devil is in the details of the third stipulation. Critics would argue that green marketing has focused more on the symptoms of consumerism rather than on its root causes, a centuries-old "productivist" discourse (Smith 1998).

With respect to developing countries, mainstream marketing thought is compatible with the neoliberal argument that economic growth is the best way for these countries to protect their environments in the longer run (Irwin 2002). Rich countries take better care of their air, water, and soils than do poor countries, and short-term trade-offs – some environmental losses in exchange for economic growth – eventually result in more money dedicated to protecting and restoring ecosystems. Furthermore, this position insists that private ownership of resources – the privatization of water services is currently a hotly debated topic (*The Economist* 2003c) – often fosters better conservation than public ownership. It is not in the economic self-interest of individual owners to squander revenue-producing resources. In contrast, no one has an incentive to husband common property, which results in overuse and destruction, also known as the "tragedy of the commons" (Shultz and Holbrook 1999). A nasty discovery that followed the overthrow of European Communism was just how badly the environment had been ruined by state-run, coal-burning, capital-intensive industries.

International trade has no direct relationship to environmental problems: "Environmental damage results from poor environmental policies, not poor trade policies" (Irwin 2002, p. 48). In some cases, government subsidies and protectionism that subvert free trade have promoted overfishing, accelerated deforestation, and intensified use of pesticides and fertilizers (Irwin).

Ideological Common Ground

Antiglobal and marketing advocates mostly agree on what marketing does in developing countries: Marketing sells global cultural products, it values IP rights, it promotes fast foods and GM technology, and it engenders the spread of rich countries' consumerism. Differences stem from how the two sides evaluate the consequences of marketing actions for developing countries. Yet because even these plainly divergent philosophies share some common ground, this section explores areas of ideological compatibility.

Undertheorized Consumer Agency

Issues of localization cut across all four challenges to marketing in developing countries. Antiglobal thinking champions the concept of "subsidiarity" or "favoring the local whenever the choice exists" (Cavanagh and Mander 2002, p. 107). International marketing texts also stress the need for localization through careful adaptation of the marketing mix. However, not unlike the muckraking critics of advertising in the postwar United States who portrayed buyers as relatively defenseless against the wiles of Madison Avenue (Packard 1957), antiglobalization theory tends to overspecify business-to-buyer influences and underestimate consumer resistance. Similarly, international marketing thought overemphasizes marketer-driven adaptation of the marketing mix – recall Cateora and Graham's (2005) and Czinkota and Ronkainen's (2004) discussion of adaptation and cultural change – and gives short shrift to consumer-driven initiatives. Both sides undertheorize consumer agency.

In *Golden Arches East: McDonald's in East Asia*, Watson (1997) and his colleagues use ethnographic methods to investigate McDonald's in five East Asian cities (date of the first restaurant is in parentheses): Tokyo (1971), Hong Kong (1975), Taipei (1984), Seoul (1988) and Beijing (1992). In each of these cities, McDonald's entry coincided with rising affluence, a focus on married couples, lower birthrates, and children as consumers. Cultural changes brought about by this new product/service form included a greater stress on kitchen and dining-area cleanliness, an acceptance of queuing, more equality between female servers and male customers, individual ordering, self-provisioning, and the use of hands to eat. McDonald's introduced American values, but would many antiglobalists object to sanitation or gender equality?

As anthropologists, these researchers did not set out to be apologists for marketing. Yet they found plenty of evidence of both intended localization and spontaneous consumer agency. When franchises, as opposed to company-owned stores, were introduced, host-country nationals became owners. They also adapted menus to cater to local tastes, such as featuring "Teriyaki McBurgers" in Japan. Furthermore, consumers themselves actively participated in localizing this global brand. In Tokyo, McDonald's became a place for teenagers to snack and hang out after school, and in Seoul these fast-food restaurants developed a reputation as a place that was friendly to women in part because they did not serve alcohol beverages and thus attract rowdy Korean men (Watson 1997). A comparative study of young KFC customers in China and the United States also found both company- and consumer-driven fast-food localization (Witkowski, Ma and Zheng 2003).

Researchers have found plenty of additional empirical evidence of developing countries' consumers adapting all types of products to their own special needs. Turks have used household appliances in innovative ways – ringer washers for making butter, ovens for drying clothes, and dishwashers for cleaning muddy spinach (Ger and Belk 1996). Indians have imparted different uses and cultural meanings to motor scooters (e.g., as a kind of family "station wagon") than have owners in Italy and Britain (De Pyssler 1992). In popular music, Jamaicans created the reggae genre by combining elements of African music with American jazz. The steel bands of Trinidad originated when resourceful musicians recycled metal barrels discarded by oil companies (Cowen 2002). As Ger (1997 111) aptly states, "Consumption can be liberating and empowering by creatively affirming identity and/or by expressing resistance through recontextualization of the meaning of goods." Through the process of "transnationalism," popular culture becomes deterritorialized. People, products, and ideas cross national borders and are no longer identified with a single place of origin. To children in Beijing, "Uncle McDonald" (i.e., Ronald) is as Chinese as the mythical characters of their folklore (Watson 1997).

By refocusing attention on the consumer as an active producer of meaning, ideological differences between antiglobal and marketing become less pronounced. Both ideologies must more fully recognize that individual consumers can resist and reinterpret marketing activities and choose to remake products and service interactions for their own ends. Consumer groups and their worldwide federation, Consumers International, provide forums for wielding political influence and perhaps finding legal remedies for grievances (Mayer 1998). At the extreme, consumers can organize boycotts of stores and brands and engage in guerilla tactics, such as defacing billboards and 'culture jamming' (Klein 1999).

Social Marketing and Collective Welfare

Observers have taunted the antiglobalization movement because in many ways, such as raising funds, organizing protests, and spreading the message, activists have proved quite adept at the art of political marketing. "It's ironic that people should rack up the frequent-flier miles while touting the virtues of localism – writing books and running institutes while telling the masses that they should stay home and tend to their lentils" (Henwood 2003, p. 169). Perhaps this remark is a cheap shot, but it underscores an openness to marketing when it can be harnessed for advancing an antiglobal agenda for poor countries' development. Stated differently, social and nonprofit marketing or, literally, marketing for developing countries constitutes a second site of common ground between antiglobal and marketing thought.

Marketing ideas have been applied to family planning, recycling, and microcredit programs with some success, albeit with nagging issues of appropriate target selection and incentive design (Dholakia 1984; Dholakia and Dholakia 2001). Marketing approaches have also infused fundraising, the promoting of appropriate technologies, and the exporting of tangible goods and tourism. Highly esteemed aid organizations, such as Oxfam International (www.oxfam.org) and Medecins Sans Frontieres (www.doctorswithoutborders.org), use their Web sites and supporting media to solicit donations, volunteer time, and support advocacy campaigns. Oxfam's planners conceive of their organization as a brand and stress coordination across the 12 different units in both meaning creation through visual images and the use of media (Oxfam International 2004). This is sophisticated marketing strategy and management reminiscent of the field of marketing aesthetics (Schmitt and Simonson 1997).

Marketing can also facilitate development through the deliberate export of local culture. Bosu (1995) presents a conceptual framework that shows how different combinations of consumption desires, craft attributes, intermediaries and producing organizations constitute three key marketing flows. Marketing can support these flows through export assistance, packaging and promotion expertise, and management training. Ten Thousand Villages, a nonprofit company that the Mennonite Central Committee runs, has more than 180 retail outlets in North America that sell arts and crafts from developing countries. Other organizations, such as the Fair Trade Foundation based in London or the Fair Trade Federation based in Washington, D.C., link low-income producers with distributors and educate buyers about the importance of purchasing fairly traded products, which support living wages and safe and healthy working conditions.

Tourism is another form of exporting local culture, though, as with many other services, it must be consumed at the site of production. A sizable segment of visitors to developing countries is motivated by a real desire to experience these cultures, both historical and contemporary. To satisfy these tourists, it is necessary to maintain those cultural differences that impart a sense of authenticity and simultaneously build a modern infrastructure that is capable of meeting travelers' needs. Belk and Costa (1995) list several benefits to the host country, including increased employment, incentives for education, hard currency and a stimulus to entrepreneurial activity, conservation, and preservation of local culture. Yet whether marketing arts and crafts for export or marketing a destination to inbound visitors, some things will change. By virtue of their connections to outside forces, sources of authenticity are eroded away (Barber 2003). Worse, cross-cultural contacts may degenerate into one-sided relationships in which rich world collectors and visitors inadvertently impose forms of cultural imperialism through their purchasing power (Belk 1993; Belk and Costa 1995). To the most zealous antiglobal advocates, market-driven culture may inexorably favor the masses, the mediocre and the superficial.

In general, however, social marketing fits nicely into the antiglobal worldview. A paramount concern of antiglobal thought is the moral imperative of improving poor countries' human development, which, as defined in the *United Nations Human Development Index* (United Nations Development Programme 2004), includes health and education factors, typically a concern of governments, in addition to gross domestic product per capita. Social marketing involves collective welfare and welfare exchanges, not merely the satisfaction of personal wants through market exchange (Brenkert 2002). Welfare is a matter of social definition as obtained through processes of social argumentation and justification. It is not simply an individual or subjective matter. Thus, society determines social marketing goals – that is, a theory of human nature held by those who sponsor social marketing programs (Brenkert 2002).

Social marketing should also appeal to the antiglobal left because programs are so often funded by government agencies and nonprofit organizations rather than by transnational corporations. However, Brenkert (2002) notes some ethical dilemmas that face social marketing, including paternalism and asymmetric moral relationships with targets, both of which actually may be more pronounced than in commercial marketing. Moreover, the sponsors of social marketing may not be above reproach and may even be using its techniques to perpetuate unjust systems. Finally, social marketing projects might affect (and possibly undermine) local cultures as much as does international marketing. For example, empowering women through education, family planning, and microcredit loans may be a desirable outcome, but it is also culturally disruptive (Dholakia and Dholakia 2001).

The Primacy of a Customer Orientation

As I stated in the introduction, a reason for seriously investigating the antiglobalization critique is because it may contain lessons for commercial marketing in developing countries. Ironically, antiglobal ideology insists that marketing practice adhere to marketing principles. If a customer orientation is indeed marketing's most cherished tenet, then this should be the bullet-proof standard for operating in developing countries. The following recommendations for serving consumer needs are drawn from the antiglobal positions on the four challenges to marketing:

1. Marketing cultural products in developing countries requires both awareness and acceptance of the cultural identities of local consumers. Large companies from rich countries

have a depth of resources that give them outsized power compared with local cultural producers. Thus, marketing must not only adapt to different conditions but also find ways to minimize its cultural footprint in developing countries.

2. Corporations must acknowledge communal rights to traditional knowledge and avoid expropriating and then monopolizing them. Their capital stock of information and technology should be shared with poor countries (Cavanagh and Mander 2002).

3. Companies must offer affordable pricing for pharmaceutical customers and develop controls over distribution to prevent gray markets from diverting drugs away from those who depend on them. Serving poor communities on their own terms can still be profitable (Prahalad and Hammond 2002).

4. Companies should encourage consumer demand for legitimate products rather than counterfeits or pirated copies through strategic marketing, such as expanding and improving theatrical facilities in developing countries (Eller 2002). Heavy-handed and largely ineffective legal actions should be avoided. Instead, firms, industry associations and governments should finance promotional campaigns that engender ethical consumer decision making by taking into account the levels of moral reasoning among audiences (Nil and Shultz 1996).

5. Although marketing thought recognizes that purchasing decisions are influenced by all sorts of impulses, the greatest ideal remains that of a rational consumer. Thus, buyers should be educated so that they make informed choices. Marketers should not wait for government mandates but instead voluntarily provide information about products. The selling of fast and GM foods requires visible and understandable nutritional and content labeling. Best marketing practices should be applied everywhere.

6. Firms that operate in emerging markets must carefully analyze and mitigate the environmental consequences of their marketing activities. Hart (1997) describes a policy of "product stewardship," whereby companies design products mindful of the possible impacts throughout the entire life cycle of the product, especially at the disposal and recycling stage. This idea should be extended to other facets of the marketing mix – for example, in the form of "distribution stewardship" and "promotional stewardship" in which local environmental considerations enter into decision making.

Further Ideological Divisions

Antiglobalization activists may never find much sympathy for commercial marketing in developing countries. Not only is there a wide gap between deeply held political views, but mutual animosities have also had too long of a history to be easily ameliorated. Those who support import substitution and other protectionist approaches to development were on the defensive for much of the 1980s and 1990s. It undoubtedly hurt to observe cherished policies rejected in favor of an openness to trade and an onrush of international marketing. Now that the antiglobal backlash is once again receiving media coverage and finding political traction, intellectual self-confidence seems to be returning. Similarly, as the once ascendant ideas of international marketing are taken to task, the natural tendency may be for thinking to become defensive and rigid.

In the light of its antiglobal critics, the field of marketing may suffer from guilt by association. Although the early development of marketing thought had German influences (Jones and Monieson 1990), throughout much of the twentieth century academic marketing was an overwhelmingly American enterprise. Only since approximately 1980 has the discipline attracted a truly worldwide following (Wilkie and Moore 2003). Similarly, in the realm of day-to-day marketing practice, the United States has been on the fore-front of everything from chain stores and shopping centers; to radio and television advertising; to credit cards, telemarketing, and Internet sales. As a field, marketing carries an unmistakable stamp of American culture.

American brands have inordinate power worldwide and, perhaps not surprisingly, receive the greatest amount of criticism. Interbrand Corporation and *Business Week's* (2004) annual survey of the world's 100 most valuable brands – defined as the net present value of the future stream of profits the brand will deliver – finds that 8 of the top 10 and 58 of the top 100 are based in the United States. Johansson (2004) believes that youth-oriented brands that are sold on the basis of convenience, low price, and brand image – such as Coca-Cola and McDonald's – are the most likely to be attacked by antiglobalists, many of whom are themselves quite young. Japanese and European brands are disparaged far less frequently, and those that are, such as Absolut Vodka, Adidas, Benetton, and the Body Shop (see Klein 1999), resemble the kinds of American brands under assault. All of these brands have a prominent visual presence that may be partly responsible for the critical backlash.

Because of its economic, military, and cultural power – not to mention specific foreign policies, such as unwavering support of Israel and the occupation of Iraq – the United States today provokes intense resentment (Chua 2004; Friedman 1999). Recent surveys show that mistrust and other negative feelings toward the United States are wide-spread and growing stronger (Pew Research Center 2004). Antiglobalization activists are often the most critical of all: "In an uncanny repetition of the way that Continental reactionaries regarded liberal, globalist, 'Jewish' Great Britain a century ago, nearly all antiglobalists focus on 'the Great Satan'" (Micklethwait and Wooldridge 2000, p. 275). McDonald's restaurants have been vandalized and boy-cotted not only because of what the company does – few multinationals take as many pains to localize their marketing mix (*The Economist* 2001, *Foreign Policy* 2001) – but also because of where it originates. Thus, America's increasingly poor image around the world would seem to increase antiglobal aversion to marketing (Johansson 2004).

Conclusion

With an intellectual history that can be traced back to the end of World War II, the antiglobalization critique of marketing in developing countries has gained momentum in recent years. I have shown how the antiglobal and marketing worldviews lead to different positions on the issues of local culture, IP, food safety and the environment. Yet the divide need not widen further. Antiglobal thought must acknowledge that its cherished principle of subsidiarity – favoring the local – not only is consistent with the marketing emphasis on adaptation but also can be realized by consumers themselves. Moreover, as the examples from Oxfam International and other aid organizations suggest, marketing theory and management can make vital contributions to the economic development of poor countries. Concepts such as segmentation, target marketing and the deft use of the promotional mix can help alleviate poverty, improve the environment, and perhaps create more democratic and just societies.

Business marketers have a moral obligation to adhere to the principle of a customer orientation. Ethical marketing means designing products that are specifically suited to the needs of low-income consumers. It means better alignment of prices with the ability of impoverished consumers to pay. It means the introduction of more efficient channels of distribution and, through well-conceived information campaigns, the creation of more sophisticated and informed consumers. Marketers must be keenly aware that their conduct in developing markets has social, economic, and environmental consequences for local consumers. The principle of "do no harm" must be taken seriously. Finally, it is prudent to remember that poor countries can become breeding grounds for resentments that may turn violently against people everywhere. Alleviating these conditions is a global interest.

Notes

1. Founded in 1994, the IFG represents 60 organizations in 25 countries. According to Henwood (2003, p. 160), the IFC "has appointed itself the intellectual leader of what is unsatisfactorily called the antiglobalization movement." Thus, the IFG report *Alternatives to Economic Globalization: A Better World Is Possible* (Cavanagh and Mander 2002), which a 19-person drafting committee prepared, is a major source, though not the only source, used to represent the antiglobalization position.
2. *The United Nations Human Development Index* (United Nations Development Programme 2004) ranks 177 countries as follows: countries 1–55 have "high human development," countries 50–141 have "medium human development," and countries 142–177 have "low human development." Among the top group are countries such as Argentina (No. 34), Poland (No. 35), Cuba (No. 52), and Mexico (No. 53), though most observers would consider these countries still developing. Therefore, this article defines developing countries as those that rank from 31 to 177 on the index.
3. Throughout the past century, there have been many different schools of marketing thought – functions, commodities, institutions, managerial, and macromarketing to name a few (Shaw

and Jones 2005; Wilkie and Moore 2003) – and individual educators, scholars, and practitioners have held diverse personal views. Nevertheless, core assumptions and principles of the managerial perspective predominate. They are embedded within contemporary marketing texts, which naturally follow mainstream thought, and constitute a reasonably coherent political philosophy.

4. Globalization has stirred up animosity among right-wing nativists who oppose the influx of immigrants from and the outsourcing of factory and service jobs to developing countries and worry about national identity and sovereignty (Buchanan 2002). Globalization also upsets religious conservatives. The destruction of the World Trade Center on September 11 by Muslim fanatics was, among other things, an attack on a prominent symbol of global capital. Such people do not share the humanistic social ideology that characterizes the heart of the antiglobalization movement.

5. Somewhat ill defined in the antiglobalization literature, the term "local culture" is used chiefly to mean culture outside the developed world. Watson (1997, p. 9) offers a more general definition of local culture as "the experience of everyday life as lived by ordinary people in specific localities." In accordance with Watson's definition, Greenwich Village and Hollywood would also qualify as local cultures, but because these places, especially the latter, are considered cultural exporters, Watson's sense is somewhat inconsistent with the antiglobal challenge to marketing.

References

Adler, Carlye (2003), "Colonel Sanders' March on China," *Time Asia Magazine*, (November 24), (accessed November 7, 2004), [available at http://www.time.com/time/asia/magazine/printout/0,13675,501031124-543845,00.html].

Barber, Benjamin R. (1995), *Jihad Vs. McWorld*. New York: Times Books.

—— (2003), "Brave New McWorld," review of *Creative Destruction: How Globalization Is Changing the World's Cultures*, by Tyler Cowen, *Los Angeles Times*, (February 3), R3, R4.

Baughn C. Christopher and Mark A. Buchanan (2001), "Cultural Protectionism," *Business Horizons*, 44 (November–December), 5–15.

BBC News (2000), "West Exports Obesity to Developing World," (September 26), (accessed November 7, 2004), [available at http://news.bbc.co.uk/1/hi/health/943783.stm].

—— (2003), "Brazil GM Crop Plan Challenged," (October 4), (accessed November 7, 2004), [available at http://news.bbc.co.uk/2/hi/americas/3163522.stm].

Belk, Russell W. (1993), "Third World Tourism: Panacea or Poison? The Case of Nepal," *Journal of International Consumer Marketing*, 5 (1), 27–68.

—— (1995), "Hyperreality and Globalization: Culture in the Age of Ronald McDonald," *Journal of International Consumer Marketing*, 8 (3–4), 23–37.

—— (2003), "What's Wrong with Globalism and What's to Be Done About It?" in *Globalization, Transformation, and Quality of Life: The Proceedings of the 8th International Conference on Marketing and Development*, Clifford J. Shultz II, Don R. Ratz, and Mark Speece, eds. Rijeka, Croatia: Faculty of Economics, University of Rijeka, 661–70.

—— and Janeen Arnold Costa (1995), "International Tourism: An Assessment and Overview," *Journal of Macromarketing*, 15 (Fall), 33–49.

Bhagwati, Jagdish (2004), *In Defense of Globalization*. New York: Oxford University Press.

Bone, Paula Fitzgerald and Karen Russo France (2003), "International Harmonization of Food and Nutrition Regulation: The Good and the Bad," *Journal of Public Policy & Marketing*, 22 (Spring), 102–110.

Bosu, Kunal (1995), "Marketing Developing Society Crafts: A Framework for Analysis and Change," in *Marketing in a Multicultural World: Ethnicity, Nationalism, and Cultural Identity*, Janeen Arnold Costa and Gary J. Bamossy, eds. Thousand Oaks, CA: Sage Publications, 257–98.

Boudreaux, Richard (2004), "Mexicans Living in One of the Fattest of the Lands," *Los Angeles Times*, (May 20), A5.

Bowman, Shanty A., Steven L. Gortmaker, Cara B. Ebbeling, Mark A. Pereira, and David S. Ludwig (2004), "Effects of Fast-Food Consumption on Energy Intake and Diet Quality Among Children in a National Household Survey," *Pediatrics*, 113 (January), 112–18.

Boze, Betsy V. and Charles R. Patton (1995), "The Future of Consumer Branding as Seen from the Picture Today," *Journal of Consumer Marketing*, 12 (4), 20–41.

Brenkert, George G. (2002), "Ethical Challenges of Social Marketing," *Journal of Public Policy & Marketing*, 21 (Spring), 14–25.

Buchanan, Patrick J. (2002). *The Death of the West: How Dying Populations and Immigrant Invasions Imperil Our Country and Civilization*. New York: St. Martins Press.

Buckley, Chris (2003), "Helped by Technology, Piracy of DVD's Runs Rampant in China," *The New York Times*, (August 18), C9.

BusinessWeek (2004), "The 100 Top Brands," (August 2), 64–71.

Caballero, Benjamin (2001). "Introduction," in *Obesity in Developing Countries: Biological and Ecological Factors: Proceedings of Experimental Biology 2000*, Benjamin Caballero and Najat Mokhtar, eds. *Journal of Nutrition*, 131 (Supplement), 866S–70S.

Caslione, John A. and Andrew R. Thomas (2000), *Growing Your Business in Emerging Markets: Promise and Perils*. Westport, CT: Quorum Books.

Cateora, Philip R. and John L. Graham (2005), *International Marketing*, 12th ed. New York: McGraw-Hill/Irwin.

Cavanagh, John and Jerry Mander, eds. (2002), *Alternatives to Economic Globalization: A Better World is Possible*. San Francisco: Berrett-Koehler Publishers.

Chua, Amy (2004), *World on Fire: How Exporting Free Market Democracy Breeds Ethnic Hatred and Global Instability*. New York: Anchor Books.

Cohn, Theodore H. (2003), *Global Political Economy: Theory and Practice*, 2d ed. New York: Addison Wesley.

Cowen, Tyler (2002), *Creative Destruction: How Globalization Is Changing the World's Cultures*. Princeton, NJ: Princeton University Press.

Crane, Andrew (2000), "Marketing and the Natural Environment: What Role for Morality?" *Journal of Macromarketing*, 20 (December), 144–54.

Cundiff, Edward W. (1982), "A Macromarketing Approach to Economic Development," *Journal of Macromarketing*, 2 (Spring), 14–19.

Czinkota, Michael R. and Ilkka A. Ronkainen (2004), *International Marketing*, 7th ed. Mason, OH: South-Western.

Dahlburg, John-Thor (1995), "Cola Invasion Stirs Up India's Nationalist Feelings," *Los Angeles Times*, (February 15), H1, H4.

De Pyssler, Bruce (1992), "The Cultural and Political Economy of the Indian Two-Wheeler," in *Advances in Consumer Research*, John F. Sherry and Brian Sternthal, eds. Provo, UT: Association for Consumer Research, 437–42.

De Soto, Hernando (2000), *The Mystery of Capital: Why Capitalism Triumphs in the West and Fails Everywhere Else*. New York: Basic Books.

Dholakia, Nikhilesh and Ruby Roy Dholakia (1982), "Marketing and the Emerging World Order," *Journal of Macromarketing*, 2 (Spring), 47–56.

—— and —— (1984), "Missing Links: Marketing and the Newer Theories of Development," in *Marketing in Developing Countries*. G.S. Kindra, ed. New York: St. Martin's Press, 57–75.

Dholakia, Ruby Roy (1984), "A Macromarketing Perspective on Social Marketing: The Case of Family Planning in India," *Journal of Macromarketing*, 4 (Spring), 53–61.

—— and Nikhilesh Dholakia (2001), "Social Marketing and Development," in *Handbook of Marketing and Society*, Paul N. Bloom and Gregory T. Gundlach, eds. Thousand Oaks, CA: Sage Publications, 486–505.

Dolan, Paddy (2002), "The Sustainability of 'Sustainable Consumption,'" *Journal of Macromarketing*, 22 (December), 170–81.

Drahos, Peter and Ruth Mayne (2002), *Global Intellectual Property: Knowledge, Access and Development*. Basingstoke, UK: Palgrave Macmillan.

Duda, Lauren M. and Terrence H. Witkowski (2003), "Piracy of U.S. Motion Pictures in Developing Countries: Conduct, Remedies, and Future Prospects," in *Globalization, Transformation, and Quality of Life: The Proceedings of the 8th International Conference on Marketing and Development*, Clifford J. Shultz II, Don R. Ratz, and Mark Speece, eds. Rijeka. Croatia: Faculty of Economics. University of Rijeka, 14–25.

Duhaime, Carole P., Ronald McTavish, and Christopher A. Ross (1985), "Social Marketing: An Approach to Third-World Development," *Journal of Macromarketing*, 5 (Spring), 3–13.

Eckhardt, Giana M. and Michael J. Houston (1998), "Consumption as Self-Presentation in a Collectivist Society," in *Asia Pacific Advances in Consumer Research*, Vol. 4, Keneta Hung and Kent Monroe, eds. Provo, UT: Association for Consumer Research, 52–58.

—— and —— (2001) "To Own Your Grandfather's Spirit: The Nature of Possessions and Their Meaning in China," in *Asia Pacific Advances in Consumer Research*, Vol. 4, Paula Tidwell and Thomas Muller, eds. Valdosta, GA: Association for Consumer Research, 251–57.

The Economist (1999), "Business: VCDs Killed the Kung Fu Star," (March 20), 67.

—— (2001), "Where's the Beef?" (November 3), 70.

—— (2002a), "Intellectual Property," (September 14), 13–14, 75–76.

—— (2002b), "Marx After Communism," (December 21), 17–19.

—— (2002c), "Why Naomi Klein Needs to Grow Up," (November 9), 70.

—— (2003a), "Asia's Consumers: A Billion Boomers," (October 11), 68.

—— (2003b), "New Cinema: Korea's Turn," (October 25), 77.

—— (2003c), "Water Privatisation: Raise a Glass," (March 22), 68.

Eller, Claudia (2002), "To Russia with Theaters (and Digital Sound)," *Los Angeles Times*, (June 25), C3.

Embassy of India (2004), "Intellectual Property Rights in India," (accessed November 7, 2004), [available at http://www.indianembassy.org/policy/ipr/ipr_2000.htm].

Foreign Policy (2001), "McAtlas Shrugged," (May–June), 26–37.

Friedman, Thomas L. (1999), *The Lexus and the Olive Tree: Understanding Globalization*. New York: Farrar, Strauss and Giroux.

Fuller, Donald A. (1999), *Sustainable Marketing: Managerial-Ecological Issues*. Thousand Oaks, CA: Sage Publications.

Ger, Güliz (1992), "The Positive and Negative Effects of Marketing on Socioeconomic Development: The Turkish Case," *Journal of Consumer Policy*, 15 (3), 229–54.

—— (1997), "Human Development and Humane Consumption: Well-Being Beyond the 'Good Life,'" *Journal of Public Policy & Marketing*. 16 (Spring). 110–15.

—— and Russell W. Belk (1996), "I'd Like to Buy the World a Coke: Consumptionscapes of the 'Less Affluent World,'" *Journal of Consumer Policy*, 19 (3), 271–304.

Hart, Stuart L. (1997), "Beyond Greening: Strategies for a Sustainable World," *Harvard Business Review*, 75 (January–February), 66–77.

Harvey, Michael G. (1995), "The MNCs' Role and Responsibility in Deforestation of Tropical Forests," *Journal of Macromarketing*, 15 (Fall), 107–127.

Henwood, Doug (2003), *After the New Economy*. New York: The New Press.

Heritage Foundation (2004), 2004 Index of Economic Freedom, (accessed November 7, 2004). [available at www.heritage.org/research/features/index].

Hirschman, Elizabeth C. (1986), "Marketing as an Agent of Change in Subsistence Cultures: Some Dysfunctional Consumption Consequences," in *Advances in Consumer Research*, Vol. 13, Richard Lutz, ed. Provo, UT: Association for Consumer Research, 99–104.

Hollander, Stanley C., Kathleen Rassuli, D.G. Brian Jones, and Laura Farlow Dix (2005), "Periodization in Marketing History," *Journal of Macromarketing*, 25 (1), forthcoming.

Hung, C.L. (1984), "Economic and Market Environment: The Case of Hong Kong," in *Marketing in Developing Countries*, G.S. Kindra, ed., New York: St. Martin's Press, 95–114.

International Intellectual Property Alliance (2004), "Copyright and Trade Issues," (accessed November 7, 2004), [available at www.iipa.com/special301.html].

International Society of Marketing and Development (2004), "International Society of Marketing and Development," (accessed November 7, 2004), [available at http://www.bsu.edu/xtranet/ISMD/org.html].

Iritani, Evelyn (2003), "Bootleggers Raise Stakes in China's Piracy Fight," *Los Angeles Times*, (July 20), C1, C4.

Irwin, Douglas A. (2002), *Free Trade Under Fire*. Princeton, NJ: Princeton University Press.

Jameson, Fredric (2000), "Globalization and Strategy," *New Left Review*, (July-August), 49–68.

Johansson, Johny K. (2004), *In Your Face: How American Marketing Excess Fuels Anti-Americanism*. Upper Saddle River, NJ: Pearson Education.

Jones, D.G. Brian and David D. Monieson (1990), "Early Development of the Philosophy of Marketing Thought," *Journal of Marketing*, 54 (January), 102–113.

Joy, Annamma and Melanie Wallendorf (1996), "The Development of Consumer Culture in the Third World: Theories of Globalism and Localism," in *Consumption & Marketing: Macro Dimensions*, Russell W. Belk, Nikhilesh Dholakia, and Alladi Venkatesh, eds. Cincinnati, OH: South-Western College Publishing, 104–142.

Kaynak, Erdener (1986), *Marketing and Economic Development*. New York: Praeger Publishers.

Kilbourne, William, Pierre McDonagh, and Andrea Prothero (1997), "Sustainable Consumption and the Quality of Life: A Macromarketing Challenge to the Dominant Social Paradigm," *Journal of Macromarketing*, 17 (Spring), 4–24.

Klein, Naomi (1999), *No Logo: Taking Aim at the Brand Bullies*. New York: Picador USA.

Klein, Thomas and Robert W. Nason (2001), "Marketing and Development: Macromarketing Perspectives," in *Handbook of Marketing and Society*, Paul N. Bloom and Gregory T. Gundlach, eds. Thousand Oaks, CA: Sage Publications, 263–97.

Kotler, Philip (1988), "Potential Contributions of Marketing Thinking to Economic Development," in *Research in Marketing, Supplement 4: Marketing and Development: Toward Broader Dimensions*, Erdogan Kumcu and A. Fuat Firat, eds. Greenwich, CT: JAI Press. 1–10.

——, Somkid Jatusripitak, and Suvit Maesincee (1997), *The Marketing of Nations: A Strategic Approach to Building National Wealth*. New York: The Free Press.

Kraul, Chris and Lorenza Munoz (2003), "Mexico Says It's a Wrap," *Los Angeles Times*, (November 12), E1, E4.

—— and Kenneth R. Weiss (2003), "Baja Marinas Project Okd," *Los Angeles Times*, (November 8). A3.

Lee, Hyang-jin (2004), "Korean Cinema's Success and Future," *The Korea Times*, (February 18), (accessed November 7, 2004), [available at http://times.hankooki.com/lpage/special/200402/kt2004021820384711490.htm].

Lessig, Lawrence (2002), *The Future of Ideas: The Fate of the Commons in a Connected World*. New York: Vintage Books.

Levitt, Theodore (1983), "The Globalization of Markets," *Harvard Business Review*, 61 (May–June), 92–102.

Lindsey, Brink (2002), *Against the Dead Hand: The Uncertain Struggle for Global Capitalism*. New York: John Wiley & Sons.

Lomborg, Bjorn (2000), *The Skeptical Environmentalist: Measuring the Real State of the World*. Cambridge, UK: Cambridge University Press.

Magretta, Joan (1997), "Growth Through Global Sustainability: An Interview with Monsanto's CEO, Robert B. Shapiro," *Harvard Business Review*, 75 (January–February), 78–88.

Martorell, Reynaldo (2001), "Obesity" (accessed November 7, 2004), [available at http://www.ifpri.org/2020/focus/focus05/focus05_07.htm].

Mayer, Robert N. (1998), "Protectionism, Intellectual Property, and Consumer Protection: Was the Uruguay Round Good for Consumers?" *Journal of Consumer Policy*, 21 (2), 195–215.

Micklethwait, John and Adrian Wooldridge (2000), *A Future Perfect: The Challenge and Hidden Promise of Globalization*. New York: Crown Publishers.

Mroue, Bassem (2002), "Arab Countries Boycott U.S. Goods Over Mideast Policies," *Los Angeles Times*, (July 29), C3.

Nil, Alexander and Clifford J. Shultz II (1996), "The Scourge of Global Counterfeiting," *Business Horizons*, 39 (November–December), 37–42.

Oxfam International (2004), "Toward Global Equity: Strategic Plan, 2001–2004," (accessed November 7, 2004), [available at http://www.oxfam.org/eng/about.htm].

Packard, Vance (1957), *The Hidden Persuaders*. New York: Pocket Books.

People's Daily Online (2000), "Survey Shows Ten Most Favored Brands of Chinese." (July 1), (accessed November 7, 2004), [available at http://english.peopledaily.com.cn/english/200007/01/eng20000701_44397.html].

Pew Research Center (2004), "A Year After Iraq War: Mistrust of America in Europe Ever Higher, Muslim Anger Persists," (accessed November 7, 2004), [available at http://people-press.org/reports/display.php3?ReportID=206].

Prahalad, C.K. and Allen Hammond (2202), "Serving the World's Poor, Profitably," *Harvard Business Review*, 8 (September), 48–57.

Ross, Emma (2004), "Developing Countries Reject Obesity Plan," *Associated Press Online*, (February 9), (accessed November 7, 2004), [available at http://www.lexis-nexis.com].

Russell, Mark (2004), "Troubled Seoul," *Hollywood Reporter. com*. (May 25), (accessed November 7, 2004), [available at http://www.hollywoodreporter.com/thr/international/feature_display.jsp?vnu_content_id=1000518156].

Said, Edward W. (1979), *Orientalism*. New York: Vintage Books.

—— (1993), *Culture and Imperialism*. New York: Vintage Books.

Savitt, Ronald (1988). "The State of the Art in Marketing and Development," in *Research in Marketing, Supplement 4: Marketing and Development: Toward Broader Dimensions*, Erdogan Kumcu and A. Fuat Firat, eds. Greenwich, CT: JAI Press, 11–17.

Schlosser, Eric (2001), *Fast Food Nation: The Dark Side of the All-American Meal*. Boston: Houghton Mifflin.

Schmitt, Bernd H. and Alex Simonson (1997), *Marketing Aesthetics: The Strategic Management of Brands, Identity and Image*. New York: The Free Press.

Scholderer, Joachim, Ingo Balderjahn, Lone Bredahl, and Klaus G. Grunert (1999), "The Perceived Risks and Benefits of Genetically Modified Food Products: Experts Versus Consumers," in *European Advances in Consumer Research*, Vol. 4. Provo, UT: Association for Consumer Research, 123–29.

Shaw, Eric H. and D.G. Brian Jones (2005), "A History of Marketing Schools of Thought," *Marketing Theory*, 5 (3), forthcoming.

Sheridan, Mary Beth (1998), "Congresswoman Seeks to Light Up Future of Mexican Cinema," *Los Angeles Times*, (November 15), A3.

Shiva, Vandana (2000), "War Against Nature and the People of the South," in *Views from the South: The Effects of Globalization and the WTO on Third World Countries*, Sarah Anderson, ed. San Francisco: International Forum on Globalization.

Shultz, Clifford J. and Morris B. Holbrook (1999), "Marketing and the Tragedy of the Commons: A Synthesis, Commentary, and Analysis for Action," *Journal of Public Policy & Marketing*, 18 (Fall), 218–29.

Singer, Peter (2002), *One World: The Ethics of Globalization*. New Haven, CT: Yale University Press.

Smith, Toby M. (1998), *The Myth of Green Marketing: Tending Our Goats at the Edge of Apocalypse*. Toronto: University of Toronto Press.

Tunstall, Jeremy (1977), *Media Are American*. New York: Columbia University Press.

United Nations Development Programme (1998), *Human Development Report 1998*. New York: United Nations Development Programme.

—— (2004), *Human Development Report 2004*. New York: United Nations Development Programme.

Watson, James L., ed. (1997), *Golden Arches East: McDonald's in East Asia*. Stanford, CA: Stanford University Press.

White, Livingston A. (2001), "Reconsidering Cultural Imperialism Theory," *Transnational Broadcasting Studies: TBS Archives*, 6 (Spring–Summer), (accessed November 7, 2004), [available at http://www.tbsjournal.com/Archives/Spring01/white.html].

Wilkie, William L. and Elizabeth S. Moore (2003), "Scholarly Research in Marketing: Exploring the '4 Eras" of Thought Development," *Journal of Public Policy & Marketing*, 22 (Fall), 116–46.

Witkowski, Terrence H., Yulong Ma, and Dan Zheng (2003), "Cross-Cultural Influences on Brand Identity Impressions: KFC in China and the United States," *Asia Pacific Journal of Marketing and Logistics*, 15 (1–2), 74–88.

Wood, Van R. and Scott J. Vitell (1986), "Marketing and Economic Development: Review, Synthesis, and Evaluation," *Journal of Macromarketing*, 6 (Spring), 28–48.

Woodruff, David (2001), "Just Say No," *The Wall Street Journal* (October 1), R4.

World Health Organization (2003), "Diet, Nutrition and Prevention of Chronic Diseases," WHO Technical Report Series 916, (accessed November 7, 2004), [available at http://www.who.int/nut/documents/trs_916.pdf].

Yan, Yunxiang (2000), "Of Hamburger and Social Space: Consuming McDonald's in Beijing," in *The Consumer Revolution in Urban China*, Deborah S. Davis, ed. Berkeley: University of California Press, 201–225.

Yergin, Daniel and Joseph Stanislaw (2002), *The Commanding Heights: The Battle for the World Economy*. New York: Simon & Schuster.

Zane, Damian (2003), "Ethiopia War of GM Seeds," *BBC News*, (June 24), (accessed November 7, 2004) [available at http://news.bbc.co.uk/go/pr/fr/-/1/hi/business/3016390.stm].

13
On Negotiating the Market?

Mark Tadajewski[1] and Douglas Brownlie[2]

[1]*University of Leicester and* [2]*University of Stirling*

For most of the last century, the steady improvement in our ability to consume has been treated as a proxy for 'social progress' (Klein and Leiss, 1978: 5). Related to this is the issue of materialism, that is, the idea that possessions are likely to provide us with a source of happiness and general fulfilment. This materialistic emphasis has not notably abated, despite apparently high levels of interest among certain groups in protecting the environment. 'There is little indication', Belk has recently noted, 'that we are ready to sever our attachments to things and become more identified by our attachments to people. We cling to an identity forged in the crucible of materialism' (Belk, 2007: 136) at least in affluent parts of the world.

As Schudson has remarked, it is relatively easy to problematise consumer culture. After all, how would we all like to be 'remembered on our gravestones': as a good, thoughtful student, a good son or daughter, 'Beloved parent. Cherished spouse. Devoted friend. Something like "citizen of the world" would be nice, too, or simply "citizen," would it not? Compare that to "he shopped till he dropped" or "a consumer of exquisite taste" or "she could always find it wholesale." These do not have quite the same ring to them' (Schudson, 2007: 237). But, even so, while it is easy to call attention to the seemingly endless desire exhibited by consumers to purchase large quantities of products, not all consumer behaviour can be considered wholly self-interested (Hudson and Hudson, 2003; Scitovsky, 1992; Schor, 2007; Shankar *et al.*, 2006). Much consumer behaviour represents gift-giving. We value those products we have been given either through inheritance or that were received as gifts, most highly (Schudson, 2007).

The idea that increases in our economic welfare have not made people any 'happier as a result' (Scitvosky, 1992: 135) has motivated a growing cohort of individuals to find alternative ways to express their identity, most notably, through their avoidance of consumption and by the affirmation of relationality with the natural environment. Before we examine these issues in more detail, let us briefly pause to consider the question of whether consumers can actually escape the market.

Arnould (2007), in response to the issue of whether consumer citizens could escape the market, argues that 'implied' in such arguments 'is the notion of agency – the physical or mental ability, skill or capacity that enables actors to do something. The actor is presumed to proceed under his or her own volition, or at least without the permission of another' (Arnould, 2007: 97). Arnould juxtaposes this affirmative vision of agency with 'some contemporary writing about the prospects for autonomous consumer action' (Arnould, 2007: 97). What he appears to do here is blur the distinction between agency and autonomy. Here we prefer to demarcate the two but can appreciate the difficulty which confronts those interested in critical perspectives with regard to these terms.

Adorno (1989), for example, describes the 'ego-weakness' of individuals in contemporary society and the incessant drilling of conformist behaviours into each person. By contrast, he sees hope for individuals to demonstrate their autonomy from the effects of the culture industries in the sense that there are 'autonomous, independent individuals who judge and decide consciously for themselves' (Adorno, 1989: 135). Likewise, Fromm devotes considerable attention to autonomy, and describes how marketing and sales promotion can 'smother and kill the critical capacities of the customer like an opiate or outright hypnosis' (Fromm, 1941/2002: 111). In equal measure, he stresses how a consumer's critical thinking abilities can be awakened and the role of the consumer movement in this educative function (cf. Kozinets and Handelman, 2004).

While some of the critical theoretic sentiment noted above can be interpreted as pessimistic, the comments do indicate some role for individual agency, as we conceive it. In reflecting on the nature of the subject, we thus need to distinguish autonomy from agency. Autonomous subjects should be able to select their own lifestyle, consumption options and belief systems regardless of the influence of a given socio-historical context. In other words, autonomous subjects do not have their lives dictated to them by any external force. Contrasting this with agency, Bevir (1999) maintains that agents are born into a world that pre-exists them and therefore exerts some formative influence on their development, along with existing political, economic and technological systems. Such regimes of power/knowledge do not determine how an individual life will be structured. However, given that we are born into a particular society, in a specific socio-historical context, the difficulties of envisioning a society different to the present order should not be underestimated, nor should the practicalities of negotiating a space within our 'promotional culture' (Lazarsfeld, 1941). As Wright (2006) notes,

> People are born in societies that are always already made, whose rules they learn and internalize as they grow up. People are preoccupied with the daily tasks of making a living, and coping with life's pains and pleasures. The idea that the social world could be deliberately changed for the better in some fundamental way strikes them as far-fetched – both because it

is hard to envisage some dramatically better yet workable alternative, and because it is hard to imagine successfully challenging the structures of power and privilege in order to create it. Thus even if one accepts the diagnosis and critique of existing institutions, the most natural response is probably a fatalistic sense that not much could be really done to really change things. (Wright, 2006: 98)

But certain groups have attempted to rethink their relationship with the environment and their fellow human beings, leading them to attempt to limit their participation in market-place activities. They have attempted to challenge what some postmodern marketing scholars identify as the almost hegemonic nature of the market (e.g. Holt, 2002; Kozinets, 2002), by adopting other life-narratives as central to their own life-world (e.g. responsible citizenship, Earth Mother etc.). As Thompson (2004: 173) argues, there are no clear boundaries between the market and emancipatory spaces. But there are ways that consumers can adopt other socio-political agendas. Some groups attempt to move beyond the circuits of global capital and market relations (Thompson, 2004), refusing the label consumer at all, preferring instead 'non-consumerist' (Abela, 2007) 'Freegan' (Cruz, 2007) or 'conserver', as the chapter by Dobscha and Ozanne highlights most vividly.

This shift toward downsizing our consumption levels is not, as we might otherwise think, a new phenomenon. We could recall the comments by O'Shaughnessy and O'Shaughnessy in their chapter where they noted that the 'thrust of most of the world's religions is anti-materialistic . . . Consumption and possession-driven hedonism find no support . . . and much condemnation'. Likewise, Henry David Thoreau's nineteenth century critique of materialism was equally clear in its implications, calling for us to 'simplify, simplify'. Thoreau's pointed question: 'What is the use of a house if you haven't got a tolerable planet to put it on?' – '[still] demands concerted attention in the political and economic climate of the early twenty-first century' (Shah et al., 2007: 6).

Historically speaking, 'since the end of the Cold War' there has been a growth in alternative views to the 'ideology of consumption' that is facilitated by marketing and supported by neoliberalism. As Kilbourne et al. (1997: 6) note, the 'Greens are fashioning a vocabulary deeply critical of consumerism and economic globalization'. Rather than completely escaping the marketplace, the more radical forms of green consumer behaviour might be better thought of as engaging in the interstitial transformation of capitalism and the market economy (e.g. Moisander and Personen, 2002). What we mean by this is that these radical green movements 'seek to build new forms of social empowerment in the niches, spaces and margins of capitalist society, often where they do not seem to pose any immediate threat to dominant classes and elites' (Wright, 2006: 122).

Some marketing scholars have been less affirmative about such attempts to negotiate the marketplace through, for example, individual or communal attempts to define a lifeworld as free from consumption and materialism as possible. Others are more positive, suggesting that it might be possible to identify a social space beyond commercial market-exchanges

(Firat and Venkatesh, 1995). Still others have claimed that consumers cannot really escape the market because they are always to some extent dependent on market mechanisms (Kozinets, 2002), even if they want to live a 'simple life' (Saren, 2007).

Even the individual who prefers to view themselves as an 'anticonsumer' cannot apparently escape the market. As Schor suggests, this behavioural choice has become an 'advertised and marketed lifestyle, with magazines, courses, clothes, and accoutrements to promote simplicity and a rejection of consumption' (Schor, 2007: 25). However, simply because particular lifestyles are marketed in this way, does not mean that individuals whose lifestyles have been co-opted are still constrained by the market (cf. Thompson and Coskuner-Balli, 2007). By not consuming, they are 'escaping' the market; by satisfying their requirements via a means other than buying, they are outside of market exchanges (Firat, 1985; Lippke, 1990; Morgan and Trentmann, 2006).

Those who support the creation of 'reflexively defiant' consumers are more optimistic about individuals negotiating the marketplace in an 'unmystified' manner (Murray and Ozanne, 2006). Ozanne and Murray (1995) have suggested that consumers can form 'a different relationship to the marketplace in which they identify unquestioned assumptions and challenge the status of existing structures as natural. Through reflection, the consumer may choose to defy or resist traditional notions of consumption, become more independent from acquisition and disposition systems, or define their own needs independent from the marketplace' (Ozanne and Murray, 1995: 522). By drawing attention to the ideological presuppositions that underwrite detrimental attitudes towards the environment, for instance, it is hoped that less exploitative relations between humans, non-humans and the natural environment can be fostered, although this is a position not likely to be supported by existing market institutions and their attendant 'power elites' (Kilbourne, 1995; Mills, 1956).

We should not, therefore, be fatalistic about escaping the market. But we should recognise the difficulties of negotiating the market. Historically, it has been easy to pour scorn on those who adopt alternative lifestyles, without calling for the overthrow of the market system. Such lifestyle choices have often 'been 'disparaged' by radical socialists 'as palliative or merely symbolic, offering little prospect of serious challenge to the status quo. Yet, cumulatively, such developments can not only make a difference in people's lives, but potentially constitute a key component of enlarging the transformative scope for social empowerment in the society as a whole' (Wright, 2006: 122). Again, there are numerous radical social movements from those associated with the World Social Forum to the 'anti-globalisation movements . . . from the Chiapas to Bolivia' that demonstrate the power of radical political and social contestation (Therborn, 2007).

Closer to home, however, while we may all want to make the world a better place for present and future generations, pragmatically there are various factors that might prevent us from being as green or ethical in our consumption habits as we would like. As Irvine and Ponton (1988: 7) note, 'For many, the sheer pressure of "getting on" with the routines of everyday life blots out deeper [environmental and consumption] issues. Others may see the dangers, but feel helpless. Some genuinely cannot see what it has got to do with them, while others say "eat, drink and be merry"'. Even environmental activists feel tension between their belief system and their everyday consumption practices. Consider the following anecdote from Doug McKenzie-Mohr (McKenzie-Mohr and Smith, 1999: 1):

> During the spring, summer and fall I bike to work. However, in the winter, which in Fredericton stretches from November through to early April, I take the taxi. I know that automobiles are a principal source of carbon dioxide emissions that lead to global warming, so why don't I walk to work or take the bus? To walk to work takes approximately 30 minutes. While the exercise would be good for me, I would rather spend that time with my family. As for the bus, there is no direct bus route from our house to the university – making it slower to take the bus than it is to walk. Finally, the taxi costs only marginally more than bus fare, making it an even easier choice to take the taxi. While I am concerned about the possibility of global warming, my behavior for six months of the year is inconsistent with my concern.

In reality, many consumers in Western nations want for very little. Most of us have enough food, clean water and cheap clothes. We may be aware of the undesirable externalities of our consumption choices or the labour conditions in so-called Export Processing Zones (Klein, 2000) and yet our ability to act on our beliefs will remain constrained by our own financial situation, cognitive capabilities and the amount of free time we possess. As Abela (2007), Desmond (1998) and Hudson and Hudson (2003) point out, marketing activities exacerbate cognitive distance and commodity fetishism: 'Modern manufacturing, packaging, and distribution technologies facilitate the separation of (more easily available) benefits from the more concealed devices that produce the benefits, allowing us to consume while being (apparently) removed from the context and consequences of our consumption on ourselves, others and the environment' (Abela, 2007: 7). Even awareness of the impact of our consumption habits does not ameliorate such issues as Martin Parker (2007) has illustrated.

Stoke-on-Trent in the United Kingdom, according to Parker, is a city with its fair share of social problems. Incomes are lower than the national average, and no wonder, says Parker, 'that people were keen on the idea of buying clothes for £4, and that there were letters to the [news] paper thanking Primark for its bargains' (Parker, 2007: 183). He describes a discussion that he had with his teenage daughter about the clothes in Primark and why they cost so little; her response being that people in less developed countries were forced to take badly paid jobs because there was no other work available. His daughter admits she feels bad about purchasing such clothes. However, as Parker notes, this is an abstract guilt and there

> ... is a complex interplay of different senses of proximity here – physical, national, racial, occupational, and so on ... If I can see pain, I am more likely to resonate with it myself. Zoe

understands that garment workers in Bangladesh get paid around £17 per month for working 60-90 hours a week, and she feels guilt. She also understands that this is a part of a system of international capitalism that she, a girl in Stoke-on-Trent, can do little about. So, the guilt is abstract, almost impersonal. The afternoon after we talked, she went to Primark with her friend and bought a very nice winter coat for £8. (Parker, 2007: 183)

So, when we assert that consumers cannot 'escape' the market, we should recognise that many consumers have found ways to live within the interstices of capitalist market economies that enable them to live a life that they find more satisfying. Negotiating the marketplace is, as we suggested earlier, complex, especially in light of extended supply chains that characterise the structure of many market economies (see Thompson, 2004: 173–174).

Turning to the chapters that follow: marketing scholars have, as Van Dam and Apeldoorn note in their chapter, attempted to articulate a limited numbers of ways that it could be possible to limit the impact of the externalities of marketing activities on the environment. Via a detailed historical account of the emergence of ecological and green marketing they demonstrate that marketing theory devotes little, if any, attention to the environmental and societal impact of the exchange process.

One way that marketing could take account of the environment, they suggest, would be to factor the real environmental cost of production, distribution and so forth into the prices paid by consumers for products. This approach, they demonstrate, is fundamentally flawed in practice. Regardless of consumers espousing their willingness to purchase environmentally sound products, in reality only a small number of consumers are willing to pay a premium for such products (Kempton *et al.*, 1996) or understand environmental issues in all their complexity, perhaps understandably (Guy and Shove, 2000; Tadajewski and Wagner-Tsukamoto, 2006; Wagner-Tsukamoto and Tadajewski, 2006). More radically, Van Dam and Apeldoorn assert that if marketing was to be truly ecologically sustainable it would need to be regulated more strictly and this is a view that would not be popular in the business community (for the consumer view see Kempton *et al.* (1996: Chapter 6)).

By contrast to the comments by Saren (2007) and Schor (2007) that consumers will find it difficult to escape the market even if they are interested in living the 'simple life', Dobscha and Ozanne provide a compelling insight into a group of consumers who do just this, limiting their involvement in marketplace activities in order to affirm their relationship with the natural environment. They draw upon ecofeminist theory to discuss how the women that they talked to functioned as change agents, encouraging their families, friends and colleagues to modify their consumption levels in a more sustainable manner.

In addition, Dobscha and Ozanne's paper also highlights how marketing managers are not the only stakeholders for academic research in marketing. They demonstrate this by detailing the implications of their work for environmental groups, regulatory agencies, consumers and for marketing managers. The positive nature of their conclusions serves to reinforce the view that consumers can exhibit a high level of 'reflexively defiant' agency by refusing to engage in culturally sanctioned and supported levels of consumption (Ozanne and Murray, 1995).

References

Abela, A.V. (2007) 'Marketing and Consumerism: A Response to O'Shaughnessy and O'Shaughnessy', *European Journal of Marketing* 40(1/2): 5–16.

Adorno, T.W. (1989) 'The Culture Industry Revisited', in S.E. Bronner and D.M. Kellner (eds) *Critical Theory and Society: A Reader*, pp. 128–135. New York: Routledge.

Arnould, E.J. (2007) 'Should Consumer Citizens Escape the Market', *The Annals of the American Academy of Political and Social Science* 611(May): 96–111.

Belk, R. (2007) 'Why Not Share Rather than Own?', *The Annals of the American Academy of Political and Social Science* 611(May): 126–140.

Bevir, M. (1999) 'Foucault and Critique: Deploying Agency Versus Autonomy', *Political Theory* 27(1): 65–84.

Cruz, G. (2007) 'The 10 Best Buzzwords', *Time Magazine*. December 24: 43.

Desmond, J. (1998) 'Marketing and Moral Indifference', in M. Parker (ed.) *Ethics and Organizations*, pp. 173–196. London: Sage.

Firat, A.F. (1985) 'A Critique of Orientations in Theory Development in Consumer Behavior: Suggestions for the Future', *Advances in Consumer Research* 12(1): 3–6.

Firat, A.F. and Venkatesh, A. (1995) 'Liberatory Postmodernism and the Reenchantment of Consumption', *Journal of Consumer Research* 22(December): 239–267.

Fromm, E. (1941/2002) *The Fear of Freedom*. London: Routledge.

Guy, S. and Shove, E. (2000) *A Sociology of Energy, Buildings and the Environment*. London: Routledge.

Holt, D. (2002) 'Why Do Brands Cause Trouble? A Dialectical Theory of Consumer Culture and Branding', *Journal of Consumer Research* 29(June): 70–90.

Hudson, I. and Hudson, M. (2003) 'Removing the Veil? Commodity Fetishism, Fair Trade, and the Environment', *Organization & Environment* 16(4): 413–430.

Irvine, S. and Ponton, A. (1988) *A Green Manifesto: Policies for a Green Future*. London: Optima.

Kempton, W., Boster, J.S. and Hartley, J.A. (1996) *Environmental Values in American Culture*. Cambridge: MIT Press.

Kilbourne, W.E. (1995) 'Green Advertising: Salvation or Oxymoron?', *Journal of Advertising* 24(2): 7–19.

Kilbourne, W.E., McDonagh, P. and Prothero, A. (1997) 'Sustainable Consumption and the Quality of Life: A Macromarketing Challenge to the Dominant Social Paradigm', *Journal of Macromarketing* Spring: 4–24.

Klein, N. (2000) *No Logo*. London: Flamingo.

Kline, S. and Leiss, W. (1978) 'Advertising, Needs and "Commodity Fetishism"', *Canadian Journal of Political and Social Theory* 2(1): 5–30.

Kozinets, R.V. (2002) 'Can Consumers Escape the Market? Emancipatory Illuminations from Burning Man', *Journal of Consumer Research* 29(1): 20–38.

Kozinets, R.V. and Handelman, J.M. (2004) 'Adversaries of Consumption: Consumer Movements, Activism, and Ideology', *Journal of Consumer Research* 31(December): 691–704.

Lazarsfeld, P.F. (1941) 'Remarks on Administrative and Critical Communications Research', *Studies on Philosophy and Social Science* 9: 2–16.

Lippke, R.L. (1990) 'Advertising and the Social Conditions of Autonomy', *Business & Professional Ethics Journal* 8(4): 35–58.

McKenzie-Mohr, D. and Smith, W. (1999) *Fostering Sustainable Behavior: An Introduction to Community-Based Social Marketing*. Gabriola Island: New Society.

Mills, C.W. (1956) *The Power Elite*. London: Oxford University Press.

Moisander, J. and Personen, S. (2002) 'Narratives of Sustainable Ways of Living: Constructing the Self and the Other as a Green Consumer', *Management Decision* 40(4): 329–342.

Morgan, B. and Trentmann, F. (2006) 'Introduction: The Politics of Necessity', *Journal of Consumer policy* 29: 345–353.

Murray, J. and Ozanne, J.L. (2006) 'Rethinking the Critical Imagination', in R. Belk (ed.) *Handbook of Qualitative Research Methods in Marketing*, pp. 46–55. Cheltenham: Edward Elgar.

Ozanne, J.L. and Murray, J.F. (1995) 'Uniting Critical Theory and Public Policy to Create the Reflexively Defiant Consumer', *American Behavioral Scientist* 38(4): 516–525.

Parker, M. (2007) 'As Far as the Eye Can See', *Critical Perspectives on International Business* 3(2): 182–184.

Saren, M. (2007) 'Marketing is Everything: The View from the Street', *Marketing Intelligence and Planning* 25(1): 11–16.

Schor, J. (2007) 'In Defence of Consumer Critique: Revisiting the Consumption Debates of the Twentieth Century', *The Annals of the American Academy of Political and Social Science* 611(May): 16–30.

Schudson, M. (2007) 'Citizens, Consumers, and the Good Society', *The Annals of the American Academy of Political and Social Science* 611: 236–249.

Scitovsky, T. (1992) *The Joyless Economy: The Psychology of Human Satisfaction*, Revised Edition. New York: Oxford University Press.

Shah, D.V., McLeod, D.M., Friedland, L. and Nelson, M.R. (2007) 'The Politics of Consumption/The Consumption of Politics', *The Annals of the American Academy of Political and Social Science* 611: 6–15.

Shankar, A., Whittaker, J. and Fitchett, J. (2006) 'Heaven Knows I'm Miserable Now', *Marketing Theory* 6(4): 485–505.

Tadajewski, M. and Wagner-Tsukamoto, S. (2006) 'Anthropology and Consumer Research: Qualitative Insights into Green Consumer Behavior', *Qualitative Market Research: An International Journal* 9(1): 8–25.

Therborn, G. (2007) 'After Dialectics: Radical Social Theory in a Post-Communist World', *New Left Review* 43(Jan/Feb): 63–114.

Thompson, C.J. (2004) 'Marketplace Mythology and Discourses of Power', *Journal of Consumer Research* 31(June): 162–180.

Thompson, C.J. and Coskuner-Balli, G. (2007) 'Countervailing Market Responses to Corporate Co-optation and the Ideological Recruitment of Consumption Communities', *Journal of Consumer Research* 34(2): 135–152.

Wagner-Tsukamoto, S. and Tadajewski, M. (2006) 'Cognitive Anthropology, Bricolage and the Problem Solving Behaviour of the Green Consumer', *Journal of Consumer Behaviour: An International Review* 5(3): 235–244.

Wright, E.O. (2006) 'Compass Points: Towards a Socialist Alternative', *New Left Review* Sept-Oct: 93–124.

14
Sustainable Marketing*

Ynte K. van Dam[1] and Paul A.C. Apeldoorn[2]

[1]*Agricultural University Wageningen, The Netherlands*
[2]*Lexmond Milieu-Aduiezen, Bodegraven, The Netherlands*

ABSTRACT *In order for marketing to play a role in sustainable economic development, a critical reassessment of marketing theory is required. Both the "societal marketing" of the 1970s and contemporary "green marketing" are efforts to improve the relationship between marketing and the natural environment. Taken alone, however, either approach provides but a partial analysis of the problems that are involved. Starting from the assumptions and limitations of economic and cognitive approaches to marketing and from the dilemmas between micro-marketing objectives and macromarketing goals, marketing is shown to have an inherent drive toward unsustainability. Sustainable marketing requires finding optimal regulatory frameworks for governing the role of marketing within a confined ecological space.*

> We're the other kind,
> we're the kind that gives people
> what they know they really need,
> not what we think they ought to want. (T. Pratchett, *Witches Abroad*)

Since the beginning of the 1970s, interest in the environmental effects of economic activity has waxed and waned. In recent years there has been widespread and growing support for "sustainable economic development." Despite this support, there seems to be little precision as to the concept. Cairncross (1991) notes that "the appeal of the phrase is that it means so many different things to different people" (p. 47).

---

* Article originally published in the *Journal of Macromarketing* (1996); 16(2) 45–56; Reproduced by permission of Sage Publications.

The Brundtland report (WCED 1987) defines sustainable development as that which "meets the needs of the present without compromising the ability of future generations to meet their own needs" (p. 8). Even so, there is "much room for, and danger of, its being supported while business and industries . . . and environmental degradation continue unabated" (Slocombe and Van Bers 1991, p. 11).

Shearman (1990) points out that the implications of sustainability are to be found in the modifications and contradictions that become apparent when the consequences of sustainable development are considered within a particular context. Thus, the meaning of sustainable marketing becomes apparent when the concept of sustainability is elaborated upon within the framework of marketing theory.

In both economics and the human sciences, the discussion of environmental issues has prompted a reassessment of premises and theory. Examples can be found in environmental (Tietenberg 1994) and ecological (Martinez-Allier 1990) economics and in the New Environmental Paradigm (Buttel 1987) in sociology. Marketing has reflected these discussions but refrained from a comparable reassessment. The current interest has led to an exuberance of books on green marketing (Peattie 1992; Ottman 1992), greener marketing (Charter 1992), or environmental marketing (Coddington 1992). Two decades earlier, ecological marketing (Fisk 1974; Henion and Kinnear 1976) was the focus of attention.

The multitude of concepts relating marketing to the natural environment requires a curtailment of meanings. Both ecological marketing and green marketing start from the necessity of combining profit making for private companies with sustainable environmental quality for society in general. The treatment of the issue shows a difference in Zeitgeist. *Ecological marketing* focuses on the acknowledgment of an impending ecological crisis and the willingness and ability of marketers to assume responsibility for avoiding this doom (Fisk 1974). In essence, this is a societal marketing approach. *Green marketing* focuses on market pull and legislative push toward improved, environmentally friendly corporate performance. In essence, this is a conventional micromarketing approach. This article introduces the concept of *sustainable marketing*, which is marketing within, and supportive of, sustainable economic development. All three concepts linking marketing to the environment (ecological, green and sustainable) are subsumed herein under the label *environmental marketing*.

Organization of the Article

Marketing has its foundations in both economics and the human sciences. The next section highlights the key issues of the ecological discussion within both of those disciplines. The discussion then turns to past views on the relationship between marketing and the environment, from within both marketing and the conserver society movement. These views are critiqued and pitted against the dominant consumption ethos of their time. After this, the current green marketing approach is explored.

These discussions lead to the conclusion that marketing is subject to internal pressures toward expansion and externalization of costs. Regulation therefore is required to contribute to sustainable economic development, many claims to the contrary notwithstanding. Because of the inevitability of regulation, research should be directed at finding optimal regulatory frameworks and conditions supportive of sustainable marketing.

An important distinction to keep in mind throughout the article is the difference between general marketing theory and corporate marketing management. Although both are part of the same market system, they operate at different levels. They easily lose their validity when transposed, as in the field of consumer behavior, where the general theory provides an ideology whose basic assumptions are rejected in daily practice (Benton 1985; Dholakia and Dholakia 1985).

Ecological Discussion Within Marketing

The two key elements of the ecology discussion in both economics and social theory are imperfect knowledge and the unwanted outcomes of rational choice. Economic theory tends to emphasize the former, while social theory focuses on the latter. This distinction is not exclusive, however, and the following sections approach each issue from both sides.

Imperfect Knowledge

The notion of sustainable development adds a new dimension to the economic concept of scarcity. Besides balancing interpersonal needs and intrapersonal needs, economics now also has to deal with balancing intergenerational needs. As a result, environmental economics entails a broadening of scope to include non-priced natural resources, the economic effects of underpricing of natural resources and economic reactions to environmental degradation.

The neoclassical approach in environmental economics focuses on valuing environmental functions in order to establish correct price signals, which reflect scarcity (Tietenberg 1994). The emphasis is on the "correction" of market prices through the internalization of external costs and reliance on the market mechanism to achieve optimal equilibrium. If all externalities were internalized in prices, the resulting "efficient market" would optimize market transactions in terms of both the use of environmental resources and the satisfaction derived from consumption. Accordingly, a market-based, sustainable economic development should be feasible. This line of argument has been criticized at some fundamental points, however, by two other theoretical streams.

Institutional economics questions the possibility of valuation and "efficient markets" because of imperfect or inadequate information. Completely unknown resources (such as genetic variation in ecosystems) and unknown feedbacks are examples of the latter. The unknown extent of the vulnerability of ecosystems to pollution or destruction (for example, by heavy metals, of the ozone layer) or the valuation of ecosystems illustrate the former. According to this view, an *objectively correct* price signal is therefore a virtual impossibility. Because any decision to give a present value to (future needs for) an exhaustible resource is a *political* decision involving a rate of discount and a time horizon, "market economics cannot by itself provide a guide for a rational intertemporal allocation of resources and waste" (Kapp 1983, cited in Martinez–Allier 1990, p. xxii). The market mechanism therefore must be confined by non-market (institutional) choices that form the basis of sustainable economic development.

The third approach in environmental economics is based on material flows, leading to the establishment of indices of sustainability, for example, in the form of critical loads (Daly 1992). Whereas the neoclassical perspective tries to incorporate the environment within the economic system, this approach starts from the principle that economics is a part of the environmental system. Daly (1992) recognizes three independent policy goals in economics: allocation, distribution, and scale. *Allocation* refers to the relative division of the resource flow among alternative product uses. *Distribution* refers to the relative division of the resource flow among alternative people (including future generations). *Scale* refers to the physical volume of the flow of raw materials from the environment and of waste back to the environment, relative to the fixed size of the ecosystem. It should be noted that the scarcity of resources, a basic axiom of traditional economic theory, is included in this model as an endogenous variable.

Efficient allocation is brought about by relative market prices, governed by economic mechanisms of supply and demand. Distribution is brought about by transfers (taxes and welfare payments) based on a political decision reflecting a just distribution of the newly created assets. Scale is to be determined by absolute limits to the use of ecological functions (resources as well as waste disposal) that are based on political decisions reflecting the estimated long-term capacity of the ecological system. The latter two instruments (transfers and limits) are of a noneconomic character, and only the former (prices) is subject to the laws of market economics. According to this third approach, both the market mechanism and its nonmarket confinements are controlled by political decisions reflecting the limits to the use of environmental resources and the dependence of the economic systems on the ecological environment. Both the high societal relevance and the high uncertainty of these decisions place them in the political realm.

These three approaches share the view that the price mechanism is suitable to optimize the allocation of any quantity of resources. The neoclassical model also depends on the price mechanism to optimize the scale of resource use. The two alternative models observe that this price mechanism will optimize neither the distribution of assets nor the scale of economic activities.

The imperfection of knowledge is explained in psychological terms as well. The rationality of individual human behavior with respect to environmental issues is bounded by the scale of ecological processes in general. The human perceptual system is tuned to processes that occur on a human scale (see Gibson 1979). This means that only processes limited in time span, size and location are perceptible. Most ecological processes, however, including environmental degradation, occur on a humanly imperceptible scale. Even though some of these processes can be, and are, rendered perceptible by science or the mass media, their absolute scale is of a level to which individuals can hardly relate. Environmental consequences of individual behavior therefore are primarily a matter of belief, while personal consequences are directly experienced (see Darby and Karni 1973). Whether we are concerned with daily household disposal building up to a nationwide waste problem (Lodge and Rayport 1991) or with individual contributions to a global greenhouse effect, ecological problems can only be noted as "consequences of consequences," implying prolonged and indirect feedback loops between ecological damage and individual behavior.

The paradigmatic model of rational intentional behavior is based on perceived consequences and the strength of belief in those consequences (Fishbein and Ajzen 1975). Many personal consequences of behavioral choices can be seen directly, while most ecological consequences are either imperceptible or perceived only indirectly. Ecological consequences are said to occur during the next century and to be contingent on the choices of entire communities, while personal consequences are dependent only on personal choice and will be felt at short notice. It seems that the paradigmatic rational decision maker has to pit known, short-term, personal outcomes against possible, long-term, societal outcomes, so the tendency of personal consequences of behavior to outweigh ecological consequences is only rational.

Social Dilemmas

Within the human sciences, environmental problems can be explained as social dilemmas in which individual rational behavior (that is, acting without restraint to maximize short-term gain) causes long-range damage to the entire society, including the individual. Dawes (1980) has suggested that the term *social dilemma* be used to encompass "commons dilemmas" (Hardin 1968), "social traps" (Platt 1973), and "prisoner dilemmas" alike, since all share common characteristics. Their central aspect is the conflict between microscopic and macroscopic levels, in which the combination of individual optimal choices leads to collective suboptimal consequences.

Within the objective of profit or utility maximization, any actor is tempted to shift from priced to nonpriced or underpriced resources (be they exhaustible or not) and to externalize costs as much as possible. As individual actors increase their personal welfare at the cost of society in general, society as a whole – including every individual actor – is driven to collapse by the accumulated externalized costs.

These dilemmas show at both sides of the market. On the demand side, individual consumers increase their welfare by increasing their level of consumption. The mechanisms underlying this consumption ethos will be treated later; here it suffices to note that this individual rationality to enjoy the fruits of consumption leads to a collective overconsumption, which generates such unwanted and negatively valued side effects as excessive waste and environmental deterioration. Because the focus of this article is marketing, not consumer behavior, the social dilemma occurring at the supply side of the market will be treated more extensively.

Although marketing theory states that producers strive toward optimal – not maximal – levels of production, a social dilemma still occurs. Suppose there is full awareness of the ecological damage of production, the avoidance of which entails costs upon a producer that are not offset by higher efficiency (Walley and Whitehead 1994). Suppose furthermore that most consumers are unwilling to pay a substantial premium for environmentally less damaging products while cheaper alternatives are available (Grunert 1992; Moore 1993). Full internalization of ecological costs then prices a product out of the market, to the benefit of products with externalized ecological costs. Therefore, for each individual producer it is attractive, or even essential, to externalize at least some of these ecological costs. Besides, at any given time consumers are concerned about only a limited number of environmental issues. Marketing textbooks stress that neither time nor energy should be spent on product features that are of no importance to the consumer. This view does not preclude attention to future demands or future environmental constraints, but in practice attention is limited to demands and constraints that can reasonably be expected in the short term, and that can be met profitably. Therefore, ecological restrictions that are not explicitly mirrored in consumer demand and or enforced by political, social, or consumer action will not be incorporated into production or marketing behavior.

A comparable conclusion can be drawn from the economic theory of competition, which implies that the forces of competition lower prices by increasing supply until marginal costs equal marginal revenues (Chamberlin 1946; Robinson 1948). A monopolist will restrict supply to a quantity that achieves maximum profit. In a competitive market this monopoly quantity would achieve maximum profit for the aggregated suppliers as well; however, even if each supplier is fully aware of this optimal monopoly quantity and of the price-lowering effects of exceeding this quantity, aggregate supply will exceed the monopoly quantity (see Gibbons 1992). This common knowledge lies at the heart of antitrust legislation around the world.

The same basic mechanism will apply when an optimum quantity of supply is determined by constraints to environmental dependency. In this case, additional resources are available, but in order to preserve the environment they should not be used. Whenever the ecological limitations to economic activity warrant an aggregate supply that is below the competitive equilibrium quantity, the market price will be above the equilibrium price. Each supplier will then receive a market revenue at which it will be efficient to raise the supplier's production. This leads to an economic drive to increase production until the market is cleared at equilibrium price. Aggregate supply will then exceed the ecological constraints, leading to ecological degradation.

Restriction of the supply below equilibrium level can be achieved by arrangements among producers, by allocating fixed quotas to producers, by taxation, or by allocating tradable "environmental use permits" to the market. The former two solutions imply a departure from the ideology of perfect competition, and all but the first imply rigorous legislation and registration of actual levels of supply or environmental dependency (for example, energy input, emission levels). The merits of each policy and the possibility of other forms of restriction remain to be studied from a marketing perspective.

For marketing theory this would mean a shift in focus from competitive strategy and its economic grounds (such as profit, cost, and market potential) toward restricted competition that balances corporate objectives, like market share, with societal objectives, like sustainability. Policy instruments, such as tradable permits, preserve market efficiency at the cost of much regulation and expensive (governmental) administration, but their applicability to large-scale regulation of widely used products is limited. Conversely, arrangements among suppliers reduce administrative expenses at the cost of competitive efficiency.

Past Views on Marketing and Environmental Problems

Within both marketing theory and a wider social framework, the relationship between production and consumption, on the one hand, and environmental deterioration, on the other hand, has been subject to critique. The following discussion briefly presents and critiques both the ecological marketing view and the conserver society movement perspective.

Ecological Marketing

Shuptrine and Osmanski (1975) draw attention to the ideological shift that occurred around 1970. Lazer (1969) still recommended that

> one of marketing's roles may be to encourage increasing expenditures by consumers of [money] and time to develop themselves socially, intellectually, and morally . . . [and to encourage that] new consumption standards should be established, including the acceptance of self-indulgence, of luxurious surroundings, and of nonutilitarian products. (p. 4)

Contrary to this, Dawson (1971) predicted that during the 1970s there would be increasing attention to

> "Should it be sold? Is it worth its cost to society?" despite the fact that marketing might feel more comfortable focusing on *"Can it be sold?"* (p. 68)

This *societal approach* within marketing is reflected in the major monographs of that era on ecological marketing (Fisk 1974; Henion and Kinnear 1976), which stress how marketers could, and most likely would, change their practices because of their recognition of an impending ecological crisis. In these texts the willingness and ability of marketers to react positively to information about the state of the environment is hardly disputed. The necessity of prices reflecting all ecological costs is stressed, but the limitations of this approach, as evident from the previous section on imperfect knowledge, are neglected. The impossibility of exercising the ecological perspective in a competitive environment, as evident from the discussion of social dilemmas, is recognized (Fisk 1974), but how a realistic market situation can be reached, in which all environmental costs are internalized, is never spelled out.

The same line of argument is typically followed in studies of the ecologically or environmentally concerned consumer (see Van Liere and Dunlap 1980; Antil 1984). Because the prime motive of the marketing function lies in consumer needs and wants, these needs and wants, and the decisions made by consumers to fulfill them, have frequently been taken as a starting point for marketing to reach sustainability.

> Since the outcome [of current marketing practice] (resource depletion and uniform distribution of materials on earth) runs counter to human wants [that is, a sound natural environment], recycling and anti-entropic marketing *must* ultimately emerge as a means of sustaining ecolibrium. (Fisk 1974, p. 67; italics ours, pun his)

Henion and Kinnear (1976) introduced the Ecologically Concerned Consumuser (ECC; another pun), who is educated and stimulated by government and marketing organizations. These ECCs are well aware of the long-distance and long-term effects of their behavior and are eager to engage in responsible consumption.

These models of both consumer and producer behavior, in which moral motives and rational abilities to act in an environment-friendly way are decisive, lead both authors to the logical conclusion that the market forces of supply and demand *will* impose their own limits (Fisk 1974; Henion and Kinnear 1976) and thus curb the environmental impact. The fundamental flaw in this line of argument, however, is that in reality the generally recognized *need* for environment friendliness, or sustainability, is not reflected in a comparably general consumer *want* or *demand*. Even worse, the consumer segments most supportive of environment friendliness are at the same time the ones least inclined to give up their consumptive aspirations and least supportive of collective measures to protect the environment (Uusitalo 1990). Indeed, the idea of self-regulating processes existing within marketing was immediately criticized (Kangun 1974). Still, concerning self-regulating producer behavior, White (1981) states that

> awareness that macro impacts (*among which environmental effects*) are present in actions and transactions by the firm is growing and will be an increasingly important aspect of future management responsibility. (p. 11)

While individual companies like DuPont and 3M show signs that this awareness is indeed growing, mainstream marketing theory still hardly pays little attention to the environmental impacts of the exchange process (Kotler 1994; Mercer 1992). Diagrams of the marketing environment typically leave aside any physical transactions with the natural environment. Only sporadically do they incorporate disposal flows.

Even though the existence of absolute limits to physical transactions with the environment has been acknowledged (Henion and Kinnear 1976; Reidenbach and Oliva 1983; Kangun 1984), the relevance of those limits to corporate marketing policy is systematically ignored. Observations on how marketing could contribute to reaching sustainability tend to start by taking the present situation for granted and then continue with a discussion of the better products, better distribution, and better consumption styles that marketing could deliver (see, for example, Henion and Kinnear 1976; Reidenbach and Oliva 1983). The contribution marketing has made and is making to the current economic system, which is far out of balance with nature, remains underexposed. Perhaps the present quantity of material goods could be produced and processed in a sustainable way, but the Brundtland report (WCED 1987) and scores of other sources state that this is not being done at the moment.

Conserver Society Movement

An ambitious approach to environmental problems is offered by the *conserver society movement*, which focuses on the changes in the social fabric that would be required to promote, facilitate, or ensure ecologically conscious producer and consumer behavior (Shapiro 1978). The conserver society movement attempts to translate the societal need for less wasteful production and consumption into a set of prescriptive policies. Depending on the scenario chosen, the conserver society should strive toward Reform of Inefficient Consumption Habits (RICH), Zero Artificial Needs Growth (ZANG), or Negative Artificial Needs Growth (NANG). Marketing's role is to convince consumers that they can derive more satisfaction from purchasing less of a company's products. Unlike ecological marketing, the conserver society movement does not expect that the mere awareness of environmental problems will inevitably induce behavioral changes; these must be enforced by full internalization of costs (within RICH) or by governmental regulation of the availability of products (within ZANG and NANG). Unfortunately, the key issue of who decides which habits are inefficient or which needs are artificial is not elaborated upon. Nevertheless, Shapiro (1978) concludes that neither the reduction of economic activities to a prescribed level, nor even the stabilization of such activities to save the environment, can be attained without government regulation and social engineering.

The prevailing consumption ethos has proven, however, to be a strong, opposing trend preventing widespread acceptance of conserver ideas. Sklair (1991, 1992) considers the taken-for-granted culture – ideology of mass consumption to be the central problem of our civilization. At a macroscopic level, Campbell (1987) also considers the key question of consumer behavior to be, not how or what people consume, but "how individuals manage to develop a regular and endless programme of wanting in relation to new goods and services" (p. 58). Existing theories of consumer behavior do not concentrate on this subject, suggesting that it results from exposure to the media, the stimulation of emulative desires, or an inherent drive of the human being; they concentrate instead on the rationality of product choice within an accepted framework of wants and tastes.

Several explanations are offered for the never-ending urge to overconsume in modern Western society. Rassuli and Hollander (1986) make a distinction between external facilitating, external socioenvironmental and internal motivating factors, which jointly provide the conditions for a consumer society. No one factor is sufficient, and some necessary elements are both cause and result of the process. For example, marketing and advertising tend to follow general consumption trends while at the same time propagating a materialistic life-style, thus inducing general consumptive desires (or the propensity to consume). In-depth studies of samples of these factors are referred to in Rassuli and Hollander (1986). Furthermore, recent studies are available on induced scarcity, emulative consumption, and conspicuous consumption (see, for example, Mason 1981; Xenos 1989) and on modern hedonistic consumption drives (Campbell 1987; Belk 1988a). The shift from utilitarianism to hedonism and the parallel shift from satisfaction to (insatiable) pleasure as the goal of consumption are noted by Skinner (1986), as well.

Both ecological marketing and the conserver society approach have been overwhelmed by this consumption ethos (Campbell 1987; Xenos 1989). The psychological role of possessions and materialistic consumption (Belk 1988b) have been greatly underestimated by the proponents of ecological marketing and conserver thinking.

In the late 1970s and the early 1980s, public (and marketing) interest in the environment declined, as reflected by the sudden drop in environment-related entries in the *Journal of Marketing* after 1975. During the same period, however, environmental policies were institutionalized. Most governments established a department of environmental affairs, and environmental policies were prepared and adopted (Cairncross 1991). Although concern with ecological issues within marketing theory declined, individual firms were increasingly likely to encounter stricter environmental regulations.

How did the corporate practice of marketing respond to this challenge? Instead of building on the societal approach of ecological marketing, practitioners stuck to conventional objectives within a new regulatory framework, reflected by the concept of green marketing; this choice of perspective ignores the essential macroscopic character of sustainability, which cannot be easily reduced to a micromarketing issue.

Green Marketing: A Micro Solution for a Macro Problem

Within marketing theory, the support for sustainability currently is reflected in the rise of *green marketing* (*Advertising Age* 1991). There is no single definition of the concept, but most of the literature describes how companies adapt to the increasing consumer demand for environmentally friendly products (see, for example, Charter 1992; Ottman 1992; Peattie 1992). A major difference between ecological and green marketing is that the societal and moral motives of the former are replaced in the latter by market pressures. In ecological marketing, environment friendliness is a matter of moral decency; in green marketing, it is a marketing tool.

> As society becomes greener . . . the demand for greener goods and services will rise. To meet these new needs marketing will have to become increasingly green, leading companies and other organisations towards sustainable management. (Peattie 1992, p. 85)

The proactive elements of ecological marketing are being abandoned in favor of a responsive attitude, and ecological issues are converted from a societal challenge into a marketing problem. This is both a strength and a weakness; the appeal of ecological issues to marketing companies has increased, but the macroscopic character of the issues is ignored. Undoubtedly, green marketing has helped and is helping to slow the deterioration of the environment, whether by product improvement or by providing environmental services. This notwithstanding, the concept of sustainability within the framework of marketing implies more than adding a new element of competition. It is doubtful that our present ways of doing business can be compatible with sustainable development. The case for business continuing as it is yet being sustainable looks increasingly suspect (Gray 1994).

Green marketing, as the term is currently employed, remains restricted to a limited number of companies that cater to the needs of a limited number of "green" consumers by offering a limited number of "green" products (see Charter 1992; Ottman 1992; Peattie 1992). From the viewpoint of sustainability, however, it does not suffice to analyze "to what extent the greening of business operations could be profitable and act accordingly"

(Peattie 1992), as this allows for the supply of nongreen products whenever these are (more) profitable. Sustainability, as a societal goal, includes all producers and consumers, willing or not, and requires a change in virtually everyone's behavior. Contrary to green marketing, sustainable marketing is a macromarketing concept.

Unsustainable Marketing

A market-based solution to environmental problems could be feasible if, but only if, environmental costs could be translated to the market as prices. The price setting of environmental functions differs from the common market transaction, however, because there is no actor producing environmental functions at prices that render optimal profit. The price of natural resources also differs from the rent of capital, as natural resources are not a set of assets to be turned into a source of profit (Ponting 1991). Price signals in relation to the environment cannot be posed by the market itself but are based, necessarily, on political decisions (Faber, Stephan, and Michaelis 1989). (Both the need for and the arbitrary character of imposed prices were discussed previously, in relation to imperfect knowledge.)

The economic mechanism that brings about consumer benefits under conditions of free competition is also responsible for the ecological challenge to marketing. This paradoxical effect is contingent on the existence of positive and negative externalities. Individual decisions regarding wealth may result in the collective wealth of nations, as Adam Smith surmised; likewise, individual decisions regarding environmental health may result in sustainable economies. This does not prevent environmental efficiency from having negative results on competitiveness and economic development, however. It is said that in the long run the principles of economic growth and environmental quality could reinforce each other (Kleiner 1991), but "not a single empirical analysis lends convincing support to that view" (Stavins 1994).

A solution of environmental problems based on rationality could be feasible, provided that all information could be processed and provided and that environmentally beneficial actions would carry with them personal gains. The ideal-typical approaches to ecological marketing and ecologically conscious consumer behavior are based on the idea of altered behaviors resulting from full understanding of environmental problems. These approaches ignore the complexity of ecological systems and the limitations of human cognition; together these result in a very limited understanding of environmental problems. People are not sufficiently informed about how their behavior affects the ecology, and the human mind is not designed to cope with the vastness of these issues. It would seem that the concept of fully informed, rational producers and consumers provides a weak basis on which to found a theory of sustainable marketing. The ecological marketing approach properly observes that environmental marketing should not be dependent on consumer demand, but it overestimates the willingness of producers to engage in environment-friendly production.

Conversely, green marketing rightly assumes that producers are market driven but over-estimates the consumer demand for environmentally benign products. Apparently, some kind of external regulation of the marketing system is indispensable.

Fisk (1974) warns that the adoption by firms of ecological criteria, as well as monetary criteria, requires regulation of all national and international competition, including the production of substitutes. Experiences in the formerly centralized economies of Eastern Europe, however, show that even strict regulation of the economy does not prevent large-scale environmental destruction. Still, this is not a proven case against regula-tion, but an indication that considerable study must be directed at finding optimal regulatory frameworks. A major issue in marketing theory always has been how to avoid government regulation. Fisk (1974) strongly opposes the regulation of market behavior, following Hardin's (1968) "mutual coercion mutually agreed upon" dictum. Henion and Kinnear (1976) suggest that the main task of the government would be to increase the number of Environmentally Concerned Consumusers through educa-tion. Such action, they suggest, would render further regulation obsolete, and ecological marketing would take the place of ecological regulation. Reidenbach and Oliva (1983) state that

> the proliferation of government-controlled macro agencies charged with the responsibility of regulating the transformation process brings with it a concomitant reduction in social and economic freedom. (p. 39)

Despite these objections to regulation, which represent "the old ways of fighting, ignoring, and hamstringing any and all environmental regulatory efforts" (Walley and Whitehead 1994), there is no escaping the social dilemma in which marketing managers and theorists are trapped. The need for regulation cannot be rationalized away.

Marketing in Sustainable Economic Development

Economic products and services can be viewed as environmental functions (de Groot 1994), like natural resources and waste-degrading capacities, that have been transformed by human actors. The task of marketing is to achieve optimal satisfaction of consumer wants by allocating the use of environmental functions in the shape of products or services, without exceeding externally determined limits.

The current wisdom appears to be that environmental improvements in products and production are the best way to increase a company's efficiency and profitability (Porter 1991; Gore 1993). Such win–win optimism has been seriously criticized (Walley and Whitehead 1994), however, and ignores the original rationalism behind environmental deterioration. Furthermore, it ignores the serious costs that will arise once we come to the end of the easy solutions to obvious problems of dissipation and inefficiency.

Sustainable marketing is not primarily concerned with such obvious and real examples of win–win solutions as those of 3M or DuPont. Sustainable marketing should contribute to finding feasible trade-offs between business and environmental concerns. Sustainable marketing is, among other things, an appeal to lengthen corporate time horizons (see Kleiner 1991) and to value continuity over profit. Most importantly, sustainable marketing is an appeal to accept the limitations of marketing philosophy and acknowledge the necessity of regulatory constraints to the market mechanism. Within these constraints, marketing can prove its efficiency, but it can never effectively pose these constraints itself.

With the acceptance of the inevitability of some form of governmental control and restriction, the discussion within marketing theory could be advanced from the level of *How to Avoid Regulation* to the level of *How to Organize the Necessary Limitations*. As that discussion fosters understanding of the role of marketing within a confined ecological space, a theory of sustainable marketing that supports sustainable economic development can be built. With regard to sustainable economic development, marketing can be part of the problem or part of the solution. Being part of the solution requires both a corporate and a collective commitment to sustainable marketing.

Future Perspective

Although some sort of control is indispensable for sustainable marketing, the character of regulation will differ by country, depending on the stage of market development and on political and cultural differences. Some countries may favor legislation, while others may prefer less rigorous intervention for a specific environmental problem. For example, reduction of packaging waste is enforced by legislation in Germany, while the same end is pursued by a covenant between government and industry in the Netherlands. Likewise, certain toxic emissions are limited by prohibitive legislation in some European countries, while the United States depends on tradable permits.

Furthermore, it should be kept in mind that regulation may be a necessary, but not a sufficient, condition for a sustainable market economy. Especially in developing countries, poverty and an inadequate judicial system may be far more important causes of environmental deterioration, and the curtailment of economic freedom has not prevented environmental catastrophes in the former Eastern bloc countries.

The disadvantages and limitations of legislation in relation to marketing are extensively treated by Harris and Carman (1983, 1984; Carman and Harris 1986). They observe that both recognizing an environmental problem as a market failure and identifying desirable solutions are embedded in ideological convictions. Thus, staunch advocates of economic growth may view environmental protection as a failure because there is too much of it; conservationists may also view environmental regulations as a failure because there is too little of it (Carman and Harris 1986, p. 54)

Depending on the environmental problem at hand either may be right. One-sided reliance on either free-market processes or restrictive legislation is equally counterproductive. Due to the character of environmental problems, however, within marketing theory the economic aspects systematically tend to be overrated, while the merits of legislation are underestimated.

Marketing, even sustainable marketing, will not offer the final solution to the current problem of unsustainability. Nevertheless, insight into the merits and limitations of sustainable marketing, controlled and directed by a balanced system of regulations and laws – incentives and punishments – would be a major step toward sustainable economic development.

References

Advertising Age (1991). "Thinking Green Gets Complicated: Green Marketing Special Report." October: 28.

Antil, J.H. (1984). "Socially Responsible Consumers: Profile and Implications for Public Policy." *Journal of Macromarketing*, 4 (Fall): 18–39.

Belk, R.W (1988a). "Capturing Consumer Culture." *Journal of Macromarketing*, 8 (Fall): 46–51.

—— (1988b). "Possessions and the Extended Self." *Journal of Consumer Research*, 15 (September): 139–68.

Benton Jr., R. (1985). "Alternative Approaches to Consumer Behavior." In *Changing the Course of Marketing: Alternative Paradigms for Widening Marketing Theory*, edited by N. Dholakia and J. Arndt. Research in Marketing series, Supplement 2. Greenwich, CT: JAI Press, pp. 197–218.

Buttel, F.H. (1987). "New Directions in Environmental Sociology." *Annual Review of Sociology*, 13: 465–88.

Cairncross, F. (1991). *Costing the Earth*. London: Economist Books.

Campbell, C. (1987). *The Romantic Ethic and the Spirit of Modern Consumerism*. Oxford: Basil Blackwell.

Carman J.M., and R.G. Harris (1986). "Public Regulation of Marketing Activity, Part III." *Journal of Macromarketing*, 6 (Spring): 51–64.

Chamberlin, E.H. (1946). *The Theory of Monopolistic Competition*. Cambridge, MA: Harvard University Press.

Charter, M. (1992). "Introduction." In *Greener Marketing: A Responsible Approach to Business*, edited by M. Charter. Sheffield, England: Greenleaf Publishing.

Coddington, W. (1992). *Environmental Marketing*. New York: McGraw–Hill.

Daly, H.E. (1992). "Allocation, Distribution, and Scale: Towards an Economics That Is Efficient, Just, and Sustainable." *Ecological Economics*, 6: 185–93.

Darby, M.R., and E. Kami (1973). "Free Competition and the Optimal Amount of Fraud." *Journal of Law and Economics*, 16 (April): 67–88.

Dawes, R.M. (1980). "Social Dilemmas." *Annual Review of Psychology*, 31: 69–193.

Dawson, L.M. (1971). "Marketing Science in the Age of Aquarius." *Journal of Marketing*, 35 (July): 66–72.

de Groot, R.S. (1994). "Evaluation of Environmental Functions as a Tool in Planning, Management, and Decision-Making." Thesis, Agricultural University Wageningen.

Dholakia, N., and R.R. Dholakia (1985). "Choice and Choicelessness in the Paradigm of Marketing." In *Changing the Course of Marketing: Alternative Paradigms for Widening Marketing Theory*, edited by N. Dholakia and J. Arndt. Research in Marketing series, Supplement 2. Greenwich, CT: JAI Press, pp. 173–85.

Faber, M., G. Stephan, and P. Michaelis (1989). *Umdenken in der Abfallwirtschaft*. Berlin: Springer Verlag.

Fishbein, M., and I. Ajzen (1975). *Belief, Attitude, Intention, and Behavior*. Reading, MA: Addison Wesley.

Fisk, G. (1974). *Marketing and the Ecological Crisis*. London: Harper and Row.

Gibbons, R. (1992). *A Primer in Game Theory*. Hemel Hempstead: Harvester Wheatsheaf.

Gibson, J.J. (1979). *The Ecological Approach to Visual Perception*. Boston: Houghton Mifflin.

Gore, A. (1993). *Earth in Balance: Ecology and the Human Spirit*. New York: Penguin.

Gray, R. (1994). "The Challenge of Going Green." *Harvard Business Review*, 72 (July–August): 46–7.

Grunert, S.C. (1992). "Everybody Seems Concerned about the Environment: But Is This Concern Reflected in (Danish) Consumer's Food Choice?" In *European Advances in Consumer Research*, vol. 1, edited by G.J. Bamossy and W.F. van Raaij. Provo, UT: Association for Consumer Research, pp. 428–33.

Hardin, G. (1968). "The Tragedy of the Commons." *Science*, 162: 1, 243–8.

Harris R.G., and J.M. Carman (1983). "Public Regulation of Marketing Activity, Part I." *Journal of Macromarketing*, 3 (Spring): 49–58.

—— (1984). "Public Regulation of Marketing Activity, Part II." *Journal of Macromarketing*, 4 (Spring): 41–52.

Henion II, K.E., and T.C. Kinnear, eds. (1976). *Ecological Marketing*. Chicago: American Marketing Association.

Kangun, N. (1974). "Environmental Problems and Marketing: Saint or Sinner?" In *Marketing Analysis for Societal Problems*, edited by J.N. Sheth and P.L. Wright. Urbana: University of Illinois Press, pp. 250–70.

—— (1984). "Marketing and the Entropy Process: A New World View." Paper presented at an American Marketing Association conference.

Kleiner, A. (1991). "What Does It Mean to Be Green?" *Harvard Business Review*, 69 (July–August): 38–47.

Kotler, P. (1994). *Marketing Management*, 8th ed. Englewood Cliffs, NJ: Prentice Hall.

Lazer, W. (1969). "Marketing's Changing Social Relationships." *Journal of Marketing*, 33 (January): 3–9.

Lodge, G.C., and J.F. Rayport (1991). "Knee Deep and Rising: America's Recycling Crisis." *Harvard Business Review*, 69 (September–October): 128–39.

Mason, R.S. (1981). *Conspicuous Consumption: A Study of Exceptional Consumer Behaviour*. Farnborough, England: Gower.

Martinez–Alier, J. (1990). *Ecological Economics: Energy, Environment, and Society*. Oxford: Basil Blackwell.

Mercer, D. (1992). *Marketing*. Oxford: Blackwell.

Moore, K. (1993). "An Emergent Model of Consumer Response to Green Marketing." In *Marketing for the New Europe: Dealing with Complexity*, 2 vols., issue 22, edited by J. Chias and J. Sureda, proceedings of the 22d annual conference of the European Marketing Academy. Barcelona: Escola Superior d'Administracio i Direccio d'Empreses, pp. 955–74.

Ottman, J.A. (1992). *Green Marketing*. Lincolnwood, IL: NTC Business Books.

Peattie, K. (1992). *Green Marketing*. London: Pitman.

Platt, J. (1973). "Social Traps." *American Psychologist*, 28 (8): 641–51.

Ponting, C. (1991). *A Green History of the World: The Environment and the Collapse of Great Civilizations*. London: Penguin Books.

Porter, M.E. (1991). "America's Green Strategy." *Scientific American*, 264 (April): 98.

Rassuli, K.M., and S.C. Hollander (1986). "Desire – Induced, Innate, Insatiable?" *Journal of Macromarketing*, 6 (Fall): 4–24.

Reidenbach, R.E., and T.A. Oliva (1983). "Toward a Theory of the Macro Systemic Effects of the Marketing Function." *Journal of Macromarketing*, 3 (Fall): 33–40.

Robinson, J. (1948). *The Economics of Imperfect Competition*. London: Macmillan and Company.

Shapiro, S.J. (1978). "Marketing in a Conserver Society." *Business Horizons*, 21 (2): 3–13.

Shearman, R. (1990). "The Meaning and Ethics of Sustainability." *Environmental Management*, 14 (1): 1–8.

Shuptrine, F.K., and F.A. Osmanski (1975). "Marketing's Changing Role: Expanding or Contracting?" *Journal of Marketing*, 39 (April): 58–66.

Skinner, B. (1986). "What Is Wrong with Daily Life in the Western World?" *American Psychologist*, 41 (5): 568–74.

Sklair, L. (1991). *Sociology of the Global System*. London: Harvester.

—— (1992). "'Consumer Behavior': Research Programs – Ideological Concepts." Discussion presented at the Association for Consumer Research European Conference, held 11–14 June in Amsterdam.

Slocombe, D.S., and C. Van Bers (1991). "Seeking Substance in Sustainable Development." *Journal of Environmental Education*, 23 (1): 11–8.

Stavins, R.N. (1994). "The Challenge of Going Green." *Harvard Business Review*, 72 (July–August): 38–9.

Tietenberg, T. (1994). *Environmental and Natural Resources Economics*. 4th ed. New York: Harper Collins.

Uusitalo, L. (1990). "Are Environmental Attitudes and Behaviour Inconsistent? Findings from a Finnish Study." *Scandinavian Political Studies*, 13 (2): 211–26.

Van Liere, K.D., and R.E. Dunlap (1980). "The Social Bases of Environmental Concern: A Review of Hypotheses, Explanations and Empirical Evidence." *Public Opinion Quarterly*, 44 (Summer): 181–97.

Walley, N., and B. Whitehead (1994). "It's Not Easy Being Green." *Harvard Business Review*, 72 (May–June): 46–52.

WCED (1987). *Our Common Future*. Oxford: Oxford University Press, for the World Commission on Environment and Development.

White, P.D. (1981). "The Systems Dimension in the Definition of Macromarketing." *Journal of Macromarketing*, 1 (Spring): 11–3.

Xenos, N. (1989). *Scarcity and Modernity*. London: Routledge.

15

An Ecofeminist Analysis of Environmentally Sensitive Women Using Qualitative Methodology: The Emancipatory Potential of an Ecological Life*

Susan Dobscha[1] and Julie L. Ozanne[2]

[1]*Bentley College and* [2]*Virginia Polytechnic Institute and State University*

ABSTRACT *Using depth interviews and observations, the authors empirically examine market activities of women who care deeply about nature. Interpreted in the light of ecofeminist theory, the data suggest that these women are forging an ecological self that affects their view of consumption and the marketplace. Leading ecological lives, the women challenge traditional notions of feminine consumption and are a force for change in their relationships with family, friends, the workplace, and the community. These data dispute conventional notions of environmentalism and green consumption; they support and extend an ecofeminist notion of the ecological self as a nondominating path of change. The authors outline implications for relevant stakeholders.*

* Article originally published in the *Journal of Public Policy and Marketing* (2001); **20(2)** (Fall): 201–214. Reproduced by permission of the American Marketing Association.

"Consume less" may become the final frontier of the consumer-rebel, the consumer who does not merely seek living space within the present system or use the products of the system to express disaffection and protest, but decides that "enough is enough," that anything less than a frontal assault on the core assumption of consumerism is inadequate.

Gabriel and Lang 1995, p. 149

T he goal of this article is to explore a group of women who protest consumerist society by consuming less to affirm their relationship to the earth. Within consumer research, interest in consumer rebellion is growing. Since Peñaloza and Price (1993) first presented their general typology of consumer resistance, researchers have examined consumer resistance to marketing (Dobscha 1997; Ritson and Dobscha 1998), advertising (Elliott and Ritson 1997), technology (Mick and Fournier 1998), and fashion (Thompson and Haytko 1997). These studies primarily view consumers' resistance as acts of defiance and reappropriations of control from a marketplace that is not designed for these particular consumers (de Certeau 1984). In general, researchers conclude that these defiant consumers can be brought back into the fold of the marketplace if their needs are truly met.

The women in this study affirm their relationship to the natural environment within the marketplace. Meeting the needs of these women, unlike those of other resistors, would require radical changes in the marketplace. The green marketing literature, however, emphasizes a managerial perspective on the relationship between consumers and the environment (e.g., Scherhorn 1993; Schwepker and Cornwell 1991) and primarily studies this relationship from a logical empiricist paradigm (e.g., Aaker and Bagozzi 1982; Shrum, McCarty, and Lowrey 1995; Zikmund and Stanton 1971). This approach holds that green consumers can meet their needs in the current marketplace. Kilbourne and Beckman (1998, p. 524) suggest that such an approach has yielded "marginal progress after twenty-five years" and call for a new paradigm.

This article breaks from traditional research and uses a feminist approach to examine the role of consumption in the lives of people who deeply regard nature. In particular, we use the ecofeminist paradigm to investigate the emancipatory potential of affirming one's relationship to nature and the impact this relationship has on consumption. We first explore the philosophical connection between women and nature to better understand how this link influences behavior, both inside and outside the marketplace. Next, we examine a group of women who care deeply about nature, and we trace the impact of this relationship on their sense of self and social connections. Finally, we outline implications for four major stakeholders: regulators, environmental action groups, consumers, and marketers.

Although we acknowledge that race, class, and nationality are strong mediators of the human–nature link (Bryant and Mohai 1992; Bullard 1990; Krauss 1993), for practical reasons, we chose to limit our study to white women even though other groups warrant attention. Similarly, although men's relationship to nature is certainly of interest, women are often found at the forefront of environmental movements. Many different groups of women are protesting the environmental degradation that is endemic in their everyday lives: rural Himalayan women successfully challenging a multinational corporation (i.e., the Chipko tree-hugging movement), Micronesian women fighting against atmospheric nuclear weapons testing, English women protesting in Greenham Common against storing nuclear missiles, Native American women researching toxicity in their breast milk from local produce, and rural Kenyan women planting millions of trees to conserve soil and water, to name but a few examples (Krauss 1993; Merchant 1992). Some researchers suggest that, in part, women engage in local activism because women and children are "ecological markers" and show signs of disease first (i.e., children because of their low body weight and women because their bodies are unhealthy environments for their unborn infants). Women are also the primary organizers and maintainers of households, and therefore they may be more likely to see the detrimental effects of pollution and toxic materials on the health of their families (Gibbs 1982; Pettus 1997). Moreover, women still perform the vast majority of household shopping (Yankelovich Marketing Research Group 1993) and are arguably the decision makers with great potential for impact in the marketplace.

We initially chose to explore women's connection to nature to discern how this link influences their product choices, consumption, and disposal. Yet as the study progressed, we broadened the focus to explore this connection as it exists throughout the women's daily lives, in which consumption plays a modest, yet complicated role. Ecofeminism, which we discuss next, offers a theoretical framework from which to view the women's everyday activities. We then describe the feminist methodology employed in this study. Finally, we organize the substantive findings into three sections, which present the women's relationship to nature, their marketplace behaviors, and the changes that arise in the women and their communities because of their connection to nature. In conclusion, we discuss implications for four relevant stakeholders.

Ecofeminism

Ecofeminism, first described by d'Eaubonne in 1974, encompasses the work of academics and activists and includes researchers working in fields as diverse as philosophy, politics, history, and literary analysis (Warren 1990). Just as no single version of feminism exists (Bristor and Fischer 1993), no single authoritative approach to ecofeminism can be found, and at times, the differences among various ecofeminists are vast (Lahar 1991; Merchant 1992; Warren 1987). Nevertheless, most ecofeminists still agree with the thesis of the germinal work of Rosemary Ruether (1975), who suggested that the social structures that dominate women are the same structures that dominate nature. Therefore, women should align themselves with nature to transform a system that devalues and potentially harms them both.

The ecofeminist paradigm stands at the intersection of feminist and ecological thought. Feminists first argued that patriarchal hierarchies, which were implicated in the oppression of women, also played a role in the domination of nature. Whereas feminists first used the analysis of philosophical dualism to understand oppression, ecofeminists have used these same analyses of oppression to understand the domination of nature. Stated briefly, philosophical dualism is when differences, such as the differences between masculine and feminine, are treated as a hierarchy and one side of the dualism is valued over the other side (e.g., masculine traits are valued over feminine traits). Sets of these dualisms form ideological systems that are interconnected (e.g., men/culture/public), reinforcing domains that are valued over the underside of the dualisms (e.g., women/nature/private). But most important, these interconnected hierarchies shape social practices. Ecofeminist theorists believe that this logic of domination is used to devalue both women and nature (for an analysis of the logic of domination, see Plumwood 1993; Warren 1990).

Beyond this basic position, ecofeminists diverge (for a collection of positions, see Diamond and Orenstein 1990). For example, historical examinations trace the roots of philosophical dualism to Greek philosophy (Plumwood 1993) and the ascension of Baconian science (Merchant 1980) and argue that a causal link exists between dualistic thinking and the exploitation of women and nature (Spretnak 1990; Warren 1990). Sociolinguistic work investigates the way that language structures relationships between women and nature (Roach 1991). Ethical approaches seek to develop different ethical bases for practices that affect both women and nature (Warren and Cheney 1991).

Moreover, the theoretical positions in ecofeminism mirror those found in feminism (Bristor and Fischer 1993; Jaggar 1983; Merchant 1992; Warren 1987). For example, liberal ecofeminists seek to work within the existing social order to make laws and practices more environmentally friendly (e.g., the legal protection of endangered animals). Cultural ecofeminists suggest that women are different from men both biologically and socially. However, problems arise when the feminine and nature are devalued. They seek to celebrate women and nature and highlight issues such as the influence of environmental degradation on women's reproductive systems (Merchant 1992). More radical forms of ecofeminism attack both of these approaches because they both shore up the status quo and leave the dualistic structures in place (i.e., privileging the feminine over the masculine is still oppressive). Radical ecofeminists seek to dismantle the patriarchal systems that subjugate both women and nature (Daly 1978). Finally, Third World ecofeminists focus on how the global economic shifts influence the everyday lives of indigenous women (Shiva 1989).

Ecofeminism is just one of many environmental discourses—such as ecology, reform environmentalism, and deep ecology—that differ in their basic assumptions and their substantive emphases. For example, the works of Thoreau, Emerson, Marsh, and Muir sparked the first ecology movement in modern Western society (Shrivastava 1994). These writers were naturalists who viewed the conception of the human community as anthropocentric and argued that preserving nature was essential for preserving human community. Ecology then arose as a branch of biology that dealt with the interdependence of organisms and made central the "whole systems" ideology.

Reform environmentalism shifted the focus toward industrialism and the pollution created by the widespread use of chemicals and pesticides (World Commission on Environment and Development 1987). This discourse was fueled by Rachel Carson's influential study of environmental pollution and forced policymakers to enact new environmental regulations (Carson 1962). Deep ecology developed in opposition to these mainstream environmental movements. Deep ecologists reject anthropocentrism, the idea that nature exists strictly for human welfare, and espouse the idea of ecological egalitarianism. Nature is assumed to have the same rights to exist and flourish as humans have (Ehrenfeld 1978; Naess 1987).

Ecofeminists build on this critique of anthropocentrism and emphasize the interdependency of the social and natural worlds. Ecofeminists differ from deep ecologists by critiquing the concept of "vital human needs" as possibly being justified by the values of patriarchal culture. Ecofeminists seek nondominating relationships among all living things. Nature exists not as an abstract concept but rather in the everyday lived experiences of every human.

McDonagh and Prothero (1997) first delineated ecofeminism within marketing and suggested that it had important implications for marketing practices. Although many versions of ecofeminism exist, our approach most closely aligns with critical ecofeminists such as Warren (1990) and Plumwood (1993). To date, no empirical research in marketing or ecofeminism examines whether nondominating relationships to nature specifically lead to different marketplace behaviors. We examined the relationship between a group of women, who care deeply about nature, and their marketplace behaviors. After describing the methodology, we articulate the informants' relationship to nature and then explore how this relationship affects their consumption and life more broadly.

Methodology

Because the goal of this research is to understand certain women's lives and personal relationships to the natural environment (De Vault 1991; Sherwin 1992; Smith 1987), we used a feminist methodology. Across two phases of data collection, we used three qualitative methods: (1) participant observation, (2) multiple interviewee-guided interviews, and (3) autoelicitation using photographs (Belk, Sherry, and Wallendorf 1988; Heisley and Levy 1991).

Feminist researchers employ many of the same data-gathering techniques as are used in positivistic and interpretive paradigms. However, these techniques are embedded in a feminist paradigm, and therefore the data-gathering techniques change. Moreover, whereas the goal of the interpretive paradigm is to seek understanding (Hudson and Ozanne 1988), for the feminist, understanding is the penultimate goal; the ultimate goal is social change guided by theory (i.e., praxis). As Reinharz (1992, p. 240) states, "Feminism is a perspective, not a method . . . Feminist research aims to create social change, represent human diversity, includes the researcher as person, and attempts to develop special relations with the people studied."

In addition to different goals, these approaches make different assumptions. For example, like all researchers, feminists worry about the quality of their data; however, feminists assume that data quality often improves when the research relationship improves and when the voices of the informants are used throughout the research process. Therefore, consistent with feminism, we attempted to hear and preserve the participants' voices during all stages of data collection and analysis (Bristor and Fischer 1993; Hudson and Ozanne 1988), minimize power relations between researcher and participant (Hirschman 1993), and build trust through multiple interviews and the free exchange of information (Oakley 1981). The details of this approach follow.

The first phase of the data collection consisted of the first author conducting a participant observation of a local environmental action group. This experience provided a crucial understanding of local environmental issues and access to a network of environmentalists. We learned the group's language and the local threats members encountered, and we met the people who were most willing to vocalize their strong connection to the environment. Over a yearlong period, field notes were taken at eight different meetings. The size of the meetings averaged approximately 50 people; the participants were white, the vast majority were women, and their ages ranged from 30 to 70 years of age. Initial contact was made with several of the women who eventually participated in this study (see Table 1).

During the second phase of the data collection process, we conducted interviewee-guided interviews, observations, and autoelicitation with nine women. Feminist researchers often rely on open-ended interviews, because this approach gives the participants the power to structure their feelings and thoughts (Reinharz 1992). Giving participants control in the interview is consistent with the feminist goal of attempting to minimize power imbalances between researchers and participants (Hirschman 1993). In addition, interviews were usually conducted in the women's homes, where they might feel most at ease. Conducting three separate interviews with each woman had a range of benefits: Initial themes were explored at greater length, additional data were collected, feedback from the participants was received, and misunderstandings were corrected. Three interviews gave more opportunity for rapport to develop within the research relationship. In some cases, this increased intimacy led to a level of confidence in which personal and private information was shared. Some feminists suggest that the quality and depth of data improve when trust and intimacy

Table 1 Profiles of Women in Study

Name	Demographic Information	Affiliation
Robin	White, late 30s, married Currently working in the home Two young children College degree in environmental engineering	Member, national women's association Coordinator, joint meeting of national women's organization and local environmental group
Laura	White, mid-40s, married Works for local natural history museum No children College degree in natural science	Board member, local environmental group Volunteer, local bird-watching club Volunteer, stream-watching club
Terry	White, early 40s, married Works for regional recycling co-op Two adult children not living at home High school degree	Founder and coordinator, recycling co-op
Ann	White, early 50s, single Works as researcher at university Two adult children not living at home College degree	Member and former president, national environmental organization Member, local environmental group
Helen	White, early 70s, married Several adult children not living at home College degree in biology	Member, local bird-watching club Contributor, newsletter for children with disabilities
Margaret	White, late 60s, divorced Works at book publishing company Several adult children not living at home College degree	Former member, national environmental organization
Rachel	White, mid-30s, married Works as organic farmer and cook for vegetarian restaurant College degree	Grows and sells organic produce at local farmer's market
Cathy	White, early 50s, divorced Works at a research clearinghouse Two adult children not living at home	Member, national environmental organization Member, local environmental group Member, Bahai Faith
Dana	White, mid-20s, married Works as coordinator for recycling center Two young children College degree	Coordinator and educator, county recycling center Member, local environmental group

exist between the researcher and the informant (Oakley 1981; Reinharz 1992). Although the informants were assured of confidentiality and told the purpose of the study, no tangible incentives were given for participation. Participants were allowed full access to the notes, recorded interviews, and results.

Identification of respondents began with a year long participant observation of a local environmental action group. The principal researcher gained access to several women who served on the board of this group, and in turn they provided the researcher with names of other women in the community who were involved in other environmental groups. Women were chosen solely if during initial contact they stated that their relationship to nature was important to them. All of the women were involved with the environment through their jobs and/or participation in voluntary organizations.

As recommended by McCracken (1988), "grand tour" questions were created to introduce the broad topic of the study to the participants. Examples of these grand tour questions are, "What is your relationship to the environment?" "What are your thoughts about the environment?" and "When did you start feeling/thinking this way?" These questions guided the first interview. The analysis of the text from the first interview served as a guide to the second interview, and emergent themes from the first interaction were clarified and validated. The third interview then served as an informal conversation in which issues from the second interview were explored and any other topics deemed important or interesting by the participant were attended to in depth. The women's comments on the transcripts were incorporated into the final analysis.

The women were encouraged to tell their stories in any manner they chose, and questions of elaboration or clarification were asked. No attempt was made to stop digressions (i.e., when women seemed to go off the topic), and these digressions often yielded valuable information in light of later analyses.

Finally, autodriving was employed, in which photographs were used as projective stimuli during the interview (Heisley and Levy 1991). Participants or the researcher photographed areas in the women's homes or possessions that were related to their environmental concerns. Typically, photographs were taken during the second interview and then discussed during the third interview.

Each woman was interviewed three times for one to three hours. Each interview was taped on a hand-held cassette recorder and transcribed verbatim. Field notes were taken after each interview to record the researcher's observations that were not captured in the interviews. A total of 38 hours of interview data was transcribed into 715 pages of text. In addition, more than 50 pages of field notes were also taken, transcribed, and included in the data analysis.

We analyzed the data using a hermeneutical and feminist method. First, we created a text around each participant. During this first stage of analysis, each woman was considered an individual, and the analysis was driven by her words. Second, we analyzed the data as a whole. The goal at this stage was to make connections among the women and create an interpretation that transcended the individual women's stories without losing the women's voices. The interpretation is an amalgam of the data. In the analysis, we attempt to maintain the voices of the participants while creating a new, integrative text that is more illuminating than the nine separate voices.

Emergent Themes and Interpretations

Prior green marketing research has focused on determining the characteristics of the socially conscious consumer (e.g., Anderson and Cunningham 1972); assessing consumers' perceptions of business (e.g., Scherhorn 1993); and measuring the influence of perception, attitudes, and incentives on green consumption (e.g., McCarty and Shrum 1994). Guided by logical empiricist methods, this research is generally based on three assumptions: (1) Green consumers use primarily rational decision processes to make product choices (e.g., Ellen 1994), (2) consumers are generally homogeneous in their response to environmental-based product claims depending on their socioeconomic status or race (e.g., Shrum, McCarty, and Lowrey 1995), and (3) consumers' product choices can be understood in isolation from the rest of their daily lives (e.g., Granzin and Olsen 1991).

Our study follows Fisk's (1973) notion that consumption contributes to rather than solves the problem of environmental degradation (Kilbourne 1995; Kilbourne, McDonagh, and Prothero 1997; McDonagh and Prothero 1997; Thogerson and Grunert-Beckman 1996). Our study suggests a vision of the environmental consumer that resonates with Fisk's conjecture. The breadth and depth of the women's green living indeed affected their action within the marketplace. Nevertheless, green living does not center on green consuming—instead, the women seek to live outside the marketplace and reluctantly enter the marketplace only when other nonmarket options are exhausted. These consumers live, shop, and buy on the basis of a complex and strong relationship to nature, a relationship that leads them to question the problem-solving ability of the marketplace.

The oppositional nature of the women's relationship to the market acts as a relief against which we explore the ecological self. We investigate how the ecological self is maintained within the ecological life that the women create for themselves and their families. Then, we discuss how the ecological life stands as a force for change in public and private domains.

The Ecological Self
"I Am Not a Consumer"

The women refuse to be defined as consumers, and therefore we respectfully no longer refer to them as consumers. Consistent with its original meaning, "consuming" is viewed as using up, squandering, and wasting (Gabriel and Lang 1995). In the following passage, Terry makes the point that defining people as consumers amplifies environmental problems:

> So consumerism, whether it's green, purple, brown, or yellow, I think is an issue that needs to be confronted, rather than simply repainted. And I think, I define, obviously when you buy something and you use it, you have consumed. But I think the concept of humans as consumers, or Americans in any case as consumers, is something that needs to be dismantled. We are not consumers. We should not be consumers. We should use things when we need to use them, but we should question much more what exactly it is we need to use, and I think we need to get out of the consumer "buy more, buy more" mindset.

The women's stances on consumption are also consistent with previous definitions of consumption as a disease that causes suffering and devours the body earth. Most of the women were disgusted by uncontrolled development that "devastated" the land (Ann) and "tore up" local habitats (Helen). The dominant consumer culture that encourages acquisition, use, and disposal is in opposition to the women's views, because this behavior translates into environmental degradation. This metaphor of consumption as a disease had a powerful orienting force on the women as they negotiated the marketplace (Zaltman, LeMasters, and Heffring 1982).

The women do not see themselves or their friends as consumers; they are conservers:

> They [friends] are not consumers . . . I mean, I could go through my cupboards and tell you, this bottle of this lasted me two years. And this has lasted me six months and will last me more. Things that I used to use, the more I learn and the more I think about, I think, well, I don't really need this. (Laura)

The women create alternative visions of themselves as conservers and attempt to protect the local habitat that supports them by casting aside the material clutter in their lives.

An Interconnected Nonhierarchical Relationship

The women view humans and the natural world as part of one system, each part relying on the other part for support. As Margaret says, "You sort of feel like you are one with nature. You're a part of an ongoing life." Humans and nature are interdependent—their fates are entangled. Therefore, dualistic ideas, such as culture/nature or human/nature, in which one part of this system dominates another part, are inconsistent with these women's views:

> Well, my relationship with nature is that I am part of it. I don't see any separation between what we call the natural environment and human beings except we human beings have built on it . . . There is unity throughout the entire creation and nothing exists separately from the whole . . . So I never ever thought any other way; I've never understood the idea that humans have dominion over nature. (Cathy)

Similar to the river guides in Arnould and Price's (1993) study, the women commune with nature and believe that their physical and emotional well-being are tied to nature:

> But I did notice a kind of a lift when the sun came out. When I spend time outdoors, I always feel a lot different than when I spend a lot of time indoors. Sleep outside or spend a lot of time, a whole day, outside. It's a really different feeling than when you live in the house. (Robin)

Moreover, nature and culture are intertwined, and the experience of nature often takes place as a cultural activity (Arnould and Price 1993). Many of the women engage in bird-watching expeditions in which they take members of the local community to look at birds in their natural habitats. These outings are educational in scope and social in purpose.

Nature as Separate and Heterogeneous

Although the women view themselves as interconnected, they also respect nature as a separate entity that does not merely exist for the needs and pleasures of the women (this view is in opposition to the anthropocentric assumptions made by deep ecologists):

> That time in the woods really opened my mind to some things that I hadn't really been aware, and really basically, it was just really feeling like I needed to learn to be a lot more gentle in my relationship to the earth and much more conscious about what I do with my garbage and what I spent my money on. Just how I lived, how I walked, even how I walked in the woods. *Where I put my feet.* I mean it is just everything. Affect every aspect, and I felt such a strong connection to the earth at that point. And it has never really left me since that time. (Rachel)

The women recognize that just as nature does not exist to serve them, human ends and natural ends are not equivalent. Hurricanes, tornadoes, mudslides, and El Niño all occur despite the culturally dominant belief that nature can be controlled for the good of society. The ecological self incorporates this element in the form of reverence or deference to the unruly and unpredictable natural world (Arnould and Price 1993).

Nature is not viewed as monolithic. Quite to the contrary, nature is seen as diverse. Margaret notes the rich diversity of nature as well as the different accompanying problems:

> In some ways the desert is more fragile than the coast or glades. Although I don't know if there is anything more fragile than the glades. And then we hiked and traveled in the Rockies, the Canadian Rockies, and that's a different kind of fragile environment. So you just become aware that different environments have different problems.

Omnipresent and Multifaceted

All the women spoke in varying degrees about how the natural world is ubiquitous in decisions as mundane as "what I do with my garbage" and as important as delivering babies and worshipping. Moreover, their relationship to nature is one of the most central relationships in their lives. Cathy finds herself in awe of nature and sees nature as a "miracle to me. I mean, I just revere it. I think it's absolutely wonderful."

At first it is tempting to view nature as part of the women's extended self (Belk 1988). The concept of the extended self maintains that possessions act as a reflection of a person's identity. In this case, nature cannot be considered part of the women's extended self, because the women believe that nature cannot be possessed and that nature serves its own ends that do not equate to human goals. Furthermore, as is clear in the next section, the women maintain the ecological self by minimizing their relationship to goods, in contrast with Belk's notion of the extended self as being maintained by goods.

In summary, these women define the self as a "self-in-relationship," which is consistent with Plumwood's (1993, p. 154) theoretical conjecture that a mutual or relational self underlies the ecological self and influences relationships to other living organisms:

> The ecological self can be viewed as a type of relational self, one which includes the goal of the flourishing of earth others and the earth community among its own primary ends, and hence respects or cares for these others for their own sake. Concepts of care, solidarity and friendship present alternatives to the instrumental mode within existing liberal societies.

The women care deeply about nature and view themselves as conservers of nature. However, they neither overly separate themselves from nature (i.e., the logic of domination) nor consider themselves in total continuity with nature. Hypercontinuity contains its own pitfalls. People who perceive no separation between themselves and nature may inaccurately perceive that their needs and nature's needs are one and the same (Plumwood 1993). The women operate toward nature as though it is different, yet they still trace interconnections between themselves and nature. These women offer empirical support for the notion that a mutual self underlies a theory of difference that is nonhierarchical and nondominating (Gaard 1993; Gruen 1993).

Living the Ecological Life

If the needs of nature and humans are in conflict, these different needs must be balanced. Therefore, the women regularly question how they balance these needs. To remain true to their ecological selves, their lives consist of an ongoing series of critical moments in which the needs of humans and nature are negotiated. Nevertheless, their persistent questioning is not aimed at finding "the solution." They understand that human life, of necessity, negatively affects nature. They use the available information at hand and strike the best possible balance. They dwell on weighty environmental issues, regret the inadequate balances, and savor the clever trade-offs. Unlike the traditional environmentally conscious consumer who seeks to shop differently, these women seek to live differently. This vision is fueled by their profound skepticism of business and marketing practices.

Cynicism of Business and Marketing

All the women distrust business and marketing practices and could be labeled "marketing heretics" (Ritson and Dobscha 1998). The intensity of the distrust ranges from skepticism to hatred. Ann calls advertising an "evil in our society." Cathy explicitly states her cynicism:

> In particular the plastic companies have been, in my opinion, . . . very abusive of the public trust. They have been offering a lot of half information and half truths. *And again that is why I always try to instill in people [the need to] question.* Especially when it comes out really smooth and slick and if they have an 800 number for free, why are they doing that? If they are doing that, there is only one thing, I hate to sound cynical, but there is only one thing that motivates any industry—the bottom line. (emphasis added)

Environmental products and claims are particularly scrutinized. Laura is bothered by the improper use of the "green" product symbol. She states, "It just bugs me that people are using, using the guise of being environmentally friendly when it really hasn't changed anything." Dana similarly questions the environmental claims of companies:

> Because a lot of companies try to make themselves out to be these green companies when they are not. Diapers, biodegradable diapers was a big one. And what were some others? Yeah, like aseptic packaging advertising. You know, recycling advertising that you are seeing now. Like those little juice boxes and how they are going to be recyclable. It's coming soon to your locality. That's a crock of bull!

Occasionally, the women take joy in the marketplace when buying something second-hand at a garage sale or finding a product that meets their strict criteria: "Well, what I use in the laundry room is Sears detergent . . . It doesn't have dyes, perfumes, and it doesn't have bleach" (Robin).

Marketplace decisions may appear to be these women's chief concerns, but these decisions are merely a few of myriads of daily trade-offs. Decisions about whether to drive, walk, or take public transportation may be low involvement for most people, but these women consider the environmental impact of these choices. Cathy relates her dilemma this way: "In fact, I hate driving. I would like to have no car if I could, but I find it inconvenient in this country. And that's what bothers me too. I don't know why more people don't walk." Similarly, Robin complains about the trade-off between country living that brings her closer to nature and the related transportation problems:

> And also deciding to live out here was a difficult [decision] environmentally because of course we use our cars a lot more. My car is, I drive a lot and I like to drive and we drive when we travel. And our car is the worst that we do to the environment. For one thing we buy it. God knows, what happened to the environment while our car was manufactured, probably a lot. And then, I drive into town three or four times a day. When I lived in town there would be a lot of times where I would choose to walk. And when I did [drive], I wouldn't have to drive as far.

Helen handles the issue of driving by bundling as many errands as possible into one trip. Rachel discusses the balance she strikes between her needs and nature's:

> We have shitty [old and scratched] cars . . . [Cars] are really not a good idea because I think people should be, we should have a way of protesting: that is, just buy used cars and hardly drive. Drive as little as possible. And make the cars last as long as possible. And not spend a lot of money on them. We try to spend the least amount of money on cars. We change the oil ourselves and as much of the repairs we do ourselves. I do, actually, most of the work on the cars. I took some auto mechanic classes when I was younger.

Thus, Rachel seeks to use cars that already exist, ignores the surface patina, maintains the car herself, and uses the car infrequently. All the women complain that driving is an activity in which a good balance is difficult to achieve. Many of the women blame society (e.g., government not being dedicated to public transportation), but others blame their own laziness or reliance on this mode of transportation. The women's views stand in stark contrast to the dominant social meanings of the car as sign of freedom and control (Kunstler 1996).

Cleaning is another domain of questioning. The women with children are concerned about environmental contaminants that might come in contact with their children or otherwise compromise their immature systems. Robin and Dana describe the dilemma:

> If I'm toilet training, this always happens when I'm toilet training a child, you don't want to sit their bottom on a toilet seat that's just been cleaned with Lysol. (Robin)

> Well, you've got little kids around. And you start thinking about those fumes. You know, when you have all these warnings on there about the ventilation needed. You're in the bathroom with no window. You start to, there are health concerns there too. I think that is why women

are much more connected to it that way. Well, I think women are more connected to the environment in general than men are. (Dana)

As the primary caregivers, the women question the risk that household products introduce into the household. Social norms are consistently violated as the women challenge the dominant notions of cleanliness and housekeeping.

Dismantling the Consumer

Our informants make consumption less central by shifting their household consumption patterns. They do without many of the conveniences that average consumers take for granted. For example, Robin avoids all flea and tick products for her animals. Rachel, Laura, Cathy, Margaret, and Helen do not use chemical pesticides or fertilizers for their lawns. Laura and Rachel never eat at restaurants where the leftovers are packaged in Styrofoam. Dana and Terry never buy prepackaged vegetables that are covered in nonrecyclable shrink-wrap. The women eschew products like dryer sheets and do not use a dryer in the warmer months. They also avoid many paper products (e.g., cups, plates, towels, napkins). Although the average consumer may engage in some of these activities, these women were perhaps more consistent and intense in their avoidance.

Although some of the refusals create hardship, our informants also believe that goods such as panty hose, junk food (e.g., Cheez Whiz), garbage disposals, and paper products are useless and easily forgone: "I always hear about these new gadgets like... voice-activated phone cards and stuff that I don't really see. Stuff like that I don't really understand why is that so great?" (Terry). Similarly, Laura states, "Why do we buy so many things in our society that we just don't really need?" When the women cannot do without a product, they simply use less:

> For instance, if I bought a can of environmentally friendly cleanser that cleans sinks and tubs, I mean I would use a can a year. I clean the kitchen sink every day but you just need a tiny sprinkle. It literally lasts me a year, same with dish detergent. Um, I probably buy a 22 ounce bottle of dish detergent a year, maybe two a year. And I'll watch other people wash their dishes and I'll bet you they buy one every two weeks. (Laura)

Another reasonable alternative to avoidance is to buy secondhand goods, as Terry states: "All the clothes I buy, I buy at the thrift store. Partly because I am a cheapskate and partially because the clothes already exist and they are perfectly good stuff. I don't need to buy new ones, which make a demand for more to be made." Helen creates collage light switch covers from pictures in magazines and newspapers and constructs clothing out of unused clothing: "Then I decided I would use the ties, like this is a tie, that's a tie, and then I had some kerchiefs that I liked that I never use anymore. So I decided I would use them. . . . So that's a recycled coat that's getting a recycled lining."

The needs of the earth place limits on the women. They avoid certain products, use products sparingly, and purchase goods secondhand if possible. In Peñaloza and Price's (1993) framework of resistance, radical acts involve altering product meaning, but the women here are more radical in their desire to avoid and limit marketplace solutions. These acts are part of a larger pattern of living. For these women, living the ecological life means that nature plays a force in the way they define themselves and their relations to others.

The Ecological Life as a Force of Change

Changing One's Self

In the marketplace, merchants facilitate consumption: convenient retail locations and hours; one-stop shopping; layaway plans; easy credit terms; shopping by mail, television, or computer; and so forth. For those seeking to build an environmentally sensitive life, less scaffolding exists. Therefore, living the ecological life requires many acts of creating, building, and foraging. Terry chronicles her own transformation process:

> I remember television shows that I watched when I was a kid that stuck with me. That had an effect, like Swiss Family Robinson type shows where they dealt with what they needed. Normally, naturally. They needed a wash basin. Well, there is a giant seashell down by the shore to bring it up and set it up. They needed to move water. Well there was a spring uphill. They got bamboo pipes and they fit them together and ran it down. And that attracted me . . . So, mechanization, technology that did not rely on flipping a switch and things that did encourage ingenuity and creativity simply always attracted me.

The women become inventors. For example, Terry created her own grain grinder from discarded pieces of machinery and parts she purchased secondhand (thus not contributing to overall increases in production):

> This is one of my mad scientist projects. [For these projects] my mind is occupied most of the time and every once in a while my body gets to be occupied. It's an exercise bike that I got at the Thrift Store. Couldn't beat the price. Right now the wheel is mounted to a grain grinder so that you can sit comfortably and pedal and with two pulley belts it will transfer what you are pedaling up to the wheel on the grain grinder so you can be pouring the grain in and it will be grinding it into flour and it will be very easy as opposed to doing it by hand which is quite tedious.

Terry solved her grain-grinding problem and makes homemade bread with the flour (again avoiding the purchase of processed bread). Living the ecological life means that the women develop their creativity and ingenuity when viable alternatives to their problems do not exist.

Rachel's inventiveness is demonstrated in her knack for foraging. Foraging is a way of life for people living on the economic fringes of a wealthy, postindustrial society (Hill and Stamey 1990). However, Rachel and her husband do not forage for survival; they forage to sustain themselves without contributing to a consumerist society. Foraging combines the wily and scrappy craftiness of a thief with the originality of an inventor (Ritson and Dobscha 2001). Here, Rachel describes why she engages in "dumpster diving":

> We are kind of like scavengers; that's one way of putting it. That's one thing you can do in this country. Because this is such a fat country, there is so much that you can live off the pickings that [are] left over. So that is one thing that we do.

A good instance of Rachel's ingenuity is found on her organic farm. She and her husband constructed a passive solar greenhouse using only materials found in people's garbage. The door to the greenhouse is from a bathroom shower, and the wood is refuse from people's home improvement projects. Two-liter soda bottles that they found in recycling bins around town contain water that heats the greenhouse.

Ann uses dog food bags for garbage bags and Cathy uses jars for glasses. Rachel and her husband make their own beer, wine, and soap. Robin and Dana use trash as raw materials for their children's school and art projects:

> Well, milk jugs we reuse a lot; we use them for watering cans or storage cans. Projects, like, [my son] built a tornado . . . We probably don't end up throwing away any of our milk jugs until they are pretty dilapidated. (Robin)

> And [my daughter's] pencil holder, she made with an old soup can. Construction paper around it, looks like an elephant . . . She'll do things like that all the time. Beer bottles with, like a western guy uniform on there or something. She's really good at reusing stuff. She doesn't like to throw anything away. (Cathy)

Many of the women precycle; that is, they only buy goods in packages that can be recycled efficiently. One of the women joined a group in order to buy in bulk. Although many people reuse products, the intensity with which the women reuse products bears note. Laura says, "I use aluminum foil so many times that I don't feel too guilty about that and then recycle it when it's totally falling apart. I had the same roll of aluminum foil for about ten years." Similarly, Helen states, "When I buy plastic bags, we wash them and reuse them. Don't just throw them out, which I used to do." She also used to buy pads of paper for notes and lists; now she uses old papers that were to be recycled. Cathy reuses envelopes by scratching out the old address and putting in new ones.

Although research exists on creativity in solving consumption-related problems (Hirschman 1980), the findings here are consistent with Schau's (2000) suggestion that consumer imagination is the transformation of goods into consumer identities. In this case, however, perhaps greater manipulation, effort, and originality are needed to take refuse and transform it into an object that affirms an ecological, conserver identity. The women invent new solutions and ways of consuming and disposing to affirm their deep connection to nature. The domain of consumer creativity needs to be expanded to include these inventions that occur throughout the exchange process.

Changing Feminine Consumption

Women are bombarded with advertisements describing the essentiality of products to their well-being. From deodorant to clothing, women are told that products can and do enhance the way they are regarded as women. In light of their relationship with nature, the women in the study have rethought their feminine consumption.

Instead of accepting the convenient, yet wasteful, feminine hygiene products (i.e., tampons and pads), Rachel employs reusable cloths for her menstruation:

> Why do we need that so much when what we really need is a way to conserve, to take care of our planet? That seems to me to be most important and it's hard for me to understand why it isn't to other people. It doesn't seem to be. People want to have convenience; they don't want to have to deal with their messes. They just want it all to [go away], a good example for me is that, I don't know if this is going to gross you out or not, but feminine hygiene products like disposable feminine napkins and tampons and all that—I don't use those. I use cloths and I wash them out. I have been doing that for a long time and it's not a big deal to me anymore. I just don't even think twice about it. So I go to the store and I look in the aisle full of all that shit, wrapped in plastic and it really kind of freaks me out that this is what everybody is using and its all just going into the landfill.

Rachel views human disconnection from the planet's health as synchronous with the disconnection people have from their own personal waste—whether bodily or household.

The women in this study also question feminine consumption in the area of housekeeping. Despite changing roles, housework is still generally viewed as women's work (DeVault 1991). The goal of housework is to present a public masterpiece of efficiency and cleanliness (Cowan 1987; DeVault 1987). This work of "keeping house" traditionally requires the use of chemical solutions to maintain the level of cleanliness instilled in most women by their mothers. Cleaning often involves covering up nature as manifested by dirt, odors, bugs, and the like (Gruen 1993).

Many of the women in this study substitute more benign alternatives (e.g., baking soda, vinegar) for harsh and toxic cleansers. Others, in a more radical move, challenge traditional norms of cleanliness. Robin questions ideas regarding cleanliness when she uses no pesticides: "We put up with a lot of spiders and ants." The women who were concerned about water issues chose to shower less regularly. Laura states, "Some people think they have to wash their sheets every week. Heck, we're fairly clean when we get in them...Or my towels, I dry myself when I've just taken a shower. Why would I have to wash my towel?" Robin labels this as a new norm of "letting things go." She states, "Like I'll use toilet bowl cleaner not regularly, but when things start to grow." Cathy says:

> I'll let things go. I haven't cleaned my toilet all the time. I'll let it go. I have well water here and I have iron bacteria, so I get this orange fill. And it is completely harmless and it doesn't smell. I mean there is absolutely no, you know, it's not bad. So I'll let that go until I can't stand it, and then I squirt some of that stuff on it and clean it, but rather than every time, cause every time you clean it you have to flush it, which is wasting a couple of gallons of water. So, I just don't do it. And I think, well, if somebody is bothered by my orange toilet bowl, well, that's too bad.

Robin and Cathy acknowledge that this norm collides with traditional norms, which is apparent from the social disapproval they receive from their mothers. Both Cathy and Robin's mothers are traditional housekeepers with myriad chemicals in their arsenals. Here, Robin discusses her gradual shift away from her mother's style of cleaning:

> Cleaning bathrooms and bathtubs concerned me right away that I was, I used the same chemicals basically that my mother did, and it concerned me that I was gonna be bathing my child in the bathtub that had just been cleaned with Clorox or Lysol or something like that. So I tended to not clean very much, like for a long time I just used Windex because it was easy and pretty inexpensive and it seemed to clean just about everything.

Terry argues that manufacturers should be proactive in eliminating chemicals from household cleansers, thus creating safer homes and a better environment. Terry discusses the contradictions of bringing in hazardous materials to clean the home:

> Wait a minute, household hazardous waste, it's in the grocery store. It comes into the town in a semi truck. Huge, big semi truck. Tons of stuff. And it's not a problem. It's there, on the shelf, on the backside of the baby food aisle. And I can go in there and I can buy it. I can put it on the same little conveyor things that goes across the little thing to the little laser

scanners so that it can tell the people what it is and keep their inventory straight. And I can bring it home, but the minute I open it up and start using some of it, if I want to throw some of it away, it's now household hazardous waste.

Another traditional area of women's work is gift giving (Fischer and Arnould 1990; Sherry 1983). All the women stated that they reuse wrapping paper, even if it means being teased by their friends and coworkers. Helen states, "But it just seems like such a waste because some of it doesn't get wrinkled, soiled or whatever. You can press it." Likewise, Dana reuses wrapping paper: "We save things like wrapping paper and bags and ribbons and all that wrapping sort of stuff... We reuse a lot of stuff like that." This activity enables the women to engage in gift giving while not creating unnecessary waste. In addition, the women have rethought the gifts they exchange. Dana used her gift as a socializing force (Otnes, Lowrey, and Kim 1993) when she gave her in-laws recycled note pads as stocking stuffers. These actions often evoke teasing from family and friends: "People used to laugh at me. In fact, one Christmas I got a big box, ... and it was everyone's paper sacks... because I always fold up my bag and take it back and use it again" (Helen). The women's tenacity in the face of this social disapproval is additional evidence of the strength of their connection with nature.

Changing the Community

A moderately high level of mainstream environmentalism characterizes the women's local community, but the women seek to extend these ideas. The most direct form of education and socialization occurs within the family. Margaret suggests that if you cultivate sensitivity to the natural world in children, "they are more likely to [protect the earth] when they grow up and are running their own households." Cathy's children did exactly what Margaret suggested: "Now my son is a biologist, and he is going to be teaching biology. So I passed it on. My daughter also just loves animals, nature. So I think that's an accomplishment to me because I see so many kids who are unaware and careless and I'm glad mine aren't." This socialization primarily took the form of fostering a deep love for nature in their children.

In addition to socializing their own families, the women also work for change in their local schools. Some of the women volunteer at the schools to present more alternatives to recycling and a different view of nature. The women also engage in formal and informal adult education. Informal strategies involve teaching by example: "People say, 'Why are you doing that?' and then you can explain... , and that does have tremendous material consequences" (Cathy). Formal strategies involve teaching structured classes. In stark contrast to the traditional approach that more information will translate into action (Cornwell and Schwepker 1995; Pickett, Kangun, and Grove 1993), the women try to develop people's connections to nature in hope that this approach will inspire change.

Another way the women work to improve their communities is by creating ecological spaces. Workspaces, for example, raise problems for the women. For example, Laura implemented a program in which employees use both sides of the paper in printing drafts. Rachel instituted a composting plan at the restaurant where she works and uses the waste to enrich her farmland.

The work of building ecological spaces began at home and continued into the workplace, but it did not end there. The most challenging task involved preserving public ecological spaces. In the eyes of the women, the ecological spaces over which they have least control—public land, national parks, and government-owned land—are rapidly deteriorating or disappearing. Helen describes the problem:

> I mean, people are finding that they want to go out and be in the, among trees and without a lot of other people around, without houses and everything. And they find there are so few places to go that these places are getting crowded. Like the national parks. Where are you going to go to be alone . . . just be in awe of the beauty of the world, etc.? And there are getting to be fewer and fewer places like that, and I think people are getting upset about that.

Dana speaks of the loss of ecological space at the hands of human-made catastrophes: "Just thinking about the oil spill. I think that was really upsetting. Feel a loss of the animals and their habitat . . . It's carelessness, stupid mistakes that can have huge impacts. And create huge losses."

The women's community action extends into protecting the environmental health of public spaces. Robin and her family and Laura are actively involved in stream watching—adopting and caring for a stretch of stream. And the women's concept of community extends to include the national and global environmental problems:

> We believe very strongly that there are two very important issues, most important issues today, and one of them is the environment and the other one is overpopulation. Because we feel that the overpopulation is affecting the environment negatively and, of course, if the environment goes, then not only do we go, but all, you know, the other species that depend on that particular environment will be affected also. (Helen)

An Interpretation

The conceptualization of self that underlies the relationship between these women and nature is the mutual self; this self-in-relation-to-nature is powerful and encompassing. The data indicate that this mutual self leads to nondominating paths and fosters a life of respect and constraint toward the natural world. In what Benjamin (1988) calls the "dance of interaction," the 'other' places constraints on the mutual self. For example, a parent seeks to have a child thrive both for the parent's sake and for the child's sake. In much the same way, the women seek to constrain themselves so that both they and the earth can flourish. The women live this ecological life, which includes questioning the taken-for-granted assumptions that underlie their daily decisions. Specifically, living the ecological life means making consumption a less central component of life. However, this constrained consumption is rarely a hardship and is often the source of satisfaction and liberation.

The women enter the marketplace when they find both problems and opportunities. Marketplace perils include questionable marketing tactics and wasteful practices, but satisfaction is found in buying local organic products at a roadside stand; purchasing things secondhand; or finding a product that fits their strict criteria for acquisition, use, and disposal. Still, these women experience more frustration within the marketplace than within nature.

Implications for Relevant Stakeholders

Implications for Marketing Managers

A challenge facing marketing managers is whether this consumer frustration can be translated into empowering acts. It may be in companies' enlightened self-interest to respond (Murray and Ozanne 1991). An ecologically friendly marketplace would include pricing that estimates the environmental costs, less packaging and the use of more recyclable materials, advertising that has environmentally accurate information, and bulk purchasing to reduce packaging. More radical forms of eco-markets would encourage less consumption, local products and markets, and systems of barter (e.g., Local Exchange Trading Systems, the Ecovillage) (see Gabriel and Lang 1995).

For marketers that pursue this unique yet growing segment, establishing trust is a considerable obstacle. As Ottman (1997, p. 183, emphasis in original) states, "The backlash to marketers' questionable green-marketing activities of the early 1990's taught us a valuable lesson: consumers' environmental concerns cannot be exploited by merely communicating superficial product tweaks and regulatory-driven corporate responses... [I]t's not enough to talk green; companies must *be* green." A genuine greening of internal operations and corporate culture requires employee participation; reassessment and improvement of manufacturing processes; and a revision of marketing practices such as labeling, packaging, and product developments that reflect environmental values.

One way to construct trust with consumers is for companies to engage in environmental audits. Many companies, such as Texaco and Xerox, already conduct external environmental auditing and provide detailed reports of the findings to their relevant stakeholders. These audits "assess current performance and set benchmarks upon which to measure progress" (Ottman 1997, p. 184). Similarly, the demand for third-party green certification of wood products is growing. This guarantee that wood is grown and harvested in sustainable ways offers a strategic tool in the marketplace. It is estimated that between 16 and 25 million people would purchase certified wood products and are willing to pay a price premium (Ozanne and Smith 1998; Ozanne and Vlosky 1997).

Establishing consumer relationships based on trust has long-term benefits (Ganesan 1994). For example, the Body Shop weathered a public relations storm when some of its environmental claims were attacked. Although stock prices dipped, the clientele remained loyal to the company because a trusting relationship had been established (Sillanpaa 1998). Two other companies pursuing a successful ecological approach are Tom's of Maine and Patagonia. Tom's of Maine's mission is to treat all humans, animals, and nature with respect and dignity. To achieve this goal, it seeks quality employee relations, donates profits to ecologically based charities, creates products using the most benign ingredients and processes, and expresses its ethos in all its marketing communication (Briskin and Peppers 2001). Similarly, Patagonia donates money to conservation groups, reduces waste and harmful chemicals in its manufacturing processes, uses recycled materials and organically grown cotton, reduces suppliers' waste, and has a no-growth strategy (Reinhardt 1998; www.patagonia.com). All three of these companies offer products and operational practices that are consistent with the values of consumers, such as the women in this study, who view themselves as conservers.

Implications for Environmental Groups

If marketing practitioners must struggle to build trust within customer relationships, environmental groups stand in a unique position relative to the consumer–manufacturing dyad. Research suggests that consumers are most likely to trust environmental groups as a source of information on environmental certification over independent third-party groups or the government (Ozanne and Vlosky 1997). Therefore, environmental groups might develop environmental seals of approval that consumers could use to simplify their decision-making strategies.

This study also provides evidence for rethinking the way environmental groups go about enacting their goals. Although consumer education plays an important role in fostering social change, the message may need to be expanded. Data on the alarming rates of deforestation, greenhouse gases in the atmosphere, or species extinction may not be the most effective message for translating public environmental concern into action. Our results suggest that working to build multifaceted relationships among people and nature may foster the development of a mutual self that can constrain consumption and increase environmentally responsible behaviors. Instead of focusing on increasing recycling and other behaviors, a more effective strategy for change may be to amplify the importance of nature in people's lives through direct and local contact. Therefore, environmental policy programs should stress hands-on interventions (e.g., bringing urban children to rural areas, watching and counting whales, erecting bluebird trails, monitoring streams) that illuminate ecological diversity and the interconnectedness of all things on earth. Programs that foster the mutual self may have a rippling effect into other facets of consumers' everyday lives, including acquisition, use, and disposal of consumer goods.

This self-in-relation-to-nature may already exist for many groups in society. For example, the river guides in Arnould and Price's (1993) study exhibit the mutual self and tried to foster this relationship with nature among the participants. Thus, the task before environmental groups may be to identify people who already possess this relationship to nature, work toward the goal of raising consciousness about this relationship, and then use this relationship to motivate moderation in consumption. Recreational activities as wide-ranging as hiking, boating, golfing, gardening, and biking all have varying degrees of contact with nature. These preexisting relationships to nature might be amplified through local demonstrations that enable people to experience nature differently. Consider the impact of transforming a section of a golf course with native plantings. From an economic standpoint, cost savings might be realized in terms of labor, water, pesticides, and fertilizers. However, environmental benefits may also be reaped, as native fauna inhabit these nontraditional golfing spaces. In contrast to sterile monoculture greens, native habitats would have greater color, movement (e.g., butterflies), and form. The results here suggest that the firsthand experience of natural diversity might affect people's behavior. Ideally, golfers might apply these firsthand insights to landscaping their own homes and businesses.

Similarly, our findings suggest that teaching children at a young age about the environment fosters stronger commitment to the environment in adult life. Environmental groups might form partnerships with local schools and create community gardens in local schoolyards so that children grow up in daily contact with nature, knowing firsthand the joy of a diverse habitat.

Implications for Regulatory Agencies

The women in this study experience government regulation of nature very differently than the average consumer. For example, many of the informants believed that the government's preservation strategies lacked vision and scope. The national parks system, though providing a "natural" haven for many tourists during the vacation months, stands as an example of our culture's disconnection with the natural that exists within everyday life. Long lines to get into the parks, massive overcrowding of campsites, and excessive amounts of waste are common occurrences in these destinations that are specifically constructed and designed for experiencing the "great outdoors."

Government regulators should look more carefully at how they package and promote nature. For many people, nature becomes a destination rather than something that exists in their everyday lives. People's disconnection from the local environs that surround their houses, towns, and adjacent communities has important ramifications. If local environs are perceived as less exotic and majestic, they may also be perceived as less worthy of conservation efforts. Fostering connections to local environmental wonders may deepen citizens' commitment to preserving those areas that most affect their everyday quality of life.

Furthermore, regulators must consider the weaknesses in the current environmental guidelines. The Federal Trade Commission guidelines of 1996 (cited in Ottman 1997, pp. 215–38) provide a good starting point, but they are largely overlooked by organizations. Moreover, these guidelines have shifted a disproportionate amount of the responsibility to consumers by providing waste disposal guidelines while often ignoring the wasteful manufacturing processes that contribute to environmental degradation. These guidelines are useful for consumers who want to make minor changes in their consumption patterns in order to shop their conscience. However, they provide little relief for the consumers who, like the women in this study, seek to become conservers. Furthermore, although these guidelines relieve the burden consumers feel when shopping for household goods, they also reinforce the "consume differently" discourse that contributes to the maintenance of the high levels of consumption that are unique to North America yet are devastating globally. More public discourse on consuming less and on alternatives to consumption needs to be encouraged (Ozanne and Murray 1995).

For example, many plastic containers that are nationally marketed have "recycle" symbols. However, collection sites are not always available to customers who buy these containers. Therefore, to avoid deception, regulators have recommended that the statement "Check to see if recycling facilities exist in your area" be included on the bottle's packaging (Ottman 1997). This recommendation lays a major onus of responsibility on the consumer, who must first actively separate this bottle from others in the recycling bin, check with the local environmental regulation agency to determine whether such a facility exists, and then throw the bottle away when no such facilities exist. Regulators need to shift more responsibility to manufacturers not just to label their products properly but also to produce products that are easily recyclable within a majority of markets.

Implications for Consumers

The mutual self is the basis for an empowering way of life in which people question the role of consumption in their lives, dismantle unnecessary consumption, and become conservers. The notion of citizen as conserver provides a potentially powerful metaphor that links the ecological self to the marketplace (Lakoff and Johnson 1980; Zaltman, LeMasters, and Heffring 1982). This citizen-as-conserver metaphor highlights an oppositional meaning to the concept of consumer, which is a foundational concept in the field of marketing.

Contrary to the assumption that consumption in a mass-market economy leads to a better quality of life, the women in this study have found freedom in conserving. By enacting the mutual self, they feel a greater sense of control and power, because they are neither dominating nor being dominated. The women have transformed themselves and the communities around them, even if the steps they take are small—cleaning a stretch of stream, providing a child with an alternative viewpoint, or becoming critically reflexive in the household choices they make.

These women view consuming as a regrettable activity and only enter the marketplace reluctantly. Questions remain: Are these women part of a growing trend, or are they a marginal group? In the best-selling book, *Your Money or Your Life* (Dominguez and Robin 1992), the excessive focus on money and consumption is cited as a primary cause of the marketplace dependency in the United States and people's loss of control over their lives. In the voluntary simplicity movement that is spreading from its origins in the Pacific Northwest (Andrews 1997), the message offered is that if people discard unnecessary material clutter from their lives, they will live more "inwardly rich" lives (Elgin 1993, p. 25). Finally, Schor (1998) identifies the growing number of downshifters, upscale and educated adults who have decided to downshift from the fast-paced life of corporate America to less stressful jobs and schedules. Although downshifters do not reject consumption out of hand, they consume differently in order to live within more modest means. They choose less demanding and economically rewarding jobs, so they have more free time to pursue family, creative, and natural activities. Schor estimates that downshifters represent approximately 15% of the U.S. population.

Thus, growing numbers of U.S. citizens are already changing their "consuming" lifestyles to gain control over their chaotic lives. Gabriel and Lang (1995, p. 151) suggest that this act may ultimately be the most radical form of protest: "Yet, it is these largely invisible rebels who may in the long run provide the greater, if not the only challenge to consumerism. By saying 'No,' they may force a questioning of the core assumptions of consumerism and open up a range of choices that are currently invisible." The women in this study find that consuming less makes them feel greater control over their homes and their families and enables them to affirm the values they hold dear. Although this empowerment occasionally brings hardships, complications, and socially deviant behaviors, the women find satisfaction in enacting and maintaining their deep connections to nature.

References

Aaker, D.A. and R.P. Bagozzi (1982), "Attitudes Toward Public Policy Alternatives to Reduce Air Pollution," *Journal of Public Policy & Marketing*, 1, 85–94.

Anderson, Thomas W., Jr., and William H. Cunningham (1972), "The Socially Conscious Consumer," *Journal of Marketing*, 36 (July), 23–31.

Andrews, Cecile (1997), *The Circle of Simplicity*. New York: Harper Collins.

Arnould, Eric J. and Linda L. Price (1993), "River Magic: Extraordinary Experience and the Extended Service Encounter," *Journal of Consumer Research*, 20 (June), 24–45.

Belk, Russell W. (1988), "Possessions and the Extended Self," *Journal of Consumer Research*, 15 (September), 139–68.

——, John F. Sherry Jr., and Melanie Wallendorf (1988), "A Naturalistic Inquiry into Buyer and Seller Behavior at a Swap Meet," *Journal of Consumer Research*, 14 (March), 449–70.

Benjamin, Jessica (1988), *The Bonds of Love: Psychoanalysis, Feminism and the Problem of Domination*. London: Virago.

Briskin, Alan and Cheryl Peppers (2001), "Soul and Work: Back to the Future," *The Journal for Quality and Participation*, 24 (1), 6–14.

Bristor, Julia and Eileen Fischer (1993), "Feminist Thought: Implications for Consumer Research," *Journal of Consumer Research*, 19 (March), 518–36.

Bryant, B. and P. Mohai, eds. (1992), *Race and Incidence of Environmental Hazards*. Boulder: Westview Press.

Bullard, R.D. (1990), *Dumping in Dixie: Race, Class, and Environmental Quality*. Boulder: Westview Press.

Carson, Rachel (1962), *Silent Spring*. Greenwich, CT: Fawcett Press.

Certeau, Michel de (1984), *The Practice of Everyday Life*. Berkeley, CA: University of California Press.

Cornwell, T. Bettina and Charles H. Schwepker Jr. (1995), "Ecologically Concerned Consumers and Their Product Purchases," in *Environmental Marketing: Strategies, Practice, Theory, and Research*, Michael Jay Polonsky and Alma T. Mintu-Wimsatt, eds. New York: The Haworth Press, 119–54.

Cowan, Ruth Schwartz (1987), "Women's Work, Housework, and History: The Historical Roots of Inequality in Work-Force Participation," in *Families and Work*, Naomi Gerstel and Harriet Engel Gross, eds. Philadelphia, PA: Temple University Press, 164–77.

Daly, Mary (1978), *Gyn/ecology: The Metaethics of Radical Feminism*. London: Women's Press.

d'Eaubonne, Françoise (1974), "Feminism or Death," in *New French Feminisms: An Anthology*, Elaine Marks and Isabelle de Courtiuron, eds. New York: Shocken Books, 64–67.

De Vault, Marjorie L. (1987), "Doing Housework: Feeding and Family Life," in *Families and Work*, Naomi Gerstel and Harriet Engel Gross, eds. Philadelphia, PA: Temple University Press, 178–91.

—— (1991), *Feeding the Family: The Social Organization of Caring as Gendered Work*. Chicago: University of Chicago Press.

Diamond, Irene and Gloria Feman Orenstein, eds. (1990), *Reweaving the World: The Emergence of Ecofeminism*. San Francisco: Sierra Club Books.

Dobscha, Susan (1997), "The Lived Experience of Consumer Rebellion Against Marketing," in *Advances in Consumer Research*, Vol. 25, Joseph W. Alba and Wesley Hutchinson, eds. Provo, UT: Association for Consumer Research, 91–97.

Dominguez, Joe and Vicki Robin (1992), *Your Money or Your Life*. New York: Penguin.

Ehrenfeld, D.W. (1978), *The Arrogance of Humanism*. New York: Oxford University Press.

Elgin, Duane (1993), *Voluntary Simplicity*. New York: Quill.

Ellen, P.S. (1994), "Do We Know What We Need to Know? Objective and Subjective Knowledge Effects in Pro-ecological Behaviors," *Journal of Business Research*, 30 (1), 43–52.

Elliott, Richard and Mark Ritson (1997), "Poststructuralism and the Dialectics of Advertising: Discourse, Ideology, Resistance," in *Consumer Research: Postcards from the Edge*, Stephen Brown and Darach Turley, eds. London: Routledge, 190–217.

Fischer, Eileen and Stephen J. Arnold (1990), "More Than a Labor of Love: Gender Roles and Christmas Gift Shopping," *Journal of Consumer Research*, 17 (December), 333–45.

Fisk, George (1973), "Criteria for a Theory of Responsible Consumption," *Journal of Marketing*, 37 (April), 24–31.

Gaard, Greta (1993), "Living Interconnections with Animals and Nature," in *Ecofeminism: Women, Animals, Nature*, Greta Gaard, ed. Philadelphia: Temple University Press, 1–12.

Gabriel, Yiannis and Tim Lang (1995), *The Unmanageable Consumer*. London: Sage Publications.

Ganesan, Shankar (1994), "Determinants of Long-Term Orientation in Buyer–Seller Relationships," *Journal of Marketing*, 58 (April), 1–19.

Gibbs, Lois (1982), *Love Canal: My Story*. Albany, NY: State University of New York Press.

Granzin, K.L. and J.E. Olsen (1991), "Characterizing Participants in Activities Protecting the Environment: A Focus on Donating, Recycling and Conservation Behavior," *Journal of Public Policy & Marketing*, 16 (1), 110–25.

Gruen, Lori (1993), "Dismantling Oppression: An Analysis of the Connection Between Women and Animals," in *Ecofeminism: Women, Animals, Nature*, Greta Gaard, ed. Philadelphia: Temple University Press, 60–90.

Heisley, Deborah D. and Sidney J. Levy (1991), "Autodriving: A Photoelicitation Technique," *Journal of Consumer Research*, 17 (December), 257–72.

Hill, Ronald Paul and Mark Stamey (1990), "The Homeless in America: An Examination of Possessions and Consumption Behaviors," *Journal of Consumer Research*, 17 (December), 303–21.

Hirschman, Elizabeth (1980), "Innovativeness, Novelty Seeking, and Consumer Creativity," *Journal of Consumer Research*, 7 (December), 283–95.

—— (1993), "Ideology in Consumer Research, 1980 and 1990: A Marxist and Feminist Critique," *Journal of Consumer Research*, 19 (March), 537–55.

Hudson, Laurel Anderson and Julie Ozanne (1988), "Alternative Ways of Seeking Knowledge in Consumer Research," *Journal of Consumer Research*, 14 (March), 508–21.

Jaggar, Alison M. (1983), *Feminist Politics and Human Nature*. Totowa, NJ: Rowman and Allanheld.

Kilbourne, William E. (1995), "Green Advertising: Salvation or Oxymoron?" *Journal of Advertising*, 24 (2), 7–19.

—— and Suzanne C. Beckmann (1998), "Review and Critical Assessment of Research on Marketing and the Environment," *Journal of Marketing Management*, 14 (6), 513–32.

——, Pierre McDonagh, and Andrea Prothero (1997), "Sustainable Consumption and the Quality of Life: A Macromarketing Challenge to the Dominant Social Paradigm," *Journal of Macromarketing*, 17 (1), 4–24.

Krauss, Celene (1993), "Women and Toxic Waste Protests: Race, Class and Gender as Resources of Resistance," *Qualitative Sociology*, 16 (3), 247–62.

Kunstler, James Howard (1996), *Home from Nowhere*. New York: Simon and Schuster.

Lahar, Stephanie (1991), "Ecofeminist. Theory and Grassroots Politics," *Hypatia*, 6 (Spring), 28–45.

Lakoff, George and Mark Johnson (1980), *The Metaphors We Live By*. Chicago: University of Chicago Press.

McCarty, J.A. and L.J. Shrum (1994), "The Recycling of Solid Wastes: Personal Values, Value Orientations, and Attitudes About Recycling as Antecedents of Recycling Behavior," *Journal of Business Research*, 30, 53–62.

McCracken, Grant (1988), *The Long Interview*. Newbury Park, CA: Sage Publications.

McDonagh, Pierre and Andrea Prothero (1997), "Leap-Frog Marketing: The Contribution of Ecofeminist Thought to the World of Patriarchal Marketing," *Marketing Intelligence & Planning*, 15 (7), 361–88.

Merchant, Carolyn (1980), *The Death of Nature*. San Francisco: Harper and Row.

—— (1992), *Radical Ecology: The Search for a Livable World*. New York: Routledge.

Mick, David Glen and Susan Fournier (1998), "Paradoxes of Technology: Consumer Cognizance, Emotions, and Coping Strategies," *Journal of Consumer Research*, 25 (2), 123–43.

Murray, Jeff B. and Julie L. Ozanne (1991), "The Critical Imagination: Emancipatory Interests in Consumer Research," *Journal of Consumer Research*, 18 (September), 129–44.

Naess, A. (1987), *Ecology, Community and Lifestyle: Ecosophy T*. Cambridge: Cambridge University Press.

Oakley, Anne (1981), "Interviewing Women: A Contradiction in Terms" in *Doing Feminist Research*, H. Roberts, ed. Boston: Routledge and Kegan Paul, 30–61.

Otnes, Cele, Tina M. Lowrey, and Young Chan Kim (1993), "Gift Selection for Easy and Difficult Recipients: A Social Roles Interpretation," *Journal of Consumer Research*, 20 (September), 229–44.

Ottman, Jacquelyn (1997), *Green Marketing: Opportunity for Innovation*, 2d ed. Chicago: NTC Business Books.

Ozanne, Julie L. and Jeff B. Murray (1995), "Uniting Critical Theory and Public Policy to Create the Reflexively Defiant Consumer," *American Behavioral Scientists*, 38 (February), 516–25.

Ozanne, L.K. and P.M. Smith (1998), "Segmenting the Market for Environmentally Certified Wood Products," *Forest Science*, 44 (3), 379–89.

—— and R.P. Vlosky (1997), "Willingness to Pay for Environmentally Certified Wood Products: The Consumer Perspective," *Forest Products Journal*, 47 (6), 39–48.

Peñaloza, Lisa and Linda L. Price (1993), "Consumer Resistance: A Conceptual Overview," in *Advances in Consumer Research*, Vol. 20, Leigh McAlister and Michael L. Rothschild, eds. Provo, UT: Association for Consumer Research, 123–28.

Pettus, Katherine (1997), "Ecofeminist Citizenship," *Hypatia*, 12 (3), 132–56.

Pickett, G.M., N. Kangun, and S.J. Grove (1993), "Is There a General Conserving Consumer? A Public Policy Concern," *Journal of Public Policy & Marketing*, 12 (2), 234–43.

Plumwood, Val (1993), *Feminism and the Mastery of Nature*. London: Routledge.

Reinhardt, Forest (1998), "Environmental Product Differentiation: Implications for Corporate Strategy," *California Management Review*, 40 (4), 43–73.

Reinharz, Shulamit (1992), *Feminist Methods in Social Research*. New York: Oxford University Press.

Ritson, Mark and Susan Dobscha (1998), "Marketing Heretics: Resistance Is Not Futile," in *Advances in Consumer Research*, Vol. 26, Eric Arnould and Linda Scott, eds. Provo, UT: Association for Consumer Research, 159.

—— and —— (2001), "The Free State: An Ethnographic Study of a Counter Culture of Consumption," working paper, London Business School.

Roach, Catherine (1991), "Loving Your Mother: On the Woman–Nature Relation," *Hypatia*, 6 (1), 46–59.

Ruether, Rosemary Radford (1974), *New Woman New Earth*. Minneapolis: Seabury Press.

Schau, Hope Jensen (2000), "Consumer Imagination, Identity, and Self-Expression," in *Advances in Consumer Research*, Vol. 27, Mary Gilly and Joan Meyers-Levy, eds. Provo, UT: Association for Consumer Research, 50–56.

Scherhorn, G. (1993), "Consumer's Concern About the Environment and Its Impact on Business," *Journal of Consumer Policy*, 16 (2), 171–91.

Schor, Juliet B. (1998), *The Overspent American*. New York: Basic Books.

Schwepker, C.H., Jr., and T.B. Cornwell (1991), "An Examination of Ecologically Concerned Consumers and Their Intention to Purchase Ecologically Packaged Products," *Journal of Public Policy & Marketing*, 10 (2), 77–101.

Sherry, John F., Jr. (1983), "Gift-Giving: An Anthropological Perspective," *Journal of Consumer Research*, 10 (September), 157–68.

Sherwin, Susan (1992), "Philosophical Methodology and Feminist Methodology: Are They Compatible?" in *Women, Knowledge, and Reality: Explorations in Feminist Philosophy*, Ann Garry and Marilyn Pearsall, eds. Boston: Unwin Hyman, 21–23.

Shiva, Vandana (1989), *Staying Alive: Women, Ecology and Development*. London: Zed Books.

Shrivastava, Paul (1994), "CASTRATED Environment: GREENING Organizational Studies," *Organizational Studies*, 15 (5), 705–26.

Shrum, L.J., J.A. McCarty, and T.M. Lowrey (1995), "Buyer Characteristics of the Green Consumer and Their Implications for Advertising Strategy," *Journal of Advertising*, 24 (2), 71–82.

Sillanpaa, Maria (1998), "The Body Shop Values Report: Toward Integrated Stakeholder Auditing," *Journal of Business Ethics*, 17 (13), 1443–56.

Smith, Dorothy E. (1987), *The Everyday World as Problematic*. Boston: Northeastern University Press.

Spretnak, Charlene (1990), "Ecofeminism: Our Roots and Flowering," in *Reweaving the World: The Emergence of Ecofeminism*, Irene Diamond and Feman Orenstein, eds. San Francisco: Sierra Club Books, 3–14.

Thogerson, J. and S.C. Grunert-Beckman (1996), "Values and Attitude Formation Towards Emerging Attitude Objects: From Recycling to General Waste Minimizing Behavior," in *Advances in Consumer Research*, Vol. 24, M. Brucks and D.J. MacInnis, eds. Provo, UT: Association for Consumer Research, 182–89.

Thompson, Craig J. and Diana L. Haytko (1997), "Speaking of Fashion: Consumers' Uses of Fashion Discourses and the Appropriation of Countervailing Cultural Meanings," *Journal of Consumer Research*, 24 (1), 15–42.

Warren, Karen J. (1987), "Feminism and Ecology: Making Connections," *Environmental Ethics*, 9 (1), 3–20.

—— (1990), "The Power and the Promise of Ecological Feminism," *Environmental Ethics*, 12 (Summer), 125–46.

—— and Jim Cheney (1991), "Ecological Feminism and Ecosystem Ecology," *Hypatia*, 6 (Spring), 179–97.

World Commission on Environment and Development (1987), *Our Common Future*. New York: Oxford University Press.

Yankelovich Marketing Research Group (1993), results as reported in the *Wall Street Journal*, (February 7), H1, H4.

Zaltman, Gerald, Karen LeMasters, and Michael Heffring (1982), *Theory Construction in Marketing*. New York: John Wiley & Sons.

Zikmund, William G. and William J. Stanton (1971), "Recycling Solid Wastes: A Channels-of-Distribution Problem," *Journal of Marketing*, 35 (July), 34–39.

16
Past Postmodernism?

Mark Tadajewski[1] and Douglas Brownlie[2]

[1]*University of Leicester and* [2]*University of Stirling*

T he chapters that conclude this volume will introduce a number of provocative ways to rethink marketing theory and practice. These papers will hopefully provide interested students and academics with a range of perspectives that they might draw upon in their own research endeavours, whether this is a small project for a specific course, or if it is a much larger piece of academic work. As the contributors in the pages that follow would testify, these papers are simply starting points for more in-depth reading.

What will probably be obvious is that there is no chapter that deals solely with postmodernism. The question that might be posed then, are we suggesting that marketing should move beyond postmodernism? To be sure, we can appreciate the fact that much postmodern theorising has directed our attention to issues relating to gender, sexuality and ethnicity in marketing and consumer research. It follows, therefore, that we agree with the sentiment espoused by Calás and Smircich (1999: 658) who in response to the question of whether we were 'past postmodernism' were careful to note that while 'there is still much work to be done in organization studies through postmodern analytics', other approaches may present equally fruitful lines of inquiry.

In this regard they list Foucauldian genealogies, Derridean deconstructions, postcolonial analyses, Actor Network Theory and Feminist perspectives. Of these, three appear in this collection, namely a starting point for a Foucauldian genealogical analysis, Feminist theoretical analysis and a chapter influenced by postcolonial theory. We think, like those scholars who have tried to engage with postmodern theory in more depth (see Linstead, 2005), that continued engagement with postmodern thought can be valuable. However, like Morgan (2003), we have serious reservations about the level of critique that is found in postmodern marketing thought. We would go further than this, going so far as to question the view that our world can really be said to be postmodern.

Like Calhoun (1993) we are not convinced that postmodernism represents the epochal shift or the new paradigm that others contend (e.g. Firat and Dholakia, 2006). This, we might expect, given that Chia (1995: 580) underscored the point that the postmodern 'is not locatable through the framing of a simple succession of historical periodizations'.

However, we cannot get away from the fact that the 'two basic organizing forces in modernity – capitalism and bureaucratic power – have hardly begun to dissolve' (Calhoun, 1993: 77). 'The postmodernization of the world is', as Therborn (2007) puts it, 'very uneven'.

More seriously, we are concerned with the incorporation of postmodernism and the elision that we see accompanying it in marketing in relation to the shifting nature of capitalism. In reference to the work of Brown (1995, 1998a), Morgan signals the limitations of postmodern critique. Acknowledging that postmodernism has posed certain challenges to the dominant logical empiricist paradigm in marketing, Morgan still remains concerned about

> . . . what sort of critical edge exists in this type of postmodernist analysis. Brown and his colleagues clearly represent a challenge to the dominant orthodoxy by their refusal to play the positivist game of hypothesis development and testing. Yet it is a limited sort of critique by virtue of its seeming unwillingness to engage with the economic organization of markets and marketing or the social and ecological impacts of mass consumerism. (Morgan, 2003: 118)

Brown (1995, 1998a) does, of course, make reference to the problematic nature of progressive modernist narratives and draws attention to the negative externalities of scientific progress. While we must appreciate, as Fromm reminds us, the fact that 'by virtue of his reason' humankind has 'built a material world the reality of which surpasses even the dreams of fairy tales and utopias' (Fromm, 1947/2003: 2), the Enlightenment also has its dark side (e.g. Gadamer, 1990). Brown (1995, 1998a) flags up issues like the destruction of the natural environment and the development of weapons of mass destruction as the negative effects of the Enlightenment project.

What does seem to be uncritically accepted by postmodern scholars in marketing is the elevation of 'liberatory' consumption over production (e.g. Firat and Dholakia, 2006; Firat and Venkatesh, 1995). This move marginalises production to a degree that we think is untenable throughout most of the world today. It is also a move that earlier critical marketers and consumer researchers sought to avoid. Firat and Dholakia, for instance, noted that the consumption 'patterns of individuals or groups evolve in consonance with, and reinforce, the productive roles of these individuals or groups' (Firat and Dholakia, 1982: 9).

The idea that consumers experience a level of individual freedom through their consumption is, nonetheless, one that is often reiterated (Arnould and Thompson, 2005; Kilbourne *et al.*, 1997; Thompson and Coskuner-Balli, 2007; Varman and Vikas, 2007). Many of those affiliated with postmodern thought in marketing gesture to the protean nature of the individual self (Brown, 1998b), while tempering their analysis with a nod to the powerful roles played by corporations and market forces in structuring everyday life (Firat and Dholakia, 2006; Firat and Venkatesh, 1995). It is the latter feature of contemporary society that we believe still retains much directive, even dictatorial force, in developing economies.

People in developed (Ehrenreich, 2002; Micheletti and Stolle, 2007) and developing economies (Klein, 2000; Varman and Vikas, 2007; Vikas and Varman, 2007) cannot all engage in the kinds of 'liberatory consumption' lauded in postmodern marketing scholarship because wealth is not equally distributed throughout the globe. We would do well to remember that our ability in advanced industrial economies to select from a vast range of cheap consumer goods is predicated on 'the systemic exploitation of subaltern groups and nation states at the periphery of the global system . . . This is a *fundamental pre-requisite* for *consumer revolution to take place in the richer countries*' (Varman and Vikas, 2007: 123; emphases in original).

Rather than elevating consumption over production, the two are, for many, firmly co-determined. To take one example that problematises the inappropriate separation of the two, Varman and Vikas (2007) examined the relationship between consumption and individual freedom. Drawing on research conducted in the North Indian city of Kanpur, they highlighted the 'wretched living conditions of subaltern consumers' and their inability to engage in extensive consumption. For these individuals, it is their powerlessness in the production (work) sphere that curtails, almost to nothing, their consumption behaviours. The reasons are primarily structural:

> These subaltern groups do not have any legal protection, despite existing government laws, to ensure payment of minimum wages. Inefficient and corrupt government machinery fails to provide any protection for these workers against exploitation by their employers. This group puts in long working hours, without any system of over-time payment. These subaltern groups lack employment guarantees, which make them particularly vulnerable to exploitation. (Varman and Vikas, 2007: 125)

These workers are not in a position to increase their wages or improve their working conditions. And this has a direct impact on their ability to consume. Far removed from the 'fluidity of the postmodern self' (Brown, 1998b: 261), these

> . . . subaltern consumers struggle to make their two ends meet [sic] and they live in shanty houses surrounded by extremely unhygienic conditions. These houses are also overcrowded with little personal space for their inhabitants. Food consumption just about meets the bare minimum requirement that is necessary for the biological survival of this group of consumers. These wretched living conditions lead to frequent outbreak of diseases, which further worsen

the lives of these consumers. Our data show that most of these subaltern consumers barely possess a set or two of clothing, which are just about adequate to cover their bodies. Low levels of access in the areas of food, clothing and shelter, provide a powerful, albeit tragic, description of unfreedom for this subaltern consumer group. (Varman and Vikas, 2007: 126)

Equally concerning is the extent to which unfettered markets and ethically dubious marketing practices appear to prevail. In a study of the selling of an intoxicant (correcting fluid) to homeless children, Vikas and Varman (2007) again draw attention to the interrelationships between structural changes in economies stimulated by changes in the nature of capitalism, notably via the influence of the IMF and their structural adjustment programs in India, which led to an increase in rural poverty levels, along with declining employment opportunities. The homeless children Vikas and Varman interviewed are, they suggest, 'a result of a social order, which is increasingly dependent on markets' (Vikas and Varman, 2007: 198). These children lead precarious lives on the poverty line, fearing for their safety and spending whatever money they earn as quickly as possible, so as to avoid having it stolen from them by larger children and adults.

Free-market rhetoric and returns to stockholders were vocalised, nonetheless, as most important to the producers and retailers who were selling the intoxicant products to homeless children: 'One of the dealers of the product told us that the firm and the managers should not be blamed as they were not encouraging these children to consume the product as an intoxicant' (Vikas and Varman, 2007: 200). Vikas and Varman find such assertions of consumer sovereignty distinctly objectionable. They firmly state their opinion about what should be done in this case:

> At a micro-level, the drug abuse by these children is clearly problematic and managers have to put an end to it by restricting sales around the railway station. Their *duty* is to re-visit the marketing strategy and to make amends to discourage such deviant consumption. This can either happen by changing [the] constituents of the product e.g. in some countries, mustard oil is mixed in solvent based correcting fluid to discourage abusers, or by stopping supplies to the retail outlets around the railway station. (Vikas and Varman, 2007: 200; emphasis in original)

To state what is perhaps obvious, while we agree that postmodernism has presented a challenge to mainstream marketing thought, it overstates the degree to which all persons in this world have been beneficiaries of the changing nature of capitalism. Of course, globalisation and the arrival of information technology have impacted on some consumers' lives. But recognition of these changing features of contemporary society should not blind us to the fact that the apparent postmodernisation of the Western world is predicated on the maintenance of a subaltern population who produce those beautifully marketed goods that we can purchase at relatively low prices.

The idea that consumption has become the overriding concern of many people is further questioned by Rothstein (2005). When studying the inhabitants of San Cosme Maztecochco in Mexico, she notes that except for the relatively successful, 'most people do not invest much (financially or emotionally) in consumption for identity' (Rothstein, 2005: 300). In the case that she examined over a period of 30 years, 'identity' structure 'was derived from "flexible production"'. Clarifying this point Rothstein writes, 'Although what and how they consume is part of their new conception of themselves, it is more complex than that. When people in San Cosme talk about how the community has changed, they do not stress the big new houses, clothes, or more frequent and more elaborate ritual celebrations. They stress the roads, cars, bus service and taxis that link them now, [to] the availability of wage (work) in the garment workshops' (Rothstein, 2005: 299). This, and the work mentioned above, in other words, seriously calls into question much postmodern marketing research. It is for this reason that we do not devote a chapter in this section to postmodern marketing (see Brown, 1995).

What we do include are chapters that attempt to transgress the boundaries of marketing and consumer research in innovative ways. We should note that these papers do not cohere into any unified world view. There is no one image of critical marketing that comes through in each and every paper, suffice to say that there are some shared themes relating to the value of critique, reflexivity, agency and resistance. These papers should not be read as defining what the boundaries of critique in marketing will, in perpetuity, represent.

The chapter by Gould is an exemplar of a limit attitude and also emblematic of the unswerving stance of the critic discussed by Said (1996) and of the parrhesiastes detailed by Foucault (2001). Gould is an iconoclastic member of the consumer research fraternity. As Arnould and Thompson (2005: 870n1) point out, his work has served 'an important function within the CCT tradition by periodically testing its epistemic boundaries, calling for renewed reflections on the relationships between the knower and the known, and forcing reconsideration of status quo paradigmatic conventions'.

In his chapter, Gould argues that introspection and critical marketing are firmly inter-twined. The reason why introspection has perhaps not been commodified or co-opted in the service of marketing management is, we might suspect, because sample sizes of one do not impress in the boardroom. Such criticism does not deter Gould who makes a compelling case why introspection is valuable as part of thinking critically *in* and *of* marketing and consumer research.

Next we have a chapter that draws upon the autonomist Marxist tradition. Marxist-informed approaches are unusual in marketing and some scholars have gone so far as to simply ignore the contribution of this rich theoretical area (see Lee and Murray, 1995). By contrast to the more affirmative paper by Gould where he highlights the central role of reflexivity and consumer agency in consumption practice, Arvidsson is concerned to examine issues related to co-optation, agency and resistance, notably in relation to brand management. In a nuanced analysis, Arvidsson examines the incorporation of cultural studies – or rather the theoretical emphases found in much cultural and literary critical work – into marketing.

He argues that consumption has not displaced production as the driving force of society. Extending this point further, he notes how the main 'value-driver' of consumer culture is the immaterial production of information. In introducing the concept of immaterial labour Arvidsson draws upon the work of Lazzarato who discussed immaterial labour in terms of the production of 'the informational and cultural content of the commodity' (Lazzarato, 1996: 133). Those involved in such productive exercises include individuals who attempt to define cultural and artistic standards such as advertising executives and other so-called 'creatives'.

To give this a more concrete basis, advertisers are interested in defining their brand in such a way that it appeals to their target consumers, guiding consumer norms through the development and diffusion of a specific lifestyle. Advertising executives and other creative individuals are involved in this process because of their 'symbolic-analytical services' (Hardt and Negri, 2000) that should hopefully develop a given campaign or media 'event' so that a particular product and advertising campaign can cultivate affect in their target market and beyond.

Arvidsson describes consumption as a form of immaterial labour, whereby the tactics of brand managers do not serve to 'discipline', consumers. Brand management is not a repressive force, but is intended to program consumers to use brands in specific ways. Consumers can, of course, resist any brand management strategies. And there is, as we would expect, some ambiguity in brand imagery, so that it remains unclear how particular products such as a BMW or Mercedes car 'are supposed to enter social relations' (Arvidsson, 2006: 245). Brand managers will, nonetheless, as the recent case of Apple stands as testament (see Shankar et al., 2006), attempt to 'police' their media image, defending the product against 'undesirable uses' or negative commentary (Arvidsson, 2006).

In a sophisticated argument, Arvidsson views consumer agency as a potentially productive force that can be used by companies in the process of the co-production of consumer experiences. In other words, consumers can and occasionally will use products in unanticipated ways. This can quite naturally be beneficial to an organisation who can then use consumer agency as a productive resource, using the consumer life-world as a living laboratory to be studied and commodified.

For Arvidsson, consumers can exhibit a certain degree of agency regarding their use of a given brand, but we should remember that the primary aim of brand management, he submits, is to ensure that consumers' use and understanding of brand meaning is channelled in very specific directions, so that they reproduce and further diffuse a dominant cultural pattern (cf. Thompson, 2005; Thompson and Arsel, 2004). Consumer agency is thus programmed in much the same way as the code in a computer program works to delimit the boundaries of appropriate movement choices for the central character.

In this case, cultural studies theory has been brought into marketing in a defanged way. It is no longer used to sketch out viable political responses to the culture industries, but can be used to support them (see Thompson *et al.*, 2006). This is clearly an argument that will be controversial given the valorisation of agency routinely found in consumer research, but which, even so, can function as another tool for marketers to use in the surveillance of their consumer populations. Cultural and literary theory has, in other words, become a potentially oppositional force co-opted by administrative, business interests.

Pauline Maclaran and Lorna Stevens have been at the forefront of feminist theorising in the United Kingdom for some time now. In a characteristically innovative paper they examine the role of theory in the marketing academy. Scholars are often expected to provide a contribution to theory, if their research is to appear in the top-tier of marketing publications such as the *Journal of Marketing* or *Journal of Consumer Research*. Maclaran and Stevens, by contrast, question the value attributed to theory and make the case that demands for theory can serve to reinforce the status quo in the academy, as well as reinforcing the theory–practice divide still further. Their critique does not stop here. It is also affirmative in providing a number of ways that scholars could possibly avoid exacerbating the theory–practice divide that Maclaran and Stevens describe; but not necessarily in an uncritical fashion, that is, by producing knowledge for marketing managers. Marketing management could equally be taken as the object of interest by critical marketing scholars.

In the next chapter Gavin Jack argues for the greater interconnection between theory, method and politics. Like Calás and Smircich (1999), he sees postcolonial theory as a fruitful way for re-politicising marketing scholarship; a politicisation that the use of interpretive methods can serve to undermine. We might recall that Jack and Westwood (2006) have previously made the case that there are a number of deficiencies in mainstream management thought that the inclusion of interpretive research, which is usually associated with qualitative methods, serves to reinforce. Specifically, while traditionally it is believed to be a benefit of qualitative and interpretive research that these studies take the respondents' point of view regarding any given consumption phenomenon, this local focus can itself be problematic from a critical perspective.

With reference to ethnography and interpretive research Jack and Westwood (2006) argue that

> . . . interpretivist research can result in mere "redescription" of the status quo of social and organizational life rather than a critical inspection of it. It is a criticism mounted, for example, by those within the radical humanist/structuralist paradigms who accuse interpretivists of reinforcing the status quo by ignoring the exercise of power . . . Ignoring these properties of social reality makes it impossible to change them for the betterment of the participants with whom the researcher engages. (Jack and Westwood, 2006: 486)

Jack's chapter introduces marketing scholars and students to postcolonialism; a task which very few have attempted. Drawing from its theoretical base, he highlights contemporary colonial and neo-colonial inflections of marketing and promotional practice, arguing that 'postcolonial theory can raise political and ethical questions about the role of marketing practice in organising problematic racial differences, and concomitantly of marketing theory in effectively erasing these key questions from the parameters of its recent debates'. Jack's approach, like many others in this collection, is partly historical. He goes further than this to show how marketing practice today reinforces a colonial mentality in ways that we might find distasteful. In doing this he raises a number of important questions that as scholars we should not shy away from; certainly, his representation of tourism marketing makes uncomfortable reading and will encourage students to think differently about this activity.

Coming to the end of this collection, it is appropriate to briefly review the terrain we have negotiated. We have outlined how critical marketing has historically developed, brought in appropriate historical papers that have challenged the representation of marketing, connected this with recent work in consumer research that directed attention to the historical development of this area and how certain debates were marginalised due to politics and a restricted view of the cognitive revolution. Then we turned our attention to the relationship between marketing and society, specifically in relation to marketing's role in perpetuating a 'consumer society'.

In a development of this theme, this collection brought together key scholarship that attempted to question marketing theory in relation to its inherent drive towards unsustainability and highlighted the ways in which 'conservers' can and do escape the market. Finally, we drew together a range of approaches that in their own unique ways sought to push marketing beyond its performative, managerial, positivist boundaries. If this book has made academics or students think differently about the way in which marketing engages with critique, then it will have achieved its goal.

References

Arnould, E.J. and Thompson, C.J. (2005) 'Consumer Culture Theory (CCT): Twenty Years of Research', *Journal of Consumer Research*, 31(4): 868–882.

Arvidsson, A. (2006) 'Brands: A Critical Perspective', *Journal of Consumer Culture* 5(2): 235–258.

Brown, S. (1995) *Postmodern Marketing*. London: Routledge.

—— (1998a) *Postmodern Marketing Two*. London: International Thompson Business Press.

—— (1998b) 'The Unbearable Lightness of Marketing: A Neo-Romantic, Counter-revolutionary Recapitulation', in S. Brown., A.M. Doherty and B. Clarke (eds) *Romancing the Market*, pp. 255–277. London: Routledge.

Calás, M. and Smircich, L. (1999) 'Past Postmodernism? Reflections and Tentative Directions', *Academy of Management Review* 24(4): 649–671.

Calhoun, C. (1993) 'Postmodernism as Pseudohistory', *Theory, Culture and Society* 10(1): 75–96.

Chia, R. (1995) 'From Modern to Postmodern Organizational Analysis', *Organization Studies* 16(4): 579–604.

Ehrenreich, B. (2002) *Nickel and Dimed: Undercover in Low Wage USA*. London: Granta.

Firat, A.F. and Dholakia, N. (1982) 'Consumption Choices at the Macro Level', *Journal of Macromarketing* 2(Fall): 6–15.

—— (2006) 'Theoretical and Philosophical Implications of Postmodern Debates: Some Challenges to Modern Marketing', *Marketing Theory* 6(2): 123–162.

Firat, A.F. and Venkatesh, A. (1995) 'Liberatory Postmodernism and the Reenchantment of Consumption', *Journal of Consumer Research* 22(3): 239–267.

Foucault, M. (2001) *Fearless Speech*. Ed. J. Pearson. Los Angles: Semiotext(e).

Fromm, E. (1947/2003) *Man For Himself*. London: Routledge.

Gadamer, H.-G. (1990) 'Reply to My Critics', in G.L. Ormiston and A.D. Schrift (eds) *The Hermeneutic Tradition: From Ast to Ricoeur*, pp. 273–297. Albany: State University of New York Press.

Hardt, M. and Negri, A. (2000) *Empire*. Cambridge: Harvard University Press.

Jack, G. and Westwood, R. (2006) 'Postcolonialism and the Politics of Qualitative Research in International Business', *Management International Review* 46: 481–501.

Kilbourne, W.E., McDonagh, P. and Prothero, A. (1997) 'Sustainable Consumption and the Quality of Life: A Macromarketing Challenge to the Dominant Social Paradigm', *Journal of Macromarketing* Spring: 4–24.

Klein, N. (2000) *No Logo*. London: Flamingo.

Lazzarato, M. (1996) 'Immaterial Labour', in P. Virno and M. Hardt (eds) *Radical Thought in Italy: A Practical Politics*, pp. 136–146. Minneapolis: University of Minneapolis Press.

Lee, R.G. and Murray, J.B. (1995) 'A Framework for Critiquing the Dysfunctions of Advertising: the Base-Superstructure Metaphor', *Advances in Consumer Research* 22: 139–143.

Linstead, S. (ed.) (2005) *Organization Theory and Postmodern Thought*. London: Sage.

Micheletti, M. and Stolle, D. (2007) 'Mobilizing Consumers to Take Responsibility for Global Social Justice', *The Annals of the American Academy of Political and Social Science* 611(May): 157–175.

Morgan, G. (2003) 'Marketing and Critique: Prospects and Problems', in M. Alvesson and H. Willmott (eds) *Studying Management Critically*, pp. 111–131. London: Sage.

Rothstein, F.A. (2005) 'Challenging Consumption Theory: Production and Consumption in Central Mexico', *Critique of Anthropology* 25(3): 279–306.

Said, E.W. (1996) *Representations of the Intellectual*. New York: Vintage.

Shankar, A., Cherrier, H. and Canniford, R. (2006) 'Consumer Empowerment: A Foucauldian Interpretation', *European Journal of Marketing* 40(9/10): 1013–1030.

Therborn, G. (2007) 'After Dialectics: Radical Social Theory in a Post-Communist World', *New Left Review* 43(Jan/Feb): 63–114.

Thompson, C.J. (2005) 'Consumer Risk Perceptions in a Community of Reflexive Doubt', *Journal of Consumer Research* 32(September): 235–248.

Thompson, C.J. and Arsel, Z. (2004) The Starbucks Brandscape and Consumers' (Anti-Corporate) Experiences of Glocalization', *Journal of Consumer Research* 31(December): 631–642.

Thompson, C.J. and Coskuner-Balli, G. (2007) 'Countervailing Market Responses to Corporate Co-optation and the Ideological Recruitment of Consumption Communities', *Journal of Consumer Research* 34(2): 135–152.

Thompson, C.J., Rindfleisch, A. and Arsel, Z. (2006) 'Emotional Branding and the Strategic Value of the Doppelgänger Brand Image', *Journal of Marketing* 70(1): 50–64

Varman, R. and Vikas, R.M. (2007) 'Freedom and Consumption: Toward Conceptualizing Systemic Constraints for Subaltern Consumers in a Capitalist Society', *Consumption, Markets and Culture* 10(2): 117–131.

Vikas, R.M. and Varman, R. (2007) 'Erasing Futures: Ethics of Marketing an Intoxicant to Homeless Children', *Consumption, Markets and Culture* 10(2): 189–202.

17

Introspection as Critical Marketing Thought, Critical Marketing Thought as Introspection

Stephen J. Gould

Baruch College, City University of New York

ABSTRACT *It is hard to escape oneself; yet, it seems in critical marketing thought, ironically just as much perhaps as in marketing science, thinkers tend to attempt to do just that. In this chapter, I challenge that effort by considering the links and uses of introspection in relation to the critical. In so doing, I engage you, the reader, in a number of critical-introspective exercises (thought experiments) designed to enable you to explore for yourself, in a very intimate way, what I am saying.*

Introduction

Both introspection and critical marketing remain contentious, misunderstood topics in marketing thought, not to mention across a wide variety of academic fields. Indeed, regarding introspection, I believe that because of such issues its uses and expression have not even come close to realising its full potential. But beyond these issues, there is much more to newly explore and develop. At the same time, I find critical theory and thought in marketing are also controversial, definitionally-charged and particularly lacking a coherent introspective-reflexive perspective. Thus, while researchers sometimes recognise the personal subjectivity present in their own critical practices, they nonetheless do not fully reflect about it introspectively or integrate it in a way that demonstrates how it informs their work. Certainly, it has always been a critical practice of mine in both my work and personal life to break out of the cultural mode that I seem to be fixed in by engaging in an unrelenting reflexive critique of my own Western culture and various other cultures I encounter.

As delineated specifically in consumer research by Murray and Ozanne (1991), critical theory and research stems from an understanding of consumer issues derived from the work of the Frankfurt School. This school postulated socially and materially constructed constraints on behaviour, which can be addressed through research informed by the analysis of intersubjective understandings and historical-empirical considerations (e.g. Hetrick and Lozada, 1994; Murray and Ozanne, 1991). As was noted in Chapter 1, beneficial social change is the goal. Thus, while I find much to applaud in the efforts to move in the directions critical theory has laid out, I feel no special attachment to these received forms.

Moreover, though there is much to consider, I would say that for our purposes here I construe 'emancipation' more broadly than it is applied in critical theory, so that it is not restricted to Western social issues as such. Instead, I relate it to the 'liberation' of mind, as a psycho-cultural construction informed by disparate Buddhist and other Asian and Western thought. I construe social issues in that context such that certain problems of the world are constructed as problems of mind (e.g., social biases are mental misapprehensions which may be liberated through various applications of mindfulness). Indeed, Kincheloe and Maclaren (2003) hold in their reconfigured view of critical theory that the 'psychic' is not separated from the sociopolitical realm, much as Fromm argued (see also Fromm 1942/2002; 1976/2007).

Reflecting an introspective-like position in this regard, Gramsci (2001) understood critical philosophy as a form of self-criticism or even autobiography. Kincheloe and Maclaren (2003) take such a perspective as a way to view and come to investigate one's own, often hidden interpretive processes. As Alvesson and Sköldberg (2004) note, research driven by critical theory must involve self-reflection. One starts where one is (Derrida, 1997), considers the issues of how the self embedded in culture can critique itself (Altman, 1995), and how critical thought and theory can be deployed in terms of disclosive possibilities of new self-understanding (Kompridis, 2005).

For me, societal deficits in their broadest configuration constrain the idea of emancipation by preventing people from reaching that goal. So while I find much to agree with in terms of the issues raised by critical theory (e.g., poverty, hegemonic dominance, human rights), I deal with them in terms of how they hinder people from achieving self-realisation in consciousness terms. I must admit that what self-realisation is differs widely for different people and cultures in such terms as whether it exists, is possible or even necessary; what it constitutes; its spiritual nature or not; or even what constitutes any such spiritual link. Thus, looking at myself, for instance, as I constitute a 'site of meaning' what I have understood as self-realisation necessarily has changed as I 'self-realise'. For example, while I engage in specific meditative practices aimed at self-realisation, my intellectual and embodied experiences of various aspects of consciousness continue to evolve. So, despite the lack of one essentialised meaning of self-realisation, I nonetheless apply it as a goal in constructing critical thought. However, even if my particular, though not altogether idiosyncratic construction of 'emancipation' is not quite how some of you conceive it, I tend to think that we can agree that the lack of an introspectively-informed linking of conscious-ness issues (e.g., empathetic awareness, interpreting our own perspectives-motivations) to social deficits is a 'critical' *aporia* in our critical theorising.

In that regard, I argue that introspection concerning one's own subjectivity is a key, if not the key to the construction and comprehension of critical thought (i.e., authors write and readers read in ways that are both self- and culturally-embedded). By introspecting on one's subjectivity, I mean looking within yourself and watching your thoughts and feelings to follow how your own viewpoints arise, what conflicts in your views may be in evidence, and what your views seem to be aiming at. Perhaps, most precipitously in this inquiry, I ask *why* I'm taking this particular critical viewpoint at this time and am trying to find out as openly and honestly as I dare or am able. Of course, there is a bit of an infinite regress here since I can ask why I am asking why and so on. Nonetheless, however you proceed, you are providing a critical reading of yourself, something I believe is a useful point of departure or stop along the way in your critical endeavours.

There are two sides to this argument: introspection as critical thought and critical thought as introspection. On the one hand, by its very controversial presence, researcher-conducted introspection constitutes a critical approach in its challenges to the status quo. Applications tend to stimulate fault-line thinking and provoke paradigmatic challenges to the marketing field. Conversely, while critical thought is generally constructed in terms of cultural critique, it is infected with introspective reflexive aspects that all too often are erased or ignored in ways ironically not that much different from scientific approaches which strive for 'objectivity'. I argue, by contrast, that the relationship between critical marketing and introspection is symbiotic, if not an embodiment of one phenomenon.

Introspection as critical marketing thought means that when one engages in some form of it, one is taking a critical position in the field, relative to everyone else, including other introspectors. For example, when various people, such as Stephen Brown, Peter Earl, Morris Holbrook and I, among others, engage in an act of introspection, we are staking out a position, making claims and applying introspection in ways that while ostensibly similar also differ meaningfully from each other. We reflect different narrative styles, explore different issues and otherwise aim to distinctively investigate consumer thought. And this is not to even consider all the different styles of others who – informed by implicit, if not explicit, introspective insight – apply various other theoretical and research approaches.

Extending from there, critical thought as introspection is perhaps even more controver-sial. In the first instance, dealing with explicit introspection, the marketing field tends to view introspection as a sort of marginalised outlier. But now I consider something even more dangerous. In this regard, I argue that the same sort of analysis that I apply to introspectors applies to all critical marketing thought, if not to all academic thought in marketing, whether it be from CCT (Arnould and Thompson, 2005) or even from such 'positivist-scientific' theoretical approaches as Behavioural Decision Theory (BDT). This is a crowded statement that needs some unpacking. First, we generally acknowledge that at least some CCT thinkers are engaging in critical thought, but may not recognise other researchers as doing so. However, if we consider critical activity as making distinctions (Gramsci, 2001), we can define critical thought as taking a position in the field on some issue with a more or less explicit and distinction-based critique. Then we can take an expansive view of critical thought without overlooking the significance of explicitly designated critical thought and theory.

Taking this expansive view allows us to contemplate the idea that all thought is to varying degrees informed by reflexive introspection and that it can be so investigated. Moreover, subjectivity-objectivity and related issues of voice, 1st person–3rd person, may be seen to reflect either the presence or erasure of the introspective perspective (Derrida, 1997). It can be further argued that the idea of critical thought or at least taking a critical position is erased in 'objective' scientific endeavours but that a trace of it remains in that domain nonetheless. As may be obvious, the very act of studying or advancing an argument involves the psychic investment of one's self, one's theoretical and methodological stance, and position in the academy, not to mention the world, even if one shudders at the thought.

To explore these issues, I will separately discuss the two perspectives, namely introspection as critical marketing thought and critical marketing thought as introspection. In addition, throughout I will draw on my own introspective experiences and engage the reader in the process through a series of critical-introspective exercises in which she can critically examine for herself whether what I am saying 'makes sense to her or not'. In other words, I directly inscribe reader response in the form of your own critique and position into this chapter, even if I do not know what it is. The paradoxical aim is to suspend judgement in order to improve one's ability to be 'critical'. Finally, I conclude with a conclusion that is not a conclusion.

Introspection as Critical Marketing Thought

Introspection in some guise or other has a long history in Western culture. In recent psychological thought, erasure of this history is especially pronounced as evidenced by the title of one book on the topic, *The Disappearance of Introspection* (Lyons, 1986). Much of this has to do with an evolution over time in which behaviorism challenged introspection in early 20th century psychology. On the other hand, Elshof (2005) writing in a philosophical-epistemological vein with links to psychology, emphatically calls his book *Introspection Vindicated*.

The application of introspection in marketing thought has a quite different genealogy and while reflecting various ties to a long qualitative-interpretive tradition (e.g., Tadajewski, 2006), it can generally be tied to early work by Gould (1991) and several papers by Holbrook (1995). It was my paper which sparked a great deal of controversy for many reasons, not the least of which was that it was published in a leading journal, the *Journal of Consumer Research*. From its publication, there emerged an evolving reactive genealogy that continues to this day, including Wallendorf and Brucks' (1993) reaction, my own further response (Gould, 1995) and the work of others.

In particular, I used introspection (Gould, 1991) to study and express my lived experience regarding my own self-perceived vital energy and consumption practices in phenomenological-consciousness and narratological terms. The idea of using myself as a 'relatively unique' case which I could study in a 'deeper and richer' way was paramount in this process (Gould, 1991: 201). In response, Wallendorf and Brucks (1993) questioned the validity of introspection in 'scientific' terms of what can be detected or claimed and further sought to move beyond what they saw as the limits of one researcher, such as myself, conducting introspection. I responded to their critique by further elaborating when 'researcher introspection' might make a contribution and emphasised that the researcher was perhaps best positioned, at certain times, to mindfully explore consumption because she could follow herself in vast detail over time, both concurrently and retrospectively, while simultaneously examining existing theory and thought (Gould, 1995).

I might add that while there are many issues to consider, I stand by that view today, though I would further develop it by asserting more strongly that any particular introspectively-informed narrative may be of interest to consumer researchers, depending on its insights, whether it is 'scientifically-based' or not. Moreover, I think we can much more deeply explore the theoretical conception of the researcher-introspector as the joint embodiment of the emic (the perspective of the one observed) and the etic (the perspective of the researcher doing the observing). If I develop themes concerning myself or have a theory about my own consumption, which may interest other researchers, all limitations of self-biases or the privileging of the self notwithstanding, does this process not reflect what we all do as researchers, as consumers? Is it not worthy of exploration? In any case, encompassing these issues and divergences as time has passed, work on introspection has continued in two ways: (1) critiques of it, especially of Gould (1991), and (2) applications of it in terms of researcher introspection or as a part of an interviewing process.

In any case, it appears impossible to apply introspection as a research method without dealing with it as a critical theory artifact. Accordingly, when considering the genealogy of introspection and its various critiques, one has to note the Zeitgeist in 1991. Much of the research of that time was done by people whose backgrounds were largely 'positivist', even as they tried to offer alternatives. Thus, Gould (1991) and much other interpretive work of the period was grounded in psychologically oriented research which included phenomeno-logical and psychoanalytic perspectives. As things developed, interpretive researchers tended to move toward more macro-cultural perspectives as captured in the CCT project which involves various ethnographic, cross-cultural, narrative, postmodern and poststructural theories and applications (Arnould and Thompson, 2005); in fact, many of the later critiques of Gould (1991) reflected that evolving perspective though my work did in fact embody an all but ignored Asian-derived cultural critique of Western culture and scientific thinking. The reason this may have been ignored is because the introspection I applied involved various thought-watching, meditative and energy-awareness techniques which were micro-psychological in application, but macro-critical in reflecting an entirely different cultural perspective on both consumer behaviour and consumer research. In this regard, I constructed consumer narrative as situated in introspective consciousness and awareness of embodiment. To better consider these processes try the following introspective-critical exercise:

Exercise 1: Thoughts and Narrative

> Watch your thoughts, emotions and bodily sensations as they flow by without trying to control them. Later take a product you use. Watch your thoughts, emotions and sensations as you use (imagine using) it. Register as much detail as possible. Also note what narratives arise. Conversely, start with a narrative about your use of a product and see how it is invested with thoughts, emotions and sensations.

Further, consider the existence of different styles of introspection. I have tried in recent papers to clarify the situation by indicating that introspection may be seen in two major forms: narrative introspection through which a researcher tells her story, and metacognitive introspection which focuses on the psychological-phenomenological processes of internal mental-sensory focusing, that is, an introspective awareness of one's own thought (Gould, 2006). Most introspection by researchers in consumer research has been of the narrative variety. However, as I suggest in my own case, one may apply both approaches as when one utilises self-observations, both in real-time and retrospectively, to construct personal narratives. For example, even in recalling certain energetic experiences related to using products, I may relive many of the same feelings I had before (e.g., 'slowly sipping this tea enables me to enter a calm meditative space'; 'the party music makes me jump out of my usual introverted self and exhibit my spinning dance which captures everybody's attention'). Thinking in terms of living and reliving brings a new dimension to introspection, which incorporates elements of narrative and metacognition, as well as real-time and retrospective introspection.

Framing these sorts of issues in terms of science versus art as many do may, nevertheless, be harmful. There may also be confusion because while some issues concerning introspection can be thought of in terms of unconscious versus conscious states, there are also issues of what is revealed (private versus public discourse) and how emerging thoughts and feelings are inscribed in discourse and narrative which introspectors can investigate. The point is not to get bogged down in scientific-poststructural debates, but rather that we make sense of metacognitive introspections through narrative introspections which are constructed of metacognitions and so on.

Given the controversies over introspection and particularly how it is constructed metacognitively and self-consciously by consumer researchers, it is fair to ask why do any researchers even engage in introspection and just as importantly why do they differ in style and content from others? Hirschman (1985) suggested one possible perspective. She took a Jungian personality approach to four researchers and showed how they differed based on their propensities. Interestingly three of those researchers in her study were interpretive (Russell Belk, Morris Holbrook, Sidney Levy) and yet differed in their research approaches. Such an approach might be extended to consider how and why some researchers engage in introspection in their research and why others don't. As a field, we have enough situating observation points and a number of us have reflexively commented on our own or others' introspection: Holbrook has been associated with a Romantic-lyrical, very personal introspection. Stephen Brown views the entertainment value of introspection, even as it informs. Peter Earl uses introspection to consider economic theory, based on his own experiences. I have tried to focus on theory even as I have embraced what some regard as the sensational. As time has gone on, these researchers have interacted either in person or in print so that various reflexive synergies have evolved over time. It is a continuing saga. In that vein and based on Hirschman's idea of different personalities taking different approaches, try the following exercise.

Exercise 2: Introspective Style

Continuing the thought-watching from Exercise 1, explore how your way of approaching the world manifests in your work. Notice, for instance, the different styles of introspection (e.g., Romantic-lyrical (Holbrook, 1995) or satirical (Brown, 1998)), and see if you are trying to be entertaining. Examine your thoughts and feelings. As per Brown (2006a) are you really entertaining and/or does your work entail controversy? Were you trying to be controversial? Are you deadpan? Are you ironic or tongue-in-cheek? Now examine how whatever style you bring to critical thought might impinge on the content of that thought. Note how your temperament expresses itself in your work and thought. Do you change with mood swings? What does this say about essentialising oneself? Is it hard to do even if you want to?

In my own continuing work, I am very conscious of what the others have done and reflect that in my present work. I know my own genealogy the best, at least as I construct it – others may and do construct it quite differently. Thus, I will use it to exemplify how I see introspection as applied in marketing as a critical approach. First of all when I wrote Gould (1991: 194), I took the position from the outset that

> Much of consumer research has failed to describe many aspects of my own consumer behavior, especially the everyday dynamics of my pervasive, self-perceived vital energy.

This meant and continues to mean to me that there was much of my own behaviour that was not even conceived of in consumer research. This related to vital energy and other practices of everyday life. I also thought that I was tapping into what could be an alternative to Western cultural and academic paradigms as well as to both positivist and interpretive approaches in particular. In that, I reflected an Asian-based approach involving various yogic-meditational practices and discourses. While to explain this approach in great detail is well beyond the scope of this chapter, let me say by way of a brief explanation that I take an encompassing time (over millennia) and space view of Asian culture from India through Tibet, China to Japan. I am constructing this view experientially, based on face-to-face encounters with many and various Asian yogic-meditational teachers and practitioners, over 30 years of personal practice and study, and my own academic endeavours in dealing with Asian-Western perspectives (e.g., Gould 1991, 1995). It involves an incessant focus on understanding and engaging consciousness and vital energy through various practices largely inconceivable in the West until recently and at that, only on a limited basis. Of course, these practices and understandings varied across these Asian time-spaces, but for many of my purposes in writing about them I treat them in terms of one meaning site and phrase, 'Asian-based', to distinguish them from 'Western-based'. In other contexts, I would make more fine-grained distinctions, practice by practice, within as well as between specific Asian cultures and so on. However, I do not want to dwell on this Asian-based aspect here per se, but use it to emphasise how literally 'foreign' my approach has been to most researchers of whatever stripe, as well as to show how it informs and constructs my introspection and critical thinking.

How did I get there? I am a child of the sixties. As an undergraduate in that era, I got interested in Asian meditative-yogic practices. I also embraced many aspects of the hippy lifestyle. That in itself made me think of myself as a 'cultural warrior'. My lifestyle stood thus in opposition to the mainstream culture though we could, I'm sure, problematise the nature of that opposition (e.g., considering what constitutes insider and outsider status). Later in the seventies as I attempted to pick up the pieces from a broken career path, I joined academia, first as an MBA student and later as a PhD student. But even then I saw myself as outside the mainstream and was trying to fit in at least outwardly, while not capitulating inwardly. I gravitated to marketing because I thought it would be more fun and stimulating than most other fields.

I brought myself into my research. From the beginning, I reflected my Asian-based perspective where I could, as well as other socially-oriented approaches which I hoped would inform people. I did not have a notion of attempting introspection until I had a paper which studied vital energy in a Tibetan context rejected at *JCR*. I wrote that paper as a kind of participant-observation ethnographic piece although I had no real idea of method. I invented method and wrote based on my experiences with Tibetans and their 'energy-culture'. There was nothing formal. So while the paper actually drew a revision request (risky though) it was eventually rejected. So partly at the suggestion of Elizabeth (Beth) Hirschman, my colleague at Rutgers at that time, and based on my own culture-challenging inclinations, I decided to undertake an introspective piece. I felt that I could not be attacked for a lack of formal ethnography. I said to myself, 'How could they challenge me telling my own story and what I knew about vital energy practices? I experienced what I experienced'.

So, in any case, my work was paradigmatically, culturally and methodologically critical in its inception – not to mention the provocative sexual element which is always forbidding. I knew this and took a stance that threw down the gauntlet to complacent, traditional research. Still, I was restrained by various overt and covert censorship practices and much was lost along the way on the proverbial cutting room floor.

The 1991 paper by itself has engendered a whole genealogy of critique. There is that infamous sequence discussed above, with Wallendorf and Brucks (1993) taking on my work, followed by my response (Gould, 1995). But so many others have used the paper as a talking point for situating both introspection and interpretive work in general (Gould, Forthcoming). So I argue that introspection, especially so-called researcher introspection, comprises critical thought by its very existence. Although I took no such explicit position in 1991, I can easily embrace it as what I was doing in terms of contesting key assumptions in consumer research, as well as Western culture in general. Today my particular challenges to the field remain, as do those of other introspectors.

One major critical element stems from what marketing is. Among other things, it is a process of reaching mass segments of people, as large as they can be in most cases. On the other hand, introspection by the researcher is seen as idiosyncratic, and ungeneralis-able, and quite non-commodifiable. I think this sort of thinking permeates our research community. In Gould (1991), I actually made some links regarding vital energy to the use of the word 'energy' in advertising while acknowledging that much of what I was writing may not extend to everyone: 'Clearly not all consumers behave precisely in the same way that I do, but all nonetheless have ordinary ways they cope with their energy ups and downs and manage their consumption experience' (1991: 205).

Lost in all this were certain elements of individual uniqueness, levels of experience and the like which were erased in the writing, review and subsequent readings of this work. Nowadays perhaps a more nuanced, poststructural reading would embrace particular sites of meaning, such as, for example, my own experiences, cultural orientation, discourses and practices, and thus engender the critical perspective my work intended by challenging the norms of academic science, the limitations of marketing and consumer research and

Western culture, itself. If we are a field of theory and research, then such understanding should be considered. If there were only a few surviving members of a species, a biologist would not exclude it from further research. If anything, the rare species is evidence for broader phenomena in the overall population-ecology of species. Yet, in marketing theory, this seems not to be the case. In fact, my own critical reading of the reading of my 1991 paper and what followed suggests that many construed it in terms of established paradigms, whether positivistic or interpretive, but failed to construe most of its meanings the way I intended or to appreciate the cultural critique it entailed.

Critical Marketing Thought as Introspection

The other side of the coin is to consider critical marketing theory and thought as intro-spective. In general, it has been recognised that researchers contemplate their own position in any research they conduct. And I would argue that considering how personal narratives inform our perspectives is a source of strength, not weakness (though I also recognise limitations all around). For example, Kincheloe and Maclaren (2003: 453) state

> Research in the critical tradition takes the form of self-conscious criticism – self-conscious in the sense that researchers try to become aware of the ideological imperatives and epistemological presuppositions that inform their research, as well as their own subjective, intersubjective, and normative reference claims.

Kincheloe and Maclaren (2003: 438) also suggest that poststructural psychoanalysis, which considers fantasy and imagination in relation to sociocultural and psychological meaning and moves beyond various patriarchal, bourgeois, ethnocentric and misogynist practices, might be useful in empowering critical researchers 'to dig more deeply into the complexity of the construction of the human psyche'. I think introspective work can help here too and find that the privileging of the macro levels of analysis at the expense of the micro levels may be a fatal shortcoming of much critical thought. Consider the construction and expression of consciousness. It is very much informed by culture; and differences between Asian and Western perspectives are noteworthy in this regard. For example, Asians often deal with a number of states of consciousness not usually recognised in the West (e.g., awareness of energy moving through invisible but felt channels in the body).

However, for researchers to study these states, they need not only study macro-cultural differences or consciousness discourses, but they also need to assess micro phenomena such as those embodied in individual difference psychology, personal meaning construction and practices, and functional magnetic resonance imaging (fMRI) (which is used to examine neural activity in the brain). These latter are areas where introspection in particular may be especially useful in terms of revealing inner processes and in the case of psychophysiological phenomena, such as fMRI, in matching them to these processes. Thus, when Derrida (1991), for instance, explores consciousness (as well as the unconscious) which he ties into subjective existence in general, how are we to read him, much less investigate it without engaging our own subjectivity through introspection? There may be much that is undecidable in delimiting the personal and cultural, but reductionism in any direction, and especially what I read as the over-privileging of certain cultural constructions (e.g., gender or class), masks other effects.

Psychological-cultural research, to take an example, theorises about identity salience in which various cultural phenomena become a subject of focus for individuals and evoke different aspects of their identity at different times (Oyserman *et al.*, 1998). On that basis, we may be led to ask, what self-collectivities, such as gender, ethnicity or class become apparent during thought? For instance, I personally am aware of various cultural issues concerning class, race and the like which are dominant themes in much critical thought. However, while I am fully aware of and informed by these, my own critical thought much as it is unfolding here, stems from my critique of consciousness as Exercise 3 reflects.

Exercise 3: Is What You Are Who You Are?

Look at your cultural and social background and current environment. How does being a woman or man influence what you write? Play with any other variables, including class, age, etc. Trace changes over time and consider them. Can you find anything *essential* about your social collectivities that stay with you in your consciousness? Or is it all in flux? Look at older work of yours. What do you think of it now and what influences your changes in attitudes toward it in terms of collectivities versus other life aspects (e.g., experiences accounted for by elements of personal consciousness and narrative)? Bring this exercise into considering how critical thought in marketing might embody and employ introspection, whether explicitly with an acknowledgement of using it or tacitly without formal acknowledgement.

The culturally constituted collectivities in the exercises constitute an external, often tacit influence on our inner introspections. A key issue to explore in this regard is the relationship of introspection and reflexivity. Introspection is largely viewed as an internal act while reflexivity involves a relationship between the external and internal, a going back and forth between the two. Of course, disentangling what is external and internal is problematic since people both internalise what is external, such as cultural norms about collectivities, and externalise the internal in their projections on the world. Nonetheless, these are the processes that constitute the reflexivity employed in critical thought and they are perhaps best revealed through introspection.

Unfortunately, I think that the controversies over introspection such that it seems toxic to many may have curtailed any thought about its relationship to reflexivity, itself, an undeveloped topic. For instance, Schroeder (2007), to his credit, discusses the explicit link between 'researcher reflexivity' and critical marketing. However, 'critically', he does not mention introspection nor deal at length with how he would actually deal with how his own viewpoint and experience would condition his critical analysis. He does discuss his own personal experience as a preface but more explicit introspection about how he arrived at his positions throughout might have been useful. It would appear that often people state who they are autobiographically and/or their assumptions as a preface but fail to more deeply probe how that informs their work. For all the embrace of poststructuralism and subjectivity, it seems that critical thought still implicitly applies a positivist paradigm of separating out the subjective from the objective, even as there is some attempt to disguise this. Consider this for yourself in the next exercise.

Exercise 4: Objectivity and Subjectivity

Ponder how you perceive your own views on objectivity and subjectivity. Take a topic you are working on with critical theoretical implications. As you engage this topic watch the process of selectivity you go through. How do you select what to include or not? What is your 'objective' (your 'subjective')? Watch your thoughts. How much do you seem to say, 'I think', 'I believe', etc.? Can you distinguish objectivity and subjectivity? How objective or subjective are you when doing that? Does such introspecting increase your objectivity or make it apparent how much farther away from it you are than you even imagined? How does new 'outside' information change your perspective? Watch how your personal aspects mix with this new information. Is it like flour and water or oil and water? Play with the hermeneutic (in going back and forth interpreting between the various informational, textual and experiential elements constituting subjective and objective perceptions) and liminality (encountering your borders of understanding and experience and bouncing off or through them in a vast variety of ways) to develop a still more critical perspective.

How we engage research topics and decide what to investigate are personal decisions, which should be assessed for their underlying personal elements; 'I' as researcher am embedded in the cultural environment that is at issue. To explore these issues without accounting for either oneself or the cultural environment can be a fatal omission. Yet, the practice seems to be in critical theory development, as well as in other research, to ignore oneself, to erase it as if it were not there. This may be due to our scientific heritage and/or it may be that we privilege culture so much as to ignore the reflexive role of the researcher. My own introspective experience indicates to me that both reductions lead to undernourished analyses. This is most notably the case for critical analysis, CCT and the like because one is writing what one is thinking. But one is being very self-censorial and may not be going deeper into how this thinking emerges from oneself.

A related issue concerns the introspective-extrospective perspective. As I observe, people appear to take an extrospective view when considering critical theory, i.e., they look outside themselves. Of course, in matters cultural and historical, one must account for the external. However, how one constructs that is embedded in one's own mindset. To understand how one comprehends even the most remote external events, one needs to look within. Western culture with its largely external focus often fails to grasp that point, at least relative to Eastern culture where various meditative techniques focus one more inwardly. While in some ways this is a crude generalisation and there are many exceptions, it serves to make the point that critical thought privileges the external analysis of events over their internal construction.

Similarly, I argue that research in marketing (as well as other fields) takes an extrospective stance. This is also a product of commodification in which internalised capacities for regulating and pleasuring the self are ignored to focus outwardly on external goods. In this I follow metaphorically and literally the idea of Chinese medicine that one turns to external healing, in the form of pills for instance, only when one cannot heal oneself through self-regulating the body internally-mentally such as through *Chi Gung*, a set of Chinese energy practices involving physical movements governed by and in conjunction with the mental channelling of healing and transformational energy throughout the body. However, the heritage of marketing is predicated on the reverse approach and privileges an external focus in which the consumer is directed to buy products from outside herself in the market economy rather than applying internal processes or trusting self-reliance. While this is not altogether bad in many areas of consumption (you, the reader, decide which ones), it does serve, whether intentional or not, to turn the individual away from internalised self-regulation. For example, instead of using internal *Chi Gung* or yogic means to heal a headache or other problems, many of us turn to external pain relievers such as aspirin, without even the awareness of other solutions. Research follows accordingly.

To elaborate further on this extrospective vein, we are always reading Derrida, Foucault, etc. as well as each other in the marketing field. We extrospectively build our cases on what these people write. But epistemologically, we are also looking inside – what Derrida says seems right to me or not. We are the decision makers, we are the readers of Derrida's text, not Derrida. We are developing a position and seeking support for it based on our own understanding. Unfortunately, we have erased much of this in analysis and formal writing though I'm sure you all recognise it. Therefore, just as with introspection, critical theorists and others have their own styles of writing and thought which come through and are often recognisable even if their names are not attached. Most importantly for critical analysis, we need to ask where their thoughts come from.

To summarise, introspection is a superb tool for establishing a reflexive perspective on reading 'external' culture and self. Practising critical theorists should introspectively examine their reflexive relationship with the culture around and embodied in them. This can be done on an individual as well as collective basis to assess how these processes evolve. Exercise 5 may be suggestive in this regard.

Exercise 5: Culture and Self

Is the self an outpost of culture? Watch your reactions to various manifestations of culture, such as everyday discourse; various practices in which you engage, especially as contrasted with those of others; and media use. Do you merely reproduce culture in these particular manifestations and expressions, i.e., being more produced than producing? Or do you actually produce culture, i.e., something new or different? Are your self and culture simultaneously produced, synchronously reflexive in relation to each other? Consider (cross)cultural phenomena such as hybridisation. When you encounter something new from another culture such as a new perspective or discourse, where does it go within you? Does it hybridise or does it somehow manifest as another of your multiple selves? Which selves express themselves when you critically assess something?

The Conclusion which is not a Conclusion

Critical thought in marketing is by and large considered in terms of macro phenomena. Though such thought is suffused with the personal, it mostly seems to be erased from the critical narratives theorists weave. While hardly ignoring extrospective-macro phenomena, I have argued that self phenomena reflexively inform what any one thinker brings to her understanding of the 'broader world'. I am very much inclined to agree with Brown (2006b: 450) that 'penning autobiographical essays about consumer behaviour may do more to raise consumer consciousness than all the huffing and puffing by prominent anti-capitalist campaigners'. One can extrapolate this sort of thinking to virtually any research, theory or critical thought. At the same time, I am not prepared to make any overly totalising-reductionist statements in this regard, it should suffice to say that one must recognise that one's own critical thought is informed by one's self-narrative.

Applying insights from introspection as I practise it, I have not tried so much to convince you one way or the other, as to provide a way for you to ponder yourself about what I am suggesting through critical-introspective exercises which point out some of the issues involved. Perhaps there is no real conclusion to all this – you likely will not find one easily essentialised point. Moreover, were all of us to communicate about our efforts (which I hope will happen), we would most certainly find that we had taken different paths, even as perhaps some commonalities are also found. Still, I do think that focusing on our own critical thought in this way changes our perspective and puts oneself in the narrative loop.

It is true that various poststructural/critically informed thinkers may have attempted to explicitly recognise subjectivity and each individual as a singularity and particular site of meaning. But as we are all perhaps too familiar with the idea of cultural construction which indicates that meaning is produced by culture, that culture, itself, is produced and that there is no essence to be found, it would seem that the concept of personal cultural construction, allowing for the idea that there are such things as personal cultures, would be a parallel, if intermeshed universe. Our personal cultures consist of the meanings, discourse, rituals and practices we hold and engage in. They link to other levels of culture, generally so seamlessly that we do not think of ourselves as a 'culture'. Consider private discourses, for example. These involve the things we say and think to ourselves without revealing them to others. Or think of the things we do without others knowing of them or at least valuing them in the same way. Introspection makes some of these aspects more transparent. Contemplate one final illustrative exercise in which you critically read your own work, employing both introspection and a bit of literary criticism (Stern, 1989).

Exercise 6: Critically Reading Your Own Work

Take a piece of your writing (it may be a current piece and at other times you may look retrospectively at your own published work) and read it through with special attention to the personal feelings and thoughts it brings up. Sometimes do this with more intention, that is, look for these things. Other times, let them arise spontaneously as you read and/or in other situations, such as post-reading. What do these feelings and thoughts tell you about the work and yourself? Does your work take a position and in any way link to explicit critical theory or seek in some way to improve the world? Do these points matter to you? Does looking in this way change your understandings and perceptions? Certainly in literary criticism, we consider the idea of authorial intent. What were/are you as author intending in your writings? At the same time, you are a reader of your own work here – reader response. How do you respond to what you have said? How do you feel when you think of others reading your work? How have your views and therefore reading of any particular piece of yours changed? Read the work of others who cite/discuss your work. Do they get it? Does your authorial intent have any connection to their reader response, even to your own?

Based on this reflexive introspection, we can deconstruct the various dichotomies critical thinkers face (or often erase) as examples of liminality and différance (differing and deferring (Derrida, 1991)) including internal–external, introspective–extrospective, personal–cultural, narrative–metacognitive, objective–subjective, authorial intent–reader response and so on. While deconstruction is itself a problematic, if not unstable term subject to its own deconstruction, I use the term here adapting it from one of Derrida's (1991) discussions of it. I engage, if not practice in that regard, a displacement of one system of critical thought (what might be construed as 'classical') by another view, if not system. What is being displaced is a system of critical thought *sans* the self. What is being proffered instead is critical thought where the critical thinker's self shares or takes centre stage and even perhaps the starring role. The dichotomies or oppositions become the battleground for intervention, for revealing, for deferring one pole of the dichotomy to the other and back, and thus for contesting.

Considering the personal–cultural, for instance, suggests that critical thought has deferred to (focused too much on) the latter (cultural determinism) while ignoring the implications of the former. One necessarily reads the cultural through the personal lens. The converse is also true and a deconstructive hermeneutic is set up in which one reflexively goes back and forth between the two. Of course, this in itself is reductionist and the boundary between the two is perhaps unfindable. What is inscribed in what? Nonetheless, thinking in this way, especially informed by an introspective consciousness and thought exercises, may provide new insights and perspectives that would otherwise have been ignored.

References

Altman, N. (1995) *The Analyst in the Inner City: Race, Class and Culture Through a Psychoanalytic Lens*. Hillsdale: The Analytic Press.

Alvesson, M. and Sköldberg, K. (2004) *Reflexive Methodology*. London: Sage.

Arnould, E.J. and Thompson, C.J. (2005) 'Consumer Culture Theory (CCT): Twenty Years of Research', *Journal of Consumer Research*, 31(4): 868–882.

Brown, S. (1998) *Postmodern Marketing 2*. London: International Thompson Business Press.

—— (2006a) *The Marketing Code*. Singapore: Marshall Cavendish Business.

—— (2006b) 'Autobiography', in R.B. Belk (ed.) *Handbook of Qualitative Methods in Marketing*, pp. 440–452. Cheltenham: Edward Elgar.

Derrida, J. (1991) *A Derrida Reader: Between the Blinds*. New York: Columbia Press.

—— (1997) *Of Grammatology*. Baltimore: The Johns Hopkins University Press.

Elshof, G.T. (2005) *Introspection Vindicated: An Essay in the Defense of the Perceptual Model of Self Knowledge*. Aldershot: Ashgate.

Fromm, E. (1942/2002) *The Fear of Freedom*. London: Routledge.

——. (1976/2007) *To Have or to Be?* New York: Continuum.

Gould, S.J. (1991) 'The Self-Manipulation of My Pervasive, Perceived Vital Energy through Product Use: An Introspective-Praxis Perspective', *Journal of Consumer Research*, 18(2): 194–207.

—— (1995) 'Researcher Introspection as a Method in Consumer Research: Applications, Issues and Implications', *Journal of Consumer Research* 21(4): 719–722.

—— (2006) 'Unpacking the Many Faces of Introspective Consciousness: A Metacognitive-Poststructuralist Exercise', in R.B. Belk (ed.) *Handbook of Qualitative Methods in Marketing*, pp. 186–197. Cheltenham: Edward Elgar.

—— (forthcoming) 'An Introspective Genealogy of My Introspective Genealogy', *Marketing Theory*.

Gramsci, A. (2001) *Selections from Cultural Writings*. London: ElecBook.

Hetrick, W.P. and Lozada, H.R. (1994) 'Construing the Critical Imagination: Comments and Necessary Diversions', *Journal of Consumer Research* 21(3): 548–558.

Hirschman, E.C. (1985) 'Scientific Style and the Conduct of Consumer Research', *Journal of Consumer Research* 12(2): 225–239.

Holbrook, M.B. (1995) *Consumer Research: Introspective Essays on the Study of Consumption*. Thousand Oaks: Sage.

Kincheloe, J.L. and Maclaren, P. (2003) 'Rethinking Critical Theory and Qualitative Research', in N.K. Denzin and Y.S. Lincoln (eds) *The Landscape of Qualitative Research*, pp. 433–488. Thousand Oakes: Sage.

Kompridis, N. (2005) 'Disclosing Possibility: The Past and Future of Critical Theory', *International Journal of Philosophical Studies* 13(3): 325–351.

Lyons, W. (1986) *The Disappearance of Introspection*. Cambridge: The MIT Press.

Murray, J.B and Ozanne, J.L. (1991) 'The Critical Imagination: Emancipatory Interests in Consumer Research', *Journal of Consumer Research* 18(2): 129–144.

Oyserman, D., Sakamoto, I. and Lauffer, A. (1998) 'Cultural Accommodation: Hybridity and the Framing of Social Obligation', *Journal of Personality and Social Psychology* 74(6): 1606–1618.

Schroeder, J.E. (2007) 'Critical Marketing: Insights for Informed Research and Teaching', in M. Saran., P. Maclaran., C. Goulding, A. Shankar and M. Caterall (eds) *Critical Marketing: Defining the Field*, pp. 18–28. Amsterdam: Butterworth-Heinemann.

Stern, B.B. (1989) 'Literary Criticism and Consumer Research: Overview and Illustrative Analysis', *Journal of Consumer Research* 16(December): 322–334

Tadajewski, M. (2006) 'Remembering Motivation Research: Toward an Alternative Genealogy of Interpretive Consumer Research', *Marketing Theory* 6(4): 429–466.

Wallendorf, M. and Brucks, M. (1993) 'Introspection in Consumer Research: Implementation and implications', *Journal of Consumer Research* 20(3): 339–359.

18
The Function of Cultural Studies in Marketing: A New Administrative Science?

Adam Arvidsson

University of Copenhagen

ABSTRACT *Over the last two decades, the marketing discipline has absorbed much of the canon of traditional cultural studies, particularly through the work of interpretive consumer researchers or, as they appear to have re-branded themselves, Consumer Culture Theoretics. Today many leading marketing journals feature material that is surprisingly similar to what cultural studies scholars produced in the 1980s. But what is the function of cultural theory within marketing? This chapter traces the history of marketing's critical, cultural turn. It argues that the absorption of cultural theory has not only been a result of academic fads and campus politics. Rather, traditional cultural theory works surprisingly well as a discursive framework for the administration of contemporary informational capitalism. It seems that cultural studies is on its way to becoming a new 'administrative science'. Indeed, the trajectory of academic marketing discourse can be understood as part of a general incorporation of critique or capitalist 'capture of cool'.*

Introduction

One of the most interesting, and for many academics, astonishing scholarly developments in the last few decades, has been the almost wholesale incorporation of the theoretical canon, methodological apparatus, and general worldview of cultural studies into marketing. Through the influential subfields of 'Critical Consumer Reasearch' (Murray and Ozanne, 1991), 'Consumer Culture Theory' (Arnould and Thompson, 2005) and 'Postmodern Marketing' (Brown, 1995; Firat and Venkatesh, 1995), cultural studies have been firmly inscribed within the publishing and career machine of the academic discipline of marketing (Cochoy, 1999; Smithee, 1997). The 'critical' subfield now has its own conferences, its own journals, its own luminaries and citation networks, and it exercises some influence on teaching and research in business schools across the world. For traditional cultural studies practitioners and people who self-identify as 'critical social theorists' this situation is deeply ironic. After all, cultural studies had originally emerged as a champion of all that marketing and consumer culture supposedly was not: agency, resistance and subjectivity. And in the 1970s cultural studies was often proposed as a progressive alternative to the conservative and complacent 'administrative research' that had dominated market and audience research since the days of Paul Lazarsfeld (Gitlin, 1978). Now it appears the tables have turned, and the cultural studies tradition has become an important reference point for marketing, the role of which is to develop theories and methods for the successful administration of consumer capitalism. Cultural studies, it seems, has become part and parcel of the very administrative machinery it once rose to challenge.

The reasons behind this incorporation of cultural studies into marketing are complex, but three obvious developments come to mind. First, it had to do with the internal crisis of marketing as an academic discipline. As Østergaard (1997) has shown, academic marketing went through something of an identity crisis in the face of the social movements and general anti-capitalist sentiment of the 1970s, and began to question its scope and identity. No longer simply the discipline of 'scientific salesmanship', marketing attempted to position itself as one of the social sciences concerned with issues of more general relevance, like 'exchange' (Bagozzi, 1974).

This broadening of marketing was followed by the interpretive turn in the 1980s, where hitherto dominant models like the information processing view of the consumer were challenged by a host of new theories from the humanities and the social sciences, such as symbolic interactionism (Hirschman and Holbrook, 1981), anthropology (Levy, 1981, McCracken 1988), semiotics (Mick, 1986), history (Hollander and Savit, 1983) and phenomenology (Thompson et al., 1989). This incorporation of theory from the humanities and the social sciences naturally led to an interest in cultural studies, which, at the time, was affirming itself as a new unified theoretical framework. Cultural studies thus offered marketing scholars a way to 'sidestep' the critique of capitalism and consumerism by incorporating its more digestible elements (cf. Boltanski and Chiapello, 1999).

Second, the cultural studies tradition had itself become more compatible with the didactic and research needs of business schools, and less hostile to consumer culture per se. Indeed, the strong disgust for the 'candy-floss world of commodity culture' that marked pioneers like Richard Hoggart (1957) began to temper with the early studies of subcultures from the 1960s (Hall and Jefferson, 1975). Stuart Hall's (1973) influential encoding/decoding model further stressed the role of consumption as the privileged site in which the subject could escape from and resist its enslavement under the capitalist system and acquire some 'agency'. With the studies of subcultures and media audiences in the late 1970s and the 1980s, resistance and agency came to be considered an aspect of consumption in general, from punks pinning swastikas to their motorcycle jackets (Hebdidge, 1979), through housewives reading pulp novels to ordinary people watching television (Radway, 1984) or just window shopping (Fiske, 1989).

Although the new enthusiasm for consumption was heavily criticised for its uncanny resemblance to contemporary neoliberal rhetoric (McGuigan, 1992; Slater, 1997, cf. Williamson, 1985), the centrality of consumption as a locus of agency was further strengthened with the subsequent influence of feminism and poststructuralism, which significantly reduced the importance of the Marxist tradition within cultural studies and, with that, the amount of structural determination attributed to consumer practices. To feminists and poststructuralists alike, there was a need to criticise previous (Marxist) notions of the market as 'an impassive monolith' or of consumption as subordinate, feminised and passive (Nava, 1997), primarily because such conceptions in themselves seemed to perpetuate undesirable patterns of male or structural dominance, and discourage that 'power of identity' which had remained with 1980s Anglo-Saxon 'identity politics' as the last hope for progressive transformation.

As a substitute it became important to show how consumption was a space where resistance could be enacted with some degree of freedom and where women, youth, gays, ethnic minorities and eventually people in general were empowered to some degree. By the late 1980s cultural studies had already developed a conceptualisation of consumption that was compatible with the outlook and interest of marketing: consumption was understood as (the perhaps last) site in which people could exercise agency and valorise their own choices and identities. After all, as Paul Willis remarked, 'commercial cultural commodities is all that most people have' (Willis, 1990: 26).

Third, and on a more cynical note, cultural studies provided a way for marketing academics to legitimise their discipline in relation to the campus radicalism and the 'culture wars' that marked American universities in the 1990s (Readings, 1997). It enabled them to sign up with consumers rather than managers, bringing in the consumer perspective and taking their meaningful practice seriously. Taking this 'critical' approach would enable marketing to engage with the social world, or even to become 'a social science discipline of some relevance to the human condition on this planet', to quote an early manifesto (Firat et al., 1987: xvi). Judging from one of the many journal issues devoted to 'postmodern marketing' this entailed opening up to diversity (Firat et al., 1994), feminism (Fischer and Bristor, 1994), different kinds of gendered agency (Peñaloza, 1994) or even the Dionysian complexity of human life as such (Süredem, 1994). Firat's and Venkatesh's influential and theoretically ambitious 1995 article on 'Liberatory Postmodernism' offers a good illustration of how the argument went. Marketing should employ the deconstructive potential of what they simply called 'postmodernism' (more or less the reading-list of your average contemporary 'lit crit' graduate student) towards a series of 'micro-emancipatory ends'. This would eventually serve to undermine the 'unilateral logic of the market' (1995: 245) and liberate consumption from the modernist horrors of 'production, order, coherence and systematic and scientific thinking' (1995: 250).

Cultural 'Theory' and its concomitant identity-politics agenda offered a way to think of marketing as a sort of critical and progressive enterprise. If identity, rather than inequality, was now the issue, then surely helping people to construct their own identities through consumer goods was a progressive practice, as long as one avoided 'the reductionism (sic) of all consumption into a single logic, namely, the market logic' (1995: 239). This way, adapting the language of cultural studies enabled marketing professors to join the ranks of the 'tenured radicals' that appeared on American campuses, and to take part in the general emphasis on identity politics and political correctness of the Clinton years. Finally, cultural studies had been established as the key worldview of the new 'Bobo' (Brooks, 2001) or 'Creative' (Florida, 2002) managerial class that dominated the advertising and marketing profession (in particular, key new figures like the 'account planner' (Frank, 2001)), and who formed, at least in theory, an extended audience for academic marketing scholars.

But it would be superficial to see the marriage of cultural studies and academic marketing as simply an effect of disciplinary crisis, campus quarrels or cultural fads. Arguably this phenomenon should be understood as part of the larger movement towards the incorporation (or 'subsumption') of culture within contemporary 'cognitive' (Moulier-Boutang, 1997) or 'informational' (Dyer-Withford, 1999) capitalism in general. This movement ranges from the ubiquitous 'branding' of public space, through corporate sponsorship of education and the arts, the growing use of culture as a management tool (Arvidsson, 2006a; Klein, 2000) to recent 'netarchic' (Bauwens, 2005) practices like user led innovation systems (von Hippel, 2006), 'cool hunting', and Web 2.0 business models, like YouTube or MySpace, that aim directly at appropriating and valorising what cultural studies considered the most valuable source of anti-systemic opposition: consumer agency and resistance (Scholtz, 2007). In other words, there seems to be a strong compatibility between the outlook and ontology of cultural studies and the logic of value that marks contemporary cognitive capitalism (cf. Hardt and Negri, 2004; Liu, 2006). This, I would suggest, constitutes the deep structural reason behind the much observed compatibility between cultural studies and 'cool' capitalism.

Postmodern marketing scholars are not the first to take an interest in culture and agency, that is, an interest in the (relatively) autonomous and (largely) unpredictable practices of ordinary subjects. True, early management philosophy regarded such unpredictable agency as an unproductive disturbance. Its main thrust was to eliminate practices that were not directly prescribed by the functional role each individual was to assume in relation to the overall valorisation process. With Taylorism (Scientific Management) this entailed reducing the diffuse and interactive productive practices of workers to a number of clearly specified job descriptions, and the elimination of traditional forms of worker interaction (talking, singing, drinking) in favour of new machinic forms of interaction mediated by the assembly line (Braverman, 1974). For early marketing, this meant structuring consumer tastes in favour of a modern and 'rational' consumption norm (Aglietta, 1978) or 'code of value' (Baudrillard, 1970/2001) mediated by advertising and the accompanying commercial media system (chiefly women's magazines, and later, television). The main idea was to make the formation of consumer desires unfold through the machinery of commodities and communications media; to implode sociality and agency within the 'system of objects', to use Baudrillard's early diagnosis. Consequently, the main object of communications and market research was 'attention', not 'culture'. This is nicely illustrated by Dallas Smythe's theory of the 'audience commodity' (published in 1981 but developed in relation to the vanishing Fordist consumer economy).

To Smythe, the value of an audience simply consists in its ability to realise a desire for the objects and lifestyles suggested by the particular medium (in this case television) that they were watching. As the Fordist factory worker was reduced to a mere appendage to the machinery of the Taylorist assembly line, the consumer, in Smythe's version, as well as in actual Fordist market and audience research in general, was captured by and reduced to a mere appendage by advertising, television and 'The Media' in general (after all the main strategy of advertising until the 1950s was 'repetition'). What happened in between these situations of media capture, in unstructured forms of consumer interaction or 'agency' was, with some exceptions, of little or no interest.

Attention to what consumers did in between moments of media capture only really developed in the late 1950s with motivation research, a form of interpretive, qualitative inquiry pioneered by, among others, Ernest Dichter (1960), Sidney Levy (1959) and Pierre Martineau (1957). Motivation research was not simply a new methodology of market research. Ultimately it contained a whole new conception of how consumers interacted with goods and media, and hence, how desire, demand and ultimately, value was generated (see Tadajewski, 2006). The main point of motivation research was that consumers actually produced part of the utility of a good by putting it to meaningful uses that were particular to their own life-situation. The motivation researchers began to argue that consumers used goods as social tools that allowed them to construct the social, symbolic and affective relations that made up both their own identities and the context in which they derived meaning and value from goods.

Along with his colleagues, Dichter argued that this new condition had resulted from an important transformation in the relations between people and goods. First, the radical transformations that American society underwent in the post-War years had served to undermine an older, more tradition-oriented and supposedly more utilitarian consumer culture. This had tended to destabilise both the meaning of consumer goods, and the make up of consumer motivations. People (at least within the new middle class) were now free to articulate their own styles of life by means of goods. 'Wanting to be different', Martineau (1957: 157) argued, was the new ethos. Second, the new more encompassing media landscape (dominated by television), the new consumer culture with its shopping malls and supermarkets, and the sheer abundance of new goods and gadgets had empowered consumers in unprecedented ways.

Motivation research saw consumption and the generation of consumer needs and desires as a continuous activity, as part of the ongoing and (relatively) autonomous production of life, and not just as an effect of particular forms of media capture. It paid attention to what consumers did and thought in between moments of media capture. And these moments themselves were understood as less frequent and less intense, as consumers now were considered to have been freed from the powerful grip of *particular* media channels (although not from *media culture* in general). Motivation research focused on how consumers used the resources put at their disposal by the new consumer and media culture in producing their own sign- and use-values for goods. It formed the foundation for cultivating the productive potential of consumer agency.

While Dichter and motivation research were largely shunned by academic marketing, it did have a substantial impact on commercial market research where qualitative methods were already prominent in the 1960s (Tadajewski, 2006). It also paved the way for psychographics or 'lifestyle segmentation' which was to modify the ontology of market research in the 1970s. Rather than presupposing, as previous research had done, that a particular demographic or economic position – a particular structural role, to use then contemporary sociological terms – would determine a particular set of values and desires, psychographics undertook the periodic surveillance of a mobile consumer culture, where consumers produced new and different configurations of values, tastes and consumption patterns, known as 'lifestyles'. Psychographics thus constituted a systematic reversal of the role of consumer agency: no longer a problematic disturbance to be eliminated, it now functioned as a productive resource to be surveyed and appropriated.

The interesting point from our perspective is that these developments can be (and were at the time) understood as reactions to a collapsing Fordist order. Postmodern marketing theorists make this point too. For example, Firat and Schultz (1997) argued that traditional market segmentation approaches needed to be deconstructed because consumers are now 'too fragmented' and lack 'the unified selves' that supposedly made them susceptible to traditional segmentation techniques and marketing frameworks. This view is often presented in emancipatory terms. From Dichter to more recent postmodern theorists the disorganisation of the Fordist (modernist) order constituted an unprecedented occasion for helping consumers to emancipate themselves from the command of advertising and consumer culture and realise their own identities (Fischer and Bristor, 1994; Peñaloza, 1994). From a less idealistic perspective, however, this immediately seems more ambiguous. Could it be that such liberations of deep subjective freedoms, together with the theoretical construct for accomplishing this – in this case, postmodern marketing – is part of a movement towards an even deeper and more detailed subsumption of agency, affect and subjectivity? What, in that case, could be the function of cultural studies within such a new administrative project?

I

The reliance on (relatively) autonomous and (largely) unpredictable ordinary practice, on agency for short, as a productive force, is precisely what characterises contemporary informational capitalism. This mode of production is characterised by the subordination of the production of commodities to the circulation of information (Dyer-Withford, 1999; Moulier-Boutang, 1997; Vercellone, 2006). This does not mean that material production is obsolete, unimportant or fading away, but that the strategic issue, and consequently the main 'value-driver' becomes the immaterial production of information. The production of information is not simply a matter of knowledge-production (as in patents and intellectual property rights), it also includes affective production and social production.

'Affective production' entails the production of new bodily and emotional relations. Examples could be the production of consumer experiences (as in retail brandscapes and call centres), love, sexuality and care, as in the growing service and sex industries, or the booming sector of internet dating sites (Arvidsson, 2006b; Fortunati, 2007), as well as the more diffuse processes that produce new forms of life and new processes of production and consumption, like, for example, consumers co-producing a brand-experience (cf. Fournier, 1998). 'Social production' entails the production of more or less enduring forms of social relations. Key examples here would be the self-organising project team, the autonomous professional working on his or her 'network' (Wittel, 1999), or, for that matter, the entire managerial class that occupies itself with coordinating the immensely complex production processes that underlie today's global economy. When such processes of cognitive, affective and social production come to actually produce the valuable immaterial content of commodities, they become forms of immaterial labour.

The interesting thing about immaterial labour is that its most important resource is the generic human capacity to 'produce [the] common world through communication and interaction' (Arendt, 1958). This way 'the production of information' is better defined as the production of new and different forms of life (cf. Hardt and Negri, 2004). Immaterial labour is, in other words, *Cultural Production*; it produces a common culture in the form of an ethically relevant social world (however transitory and unstable). The real value of immaterial labour is its ability to produce stability in a world of flux: the team as a relatively stable process of production in the flexible organisation, the brand as a relatively stable axis of consumption in a complex and mobile consumer culture.

The centrality of immaterial labour to contemporary capitalism has to do with the fact that today this generic human capacity to engage in cultural production has been substantially empowered by the massive socialisation of new vectors of communication and interaction: media technologies, consumer goods, information and communication technologies and the global 'Media Culture' (Kellner, 1995) that these objects have enabled. These resources work as a commonly available productive resource – what Marx called a 'General Intellect' – that can be employed to vastly enhance the affective, social or cognitive productivity of a particular interaction. (Example: I can use LinkedIn to extend my social network; computer-aided design systems enable engineers to share knowledge on a global scale; teenagers form Norway and Korea can use MTV to create a common identity and so forth.)

Now, immaterial labour is essentially Cultural Production. This socialisation of the means of immaterial production has led to a massive empowerment of ordinary life practices, of agency, to the point that these now constitute a valuable externality, not only for the creative industries (that have engaged in cool hunting since the 1980s) but increasingly for consumer-oriented companies in general (as evidenced by the present popularity of user-led innovation schemes). Indeed, this technological and symbolic empowerment of consumer agency has led to a situation where such external and (relatively) autonomous practices have become more productive and innovative than the corporate production processes originally intended to replace them.

This happened to symbolic and stylistic innovation in the 1960s, where street style established itself as the innovation leader (Polhemus, 1994). It has since also happened to some forms of technological innovation, as illustrated by the decisive role of amateurs or 'hackers' in constructing the technological platform of the internet, and the present 'success of Open Source' (Weber, 2004). This socialised productive potential has, subsequently, been further radicalised with recent diffusions of fast, networked information and communication technology. First, because these technologies empower the productive potential of such agency by improving on the means of immaterial production, they become the means for the distribution, information retrieval and the organisation of the productive process that are (virtually) freely available to people on the right side of the digital divide. Second, and importantly, these technologies render the surplus (or culture) thus produced immediately public, visible and hence open for appropriation. The evasive cultural studies category of the popular is now immediately and clearly visible as it is put to work on Second Life, YouTube and in the blogsphere (Lovink, 2007). The consequences of this are a blurring of the boundary between life and work. This is true from a phenomenological point of view, where the versatility of the networked computer means that

> . . . both work and play take place on the same machine; this might seem trivial, but it isn't. The fact that we use the same technology to fill out our spreadsheets and to play World of Warcraft, and that we easily can alt+tab between the two apps merges the spheres of work and play even more solidly. And once you have played WoW for a while you actually start

filling out spreadsheets to track your progress. And you will start thinking about business strategies in terms of raids, loot and mobs. (Kane, 2007)

But it is also true from an economic point of view, where the boundaries between an organisation and its environment are becoming less clear; where what matters more and more are things that cannot be directly commanded or included in a job description (commitment, the right values or attitude, reputation, buzz, consumer enthusiasm). After all, you cannot order somebody to be 'creative' or 'cool'! Things that used to remain outside of the equation, or only touch it marginally, that is, the private attitudes, thoughts and feelings of employees and other stakeholders, as well as the attitudes of consumers, now acquire a directly productive role. Consequently, the key to value and profits becomes not just (or even primarily) the organisation of productive processes, but also the organisation of social processes: of flows of communication and interaction that unfold outside of the organisation, the organisation of life. This way, as Douglas Holt (2004) argues, brand management (and management in general) is becoming a form of social activism!

II

As it developed in the post-War years, cultural studies was a reaction to two secular tendencies: the growing mediatisation of everyday life by means of new media technologies, commodities and consumer culture, and the declining ability of the establishment to command these processes, and mobilise the new forms of life that were emerging by means of the commodity culture. In fact, the pioneers of cultural studies like Raymond Williams and Richard Hoggart were working class boys, who did not share the elitist dismissal of actual working class practice that prevailed within the educated Left. They insisted, instead, on the liberatory potential of actually lived working class culture, and on its capacity to produce resistance. Inspired by the Gramscian notion of the 'organic intellectual' and shaped by their experience with working class adult education students in the 1940s and 1950s, early cultural studies scholars saw their task as that of studying the lived culture of the subordinate groups, not simply in order to document it, but in order to help it articulate itself as an alternative to the now hegemonic mass culture produced by the culture industries (Williams, 1983; cf. McGuigan, 1992: 21–44). Its method of inquiry was thus linked to a particular *activist imperative*. And although cultural studies has since 'autonomized itself into a school of thought' (McGuigan, 1992: 39) – a more or less reified academic discipline with (barring a few exceptions) little engagement with practical realities – this activist imperative has remained a vital aspect of its epistemological outlook.

To engage with 'Cultural Studies' thus means – methodologically and theoretically, in my opinion – to look for and identify the capacity of subjects to produce a resistance, alternative or excess in relation to the given conditions that they face. It means finding ways to empower that potential, helping it to organise itself, to come out as a political force. But as contemporary theories of power have shown, empowerment is an ambiguous thing. In part, it is a matter of strengthening the potential, agency and capacity for self-government on the part of a particular group of people.

But, on the other hand, this empowerment always moves within a particular context that empowers in a specific direction. Thus the language of cultural studies, although open to the creativity and potential of the new forms of life that emerged out of 1960s and 1970s commodity culture, always sought to empower these in the direction of articulating a fairly particular political self-understanding, clothed in the Gramscian soft-Marxism of the New Left. Now, such strategies of activist, selective empowerment are, as Holt (2004) suggests, becoming the *modus operandi* of contemporary management.

Given that external life processes cannot be directly commanded, that you cannot order someone to be creative or cool, power works by designing a context in which such processes evolve in the right direction, where people themselves strive to become creative or cool. It is an instance of power becoming 'ontological' rather than 'epistemological', to use Scott Lash's (2007) recent distinction. Older forms of 'epistemological' power were based on the power/knowledge nexus identified by Foucault in *Discipline and Punish*, and characterised by scientific discourses (or, in a more contemporary example, like those of Lazarsfeldtian media and market research). These discourses contained a particular model of life, which was subsequently imposed on its subjects through the institutional means at its command (in this case advertising and consumer culture at large). Ontological power (which, as a concept, is closer to Foucault's later work on biopolitics), on the other hand, does not build on representative knowledge, but on activist interventions, able to program, design and build a reality where particular forms of actions and attachments have been pre-ordained. It looks less like the 19th century school and more like a videogame: Lara Croft is free to do what she wants, but only certain actions make sense and add to the pleasure of the experience.

As I have argued elsewhere (Arvidsson, 2006a), contemporary brand management provides a good illustration of this *modus operandi*. The brand is essentially a mechanism for the reproduction of a particular pattern of affect and community, of culture, for short. The status and function of the brand has changed radically in this respect. While brands originated as symbols of products (or producers) that would enable consumers to differentiate between virtually identical mass produced goods, cutting edge brands today tend to function more as a kind of social media. They stand less for a product (often they stand for a wide range of products) and more for a particular cultural pattern – a particular experience or mode of relating – which is reproduced in a wide variety of different situations, involving many different actors. This is perhaps most evident in the case of recent successes like Facebook, Myspace and YouTube. There, the ability to accumulate value (chiefly on financial markets) is directly based on the ability to accumulate the kinds of attention, affect and community – the culture for short – that consumers themselves produce.

The trend is for more mainstream brands to move in the same direction, to that described above. What this means in practice is that there is greater emphasis on 'customer based brand equity' (Kellner, 1995) and a concomitant recognition of the active role of consumers in contributing to brand value, along with attention to the sensorial or experiential aspects of brand management. The net result of this is an expansion of the number of dimensions through which consumers can be involved with brands and a growing emphasis on attention and affect in the calculation and establishment of brand value (Arvidsson, 2006a). At least for some high profile brands, financial values directly build on the ability to mobilise consumer agency in generating attention and affect – an ethical surplus (discussed below) (Lazzarato, 1997). This way brand values tend to build ever more directly on a selective activation of consumer agency.

It is important to emphasise the selective nature of this activation. Consumers are free to do what they want with the brand, but the point of contemporary brand management is to make sure that that freedom evolves in particular directions, with consumers producing and reproducing a particular cultural pattern. Like cultural studies in its earlier more politically oriented incarnation, brand management is about inserting a particular program into the social that empowers it from below, by means of the language, artifacts or self-understandings that it uses to articulate itself, and pushes it in the direction of reproducing highly particular outcomes. This, I think, is the context in which we should read Holt's appeal for managers to function as 'cultural activists'.

III

So, the structural reasons behind the current union of marketing (and management) with cultural studies are two-fold. First, the condition of informational capitalism has made autonomously produced culture, what cultural studies used to call 'agency', an important and potentially valuable productive force. Second, the way such 'agency' is appropriated is through selective empowerment, rather than through discipline. The originally political practice of activism and the administrative practice of management have thus fused together. Management has, as Christian Marazzi (1999) suggests, become a matter of what Max Weber called 'political entrepreneurship'. Cultural studies owes its popularity to the fact that it provides a language and a methodology that is able to both identify and operationalise the productive element in such autonomous immaterial productive processes (their 'agency'), and to motivate and justify an activist approach to it.

Conclusion

What, then, does this mean for the critical potential of cultural studies, marketing and social science in general? Is critique impossible when its very vocabulary has been appropriated as yet another language of power and, in true Adornian fashion, made to strengthen what it once rose against? There is, of course, some salience to such a perspective. The Orwellian reality behind claims for the emancipating potential of consumer agency or postmodern consumer culture as such, is reliant on a massive increase in the size and scope of the surveillance systems deployed to administer contemporary consumer capitalism. The activist approach to brand management is only possible with massive amounts of consumer data that allow the activist manager to make real time adjustments in her programme, so that consumers always recognise the brand not just as something that gives meaning and significance, but as providing the kinds of meaning and significance that they always already wanted.

In this way, the necessary pre-structuring of agency that is a component of this *modus operandi*, is also, effectively, an elimination, or at least significant restriction, of agency. From this perspective, theoretical and methodological developments, whether in marketing or cultural studies, that aim at uncovering and thus empowering such agency also have the dialectical consequence of producing new surveillance tools that contribute to the efficiency of its subsumption. In any case, posing freedom and subjectivity as an antithesis to power, as many enthusiastic critical marketing scholars have done, is antiquated at a time where power mainly works through freedom, not against it (cf. Rose, 1999). To put it in more political terms: the contradiction today does *not* stand between the potential freedom and agency of consumers and the administrative discipline of consumer capitalism. Rather, the administration of consumer capitalism largely unfolds through the encouragement of such freedom and agency. It is by self-administering one's own consumer agency that one becomes a successful consumer. Success, in these terms, is determined by cultivating an individual taste, look or bundle of experiences, and *not* by following fashion. If freedom used to mean emancipation from work in the 1970s, today, for a growing number of people, and for consumers in particular, it means hard immaterial labour.

The contradiction unfolds elsewhere. It is progressively more clear that value and profits within contemporary consumer capitalism rest on the ability to translate the products of unstructured consumer agency into forms of programmed consumer agency: to ensure that a new trend becomes part of a brand, to see that networking and 'friending' unfolds on a particular site or platform. Indeed, we are in fact dealing with two different economies. One monetary economy that deals in measurable values and is organised according to monetary incentives; the other is an ethical economy that moves according to entirely different motivations. (Most people who contribute to the enormous wealth of contemporary social wealth production, in Web 2.0, in peer to peer production, in the formulation of new fashion and music styles, are not in it for the money but are motivated by ethical ambitions such as to make friends, expand networks and gain respect.) We are also seeing how this ethical economy is beginning to acquire the ability to self-organise. Networked information technologies make it possible to transform peer recognition into new currency systems (like trustmetrics) that can empower the ability of this economy to self-organise and de-link from the monetary economy of consumer capitalism. The task facing a truly critical (or at least progressive) marketing would be to abandon an outdated and today largely ideological embrace of 'agency' to investigate what kinds of programme could effectively aid and empower the autonomy of this ethical economy; to turn back to viewing marketing as a societal practice; a practice that builds the basis for the post-capitalist order.

References

Aglietta, M. (1978) *A Theory of Capitalist Regulation*. London: New Left Books.

Arendt, H. (1958) *The Human Condition*. Chicago: University of Chicago Press.

Arnould, E.J. and Thompson, C.J. (2005) 'Consumer Culture Theory (CCT): Twenty Years of Research', *Journal of Consumer Research*, 31(4): 868–882.

—— (2006a) *Brands: Meaning and Value in Media Culture*. London: Routledge.

—— (2006b) 'Quality Singles: The Work of Fantasy in Internet Dating', *New Media and Society* 8(4): 671–690.

Bagozzi, R.P. (1974) 'Marketing as an Organized Behavioral System of Exchange', *Journal of Marketing* 38: 77–81.

Baudrillard, J. (1970/2001) 'Consumer Society', in M. Poster (ed.) *Jean Baudrillard. Selected Writings*, pp. 207–224. Cambridge: Polity Press.

Bauwens, M. (2005) 'The Political Economy of Peer Production', *Ctheory*. Available at http://www.ctheory.net

Boltanski, L. and Chiapello, E. (1999) *Le Nouvel Esprit du Capitalisme*. Paris: Gallimard.

Braverman, H. (1974) *Labor and Monopoly Capital*. London: Monthly Review Press.

Brooks, D. (2001) *Bobos in Paradise: The New Upper Class and How They Got There*. New York: Thorndike Press.

Brown, S. (1995) *Postmodern Marketing*. London: Routledge.

Cochoy, F. (1999) *Une Histoire du Marketing*. Paris: Editions de la Decouvèrte.

Dichter, E. (1960) *The Strategy of Desire*. New York: Doubleday.

Dyer-Withford, N. (1999) *Cyber-Marx: Cycles and Circuits of Struggle in High Technology Capitalism*. Urbana: University of Illinois Press.

Firat, A.F., Dholakia, N. and Bagozzi, R. (1987) 'Introduction', in A.F. Firat, N. Dholakia and R.P. Bagozzi (eds) *Philosophical and Radical Thought in Marketing*, pp. xiii-xxi. Lexington: Lexington Books.

Firat, A.F. and Schultz, C.J. (1997) 'From Segmentation to Fragmentation: Markets and Marketing Strategy in the Postmodern Era', *European Journal of Marketing* 31(3/4): 183–207.

Firat, A.F. and Venkatesh, A. (1995) 'Liberatory Postmodernism and the Reenchantment of Consumption', *Journal of Consumer Research* 22(4): 239–266.

Firat, A.F., Sherry, J.F. and Venkatesh, A. (1994) 'Postmodernism, Marketing and the Consumer', *International Journal of Research in Marketing* 11(4): 311–316.

Fischer, E. and Bristor, J. (1994) 'A Feminist Poststructuralist Analysis of the Rhetoric of Marketing Relationships', *International Journal of Research in Marketing* 11(4): 317–331.

Fiske, J. (1989) *Reading the Popular*. London: Routledge.

Florida, R. (2002) *The Rise of the Creative Class*. New York: The Free Press.

Fortunati, L. (2007) 'Immaterial Labor and its Machination', *ephemera: theory and politics in organization*, 7(1): 139–157.

Fournier, S. (1998) 'Consumers and their Brands: Developing Relationship Theory in Consumer Research', *Journal of Consumer Research* 24(4): 343–373.

Frank, T. (2001) *One Market Under God. Extreme Capitalism, Market Populism and the End of Economic Democracy*. London: Secker & Warburg.

Gitlin, T. (1978) 'Media Sociology: The Dominant Paradigm', *Theory and Society* 6: 205–253.

Hall, S. (1973) *Encoding and Decoding in Television Discourse*. Birmingham: Institute for Cultural Studies.

Hall, S. and Jefferson, T. (eds) (1975) *Resistance through Rituals*. London: Hutchinson.

Hardt, M. and Negri, A. (2004) *Multitude*. New York: Penguin.

Hebdidge, D. (1979) *Subculture: The Meaning of Style*. London: Methuen.

Hirschman, E. and Holbrook, M.B. (1981) *Symbolic Consumer Behavior*. Ann Arbor: Association of Consumer Research.

Hoggart, R. (1957) *The Uses of Literacy*. London: Penguin.

Hollander, S. and Savit, R. (eds) (1983) *First North American Workshop on Historical Research in Marketing*. East Lansing: Michigan State University.

Holt, D. (2004) *How Brands Become Icons: The Principles of Cultural Branding*. Boston: Harvard Business School Press.

Kane, P. (2007) *Notes towards a theory of Ludocapitalism*, posting, Institute for Distributed Creativity List, 9/5, 2007, available at https://lists.thing.net/pipermail/idc/ [accessed 19 November 2007]

Kellner, D. (1995) *Media Culture: Cultural Studies, Identity and Politics Between the Modern and the Postmodern*. London: Routledge.

Klein, N. (2000) *No Logo*. London: Flamingo.

Lash, S. (2007) 'Power after Hegemony: Cultural Studies in Transition', *Theory, Culture and Society* 24(3): 55–78.

Lazzarato, M. (1997) *Lavoro Immateriale*. Verona: Ombre Corte.

Levy, S. (1959) 'Symbols for Sale', *Harvard Business Review* 37(4): 117–124.

—— (1981) 'Symbols, Selves and Others', *Advances in Consumer Research* 9: 542–543.

Liu, A. (2006) *The Laws of Cool: Knowledge Work and the Culture of Information*. Chicago: University of Chicago Press.

Lovink, G. (2007) *Zero Comments*. London: Routledge.

Marazzi, C. (1999) *E il denaro va*. Turin: Bollati Boringheri.

Martineau, P. (1957) *Motivation in Advertising*. New York: McGraw-Hill.

McCracken, G. (1988) *Culture and Consumption: New Approaches to the Symbolic Character of Consumer Goods and Activities*. Bloomington: University of Indiana Press.

McGuigan, J. (1992) *Cultural Populism*. London: Routledge.

Mick, D.G. (1986) 'Consumer Research and Semiotics: Exploring the Morphology of Signs, Symbols and Significance', *Journal of Consumer Research* 13(3): 196–213.

Moulier-Boutang, Y. (1997) *Le Capitalisme Cognitif: La Nouvelle Grande Transformation*. Paris: Éditions Amsterdam.

Murray, J.B. and Ozanne, J. (1991) 'The Critical Imagination: Emancipatory Interests in Consumer Research', *Journal of Consumer Research* 19(3): 129–144.

Nava, M. (1997) 'The Framing of Advertising', in M. Nava, A. Blake, J. McRury and B. Richards (eds) *Buy this Book! Studies in Advertising and Consumption*, pp. 34–50. London: Routledge.

Østergaard, P. (1997) *Trk af marketing disciplinens epistemologiske udvikling: En periodisering af amerikansk marketingteoris historie med fokus på accepten af de kvalitative metoder.* Odense: Odense Universitets Trykkeri.

Peñaloza, L. (1994) 'Crossing Boundaries/Drawing Lines: A Look at the Nature of Gender Boundaries and their Impact on Marketing Research', *International Journal of Research in Marketing* 11(4): 359–379.

Polhemus, T. (1994) *Street Styles.* London: Victoria and Albert Museum.

Radway, J. (1984) *Reading the Romance: Women, Patriarchy and Popular Literature.* Durham: University of North Carolina Press.

Readings, B. (1997) *The University in Ruins.* Harvard: Harvard University Press.

Rose, N. (1999) *The Powers of Freedom.* Cambridge: Cambridge University Press.

Scholtz, T. (2007) 'What the MySpace Generation Should Know about Working for Free'. Available: http://www.re-publish.net.

Slater, D. (1997) *Consumer Culture and Modernity.* Cambridge: Polity.

Smithee, A. (1997) 'Kotler is Dead!', *European Journal of Marketing* 31(3/4): 317–325.

Smythe, D. (1981) *Dependency Road: Communications, Capitalism, Consciousness and Canada.* Norwood: Abbex.

Süredem, A. (1994) 'Social De(re)construction of Mass Culture: Making (non)sense of Consumer Behaviour', *International Journal of Research in Marketing* 11(4): 423–443.

Tadajewski, M. (2006) 'Remembering Motivation Research: Toward an Alternative Genealogy of Interpretive Consumer Research', *Marketing Theory* 6(4): 429–466.

Thompson, C.J., Locander, W.B. and Pollio, H.R. (1989) 'Putting Consumer Experience Back into Consumer Research: The Philosophy and Method of Existential-Phenomenology', *Journal of Consumer Research* 16(2): 133–147.

Vercellone, C. (ed.) (2006) *Capitalismo Cognitivo.* Rome: Manifestolibri.

Von Hippel, E. (2006) *Democratizing Innovation.* Cambridge: MIT Press.

Weber, S. (2004) *The Success of Open Source.* Cambridge: Harvard University Press.

Williams, R. (1983) *The Year 2000.* London: Pantheon Books.

Williamson, J. (1985) 'Consuming Passions', *New Socialist* February: 19–20.

Willis, P. (1990) *Common Culture: Symbolic Work at Play in the Everyday Cultures of the Young.* Milton Keynes: Open University Press.

Wittel, A. (1999) 'Towards a Network Sociality', *Theory, Culture and Society* 18(6): 51–76.

19
Thinking through Theory: Materialising the Oppositional Imagination

Pauline Maclaran[1] and Lorna Stevens[2]

[1]*Keele University and* [2]*University of Ulster*

Like so many words that are bandied about, the word theory threatens to become meaningless. Because its referents are so diverse – including everything from minor working hypotheses through comprehensive but vague and unordered speculations, to axiomatic systems of thought – use of the word often obscures rather than creates understanding. (Merton, 1949/1968: 39)

ABSTRACT   *In academia we often take the word theory for granted and presume it is a desirable, if not essential, goal of our research and writing. Drawing on feminist debates, this chapter highlights how theory can be used to reinforce status and power relations, creating major divides between theory and practice. It explores how critical marketers can avoid some of these pitfalls by generating theory that derives from practice and concentrates on embodied experience together with the collective construction of knowledge.*

Introduction

As Merton highlights, the word 'theory', despite its diminutive size, carries more than its fair share of academic baggage. Many authors have highlighted its ambiguous status, and how the tools of our trade, namely our concepts and frameworks, developed in ways that mask the power relations embedded in them. Feminists, together with postmodern and poststructuralist thinkers, have criticised the practices of 'grand', 'high' or 'general' theory. They have shown how often this deceives through theoretical discourses that claim to be 'neutral' in respect of class, gender, sexuality or race, but in fact are laden with the predilections of a privileged patriarchal value system.

In order to challenge this value system, feminists have tended to analyse the local, specific and material, emphasising the activist, practical or experiential aspects of their findings. Often they have derided theory altogether, seeing it as a masculine game that privileges words over action and addresses an elite, usually academic, audience in ways that are inaccessible to others.

Yet, in the marketing academy we constantly justify ourselves through recourse to theory, and are always at pains to establish our 'theoretical positioning'. Without a strong, substantive and fixed foundation we feel that our work will be ridiculed, or relegated to the 'descriptive' dustbin. And so we wrap our work in theories, but like the story of the emperor's new clothes, we may thereby collude with the emperor in weaving a web of deception, loath to challenge this appearance of academic rigour and respectability, or to design an alternative and better-fitting mode of academic 'dress'.

In this chapter we explore the quest for theory and set it in the context of the many feminist debates on the topic. First, we problematise the assumption that theory is in itself a good thing, and examine the divides that are created between theory and practice, research and education. Then, we consider the potential for critical marketers to generate theory in ways that avoid past pitfalls. Our argument, overall, is that if theory is relocated in everyday practices and material realities it can become an act of agency that opens up a dynamic space for the critical voice to create theory for emancipatory ends.

The Uses and Abuses of Theory

We begin by exploring in a little more detail some of the meanings that lie behind the word theory. In everyday parlance we use the word in a speculative sense to offer an explanation about events or behaviours that are not entirely obvious (I have a theory that she doesn't like him because...). In academic parlance, however, the word theory *usually* loses its speculative connotations and emphasises its explanatory power. Academic theory is more than just a system of hypotheses, it has to have analytical significance, explaining the 'complex relationships of a systematic kind among a number of facts' (Culler, 1997: 4).

Of course, scholars will have different views of what constitutes theory, depending on their philosophical orientation. Interpretivists often see theory as more of a process that tells a story about the data, as illustrated by Golden-Biddle and Locke's (1997) notion of a 'theorized storyline'. Here, the process of theorising consists of activities like abstracting, generalising, relating, selecting, explaining, synthesising and idealising (Sutton and Shaw in Price, 2007). In contrast, those from a more positivistic orientation see theory as a systematic and rigorous structure that explains and predicts the behaviour of phenomena and enables the production of law-like generalisations (Hunt, 1991).

From both perspectives, however, there is common agreement that theories offer explanations of the physical and social worlds around us that can lead to deeper understandings of how and why things happen in the ways that they do. In essence, and at its most basic, theory is really an organised way to think about a topic. Theory's building blocks are its underlying concepts and definitions, the unstated assumptions which Minow (1990) warns us against, as they are often normative and shared amongst a particular, and often privileged, group of individuals.

And this is why we also need to be suspicious of theory. Just like the use of metaphor, theory both broadens our minds and ties us in to particular ways of thinking, skewing our perspectives in ways that often go unquestioned and unrecognised. It can thus be used to reinforce existing power relations, and to maintain the status quo both within, and outside of, the academy since 'some groups will have greater opportunity to own or control the means of production, their interests will inevitably be reflected in what is considered "legitimate" knowledge' (Murray and Ozanne, 1997: 62).

The role of critical theory is to question taken-for-granted underpinning assumptions, and to act as a 'pugnacious critique of common sense norms' (Culler, 1997: 3). Yet, critical theory too has often been shown to be just as exclusive as it tries to be inclusive, just as prescriptive, and indeed, proscriptive, as the theory it tries to overturn. The postmodern critique called into question the notion of grand theory and exposed the pitfalls of meta-narratives, changing our ideas of what critical theory is or could be. Although sometimes perceived to be under the critical theory umbrella, many feminists feel little affinity with critical theory per se, seeing it as a body of thinking that is largely male-dominated, and they remain resistant to the notion of being defined as 'a sub-branch of a sub-branch of traditional theory' (Walby, 2000: 237). Feminist theory is seen by most feminists as being much more wide-ranging because it draws from the full range of social sciences and beyond. However, there are signs of a place for feminism in the 'reconceptualised critical theory' that Kincheloe and McLaran (2000: 296) propose, that acknowledges 'the movement of feminist theoretical concerns to the center of critical theory with the inclusion of race and gender alongside class'.

One of the reasons that many feminists still remain deeply critical of theory is that there is often a bifurcation between theory and practice, with the former being located in remote (and privileged) academic ivory towers, whilst the latter is relegated to the mundane (and de-privileged) realities of everyday experiences (Stanley and Wise, 2000). We know this, of course, in our own discipline, where marketing's crisis literature has fully documented the void between marketing theories and the world of those who practise marketing (Brown, 1995; Brownlie and Saren, 1992). In focusing our research on theoretical issues we have tended to look at the logical, objective side of being a marketing practitioner, and we have overlooked the emotional, subjective side that actual marketing practice involves (Maclaran and Catterall, 2000). Furthermore, the gap between theory and practice can be perceived as one that perpetuates class elitism and supports dominant class interests:

> It is evident that one of the many uses of theory in academic locations is in the production of an intellectual class hierarchy where the only work deemed truly theoretical is work that is highly abstract, jargonistic, difficult to read, and containing obscure references that may not be at all clear or explained. (bell hooks 1991: 4)

Referring to theory as 'a narcissistic self-indulgent practice', bell hooks (1991) accuses theory of being produced for a small, exclusive academic audience, and of failing to contribute to political progression or real life concerns. bell hooks practises what she preaches, writing in a highly accessible and comprehensible style that refuses to use academic conventions such as references or obscure academic vocabulary. In a world where literacy and numerical skills still elude a large percentage of the population, published theories can have little impact, hooks (1991) argues, unless they can also be shared in everyday conversation and used in this way to educate the public.

Theory can thus be used to suppress, silence and devalue other theoretical voices and subvert the very movement to which it pays lip-service. In this way it can be a source of intimidation, not just between academics and practitioners, but also among academics, who frequently use it as a way to upstage and undermine their peers. Take, for example, the use of excessive citations to indicate familiarisation with the theories of others as a way of pre-empting debate, or citing an obscure theorist to confound or confuse. Grey and Sinclair (2006) beautifully illustrate some of these intimidation processes in an article that takes to task exactly this type of academic practice, as they reminisce on a session at the *Critical Management Studies Conference*:

> We are five minutes in and I'm beginning to feel dizzy. It isn't my hangover – paradoxically, that's slightly better – but I'm dizzy with names. Foucault and Derrida have been dismissed as old hat, Zizek as a suspect popularist, Deleuze – no I haven't been paying attention, I am not sure whether he is in favour or out. Hardt and Negri show promise but have essentialist 'tendencies'... Now we are in the question and answer session (the Chair tells us it is a discussion, but she is being wildly optimistic). Z has obviously had the same insight into the speaker's intentions as I have. But his response is different to mine. His question seems to be designed to show what none of us thought possible: Z has read even more than the speaker. He brings the heavyweights into our unprepossessing room. Forget Habermas, what about Hegel? And Z has a good line in obscurity. Foucault has been dismissed, but what about Fichte? (The speaker sniffs: 'I wouldn't call Fichte particularly obscure'). But Z has a more subtle weapon in his armoury. For the really class act – and Z is nothing if not a class

act – reclaims the previously fashionable, just to show that he is not in thrall to fashion. So Gramsci, Poulantzas and even poor old Marx make their momentary bows before us. (Grey and Sinclair, 2006: 444)

Like babes in arms, we academics feel naked and insecure when we aren't swaddled in our comforting theories, which make us feel secure and shield us from the onslaughts of our academic colleagues and the 'real', potentially hostile world beyond. Theory can empower us and make us believe ourselves to be masters (and mistresses) of our own (research) universe, as we discover concepts to organise and understand phenomena. A focus on the development of theory remains one of the key ways to be taken seriously in academic research. It is a crucial part of the paradigm wars, and it is no coincidence, that in seeking to have a more significant impact on mainstream consumer research, many interpretivist researchers have now banded together under the label of CCT (Arnould and Thompson, 2005), in an attempt to lend gravitas to a previously marginal, and potentially subversive fringe.

The Gender Biases of Theory

It is exactly on account of this desire for 'mastery' that feminists have resented male-centred theories that work to marginalise women culturally, economically, sexually and socially. Although in one way the postmodern emphasis on the socially constructed nature of the categories men and women supported feminist thinking, in another way it decentred the notion of the subject, just as women were realising themselves and fully becoming subjects. This makes feminists deeply suspicious of what is frequently seen as yet another variant of malestream research (Hartstock, 1990 in Buker, 1991). Add to this the fact that most philosophers and social theorists are male, and we can begin to understand why many feminists remain hostile to theory. Male social and philosophical theories often have deep gender biases built into them. For example, Bourdieu's (1984) study of food and taste, *Distinction*, can be critiqued because women are positioned as signifying social and cultural capital for men, rather than accruing it in their own right, i.e. women are conceptualised as 'capital-bearing objects', rather than as 'capital-accumulating subjects' (Lovell, 2007: 20). In addition, women's contributions have often been overlooked entirely or, as in the case of Simone de Beavoir and Jean-Paul Sartre, accorded a supporting role in the development of their male partner's thinking (Witt, 2006).

When it comes to business research, we see a similar pattern. Gamber's 1998 study of the history of small businesses in the 19th century reveals how American women who ran small businesses were not acknowledged in the mainstream business literature of that time. These business women included purveyors of food and lodging, brothel keepers, proprietors of grocery and variety stores, dealers of books and newspapers, tobacconists, jewellers, midwives, fortune tellers and body embalmers. Their omission from history has been largely due to three factors: (1) the assumption that business is a masculine endeavour; (2) the use of models that exclude such small enterprises; and (3) a lack of interest in female entrepreneurship shown by historians (Gamber, 1998). In effect these women were written out of history and, in turn, out of business theory.

Similarly, Cooke (1999) has shown how, in recent years, women have been written into the histories of organisation development where previously their 'contributions' were unrecorded, underlying how history itself is socially constructed, partial, and protective of dominant, prevailing interests. And marketing too is not exempt from this selective, editing out process. Women's influence on marketing theory and practices has only recently begun to be examined. Zuckerman and Carsky (1990) examined the contribution of home economists (predominantly women) to our understanding of consumer behaviour. Scanlon (1995) highlighted the hitherto invisible presence of women in advertising in the twentieth century, and McDonald and King (1996) acknowledged the previously unacknowledged women amongst the founders of the Market Research Society in Britain in the 1940s.

Marketing theory itself has been shown to be gendered in many unarticulated and unrecognised ways (Stern, 1992; Bristor and Fischer, 1993; Hirschman, 1993; Joy and Venkatesh, 1994). For example, much theorising around the consumer has been underpinned by a machine metaphor to characterise human behaviour that is also inherently gendered in its assumptions. This metaphor has for a long time privileged the mind and cognitive activity (assumed male) over the body and emotions (assumed female). Furthermore, the ubiquitous conceptualisation of the consumer as female and the producer as male in marketing discourse has underpinned much theorising in marketing (Fischer and Bristor, 1994).

The Rejection of Theory

On account of these inbuilt gender biases, certain feminists have turned against the very idea of 'theory'. Buker (1991) writes that postmodern feminists challenge the notions of theoretical 'groundings' and 'foundations', as fixed images that constrain and contain; images that are static, immovable facades, which offer no possibility of shift or flux. Instead she advocates a story metaphor, which opens up a 'play of difference' discourse, and thereby rocks theory's theoretical foundations. Buker argues that this enables us to 'take on civic responsibilities as continuous struggles for justice' (1991: 244). This call to the power and politics of language, speech and symbolism is also addressed by bell hooks (1991). She believes that communication (via various media) and using a range of writing, speeches and literary styles, is the key to developing healthy communities of what she refers to as 'enlightened witnesses' in our society. Other feminist detractors (e.g. Showalter, Baym and Marcus) also argue that theory is masculine, conceiving of it as 'tougher, more rigorous than the subjective and intuitive critical practices' (Finke, 1991: 260). They see it as inherently misogynistic to the extent that they accuse feminist theorists of selling out, 'phallic feminists' according to Baym (1984), who structure their arguments with male-centred theories such as deconstruction or Marxism. hooks (1991), in particular, highlights how certain feminist academics have formed alliances with white male peers to define what is theoretical and what is not. She argues that these alliances work to devalue the critical insights offered by black women about their own situations. Moreover, she maintains that much feminist theory, in seeking to legitimise itself in terms of the ruling, male-dominated powers, often uses the same ploys that other feminists critique, namely power plays of language and so forth. This, she argues, only serves to make her students feel humiliated at their lack of understanding, and their inability to connect what they are learning to their everyday lives.

Berg (1991), in her discussion of women literary theorists, argues that contrary to the perceived wisdom that women cannot do theory, women do do theory, but they do it differently from men and thus their work is written out over time. One reason for this, she argues, is that women literary theorists such as Louise Rosenblatt stress the interconnectedness of art and life, and our emotional engagement with and commitment to texts. They thus conflate intellectual with emotional involvement. Women literary theorists, she argues, typically place themselves personally at the centre of the act of reading and, in so doing, reading is positioned as 'a social as well as an aesthetic experience' (1991: 186). Another reason is that male literary theorists stress their 'universal' credentials, 'veiling their self-absorption in universal drapery' (1991: 191). It is this emphasis on the personal, then, that makes it easy for the academic canon to 'discredit and overlook the work of women in theory' (1991: 191). Berg suggests that it is only by seeking to uncover a hitherto erased female line of theory that can we begin to understand why women are ignored by the academic canon.

Such feminist stances can, of course, also reinforce, and even reify, culturally constructed differences between men and women's ways of thinking, i.e. masculinity, science, rationality and objectivity versus femininity, art, intuition and subjectivity (Finke, 1991). In seeking a solution to this theoretical impasse, Baym (1984) advocates a pluralism of theoretical perspectives, where different interpretations of phenomena can exist in harmony with each other, complementary to, rather than competing with or invalidating one another. Yet, as Finke (1991) highlights, pluralism is, somewhat naively and idealistically, based on the erroneous assumption that ideas compete equally in 'a free marketplace of ideas'. Following Kuhn (1962), we know that this is not so, and that this position masks the power relations that exist, and that usually work to defend the status quo and dominant interests. Within marketing, Tadajewski (2006: 186) has examined the social, economic and institutional logic underpinning theory production in marketing, and has exposed the power relationships that have influenced the development of marketing theory:

> Far from intellectual debate being a forum where ideas are judged solely on their merit the production and effective marketing of theory necessitates that theory is marketed so that it negotiates the practices of exclusion which admit only certain forms of research into the canon while pushing other material to the margins of marketing theory.

In addition, pluralism can also serve to protect the centre of mainstream thinking and to ensure the marginality of its critics: 'Pluralism is the method employed by the central authorities to neutralize opposition by seeming to accept it. The gesture of pluralism on the part of the *marginal* can only mean capitulation to the centre' (Spivak in Finke, 1991: 257; emphasis in original).

Pluralism itself can end up as being as authoritative and exclusive as the centre that it seeks to critique. We have argued elsewhere that the pluralism advocated by postmodernism has worked to stifle critique by encouraging conceptions of gender as just another ludic element of an identity that can be altered at will in the marketplace (Catterall *et al.*, 2005). This ignores the material realities of disadvantaged consumers, a large percentage of whom are women who have limited choices in the marketplace. Moving analyses away from the dichotomous categories of women and men, the postmodern critique revealed many discourses of femininities and masculinities that vary according to particular times and places. The postmodern emphasis on discourse and relativism militates against political action, and does little to challenge the norms or change the status quo. The postmodern decentring of the subject remains problematic for feminists, although Buker (1991) highlights how it may not be possible to decentre the female subject and thus promote her agency because she has not yet been fully centred as a subject. It is problematic too, because the categories of men and women are still used as organising categories for many facets of social, economic and institutional structures that impact on individuals' everyday lives. So, whilst postmodern theorising has made valuable points about the intersections of class, race, gender and sexuality, and the need to refrain from theorising gender inequality at too abstract and general a level, by situating everything in discourse, it also masks the material realities that marginalised groups experience.

Nor is it just feminists and postmodernists who have challenged theory. In organisation studies, Van Maanen (1988) argued for a 10-year moratorium on theoretical papers of organisational life on the grounds that the field needed many more descriptive narratives first before sound theories could be developed. His argument was that, often, as we move from the concrete to the abstract in our quest for theory-building, we leave behind the richness of the context of our study, a richness that may give others new insights into the phenomena and generate stronger theory over time. Carrying out abstraction too quickly may also ruin the chance to 'build cumulative theory from small but comprehensible events' (Sutton and Straw, 1995: 383). Moving away from the context is of particular concern to feminists because too much abstraction can mean that the worlds of informants are left behind, forgotten, or even sacrificed to academic progression. To actually succeed in bringing about change requires a focus on the concrete context for action. More recent anti-theory calls within organisational studies have echoed feminist voices in critiquing theory as a self-serving practice, which changes with the current fashion and is carried out by academics who are detached from the worlds on which they pronounce (Parker, 2002a, 2002b).

In Search of the Oppositional Imagination

So how can critical marketers generate theory in ways that avoid the pitfalls that we have just discussed? We believe that a solution lies in engaging and theorising more at the level of practice. For example, although some critical marketers reject the relevance of the worlds of marketing practitioners (Bradshaw and Firat, 2007), Svensson (2007) argues that it is important to explore the human side of marketing in order to develop theories on the nature of marketing work that will counter mainstream marketing management applications. Accordingly, he draws attention to the social and discursive nature of doing marketing work and the practices involved therein.

Theory that derives from a study of practice tries to explain the way phenomena occur in practice and also attempts to bridge the perceived theory/practice divide. In particular it focuses on the practices ('routinised types of behaviour' (Reckwitz, 2002: 249) – that include both doing and saying) around which individuals express and share meanings in their personal activities and identity construction. Practice theory looks at how such meanings are produced and reproduced in an evolving dialectic between everyday life and wider cultural forces. As such it 'situates the sociohistorical function of persons as students, as women, as CEOs, as African-Americans, as patriots, as at-risk students or any other identity, in wider relations of power' (Holland, 2004: 1). This type of theorising seeks to achieve a balance between theory and practice without privileging one over the other (Böhm, 2002).

Brownlie and Hewer (2007: 9) see the domain of consumer studies as the 'natural home for the critical project in marketing' and where there is already a growing body of theorising resistance as consumer practice (Holt, 2002). The spaces where consumers produce their own culture (e.g. Kozinets, 2002) are what Cocks (1981: 4) envisages as sites for the oppositional imagination, sites that contain 'life-forms that negate, if not the center's authority, at least the breadth and depth of its control'. She sees these small pockets of opposition not in isolation, but as forming crucial nodes around which we can begin to theorise the processes of opposition and resistance. By studying their commonalities and differences at a localised level we can start to expose the taken-for-granted social norms that thread power relations through everyday social interactions. For bell hooks (1991) too, such theorising is a crucial part of liberatory practice. She envisages it as something that makes sense of everyday experiences and that can be used as an intervention to challenge the status quo and question social practices that appear natural, helping us to imagine other ways of being, other possible futures.

So what can critical marketers learn from feminist scholarship in relation to the development of theory from the study of everyday practices? We believe there are four key areas in materialising the oppositional imagination for critical marketing theory, and we go on to look at each of these in turn.

The Collective Construction of Theory

Western theory construction is still dominated by the individualised (male) scholar model of research. Not having sufficient 'single-authored' works is still something that can be seen in pejorative terms and that can undermine our academic ability. Feminist scholars have long argued for the collective construction of theory, both in terms of co-creating it with other academics, but especially with research participants, so that theory has a more direct input on their lives. This also links closely with the feminist vision of 'praxis' and the ongoing theory building cycle of description – analysis – vision – strategy (for change). According to Humm (1995: 218), praxis is 'the struggle to unite theory and practice, action and reflection' in order to bring about transformation. Above all, praxis connects personal experience to social structures. Buker (1991) writes that a praxis model 'shows how genuine knowledge emerges only after we act upon our theories, to thus reform them and reform ourselves' (1991: 243).

Perceiving knowledge to be partial, subjective, situated and tied to the values of those that create it, more collective approaches to knowledge creation embrace research teams that incorporate differences of age, race, class, gender, sexuality and so forth. Moreover, if academics establish stronger linkages with each other's work, small descriptive studies may over time generate new theories. To this end, critical marketers could work to develop multi-site studies of particular topics, and establish stronger linkages with each other's existing work to more actively connect and theorise from the findings of smaller, localised studies. The current motherhood project in our field is perhaps a good example of this. This research project brings together women marketing academics from Ireland, USA, UK and Denmark to explore issues of researching motherhood, around three key issues: 'experience, empowerment and embodiment' (Prothero et al., 2006).

More Inclusive Methodologies

Pursuing a more collective approach to knowledge-building requires changes not only to content, but also to the form that theory takes. Feminist epistemologies have long reconsidered 'the relationship between knower and known to develop a method of enquiry that will preserve the presence of the subject as an activist experiencer' (Stanley and Wise, 2000: 261). Consequently they have looked for innovative methodologies that enable a more equal balance of power between researcher and researched. One way to achieve this is to focus on respondents' life-worlds and 'lived experience'. This approach has been widely embraced in women's studies and cultural studies, and increasingly in our own discipline too, notably by those of us exploring consumer culture. 'Storying the self' is a key aspect of cultural research such as this, as it enables individuals to formulate, justify and express personal experience, and give meaning to what might otherwise be experienced as fragmented and chaotic (Finnegan, 1997). Reception ethnographies, for example, explore how media are subjectively experienced by their audiences, and take 'an appreciative view' of our interaction with cultural products 'within the context of particular social situations and frames of understanding' (Rakow, 1998: 284). In so doing, the personal is broadened out to include the wider, socio-political context, thus moving from the emic to the etic (Thompson, 1996, 1997; Thompson *et al.*, 1990).

Whilst this is now commonly accepted in much interpretive research as good practice, the focus is usually on individuals' experiences, albeit within a social context. A very creative methodology that takes a more collective approach is provided by Friend and Thompson (2000), who adopt a methodology called 'memory work' to story not only the self but also others in their study of women's retail experiences. Memory work is a collective, experience-led approach to research. The method involves participants writing focused texts (structured around collectively agreed 'trigger topics') about their experiences. These stories are written in the third person in order to de-emphasise the self. These are then read, discussed and analysed in a collective research group. An important aspect of the research process is that it enables participants to unpick language and reveal the clichés, contradictions, metaphors and gaps or absences in the texts. The process enables the group to identify patterns, similarities and differences as they search for explanations of their experiences. The strength of such a research approach is that it helps change inequitable social relations by empowering everyone who is involved in the research study. It also bridges the gap between theory and experience, validates the memory writing and reflections of participants, and uncovers the different layers of meanings related to individuals' experiences. Knowledge is produced from the collective experience, and is about understanding relative truths or multiple truths, which then allows relative generalisations to occur, and ultimately leads to theory generation.

Oral as Well as Written Narratives

So can we engage more in dialogue with our informants? Critical marketers need to be prepared to directly engage with their informants and actively embrace the free flow of dialogue, debate and disagreement. We need to see language as living, mutable and evolving, rooted in real lives and 'lived' experiences. We also need to de-privilege the written word, especially those words written from a 'purely' academic perspective, as they may be far from the real, everyday reality of those we presume to research (hooks, 1991). According to Kincheloe and McLaran (2000), oppositional and insurgent researchers 'must not confuse their research efforts with the textual suavities of an avant-garde academic posturing... rather they need to locate their work in a transformative praxis that leads to the alleviation of suffering and the overcoming of oppression' (2000: 303).

An important means of bringing about equity and empathy lies in the concept of dialogue. Buker (1991) underlines the importance of dialogue in the 'praxis' process, when she observes that action is enabled by 'the words we speak or fail to speak' (1991: 242). Pearce (1997) writes that dialogic theory, which is derived from Bakhtin's notion of reciprocity in language and literature, assumes an addressee or recipient of the words of the addresser, and highlights the notion of exchange in terms of the written and spoken word, as well as the power of the addressee (or controlling text) to shape the words of the addresser or speaker. In relation to academic writing, it poses the question to whom do we address our words? It also raises the issue of why we write the way we do. Discourses function as 'a form of regulation and domination' with institutions often acting to impose 'discursive closure' (Kincheloe and McLaran, 2000: 284). The dialogic emphasises that there is a relationship between addresser and addressee, and there are also textual positions that are fluid as well as 'historically specific and politically strategic' (2000: 76).

Storytelling can be used as a key means of theorising, writes Buker (1991). By letting go of the old images of theory 'building', the story metaphor offers a more creative and 'overlapping' metaphor, which focuses on our 'telling a story about the world' (1991: 242). The emphasis here is on politicising our everyday discourse and underlines not only that the personal is political but that political action is about the words we speak (or write) or the words we fail to speak (or write). This focus also enables us to interrogate and problematise the taken-for-granted.

One way that this more accessible, democratic and inclusive emphasis expresses itself in our discipline is in the 'visual turn' that it has increasingly taken in recent years, in conjunction with the wider social sciences, particularly cultural studies. This has been evidenced most notably in our field by the growth of videography. The popularity of this medium is perhaps an acknowledgement that the written word alone may not capture the reality of cultural phenomena. It is also symptomatic of the postmodern movement from the written to the visual (Brown, 1995), the breakdown of the distinction between high culture and low culture (Brants *et al.*, 1998), as well as the increasing interest in 'the beliefs and practices of ordinary people' (Schudson, 1998: 495).

Videography has become the medium of our time, as it goes some way to show that the written word may have limited expression, whereas images and oral expression may provide a much richer means of understanding consumer behaviour and consumer culture. It also may bring about greater democracy, in that consumers may use cameras and other visual technology to gather their own data, in order to express and articulate their own experience. They are thus co-creators of meanings within research studies, in a very tangible sense. Researchers can then communicate their findings back to participants in ways that are accessible and meaningful to them. Perhaps more importantly, participants can challenge research findings, reframing research questions, and providing new, relevant answers that reflect the reality of their day-to-day lives. This more equitable relationship challenges the traditional privileging of the researcher over the researched, and replaces it with power-sharing.

Theorising from Embodied Experience

Until comparatively recently, the body was ignored in marketing and consumer research, and consumption was treated and conceptualised as a 'disembodied phenomenon' (Joy and Venkatesh, 1994). This has now changed, and there has been a growing interest in embodied experience in our discipline. This new focus is compatible with the postmodern shift from the mind to the body, and with feminist theory, which has long called for a revalidation of the (female) body. Davis (1997), for example, writes that embodied theory challenges the perception of woman as the 'other', inferior body. Instead it takes account of the individual, material body in everyday life, the ordinary and mundane, as well as the wider social and cultural theories that surround the body in contemporary culture. Contrary to nature or social constructionist theories, embodied theory conceptualises the body as both a natural, physical entity, and as something that is 'produced through cultural, discursive practices' (Pilcher and Whelehan, 2004: 9). This emphasis reclaims the feminist project of praxis, as it roots bodies in concrete social, cultural, historical, organisational and political contexts.

In consumer culture the body has become a malleable and mouldable product or commodity, and an important means of expression. Body obsession transcends gender categories and gender boundaries so that 'gender' is more akin to a performance or even a masquerade (see Butler, 1990), rather than a simple, defining and confining category of humanity and human experience. Judith Butler's approach to the gender debate argues that bodies are 'the effects of discourse', but this argument might undermine the material reality of bodies (McDowell, 1997).

The return to the body has important implications for critical marketers. It extols us to keep our research grounded in the material reality of lives, namely the tangible, physical materiality of human existence, and the political, social, cultural and natural forces that shape human consciousness and experience. In keeping with Marxist thought, the core of existence is thus conceptualised as a social process and a product of human activity and agency. This shift enables us to privilege the body over the mind, and sees the body as a site of struggle, rebellion and potential liberation. It also points to the emancipatory potential of the body in the marketplace. In a recent study of poverty, Hamilton (2007) focuses on the marketplace coping strategies employed by lone mothers with limited financial resources to enable them to provide for their families. In a related study Catterall *et al.* (2005) draw on materialist feminist theory to explore the topic and highlight the inequities inbuilt in social and political structures where production is valued over reproduction, and where women can be thus trapped in poverty by their bodies. By listening to those previously excluded from consumer behaviour research, the so-called 'non-consumers', we can develop our understanding and empathy for others, as well as rethink our taken-for-granted assumptions about the marketplace. This enables us to appreciate consumer behaviour within the marketplace, outside of the marketplace, and at the liminal zones and ragged edges of the marketplace. By focusing on the material body, we reinforce wider calls for a material turn in consumer research, where theorists are concerned to explore more fully the material dimensions of those engaged in markets and marketing practices (Parsons, 2007).

Conclusion

In this chapter we have tried to think through the problems that are associated with the development of theory, highlighting the uses and abuses that justify us treating theory with suspicion. In particular, we have illustrated how theory's frequent, inbuilt gender biases have led to its rejection by many feminists. Then, advocating a stance that derives theory from practice, we have gone in search of the oppositional imagination, exploring the ways in which we can adopt a critical perspective to unsettle the theoretical assumptions of our discipline and thus open up a space for a critical voice to emerge. Drawing on feminist research, we have advocated four key ways to materialise the oppositional imagination, without repeating the same mistakes as those we critique. Firstly, we call for a more collective emphasis in terms of how research is conducted and how theory is generated. We embrace more inclusive methodologies that are based on parity, respect, and the reality of lived experience and collective knowledge. We also advocate other, alternative means of understanding consumers: speech, dialogue, stories and videography all enable research to be relevant to people's real, lived experience. Finally, embodied theory brings our attention back to the body and the material reality of life, the social processes and political constructs that shape and mould human experience and human consciousness. The material turn is thus a crucial element of the critical marketing project. By embracing such principles we believe that we are better placed as researchers to document and record the practices and realities of the marketplace, and better equipped to develop new theories that truly reflect, describe and problematise these practices and realities.

References

Arnould, E.J. and Thompson, C.J. (2005) 'Consumer Culture Theory (CCT): Twenty Years of Research', *Journal of Consumer Research*, 31(4): 868–882.

Baym, N. (1984) 'The Madwoman and her Languages: Why I Don't Do Feminist Theory', *Tulsa Studies in Women's Literature* 3(1/2): 45–59.

Berg, T.F. (1991) 'Louise Rosenblatt: A Woman in Theory', in J. Clifford (ed.) *The Experience of Reading: Louise Rosenblatt and Reader-Response Theory*, pp. 177–195. Portsmouth, NH: Boynton/Cook Publishers.

Böhm, S. (2002) 'Movements of Theory and Practice', *ephemera: theory and politics in organization* 2(4): 328–351.

Bourdieu, P. (1984) *Distinction: A Social Critique of the Judgement of Taste*. Cambridge: Harvard University Press.

Bradshaw, A. and Firat, A.F. (2007) 'Rethinking Critical Marketing', in M. Saren, P. MacLaran, C. Goulding, R. Elliott, A. Shankar, and M. Catterall, (eds) *Critical Marketing: Defining the Field*, pp. 30–43. Oxford: Elsevier.

Brants, K., Hermes, J. and Van Zoonen, L. (eds) (1998) *The Media in Question: Popular Culture and Public Interests*. London: Sage.

Bristor, J.M. and Fischer, E. (1993) Feminist Thought: Implications for Consumer Research, *Journal of Consumer Research* 19(March): 518–536.

Brown, S. (1995) 'Life Begins at 40? Further Thoughts on Marketing's "Mid-Life" Crisis', *Marketing Intelligence and Planning* 13(1): 4–17.

Brownlie, D. and Hewer, P. (2007) 'Concerning Marketing Critterati: Beyond Nuance, Estrangement and Elitism', in M. Saren, P. Maclaran, C. Goulding, R. Elliott, A. Shankar and M. Catterall (eds) *Critical Marketing: Defining the Field*, pp. 44–68. Oxford: Elsevier.

Brownlie, D. and Saren, M. (1992) 'The Four Ps of the Marketing Concept: Prescriptive, Polemical, Permanent and Problematical', *European Journal of Marketing* 26(4): 34–47.

Buker, E.A. (1991) 'Rhetoric in Postmodern Feminism: Put-Offs, Put-Ons, and Political Plays', in D.R. Hiley (ed.) *The Interpretive Turn: Philosophy, Science, Culture*, pp. 218–244. Ithaca: Cornell University Press.

Butler, J. (1990) *Gender Trouble: Feminism and the Subversion of Identity*. New York: Routledge.

Catterall, M., Maclaran, P. and Stevens, L. (2005) 'Postmodern Paralysis: The Critical Impasse in Feminist Perspectives on Consumers', *Journal of Marketing Management* 21 (5–6): 489–504.

Cocks, J. (1981) *The Oppositional Imagination: Feminism, Critique and Political Theory*. London: Routledge.

Cooke, B. (1999) 'Writing the Left Out of Management Theory: The Historiography of the Management of Change', *Organization* 6(1): 81–105.

Culler, J. (1997) *Literary Theory: A Very Short Introduction*. New York: Oxford University Press.

Davis, K. (1997) *Embodied Practices: Feminist Perspectives on the Body*. London: Sage Publications.

Finke, L. (1991) 'The Rhetoric of Marginality: Why I do Feminist Theory', *Tulsa Studies in Women's Literature* 5(2): 252–272.

Finnegan, R. (1997) ' "Storying the Self": Personal Narratives and Identity', in H. Mackay (ed.) *Consumption and Everyday Life*, pp. 65–112. Milton Keynes: The Open University.

Fisher, E. and Bristor, J. (1994) 'A Feminist Poststructuralist Analysis of the Rhetoric of Marketing Relationships', *International Journal of Research in Marketing* 11(4): 317–331.

Friend, L.A. and Thompson, S.M. (2000) 'Using Memory-Work to Give a Voice to Marketing Research', in M. Catterall., P. Maclaran., and L. Stevens (eds.) *Marketing and Feminism: Current Issues and Research*, pp. 94–111. London: Routledge.

Gamber, W. (1998) 'A Gendered Enterprise: Placing Nineteenth-century Businesswomen in History', *Business History Review* 72(2): 188–218.

Golden-Biddle, K. and Locke, K. (2007) *Composing Qualitative Research*, Second Edition. Thousand Oaks: Sage.

Grey, C. and Sinclair, A. (2006) 'Writing Differently', *Organization* 13: 443–453.

Hamilton, K. (2007) 'Making Sense of Consumer Disadvantage', in M. Saren, P. MacLaran, C. Goulding., R. Elliott, A. Shankar and M. Catterall (eds) *Critical Marketing: Defining the Field*, pp. 178–192. Oxford: Elsevier.

Hirschman, E.C. (1993) 'Ideology in Consumer Research, 1989 and 1990: A Marxist and Feminist Critique', *Journal of Consumer Research* 19(March): 537–552.

Holland, D. (2004) 'Using Social Practice Theory to Study Identity Formation and Social Change', *Paper Presented at the Charles Colloquium on Education: Practice Theory in Social Science and Education Research*, University of Colorado at Boulder, November.

Holt, D.B. (2002) 'Why Do Brands Cause Trouble? A Dialectical Theory of Consumer Culture and Branding', *Journal of Consumer Research* 29(1): 70–90.

hooks, b. (1991) 'Theory as Liberatory Practice', *Yale Journal of Law and Feminism* 4(1): 1–12.

Humm, M. (1995) *The Dictionary of Feminist Theory*, Second Edition. Hemel Hempstead: Harvester Wheatsheaf.

Hunt, S.D. (1991) *Modern Marketing Theory: Critical Issues in the Philosophy of Marketing Science*. Cincinnati: South-Western Publishing.

Joy, A. and Venkatesh, A. (1994) 'Postmodernism, Feminism, and the Body: The Visible and the Invisible in Consumer Research', *International Journal of Research in Marketing* 11: 333–357.

Kincheloe, J.L. and McLaran, P. (2000) 'Rethinking Critical Theory and Qualitative Research', in N.K. Denzin and Y.S. Lincoln (eds) *The Handbook of Qualitative Research*, Second Edition, pp. 279–304. Thousand Oaks: Sage.

Kozinets, R.V. (2002) 'Can Consumers Escape the Market? Emancipatory Illuminations from Burning Man', *Journal of Consumer Research* 29(1): 20–38.

Kuhn, T.S. (1962) *The Structure of Scientific Revolutions*. Chicago: University of Chicago Press.

Lovell, T. (2007) 'Thinking Feminism With and Against Bourdieu', *Feminist Theory* 1(1): 11–32.

Maclaran, P. and Catterall, M. (2000) 'Bridging the Knowledge Divide: Issues on the Feminisation of Marketing Practice', *Journal of Marketing Management* 16(6): 635–646.

—— McDonald, C. and King, S. (1996) *Sampling the Univese: The Growth, Development and Influence of Market Research in Britain Since 1945*. London: NTC Publications.

McDowell, L. (1997) *Capital Culture: Gender at Work*. Blackwell, Oxford.

Merton, R.K. (1949/1968) *Social Theory and Social Structure*. New York: The Free Press.

Minow, M. (1990) *Making All the Difference: Inclusion, Exclusion, and American Law*. Ithaca: Cornell University Press.

Murray, J.B. and Ozanne, J.L. (1997) A Critical-Emancipatory Sociology of Knowledge: Reflections on the Social Construction of Consumer Research, in R. Belk, (ed.) *Research in Consumer Behavior*, pp. 57–92. Greenwich: JAI Press

Parker, M. (2002a) *Against Management: Organization in the Age of Managerialism*. Cambridge: Polity.

—— (2002b) 'No Theory', *Organization* 9(1): 181–184.

Parsons, E. (2007) 'The Evocative Power of Things: Materiality, Temporality and Value in the Consumption of Used Objects', Special Session, *European Association for Consumer Research Conference*, Milan, July.

Pearce, L. (1997) *Feminism and the Politics of Reading*. London: Arnold.

Pilcher, J. and Whelehan, I. (2004) *50 Key Concepts in Gender* Studies. Sage: London.

Price, L.L. (2007) ' "That's Interesting", but Now What?', *Presented at the Consumer Culture Theory Qualitative Workshop*, Toronto, May.

Prothero, A., Davies, A., Dobscha, S., Geiger, S., O'Donohoe, S., O'Malley, L., Patterson, M., Sorensen, E.B. and Thomsen, T.U. (2006) 'Researching Motherhood: Experience, Empowerment and Embodiment', in L. Stevens and J. Borgerson (eds) *8th Association for Consumer Research Conference on Gender, Marketing and Consumer Behaviour*, pp. 66–70. Provo: Association for Consumer Research.

Rakow, L.F. (1998) 'Giving Patriarchy its Due', in J. Storey (ed.) *Cultural Theory and Popular Culture: A Reader*, Second Edition, pp. 275–291. Hemel Hempstead: Prentice Hall.

Reckwitz, A. (2002) 'Towards a Theory of Social Practices: A Development in Culturalist Theorizing', *European Journal of Social Theory* 5(2): 245–265.

Scanlon, J. (1995) *Inarticulate Longings: The Ladies' Home Journal, Gender, and the Promises of Consumer Culture*. Routledge: New York.

Schudson, M. (1998) 'The New Validation of Popular Culture: Sense and Sentimentality in Academia', in J. Storey (ed.) *Cultural Theory and Popular Culture: A Reader*, Second Edition, pp. 495–503. Hemel Hempstead: Prentice Hall.

Stanley, L. and Wise, S. (2000) 'But the Empress Has No Clothes: Some Awkward Questions About the "Missing Revolution" in Feminist Theory', *Feminist Theory* 1(3): 261–288.

Stern, B.B. (1992) 'Feminist Literary Theory and Advertising Research: A New Reading of the Text and the Consumer', *Journal of Current Issues and Research in Advertising* 14 (Spring): 9–22.

Sutton, R.I. and Straw, B.M. (1995) 'What Theory is Not', *Administrative Science Quarterly* 40(3): 371–384.

Svensson, P. (2007) 'Producing Marketing: Towards a Social-Phenomenology of Marketing Work', *Marketing Theory* 7(3): 271–290.

Tadajewski, M. (2006) 'The Ordering of Marketing Theory: The Role of McCarthyism and the Cold War', *Marketing Theory* 6(2): 163–200.

Thompson, C.J. (1996) 'Caring Consumers: Gendered Consumption Meanings and the Juggling Lifestyle', *Journal of Consumer Research* 22(March): 388–407.

—— (1997) 'Interpreting Consumers: A Hermeneutical Framework for Deriving Marketing Insights From the Texts Of Consumers' Consumption Stories', *Journal of Marketing Research* November: 438–455.

Thompson, C.J., Locander, W.B. and Pollio, H.R. (1990) 'The Lived Experience of Free Choice: An Existential-Phenomenological Description of Everyday Consumer Experiences of Contemporary Married Women', *Journal of Consumer Research* 17(December): 346–361.

Van Maanen, J. (1988) *Tales from the Field*. Chicago: University of Chicago Press.

Walby, S. (2000) 'In Search of Feminist Theory', *Feminist Theory* 1(2): 236–238.

Witt, C. (2006) 'Feminist Interpretations of the Philosophical Canon', *Signs: Journal of Women in Culture and Society* 31(2): 537–599.

Zuckerman, M.E. and Carsky, M.L. (1990) 'Contribution of Women to U.S. Marketing Thought: The Consumers' Perspective, 1990–1940', *Journal of the Academy of Marketing Science* 18(4): 313–318.

20
Postcolonialism and Marketing

Gavin Jack

University of Leicester

ABSTRACT *In this chapter I will provide a selective introduction to postcolonialism. Specifically, I illustrate how its theoretical insights can be useful for understanding the historical and contemporary colonial and neo-colonial inflections of marketing and promotional practice. It is my contention that postcolonial theory can raise political and ethical questions about the role of marketing practice in organising problematic racial differences, and concomitantly of marketing theory in effectively erasing these key questions from the parameters of its recent debates.*

Introduction

Postcolonialism has had a profound effect on academic work across a number of disciplines in the humanities and social sciences, most notably in literary criticism, history and cultural studies. Its inception in the academy is conventionally associated with the publication in 1978 of Edward Said's monumental work *Orientalism: Western Conceptions of the Orient*.[1] Despite its popularity in other areas of social scientific inquiry, postcolonial theory has had only limited impact on the management academy. In this latter context, postcolonial work is primarily associated with a small number of researchers principally in organisation studies/organisation theory[2] and to a lesser extent in accounting.[3] The marketing academy is practically silent on postcolonialism with the recent exception of work by Patterson and Brown (2007) on Irish pubs and the briefest of mentions elsewhere by Burton (2000) and Murray (2002).[4]

The aim of this chapter is to provide a more concerted introduction to, and interesting illustrations of, postcolonialism as an analytical frame and political agenda for scholars of/in marketing and consumer research. It is structured into two key sections. The first section provides a necessarily brief entrée into postcolonial scholarship for readers unfamiliar with the terrain. The second draws upon studies from other disciplines (notably anthropology, sociology, history, cultural studies, communication studies) which have deployed postcolonialism as a vehicle for analysing topics of interest to a (critical) marketing and consumer research audience. This section presents historical and contemporary analyses of marketing and, more specifically, promotional and advertising practices from a variety of industry sectors and product categories including soap and cleaning agents, tourism and travel, food and clothing, cartoons and computer games.

Section One

Postcolonialism: Some Introductory Remarks

As with related terms like poststructuralism or postmodernism, it is customary to begin attempts that survey the salient features of postcolonialism with a statement about the impossibility of such a task. Postcolonialism, postcolonial theory and postcolonial analysis speak of a vast, ever-growing, theoretically and politically contested terrain of scholarly work with a history and complexity that eludes representation in a few sections of text. As such, I would recommend that readers consult some of the excellent introductory works to postcolonialism now available to establish some avenues of inquiry (notably Ashcroft, Griffiths and Tiffin, 1989, 2000; Gandhi, 1998; Loomba, 1998; Mishra and Hodge, 1991; Moore-Gilbert, 1997; Young, 2003). With these overviews in mind, the next port of call would be 'the classics' of postcolonial thinking. To me, these would include the early works of anti-colonial activists (e.g. Fanon, 1961/1967, 1952/1986; Memmi, 1965), the so-called 'Holy Trinity' of modern postcolonial theorists (Said, 1978, 1981, 1993; Bhabha, 1990, 1994; Spivak, 1987, 1988, 1990, 1999), key Marxist and neo-Marxist critics of the use of (French) High Theory in postcolonial studies (e.g. Ahmad, 1992; Dirlik, 1997) and other noteworthy contemporary critiques (e.g. Mohanty, 1984, 2003; Chakrabarty, 2000; Gilroy, 1993, 2005; Guha, 1982; Nandy, 1983; Trinh, 1989; Young, 1990, 2001). As I have already noted, my aim in this first section of the chapter is to sketch a broad picture of postcolonial concerns before articulating the selected theoretical materials which drive the later analysis of marketing practice.

Whilst colonisation[5] and the exercise of colonial rule has a long history, it is the formal colonial expansion of Western European nations and their conquest and physical occupation of around 85 % of the earth (Loomba, 1998) which has been the focus in postcolonial studies. According to Prasad (2003), the Western colonial regimes established from the 15th century until the first half of the 20th century differed in two central ways from previous forms of Empire. First, Western colonialism 'linked the West and its colonies in a complex structure of unequal exchange and industrialisation that made the colonies economically dependent upon the Western colonial nations' (Prasad, 2003: 5). The history of European capitalism is also therefore the history of European colonialism, with colonies used as a source of raw materials and labour power,[6] as well as a market for finished products.

Second, Western colonialism was as much about cultural and ideological subjugation as it was economic exploitation. Postcolonial work illustrates that colonisers were in the business of 'civilising the natives', of bringing modernity, 'order' and 'progress' to the putatively primitive nature of the colonised. Historical work on British colonialism, for instance, shows how the petit bourgeois morality of the Victorians, combined with the religious zeal of different branches of the Christian Church, was brought to bear on colonised peoples through the cultural and ideological work of colonial administration and its functionaries, as well as marketing and other aspects of commodity production and distribution. The discursive construction of the native as 'lacking' or 'deficient', and therefore in need of 'salvation' and 'civilisation', became a central ideological justification for the exercise of Empire.

A first key objective of postcolonial scholarship has been to investigate the motives, nature and effects of the interactions of coloniser and colonised across the variety of different colonial regimes. At the heart of this literary, historical, biographical and auto-biographical work has been a concern with particularity and local experience. Since each colonial regime (British, Dutch, French etc.) had a very different history and was played out in distinct and often contradictory ways depending on exactly where it was being exercised,[7] it is fallacious to generalise about the experience of colonisation. It would also be infelic-itous to assume that the process of colonisation was accepted and passively assimilated by local peoples without considerable struggle and active resistance. The early works of Frantz Fanon (in Algeria) and Mahatma Gandhi (in India), most notably, are works of anti-colonisation, pursued in Fanon's case through armed resistance and Gandhi's case passive and contemplative resistance to their respective French and British colonisers. A key task of postcolonial scholarship has been to discuss these forms of resistance, and also to give voice (Bhabha, 1994; Spivak, 1988) to the experiences, cultures and languages associated with the indigenous knowledge systems which colonisation attempted to dismantle and replace with Western discourse.

A second key objective of postcolonial scholarship is based on the understanding that the colonial project did not suddenly 'stop' when colonies were granted their independence. Considerable debate has ensued within postcolonial studies about the use of the prefix 'post', and whether one should deploy the term 'postcolonialism' (without hyphen) or 'post-colonialism' (with hyphen).[8] The debate has centred on two issues: first the understanding that there is no unitary date for the formal independence of colonies and hence no one point when 'post'-colonisation began (with the hyphen debate); second the understanding that, whilst colonialism as the physical occupation of a coloniser in a colonised country may have been brought to an end, economic, cultural and ideological structures connecting coloniser and colonised have not simply disappeared as a result of independence. Mutated and new forms of colonialism, covered by the term 'neo-colonialism', exist and are the object of inquiry by postcolonial scholars.[9] Current concerns with the contemporary global system of late capitalism (Young, 2001: 67) have been refracted through the discourse of neo-colonialism, especially discussions of the role of the USA as a contemporary imperial force. Bringing together these two points, it is the case that 'the continuing imprint of colonialism and anticolonialism is discernible in a range of contemporary practices and institutions, whether economic, political, or cultural' (Prasad, 2003: 5); and marketing counts as one of these. Postcolonialism can therefore be summarised as 'an attempt to investigate the complex and deeply fraught dynamics of modern Western colonialism and anticolonial resistance, and the ongoing significance of the colonial encounter for people's lives in the West and the non-West' (Prasad, 2003: 5).

Theoretical Frame

Postcolonialism deploys diverse[10] theoretical and political resources to interrogate, intervene in and transform the continued power asymmetries and effects of contemporary neo-colonialism, and other forms of imperialism. In this chapter, I draw very selectively from this theoretical diversity in order to bring analytic focus to an account of historical and contemporary marketing practice across a number of product sectors. Key to my analysis is the concept of Orientalism which is articulated in Edward Said's (1978) seminal text of the same title. The success of Said's work resides in its systematic and complex unravelling of the way in which Western scholars (historians, geographers, anthropologists, linguists, philologists) and others (travel writers, artists, curators, administrators) constructed knowledge of the 'Orient'[11] (Gandhi, 1998; Moore-Gilbert, 1997). Said explored the sets of representations (categories, classifications, images) utilised by these scholars and commentators in producing accounts of the Oriental 'other'. In doing so, he emphasised the notion of the Orient as a *cultural production* rather than a reflection of an already existing reality. For him: 'as much as the West itself, the Orient is an idea that has a history and a tradition of thought, imagery, and vocabulary that have given it reality and presence in and for the West' (Said, 1978: 5)

Orientalism is, therefore, a Western set of ontological assumptions, epistemological practices and cultural constructions which serve to create its object of study, rather than a descriptive set of methods for articulating the contours of an *a priori* reality called the Orient. In short, Orientalism is a practice of Othering where the construction of the Self is dialectically achieved through the simultaneous construction of the Other. As Easthope and McGowan (1992: 243) point out, 'what occurs in the process of the production of these knowledges is the whole fictioning of a culture or cultural meanings which is regulated in such minute ways that it comes eventually to be regarded as natural'.

This process of naturalisation means that the ideological practices required to produce these knowledges are erased or repressed, such that the effect, the orientalised other, is made to appear as a form of truth, 'free' of ideological domination or political distortion. What Said shows is that the 'naturalisation' of the knowledge of the other is neither neutral nor value-free.

The political distortions and moral condemnations that characterise Orientalism have often been articulated around the notion of 'progress'. The discourse on 'progress' that informed the colonial project suggested that some 'races' were inferior to others; colonising powers had a moral obligation to assume control and help develop lesser peoples; the knowledge systems of such people were inferior; only the 'developed' and 'educated' people of the colonising world were capable of producing valid knowledge; the 'less developed' people (the subalterns)[12] should not be allowed to speak for themselves, until judged as 'progressed'. This Enlightenment-based view of progress was, McClintock (1994) argues, one of the most tenacious tropes of colonialism. It produced, as Prasad (1997) explains, an elaborate series of hierarchical and asymmetrical binaries, which constructed the West as 'superior' and the non-West as 'inferior' as illustrated in Table 20.1 below.

Table 20.1   The Hierarchical System of Colonialist Binaries

West	Non-West
Active	Passive
Center	Margin/periphery
Civilised	Primitive/savage
Developed	Backward/underdeveloped/ Underdeveloped/developing
Fullness/plenitude/completeness	Lack/inadequacy/incompleteness
Historical (people with history)	Ahistorical (people without history)
The liberated	The savable
Masculine	Feminine/effeminate
Modern	Archaic
Nation	Tribe
Occidental	Oriental
Scientific	Superstitious
Secular	Non secular
Subject	Object
Superior	Inferior
The vanguard	The led
White	Black/brown/yellow

Source: Prasad (1997: 291)

As Ashcroft *et al.* (1995) explain, 'knowing' other people through this type of discourse underpinned imperial dominance and, more insidiously, became the mode through which the colonised were persuaded to know themselves.[13] Much of this cultural work was achieved through practices of myth-making. A key example is the 'myth of the lazy native' which was used, as Alatas (1977) carefully documents in regard to accounts of the colonial history of the Malays, Filipinos and Javanese, to 'justify compulsion and unjust practices in the mobilization of labour in the colonies. It portrayed a negative image of the natives and their society to justify and rationalize European conquest and domination' (1977: 2). Similarly with regard to Africa, the 'myth of the dark continent' has a complex history traced by Brantlinger (1985) from the years prior to 1833 when slavery was abolished in British lands up to the partitioning of Africa in the latter part of the 19th century. The myth functioned ideologically to demand that Africa, and its 'savage customs' (notably cannibalism) be colonised and thus 'civilised' and 'enlightened' on 'moral, religious and scientific grounds' (1985: 167–168).

As Brantlinger points out, at the core of this mythical ideology was a projection of European fears and desires onto this Other underpinned by a psychology of 'blaming the victim' (1985: 198) for their own colonisation. Crang (1998) notes how images of Africa (and elsewhere) in imperialist and Orientalist discourse were typically highly sexualised and feminised, a likely outcome of the fact that the fears and desires projected onto the continent were those of white, male colonialists. A fascination with male dominance, female sexual availability and the 'menace' of black sexuality lay at the heart of white colonial male fears and desire for the Other. Elements of both myths can be found in so-called discourses of tropicalisation which were a further key Orientalist discourse. Here images of the tropics lay claim to a 'lush earthly paradise, full of exotic flora and fauna . . . this Edenesque abundance is . . . held responsible for the lethargy and idleness of the tropical natives' (Prasad, 2003: 157).

Said's work has fostered the growth of so-called colonial discourse analysis; that is to say, the critical analysis of the sets of textual and visual representations, including the myths noted above, used to accomplish the work of Othering. Said's original text, and much of the analysis to which it has led, has been the source of much criticism. Most often, critics point to Said's tendency to homogenise colonial discourse and thus to ignore the divergences between British, French and Portuguese Empire for instance; to ignore resistance to colonial discourse, and thus to underplay the complex, contradictory and often ambivalent nature of the colonial encounter;[14] to sideline the gender dynamics of Empire, as well as the material/economic contexts of production for these sets of images and representations.[15] Bearing these criticisms in mind, the next section works with and against the grain of a Saidian colonial discourse analysis to surface and critically discuss the ways in which marketing and promotional practices have been centrally involved in the production and reproduction of a 'colonial project'. This has been a much neglected task by those of us in the marketing discipline.[16]

Section Two
The History of Soap and Other Imperial Commodities

'SOAP IS CIVILIZATION': Unilever Company Slogan (in McClintock, 1995: 207)

An historical approach to the study of commerce and advertising reveals the simultaneously fascinating and disturbing facets of marketing practice during colonial times. In one of the best-known pieces of postcolonial analysis *Imperial Leather: Race, Gender and Sexuality in the Colonial Conquest*, Anne McClintock (1995) presents an historical analysis of British imperialism and, more specifically, its reproduction of and constitution by the economic and cultural inter-relationships of race, gender and sexuality. A key illustrative aspect of her analysis pertains to the development of commodity culture in late 19th century imperialist Britain at the forefront of which was the soap industry. In chapter five of her book entitled 'Soft-soaping Empire: Commodity racism and imperial advertising', McClintock draws upon selected theoretical resources from socialist, psychoanalytic, feminist and postcolonial thought to account for the development and provide a critical reading of the economic and cultural organisation of soap production and advertising from 1851 to the turn of the 20th century.

As noted above, a key understanding of postcolonialism is that the development of capitalism and the development of colonisation were mutually dependent enterprises. In the case of soap, the British Empire brought together raw materials such as cotton and palmoil with the growing domestic market for soaps and clothes fuelled by the spending power of Britain's imperial middle classes who could, for the first time, afford a product until then considered a luxury. McClintock makes clear that the growth of soap advertising was not merely a reflection of the economic organisation of colonialism. Economic competition from the USA and Germany meant that British manufacturers across a number of product categories turned to advertising and promotional practices as they needed to work harder to differentiate themselves from rivals. Corporate signatures were used as branding tools and a professional class of advertisers emerged selling themselves as 'Empire builders'. These advertisers exploited the prevalence of an imperial culture in which economic expansion, national pride and racial superiority were tightly bound together. By the 1890s sales of soap soared in Great Britain as 'advertising had emerged as the central cultural form of commodity capitalism' (1995: 210).

McClintock argues, however, that the emergence of commodity production and soap advertising was not just a matter of economic organisation; it was also a matter of *cultural* organisation.[17] Following Lukács' view of commodities as threshold items between commerce and culture, McClintock suggests (1995: 207) that 'Commodity kitsch made possible the mass marketing of empire as an organized system of images and attitudes'.

Soap advertising was at the forefront of the manufacture of a sign system for Empire which was efficiently distributed and dispersed through the wide circulation of commodities. McClintock's analysis of the contents of this sign system reveals a number of disturbing facets of imperial soap advertising, which she articulates through the concept of commodity racism and using examples of adverts from leading soap producers (primarily Pears, Monkey Brand) and other cleaning and food products.

The sign system of soap advertising was based on two dominant themes of contemporary bourgeois British Victorian culture: the cult of domesticity and new imperialism. Advertisers drew upon these cultural resources to articulate soap with core middle-class values and pursuits such as monogamy (equated with 'clean sex'), industrial capital (equated with 'clean money'), class control (equated with the 'cleaning' of the working classes/the poor/the unwashed), Christianity (equated with washing in the 'blood of the Lamb') and the civilising mission at the heart of British colonialism (equated with clothing and cleaning 'the savage'). The aim of the Victorian imperial mission was to bring civilisation and progress to those it colonised, that is, about bringing light to dark, cleansing to dirt and by metonymic extension, white to black. Soap was the moral and economic salvation of Britain and as McClintock notes, it was also the 'spiritual ingredient' of the imperial mission itself, part of a Victorian obsession and fetishisation of clean white bodies and clean white clothing.

> Soap flourished not only because it created and filled a spectacular gap in the domestic market but also because, as a cheap and portable domestic commodity, it could persuasively mediate the Victorian poetics of racial hygiene and imperial progress. (McClintock, 1995: 209)

Victorian advertising thus took shape around the construction of racial difference and in her analyses, McClintock identifies four key fetishes of imperial soap (the soap itself; white clothing, especially aprons; mirrors; monkeys) which all worked with allegories of reformation, or transformation from dirty to clean, black to white, primitive to civilised. One advert for Pears' Soap printed in the book (1995: 213) comprises two 'before' and 'after' scenes which McClintock interprets as follows:

> . . . a black boy sits in the bath, gazing wide-eyed into the water as if into a foreign element. A white boy, clothed in a white apron – the familiar fetish of domestic purity – bends benevolently over his "lesser" brother, bestowing upon him the precious talisman of racial progress. (McClintock, 1995: 214)

In the advert, the second scene shows how, having used Pears' Soap, the black boy's body has changed colour: whilst his face is still black, his body is now white and the transformation is almost complete. The stigma of his racial identity has almost been washed away; his body has almost become pure. The white child, who holds a mirror in his hand in both scenes in the advert, showing the black boy his transformation, thereby becomes: 'the agent of history and the male heir to progress, reflecting his lesser brother in the mirror of European self-consciousness' (1995: 214).

The racist iconography of soap advertising was also prevalent in other product categories in which a plethora of signifiers for Britishness (e.g. Britannia and John Bull) and scenes of exploration and conquest in Africa adorned the front of biscuit tins, whisky bottles and Bovril. Huntley and Palmer biscuit tins, for instance, featured white male colonialists sitting in the middle of the jungle on biscuit crates sipping tea. Cleaning advertisements typically deployed liminal images of oceans and shorelines (1995: 220): Chlorinol bleaching soda, for instance, portrays two black boys on a boat whose sail sports the tagline 'We are going to use "Chlorinol" and be like de white Nigger'. Also in that boat is a third boy whose skin is bleached a strange white colour – the racial hybrid, bleaching soda as an agent of history. To quote McClintock: 'the whitening agent of bleach promises an alchemy of racial upliftment through historical contact with commodity culture. The transforming power of the civilising mission is stamped on the boat-box's sails as the objective character of the commodity itself' (1995: 220).

McClintock's analysis suggests that commodities are more than just imperialist symbols: they are actually agents of history. Exhibiting Marxist credentials she notes that the commodity, 'abstracted from social context and human labor, does the civilizing work of empire, whilst radical change is figured as magical, without process or social agency' (1995: 222). The distinctively racial and gendered division of labour on which these commodities trade, privileges the role of white men in history, whilst white African women are either invisible, doll-like and happy in their servitude (Lury, 1997) or sexualised, and African men passive and typically feminised. These interrelations of gender, race and sexuality form the social structure of imperial soap advertising and express a poetics of social discipline. The inscription of African bodies as dirty, undomesticated and lacking in hygiene is used to legitimise imperialists' violent reinforcement of their cultural and economic values, especially as they bolster the imperial economy.

As with any fetish item, however, the desire for it can never be fully contained, and inevitably involves excesses, conflicts, ambivalences and supplements which return to haunt the boundaries of the fictitious original. The idea that Africa was an undiscovered land with a homogeneous primitive culture disconnected from previous outside influence ignores the fact that Africans had well-established trading relationships and networks to the west and north in particular and that Europeans had been trading with Africans long before the Victorian period. Further, Africans did not passively accept the civilising missions, economic and cultural values, violence and aggression of British colonisers. Mimicry and violent attacks on British colonisers, as well as swindling and theft, all demonstrated the local capacity to resist and appropriate imperialist ideology. Finally, as much as commodity racism organised and affirmed middle-class Victorian values, it also disorganised them. McClintock thus notes a paradox at the heart of Victorian advertising: while it upheld and promoted middle-class distinctions (e.g. public v. private, paid v. unpaid work), it also transgressed them. It took intimate cleansing rituals from the home into the public sphere of advertising, and it brought scenes of Empire and colonial conquest into the home on the surfaces of tins, bars and bottles.

Getting a Bit of the Other: Tourism and Travel

To assume that the deployment of colonial discourse is a purely historical facet of marketing and advertising practice would be incorrect. Colonial discourse, and the exercise of Orientalism upon which it typically rests, continues to be reproduced in contemporary marketing practice across a number of product categories. Adverts for confectionery items like Bounty Bars or Turkish Delight, spicy snacks like Jacobs Thai Bites, in-store design and promotional catalogues for home furnishing stores like Habitat or The Pier deploy images and myths of the exotic, the ethnic, the mysterious or the bounteous Other to construct meaning for their products. Tourism and travel is a product category where the discourses of Orientalism are found in such frequent and varied forms.

Tourism discourses, according to Papen (2005: 79), are 'a set of expressions, words and behaviour as well as particular touristic structures and activities that describe a place and its inhabitants'. They play a central role in the construction of so-called place-myths (Lash and Urry, 1994) which marketers and other cultural intermediaries carry out by drawing upon a circumscribed set of symbols, and associations, a process which Rojek (1997) describes as 'dragging'. Tourism marketers are in the business of producing 'induced images' of destinations, of manufacturing what Urry (2002) most famously called the 'tourist gaze' which frames consumers' understandings and expectations of particular places and people. As Cooper (1994: 144 in Echtner, 2002: 415) notes: 'Travel brochures . . . frame the ritual acts that must be performed and the centres of 'pilgrimage' that must be visited; they orchestrate contact with the world of the Other'.

A considerable amount of academic effort has been dedicated to analysing the content and components of tourism discourse and its sets of representations as found in brochures and other promotional materials. These studies, many of which are to be found in the *Annals of Tourism Research*, clearly illustrate the perpetuation of colonial imaginary and ideology in present times (Palmer, 1994; Silver, 1993), with several focusing in particular on the growing sector of so-called Third World tourism.[18] Morgan and Pritchard (1998: 169) encapsulate neatly the core colonial dynamic of Third World tourism as follows: 'images of the Third World . . . tend to reflect a western, white male, colonial perspective', whereby 'a dynamic First World contrasts itself with a static, timeless and unchanging Third World'. Images resonate with those found by McClintock in her study of commodity racism: paradise, sensuous, unspoiled, authentic, mystical, exotic, erotic, abundant, green, curious, primitive, remote, natural, timeless, mythical. Of course, the vast majority of tourists to the Third World are from the so-called First World, and as Echtner and others have pointed out:

> Third World destinations are primarily promoted by multinational tour operators, travel agencies and other tourism corporations with origins in the First World. (. . .) This situation creates a marketing system whereby the majority of the images used to represent Third World tourism destinations are selected by First World promoters in order to cater to the needs of consumers in developed countries. (Echtner, 2002: 413–414)

Echtner (2002) presents one of the most comprehensive analyses of the images found in 115 tourist brochures for 12 selected countries representing different corners of the Third World. Using the categories of attractions, actors, actions and atmospheres to classify these materials, she found three distinct types which cast the tourist either as time-traveller, indulgent sun-seeker or adventurer, and the locals as 'fixed into archaic, subservient or savage archetypes. Such stereotyping is at the very least unrepresentative but at worst becomes demeaning and degrading' (2002: 432). Echtner (2002: 413) concludes that 'by emphasising and stereotyping certain attractions, actors, actions and atmospheres, certain overarching tourism myths are created around Third World destinations'.

In a joint publication in 2003, Echtner and Prasad further the work done in Echtner's original paper by deploying more explicitly postcolonial theory in interpreting the myths created by these brochures. They suggest that the findings point to three key 'Un'-myths in tourism marketing: the myth of the unchanged, the myth of the unrestrained, and the myth of the uncivilised. All these myths, they argue, replicate colonial discourse. The host/the Other is found to be lacking, to be in deficit compared to the Western tourist. I have reproduced their table which provides a synopsis of Third World tourism un-myths which clearly work with the kinds of colonial binary categories mentioned in the introduction to this chapter.

Table 20.2 Tourism Myths (Echtner and Prasad, (2003: 678))

Myths	Unchanged	Unrestrained	Uncivilised
The Place	Lands of Legend	Lands of Luxuriance	Lands at the Limit
The Time	Past	Present	Primordial
The Natural	Significant silence	Soft	Savage
The Built	Relics	Resorts	Significant silence
The Host	Peasant (simple/stoic)	Pleasant (serving/smiling)	Primitive (savage/surprising)
The Tourist	Explorer into the past	Exploiter into paradise	Expedition into the primitive

However, while the studies of Echtner and others provide descriptions and contextualisations of the content and components of tourist brochures, and representational dimensions of the Other, they fail to provide insight into how these are actually produced. Detailed studies of textual production offer more insight on this issue.

Lester (1992) offers us a different insight into travel, one that involves us not having to leave our armchairs. Lester critically examines the use of the Other as an exotic object in the retailer Banana Republic's mail order catalogue, a document which she sees as neatly capturing 'the restless desire and power of the modern West to collect the world' (Clifford, 1988: 196). She describes how the advert copy typically refers to the travel writing of the great travellers of the colonial past, as well as journalism and other pieces of literature, to link varied cultures to different products in the creation of the fictional and exotic Banana Republic. These fragments as well as material artifacts like African masks, toucans, palm trees, Buddhas and a frangipani formed the basis of the 1988 catalogue which Lester critically analysed. In this catalogue, Lester identified four strategies that create the exotic Other: the creation of the subject through the construction of a preferred reader; the uses of history and invented tradition from the point of view of the preferred reader; the jumbling of spatial and temporal images; and the construction of authenticity. The preferred reader is the leisure traveller, while the Third World is positioned as a bazaar in which white people can sample an assortment of exotica. The objects of the Banana Republic are people of colour in the so-called Third World who (with cues to the myth of the dark continent discussed earlier) are never shown wearing the product for sale: they are in native dress in order to speak for a cultural authenticity of a time gone by. According to Lester, these are textual strategies that propagate through commodity form: 'the subjection, exclusion and silence of the particular in this celebration of the general, the global village, One World Order' (1992: 77).

Similarly, Adams' (1984) study of ethnic tourism marketing in the case of the Toraja of Sulawesi (Indonesia) describes the 'staged authenticity' involved in the production of this tourist destination. Valene Smith defines ethnic tourism as follows: 'Ethnic tourism is marketed to the public in terms of the 'quaint' customs of indigenous and often exotic peoples' (1978: 2). Adams illustrates how, as so-called brokers of ethnicity, tour operators and their brochures deploy a small number of ethnic markers (e.g. clothing, architecture, dance, religious festivals and practices etc.), which they then exaggerate to draw appealing mental pictures of the ethnicity of the Toraja people. Adams found that the American travel agents she studied gave repeated descriptions of 'animistic funeral celebrations', 'traditional, thatched, boat-like houses', and 'dramatic buffalo sacrifices' (1984: 474). Toraja houses, rituals and the Toraja name itself became the key signifiers around which Torajan ethnicity was elaborated. These markers are used to invent ethnic authenticity for the First World tourists, but they are inaccurate distortions of the history and culture of the Toraja when measured against the anthropological record. The anthropological record shows that the Toraja have a rich and complex mythology which the brochure stereotypes, narrows down and edits out. The distinctive features of the Toraja sold in brochures are grafted on to external and visible aspects of Toraja life (e.g. houses are modified so that when tourists arrive, their expectations are immediately confirmed). This is a form of what MacCannell (1976) famously called 'staged authenticity', where authenticity is not about an original, essential cultural moment but, as noted by Silver (1993), verifies a marketed representation of something.

The problem of tourism discourse, then, is also the problem of the imperial advertising surveyed by McClintock: not only that it provides distorted and narrowed views of a place and people, but also that it turns on problematic productions of race and ethnicity which define the Other in terms of the asymmetrical binaries of the Self. Britton (1979) suggests that the reasons for the production of distorted realities lie in the fact that tourism is in part a myth of escape in which tourists do not want to be reminded of poverty and misery in the Third World context. Moreover, research has shown that the mythical and distorted realities of tourism marketing can actually reinforce negative stereotypes and encourage undesirable attitudes and behaviours whilst overseas. The confirmation of the 'myth of the lazy native' for instance forms a repetitious cycle of stereotyping that is hard to break. Finally, there is a continuity of Orientalist practice here. During colonialism Europeans invented the traditions of the locals, and provided them with a frame through which to re-narrate their customs and traditions and to distort their ethnic histories for ideological purposes. Africans came to believe that certain social structures, necessary under colonialism, were part of traditional African ways of life prior to their first contact with the West. But no indigenous society had a singular identity or set of traditions prior to contact with the West. Most were multifaceted and complex. Furthermore, the portrayal of non-white populations as stages for Western consumption suggests that natives exist primarily for the consumption of Western tourists. However, since the First World plays a dominant role in the production and control of image in the tourist industry, it is difficult to predict any changes to these cultural asymmetries.

Uta Papen's (2005) study of community-based tourism enterprises (CBTEs) in Namibia is a good example of how one can combine a neo-colonial discourse analysis with a concern for the political economic dimensions of global tourism. Based on ethnographic fieldwork, Papen describes the production and consumption of two key forms of tourism in Windhoek, the capital city: ethnotourism, and ecotourism. Her fieldwork was conducted in a black township in Windhoek called Katatura where she worked with local CBTEs owned and run by local communities. What Papen found was the structural and symbolic reproduction of a set of colonial structures and practices which replicate racially-based inequalities between white and black communities.

Papen's interest was piqued when investigating the increasing demand amongst tourists coming to Namibia for a slice of 'indigenous life', a form of ethnic tourism. One would have expected local black townships and black life to form part of this picture, but both have been consistently written out of the dominant, First-World produced tourism discourse on/in Namibia. Ethnic tourism in Windhoek was subject to two competing discourses serving two different sets of customers: 'the "white" colonial Namibia of the capital city, and the "black" Namibia of the capital's township' (2005: 88). Whilst the former discourse primarily attracts package safari tourists (typically Germans with an interest in their Namibian colonial history), the second discourse of black Namibian culture attracts younger travellers, backpackers and independent tourists. The mainstay of the Windhoek tourism market is the former category of traveller, a category which simply misses out the black townships. As Papen notes, these package tourists go 'with white Namibians or Europeans as guides focusing on "white" Windhoek and its colonial history. Some of these city tours drive through Katatura's main road, but they do not stop in the township' (Papen, 2005: 87).

The discursive bias towards white tourism in Namibia involves a writing out of racial divides in the country from advertising, and positions black Namibian life as 'culture', turning its folklore and history into heritage and thus fixing it in the past. This discursive bias maps on to a structural asymmetry in the Namibian tourist industry which further serves to marginalise local black tourism operators. Most travellers come from the First World, and book their trips overseas. These agencies typically are multinational tour operators who have links with local tour operators and other lodges and hotels, and locals therefore find it difficult to attract these tourists. Local black communities have little control over either the material flows, or the cultural flows and destination images among a large number of customers in the sector. Dominant tourism discourse and material structures are set by others and, as Papen suggests, they have little choice but to accept it. They do not have the resources (economic or capital) to explore the semiotic resources of their destinations nor to monitor their position within the discursive order.

However, Papen argues that 'community-based tourism groups are not totally without a stake in the creation and promotion of fashionable tourism discourses' (2005: 95) pointing to the government's current discourse of community development and black empowerment as offering some potentially interesting room for symbolic manoeuvre.

Picking up on this latter point, postcolonial work teaches us that to understand imperialism is also to understand struggle and resistance. Locals are rarely passive dupes or recipients of colonisers' messages. One of the shortcomings of the discourse approach to colonial analysis, then, is not only a neglect of the context of productions, but also of the reception of the text. The Adams piece above, for instance, gestures at a rather neglected aspect of her analysis: the view and perceptions of the Toraja themselves. She notes that on occasion the stereotypes created by travel agents are sometimes fed back to the native group but she does not tell us 'what happened next'. Britton (1979) cites parts of speeches from politicians of Third World countries who are aware of and frustrated at the images. He quotes the former Premier of St Vincent in 1972 speaking to local tourist people: 'One myth that needs to be exploded is the idea of the Caribbean paradise. Let us face it, there is no paradise, only different ways of life. Not that paradise has been lost, or destroyed, but that it never existed, neither here nor in the Pacific' (Britton, 1979: 324).

Evans-Pritchard (1989) conducted ethnographic work with Native Americans about their perceptions and relations to others, notably tourists. This study shows that the tourist gaze cuts both ways – that its Others are typically aware of how visiting groups see them and the stereotypes they hold. Interestingly, and contrary to some of the views taken by other researchers, Evans-Pritchard suggests that stereotypes can also serve an indigenous group positively. In short, her work demonstrates the agency, the subversion and the resistance of Native Americans, as well as the way they are actively aware of and use stereotypes for their own benefit. This is one of the rare studies that shows locals as agents of social and economic change.

Indeed there is a long history of Native American folklore and mythology that, to use Evans-Pritchard's terminology 'burlesques' the Other (1989: 89), and provides parodies and criticisms of the 'whiteman' and its impact on local communities. She notes how

> Indian responses to the whitemen have varied with the times, historically following a pattern of astonishment, messianic worship, armed revolt, and finally bitterness . . . They have caricatured the fire and brimstone of the missionaries, the financial gouging of the traders, the hypocrisy of the great white chiefs, and the credulity of the anthropologists. (Evans-Pritchard, 1989: 90)

Her own three-year fieldwork study investigated Pueblo and Navajo silversmiths in New Mexico and their perceptions and interactions with tourists visiting their shops and buying their work. The beauty of this paper is the detailed description of accounts of face-to-face interactions between the Indians and the tourists when selling crafts and arts. She suggests that there is a common set of representations of tourists that Indians have built up over time that illustrate an acute awareness of the preconceived ideas tourists have of them. This awareness informs how Indians deal with tourists in situationally-specific interactions like selling arts and crafts. Evans-Pritchard gives examples of many different types of interactions that show 'perception, expression and manipulation of stereotypes' (1989: 95) through strategies of trickstering, self-objectification, silence and various kinds of emotional reaction. She also shows the Native Indians' talents at marketing. She describes how one of the most frequent questions tourists ask local Indian artists is about the cultural significance of art, a question which assumes that they produce art for purely aesthetic, cultural or spiritual reasons, a trapping of the Other in a non-commercial sphere. Oftentimes, there is no cultural significance for the artist, but to fulfil tourists' need for a narrative and thus to turn a profit, Indian silversmiths will sometimes make one up, telling them what they want to hear. The editing and invention of tradition is not just a practice of the dominant group; it is also part of minority engagement with the economic and cultural practices of, and complex relations with, industry.

Evans-Pritchard argues that stereotypes of Native Indians propagated by tourists can 'function to defend and protect as well as to discriminate' (1989: 89); in short, they are not just negative forms of psychological attribution; they can also be mobilised to protect the privacy of the Indians. In cases such as the following, one can see why this is necessary. Evans-Pritchard describes how Native Indian Laureen responded to one American woman's comment: "'Dear, are you a real Indian? . . . I hope you don't mind my asking. But you look so American" with the retort: "'I am a buffalo'".

Postmodernism and Techno-Orientalism

A further and final contemporary example of the value of a postcolonial appreciation of marketing practice relates to the success of Japanese business practices and products in the 1980s and 1990s which spawned a particular kind of neo-colonial discourse which Morley and Robins (1992) refer to as 'techno-Orientalism'.

At this point in history, Japan posed a problem for the West in economic and cultural terms: not only were its leading corporations eroding US and European market shares and setting up factories in their backyards, there were fears, or more accurately fantasies (to use Morley and Robins' terminology), about the pernicious cultural impact of Japan in particular on the American way of life. Morley and Robins survey numerous press commentaries from the 1980s which positioned Japan as a threat, an alien culture, complex and ambiguous in the Western imagination, working behind the scenes in a 'chameleon-like' fashion to erode the economic and cultural values of America slowly but surely. Morley and Robins describe how the broader cultural theme here was one where Western modernity was being brought into question, and gesturing to a shift from 'Cocacolonization to sake imperialism' (1992: 139).

Techno-Orientalism is a marketing concern in at least two respects. First it was part and parcel of a number of media and popular culture products in the 1980s and 1990s. Morley and Robins cite the Teenage Mutant Ninja Turtles' character Shredder as one example. This character lived in the sewers, away from the light of everyday life, using ninja principles to erode American civilisation,[19] a cartoon embodiment of a wider American fear. But second, and more centrally to their argument, techno-Orientalism was a cultural production associated with the marketing success of Japanese high technology in Western markets. It stemmed from the mythology of Japan as the most machine loving nation on earth, part of which, according to Morley and Robins, involved a critique of their technology as a problematic postmodern mutation of human experience. Computer games, they suggested, were seen to embody the exotic, enigmatic and mysterious essence of Japanese particularism. They cite *Blade Runner* as an example of a film that carries this theme, as well as computer graphics that mix feudal images and high technology. Projected on to Japanese games were erotic and exotic fantasies, but also a strain of racism that reinforced views of Japanese culture, like their technologies, as cold and machine-like. Morley and Robins conclude that

> There is something profoundly disturbing in this Techno-Orientalism. Following Castoriadis, we have suggested that western xenophobia and racism are motivated by the apparent incapacity of a culture to constitute itself without excluding, devaluing and then hating the Other. (Morley and Robins, 1992: 155)

But what happens when it is no longer possible to keep the Other in an subordinate place, Morley and Robins ask? The issue is anxiety about the West's claim to a universal history through the structure of modernity.

> Japan has now become modern to the degree of seeming postmodern, and it is its future that now seems to be the measure for all cultures. And, thereby, the basis of western identity is called into question. (Morley and Robins, 1992: 141)

It was no longer Europe or the US that was the key site of modernity; Japanese technological superiority suggests they are the vanguards of postmodernity, an even more advanced stage of history. Here the non-West was reclaiming a subjectivity lost by the kinds of Orientalism that excluded them from history. Japan has destabilised the west/east modern/premodern binaries – Japan should be premodern or at least nonmodern, not postmodern. This ability of Japan to express its own history and subjectivity was facilitated by 'nihonjinron' discourses of Japaneseness, a brand of cultural nationalism which assumed Japanese superiority and uniqueness over other civilisations. One wonders how, if at all, the rise of the Indian and Chinese economies will trigger new and mutated forms of old Orientalism?

Conclusion

This chapter has aimed to provide a necessarily brief and selective introduction to post-colonialism for the marketing and consumer research community and to illustrate how its theoretical insights can be useful for understanding the historical and contemporary colonial and neo-colonial inflections of marketing and promotional practice. While the theoretical frame is largely limited to that of colonial discourse analysis, I have made attempts to round out the marketing analysis with reference to the economic and material contexts of production, as well as the ambivalent contexts of reception/consumption for the sets of texts, images and material artefacts that constitute a colonial discourse. I have demonstrated not only how marketing was central to the formal colonial projects of the 19th century, but also that it continues to play a role in the reproduction of the longstanding discourse of Orientalism. Ultimately this insight raises political and ethical questions about the role of marketing practice in organising problematic racial differences, and of marketing theory in effectively erasing these key questions from the parameters of its recent debates.

Notes

1. This convention is a problem since it leads readers to overlook the important writings and political struggles of earlier anti-colonial activists like Frantz Fanon, Aimé Césaire or Mahatma Gandhi *inter alia*. As noted in the section introducing postcolonialism, however, there is a current trend towards remembering and revaluing the insights and protests of these earlier writers as a better 'originary moment' for postcolonial studies.
2. Anshuman Prasad, Pushkala Prasad, Bill Cooke, Ali Mir, Raza Mir, Bobby Banerjee, Robert Westwood, Vanessa Chio.
3. Dean Neu, Josephine Maltby.
4. As noted by Patterson and Brown (2007).
5. There are subtle distinctions to be made between terms like imperialism, colonialism and neo-colonialism which are discussed in Young (2001). For my purposes, I view colonialism as one form of imperialism, and neo-colonialism to be a form of colonialism not based on the physical occupation and control of one nation by another but instead through other forms of economic, cultural and ideological influence.
6. Cooke (2003) argues that the principles and practices of classical management theory were importantly developed in the plantations of America's deep south. By the 1860s 38,000 managers developed effective command and control techniques for the organisation of the labour power of the millions of slaves on the plantations. That management theory and practice emerged with blood on its hands, and racism and exploitation in its minds, is expunged from conventional management history texts.
7. The British, for instance, pursued different forms of colonialism in Australia, where it worked via settlement, and India which unlike Australia had a populace and extant civilisation that required rule of a different kind.
8. See McClintock (1994) and Young (2001).
9. There is considerable tension about the postcolonial status of nations like Australia and Canada, which are former parts of the British Empire. It is argued by some that while they might have gained independence from Britain, they pursue a form of internal colonialism towards their own minorities i.e. the Aborigines in Australia and the French-speaking minority of Canada.
10. See Moore-Gilbert (1997) for an excellent comparative synthesis of the works of Said, Bhabha and Spivak.
11. Although some analysis focuses on what might typically be understood as the Orient – in effect the analysis tends to extend to everything that was not Europe.
12. The term 'subaltern' was originally coined by Gramsci to refer to those elements of society that were subject to the hegemony of the ruling class. It was adapted by a group of primarily Indian scholars to denote the general attribution of subordination of sectors of society, including colonial and neo-colonial subordination. Subaltern historians, in particular, drew attention to the difficulty of subaltern groups speaking and accounting for themselves since the spaces for such accounts and explanations were dominated by western historical and other discourses. Only those Western accounts were accepted as legitimate and valid (see for example Guha (1982) and Chaturvedi (2000)).

13. This interpolation of modes of self-knowing was very much the point of the subaltern studies project (see Guha, 1982).
14. Bhabha is noted for his psychoanalytic analyses of the colonial encounter articulated through the concepts of mimicry, hybridisation and ambivalence.
15. See Spivak for interesting articulations of the labour theory of value with feminist and deconstructive concerns.
16. Venturing an explanation for the neglect of postcolonialism in marketing, I would suggest, first, that it is an outcome of the demographics of the marketing academy and second that it is tied to the lack of poststructuralist debates in theory development debates. The rise of poststructuralist theory in the late 1970s was a key context for the successful reception of Said and subsequent scholars. Marketing rarely looks at poststructuralism and so, it seems to me, can easily avoid mention of postcolonialism.
17. McClintock cites the 1851 Great Exhibition as a crucial moment in the development of commodity culture. She cites it as the hitherto most significant example of the 'transforma-tion of collective and private life into a space for the spectacular exhibition of commodities'. She quotes Richards who described the Great Exhibition as a: 'semiotic laboratory for the labour theory of value'. Capitalism was not just becoming a dominant system of exchange, but also creating 'a dominant form of representation . . . the voyeuristic panorama of surplus as spectacle' (1995: 208). From this point on, the idea of commodity as spectacle, of the ideology of consumerism and of capitalism as an organised system of images, was born (1995: 209–210).
18. According to Echtner (2002) Third World tourism is gaining considerably in popularity, most notably in East Asia, Africa, Latin America and Micronesia. She states that about 30% of all international tourism is to Third World nations, a tripling of this figure over 20 years up to 1999.
19. US suspicion of Japan has a long cultural history stretching back to the early 20th century popularity of Fu Manchu and the Yellow-Peril literature in Europe and the US.

References

Adams, K.M. (1984) 'Come to Tana Toraja, Land of the Heavenly Kings: Travel Agents as Brokers of Ethnicity', *Annals of Tourism Research* 11: 469–485.
Ahmad, A. (1992) *In Theory: Classes, Nations, Literatures*. London: Verso.
Alatas, S.H. (1977) *The Myth of the Lazy Native*. London: Frank Cass.
Ashcroft, B., Griffiths, G. and Tiffin, H. (1989) *The Empire Strikes Back: Theory and Practice in Post-Colonial Literatures*. London: Routledge.
—— (2000) *Post-Colonial Studies: The Key Concepts*. London: Routledge.
—— (eds) (1995) *The Postcolonial Studies Reader*. London: Routledge.
Bhabha, H. (1990) *Nation and Narration*. London: Routledge.
—— (1994) *The Location of Culture*. London: Routledge.
Brantlinger, P. (1985) 'Victorians and Africans: The Genealogy of the Myth of the Dark Conti-nent', *Critical Inquiry* 12: 166–203.
Britton, R. (1979) 'The Image of the Third World in Tourism Marketing', *Annals of Tourism Research* July–September: 318–329.
Burton, D. (2000) 'Critical marketing theory: the blueprint?', *European Journal of Marketing* 35(5/6): 722–743.
Chakrabarty, D. (2000) *Provincializing Europe*. Princeton: Princeton University Press.
Chaturvedi, V. (ed.) (2000) *Mapping Subaltern Studies and the Postcolonial*. London: Verso.

Clifford, J. (1988) *The Predicament of Culture: Twentieth Century Ethnography, Literature, and Art*. Cambridge: Harvard University Press.

Cooke, B. (2003) 'The Denial of Slavery in Management Studies', *Journal of Management Studies* 40(8): 1895–1918.

Crang, M. (1998) *Cultural Geography*. London: Routledge.

Dirlik, A. (1997) *The Postcolonial Aura: Third World Criticism in the Age of Global Capitalism*. Boulder: Westview Press.

Easthope, A. and McGowan, K. (1992) *A Critical and Cultural Theory Reader*. Buckingham: Open University Press.

Echtner, C.M. (2002) 'The Content of Third World Tourism Marketing: A 4A Approach', *International Journal of Tourism Research* 4: 413–434.

Echtner, C.M. and Prasad, P. (2003) 'The Context of Third World Tourism Marketing', *Annals of Tourism Research* 30(3): 660–682.

Evans-Pritchard, D. (1989) 'How "They" See "Us": Native American Images of Tourists', *Annals of Tourism Research* 16: 89–105.

Fanon, F. (1952/1986) *Black Skin, White Masks*. London: Pluto.

—— (1961/1967) *The Wretched of the Earth*. London: Penguin.

Gandhi, L. (1998) *Postcolonial Theory: An Introduction*. Edinburgh: Edinburgh University Press.

Gilroy, P. (1993) *The Black Atlantic: Modernity and Double Consciousness*. London: Verso.

—— (2005) *Postcolonial Melancholia*. New York: Columbia University Press.

Guha, R. (1982) *Subaltern Studies 1: Writings on South Asian History and Society* (7 volumes). Delhi: Oxford University Press.

Lash, S. and Urry, J. (1994) *Economies of Signs and Space*. London: Sage.

Lester, E. (1992) 'Buying the Exotic "Other": Reading the "Banana Republic Mail Order Catalog"', *Journal of Communication Inquiry* 16(2): 74–85.

Loomba, A. (1998) *Colonialism/Postcolonialism*. London: Routledge.

Lury, C. (1997) *Consumer Culture* Polity Press, Cambridge.

MacCannell, D. (1976) *The Tourist: A New Theory of the Leisure Class*. New York: Schocken Books.

McClintock, A. (1994) 'The Angels of Progress: Pitfalls of the Term 'Postcolonialism', in F.J. Barker, P. Hulme and M. Iverson (eds) *Colonial Discourse/Postcolonial Theory*, pp. 253–266. Manchester: Manchester University Press.

—— (1995) *Imperial Leather: Race, Gender and Sexuality in the Colonial Conquest*. New York: Routledge.

Memmi, A. (1965) *The Colonizer and the Colonized*. Boston: Beacon Press.

Mishra, V. and Hodge, B. (1991) 'What is Post (-) Colonialism?', *Textual Practice* 5: 399–414.

Mohanty, C.T. (1984) 'Under Western Eyes: Feminist Scholarship and Colonial Discourses', *Boundary* 12(3): 338–358.

—— (2003) *Feminism Without Borders*. Durham: Duke University Press.

Moore-Gilbert, B. (1997) *Postcolonial Theory: Contexts, Practices, Politics*. London: Verso.

Morgan, N. and Pritchard, A. (1998) *Tourism Promotion and Power: Creating Images, Creating Identities*. Chichester: Wiley.

Morley, D. and Robins, K. (1992) 'Techno-Orientalism: Futures, Foreigners and Phobias', *New Formations* 16: 136–156.

Murray, J.B. (2002) 'The Politics of Consumption: A Re-inquiry on Thompson and Haytko's "Speaking of Fashion"', *Journal of Consumer Research* 29(3): 427–440.

Nandy, A. (1983) *The Intimate Enemy: Loss and Recovery of Self Under Colonialism*. New Delhi: Oxford University Press.

Palmer, C.A. (1994) 'Tourism and Colonialism: The Experience of the Bahamas', *Annals of Tourism Research* 21: 792–811.

Papen, U. (2005) 'Exclusive, Ethno and Eco: Representations of Culture and Nature in Tourism Discourses in Namibia', in A. Jaworski and A. Pritchard (eds) *Discourse, Communication and Tourism*, pp. 79–97. Clevedon: Channel View Publications.

Patterson, A. and Brown, S. (2007) 'Inventing the Pubs of Ireland: The Importance of Being Postcolonial', *Journal of Strategic Marketing* 15: 41–51.

Prasad, A. (1997) 'The Colonizing Consciousness and Representation of the Other: A Postcolonial Critique of the Discourse of Oil', in P. Prasad, A. Mills, M. Elmes and A. Prasad (eds) *Managing the Organizational Melting Pot: Dilemmas of Workplace Diversity*, pp. 285–311. Thousand Oaks: Sage.

—— (ed.) (2003) *Postcolonial Theory and Organizational Analysis*. New York: Palgrave Macmillan.

Rojek, C. (1997) 'Indexing, Dragging and the Social Construction of Tourist Sights', in C. Rojek and J. Urry (eds) *Touring Cultures*, pp. 52–75. London: Routledge.

Said, E. (1978) *Orientalism: Western Conceptions of the Orient*. London: Penguin.

—— (1981) *Covering Islam*. London: Vintage.

—— (1993) *Culture and Imperialism*. London: Vintage.

Silver, I. (1993) 'Marketing Authenticity in Third World Countries', *Annals of Tourism Research* 20: 302–318.

Smith, V. (ed.) (1978) *Hosts and Guests: The Anthropology of Tourism*. Oxford: Basil Blackwell.

Spivak, G.C. (1987) *In Other Worlds: Essays in Cultural Politics*. London: Routledge.

—— (1988) 'Can the Subaltern Speak?', in C. Nelson and L. Grossberg (eds) *Marxism and the Interpretation of Culture*, pp. 271–313. Basingstoke: Macmillan.

—— (1990) *The Post-Colonial Critic: Interviews, Strategies, Dialogues*. London: Routledge.

—— (1999) *A Critique of Postcolonial Reason*. Cambridge: Harvard University Press.

Trinh, T.M. (1989) *Woman, Native, Other: Writing Postcoloniality and Feminism*. Bloomington: Indiana University Press.

Urry, J. (2002) *The Tourist Gaze*, Second Edition. London: Sage.

Young, R. (1990) *White Mythologies: Writing History and the West*. London: Routledge.

—— (2001) *Postcolonialism: A Historical Introduction*. Oxford: Blackwell.

—— (2003) *Postcolonialism: A Very Short Introduction*. Oxford: Oxford University Press.

Index

3M   261, 266

Aaker, J.   133
Abela, A.V.   249
Absolut Vodka   237
Absolute reasons   174
Action concepts   163–4, 168–9
Adams, Henry C.   47
Adams, K.M.   374, 376
Adidas   237
Adler, P.S.   10
Administrative research   11, 330
Adorno, Theodor W.   2, 115, 117, 246
Advertising
  created wants   193, 194, 205
  emotional   134
  hedonism   187–90
  image-saturated environment   199–200
  positional goods   194–5
  privileging ephemeral and superficial
      values   198–9
  soap   369–72
  word-of-mouth   108–9
Aesthetic images   143–4
Affective production   335
Africa
  colonialism   367, 369–370
  social marketing   7
Agency   246
  brand management   306–8, 339
  cultural studies   331, 332–3, 335, 339,
      340
  immaterial labour   336
  motivation research   334

psychographics   334
  undertheorized consumer agency   232–3
Agricultural marketing   51–2
AIDS treatment   201, 224
Alatas, S.H.   368
Alba, J.W.   139, 145
Alderson, Wroe   4
Alexander of Hales   36
Allende, Salvador   214
Altruism   138–40
American Association for Agricultural
      Legislation   3
American Economic Association (AEA)   48
American Marketing Association (AMA)   4,
      98
Ancre Riwle   41
Andreasen, A.R.   7
Anthropology, cultural   99–100
Anti-materialism   188
Antiglobal challenges to marketing   184–5,
      211–14, 220, 236–8
  development thought, eras in history of
      214–18
  ideological common ground   232–6
  intellectual property rights *versus* human
      rights   213, 223–6
  local cultures, undermining of   219,
      220–1
  unhealthy diet and unsafe food
      technologies   219, 226–9
  unsustainable consumption   219, 229–2
Apologists   12
Apple   306
Apter, M.J.   205

Aquinas, St. Thomas   36, 37–8
Arendt, H.   335
Argentina   229
Ariely, D.   138–9
Aristotle   34–5, 39, 40
Arndt, J.   94
Arnold, M.J.   12
Arnould, Eric J.
    Consumer Culture Theory   92–3, 149
    escaping the market   248
    Gould, Stephen J.   305
    nature   281, 294
Asbury, K.   86
Ashcroft, B.   368
Association for Consumer Research   122
Association to Advance Collegiate Schools of
        Business   216
'Audience commodity'   333
Augustine, St.   35, 41
Australia   380n9
Austria   96–7
Automatic choice   145–7
Autonomy   246
Auxiliary reasons   174
Auyang, S.Y.   165

Bacon, Francis   37
Bakhtin, M.   356
Banana Republic   374
Baritz, L.   193
Barrett, L.   138, 144–5, 146
Barriers to trade   221
Bartels, Robert   30
Barter systems   292
Basic functions of marketing   58–9
Baudrillard, J.   195, 197, 333
Bauer, R.A.   119
Bauman, Z.   205, 206
Baumgartner, H.   148
Baym, N.   351
Bayton, J.A.   105
Beavoir, Simone de   349
Beckman, C.   272
Behavioural Decision Theory (BDT)   314
Behaviorism   158–9, 161, 164
    and cognitive revolution   158
    hedonism   188, 190
    introspection   314
Beliefs, ethnopsychology   163

Belk, Russell W.
    extended self   282
    global markets   218, 221
    materialism   245
    personal possessions in workplace   137
    tourism   234
Benedict, Ruth   132
Benetton   237
Benham, F.   79
Benjamin, Jessica   291
Bennett, M.R.   164, 172
Berg, T.F.   351
Berlin Handelshochschule   53
Berlin, University of   60, 61n.2
    institutional approach   47, 50
    scientific marketing management   53, 54
Bernadino, San   36
Berthold von: Regensburg   39
Bettman, J.R.   137
Bevir, M.   246
Bhabha, H.   381n14
Bharatiya Janata Party   221
Bible   39, 41
Biotechnologies   227–8, 229
Bittner, R.   164
Blake, J.K.   119
Bloch   143–4
Boas, Franz   132, 133
Body Shop   237, 293
Bogdan, R.J.   167
Bohr, Niels   161
Bolton, L.E.   139
Bosu, Kunal   234
Bounty Bars   372
Bourdieu, Pierre   190, 349
Bové, José   226
Bovril   371
Boycotts   221
Brands
    American   237
    communities   136, 138
    evolutionary biology   133
    globalization   220
    management   306–7, 337, 338–9, 340
    social status and social bonding   194
    tribal identity   136, 137
Brantlinger, P.   368
Brasel, A.   133
Brazil   228

Brenkert, George G.   235
Breyer, Ralph   4
Briley, D.A.   139
British Empire   369–72
Britt, S.H.   99, 102, 103, 105
Britton, R.   376, 377
Brown, J.R.   172
Brown, Stephen
   introspection   317, 324
   motivation research   123n2
   postcolonialism   363
   postmodernism   302, 304
Brownlie, D.   353
Brucks, M.   315, 319
Brundtland report   254, 261
Bruner, Jerome   160, 161–2, 165–67, 172
   cognitive psychology   158, 161, 165
Buker, E.A.   350, 352, 354, 356
Bureau of Business Research   56–7
Burgess, R.L.   131
Burma   214
Burrell, G.   89
Burroughs, J.E.   148
Burton, D.   363
Business-to-business marketing   189
Butler, Judith   357
'Buy Nothing Day' (BND)   206
Buzzell, R.D.   71

Cairncross, F.   253
Calás, M.   303, 309
Calhoun, C.   304
Calvinism   190
Campbell, C.
   conserver society movement   262
   fantasy and hedonism   197, 203
   moral obligations   203
   pleasure motive   203, 204
   pleasure-seeking and satisfaction-seeking,
      distinction between   192
Canada   380n9
Cargill   228
Carman, J.M.   266–7
Carnegie Foundation   116, 117
Carsky, M.L.   350
Carson, Rachel   275
Case method   55–6
Caslione, John A.   216
Cateora, Philip R.   223, 232

Catterall, M.   358
Cavanagh, John   218
   environmental problems   230
   food technologies   226
   intellectual property rights   224
   local cultures, undermining of   220
   undertheorized consumer agency   232
Censorship   221
Chamberlin, Edward   42
Chandler, Alfred   56
Chaudhuri, Nirad   201
Cherington, Paul   55
Cherniak, C.   165
Cheskin, L.   103
Chia, R.   302
Chile   214
China
   censorship   221
   counterfeiting and piracy   225
   fast-food chains   222, 226, 227, 233
   genetically modified foods   229
   neoliberalism and globalisation   217
   quotas   221
   state-directed development   214
Chlorinol   371
Choice criteria   176–7
Chrysostom, St John   35
Chua, Amy   217
Cicero   38
Clark, J.B.   47
Coca-Cola   221, 237
Cochran, G.   148
Cocks, J.   353
Cognitive capitalism   332
Cognitive decision theory   132–3
Cognitive psychology   158, 159, 161, 165
   goal-directed behaviour   165
Cognitive revolution   158, 159
Cole, Arthur   54
Collective construction of theory   354
Collective welfare and social marketing
      233–5
Collins, L.   116, 117
Colonial discourse analysis   368
Colonialism   365–7, 370, 380n5
   'progress' discourse   367–8
   tourism   375
Columbia University   47
Commodification of social life   197

'Commodity fetishism' 141
Commons 224–5
  tragedy of the 231
Commons, John R. 48
Communist planned economies 206
Community, changing the 290–1
Commuri, S. 134
Competition
  classical economics 75–6
  and consumer choice 75
  economic theory of 258
  impersonal nature of 79
  social welfare and 75–6, 77
Computer metaphor, ethnopsychology
    159, 167–8
Conclusive reasons 174
Conrad, Johannes 50
Consciousness
  construction and expression of 320–1
  reflexive 163
Conserver society movement 261–3, 280,
    295–6
Conspicuous consumption 107, 193, 194
'Constructive alternativism' 166
Consumer agency, undertheorized 232–3
Consumer Behavior Odyssey 92
Consumer Culture Theory (CCT) 92–3
  evolutionary biology 149
  experiential consumer research 118
  introspection 314, 316, 320
  motivation research 116, 120
  non-performative stance 9
  theory 349
Consumer problem 3
Consumer sovereignty
  antiglobalism 212, 223, 229
  macromarketing 68–71, 77–82
  objections to 304
Consumers International 224, 233
Consumption and consumerism
  brand management 338–9
  conspicuous consumption 107, 193, 194
  consumer resistance, see ecofeminist
    analysis of environmentally sensitive
    women
  critical marketing thought 14–15, 17
  cultural studies 330, 331–2, 340
  dismantling the consumer 285–6

globalisation as transmitting the
    consumer society 200–3
  hedonism 187–89, 190–192, 203
  ideology 12, 195, 200, 247
  'liberatory consumption' 303–5
  motivation research 333–5
  origins of research 94–7
  pressures 199–200
  symbolic consumption 150–1
  unsustainable consumption 213, 219,
    229–2
Converse, Paul D. 55, 61, 69, 97–8
Cooke, B. 350
Copeland, Melvin T. 55
Cosmides, L. 144
Costa, Janeen Arnold 234
Counterfeiting 225–6
Cox, R. 73, 74
Crang, M. 368
Created wants 193–4, 205
Critical ecofeminism 275
Critical marketing 8–10, 14–17
  as emancipatory social science? 17–18
Critical reflections on consumer research
    85–9
Critical theory 13–14, 101, 111–12,
    311–12
  1940s 10–13
  introspection 311–26
  uses and abuses 346
Critically reading your own work 325–6
"Crony capitalism" 217
Crossette, B. 201
Csikszentmihalyi, M. 203, 204, 207
Culler, J. 346, 347
Cultural anthropology 99–100
Cultural basis of ethnopsychology 167–8
Cultural determinism 132–3
Cultural ecofeminism 273
Cultural imperialism 220
Cultural production 335–6
Cultural studies 307–9, 329–41
Culture
  local 213, 220, 224–6, 234–5
  and nature, intertwining of 281
  and self 324, 325
Cusick, E.T. 52
Customer orientation, primacy of a 235–6
Cynicism of business and marketing 283–5

Cyprian, St. 41
Czinkota, Michael R. 222, 232

Dahl, D.W. 140
Daly, H.E. 256
Darwin, Charles 85, 86, 132
Davis, K. 357
Dawes, R.M. 257
Dawson, L.M. 260
De Sousa, R. 175
Deep ecology 274, 275
Definitions of marketing 3–6
Demand
    producers' response to 74–5
    transformation of wants into 73–4
Democracy
    macromarketing 77–82
    videography 358
Deng Xiaoping 216
Dennett, D.C. 163, 165–6
Depth interviewing, motivation research
    109, 110
Derrida, J. 321, 323, 325
Descartes, René 190
Descriptive statement, macromarketing
    72–5
Desmond, J. 5
Developing countries, *see* antiglobal
    challenges to marketing
Development thought, eras in history of
    214
    1945–1979 214–15
    1979–1999 214–15
    1999 217–18
Dholakia, N. 14, 302
Dialogue 356
Dichter, Ernest
    axiology 99–102
    epistemological assumptions 105–7
    experiential customer research 119–21
    Fordist order, collapse 334
    methodological assumptions 107–10
    motivation research 93–4, 96–110,
        114–16, 117, 119–22, 333, 334
    ontological assumptions 102–5
Dickinson, R. 74
Diet, unhealthy 213, 219, 226–8
Diogenes 39
Dionysius 38

Discriminatory taxation 221
Dittmar, H. 196
Division of labour 35
Dominant social paradigm 12, 13, 231
Dominguez, Joe 296
Domitian 38
Douglas, M. 195
Downshifters 296
DRD4 7–repeat allele 147–8, 151
Drolet, A. 147
Dube, L. 134
Duddy, E.A. 70–1
Dunbar, R.I.M. 86–7
Duncan, D.J. 69
Duns Scotus, John 36
DuPont 261, 266

Earl, Peter 317
Eastern Europe
    democratization 77
    environmental issues 265
Easthope, A. 366–7
Echtner, C.M. 373–4, 381n18
Ecofeminist analysis of environmentally
        sensitive women 271–5
    consumers, implications for 295–6
    ecological life as force of change 286–92
    ecological self 279–82
    environmental groups, implications for
        293–4
    living the ecological life 282–6
    marketing managers, implications for
        292–3
    methodology 275–9
    regulatory agencies, implications for
        294–6
Ecological discussion within marketing 255
    imperfect knowledge 255–7
    social dilemmas 257–9
Ecological impact of marketing, *see*
        environmental and ecological impact of
        marketing
Ecological life
    as force of change 286–91
    living the 282–6, 292
Ecological marketing 254, 259–61, 262,
        264–5
    and green marketing, difference between
        263

Ecological self 279–82
Ecological spaces, creating and preserving 291
Ecology movement 274–5
Economic history, discipline of 54
Education, and cultural indoctrination 202
Einstein, Albert 161
Eke, P.A.C. 52
Eliade, M. 197
Eliasberg, W. 107, 119
Eliot, Charles W. 53
Elshof, G.T. 314
Elster, J. 202
Ely, Richard T. 46
  institutional approach, origins of 47–9, 50, 60
  macromarketing 68
Emancipatory social science, critical marketing as an 17–18
Embodied theory 357–8
Emotional advertising 134
Emotional response patterns 145–6
Emotions
  ethnopsychology 173, 177, 178
  and rationality, link between 173
Enlightenment 302
Environmental and ecological impact of marketing 1
  antiglobalism 229–32
  customer orientation 235
  ethnopsychology 173
  see also ecofeminist analysis of environmentally sensitive women; sustainable marketing
Environmental audits 292–3
Environmental economics 255–7
Environmental groups 293–4
Environmental guidelines 295
Environmental marketing 254
Environmental policy programs 293–4
"Environmental use permits" 259
Ephemeral values, privileging 198–9
'Epistemological' power 338
Erdman, H.E. 52
Escalas, J.E. 137
Ethical ecofeminism 273
Ethical economy 340–1
Ethical guidelines 5
Ethical hedonism 190

Ethnic tourism 374–6
Ethnopsychology 88, 157–8
  action concepts 168–9
  choice criteria 176–7
  as culturally based 167–8
  as folk psychology study 158–3
  folk psychology, intention and prediction 165–6
  hermeneutics 177–80
  inter-subjective understanding, assumption of 170–1
  meaning as directing action 163–4
  methods 163
  mind as software to brain's hardware 166–7
  motives and self-interest 171–4
  operative, auxiliary, conclusive and absolute reasons 174
  reason-giving, limitations 169–70
  reasons, categories of 175–6
Evans-Pritchard, D. 377–8
Evolutionary biology 85–7, 131–3, 149
  altruism, sharing and selection for group welfare 138–40
  automatic and unconscious choice 145–7
  gender differences and mate choice 133–5
  genetics 148–9
  incorporation in consumer research 149–50
  individual differences and the DRD4 7-repeat allele 147–9
  mating strategies 135–6
  metaphor and the modular mind 143–5
  social influence and Theory of Mind 140–3
  symbolic consumption 150–1
  tribal identity 136–8
Experiential consumer research 118–21
Extended self, and ecological self 282
Extrospection 323

Facebook 339
Fair Trade Federation 234
Fair Trade Foundation 234
Fairness 139, 170
Falkner, R.P. 47
Fanon, Frantz 365

Fantasy, influence on buying decisions 175, 197–8
Farmer, R.N. 183, 184
Fast and frugal algorithms 145–7
Fay, B. 172
Featherstone, M. 197
Federal Trade Commission 295
Feminine consumption, changing 288–90
Feminism
cultural studies 331
theory 346, 347, 349–50, 352–4, 357–8
see also ecofeminist analysis of
environmentally sensitive women
Fetter, F.A. 70
Finke, L. 351
Firat, A.F.
consumption patterns 302
critical marketing thought 14, 15, 16
postmodernism 331–2, 334
Fisher, J.E. 12
Fisher, R. 134
Fisk, George 70, 74, 260, 265, 279
Fiske, J. 195
Flanagan, O. 196
Fleck, L. 122
Flinn, M.V. 141, 142, 146
Fodor, Jerry A. 144, 166
Folk psychology 158, 160–5, 166–7
reasons, categories of 175
Fonatur 230
Food security 228–9
Food technologies, unsafe 213, 219, 226–9
Foraging 287
Ford Foundation 116, 117
Fordism 333, 334
Foucault, Michel 10, 17, 305, 338
Fournier, S. 133
Fournier, V. 9, 10, 18, 185
Foxall, G. 103
France 221, 228
Frank, R.H. 193–4
Frankfurt School 11, 13, 312
Frederick, J.George 85
Free association 106, 109
Freedom 78–9, 80, 81, 82, 193
globalisation 202–3
hedonism 207
Freud, Sigmund 98–9, 106, 107, 110
Friedman, Thomas 216

Frito-Lay 228
Fromm, E. 246, 302, 312
Fuller, Donald A. 231
Fullerton, R.A. 94
Functions of marketing 58–9
Fundraising 234

Gabriel, Yiannis 272, 296
Gadamer, Hans-Georg 88–9, 178–80
Galbraith, J.K. 194
Galton, Francis 85
Gamber, W. 349–50
Gandhi, Mohandas Karamchand 365
Gardner, Howard 158, 158–60
Gay, Edwin Francis 46
institutional approach, origins of 47
scientific marketing management, origins
of 53–7, 58–9, 60
Geary, D.C. 146
Gellner, E. 202
Gender biases of theory 349–50
Gender differences, evolutionary biology
133–4, 149–50
General Systems paradigm
consumer sovereignty 70, 80
marketing effort and social
welfare 77
Genetic science 86
Genetically modified (GM) foods 171,
227–930, 232
Genetics 147–9, 151
Gentry, J.W. 134
Ger, Güliz 217–18, 233
German Historical school 30, 45,
59–60, 61
institutional approach, origins of 47–8,
50, 52, 59
scientific marketing management, origins
of 53–4, 56, 59
Germany 266
Ghana 215
Gielens, K. 147–8
Gift-giving 245
environmentally sensitive
women 290
evolutionary biology 137
social influence 140
Global warming 229–30

Globalization
  era   215–17
  hedonism-consumerism and   188, 189
  opposition to, *see* antiglobal challenges to
    marketing
  as transmitting the consumer society
    200–3
Goals of marketing   9
Goffman, Erving   196
Golden-Biddle, K.   346
Goldman, A.   163, 165
Goodman, E.   72
Gordon, R.A.   116
Gosling, J.C.B.   204
Gottdiener, M.   195
Gould, Stephen J.   305, 315–16, 318, 319
Gower, John   40
Graham, John L.   223, 232
Gramsci, A.   314, 337, 338, 380n12
Grayson, K.   139, 143
Great Exhibition   381n17
Green certification of wood
    products   293
Green consumer behaviour   247, 248
Green marketing   254, 263–4, 265, 272
  backlash   292
Green, H.E.   95
Grether, E.T.   73, 74
Grey, C.   9, 10, 18, 185, 348–9
Group welfare, selection for   138–40
Guilt cultures   202–3

Habermas, J.   87–9
Habitat   372
Hacker, P.M.S.   164, 172
Hagerty   50
Haire, M.   100
Hall, Stuart   331
Halle, University of   50
Hamilton, K.   358
Hamilton, W.D.   138
Hammond, M.B.   49
Hammurabi, Code of   39
Hardin, G.   265
Hartnack, J.   169
Harpending, H.   148
Harris, R.G.   266–7
Hart, Stuart L.   236
Hartley, R.F.   70

Harvard Business School   45, 46, 59–61
  institutional approach, origins of   47
  scientific marketing management, origins
    of   52–9
Hastings, G.   8
Hayek, F.A.von   70
Heaton, Herbert A.   54
Hedonism   184, 187–90, 203–4, 207–8
  consumerism and   192–200
  definitions and meanings   190–2
  globalization   200–3
  responsibility for   205–7
  utilitarianism and   190, 262
Hedonistic paradox   203, 204
Heidegger, Martin   178
Heider, Fritz   160
Henion, K.E., II   260, 265
Henry, Harry   115
Henwood, Doug   234
Herbst, A.   74
Herbst, Jurgen   47
Hermeneutics   87–9
  ethnopsychology   177–80
Herodotus   38, 105–6
Hertzog, Herta   93–4, 115
Hewer, P.   353
Hibbard, B.H.   48, 49, 52
Hirschman, E.C.
  experiential customer research   118–19,
    120, 122
  ideology of consumption   195
  introspection   319
  psychographics   118
  research styles   317
Historical ecofeminism   274
Historical school, *see* German Historical
    school
HIV/AIDS treatment   201, 224
Hobbes, Thomas   190
Hoggart, Richard   330, 337
Holbrook, M.B.
  experiential customer research   118–19,
    120, 121, 122
  ideology of consumption   195
  introspection   315, 317
  psychographics   118
Holland, D.   353
Hollander, S.C.   262
Holt, Douglas B.   133, 141, 337, 338, 339

Hong Kong   215, 226
Hooks, bell   348, 350, 351, 353–4
Horgan, John   159
Horkheimer, M.   13
Horowitz, D.   123n2
Housework   288–90
Howard, J.A.   161
Howell, J.E.   116
Hoyt, E.E.   70, 80
Huegy, H.W.   69
Human rights   213, 219, 223–6
Hume, David   173, 202
Humm, M.   354
Hunt, C.L.   68
Huntley and Palmer   371
Hutt, W.H.   70, 80
Hygiene
    colonialism   369–2
    environmentally sensitive women   288
Hyman, H.   202

Identity, taken from possessions   197–8
Image-saturation   199–200
Imagery, influence on buying decisions
    197–8
Imagination   191
Immaterial labour   306, 335–6, 340
Imperfect knowledge   255–7
Imperialism   369, 376, 380n5
    commodities   369–2
Import substitution programmes   215
Impulse buys   173–4
India
    Coca-Cola   221
    consumption behaviours   303–4
    counterfeiting and piracy   226
    cultural identity   220
    globalisation   201, 216
    growth   215
    intoxicant products sold to homeless
        children   304
    McDonald's   222
    motor scooters   233
    neoliberalism   216
    Patent Act   225
    state-directed development   214
    structural adjustment programmes   304
Individual differences   147–9
Indonesia   214, 217, 374–5

Industrial management, origins of   55
Informational capitalism   332, 335, 339
Ingram, J.K.   81
Innovation
    consumer resistance   285–7, 288
    desirability of   223
    evolutionary biology   144, 147, 149
    immaterial labour   336
    intellectual property rights   224
    psychological obsolescence   207
Institute of Basic Mathematics for
    Application to Business   116
Institutional approach to marketing   46–52,
    59, 60
Institutional economics   256
Inter-subjective understanding, assumption
    of   170–1
International Forum on Globalization (IFG)
    211–12, 218, 220
International Intellectual Property Alliance
    225
International Marketing Review   216
International Monetary Fund   304
International Society of/for Marketing and
    Development   218
Interpretive research   85, 91–3, 94, 101,
    111–12, 307
    folk psychology   165
    metaphor and symbolism   143
    motivation research and   119–20
    ontological assumptions   102–5
    theory   346, 347
    verstehen concept   107
Introspection   305, 311–14, 324–6
    as critical marketing thought   314–20
    critical marketing thought as   320–6
    exercises   314–20, 321–4, 325–6
Iran   221
Irreplaceable possessions   143
Irvine, S.   248–50
Irwin, Douglas A.   232
Isherwood, B.   195

Jack, Gavin   307
Jacobs Thai Bites   372
Jamaica   233
James, E.J.   47
Jameson, C.   114
Jameson, Fredric   218

Janata Dal Party   221
Japan   201–2, 233, 378–9
Jastrow, Ignaz   53
Jerome, St.   35
Jobling, M.A.   137–8
Johansson, Johny K.   220, 237
Johar, G.V.   145
Johns Hopkins University   47, 48
Johnson, E.R.   47
Johnson, J.F.   47
Jones, Edward David   3, 49–50
Jordan, Michael   200
Journal of Consumer Research (JCR)
   altruism, sharing and selection for group
      welfare   138–9
   automatic and unconscious choice
      145–6
   evolutionary biology   132, 133, 149
   gender differences and mate choice
      133–4
   Gould, Stephen J.   315, 319
   metaphor and the modular model   143–4
   social influence and Theory of Mind
      140–2
   tribal identity   136–7
   variety seeking behaviour   147–8
*Journal of International Consumer
   Marketing*   216
Journal of International Marketing   216
Joy, A.   16, 139

Kagan, Jerome   161, 173–4
Kane, P.   337
Kant, Immanuel   173
Kass, A.   207
Kass, L.R.   207
Kassarjian, H.H.   93
Kellner, D.   339
Kelly, George   166
Kentucky Fried Chicken
   adaptation to local cultures   222, 233
   advertising slogan   189
   globalisation   223, 228
Kilbourne, William E.   9, 12, 247, 272
Kin selection   138
Kincheloe, J.L.   312, 320, 347, 356
Kinley, David   49
Kinnear, T.C.   260, 265
Knies, Karl   54

Kotler, P.
   ethics and morality   82
   marketing concept   67, 71, 74, 75
   societal marketing concept   68
Kozinets, R.V.   136–7
Kraft   228
Krugman, H.E.   113
Kuhn, Thomas   29, 88, 351
Kuwait   227

Laboratory method   56, 58
Labour
   division of   35
   immaterial   306, 335–6, 340
Laczniak, G.R.   5, 6
LaFeber, W.   200
Lal, D.   201–2
Lang, Tim   272, 296
Language
   evolutionary adaptation   138
   globalization   220
Lash, Scott   338
Latin America   215, 216
Lazarsfeld, Paul   11–12, 94, 96, 330, 338
Lazer, W.   259
Lazzarato, M.   306
Le Carré, John   201
Lears, T.J.J.   15
Leipzig, University of   54
Leo the Great   35
Lester, E.   374
Levav, J.   138–9
Levitt, Theodore   79, 216
Levy, Sidney J.   94, 120–1, 333
Liberal ecofeminism   274
'Liberatory consumption'   303
Liberty, *see* freedom
Licensing   75
Lifestyle segmentation   334
'Limit attitude' towards marketing   10, 12
Literary theory   351
Local cultures
   export of   234–5
   undermining of   213, 219, 220–1
Local products and markets   292
Locke, K.   346
Loewenstein, G.   146
Lomborg, Bjorn   229
Lusch, R.F.   8

Luther, Martin   36
Lyons, William   162, 166, 314

MacCannell, D.   375
McCarthy, E.J.   71
McCarthyism   116, 123n2
McCartney, J.   188
McClintock, Anne   367, 369–71, 372
McCracken, Grant   278
McDonagh, Pierre   275
McDonald, K.   134–5
McDonald's
   adaptation to local cultures   222, 233
   antiglobalism   226, 237
   globalization   220, 227, 234–5
   "healthier" menu choices   228
Macklin, Theodore   48, 52
McGowan, K.   366–7
McGraw, A.P.   137
McGuigan, J.   337
McKenzie-Mohr, Doug   249
McLaran, P.   347, 356, 347, 356
Macromarketing   67–8
   consumer sovereignty   68–71, 77–82
   consumer wants   72–5
   democracy   77–82
   marketing concept   69–71, 79–82
   social welfare   75–7
Managerial discourse, marketing as a   2–6
Mander, Jerry   218
   environmental problems   230
   food technologies   226
   intellectual property rights   224
   local cultures, undermining of   220
   undertheorised consumer agency   232
Mao Tse-tung   216
Marcuse, H.   193
Marketing concept   67, 69–71, 77, 79–82
Marketing problem   3
Marrazzi, Christian   339
Marshall, Alfred A.   33–4, 53, 76
Martial   38
Martin, Seldin O.   57
Martineau, Pierre   92, 116, 333, 334
Martinec, R.   139
Marx, Karl   336
Marxism   307
   antiglobalism   212
   cultural studies   331

embodied theory   357
evolutionary biology   141
hedonism   189–90
persuasive hegemony of marketing system
      141
postcolonialism   369
Mate choice, evolutionary biology   133–5
Materialism   195, 245
   critiques   247
Mating strategies, evolutionary biology
      135–6
Mayo-Smith, R.   47
Mead, Margaret   132
Meaning as directing action   163–4
Médécins Sans Frontières   234
Memory work   355
Menon, G.   146
Mercantilism   37
Merton, R.K.   345
Message saturation   199–200
Metacognitive introspection   316–17
Metaphor   143–5
Mexico
   antiglobalism   217
   consumption and identity   305
   cultural identity   220
   obesity   226
   subsidies   221
   tourism   230
Michigan, University of   47, 98
Mick, D.G.   148
Micklethwait, J.   202, 237
Mill, John Stuart
   freedom   80, 81, 202
   globalization   202
   self- and other-regarding actions   193
   self-interest and social welfare   76
Miller, George   159
Minimal rationality   165
Minow, M.   347
Mishra, Pankaj   201
Mitchell, W.C.   74
Modernization theory   216
Modular mind   143–5
Monism   87, 162
Monkey Brand   370
Montaigne, Michel Eyquem de   36
Montgomery, C.   116, 117
Moon, Y.M.   140

Moore, E.S.   3–4, 6
Moorman, C.   4–5
Moran, D.   88
Morgan, G.   301, 302
Morgan, N.   372
Moriarty, W.D.   69
Morley, D.   378–9
Motherhood project   354
Motivation research   91–4, 97–8, 101,
      111–12, 121–2, 333–4
   axiology   98–102
   emergence   96–7
   epistemological assumptions   105–7
   methodological assumptions
      107–10
   ontological assumptions   102–5
   psychographics to experiential consumer
      research   118–21
   transformation   114–18
   translation, politics of   110–3
Motives and self-interest, ethnopsychology
      171–4
Mouffe, Chantal   19
Multinational corporations   183
   globalisation of consumer society   200–3
   see also antiglobal challenges to marketing
Muniz, A.M.   136
Murphy, P.E.   5, 6
Murray, J.B.   94, 143, 314, 347, 363
Murray, J.F.   248
Mutual self   291–2, 293, 294, 295, 296
Myspace   339
Myth-making, colonialism   368

Naïve empiricism   105–6
Namibia   375–6
Narratives
   critical-introspective exercise
      316–17
   and theory   352
Narrow hedonism   190, 198–9, 203
Narver, J.C.   70
National parks system   294
Nationalization   214
Native Americans   377–8
Negative Artificial Needs Growth (NANG)
      261, 262
Negotiating the market   245–51
Neo-colonialism   366, 375, 380n5

Neoclassical economics   59
   environmental economics
      255, 256
   marketing's intellectual roots   212
Neoliberalism   215–17
   antiglobalism   217
   environmental protection   232
   ideology of consumption   247
Nepal   230
Nestlé   212, 222
Netherlands   266
Newman, J.W.   109, 113, 115–16
Nicomachean Ethics   40
Nike   183, 200
Non-performative stance, critical marketing
      scholarship   9
Norman, D.A.   168
Normative issue, marketing and social
      welfare   75–7
Not-for-profit marketing   189
Nowlis, S.M.   147
Nu, U   214
Nystrom, Paul   48

O'Guinn, T.C.   136
O'Shaughnessy, J.   74
Obesity   226–7, 228–9
Objectivity critical-introspective exercise
      324–6
Obote, Milton   214
Observation   163
Obsolescence, psychological   206–7
Ohio State Workshop on consumer
      behaviour   122
Oliva, T.A.   265
Ontological denaturalisation, critical
      marketing scholarship   9
Ontological power   338
Operant conditioning   158–9
Operative reasons   174
Oppositional imagination
      353–8
Oral narratives   355–7
Orientalism   366–7, 372, 379
   tourism   375
Østergaard, P.   330
Ottman, Jacquelyn   292, 293
Oxfam International   234, 238
Ozanne, J.L.   248, 312, 347

Packaging waste   266
Packard, V.   105, 119, 123n2
Papen, Uta   372, 375–6
Paratelic mode   205
Parker, Martin   249–50
Patagonia   293
Patten, S.N.   47
Patterson, A.   363
Patterson, M.   92, 93, 94
Pearce, L.   356
Pears   370–1
Peattie, K.   263
Peñaloza, Lisa   143, 272, 286
Pennsylvania, University of   47
Personal hygiene
    colonialism   369–2
    environmentally sensitive women   288
Peters, R.   168
Peterson, W.H.   77
Pfeiffer, James   7, 8
Pham, M.T.   145–6
Pharmaceutical products   201, 224, 225,
    236
Philips, C.F.   69
Philosophic origins of marketing thought
    45–6, 59–61
    institutional approach   46–52
    scientific marketing management   52–9
Philosophical dualism   274
Pier, The   372
Pilcher, J.   357
Piracy   225–6
Plato   30
    hermeneutics   178
    sinful marketers   40, 41
    social costs of marketing   37, 39
    social welfare, contribution of marketing
        to   34
Plomin, R.   86
Plumwood, Val   275, 282
Pluralism
    Dichter, E.114
    in marketing   19, 87
    in theory   351–2
Politz, Alfred   110, 115
Pollay, R.W.   198
Pollution   229–30
Ponton, A.   248–9
Popper, Karl   166

Positional goods   194–5
    and self-identity   196
Positivism   92, 93, 101, 111–12
    theory   350
Posner, R.A.   205
Postcolonialism   307–8, 363–6, 379
    history of soap and other imperial
        commodities   369–72
    techno-Orientalism   378–9
    theoretical frame   366–8
    tourism and travel   372–8
Postmodernism   301–5
    consumer society   192
    cultural studies   331–2
    embodied experience   357
    feminism   347, 350, 352
    Fordist order, collapse   334
    high and low culture   193
    pluralism   352
    self-identity   195
    techno-Orientalism   378–9
    theory   346, 347, 352
Poststructural psychoanalysis   320
Poststructuralism   381n16
    cultural studies   331
    theory   346
Practice theory   353
Prasad, A.   364–5, 366, 367, 368, 373
Praxis   354, 356, 357
Precycling   287
Prejudice against marketing   29–30,
    33–4, 42
    marketing's contribution to social welfare
        34–7
    sinful marketers   40–1
    social costs of marketing   37–40
Price, Linda L.   272, 281, 286, 294
Pritchard, A.   372
Procter & Gamble   222
"Product stewardship"   236
Profit motive   9, 69, 71
'Progress' discourse, colonialism   367–8
Protectionism, cultural   221, 222
Prothero, Andrea   275, 354
Psychoanalysis, poststructural   320
Psychographics   117–18, 334
Psychological-cultural research   321
Psychological hedonism   190
Psychological obsolescence   206–7

Psychological theory
  and consumer research   95–6
  motivation research   98–9, 106, 107–8,
    110–3
Psychology
  cognitive   160, 161, 163, 164, 165
  ethnopsychology, see ethnopsychology
  folk   158–63, 165–7, 175
Puritanism   188
Putnam, Hilary   166

Qualitative research   92, 94, 307
  motivation research   117
Quantitative research   117
Quotas   221
  sustainable marketing   259

Rabinow, P.   86
Radical ecofeminism   274
Raghubir, P.   146
Rakow, L.F.   355
Rassuli, K.M.   262
Rationalising hedonism   190
Rawls, J.   193
Reagan, Ronald   216
Real Utopias Project   18
Reason-giving explanation   169–70, 172–3
Reasons
  absolute   174
  auxiliary   174
  categories   175–6
  conclusive   174
  operative   174
Reception ethnographies   355
Reckwitz, A.   353
Reconstructionists   12
Recycling   283, 287, 295
Reflexivity
  critical marketing scholarship   10
  and introspection, relationship between
    321–2, 323–4
Reform environmentalilsm   275
Reform of Inefficient Consumption Habits
  (RICH)   261, 262
Reidenbach, R.E.   265
Reinharz, Shulamit   276
Religious belief   202
Research in marketing, origins of   56–7
Reusing products   287–8, 290

Reuther, Walter   194
Reversal theory   205
Reverse engineering   225
Revzan, D.A.   70–1
Richard of Middletown   36
Ricoeur, P.   106
Robin, Vicki   296
Robins, K.   378–9
Rohatyn, D.   191
Rojek, C.   372
Ronkainen, Ilkka A.   222, 232
Ropke, W.   70
Roscher, Wilhelm   54, 59
Rose R.L.   141
Rose, N.   86
Rosenblatt, Louise   351
Rosenthal, E.   171
Ross, C.A.   16
Rothstein, F.A.   305
Rothwell, N.D.   110, 113
Ruether, Rosemary   273

Said, Edward
  antiglobalism   217
  critic, unswerving stance of the   305
  intellectual, function of the   17
  postcolonialism   363, 366, 369, 373
Sampson, P.   94
Sartre, Jean-Paul   349
Savitt, R.   70
Scanlon, J.   350
Schau, Hope, Jensen   288
Schleiermacher, Friedrich   178
Schlosser, A.E.   141
Schmoller, G.   54
Schoenfeld, W.A.   52
Scholasticism   36, 39, 40
Schor, J.   248, 296
Schroeder, J.E.   324
Schudson, M.   195, 198–9, 245, 356
Schultz, C.J.   334
Schumpeter, Joseph A.   35
Scientific management   332–3
Scientific marketing management, origins
  52–5, 60
  basic functions of marketing   58–9
  case method   55–6
  research in marketing   56–7
Scitovsky, T.   245

Scriven, L.E.   113
Secondhand purchases   285, 286, 292
Self and culture, critical-introspective
   exercise   324
Self-identity, taken from possessions   195–6
Self-interest   75–6, 171–4
Seligman, E.R.A.   47
Senior, W.N.   76
Sensation-seeking behaviour   134–5
September 11 attacks   239n4
Sering, Max   50
Shallice, T.   168
Shame cultures   201–2
Shankar, A.   92, 93, 94
Shapiro, S.J.   262
Sharing   138–40
Shaw, Arch W.
   basic functions of marketing   58–9
   Bureau of Business Research   56–7
   definition of marketing   4
   "external" problems of business   77
   social welfare   81
Shearman, R.   254
Sheth, J.N.   161
Shulman, D.   143
Significance, concept of   165
Silver, I.   375
Simmons, C.J.   145
Simonson, I.   147
Simplicity movement   298
Sinclair, A.   350–1
Sinful marketers   39–41
Singer, Peter   215
Skinner, Burrhus Frederic   160–1, 264
Sklair, L.   264
Smircich, L.   303, 309
Smith, Adam
   annual revenue of society   76
   consumer sovereignty and social welfare
     75
   democracy   80
   free market economy   81
   invisible hand   75
   marketing concept   68, 71
   social welfare   81–2
   unsustainable marketing   264
   Wealth of Nations publication   78
Smith, G.H.   110
Smith, N.Craig   71

Smith, Valene   374
Smythe, Dallas   333
Soap advertising, British Empire   369–72
Social bonding, positional goods for   194–5
Social class
   consumption cleavages   196–7
   declining importance   196
   mate choice   133
Social costs of marketing   37–40
Social dilemmas, environmental problems as
   257–9
Social influence   140–3
Social life, commodification of   197
Social marketers   12
Social marketing (SM)   6
   and collective welfare   233–5
   critical?   6–8
Social production   335
Social status, positional goods for   194–5
Social welfare, marketing's contribution to
   34–7
   macromarketing   75–7, 81–2
   normative issue   75–7
Socialism   206
Socially activist roles   3, 30
Societal marketing concept   68, 69
   sustainable marketing   260
Society and marketing   183–5
Sociolinguistic ecofeminism   274
Soros, George   203
South Africa, AIDS in   201
South Korea   215, 221, 233
Southeast Asia   216
Sparling, Samuel   49, 50
Spencer, Herbert   132
Sperber, D.   144
Spivak, G.C.   381n15
Spratlen, T.H.   12
Staelin, R.   116
Starbucks   221
State-directed development, era of   214–15
Stavins, R.N.   264
Steenkamp, J.-B.   147–8
Steiner, R.L.   29–30, 35–6, 40
Stern, Barbara   93
'Storying the self'   355
Storytelling   356
Strasser, Susan   206
Straw, B.M.   352

Structural adjustment programmes   7, 304
Stryker, P.   115
Subjectivity critical-introspective exercise
        324–5
Subsidies   219
Suharto, T.N.J.   217
Sukarno, Achmed   214
Superficial values, privileging   198–9
Sustainable economic development   253–4,
        265–6
    green marketing   263–4
    imperfect knowledge   255–7
Sustainable marketing   231, 253–5
    conserver society movement   261–3
    ecological discussion within marketing
            255–9
    future perspective   266–7
    micro solution for macro problem   263–4
    past views on marketing and
            environmental problems   259–61
    sustainable economic development,
            marketing in   265–6
Sutton, R.I.   352
Svensson, P.   353
Symbolic consumption   150–1
Symbolism   143–4, 197–8
Szmigin, I.   103

Tadajewski, M.   116, 351–2
Taiwan   215
Tariffs   221
Taussig, Frank W.   47, 53, 60, 69
Taxation
    discriminatory   221
    sustainable marketing   259
Taylor, Charles   162–3
Taylor, Frederick W.   55
Taylor, Henry Charles   3, 49, 50–2
Taylorism   332–3
Techno-Orientalism   378–9
Telic mode   205
Ten Thousand Villages   234
Texaco   292
Thatcher, Margaret   216
Thematic Apperception Tests   110
Theory   307, 345–6, 358
    collective construction   354
    embodied experience, theorising from
            357–8

gender biases   349–50
    inclusive methodologies   354–5
    oppositional imagination   353–4
    oral and written narratives   355–7
    rejection   350–3
    uses and abuses   346–9
Theory of Mind   140–3
Therborn, G.   302
Third World ecofeminism   274
Thomas, Andrew R.   216
Thompson, C.J.
    Consumer Culture Theory   92–3, 149
    gender differences   133
    Gould, Stephen J.   305
    market and emancipatory spaces   247
Thompson, Clarence B.   55
Thord World tourism   372–3
Thoreau, Henry David   247
Thoughts critical-introspective exercise
        316–17
Tian, K.   137, 147
Tom's of Maine   293
Tooby, J.   144
Tourism
    environmental impact   230
    exporting local culture   234–5
    postcolonialism   373–8
Trade barriers   221
Transitory appetites, satisfying   193–4
Travel, and postcolonialism   372–8
Tribal identity   136–8
Trinidad   233
Tropicalisation discourses   368
Trust, establishing   292–3
Trustmetrics   341
Turkey   233
Turkish Delight   372

Uganda   214
Unconscious choice   145–7
Undernutrition   226–7
Unhealthy diet   213, 219, 226–9
Unilever   222, 369
Uniqueness, need for   147, 151
United Nations
    Food and Agricultural Organization   228
    Group of Seventy-Seven   229
    Human Development Index   216, 235,
            238n2

United States of America
  antiglobalism   220, 221, 237
  cultural innovativeness   148
  downshifters   296
  globalisation of consumer culture   201
  imperialism   366
  innovation   148, 207
  losses through counterfeiting and piracy
    225
  motivation research   121–2n2
  obesity   226
  over-consumption   206
  techno-Orientalism   378
  toxic emissions   266
Universal hedonism   190
Unsafe food technologies   213, 219, 226–9
Unsustainable consumption   213, 219,
    229–2
Unsustainable marketing   264–5
Urry, J.   372
Utilitarianism   192, 262

Vaile, R.S.   73, 74
Van Bers, C.   254
Van Maanen, J.   352
Van Osselaer, S.   145
Variety seeking behaviour   147–8
Varman, R.   303–4
Veblen, T.   107
Velleman, J.D.   173
Venkatesh, A.   14, 331–2
Vicary, J.M.   117
Videography   356–7
Vikas, R.M.   303–4
Virtue, motive for   174

Wagner, A.   54
Walby, S.   347
Walker, H.R.   52
Wallendorf, M.   315, 319
Walley, N.   265
Wants   72–3
  created   195–6, 205
  ethnopsychology   163
Ward, L.B.   103
Warlop, L.   139
Warren, Karen J.   275
Watson, James L.   232–3, 239n5
Watson, John Broadus   158, 159

Weber, Max   339
Wehrwein, G.S.   52
Weiss, E.H.   95
Weld, L.D.H.   61n1
Welfare state   197
Wells, W.D.117–18
Westwood, R.   307
Whelehan, I.   357
White, P.D.   261
Whitehead, B.   265
Wilkie, W.L.   3–4, 116
Williams, Raymond   337
Willis, Paul   331
Winch, P.   168
Wisconsin Idea   48
Wisconsin Progressivism   48
Wisconsin, University of   45, 46, 57, 59–61
  institutional approach, origins of   47,
    48–9, 50–2
Wishes   168
Wood S.L.   141
Wood products, green certification of   293
Wooldrige, A.   202, 237
Wootens, D.B.   140
Word-of-mouth advertising   108–9
World Health Organization (WHO)   228
World Social Forum   248
World Trade Center attacks   239n4
World Trade Organization (WTO)   217
  Agreement on Trade-Related Aspects of
    Intellectual Property Rights   223
Wright, C.R.   202
Wright, Erik Olin
  emancipatory social science   18
  green consumer behaviour   247
  negotiating the market   248
  social world   246–7
Wyer, R.S.   139

Xerox   292

Yoell, W.A.   104, 119
Yorkston, E.   146
YouTube   339

Zero Artificial Needs Growth (ZANG)   261,
  262
Zuckerman, M.E.   350